T0234175

Lecture Notes in Computer Science　8606

Commenced Publication in 1973
Founding and Former Series Editors:
Gerhard Goos, Juris Hartmanis, and Jan van Leeuwen

More information about this series at http://www.springer.com/series/7407

Viktória Zsók · Zoltán Horváth
Lehel Csató (Eds.)

Central European Functional Programming School

5th Summer School, CEFP 2013
Cluj-Napoca, Romania, July 8–20, 2013
Revised Selected Papers

 Springer

Editors
Viktória Zsók
Faculty of Informatics
Eötvös Loránd University
Budapest
Hungary

Zoltán Horváth
Faculty of Informatics
Eötvös Loránd University
Budapest
Hungary

Lehel Csató
Faculty of Mathematics and Informatics
Babeş-Bolyai University
Cluj-Napoca
Romania

ISSN 0302-9743   ISSN 1611-3349 (electronic)
Lecture Notes in Computer Science
ISBN 978-3-319-15939-3   ISBN 978-3-319-15940-9 (eBook)
DOI 10.1007/978-3-319-15940-9

Library of Congress Control Number: 2015934896

LNCS Sublibrary: SL1 – Theoretical Computer Science and General Issues

Springer Cham Heidelberg New York Dordrecht London

Printed on acid-free paper

Springer International Publishing AG Switzerland is part of Springer Science+Business Media
(www.springer.com)

Preface

This volume presents the revised lecture notes of selected talks given at the fifth Central European Functional Programming School, CEFP 2013, held during July 8–20 in Cluj-Napoca, Romania at Babeş-Bolyai University, Faculty of Mathematics and Informatics.

The summer school was organized in the spirit of the advanced programming schools. CEFP involves an ever-growing number of students, researchers, and teachers from whole Europe, providing opportunities especially for students from Central- and Eastern-European countries.

The intensive programme offered a creative, inspiring environment for presentations, and for the exchange of ideas on new specific programming topics. The lectures covered a wide range of domain-specific and functional programming subjects.

We are very grateful to the lecturers and researchers for the time and effort they devoted to their talks and lecture notes. The lecture notes were each carefully checked by reviewers selected from experts. The papers were revised by the lecturers based on reviews. This revision process guaranteed that only high-quality papers were accepted for the volume.

The last five papers in the volume are selected papers of the Ph.D. Workshop organized for the participants of the summer school.

We would like to express our gratitude for the work of all the members of the Programme Committee and the Organizing Committee.

The web-page for the summer school can be found at: http://dsl2013.math.ubbcluj.ro.

December 2014

Viktória Zsók
Zoltán Horváth
Lehel Csató

Organization

CEFP 2013 was organized by Babeş-Bolyai University, Cluj-Napoca, Romania in collaboration with Eötvös Loránd University, Budapest, Hungary.

Sponsoring Institutions

The summer school was supported by the Erasmus Intensive Programme (IP) Project and the CEEPUS programme via the CEEPUS CII-HU-19 Network.

Contents

Functional Programming for Domain-Specific Languages

Jeremy Gibbons[✉]

Department of Computer Science, University of Oxford, Oxford, UK
jeremy.gibbons@cs.ox.ac.uk
http://www.cs.ox.ac.uk/jeremy.gibbons/

Abstract. Domain-specific languages are a popular application area for functional programming; and conversely, functional programming is a popular implementation vehicle for domain-specific languages—at least, for embedded ones. Why is this? The appeal of embedded domain-specific languages is greatly enhanced by the presence of convenient lightweight tools for defining, implementing, and optimising new languages; such tools represent one of functional programming's strengths. In these lectures we discuss functional programming techniques for embedded domain-specific languages; we focus especially on algebraic datatypes and higher-order functions, and their influence on deep and shallow embeddings.

1 Introduction

In his book [1], Fowler defines a domain-specific language (DSL) as

> a computer programming language of limited expressiveness focussed on a particular domain

A DSL is targetted at a specific class of programming tasks; it may indeed not be Turing-complete. By restricting scope to a particular domain, one can tailor the language specifically for that domain. Common concepts or idioms in the domain can be made more easily and directly expressible—even at the cost of making things outside the intended domain more difficult to write. The assumptions common to the domain may be encoded within the language itself, so that they need not be repeated over and over for each program within the domain—and again, those assumptions may be inconsistent with applications outside the domain.

The term 'DSL' is rather more recent than its meaning; DSLs have pervaded the history of computing. As Mernik et al. [2] observe, DSLs have in the past been called 'application-oriented', 'special-purpose', 'specialised', 'task-specific', and 'application' languages, and perhaps many other things too. The 'fourth-generation languages' (4GLs) popular in the 1980s were essentially DSLs for database-oriented applications, and were expected at the time to supercede general-purpose 3GLs such as Pascal and C. One might even say that Fortran and Cobol were domain-specific languages, focussed on scientific and business

V. Zsók et al. (Eds.): CEFP 2013, LNCS 8606, pp. 1–28, 2015.
DOI: 10.1007/978-3-319-15940-9_1

applications respectively, although they are both Turing-complete. Bentley [3] wrote influentially in his Programming Pearls column about the 'little languages' constituting the philosophy and much of the functionality of the Unix operating system: tools for programmers such as the shell, regular expressions, lex and yacc, and tools for non-programmers such as the Pic language for line drawings and a language for specifying surveys.

There are two main approaches to implementing DSLs. The historically prevalent approach has been to build *standalone* languages, with their own custom syntax. Standard compilation techniques are used to translate programs written in the DSL into a general-purpose language (GPL), or to interpret them, for execution. The syntax of the DSL can be designed specifically for the intended users, and need bear no relation to that of the host language—indeed, there may be many different host languages, as there are for SQL, or the DSL 'syntax' may be diagrammatic rather than textual.

However, implementing a new standalone DSL is a significant undertaking, involving a separate parser and compiler, and perhaps an interactive editor too. Moreover, the more the DSL is a kind of 'programming' language, the more likely it is that it shares some features with most GPLs—variables, definitions, conditionals, etc—which will have to be designed and integrated with the DSL. In the process of reducing repetition and raising the level of abstraction for the DSL programmer, we have introduced repetition and lowered the level of abstraction for the DSL implementer. That may well be a rational compromise. But is there a way of getting the best of both worlds?

The second approach to implementing DSLs attempts exactly that: to retain as much as possible of the convenient syntax and raised level of abstraction that a DSL provides, without having to go to the trouble of defining a separate language. Instead, the DSL is *embedded* within a host language, essentially as a library of definitions written in the host GPL (although it is debatable to what extent 'library' and 'language' coincide: we return to this point in Sect. 2.1 below). All the existing facilities and infrastructure of the host environment can continue to be used, and familiarity with the syntactic conventions of the host can be carried over to the DSL.

However, there are some downsides to embedding a DSL in a host language. DSL programs have to be written in the syntax of the host language; this may be clumsy if the host syntax is rigid, and daunting to non-programmer domain specialists if the host syntax is obscure. It can be difficult to preserve the abstraction boundary between the DSL its host: naive users may unwittingly invoke sophisticated language features, and error messages may be reported unhelpfully in terms of the host language rather than the DSL. Needless to say, these issues are hot research topics among those working on embedded DSLs.

Fowler [1] calls the standalone and embedded approaches 'external' and 'internal' respectively. He does this not least because 'embedded' suggests misleadingly that specialised code written in a DSL is quoted verbatim within a host program written in a GPL, with the whole being expressed in a hybrid language that is neither the DSL nor the GPL; for example, JavaServer Pages 'programs' are hybrids, consisting of HTML markup with embedded fragments of Java. (In fact, Fowler calls such hybrids 'fragmentary', and uses the term 'standalone' for pure-bred DSLs, in which any program is written in just one language, whether internal or external.) That objection notwithstanding, we will stick in this article to the terms 'standalone' and 'embedded'.

We will concentrate on embedded DSLs, only briefly making the connection back to standalone DSLs. Again, there are two main approaches to embedded DSLs, which are conventionally called *deep* and *shallow* embedding [4]. With a deep embedding, terms in the DSL are implemented simply to construct an abstract syntax tree; this tree is subsequently transformed for optimisation and traversed for evaluation. With a shallow embedding, terms in the DSL are implemented directly as the values to which they evaluate, bypassing the intermediate AST and its traversal. We explore this distinction in Sect. 2.4.

It turns out that functional programming languages are particularly well suited for hosting embedded DSLs. Language features such as algebraic datatypes, higher-order functions, lazy evaluation, and rich type systems supporting type inference all contribute. We discuss these factors in more detail in Sect. 3.

The syntax of the host language is another factor, albeit a relatively minor one: functional languages often have lightweight syntax, for example favouring the use of whitespace and layout rather than punctuation for expressing program structure, and strongly supporting orthogonality of naming in the sense that both symbolic as well as alphabetic identifiers may be used in definitions. Both of these features improve flexibility, so that an embedded DSL can have a syntax close to what one might provide for a corresponding standalone DSL. Of course, there are functional languages with noisy syntactic conventions, and non-functional languages with quiet ones, so this factor does not map precisely onto the language paradigm. We make no more of it in this article, simply using Haskell syntax for convenience.

We use a number of little examples of embedded DSLs throughout the first part of the article. We conclude in Sect. 4, with a more detailed study of one particular embedded DSL, namely Yorgey's Diagrams package [5].

2 Exploring the Design Space

In the interests of focussing on the essence of DSLs, we start with a very simple example: a DSL for finite sets of integers. This consists of a representation of sets, and a number of operations manipulating that representation:

```
type IntegerSet = ...

empty  :: IntegerSet
insert :: Integer → IntegerSet → IntegerSet
delete :: Integer → IntegerSet → IntegerSet
member :: Integer → IntegerSet → Bool
```

For example, one might evaluate the expression

$member\ 3\ (insert\ 1\ (delete\ 3\ (insert\ 2\ (insert\ 3\ empty))))$

and get the result *False* (assuming the usual semantics of these operations).

2.1 Libraries

The first approach one might take to implementing this characterisation of integer sets might be as a *library*, that is, as a collection of related functions. For example, one might represent the set as a list, possibly with duplicates and treating order as insignificant:

type *IntegerSet* = [*Integer*]   -- unsorted, duplicates allowed

empty :: *IntegerSet*
empty = []

insert :: *Integer* → *IntegerSet* → *IntegerSet*
insert x xs   = *x* : *xs*

delete :: *Integer* → *IntegerSet* → *IntegerSet*
delete x xs   = *filter* (≢ *x*) *xs*

member :: *Integer* → *IntegerSet* → *Bool*
member x xs = *any* (≡ *x*) *xs*

(Here, the standard library function $any\ p\ =\ foldr\ ((\lor) \circ p)\ False$ determines whether any element of a list satisfies predicate p.)

We have been writing code in this style—that is, collections of types and related functions—from the earliest days of computing. Indeed, compilers are so called because they 'compile' (collect and assemble the pieces for) an executable by linking together the programmer's main program with the necessary functions from the library. The problem with this style is that there is no encapsulation of the data representation: it is evident to all clients of the abstraction that the representation uses lists, and client code may exploit this knowledge by using other list functions on the representation. The representation is public knowledge, and it becomes very difficult to change it later.

2.2 Modules

The realisation that libraries expose data representations prompted the notion of *modular programming*, especially as advocated by Parnas [6]: code should be partitioned into modules, and in particular, the modules should be chosen so that each hides a design decision (such as, but not necessarily, a choice of data representation) from all the others, allowing that decision subsequently to be changed.

The modular style that Parnas espouses presupposes mutable state: the module hides a single data structure, and operations query and modify the value of that data structure. Because of this dependence on mutable state, it is a little awkward to write in the Parnas style in a pure functional language like Haskell. To capture this behaviour using only pure features, one adapts the operations so that each accepts the 'current' value of the data structure as an additional argument, and returns the 'updated' value as an additional result. Thus, an impure function of type $a \to b$ acting statefully on a data structure of type s can be represented as a pure function of type $(a, s) \to (b, s)$, or equivalently by currying, $a \to (s \to (b, s))$. The return part $s \to (b, s)$ of this is an instance of the *state monad*, implemented in the Haskell standard library as a type *State s b*. Then the set module can be written as follows:

```
module SetModule (Set, runSet, insert, delete, member) where
    type IntegerSet = [Integer]
    newtype Set a = S { runS :: State IntegerSet a }
    instance Monad Set where
        return a = S (return a)
        m >>= k = S (runS m >>= (runS ∘ k))

    runSet :: Set a → a
    runSet x = evalState (runS x) []

    insert :: Integer → Set ()
    insert x  = S $ do { modify (x:) }

    delete :: Integer → Set ()
    delete x  = S $ do { modify (filter (≢ x)) }

    member :: Integer → Set Bool
    member x = S $ do { xs ← get; return (any (≡ x) xs) }
```

Here, the type *Set* of stateful operations on the set is abstract: the representation is not exported from the module, only the type and an observer function *runSet* are. The operations *insert*, *delete*, and *member* are also exported; they may be sequenced together to construct larger computations on the set. But the only way of observing this larger computation is via *runSet*, which initialises the set to empty before running the computation. Haskell's **do** notation conveniently hides the plumbing required to pass the set representation from operation to operation:

```
runSet $ do { insert 3; insert 2; delete 3; insert 1; member 3 }
```

(To be precise, this stateful programming style does not really use mutable state: all data is still immutable, and each operation that 'modifies' the set in fact constructs a fresh data structure, possibly sharing parts of the original. Haskell does support true mutable state, with imperative in-place modifications; but to do this with the same interface as above requires the use of unsafe features, in particular *unsafePerformIO*.)

2.3   Abstract Datatypes

Parnas's approach to modular programming favours modules that hide a single data structure; the attentive reader will note that it is easy to add a *union* operation to the library, but difficult to add one to the module. A slightly different approach is needed to support data abstractions that encompass multiple data structures—*abstract datatypes*. In this case, the module exports an abstract type, which specifies the hidden representation, together with operations to create, modify and observe elements of this type.

> **module** *SetADT* (*IntegerSet, empty, insert, delete, member*) **where**
>
> **newtype** *IntegerSet* = *IS* [*Integer*]
>
> *empty* :: *IntegerSet*
> *empty* = *IS* [ ]
>
> *insert* :: *IntegerSet* → *Integer* → *IntegerSet*
> *insert* (*IS xs*) *x*   = *IS* (*x* : *xs*)
>
> *delete* :: *IntegerSet* → *Integer* → *IntegerSet*
> *delete* (*IS xs*) *x*   = *IS* (*filter* ($\not\equiv x$) *xs*)
>
> *member* :: *IntegerSet* → *Integer* → *Bool*
> *member* (*IS xs*) *x* = *any* ($\equiv x$) *xs*

Note that in addition to the three operations *insert*, *delete* and *member* exported by *SetModule*, we now export the operation *empty* to create a new set, and the abstract type *IntegerSet* so that we can represent its result, but not the constructor *IS* that would allow us to deconstruct sets and to construct them by other means than the provided operations. Note also that we can revert to a purely functional style; there is no monad, and 'modifiers' manifestly construct new sets—this was not an option when there was only one set. Finally, note that we have rearranged the order of arguments of the three operations, so that the source set is the first argument; this gives the feeling of an object-oriented style, whereby one 'sends the *insert* message to an *IntegerSet* object':

> (((((*empty* 'insert' 3) 'insert' 2) 'delete' 3) 'insert' 1) 'member' 3

2.4   Languages

One might, in fact, think of the abstract datatype *SetADT* as a DSL for sets, and the set expression above as a term in this DSL—there is at best a fuzzy line between ADTs and embedded DSLs. If one were to make a formal distinction between 'languages' and 'libraries', it would presumably be that a 'language' privileges one particular datatype whose elements represent terms in the language, with constructors that compose terms, and observers that analyse terms; a 'library', on the other hand, is just a collection of related functions, and may have no one such privileged datatype.

The *SetADT* implementation above can be seen as an intermediate point on the continuum between two extreme approaches to implementing embedded

DSLs: *deep* and *shallow embedding*. In a deep embedding, the operations that construct elements of the abstraction do as little work as possible—they simply preserve their arguments in an abstract syntax tree.

```
module SetLangDeep (IntegerSet (Empty, Insert, Delete), member) where
    data IntegerSet :: * where
        Empty ::                          IntegerSet
        Insert :: IntegerSet → Integer → IntegerSet
        Delete :: IntegerSet → Integer → IntegerSet

    member :: IntegerSet → Integer → Bool
    member Empty         y = False
    member (Insert xs x) y = (y ≡ x) ∨ member xs y
    member (Delete xs x) y = (y ≢ x) ∧ member xs y
```

Now we declare and export an algebraic datatype *IntegerSet* as the implementation of the three operations that yield a set; we have used Haskell's generalised algebraic datatype notation to emphasise their return types, even though we make no use of the extra expressive power of GADTs. The *member* operation, on the other hand, is implemented as a traversal over the terms of the language, and is not itself part of the language.

$$((((Empty \; `Insert` \; 3) \; `Insert` \; 2) \; `Delete` \; 3) \; `Insert` \; 1) \; `member` \; 3$$

Whereas in a deep embedding the constructors do nothing and the observers do all the work, in a shallow embedding it is the other way round: the observers are trivial, and all the computation is in the constructors. Given that the sole observer in our set abstraction is the membership function, the shallow embedding represents the set directly as this membership function:

```
module SetLangShallow (IntegerSet, empty, insert, delete, member) where
    newtype IntegerSet = IS (Integer → Bool)

    empty   ::                          IntegerSet
    empty            = IS (λy → False)

    insert   :: IntegerSet → Integer → IntegerSet
    insert (IS f) x = IS (λy → (y ≡ x) ∨ f y)

    delete   :: IntegerSet → Integer → IntegerSet
    delete (IS f) x = IS (λy → (y ≢ x) ∧ f y)

    member :: IntegerSet → Integer → Bool
    member (IS f) = f
```

It is used in exactly the same way as the *SetADT* definition:

$$((((empty \; `insert` \; 3) \; `insert` \; 2) \; `delete` \; 3) \; `insert` \; 1) \; `member` \; 3$$

We have only a single observer, so the shallow embedding is as precisely that observer, and the observer itself is essentially the identity function. More generally, there may be multiple observers; then the embedding would be as a tuple of values, and the observers would be projections.

In a suitable sense, the deep embedding can be seen as the most abstract implementation possible of the given interface, and the shallow embedding as the most concrete: there are transformations from the deep embedding to any intermediate implementation, such as $SetADT$—roughly,

$$elements :: SetLangDeep.IntegerSet \rightarrow SetADT.IntegerSet$$
$$elements\ Empty\qquad = [\,]$$
$$elements\ (Insert\ xs\ x) = x : elements\ xs$$
$$elements\ (Delete\ xs\ x) = filter\ (\neq x)\ (elements\ xs)$$

and from this to the shallow embedding—roughly,

$$membership :: SetADT.IntegerSet \rightarrow SetLangShallow.IntegerSet$$
$$membership\ xs = \lambda x \rightarrow any\ (\equiv x)\ xs$$

Expressed categorically, there is a category of implementations and transformations between them, and in this category the deep embedding is the initial object and the shallow embedding the final object [7]. The shallow embedding arises by deforesting the abstract syntax tree that forms the basis of the deep embedding.

Kamin [8] calls deep and shallow embedding *operational* and *denotational domain modelling*, respectively, and advocates the latter in preference to the former. Erwig and Walkingshaw [9] call shallow embedding *semantics-driven design*, and also favour it over what they might call *syntax-driven design*.

Deep embedding makes it easier to extend the DSL with new observers, such as new analyses of programs in the language: just define a new function by induction over the abstract syntax. But it is more difficult to extend the syntax of the language with new operators, because each extension entails revisiting the definitions of all existing observers. Conversely, shallow embedding makes new operators easier to add than new observers. This dichotomy is reminiscent of that between OO programs structured around the VISITOR pattern [10] and those in the traditional OO style with methods attached to subclasses of an abstract *Node* class [11]. The challenge of getting the best of both worlds—extensibility in both dimensions at once—has been called the *expression problem* [12].

2.5   Embedded and Standalone

All the approaches described above have been for *embedded* DSLs, of one kind or another: 'programs' in the DSL are simply expressions in the host language. An alternative approach is given by *standalone* DSLs. As the name suggests, a standalone DSL is quite independent of its implementation language: it may have its own syntax, which need bear no relation to that of the implementation language—indeed, the same standalone DSL may have many implementations, in many different languages, which need have little in common with each other.

Of course, being standalone, the DSL cannot depend on any of the features of any of its implementation languages; everything must be build independently, using more or less standard compiler technology: lexer, parser, optimiser, code generator, etc.

Fortunately, there is a shortcut. It turns out that a standalone DSL can share much of the engineering of the embedded DSL—especially if one is not so worried about absolute performance, and is more concerned about ease of implementation. The standalone DSL can be merely a frontend for the embedded DSL; one only needs to write a parser converting strings in the standalone DSL to terms in the embedded DSL. (In fact, Parnas made a similar point over forty years ago [6]: he found that many of the design decisions—and hence the modules—could be shared between a compiler and an interpreter for the same language, in his case for Markov processes.)

For example, suppose that we are given a type *Parser a* of parsers reading values of type *a*

type *Parser a* = ...

and an observer that applies a parser to a string and returns either a value or an error message:

runParser :: *Parser a* → *String* → *Either a String*

Then one can write a parser *program* :: *Parser Bool* for little set programs in a special syntax; perhaps "{}+3+2-3+1?3" should equate to the example expressions above, with "{}" denoting the empty set, "+" and "−" the insertion and deletion operations, and "?" the membership test. Strings recognised by *program* are interpreted in terms of *insert*, *delete* etc., using one of the various implementations of sets described above. Then a simple wrapper program reads a string from the command line, tries to parse it, and writes out the Boolean result or an error message:

```
main :: IO ()
main = do
  ss ← getArgs
  case ss of
    [s] → case runParser program s of        -- single arg
      Left b  → putStrLn ("OK: " ++ show b)    -- parsed
      Right s → putStrLn ("Failed: " ++ s)     -- not parsed
      _       → do                             -- zero or multiple args
        n ← getProgName
        putStrLn ("Usage: " ++ n ++ " <set-expr>")
```

Thus, from the command line:

```
> ./sets "{}+3+2-3+1?3"
OK: False
```

Of course, parsers can be expressed as another DSL; We will return to this example in Sect. 3.3.

3 Functional Programming for Embedded DSLs

Having looked around the design space a little, we now step back to consider what it is about functional programming that makes it particularly convenient for implementing embedded DSLs. After all, a good proportion of the work on DSLs expressed in the functional paradigm focusses on embedded DSLs; and conversely, most work on DSLs in other (such as OO) paradigms focusses on standalone DSLs. Why is that? We contend that there are three main aspects of modern functional programming that play a part: they are both useful for implementing embedded DSLs, and absent from most other programming paradigms. These are *algebraic datatypes*, *higher-order functions*, and (perhaps to a lesser extent) *lazy evaluation*. We discuss each in turn, and illustrate with more simple examples of embedded DSLs. Some parts are left as exercises.

3.1 Algebraic Datatypes

The deep embedding approach depends crucially on algebraic datatypes, which are used to represent abstract syntax trees for programs in the language. Without a lightweight mechanism for defining and manipulating new tree-like datatypes, this approach becomes unworkably tedious.

Algebraic datatypes are extremely convenient for representing abstract syntax trees within the implementation of a DSL. Operations and observers typically have simple recursive definitions, inductively defined over the structure of the tree; optimisations and transformations are often simple rearrangements of the tree—for example, rotations of tree nodes to enforce right-nesting of associative operators.

In addition to this, algebraic datatypes are also extremely convenient for making connections outside the DSL implementation. Often the DSL is one inhabitant of a much larger software ecosystem; while an embedded implementation within a functional programming language may be the locally optimal choice for this DSL, it may have to interface with other inhabitants of the ecosystem, which for legacy reasons or because of other constraints require completely different implementation paradigms. (For example, one might have a DSL for financial contracts, interfacing with Microsoft Excel at the front end for ease of use by domain specialists, and with monolithic C++ pricing engines at the back end for performance.) Algebraic datatypes form a very useful marshalling format for integration, parsed from strings as input and pretty-printed back to strings as output.

Consider a very simple language of arithmetic expressions, involving integer constants and addition. As a deeply embedded DSL, this can be captured by the following algebraic datatype:

data *Expr* = *Val Integer*
         | *Add Expr Expr*

Some people call this datatype *Hutton's Razor*, because Graham Hutton has been using it for years as a minimal vehicle for exploring many aspects of compilation [13].

Exercises

1. Write an observer for the expression language, evaluating expressions as integers.

   $$eval :: Expr \rightarrow Integer$$

2. Write another observer, printing expressions as strings.

   $$print :: Expr \rightarrow String$$

3. Reimplement the expression language using a shallow embedding, such that the interpretation is that of evaluations.

   type *Expr* = *Integer*
   val :: *Integer*   → *Expr*
   add :: *Expr* → *Expr* → *Expr*

4. Reimplement the expression language via a shallow embedding again, but this time such that the interpretation is that of printing.

   type *Expr* = *String*
   val :: *Integer*   → *Expr*
   add :: *Expr* → *Expr* → *Expr*

5. Reimplement via a shallow embedding again, such that the interpretation provides *both* evaluation and printing.
6. What interpretation of the shallow embedding provides the deep embedding? Conversely, given the deep embedding, what additional computation is needed to obtain the various interpretations we have used as shallow embeddings?
7. What if you wanted a third interpretation, say computing the *size* of an expression? What if you wanted to allow ten different interpretations? What about allowing for unforeseen future interpretations?

3.2   Generalised Algebraic Datatypes

The *Expr* DSL above is untyped, or rather "unityped": there is only a single type involved, namely integer expressions. Suppose that we want to represent both integer- and Boolean-valued expressions:

data *Expr* = *ValI Integer*
           | *Add Expr Expr*
           | *ValB Boolean*
           | *And Expr Expr*
           | *EqZero Expr*
           | *If Expr Expr Expr*

The idea is that *EqZero* yields a Boolean value (whether its argument evaluates to zero), and *If* should take a Boolean-valued expression as its first argument. But what can we do for the evaluation function? Sometimes it should return an integer, sometimes a Boolean. One simple solution is to make it return an *Either* type:

$$eval :: Expr \rightarrow Either\ Integer\ Bool$$
$$eval\ (ValI\ n)\quad = Left\ n$$
$$eval\ (Add\ x\ y)\quad = \textbf{case}\ (eval\ x, eval\ y)\ \textbf{of}\ (Left\ m, Left\ n) \rightarrow Left\ (m + n)$$
$$eval\ (ValB\ b)\quad = Right\ b$$
$$eval\ (And\ x\ y)\quad = \textbf{case}\ (eval\ x, eval\ y)\ \textbf{of}\ (Right\ a, Right\ b) \rightarrow Right\ (a \wedge b)$$
$$eval\ (EqZero\ x) = \textbf{case}\ eval\ x\ \textbf{of}\ Left\ n \rightarrow Right\ (n \equiv 0)$$
$$eval\ (If\ x\ y\ z)\quad = \textbf{case}\ eval\ x\ \textbf{of}\ Right\ b \rightarrow \textbf{if}\ b\ \textbf{then}\ eval\ y\ \textbf{else}\ eval\ z$$

This is rather clumsy. For one thing, *eval* has become a partial function; there are improper values of type *Expr* such as *EqZero* (*ValB True*) on which *eval* is undefined. For a second, all the tagging and untagging of return types is a source of inefficiency. Both of these problems are familiar symptoms of dynamic type checking; if we could statically check the types instead, then we could rule out ill-typed programs, and also abolish the runtime tags—a compile-time proof of well-typedness prevents the former and eliminates the need for the latter.

A more sophisticated solution, and arguably The Right Way, is to use dependent types, as discussed by Edwin Brady elsewhere in this Summer School. There are various techniques one might use; for example, one might tuple values with value-level codes for types, provide an interpretation function from codes to the types they stand for, and carry around "proofs" that values do indeed inhabit the type corresponding to their type code.

Haskell provides an intermediate, lightweight solution in the form of *type indexing*, through so-called *generalised algebraic datatypes* or GADTs. Let us rewrite the *Expr* datatype in an equivalent but slightly more repetitive form:

```
data Expr :: * where
    ValI   :: Integer              → Expr
    Add    :: Expr → Expr          → Expr
    ValB   :: Bool                 → Expr
    And    :: Expr → Expr          → Expr
    EqZero :: Expr                 → Expr
    If     :: Expr → Expr → Expr → Expr
```

This form lists the signatures of each of the constructors; of course, they are all constructors for the datatype *Expr*, so they all repeat the same return type *Expr*. But this redundancy allows us some flexibility: we might allow the constructors to have different return types. Specifically, GADTs allow the constructors of a polymorphic datatype to have return types that are instances of the type being returned, rather than the full polymorphic type.

In this case, we make *Expr* a polymorphic type, but only provide constructors for values of type *Expr Integer* and *Expr Bool*, and not for other instances of the polymorphic type *Expr a*.

data *Expr* :: ∗ → ∗ **where**
> *ValI* :: *Integer*   → *Expr Integer*
> *Add*   :: *Expr Integer* → *Expr Integer* → *Expr Integer*
> *ValB* :: *Bool*   → *Expr Bool*
> *And*   :: *Expr Bool* → *Expr Bool*   → *Expr Bool*
> *EqZero* :: *Expr Integer*   → *Expr Bool*
> *If*   :: *Expr Bool* → *Expr a* → *Expr a* → *Expr a*

We use the type parameter as an index: a term of type *Expr a* is an expression that evaluates to a value of type *a*. Evaluation becomes much simpler:

> *eval* :: *Expr a* → *a*
> *eval* (*ValI n*)   = *n*
> *eval* (*Add x y*) = *eval x* + *eval y*
> *eval* (*ValB b*)   = *b*
> *eval* (*And x y*) = *eval x* ∧ *eval y*
> *eval* (*EqZero x*) = *eval x* ≡ 0
> *eval* (*If x y z*) = **if** *eval x* **then** *eval y* **else** *eval z*

As well as being simpler, it is also safer (there is no possibility of ill-typed expressions, and *eval* is a total function again) and swifter (there are no runtime *Left* and *Right* tags to manipulate any more).

Exercises

8. The type parameter *a* in *Expr a* is called a *phantom type*: it does not represent contents, as the type parameter in a container datatype such as *List a* does, but some other property of the type. Indeed, there need be no *Bool*ean inside an expression of type *Expr Bool*; give an expression of type *Expr Bool* that contains no *Bool*s. Is there always an *Integer* inside an expression of type *Expr Integer*?

9. How do Exercises 2–7 work out in terms of GADTs?

3.3 Higher-Order Functions

Deep embeddings lean rather heavily on algebraic datatypes. Conversely, shallow embeddings depend on *higher-order functions*—functions that accept functions as arguments or return them as results—and more generally on *functions as first-class citizens* of the host language. A simple example where this arises is if we were to extend the *Expr* DSL to allow for **let** bindings and variable references:

> *val* :: *Integer*   → *Expr*
> *add* :: *Expr* → *Expr*   → *Expr*
> *var* :: *String*   → *Expr*
> *bnd* :: (*String, Expr*) → *Expr* → *Expr*

The idea is that *bnd* represents **let**-bindings and *var* represents variable references, so that

$$bnd\ (\text{"x"}, val\ 3)\ (add\ (var\ \text{"x"})\ (var\ \text{"x"}))$$

corresponds to the Haskell expression **let** $x = 3$ **in** $x + x$. The standard structure of an evaluator for languages with such bindings is to pass in and manipulate an *environment* of bindings from variables to values (not to expressions):

type $Env = [(String, Integer)]$
$eval :: Expr \rightarrow Env \rightarrow Integer$

The environment is initially empty, but is augmented when evaluating the body of a **let** expression. With a shallow embedding, the interpretation *is* the evaluation function:

type $Expr = Env \rightarrow Integer$

That is, expressions are represented not as integers, or strings, or pairs, but as functions (from environments to values).

Exercises

10. Complete the definition of the *Expr* DSL with **let** bindings, via a shallow embedding whose interpretation provides evaluation in an environment.
11. Look again at Exercise 7: can we define a shallow embedding that allows for unforeseen future interpretations? Hint: consider a 'generic' or 'parametrised' interpretation, as a higher-order function, which can be instantiated to yield evaluation, or printing, or any of a number of other concrete interpretations. What is common to the evaluation and printing interpretations above, and what is specific? What kinds of function is it sensible to consider as 'interpretations', and what should be ruled out?

A larger and very popular example of shallow embeddings with functional interpretations is given by *parser combinators*. Recall the type *Parser a* of parsers recognising values of type a from Sect. 2.5; such a parser is roughly a function of type $String \rightarrow a$. But we will want to combine parsers sequentially, so it is important that a parser also returns the remainder of the string after recognising a chunk; so it would be better to use functions of type $String \rightarrow (a, String)$. But we will also want to allow parsers that fail to match, so that we can try a series of alternatives until one matches, and more generally parsers that match in multiple ways; so it is better still to return a list of results:

type $Parser\ a = String \rightarrow [(a, String)]$

(Technically, these are more than just parsers, because they combine semantic actions with recognising and extracting structure from strings. But the terminology is well established.)

The *runParser* function introduced in Sect. 2.5 takes such a parser and an input string, and returns either a successful result or an error message:

$runParser :: Parser\ a \rightarrow String \rightarrow Either\ a\ String$
$runParser\ p\ s = \textbf{case}\ p\ s\ \textbf{of}$

$[(a, s)] \rightarrow$ **if** *all isSpace s* **then** *Left a*

$\qquad\qquad$ **else** *Right* ("Leftover input: " $+\!\!+ s$)

$[\,]\qquad\;\; \rightarrow Right$ "No parse"

$x\qquad\;\; \rightarrow Right$ ("Ambiguous, with leftovers " $+\!\!+ show\ (map\ snd\ x)$)

If the parser yields a single match, and any leftover input is all whitespace, we return that value; if there is a nontrivial remainder, no match, or multiple matches, we return an error message.

Such parsers can be assembled from the following small set of combinators:

$success :: a \qquad\qquad\qquad\qquad \rightarrow Parser\ a$

$failure ::\qquad\qquad\qquad\qquad\;\; Parser\ a$

$(\langle*\rangle)\quad :: Parser\ (a \rightarrow b) \rightarrow Parser\ a \rightarrow Parser\ b$

$(\langle|\rangle)\quad :: Parser\ a \rightarrow Parser\ a \qquad \rightarrow Parser\ a$

$match :: (Char \rightarrow Bool) \qquad\quad\; \rightarrow Parser\ Char$

In other words, these are the operators of a small DSL for parsers. The intention is that: parser *success x* always succeeds, consumes no input, and returns x; *failure* always fails; $p \langle*\rangle q$ is a kind of sequential composition, matching according to p (yielding a function) and then on the remaining input to q (yielding an argument), and applying the function to the argument; $p \langle|\rangle q$ is a kind of choice, matching according to p or to q; and *match b* matches the single character at the head of the input, if this satisfies b, and fails if the input is empty or the head does not satisfy.

We can implement the DSL via a shallow embedding, such that the interpretation is the type *Parser a*. Each operator has a one- or two-line implementation:

$success :: a \rightarrow Parser\ a$

$success\ x\ s\quad\; = [(x, s)]$

$failure :: Parser\ a$

$failure\ s\qquad = [\,]$

$(\langle*\rangle) :: Parser\ (a \rightarrow b) \rightarrow Parser\ a \rightarrow Parser\ b$

$(p \langle*\rangle q)\ s\quad = [(f\ a, s'') \mid (f, s') \leftarrow p\ s, (a, s'') \leftarrow q\ s']$

$(\langle|\rangle) :: Parser\ a \rightarrow Parser\ a \rightarrow Parser\ a$

$(p \langle|\rangle q)\ s\quad = p\ s +\!\!+ q\ s$

$match :: (Char \rightarrow Bool) \rightarrow Parser\ Char$

$match\ q\ [\,]\quad = [\,]$

$match\ q\ (c : s) = $ **if** $q\ c$ **then** $[(c, s)]$ **else** $[\,]$

From the basic operators above, we can derive many more, without depending any further on the representation of parsers as functions. In each of the following exercises, the answer is another one- or two-liner.

Exercises

12. Implement two variations of sequential composition, in which the first (respectively, the second) recognised value is discarded. These are useful when one of the recognised values is mere punctuation.

    $(*\rangle) :: Parser\ a \rightarrow Parser\ b \rightarrow Parser\ b$
    $(\langle*) :: Parser\ a \rightarrow Parser\ b \rightarrow Parser\ a$

13. Implement iteration of parsers, so-called Kleene plus (*some*) and Kleene star (*many*), which recognise one or more (respectively, zero or more) occurrences of what their argument recognises.

    $some, many :: Parser\ a \rightarrow Parser\ [a]$

14. Implement a *whitespace* parser, which recognises a non-empty section of whitespace characters (you might find the Haskell standard library function *Data.Char.isSpace* helpful). Implement a variation *ows* for which the whitespace is optional. For both of these, we suppose that the actual nature of the whitespace is irrelevant, and should be discarded.

    $whitespace, ows :: Parser\ ()$

15. Implement a parser *token*, which takes a string and recognises exactly and only that string at the start of the input. Again, we assume that the string so matched is irrelevant, since we know precisely what it will be.

    $token :: String \rightarrow Parser\ ()$

16. Now implement the parser *program* from Sect. 2.5, which recognises a "set program". A set program starts with the empty set {}, has zero or more insert (+) and delete (-) operations, and a mandatory final member (?) operation. Each operation is followed by an integer argument. Optional whitespace is allowed in all sensible places.

    $program :: Parser\ Bool$

3.4   Lazy Evaluation

A third aspect of modern functional programming that lends itself to embedded DSLs—albeit, perhaps, less important than algebraic datatypes and higher-order functions—is *lazy evaluation*. Under this strategy, evaluation is demand-driven, and function arguments are not evaluated until their value is needed to determine the next step (for example, to determine which of multiple clauses of a definition to apply); and moreover, once an argument is evaluated, that value is preserved and reused rather than being discarded and recomputed for subsequent uses.

One nice consequence of lazy evaluation is that infinite data structures work just as well as finite ones: as long as finite parts of the result of a function can be constructed from just finite parts of the input, the complete infinite data structure may not need ever to be constructed. This is sometimes convenient for a shallow embedding, allowing one to use a datatype of infinite data structures for the domain of interpretation. This can lead to simpler programs than would be the case if one were restricted to finite data structures—in the latter case, some terminating behaviour has to be interwoven with the generator, whereas in the former, the two can be quite separate. But we will not study infinite data structures further in this article.

A second consequence of lazy evaluation manifests itself even in finite data: if one component of a result is not used anywhere, it is not evaluated. This is very convenient for shallow embeddings of DSLs with multiple observers. The interpretation is then as a tuple containing all the observations of a term; but if some of those observations are not used, they need not be computed.

Exercises

17. Review Exercise 5, which was to define a shallow embedding interpreted as a pair, providing both evaluation and printing. Convince yourself that if only one component of the pair is demanded, only that component gets computed.
18. Here is an alternative technique for allowing for multiple observers with a shallow embedding. It is presented here using Haskell type classes; but the general idea is about having a data abstraction with an interface and a choice of implementations, and doing abstract interpretation in one of those implementations. For simplicity, let us return to Hutton's Razor

> **type** $Expr = ...$
> $val :: Integer \quad\quad \rightarrow Expr$
> $add :: Expr \rightarrow Expr \rightarrow Expr$

with two desired observers

> $eval \ :: Expr \rightarrow Integer$
> $print :: Expr \rightarrow String$

The trick is to define $Expr$ as a type class, the class of those types suitable as representations of expressions according to this little DSL. What operations must a type support, if it is to be suitable for representing expressions? It needs to have at least the val and add operations:

> **class** $Expr \ a$ **where**
> $val \ :: Integer \rightarrow a$
> $add :: a \rightarrow a \ \rightarrow a$

Of course, it is easy to define these two operations on integers:

> **instance** $Expr \ Integer$ **where**
> $val \ n \quad = n$
> $add \ x \ y = x + y$

It is also easy to define them on strings:

```
instance Expr String where
  val n   = show n
  add x y = "(" ++ x ++ "+" ++ y ++ ")"
```

Now, a term in the expression DSL has a polymorphic type: it can be interpreted in *any* type in the type class *Expr*.

```
expr :: Expr a ⇒ a
expr = add (val 3) (val 4)
```

Then evaluating and printing expressions amounts to interpreting the polymorphic type at the appropriate instance:

```
eval_Expr  :: Integer
eval_Expr = expr

print_Expr :: String
print_Expr = expr
```

Try this approach out. (You will find that you need some language extensions for the *String* instance, but the Haskell type checker should guide you in the right direction.) It is a bit of an idiosyncratic way of implementing data abstraction: the implementation is chosen implicitly by fixing a type, rather than explicitly by passing a parameter. This is a slight problem, if you want two different interpretations on the same type, such as compact and verbose printings. What can you do to work around that?

4   An Extended Example: Diagrams

We now turn to a larger example of an embedded DSL, inspired by Brent Yorgey's **diagrams** project [5] for two-dimensional diagrams. That project implements a very powerful language which Yorgey does not name, but which we will call *Diagrams*. But it is also rather a large language, so we will not attempt to cover the whole thing; instead, we build a much simpler language in the same spirit. The **diagrams** project does, however, provide a useful backend to output Scalable Vector Graphics (SVG) files, which we will borrow to save ourselves from having to reinvent one.

4.1   Shapes, Styles, and Pictures

The basics of our diagram DSL can be expressed in three simpler sublanguages, for shapes, styles, and pictures. We express them first via deep embedding. First, there are primitive shapes—as a language, these are not very interesting, because they are non-recursive.

data *Shape*
   = *Rectangle Double Double*
   | *Ellipse Double Double*
   | *Triangle Double*

The parameters of a *Rectangle* specify its width and height; those of an *Ellipse* its x- and y-radii. A *Triangle* is equilateral, with its lowest edge parallel to the x-axis; the parameter is the length of the side.

Then there are drawing styles. A *StyleSheet* is a (possibly empty) sequence of stylings, each of which specifies fill colour, stroke colour, or stroke width. (The defaults are for no fill, and very thin black strokes.)

type *StyleSheet* = [*Styling*]
data *Styling*
   = *FillColour Col*
   | *StrokeColour Col*
   | *StrokeWidth Double*

Here, colours are defined in an external library, which among other things provides a large number of colour constants named according to the W3C SVG Recommendation [14, Sect. 4.4].

type *Col* = ...
red, blue, green, yellow, brown, black ... :: *Col*

Finally, pictures are arrangements of shapes: individual shapes, with styling; or one picture above another, or one beside another. For simplicity, we specify that horizontal and vertical alignment of pictures is by their centres.

data *Picture*
   = *Place StyleSheet Shape*
   | *Above Picture Picture*
   | *Beside Picture Picture*

For example, here is a little stick figure of a woman in a red dress and blue stockings.

figure :: *Picture*
figure = *Place* [*StrokeWidth* 0.1, *FillColour bisque*] (*Ellipse* 3 3) 'Above'
      Place [*FillColour red, StrokeWidth* 0] (*Rectangle* 10 1) 'Above'
      Place [*FillColour red, StrokeWidth* 0] (*Triangle* 10) 'Above'
      (*Place* [*FillColour blue, StrokeWidth* 0] (*Rectangle* 1 5) 'Beside'
       Place [*StrokeWidth* 0] (*Rectangle* 2 5) 'Beside'
       Place [*FillColour blue, StrokeWidth* 0] (*Rectangle* 1 5)) 'Above'
      (*Place* [*FillColour blue, StrokeWidth* 0] (*Rectangle* 2 1) 'Beside'
       Place [*StrokeWidth* 0] (*Rectangle* 2 1) 'Beside'
       Place [*FillColour blue, StrokeWidth* 0] (*Rectangle* 2 1))

The intention is that it should be drawn like this:

(Note that blank spaces can be obtained by rectangles with zero stroke width.)

4.2   Transformations

In order to arrange pictures, we will need to be able to translate them. Later on, we will introduce some other transformations too; with that foresight in mind, we introduce a simple language of transformations—the identity transformation, translations, and compositions of these.

> **type** *Pos* = *Complex Double*

> **data** *Transform*
>   = *Identity*
> | *Translate Pos*
> | *Compose Transform Transform*

For simplicity, we borrow the *Complex* type from the Haskell libraries to represent points in the plane; the point with coordinates (x, y) is represented by the complex number $x :+ y$. *Complex* is an instance of the *Num* type class, so we get arithmetic operations on points too. For example, we can apply a *Transform* to a point:

> *transformPos* :: *Transform* → *Pos* → *Pos*
> *transformPos Identity*   = *id*
> *transformPos* (*Translate p*) = (*p*+)
> *transformPos* (*Compose t u*) = *transformPos t* ∘ *transformPos u*

Exercises

19. *Transform* is represented above via a deep embedding, with a separate observer function *transformPos*. Reimplement *Transform* via a shallow embedding, with this sole observer.

4.3   Simplified Pictures

As it happens, we could easily translate the *Picture* language directly into *Diagrams*: it has equivalents of *Above* and *Beside*, for example. But if we were "executing" our pictures in a less sophisticated setting—for example, if we had to implement the SVG backend from first principles—we would eventually have to simplify recursively structured pictures into a flatter form.

Here, we flatten the hierarchy into a non-empty sequence of transformed styled shapes:

type *Drawing* $= [(\textit{Transform}, \textit{StyleSheet}, \textit{Shape})]$

In order to simplify alignment by centres, we will arrange that each simplified *Drawing* is itself centred: that is, the combined extent of all translated shapes will be centred on the origin. Extents are represented as pairs of points, for the lower left and upper right corners of the orthogonal bounding box.

type *Extent* $= (\textit{Pos}, \textit{Pos})$

The crucial operation on extents is to compute their union:

unionExtent :: *Extent* → *Extent* → *Extent*
unionExtent $(llx_1 \mathbin{:\!+} lly_1, urx_1 \mathbin{:\!+} ury_1)\ (llx_2 \mathbin{:\!+} lly_2, urx_2 \mathbin{:\!+} ury_2)$
$\quad = (\textit{min } llx_1\ llx_2 \mathbin{:\!+} \textit{min } lly_1\ lly_2, \textit{max } urx_1\ urx_2 \mathbin{:\!+} \textit{max } ury_1\ ury_2)$

Now, the extent of a drawing is the union of the extents of each of its translated shapes, where the extent of a translated shape is the translation of the two corners of the extent of the untranslated shape:

drawingExtent :: *Drawing* → *Extent*
drawingExtent = *foldr1 unionExtent* ∘ *map getExtent* **where**
$\quad$ *getExtent* $(t, _, s) = $ **let** $(ll, ur) = \textit{shapeExtent } s$
$\qquad\qquad\qquad\qquad$ **in** $(\textit{transformPos } t\ ll, \textit{transformPos } t\ ur)$

(You might have thought initially that since all *Drawings* are kept centred, one point rather than two serves to define the extent. But this does not work: in computing the extent of a whole *Picture*, of course we have to translate its constituent *Drawings* off-centre.) The extents of individual shapes can be computed using a little geometry:

shapeExtent :: *Shape* → *Extent*
shapeExtent $(\textit{Ellipse } xr\ yr)\quad = (-(xr \mathbin{:\!+} yr), xr \mathbin{:\!+} yr)$
shapeExtent $(\textit{Rectangle } w\ h) = (-(^w\!/_2 \mathbin{:\!+} {}^h\!/_2), {}^w\!/_2 \mathbin{:\!+} {}^h\!/_2)$
shapeExtent $(\textit{Triangle } s)\quad = (-(^s\!/_2 \mathbin{:\!+} \sqrt{3} \times {}^s\!/_4), {}^s\!/_2 \mathbin{:\!+} \sqrt{3} \times {}^s\!/_4)$

Now to simplify *Pictures* into *Drawings*, via a straightforward traversal over the structure of the *Picture*.

$$drawPicture :: Picture \rightarrow Drawing$$
$$drawPicture\ (Place\ u\ s)\ = drawShape\ u\ s$$
$$drawPicture\ (Above\ p\ q)\ = drawPicture\ p\ `aboveD`\ drawPicture\ q$$
$$drawPicture\ (Beside\ p\ q) = drawPicture\ p\ `besideD`\ drawPicture\ q$$

All the work is in the individual operations. *drawShape* constructs an atomic styled *Drawing*, centred on the origin.

$$drawShape :: StyleSheet \rightarrow Shape \rightarrow Drawing$$
$$drawShape\ u\ s = [(Identity, u, s)]$$

aboveD and *besideD* both work by forming the "union" of the two child *Drawings*, but first translating each child by the appropriate amount—an amount calculated so as to ensure that the resulting *Drawing* is again centred on the origin.

$$aboveD, besideD :: Drawing \rightarrow Drawing \rightarrow Drawing$$
$$pd\ `aboveD`\ qd\ =\ transformDrawing\ (Translate\ (0 :+ qury))\ pd\ +\!\!+$$
$$\qquad\qquad\qquad transformDrawing\ (Translate\ (0 :+ plly))\ qd\ \textbf{where}$$
$$(pllx :+ plly, pur)\ =\ drawingExtent\ pd$$
$$(qll, qurx :+ qury)\ =\ drawingExtent\ qd$$

$$pd\ `besideD`\ qd = transformDrawing\ (Translate\ (qllx :+ 0))\ pd\ +\!\!+$$
$$\qquad\qquad\qquad transformDrawing\ (Translate\ (purx :+ 0))\ qd\ \textbf{where}$$
$$(pll, purx :+ pury)\ =\ drawingExtent\ pd$$
$$(qllx :+ qlly, qur)\ =\ drawingExtent\ qd$$

This involves transforming the child *Drawings*; but that is easy, given our representation.

$$transformDrawing :: Transform \rightarrow Drawing \rightarrow Drawing$$
$$transformDrawing\ t = map\ (\lambda(t', u, s) \rightarrow (Compose\ t\ t', u, s))$$

Exercises

20. Add *Square* and *Circle* to the available *Shapes*; for simplicity, you can implement these using *rect* and *ellipseXY*.
21. Add *Blank* to the available shapes; implement this as a rectangle with stroke width zero.
22. Centring and alignment, as described above, are only approximations, because we do not take stroke width into account. How would you do so?
23. Add *InFrontOf* :: *Picture* → *Picture* → *Picture* as an operator to the *Picture* language, for placing one *Picture* in front of (that is, on top of) another. Using this, you can draw a slightly less childish-looking stick figure, with the "arms" overlaid on the "body":

24. Add *FlipV* :: *Picture* → *Picture* as an operator to the *Picture* language, for flipping a *Picture* vertically (that is, from top to bottom, about a horizontal axis). Then you can draw this chicken:

You will need to add a corresponding operator *ReflectY* to the *Transform* language; you might note that the *conjugate* function on complex numbers takes $x :+ y$ to $x :+ (-y)$. Be careful in computing the extent of a flipped picture!

25. *Picture* is represented above via a deep embedding, with a separate observer function *drawPicture*. Reimplement *Picture* via a shallow embedding, with this sole observer.

4.4 Generating SVG

The final step is to assemble our simplified *Drawing* into some expression in the *Diagrams* language. What we need are the following:

– A type for representing diagrams.

    type *DiagramSVG* = ...

(This is actually a synonym for a specialisation of a more flexible *Diagrams* type from Yorgey's library.)

– Primitives of type *DiagramSVG*:

    rect   :: *Double* → *Double* → *DiagramSVG*
    ellipseXY :: *Double* → *Double* → *DiagramSVG*
    eqTriangle :: *Double*   → *DiagramSVG*

– An operator for superimposing diagrams:

$$atop :: DiagramSVG \to DiagramSVG \to DiagramSVG$$

– Transformations on diagrams:

$$translate \circ r2 :: (Double, Double) \to DiagramSVG \to DiagramSVG$$
$$reflectY \quad :: \qquad\qquad\qquad DiagramSVG \to DiagramSVG$$

(The latter is needed for Exercise 24.)
– Functions for setting fill colour, stroke colour, and stroke width attributes:

$$fc :: Col \quad \to DiagramSVG \to DiagramSVG$$
$$lc :: Col \quad \to DiagramSVG \to DiagramSVG$$
$$lw :: Double \to DiagramSVG \to DiagramSVG$$

– A wrapper function that writes a diagram out in SVG format to a specified file:

$$writeSVG :: FilePath \to DiagramSVG \to IO\ ()$$

Then a *Drawing* can be assembled into a *DiagramSVG* by laying one translated styled shape on top of another:

```
assemble :: Drawing → DiagramSVG
assemble = foldr1 atop ∘ map draw where
    draw (t, u, s) = transformDiagram t (diagramShape u s)
```

Note that *Shapes* earlier in the list appear "in front" of those later; you will need to use this fact in solving Exercise 23.

A *StyleSheet* represents a sequence of functions, which are composed into one styling function:

```
applyStyleSheet :: StyleSheet → (DiagramSVG → DiagramSVG)
applyStyleSheet = foldr (∘) id ∘ map applyStyling

applyStyling :: Styling → DiagramSVG → DiagramSVG
applyStyling (FillColour c)   = fc c
applyStyling (StrokeColour c) = lc c
applyStyling (StrokeWidth w)  = lw w
```

A single styled shape is drawn by applying the styling function to the corresponding atomic diagram:

```
diagramShape :: StyleSheet → Shape → DiagramSVG
diagramShape u s = shape (applyStyleSheet u) s where
    shape f (Ellipse xr yr)  = f (ellipseXY xr yr)
    shape f (Rectangle w h) = f (rect w h)
```

$$shape\ f\ (Triangle\ s) \quad = f\ (translate\ (r2\ (0, -y))\ (eqTriangle\ s))$$
$$\textbf{where}\ y = s \times {\sqrt{3}}/{12}$$

(The odd translation of the triangle is because we place triangles by their centre, but *Diagrams* places them by their centroid.)

A transformed shape is drawn by transforming the diagram of the underlying shape.

$$transformDiagram :: Transform \rightarrow DiagramSVG \rightarrow DiagramSVG$$
$$transformDiagram\ Identity \qquad = id$$
$$transformDiagram\ (Translate\ (x :+ y)) = translate\ (r2\ (x, y))$$
$$transformDiagram\ (Compose\ t\ u) \quad = transformDiagram\ t\ \circ$$
$$\qquad\qquad\qquad\qquad\qquad\qquad transformDiagram\ u$$

And that is it! (You can look at the source file `Shapes.lhs` for the definition of *writeSVG*, and some other details.)

Exercises

26. In Exercise 19, we reimplemented *Transform* as a shallow embedding, with the sole observer being to transform a point. This does not allow us to apply the same transformations to *DiagramSVG* objects, as required by the function *transformDiagram* above. Extend the shallow embedding of *Transform* so that it has two observers, for transforming both points and diagrams.

27. A better solution to Exercise 26 would be to represent *Transform* via a shallow embedding with a single parametrised observer, which can be instantiated at least to the two uses we require. What are the requirements on such instantiations?

28. Simplifying a *Picture* into a *Drawing* is a bit inefficient, because we have to continually recompute extents. A more efficient approach would be to extend the *Drawing* type so that it caches the extent, as well as storing the list of shapes. Try this.

29. It can be a bit painful to specify a complicated *Picture* with lots of *Shapes* all drawn in a common style—for example, all blue, with a thick black stroke—because those style settings have to be repeated for every single *Shape*. Extend the *Picture* language so that *Pictures* too may have *StyleSheets*; styles should be inherited by children, unless they are overridden.

30. Add an operator *Tile* to the *Shape* language, for square tiles with markings on. It should take a *Double* parameter for the length of the side, and a list of lists of points for the markings; each list of points has length at least two, and denotes a path of straight-line segments between those points. For example, here is one such pattern of markings:

$$markingsP :: [[Pos]]$$
$$markingsP = [[(4 :+ 4), (6 :+ 0)],$$
$$[(0 :+ 3), (3 :+ 4), (0 :+ 8), (0 :+ 3)],$$

$$[(4 :+ 5), (7 :+ 6), (4 :+ 10), (4 :+ 5)],$$
$$[(11 :+ 0), (10 :+ 4), (8 :+ 8), (4 :+ 13), (0 :+ 16)],$$
$$[(11 :+ 0), (14 :+ 2), (16 :+ 2)],$$
$$[(10 :+ 4), (13 :+ 5), (16 :+ 4)],$$
$$[(9 :+ 6), (12 :+ 7), (16 :+ 6)],$$
$$[(8 :+ 8), (12 :+ 9), (16 :+ 8)],$$
$$[(8 :+ 12), (16 :+ 10)],$$
$$[(0 :+ 16), (6 :+ 15), (8 :+ 16), (12 :+ 12), (16 :+ 12)],$$
$$[(10 :+ 16), (12 :+ 14), (16 :+ 13)],$$
$$[(12 :+ 16), (13 :+ 15), (16 :+ 14)],$$
$$[(14 :+ 16), (16 :+ 15)]$$
$$]$$

In Shapes.lhs, you will find this definition plus three others like it. They yield tile markings looking like this:

You can draw such tiles via the function

$$tile :: [[Pos]] \rightarrow DiagramSVG$$

provided for you. Also add operators to the *Picture* and *Transform* languages to support scaling by a constant factor and rotation by a quarter-turn anticlockwise, both centred on the origin. You can implement these on the *DiagramSVG* type using two *Diagrams* operators:

$$scale \qquad :: Double \rightarrow DiagramSVG \rightarrow DiagramSVG$$
$$rotateBy \ (^1/_4) :: \qquad DiagramSVG \rightarrow DiagramSVG$$

Then suitable placements, rotations, and scalings of the four marked tiles will produce a rough version of Escher's "Square Limit" print, as shown in the left-hand image below:

 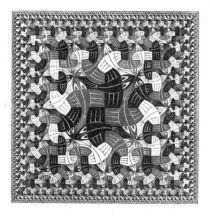

This construction was explored by Peter Henderson in a famous early paper on functional geometry [15,16]; I have taken the data for the markings from a note by Frank Buß [17]. The image on the right is the real "Square Limit" [18].

31. Morally, "Square Limit" is a fractal image: the recursive decomposition can be taken ad infinitum. Because Haskell uses lazy evaluation, that is not an insurmountable obstacle. The datatype *Picture* includes also infinite terms; and because *Diagrams* is an embedded DSL, you can use a recursive Haskell definition to define an infinite *Picture*. You cannot render it directly to SVG, though; that would at best yield an infinite SVG file. But still, you can prune the infinite picture to a finite depth, and then render the result. Construct the infinite *Picture*. (You will probably need to refactor some code. Note that you cannot compute the extent of an infinite *Picture* either—how can you get around that problem?)

Acknowledgements. I am very grateful to the organisers of the Central European Functional Programming Summer School on Domain-Specific Languages in Cluj-Napoca, Romania, for the invitation to speak at the school on the subject of FP and DSLs. My thanks go to the students who provided assistance during the practical sessions: Andrew Bate, Kwok Cheung, Bogdan Panait, and Christopher Rosset. Nick Wu and other members of the Algebra of Programming research group at Oxford made helpful suggestions on the material, and an anonymous reviewer made some suggestions to improve the presentation. This work was partially supported by UK EPSRC grant *Reusability and Dependent Types* (EP/G034516/1).

References

1. Fowler, M.: Domain-Specific Languages. Addison-Wesley, Reading (2011)
2. Mernik, M., Heering, J., Sloane, A.M.: When and how to develop domain-specific languages. ACM Comput. Surv. **37**(4), 316–344 (2005)
3. Bentley, J.: Little languages. Commun. ACM **29**(8), 711–721 (1986). Also in 'More Programming Pearls' (Addison-Wesley, 1988)

4. Boulton, R., Gordon, A., Gordon, M., Harrison, J., Herbert, J., Tassel, J.V.: Experience with embedding hardware description languages in HOL. In: Stavridou, V., Melham, T.F., Boute, R.T. (eds.) Proceedings of the IFIP TC10/WG 10.2 International Conference on Theorem Provers in Circuit Design: Theory, Practice and Experience. Volume A-10 of IFIP Transactions, pp. 129–156. North-Holland/Elsevier, Nijmegen (1992)
5. Yorgey, B.: Diagrams 0.6 (2012). http://projects.haskell.org/diagrams/
6. Parnas, D.L.: On the criteria to be used in decomposing systems into modules. Commun. ACM **15**(12), 1053–1058 (1972)
7. Wand, M.: Final algebra semantics and data type extensions. J. Comput. Syst. Sci. **19**, 27–44 (1979)
8. Kamin, S.: An implementation-oriented semantics of Wadler's pretty-printing combinators. Oregon Graduate Institute (1998). http://www-sal.cs.uiuc.edu/~kamin/pubs/pprint.ps
9. Erwig, M., Walkingshaw, E.: Semantics-driven DSL design. In: Mernik, M. (ed.) Formal and Practical Aspects of Domain-Specific Languages: Recent Developments, 56–80. IGI-Global, Hershey (2012)
10. Gamma, E., Helm, R., Johnson, R., Vlissides, J.: Design Patterns: Elements of Reusable Object-Oriented Software. Addison-Wesley, Reading (1995)
11. Cook, W.R.: On understanding data abstraction, revisited. In: OOPSLA, pp. 557–572. ACM (2009)
12. Wadler, P.L.: The expression problem. Posting to `java-genericity` mailing list (1998)
13. Hutton, G.: Fold and unfold for program semantics. In: Proceedings of the Third ACM SIGPLAN International Conference on Functional Programming, Baltimore, Maryland, pp. 280–288 (1998)
14. W3C: Scalable vector graphics (SVG) 1.1: recognized color keyword names (2011). http://www.w3.org/TR/SVG11/types.html#ColorKeywords
15. Henderson, P.: Functional geometry. In: Lisp and Functional Programming, pp. 179–187 (1982). http://users.ecs.soton.ac.uk/ph/funcgeo.pdf
16. Henderson, P.: Functional geometry. High. Order Symb. Comput. **15**(4), 349–365 (2002). Revision of [15]
17. Buß, F.: Functional geometry (2005). http://www.frank-buss.de/lisp/functional.html
18. Escher, M.C.: Square limit (1964). http://www.wikipaintings.org/en/m-c-escher/square-limit

Structured Parallel Programming with "core" FastFlow

Marco Danelutto$^{(\boxtimes)}$ and Massimo Torquati

Department of Computer Science, University of Pisa, Pisa, Italy
`marco.danelutto@unipi.it, torquati@di.unipi.it`

Abstract. FastFlow is an open source, structured parallel programming framework originally conceived to support highly efficient stream parallel computation while targeting shared memory multi cores. Its efficiency mainly comes from the optimized implementation of the base communication mechanisms and from its layered design. FastFlow eventually provides the parallel applications programmers with a set of ready-to-use, parametric algorithmic skeletons modeling the most common parallelism exploitation patterns. The algorithmic skeleton provided by FastFlow may be freely nested to model more and more complex parallelism exploitation patterns. This tutorial describes the "core" FastFlow, that is the set of skeletons supported since version 1.0 in FastFlow, and outlines the recent advances aimed at (i) introducing new, higher level skeletons and (ii) targeting networked multi cores, possibly equipped with GPUs, in addition to single multi/many core processing elements.

1 Introduction

FastFlow is an algorithmic skeleton (see Fig. 1) programming environment developed and maintained by researchers at the Dept. of Computer Science of the Univ. of Pisa and Univ. of Torino [1]. A number of different papers and technical reports discuss the different features of this programming environment [3,11,16], the kind of results achieved while parallelizing different applications [4,12,14,15,22] and the usage of FastFlow as *software accelerator*, i.e. as a mechanisms suitable to exploit unused cores of a multi core architecture to speedup execution of sequential code [7,8]. This work represents instead a tutorial aimed at instructing programmers in the usage of the FastFlow skeletons and in the typical FastFlow programming techniques.

Therefore, after recalling the FastFlow design principles in Sect. 2, in Sect. 3 we describe the (trivial) installation procedure. Then, in Sects. 4 to 9 we introduce the main features of the FastFlow programming framework: how to implement a simple "hello world" program (Sect. 4), how to manage streams (Sect. 5), how to wrap sequential code (Sect. 6), how to use explicit sharing (Sect. 7) and how to use pipelines and farm (Sects. 8 and 9). Then Sect. 10 deals with FastFlow usage as software accelerator, Sect. 11 discusses how FastFlow skeletons

---

This work has been partially supported by FP7 STREP project "ParaPhrase" (www.paraphrase-ict.eu).

V. Zsók et al. (Eds.): CEFP 2013, LNCS 8606, pp. 29–75, 2015.
DOI: 10.1007/978-3-319-15940-9_2

Algorithmic skeletons have been introduced by M. Cole in late 88 [19]. According to this original work

> The new system presents the user with a selection of independent "algorithmic skeleton", each of which describes the structure of a particular style of algorithm, in the way in which higher order functions represent general computational frameworks in the context of functional programming languages. The user must describe a solution to a problem as an instance of the appropriate skeleton.

Later on, in his algorithmic skeleton "manifesto" [20] this definition evolved as follows:

> many parallel algorithms can be characterized and classified by their adherence to one or more of a number of generic patterns of computation and interaction. For example, many diverse applications share the underlying control and data flow of the pipeline paradigm. Skeletal programming proposes that such patterns be abstracted and provided as a programmer's toolkit, with specifications which transcend architectural variations but implementations which recognize these to enhance performance.

Different research groups started working on the algorithmic skeleton concept and produced different programming frameworks providing the application programmers with algorithmic skeletons. The definition of algorithmic skeletons evolved and eventually a widely shared definition emerged stating that:

> An algorithmic skeleton is parametric, reusable and portable programming abstraction modeling a known, common and efficient parallelism exploitation pattern.

At the moment being, different frameworks exists that provide the application programmers with algorithmic skeletons. Usually, the frameworks provide stream parallel skeletons (pipeline, task farm), data parallel (map, reduce, scan, stencil, divide&conquer) and control parallel (loop, if-then-else) skeletons mostly as libraries to be linked with the application business code. Several programming frameworks are actively maintained, including Muesli http://www.wil.uni-muenster.de/pi/forschung/Skeletons/1.79/index.html, Sketo http://sketo.ipl-lab.org/, OSL http://traclifo.univ-orleans.fr/OSL/, SKEPU http://www.ida.liu.se/~chrke/skepu/, FastFlow http://calvados.di.unipi.it/fastflow, Skandium https://github.com/mleyton/Skandium. A recent survey of algorithmic skeleton frameworks may be found in [28].

Fig. 1. Algorithmic skeletons

may be nested and Sect. 12 discusses how to use "cyclic" skeletons. Eventually Sect. 13 outlines the main FastFlow RTS accessory routines and Sect. 15 outlines the major improvements to the "core" FastFlow currently being designed and implemented (high level patterns, targeting heterogeneous and distributed architectures, refactoring parallel programs).

2   Design Principles

FastFlow[1] has been designed to provide programmers with efficient parallelism exploitation patterns suitable to implement (fine grain) stream parallel applications. In particular, FastFlow has been designed

- to promote high-level parallel programming, and in particular skeletal programming (i.e. pattern-based explicit parallel programming), and
- to promote efficient programming of applications for multi-core.

---

[1] See also the FastFlow home page at http://mc-fastflow.sourceforge.net.

Efficient applications for multi core and many core

⇓

Streaming network patterns pipeline, farm, divide&conquer, ... **Arbitrary streaming networks** Lock free SPMC, MPSC, MPMC queues **Simple streaming networks** Lock free SPSC queues and general threading model (e.g. Pthread)

⇓

Multi core and many-core cc-UMA and cc-NUMA featuring sequential or weak consistency model

Fig. 2. Layered FastFlow design

The whole programming framework has been incrementally developed according to a layered design on top of Pthread/C++ standard programming framework and targets shared memory multi core architectures (see Fig. 2).

A first layer, the **Simple streaming networks** layer, provides very efficient lock-free Single Producers Single Consumer (SPSC) queues on top of the Pthread standard threading model [9].

A second layer, the **Arbitrary streaming networks** layer, provides lock-free implementations for Single Producer Multiple Consumer (SPMC), Multiple Producer Single Consumer (MPSC) and Multiple Producer Multiple Consumer (MPMC) queues on top of the SPSC implemented in the first layer.

Eventually, the third layer, the **Streaming Networks Patterns** layer, provides common stream parallel patterns. The primitive patterns include pipeline and farms. Simple specialization of these patterns may be used to implement more complex patterns, such as divide and conquer, map and reduce patterns.

Parallel application programmers are assumed to use FastFlow directly exploiting the parallel patterns available in the Streaming Network Patterns level. In particular:

- defining sequential concurrent activities, by sub classing a proper FastFlow class, the ff_node class, and
- building complex stream parallel patterns by hierarchically composing sequential concurrent activities, pipeline patterns, farm patterns and their "specialized" versions implementing more complex parallel patterns.

The ff_node sequential concurrent activity abstraction provides suitable ways to define a sequential activity that (a) processes data items appearing on a single input channel and (b) delivers the related results onto a single output channel. Particular cases of ff_nodes may be simply implemented with no input channel or no output channel. The former is used to install a concurrent activity *generating* an output stream (e.g. from data items read from keyboard or from a disk file); the latter to install a concurrent activity *consuming* an input stream (e.g. to present results on a video or to store them on disk).

The pipeline pattern may be used to implement sequences of streaming networks $S_1 \rightarrow \ldots \rightarrow S_k$ with S_i receiving input from S_{i-1} and delivering outputs to S_{i+1}. The generic *stage* S_i may be either a sequential activity or another parallel pattern. When the pipeline is used standalone (i.e. not as component of another skeleton) S_1 must be a stream generator activity and S_k a stream consuming one.

The farm pattern models different embarrassingly (stream) parallel constructs. In its simplest form, it models a master/worker pattern with workers producing no stream data items. Rather the worker consolidate results directly in memory. More complex forms including either an emitter, or a collector of both an emitter and a collector implement more sophisticated patterns:

- by adding an emitter, the user may specify policies, different from the default round robin one, to schedule tasks from the farm input stream to the workers;
- by adding a collector, the user may use workers producing some output values, which are gathered and delivered to the farm output stream by the collector component. Different policies may be implemented on the collector to gather data from the worker and deliver them to the output stream.

In addition, a feedback channel may be added to a farm, moving output results back from the collector (or from the collection of workers in case no collector is specified) back to the emitter input channel.

Specialized versions of the farm may be used to implement more complex patterns, such as:

- divide and conquer, using a farm with feedback loop and proper stream items tagging (input tasks, subtask results, results)
- MISD (multiple instruction single data, that is something computing $f_1(x_i)$, ..., $f_k(x_i)$ out of each x_i appearing onto the input stream) pattern, using a farm with an emitter implementing a broadcast scheduling policy
- map, using an emitter partitioning an input collection and scheduling one partition per worker, and a collector gathering sub-partitions results from the workers and delivering a collection made out of all these results to the output stream.

Actually, in the new versions of FastFlow—built on top of the "core FastFlow" described here—the divide&conquer and the map skeletons have been implemented in proper classes and they are provided to the application programmers as *high level* skeletons. It is worth pointing out the different usage of the core FastFlow skeletons. On the one hand, when using plain pipeline and farms (with or without emitters and collectors) to model staged or embarrassingly parallel computations actually these programming abstractions may be classified as "skeletons" according to the traditional definition of algorithmic skeletons. When using specialized versions of the farm streaming network to implement different parallel patterns, instead, the core FastFlow farm should be considered a kind fo "pattern template", being used to build new patterns rather than to provided a primitive skeletons.

2.1 FastFlow Usage Models

Concerning the usage of FastFlow to support parallel application development on shared memory multi cores, the framework provides two abstractions of structured parallel computation:

- a *skeleton program abstraction* used to implement applications completely modeled according to the algorithmic skeleton concepts. When using this abstraction, the programmer writes a parallel application by providing the business logic code, wrapped into proper ff_node subclasses, a skeleton (composition) modeling the parallelism exploitation pattern of the application and a single command starting the skeleton computation and awaiting for its termination.
- an *accelerator abstraction* used to parallelize (and therefore accelerate) only some parts of an existing application. In this case, the programmer provides a skeleton (composition) which is run on the "spare" cores of the architecture and implements a parallel version of part of the business logic of the application, e.g. the one computing a given $f(x)$. The skeleton (composition) will have its own input and output channels. When an $f(x_j)$ has actually to be computed within the application, rather than writing proper code to call to the sequential f code, the programmer may insert code asynchronously "offloading" x_j to the accelerator skeleton. Later on, when the result of $f(x_j)$ is to be used, some code "reading" accelerator result may be used to retrieve the accelerator computed values.

This second abstraction fully implements the "minimal disruption" principle stated by Cole in his skeleton manifesto [20], as the programmer using the accelerator is only required to program a couple of offload/get_result primitives in place of the single ... = $f(x)$ function call statement (see Sect. 10).

3 Installation

Before entering the details of how FastFlow may be used to implement efficient stream parallel (and not only) programs on shared memory multi core architectures, let's have a look at how FastFlow may be installed[2]. FastFlow is provided as a set of header files. Therefore the installation process is trivial, as it only requires to download the last version of the FastFlow source code from Source-Forge (http://sourceforge.net/projects/mc-fastflow/) by using svn:

svn co https://svn.code.sf.net/p/mc-fastflow/code/fastflow

Once the code has been downloaded, the directory containing the ff subdirectory with the FastFlow header files should be named in the -I flag of g++, such that the header files may be correctly found.

---

[2] We only detail instructions needed to install FastFlow on Linux/Unix/BSD machines here. A Windows port of FastFlow exist, that requires slightly different steps for the installation.

Take into account that, being FastFlow provided as a set of .hpp source files, the -O3 switch is fundamental to obtain good performances. Compiling with no -O3 compiler flag will lead to poor performances because the run-time code will not be optimized by the compiler. Also, remember that the correct compilation of FastFlow programs requires to link the pthread library (-lpthread flag). Sample makefiles are provided both within the $FF_ROOT/tests and the $FF_ROOT/examples directories in the source distribution.

4   Hello World in FastFlow

As all programming frameworks tutorials, we start with a Hello world code, that is a program simply printing a string onto the screen. We first discuss how to implement it sequentially, then we introduce a pipeline skeleton and we show how two stages may be used to print the components of a string in parallel.

In order to implement our sequential Hello world program, we use the following code, that uses a single stage pipeline:

```
1 #include <iostream>
2 #include <ff/pipeline.hpp>
3
4 using namespace ff;
5
6 class Stage1: public ff_node {
7 public:
8
9     void * svc(void * task) {
10         std::cout << "Hello world" << std::endl;
11         return NULL;
12     }
13 };
14
15 int main(int argc, char * argv[]) {
16
17     ff_pipeline pipe;
18     pipe.add_stage(new Stage1());
19
20     if (pipe.run_and_wait_end()<0) {
21         error("running pipeline\n");
22         return -1;
23     }
24
25     return 0;
26 }
```

Line 2 includes all what's needed to compile a FastFlow program just using a pipeline pattern and line 4 instructs the compiler to resolve names looking (also) in the ff namespace. Lines 6 to 13 host the application business logic code, wrapped into a class sub classing ff_node. The void * svc(void *) method[3] wraps the body of the concurrent activity. It is called every time the concurrent activity is given a new data item from its input stream. The input stream data item is passed through the svc input void * parameter. The result of the single invocation of the concurrent activity body is passed back to the FastFlow runtime returning the void * result. In case a NULL is returned, the concurrent activity

---

[3] We use the term svc as a shortcut for "service".

actually terminates itself. The application main only hosts the code needed to setup the FastFlow streaming network and to start the skeleton (composition) computation: lines 17 and 18 declare a pipeline pattern (line 17) and insert a single stage (line 18) in the pipeline. Line 20 starts the computation of the skeleton program and awaits for skeleton computation termination. In case of errors the run_and_wait_end() call returns a negative number (according to the Unix/Linux syscall conventions).

When the program is run, the FastFlow RTS accomplishes to start the pipeline. In turn the first stage is started. When the stage svc returns a NULL, the FastFlow RTS immediately terminates it and the whole program terminates.

If we compile and run the program, we get the following output:

```
1 ffsrc$ g++ -I $FF_ROOT helloworldSimple.cpp -o hello -lpthread
2 ffsrc$ ./hello
3 Hello world
4 ffsrc$
```

There is nothing parallel here, however. The single pipeline stage is run just once and there is nothing else, from the programmer viewpoint, running in parallel.

A more interesting Hello World program may be implemented using a two stage pipeline where the first stage prints the "Hello" and the second one, after getting the results of the computation of the first one, prints "world". In order to implement this behavior, we have to write two sequential concurrent activities and to use them as stages in a pipeline. Additionally, we have to send something out as a result from the first stage to the second stage. Let's assume we just send the string with the word to be printed. The code may be written as follows:

```cpp
1  #include <iostream>
2  #include <ff/pipeline.hpp>
3
4  using namespace ff;
5
6  class Stage1: public ff_node {
7  public:
8
9      void * svc(void * task) {
10         std::cout << "Hello" << std::endl;
11         char * p = new char[10];
12         strcpy(p,"World");
13         sleep(1);
14         return ((void *)p);
15     }
16 };
17
18 class Stage2: public ff_node {
19 public:
20
21     void * svc(void * task) {
22        std::cout << ((char *)task) << std::endl;
23        delete [] (char*)task;
24        return GO_ON;
25     }
26 };
27
28 int main(int argc, char * argv[]) {
29
30     ff_pipeline pipe;
31     pipe.add_stage(new Stage1());
32     pipe.add_stage(new Stage2());
```

```
33
34      if (pipe.run_and_wait_end()<0) {
35          error("running pipeline\n");
36          return −1;
37      }
38
39      return 0;
40 }
```

We define two sequential stages. The first one (lines 6–16) prints the "Hello" message on the screen, then allocates some memory buffer storing the "World" message in the buffer and sending the buffer pointer to the output stream (return command on line 14). The sleep on line 13 is here just for making more evident the FastFlow scheduling of concurrent activities. The second one (lines 18–26) just prints whatever it gets on the input stream (the data item stored after the void * task pointer of svc header on line 21), frees the allocated memory and then returns a GO_ON mark. This mark is interpreted by the FastFlow framework as something indicating: *I finished processing the current task, I give you no result to be delivered onto the output stream, but please keep me alive ready to receive another input task*. The main on lines 28–40 is almost identical to the one of the previous version but for the fact we add two stages to the pipeline pattern. Implicitly, this sets up a streaming network with Stage1 connected by a stream to Stage2. Items delivered on the output stream by Stage1 will be read on the input stream by Stage2. The concurrent activity graph is therefore:

If we compile and run the program, however, we get a kind of unexpected result:

```
 1 ffsrc$ g++ −I $FF_ROOT hello2stages.cpp −o hello2stages −lpthread
 2 ffsrc$ ./hello2stages
 3 Hello
 4 WorldHello
 5
 6 Hello World
 7
 8 Hello World
 9
10 Hello World
11
12 ^C
13 ffsrc$
```

First of all, the program keeps running printing an "Hello world" every second. We in fact terminate the execution through a CONTROL-C. Second, the initial sequence of strings is a little bit strange[4].

The "infinite run" is related to way FastFlow implements concurrent activities. Each ff_node is run as many times as the number of the input data items appearing onto the output stream, unless the svc method returns a NULL. Therefore, if the method returns either a task (pointer) to be delivered onto the concurrent activity output stream, or the GO_ON mark (no data output to the output

---

[4] And depending on the actual number of cores of your machine and on the kind of scheduler used in the operating system, the sequence may vary a little bit.

Value	Semantics
NULL	*Termination*: the svc method has been executed for the last time and will never be executed again
void * ptr	*Result*: the svc method is returning a result to be passed on onto the output stream. It will await to be called again with another input task
GO_ON	*Pass*: the svc method has been executed, no result has been generated (or in case it has been passed on through a ff_send_out but it expects to be called again with another input task)
FF_EOS	*End of stream*: this is the last value generated on the output stream. Other activities may follow, not leading to generation of more output data.

Fig. 3. Legal return values in ff_nodes

stream but continue execution), it is re-executed as soon as there is some input available (the different legal return values from an ff_node are summarized in Fig. 3). The first stage, which has no associated input stream, is re-executed up to the moment it terminates the svc with a NULL. In order to have the program terminating, we may use the following code for Stage1:

```
1  class Stage1: public ff_node {
2  public:
3    void * svc(void * task) {
4      if(task==NULL) {
5        std::cout << "Hello " << std::endl;
6        char * p = new char[10];
7        strcpy(p,"World");
8        sleep(1);
9        first = false;
10       return ((void *)p);
11     }
12     return NULL;
13   }
14 };
```

If we compile and execute the program with this modified Stage1 stage, we'll get an output such as:

```
1  ffsrc$ g++ -I $FF_ROOT hello2terminate.cpp -o hello2terminate -lpthread
2  ffsrc$ ./hello2terminate
3  Hello
4  World
5  ffsrc$
```

that is the program terminates after a single run of the two stages. Now the question is: why the second stage terminated, although the svc method return value states that more work is to be done? The answer is in the stream semantics implemented by FastFlow. FastFlow streaming networks automatically manage end-of-streams. That is, as soon as an ff_node returns a NULL–implicitly declaring he wants to terminate its output stream, the information is propagated to the node consuming the output stream. This nodes will therefore also terminate execution–without actually executing its svc method–and the end of stream will be propagated onto its output stream, if any. This is why Stage2 terminates immediately after the termination of Stage1.

The other problem, namely the appearing of the initial 2 "Hello" strings apparently related to just one "world" string is related to the fact that FastFlow does not guarantee any scheduling semantics of the ff_node svc executions. The first stage delivers a string to the second stage, then it is executed again and again. The sleep inserted in the first stage prevents to accumulate too much "hello" strings on the output stream delivered to the second stage. If we remove the sleep statement, in fact, the output is much more different: we will see on the input a large number of "hello" strings followed by another large number of "world" strings. This because the first stage is enabled to send on its output stream as much data items as of the capacity of the SPSC queue used to implement the stream between the two pipeline stages.

5   Generating a Stream

In order to achieve a better idea of how streams are managed within FastFlow, we slightly change our HelloWorld code in such a way the first stage in the pipeline produces on the output stream n integer data items and then terminates. The second stage prints a "world -i-" message upon receiving each i item onto the input stream.

Recalling the already discussed role of the return value of the svc method, a first version of this program may be implemented using the following code:

```
 1 #include <iostream>
 2 #include <ff/pipeline.hpp>
 3
 4 using namespace ff;
 5
 6 class Stage1: public ff_node {
 7 public:
 8
 9   Stage1(int n):streamlen(n),current(0) {}
10
11   void * svc(void * task) {
12     if(current < streamlen) {
13       current++;
14       std::cout << "Hello number " << current << " " << std::endl;
15       int * p = new int(current);
16       sleep(1);
17       return ((void *)p);
18     }
19     return NULL;
20   }
21 private:
22   int streamlen, current;
23 };
24
25 class Stage2: public ff_node {
26 public:
27
28     void * svc(void * task) {
29       int * i = (int *) task;
30       std::cout << "World -" << *i << "- " << std::endl;
31       delete task;
32       return GO_ON;
33     }
```

```
34  };
35
36  int main(int argc, char * argv[]) {
37
38      ff_pipeline pipe;
39      pipe.add_stage(new Stage1(atoi(argv[1])));
40      pipe.add_stage(new Stage2());
41
42      if (pipe.run_and_wait_end()<0) {
43          error("running pipeline\n");
44          return -1;
45      }
46
47      return 0;
48  }
```

The output we get is the following one:

```
1   ffsrc$ g++ -I$FF_ROOT helloStream.cpp -o helloStream -lpthread
2   ffsrc$ ./helloStream 5
3   Hello number 1
4   Hello number 2World - 1-
5
6   Hello number World -32 -
7
8   World -3- Hello number
9   4
10  Hello number 5World - 4-
11
12  World -5-
13  ffsrc$
```

However, there is another way we can use to generate the stream, which is a little bit more "programmatic". FastFlow makes available an ff_send_out method in the ff_node class, which can be used to direct a data item onto the concurrent activity output stream, without actually using the svc return way.

In this case, we could have written the Stage1 code as follows:

```
1   class Stage1: public ff_node {
2   public:
3
4     Stage1(int n):streamlen(n),current(0) {}
5
6     void * svc(void * task) {
7       while(current < streamlen) {
8         current++;
9         std::cout << "Hello number " << current << " " << std::endl;
10        int * p = new int(current);
11        sleep(1);
12        ff_send_out(p);
13      }
14      return NULL;
15    }
16  private:
17    int streamlen, current;
18  };
```

In this case, the Stage1 is run just once (as it immediately returns a NULL. However, during the single run the svc while loop delivers the intended data items on the output stream through the ff_send_out method. In case the sends fill up the SPSC queue used to implement the stream, the ff_send_out will block up to the moment Stage2 consumes some items and consequently frees space in the SPSC buffers.

6   More on ff_node

The ff_node class actually defines three distinct virtual methods:

```
1 public:
2     virtual void* svc(void * task) = 0;
3     virtual int    svc_init() { return 0; };
4     virtual void   svc_end()   {}
```

The first one is the one defining the behavior of the node while processing the input stream data items. The other two methods are automatically invoked once and for all by the FastFlow RTS when the concurrent activity represented by the node is started (svc_init) and right before it is terminated (svc_end).

These virtual methods may be overwritten in the user supplied ff_node subclasses to implement initialization code and finalization code, respectively. The svc method *must* be overwritten as it is defined as a pure virtual method.

We illustrate the usage of the two methods with another program, computing the Sieve of Eratosthenes. The sieve uses a number of stages in a pipeline. Each stage stores the first integer it got on the input stream. Then it cycles passing onto the output stream only the input stream items which are not multiple of the stored integer. An initial stage injects in the pipeline the sequence of integers starting at 2, up to n. Upon completion, each stage has stored a prime number.

We can implement the Eratosthenes sieve in FastFlow as follows:

```
 1 #include <iostream>
 2 #include <ff/pipeline.hpp>
 3
 4 using namespace ff;
 5
 6 class Sieve: public ff_node {
 7 public:
 8
 9   Sieve(): filter(0) {}
10
11   void * svc(void * task) {
12     unsigned int * t = (unsigned int *)task;
13
14     if (filter == 0) {
15       filter = *t;
16       return GO_ON;
17     } else {
18       if(*t % filter == 0)
19         return GO_ON;
20       else
21         return task;
22     }
23   }
24
25   void svc_end() {
26     std::cout << "Prime(" << filter << ")\n";
27     return;
28   }
29
30
31 private:
32   int filter;
33 };
34
35 class Generate: public ff_node {
36 public:
37
```

```
38        Generate(int n):streamlen(n),task(2) {
39          std::cout << "Generate object created" << std::endl;
40          return;
41        }
42
43
44      int svc_init() {
45          std::cout << "Sieve started. Generating a stream of " << streamlen <<
46            " elements, starting with " << task << std::endl;
47          return 0;
48        }
49
50      void * svc(void * tt) {
51          unsigned int * t = (unsigned int *)tt;
52
53          if(task < streamlen) {
54            int * xi = new int(task++);
55            return xi;
56          }
57          return NULL;
58        }
59    private:
60        int streamlen;
61        int task;
62    };
63
64    class Printer: public ff_node {
65
66        int svc_init() {
67          std::cout << "Printer started " << std::endl;
68          first = 0;
69        }
70
71        void * svc(void *t) {
72          int * xi = (int *) t;
73          if (first == 0) {
74            first = *xi;
75          }
76          return GO_ON;
77        }
78
79        void svc_end() {
80          std::cout << "Sieve terminating, prime numbers found up to " << first
81              << std::endl;
82        }
83
84    private:
85        int first;
86    };
87
88    int main(int argc, char * argv[]) {
89      if (argc!=3) {
90        std::cerr << "use: " << argv[0] << " nstages streamlen\n";
91        return -1;
92      }
93
94      ff_pipeline pipe;
95      int nstages = atoi(argv[1]);
96      pipe.add_stage(new Generate(atoi(argv[2])));
97      for(int j=0; j<nstages; j++)
98        pipe.add_stage(new Sieve());
99      pipe.add_stage(new Printer());
100
101      ffTime(START_TIME);
102      if (pipe.run_and_wait_end()<0) {
103        error("running pipeline\n");
104        return -1;
105      }
```

```
106    ffTime(STOP_TIME);
107
108    std::cerr << "DONE, pipe  time= " << pipe.ffTime() << " (ms)\n";
109    std::cerr << "DONE, total time= " << ffTime(GET_TIME) << " (ms)\n";
110    pipe.ffStats(std::cerr);
111    return 0;
112 }
```

The **Generate** stage at line 35–62 generates the integer stream, from 2 up to a value taken from the command line parameters. It uses an **svc_init** just to point out when the concurrent activity is started. The creation of the object used to represent the concurrent activity is instead evidenced by the message printed in the constructor.

The **Sieve** stage (lines 6–33) defines the generic pipeline stage. This stores the initial value got from the input stream on lines 14–16 and then goes on passing the inputs not multiple of the stored values on lines 18–21. The **svc_end** method is executed right before terminating the concurrent activity and prints out the stored value, which happen to be the prime number found in that node.

The **Printer** stage is used as the last stage in the pipeline (the pipeline built at lines 94–99 in the program **main**) and just discards all the received values but the first one, which is kept to remember the point where we arrived storing prime numbers. It defines both an **svc_init** method (to print a message when the concurrent activity is started) and an **svc_end** method, which is used to print the first integer received, representing the upper bound (non included in) of the sequence of prime numbers discovered with the pipeline stages. The concurrent activity graph of the program is the following one:

The program output, when run with 7 **Sieve** stages on a stream from 2 to 30, is the following one:

```
 1 ffsrc$ ./sieve 7 30
 2 Generate object created
 3 Printer started
 4 Sieve started. Generating a stream of 30 elements, starting with 2
 5 Prime(2)
 6 Prime(3)
 7 Prime(5)
 8 Prime(7)
 9 Prime(Prime(Sieve terminating, prime numbers found up to 1317)
10 )
11 19
12 Prime(11)
13 DONE, pipe  time= 0.275 (ms)
14 DONE, total time= 25.568 (ms)
15 FastFlow trace not enabled
16 ffsrc$
```

showing that the prime numbers up to 19 (excluded) has been found.

7   Managing Access to Shared Objects

Shared objects may be accessed within FastFlow programs using the classical pthread concurrency control mechanisms. The FastFlow program is actually a multithreaded code using the pthread library, in fact.

As an example, in order to avoid mixing parts of the strings output by different ff_nodes in a FastFlow program, we may wrap each output to the cout file descriptor with proper locks to a pthread_mutex variable. Therefore, after declaring the mutex

```
1 #include <pthread.h>
2 static pthread-mutex-t lock = PTHREAD_MUTEX_INITIALIZER;
```

we may explicitly wrap each statement printing to the console in our source code with a lock and an unlock call to the mutex:

```
1 pthread-mutex-lock(&lock);
2 std::cout << ... << std::endl;
3 pthread-mutex-unlock(&lock);
```

In other cases, a viable alternative consists in wrapping the calls operating on the shared state in properly synchronized functions. As an example, if we need to update a shared state represented by an integer value by adding or subtracting values, we may use a function:

```
1 pthread-mutex-t state-lock = PTHREAD_MUTEX_INITIALIZER;
2 int state-var = 0;
3 int update(int amount) {
4    pthread-mutex-lock(&state-lock);
5    state-var += amount;
6    pthread-mutex-lock(&state-lock);
7    return(state-var);
8 }
```

or we may consider using new C++11 features such as the std::lock_guard supporting kind of more "automatic" locking, e.g.

```
1 int update(int amount) {
2    std::lock_guard<std::mutex> lock(state-mutex);
3    state-mutex++;
4    state-var += amount;
5    return(state-var);
6 }
```

This requires compiling with the proper -std=c++11 but the lock is automatically release at the end of the scope of the state_mutex variable.

It is worth pointing out that any additional synchronization mechanism inserted in a FastFlow program interacts with the primitive, optimized synchronizations of the framework. In particular, the FastFlow programmer must be aware that:

– FastFlow ensures correct access sequences to the shared object used to implement the streaming networks (the graph of concurrent activities), such as the SPSC queues used to implement the streams, for instance.
– FastFlow stream semantics guarantees correct sequencing of activation of the concurrent activities modeled through ff_nodes and connected through streams. The stream implementation actually ensures *pure data flow* semantics.

- passing data from concurrent activity A to concurrent activity B (e.g. when stage$_i$ svc method returns a void * pointer which is passed as input parameter to the svc method of stage$_{i+1}$ in a pipeline) conceptually transfers the *capability* to operate on the pointed data from one concurrent activity to the other one.
- any access to any user defined shared data structure must be protected with either the primitive mechanisms provided by FastFlow (see above) or the primitives provided within the pthread library.

but also that

- any synchronization mechanism added in the user code may impair the efficiency achieved by the FastFlow runtime in the orchestration of the parallel activities defined by the FastFlow skeletons used in the parallel application.

8   More Skeletons: The FastFlow Farm

In the previous sections, we used only pipeline skeletons in the sample code. Here we introduce the other primitive skeleton provided in FastFlow, namely the farm skeleton.

The simplest way to define a farm skeleton in FastFlow is by declaring a farm object and adding a vector of *worker* concurrent activities to the farm. An excerpt of the needed code is the following one:

```
1  #include <ff/farm.hpp>
2
3  using namespace ff;
4
5  int main(int argc, char * argv[]) {
6
7    ...
8    ff_farm<> myFarm;
9    std::vector<ff_node *> w;
10   for(int i=0;i<nworkers;++i)
11     w.push_back(new Worker);
12   myFarm.add_workers(w);
13   ...
```

This code basically defines a farm with **nworkers** workers processing the data items appearing onto the farm input stream and delivering results onto the farm output stream. The default scheduling policy used to send input tasks to workers is the round robin one. Workers are implemented by the ff_node Worker objects. These objects may represent sequential concurrent activities as well as further skeletons, that is either pipeline or farm instances.

However, this farm may not be used alone. There is no way to provide an input stream to a FastFlow streaming network but having the first component in the network generating the stream. To this purpose, FastFlow supports two options:

- we can use the farm defined with a code similar to the one described above as the second stage of a pipeline whose first stage generates the input stream according to one of the techniques discussed in Sect. 5. This means we will use the farm writing a code such as:

```
1   ...
2   ff_pipeline myPipe;
3
4   myPipe.add_stage(new GeneratorStage());
5   myPipe.add_stage(myFarm);
```

– or we can provide an `emitter` and a `collector` to the farm, specialized in such a way they can be used to produce the input stream and consume the output stream of the farm, respectively, while inheriting the default scheduling and gathering policies.

The former case is simple. We only have to understand why adding the farm to the pipeline as a pipeline stage works. This will discussed in detail in Sect. 11. The latter case is simple as well, but we discuss it through some more code.

8.1 Farm with Emitter and Collector

First, let us see what kind of objects we have to build to provide the farm an `emitter` and a `collector`. Both `emitter` and `collector` must be supplied as `ff_node` subclass objects. If we implement the `emitter` just providing the `svc` method, the tasks delivered by the `svc` on the output stream—either using a `ff_send_out` or returning the proper pointer with the `svc return` statement— will be dispatched to the available workers according to the default round robin scheduling. An example of `emitter` node, generating the stream of integer tasks eventually processed by the farm `workers` is the following one:

```
1   class Emitter: public ff_node {
2   public:
3       Emitter(int n):streamlen(n),task(0) {}
4
5       void * svc(void *) {
6           sleep(1);
7           task++;
8           int * t = new int(task);
9           if (task<streamlen)
10              return t;
11          else
12              return NULL;
13      }
14
15  private:
16      int streamlen;
17      int task;
18  };
```

In this case, the node `svc` actually does not take into account any input stream item (the input parameter name is omitted on line 8). Rather, each time the node is activated, it returns a task to be computed using the internal `tasks` value. The task is directed to the "next" worker by the FastFlow farm run time support.

In order to provide a `collector`, we can use again a `ff_node`. In case the results need further processing, they can be directed to the next node in the streaming network using the mechanisms detailed in Sect. 5. Otherwise, they can be processed within the `svc` method of the `ff_node` subclass used to instantiate

the collector. As an example, a `collector` just printing the tasks/results it gets
from the workers may be programmed as follows:

```
1  class Collector: public ff_node {
2  public:
3      void * svc(void * task) {
4          int * t = (int *)task;
5          std::cout << "Collector got " << *t << std::endl;
6          return GO_ON;
7      }
8  };
```

With these `Emitter` and `Collector` classes defined and assuming to have a
worker defined by the class:

```
1  class Worker: public ff_node {
2  public:
3      void * svc(void * task) {
4          int * t = (int *)task;
5          (*t)++;
6          return task;
7      }
8  };
```

we can define a program processing a stream of integers by increasing each one
of them with a farm as follows:

```
1  int main(int argc, char * argv[]) {
2      int nworkers=atoi(argv[1]);
3      int streamlen=atoi(argv[2]);
4
5      ff_farm<> farm;
6
7      Emitter E(streamlen);
8      farm.add_emitter(&E);
9
10     std::vector<ff_node *> w;
11     for(int i=0;i<nworkers;++i)
12         w.push_back(new Worker);
13     farm.add_workers(w);
14
15     Collector C;
16     farm.add_collector(&C);
17
18     if (farm.run_and_wait_end()<0) {
19         error("running farm\n");
20         return -1;
21     }
22     return 0;
23 }
```

The concurrent activity graph in this case is the following one:

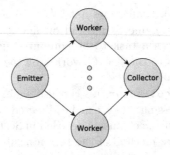

When run with the first argument specifying the number of workers to be used and the second one specifying the length of the input stream generated in the collector node, we get the expected output:

```
 1 ffsrc$ ./a.out 2 10
 2 Collector got 2
 3 Collector got 3
 4 Collector got 4
 5 Collector got 5
 6 Collector got 6
 7 Collector got 7
 8 Collector got 8
 9 Collector got 9
10 Collector got 10
11 ffsrc$
```

8.2 Farm with No Collector

We move on considering a further case: a farm with emitter but no collector. Having no collector the workers may not deliver results: all the results computed by the workers must be consolidated in memory. The following code implements a farm where a stream of tasks of type TASK with an integer tag i and an integer value t are processed by the worker of the farm by:

– computing t++ and
– storing the result in a global array at the position given by the tag i.

Writes to the global result array need not to be synchronized as each worker writes different positions in the array (the TASK tags are unique, the array is managed according a "single owner computes" rule).

```
 1 #include <vector>
 2 #include <iostream>
 3 #include <ff/farm.hpp>
 4
 5 static int * results;
 6
 7 struct task_t {
 8     task_t(int i,int t):i(i),t(t) {}
 9     int i;
10     int t;
11 };
12
13 using namespace ff;
14
15 class Worker: public ff_node {
16 public:
17     void * svc(void * task) {
18         TASK * t = (TASK *) task;
19         results[t->i] = ++(t->t);
20         return GO_ON;
21     }
22 };
23
24 class Emitter: public ff_node {
25 public:
26     Emitter(int n):streamlen(n),task(0) {}
27
28     void * svc(void *) {
29         task++;
30         task_t * t = new task_t(task,task*task);
```

```
31              if (task<streamlen) return t;
32              return NULL;
33          }
34  private:
35          int streamlen;
36          int task;
37  };
38
39  int main(int argc, char * argv[]) {
40
41          int nworkers=atoi(argv[1]);
42          int streamlen=atoi(argv[2]);
43          results = (int *) calloc(streamlen,sizeof(int));
44
45          ff_farm <> farm;
46
47          Emitter E(streamlen);
48          farm.add_emitter(&E);
49
50          std::vector<ff_node *> w;
51          for(int i=0;i<nworkers;++i)
52              w.push_back(new Worker);
53          farm.add_workers(w);
54
55          std::cout << "Before starting computation" << std::endl;
56          for(int i=0; i<streamlen; i++)
57              std::cout << i << " : " << results[i] << std::endl;
58          if (farm.run_and_wait_end()<0) {
59              error("running farm\n");
60              return -1;
61          }
62          std::cout << "After computation" << std::endl;
63          for(int i=0; i<streamlen; i++)
64              std::cout << i << " : " << results[i] << std::endl;
65          return 0;
66  }
```

The Worker code at lines 15–22 defines an svc method that returns a GO_ON. Therefore no results are directed to the collector (non existing, see lines 45–53: they define the farm but they do not contain any add_collector in the program main). Rather, the results computed by the worker code at line 19 are directly stored in the global array. In this case the concurrent activity graph is the following:

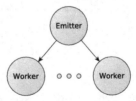

The main program prints the results vector before calling the FastFlow

start_and_wait_end()

and after the call, and you can easily verify the results are actually computed and stored in the correct place in the vector:

```
1  ffsrc$ farmNoC 2 10
2  Before starting computation
3  0 : 0
4  1 : 0
5  2 : 0
```

```
 6  3  :  0
 7  4  :  0
 8  5  :  0
 9  6  :  0
10  7  :  0
11  8  :  0
12  9  :  0
13 After computation
14  0  :  0
15  1  :  2
16  2  :  5
17  3  :  10
18  4  :  17
19  5  :  26
20  6  :  37
21  7  :  50
22  8  :  65
23  9  :  82
24 ffsrc$
```

Besides demonstrating how a farm without collector may compute useful results, the program of the last listing also demonstrates how complex task data structures can be delivered and retrieved to and from the FastFlow streaming network streams via svc void * parameters.

8.3 Specializing the Scheduling Strategy in a Farm

In order to select the worker where an incoming input task has to be directed, the FastFlow farm uses an internal ff_loadbalancer that provides a method int selectworker() returning the index in the worker array corresponding to the worker where the next task has to be directed. This method cannot be overwritten, actually. But the programmer may subclass the ff_loadbalancer and provide his own selectworker() method and pass the new load balancer to the farm emitter, therefore implementing a farm with a user defined scheduling policy.

The steps to performed in this case are exemplified with the following, relevant portions of code. First, we subclass the ff_loadbalancer and we provide our own selectworker() method:

```
1  class my_loadbalancer: public ff_loadbalancer {
2  protected:
3      // implement your policy...
4      inline int selectworker() { return victim; }
5
6  public:
7      // the ff_loadbalancer requires the maximum number of workers
8      my_loadbalancer(int max_num_workers): ff_loadbalancer(max_num_workers)
            {}
9
10      void set_victim(int v) { victim=v;}
11  private:
12      int victim;
13  };
```

Then we create a farm specifying the new load balancer class as a type parameter:

```
1  ff_farm<my_loadbalancer> myFarm(...);
```

Please note that the class ff_loadbalancer needs to know the maximum number of worker threads it has to manage. Eventually, we create an emitter that within its `svc` method invokes the `set_victim` method right before outputting a task towards the worker string, either with a `ff_send_out(task)` or with a `return(task)`. The emitter is declared as:

```
1  class myEmitter: public ff_node {
2
3    myEmitter(my_loadbalancer * lb):lb(lb) {}
4
5    ...
6
7    void * svc(void * task) {
8      ...
9      workerToBeUsed = somePolicy(...);
10     lb->set_victim(workerToBeUsed);
11     ...
12     ff_send_out(task);
13     return GO_ON;
14   }
15
16   ...
17 private:
18   my_loadbancer * lb;
19 }
```

and it is inserted in the farm with the code

```
1 myEmitter emitter(myFarm.getlb());
2 myFarm.add_emitter(emitter);
```

Another simpler option for scheduling tasks directly in the `svc` method of the farm emitter is to use the `ff_send_out_to` method of the `ff_loadbalancer` class. In this case what is needed is to pass the default load balancer object to the emitter thread and to use the `ff_loadbalancer::ff_send_out_to` method instead of `ff_node::ff_send_out` method for sending out tasks.

What we get is a farm where the worker to be used to execute the task appearing onto the input stream is decided by the programmer through the proper implementation of `my_loadbalancer` rather than being decided by the current FastFlow implementation.

Two particular cases specializing the scheduling policy in different way by using FastFlow predefined code are illustrated in the following two subsections.

8.4 Broadcasting a Task to all Workers

FastFlow supports the possibility to direct a task to all the workers in a farm. It is particularly useful if we want to process the task by workers implementing different functions. The broadcasting is achieved through the declaration of a specialized load balancer, in a way very similar to what we illustrated in Sect. 8.3.

The following code implements a farm whose input tasks are broadcasted to all the workers, and whose workers compute different functions on the input tasks, and therefore deliver different results on the output stream.

```
1 #include <iostream>
2 #include <ff/farm.hpp>
3 #include <ff/node.hpp>
4 #include <cmath>
5
6 using namespace std;
```

```
7  using namespace ff;
8
9
10 // should be global to be accessible from workers
11 #define MAX 4
12 int x[MAX];
13
14 class WorkerPlus: public ff_node {
15   int svc_init() {
16     cout << "Worker initialized" << endl;
17     return 0;
18   }
19
20   void * svc(void * in) {
21     int *i = ((int *) in);
22     int ii = *i;
23     *i++;
24     cout << "WorkerPLus got " << ii << " and computed " << *i << endl ;
25     return in;
26   }
27 };
28
29 class WorkerMinus: public ff_node {
30   int svc_init() {
31     cout << "Worker initialized" << endl;
32     return 0;
33   }
34
35   void * svc(void * in) {
36     int *i = ((int *) in);
37     int ii = *i;
38     *i--;
39     cout << "WorkerMinus got " << ii << " and computed " << *i << endl ;
40     return in;
41   }
42 };
43
44 class my_loadbalancer: public ff_loadbalancer {
45 public:
46     // this is necessary because ff_loadbalancer has non default parameters
47     ....
47     my_loadbalancer(int max_num_workers):ff_loadbalancer(max_num_workers)
        {}
48
49     void broadcast(void * task) {
50         ff_loadbalancer::broadcast_task(task);
51     }
52 };
53
54 class Emitter: public ff_node {
55 public:
56     Emitter(my_loadbalancer * const lb):lb(lb) {}
57     void * svc(void * task) {
58         lb->broadcast(task);
59         return GO_ON;
60     }
61 private:
62     my_loadbalancer * lb;
63 };
64
65 class Collector: public ff_node {
66 public:
67     Collector(int i) {}
68     void * svc(void * task) {
69         cout << "Got result " << * ((int *) task) << endl;
70         return GO_ON;
71     }
72
```

```
73
74  };
75
76
77
78  #define NW 2
79
80  int main(int argc, char * argv[])
81  {
82      ffTime(START_TIME);
83
84      cout << "init " << argc << endl;
85      int nw = (argc==1 ? NW : atoi(argv[1]));
86
87      cout << "using " << nw << " workers " << endl;
88
89      // init input (fake)
90      for(int i=0; i<MAX; i++) {
91          x[i] = (i*10);
92      }
93      cout << "Setting up farm" << endl;
94      // create the farm object
95      ff_farm<my_loadbalancer> farm(true,nw);
96      // create and add emitter object to the farm
97      Emitter E(farm.getlb());
98      farm.add_emitter(&E);
99      cout << "emitter ok "<< endl;
100
101
102     std::vector<ff_node *> w;    // prepare workers
103     w.push_back(new WorkerPlus);
104     w.push_back(new WorkerMinus);
105     farm.add_workers(w);          // add them to the farm
106     cout << "workers ok "<< endl;
107
108     Collector C(1);
109     farm.add_collector(&C);
110     cout << "collector ok "<< endl;
111
112     farm.run_then_freeze();       // run farm asynchronously
113
114     cout << "Sending tasks ..." << endl;
115     int tasks[MAX];
116     for(int i=0; i<MAX; i++) {
117         tasks[i]=i;
118         farm.offload((void *) &tasks[i]);
119     }
120     farm.offload((void *) FF_EOS);
121
122     cout << "Waiting termination" << endl;
123     farm.wait();
124
125     cout << "Farm terminated after computing for " << farm.ffTime() << endl;
126
127     ffTime(STOP_TIME);
128     cout << "Spent overall " << ffTime(GET_TIME) << endl;
129
130 }
```

At lines 44–52 a ff_loadbalancer is defined providing a broadcast method.
The method is implemented in terms of an ff_loadbalancer internal method.
This new loadbalancer class is used as in the case of other user defined sched-
ulers (see Sect. 8.3) and the emitter eventually uses the load balancer broadcast
method *instead* of delivering the task to the output stream (i.e. directly to the
string of the workers). This is done through the svc code at lines 57–60. Lines

103 and 104 are used to add two different workers to the farm. The rest of the program is standard, but for the fact the resulting farm is used as an accelerator (lines 112–123, see Sect. 10).

8.5 Using Autoscheduling

FastFlow provides suitable tools to implement farms with "auto scheduling", that is farms where the workers "ask" for something to be computed rather than accepting tasks sent by the emitter (explicit or implicit) according to some scheduling policy. This scheduling behaviour may be simply implemented by using the ff_farm method set_scheduling_ondemand(), as follows:

```
1 ff_farm <> myFarm ( ... ) ;
2 myFarm. set_scheduling_ondemand () ;
3 ...
4 farm . add_emitter ( ... ) ;
5 ...
```

The scheduling policy implemented in this case is an approximation of the auto scheduling, indeed. The emitter simply checks the length of the SPSC queues connecting the emitter to the workers, and delivers the task to the first worker whose queue length is less or equal to 1. To be more precise, FastFlow should have implemented a request queue where the workers may write tasks requests tagged with the worker id and the emitter may read such request to choose the worker where the incoming tasks is to be directed. This is not possible as of FastFlow 1.1 because it still doesn't allow to read from multiple SPSC queues preserving the FIFO order.

8.6 Ordered Farm

Tasks passing through a task-farm can be subjected to reordering because of different execution times in the worker threads. To overcome the problem of sending packets in a different order with respect to input, tasks can be reordered after collection from the workers, although this solution might introduce extra latency mainly because reordering checks have to be executed even if the packets already arrive at the farm collector in the correct order.

The default round-robin and auto scheduling policies are not order preserving, for this reason a specialized version of the FastFlow farm has been introduced which enforce the ordering of the packets.

The ordered farm may be introduced by using the ff_ofarm skeleton. The following code sketches how to use the it as a middle stage of a 3-stage pipeline:

```
1   ...
2   ff_pipeline pipe;
3   pipe . add_stage (new FirstStage ( ... ) ) ;
4
5   ff_ofarm ofarm;   // defines an order−preserving farm
6   std:: vector<ff_node *> w;
7   for ( int i =0;i <nworkers;++i ) w. push_back (new Worker ) ;
8   ofarm . add_workers (w) ;
9
10  pipe . add_stage (&ofarm ) ; // adds the farm as 2nd stage
```

```
11    pipe.add_stage(new LastStage(...));
12
13    pipe.run_and_wait_end();
```

8.7 Simplified Ways to Create Farms Using C++11

In order to simplify the creation of farm objects—and especially for simple cases—some new constructors have been introduced in the latest release of Fast-Flow.

Using these new features, the simplest way to create a farm in FastFlow is to create a function F having the signature T* F(T*, ff_node*const) where T is a generic type, and then use this function to create the workers of the farm. As an example, in the following code excerpt a farm with 5 workers, each executing the function F, is declared and run:

```
1 ff_farm<> farm((std::function<T*(T*,ff_node*const)>)F, 5);
2 farm.run_and_wait_end();
```

With this code, the default emitter and collector nodes and the default round-robin scheduling and gathering policy are automatically instantiated. As different features of the new C++11 standard are used in the implementation of this farm, to compile the example above the correct flags to used with the g++ command are:

```
1 -std=c++11 -DHAS_CXX11_VARIADIC_TEMPLATES
```

Another way to create a task-farm skeleton in FastFlow is to pass the vector of ff_nodes, the Emitter and Collector nodes (if both exist) directly as parameters of the farm constructor as in the following simple examples:

```
1  #include <vector>
2  #include <ff/farm.hpp>
3
4  using namespace ff;
5  int main() {
6      struct MyWorker: ff_node {
7          void *svc(void *t) {
8              printf("worker %d got one task\n", get_my_id());
9              return t;
10         }
11     };
12     // Emitter
13     struct Emitter:public ff_node {
14         std::function<void*()> F;
15         Emitter(std::function<void*()> F):F(F) {}
16         void *svc(void*) { return F(); }
17     };
18     const int K  = 20; // stream length
19     const int nw = 7;  // n. of workers
20     // function executed in the Emitter node
21     auto F = [K]() -> void* {
22         static int k = 0;
23         if (k++ == K) return NULL;
24         return new int(k);
25     };
26     std::vector<ff_node*> W;
27     for(int i=0;i<nw;++i) W.push_back(new MyWorker);
28
29     // farm with specialized Emitter and without collector
30     ff_farm<> farm(W, new Emitter(F));
```

```
31    farm . run_and_wait_end () ;
32
33    return 0;
34 }
```

9 More on ff_pipeline

Pipeline skeletons can be easily instantiated using the new C++11-based constructors available in the latest release of FastFlow.

The simplest way to create a pipeline of n-stage in FastFlow is to create a number of functions with signature T* (*F) (T*,ff_node*const) and/or ff_node objects and then to pass them in the correct order to the ff_pipe constructor[5]. As an example consider the following 3-stage pipeline:

```
1     struct myTask { .... }; // this is my input/output type
2
3     myTask* F1(myTask *in , ff_node*const node) {...} // 1st function
4     struct F2: ff_node {      // 2nd stage
5        void *svc(void *t) {...}
6     } F2;
7     myTask* F3(myTask *in , ff_node*const node) {...} // 3rd function
8
9     ff_pipe <myTask> pipe (F1,&F2,F3) ;
10    pipe . run_and_wait_end () ;
11 };
```

Here 2 functions getting a myTask pointer as input and return type are used as first and third stage of the pipeline whereas an ff_node object is used as middle stage. To compile the above snippet of code, the command to use is:

```
1 ffsrc$ g++ −std=c++0x −DHAS_CXX11_VARIADIC_TEMPLATES −I $FF_ROOT test .
      cpp −o test −lpthread
```

that is the same switches needed to use the new farm syntax outlined in Sect. 8.7 are needed.

Since ff_pipe accepts both functions and ff_node, it is possible to easily build "complex" streaming networks using just few commands as in the following example where ff_pipe and ff_farm skeletons are mixed together:

```
1     std::vector<ff_node*> W;
2     W.push_back(new ff_pipe <myTask>(&F2,F3)); // 2−stage pipeline , 1st worker
3     W.push_back(new ff_pipe <myTask>(&F2,F3)); // 2−stage pipeline , 2nd worker
4
5     ff_pipe <myTask> pipe(F1, new ff_farm <>(W)); // 2−stage pipeline , seq+farm
6
7     pipe . run_and_wait_end () ;
8 };
```

10 FastFlow as a Software Accelerator

Up to know we just showed how to use FastFlow to write a "complete skeleton application", that is an application whose complete flow of control is defined through skeletons. In this case the main of the C++ program written by the user is basically providing the structure of the parallel application by defining a

---

[5] The class *ff_pipe* is a wrapper of the class *ff_pipeline*.

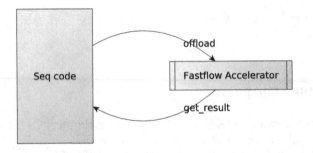

Fig. 4. FastFlow accelerator

proper FastFlow skeleton nesting and the commands to start the computation of the skeleton program and to wait its termination. All the business logic of the application is embedded in the skeleton parameters.

Now we want to discuss the second kind of usage which is supported by FastFlow, namely the FastFlow accelerator mode. The term "accelerator" is used the way it is used when dealing with hardware accelerators. An hardware accelerator—a GPU or an FPGA or even a more "general purpose" accelerator such as Tilera 64 core chips, Intel Many Core or IBM WireSpeed/PowerEN—is a device that can be used to compute particular kind of code faster that the CPU. FastFlow accelerator is a "software device" that can be used to speedup portions of code using the cores left unused by the main application. In other words, it's a way FastFlow supports to accelerate particular computation by using a skeleton program and offloading to the skeleton program tasks to be computed.

The FastFlow accelerator will use $n-1$ cores of the n core machine, assuming that the calling code is not parallel and will try to ensure a $n-1$ fold speedup is achieved in the computation of the tasks offloaded to the accelerator, provided a sufficient number of tasks to be computed are given.

Using FastFlow accelerator mode is not that different from using FastFlow to write an application only using skeletons (see Fig. 4). In particular, the following steps must be followed:

- A skeleton program has to be written, using the FastFlow skeletons computing the tasks that will be given to the accelerator. The skeleton program used to program the accelerator is supposed to have an input stream, used to offload the tasks to the accelerator.
- Then, the skeleton program must be run using a particular method, different from the `run_and_wait_end` we have already seen, that is a `run_then_freeze()` method. This method will start the accelerator skeleton program, consuming the input stream items to produce either output stream items or to consolidate (partial) results in memory. When we want to stop the accelerator, we will deliver and end-of-stream mark to the input stream.
- Eventually, we must wait the computation of the accelerator is terminated.

A simple program using FastFlow accelerator mode is shown below:

```
1  #include <vector>
2  #include <iostream>
3  #include <ctime>
4  #include <ff/farm.hpp>
5
6  using namespace ff;
7
8  int * x;
9  int nworkers = 0;
10
11 class Worker: public ff_node {
12 public:
13
14    Worker(int i) {
15       my_id = i;
16    }
17
18    void * svc(void * task) {
19       int * t = (int *)task;
20       x[my_id] = *t;
21       return GO_ON;
22    }
23 private:
24    int my_id;
25 };
26
27 int main(int argc, char * argv[]) {
28
29    if (argc<3) {
30       std::cerr << "use: "
31          << argv[0]
32          << " nworkers streamlen\n";
33       return -1;
34    }
35
36    nworkers=atoi(argv[1]);
37    int streamlen=atoi(argv[2]);
38
39    x = new int[nworkers];
40    for(int i=0; i<nworkers; i++)
41       x[i] = 0;
42
43    ff_farm<> accelerator(true);
44
45    std::vector<ff_node *> w;
46    for(int i=0;i<nworkers;++i)
47       w.push_back(new Worker(i));
48    accelerator.add_workers(w);
49
50    if (accelerator.run_then_freeze()<0) {
51       error("running farm\n");
52       return -1;
53    }
54
55    for(int i=0; i<=streamlen; i++) {
56       int * task = new int(i);
57       accelerator.offload(task);
58    }
59    accelerator.offload((void *) FF_EOS);
60    accelerator.wait();
61
62    for(int i=0; i<nworkers; i++)
63       std::cout << i << ":" << x[i] << std::endl;
64
65    return 0;
66 }
```

We use a farm accelerator. The accelerator is declared at line 43. The "true" parameter is the one telling FastFlow this farm has to be used as an accelerator. Workers are added at lines 45–48. Each worker is given its id as a constructor parameters. This is the very same code as the one used in plain FastFlow applications. Line 50 starts the skeleton code in accelerator mode. Lines 55 to 58 offload tasks to be computed to the accelerator. These lines could be part of any larger C++ program, indeed. The idea is that whenever we have a task ready to be submitted to the accelerator, we simply "offload" it to the accelerator. When we have no more tasks to offload, we send and end-of-stream (line 59) and eventually we wait for the completion of the computation of tasks in the accelerator (line 60).

This kind of interaction with an accelerator without output stream is intended to model those computations than consolidate results directly in memory. We can also assume that results are awaited from the accelerator through its output stream. In this case, we first have to write the skeleton code of the accelerator in such a way an output stream is supported. In the new version the accelerator sample program below, we add a collector to the accelerator farm (line 45). The collector simply merges the results from workers to the output stream (lines 18–24 in the code listing below). Once the tasks have been offloaded to the accelerator, rather than waiting for accelerator completion, we can ask computed results as delivered to the accelerator output stream through the bool load_result(void **) method (see lines 59–61).

```
1  #include <vector>
2  #include <iostream>
3  #include <ctime.h>
4  #include <ff/farm.hpp>
5
6  using namespace ff;
7
8  class Worker: public ff_node {
9  public:
10
11    void * svc(void * task) {
12      int * t = (int *)task;
13      (*t)++;
14      return task;
15    }
16  };
17
18  class Collector: public ff_node {
19  public:
20      void * svc(void * task) {
21        int * t = (int *)task;
22        return task;
23      }
24  };
25
26
27  int main(int argc, char * argv[]) {
28
29    if (argc<3) {
30      std::cerr << "use: "
31          << argv[0]
32          << " nworkers streamlen\n";
33      return -1;
34    }
35
```

```
36    int nworkers=atoi(argv[1]);
37    int streamlen=atoi(argv[2]);
38
39    ff_farm<> accelerator(true);
40
41    std::vector<ff_node *> w;
42    for(int i=0;i<nworkers;++i)
43        w.push_back(new Worker());
44    accelerator.add_workers(w);
45    accelerator.add_collector(new Collector());
46
47    if (accelerator.run_then_freeze()<0) {
48        error("running farm\n");
49        return -1;
50    }
51
52    for(int i=0; i<=streamlen; i++) {
53        int * task = new int(i);
54        accelerator.offload(task);
55    }
56    accelerator.offload((void *) FF_EOS);
57
58    void * result;
59    while(accelerator.load_result(&result)) {
60        std::cout << "Got result :: "<< (*((int *)result)) << std::endl;
61    }
62    accelerator.wait();
63
64    return 0;
65 }
```

The `bool load_result(void **)` methods synchronously await for one item being delivered on the accelerator output stream. If such item is available, the method returns "true" and stores the item pointer in the parameter. If no other items will be available, the method returns "false". An asynchronous method is also available with signature `bool load\_results\_nb(void **)` If no result is available at the moment the method is called, it returns a "false" value, and you should retry later on to see whether a result may be retrieved.

It is worth pointing out that the usage of FastFlow to build accelerators applies to both C++ and pure C sequential programs. In the latter case, the resulting program must be compiled using the C++ tool chain, of course, but eventually the code gets accelerated exactly as if the original sequential code was written in C++. This is because all the C++ part is confined in the FastFlow accelerator part and because the accelerator "interface" methods (the offloading and result retrieval methods) perfectly work with pure C parameters.

11 Skeleton Nesting

In FastFlow skeletons may be arbitrarily nested. Taking into account just farms and pipelines this means that farms may be used as pipeline stages, and pipelines may be used as farm workers.

As an example, you can define a farm with pipeline workers as follows:

```
1    ff_farm<> myFarm;
2
3    std::vector<ff_node *> w;
4    for(int i=0; i<nW; i++)
```

```
5        ff_pipeline * p = new ff_pipeline;
6        p->add_stage(new S1());
7        p->add_stage(new S2());
8        w.push_back(p);
9    }
10   myFarm.addWorkers(w);
```

or we can use a farm as a pipeline stage by using a code such as:

```
1    ff_pipeline * p = new ff_pipeline;
2    ff_farm <>    f = new ff_farm;
3
4    ...
5
6    f.addWorkers(w);
7
8    ...
9
10   p->add_stage(new SeqWorkerA());
11   p->add_stage(f);
12   p->add_stage(new SeqWorkerB());
```

The concurrent activity graph in this case will be the following one:

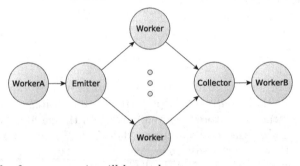

while in the former case it will be such as

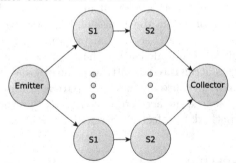

As a general rule, any skeleton may be used in any place where a ff_node is required. As more and more skeletons are added in FastFlow, more and more complex composite skeleton structures may be used.

12   Feedback Channels

There are cases where it is useful to have the possibility to route back some results to the streaming network input stream for further computation. For example, this possibility may be exploited to implement divide&conquer pattern using the task-farm: tasks injected in the farm are split by the scheduler to the workers and the resulting tasks are routed back to the scheduler to evaluate if further splitting is needed. Tasks that can be computed using the base case code, are computed by the workers and their results are used for the conquer phase, usually performed in memory.

The feedback channel in a farm or pipeline may be introduced by the `wrap_around()` method on the interested skeleton. In case our applications uses a farm pattern as the outermost skeleton, we may therefore add the method call after instantiating the farm object:

```
1  ff_farm <> myFarm;
2  ...
3  myFarm.add_emitter(&e);
4  myFarm.add_collector(&c);
5  myFarm.add_workers(w);
6
7  myFarm.wrap_around();
8  ...
```

and this will lead to the concurrent activity graph

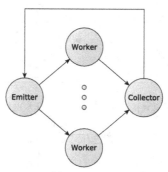

The same if parallelism is expressed by using a pipeline as the outermost skeleton:

```
1  ff_pipeline myPipe;
2
3  myPipe.add_stage(s1);
4  myPipe.add_stage(s2);
5  myPipe.add_stage(s3);
6  ...
7  myPipe.wrap_around();
8  ...
```

leading to the concurrent activity graph:

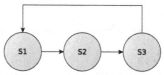

As of FastFlow 1.1, the only possibility to use the feedback channel provided by the `wrap_around` method is relative to the outermost skeleton, that is the one with no input stream. Starting with version 2.0.0, this limitation has been relaxed such that it is possible to use feedback channels (for some particular skeleton cases) where the `wrap_around` method can be called not only in the outmost skeleton but also to the last stage of a pipeline composing the application. Some of these possible cases are sketched in Fig. 5.

As an example, in the following we provide the code needed to create a 2-stage pipeline where the second stage is a farm with feedback channels between each worker and the farm emitter:

```
1      ff_farm<>     farm(F, 8);   // farm of the function F using 8 workers
2      farm.remove_collector();  // removes the default collector
3      // the scheduler gets in input the internal load-balancer
4      farm.add_emitter(new Sched(farm.getlb()));
5      // adds feedback channels between each worker and the scheduler
6      farm.wrap_around();
7
8      ff_pipe<myTask> pipe(seq, &farm); // creates the pipeline
9      pipe.run_and_wait_end();
```

In this case the emitter node of the farm receives tasks both from the first stage of the pipeline and from farm's workers. The emitter non-deterministically processes input tasks giving priority to the tasks coming back from workers.

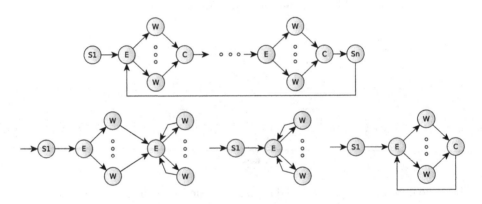

Fig. 5. Some possible FastFlow schemas with feedback channels.

13   Run Time Routines

Several utility routines are defined in the FastFlow runtime. We recall here the main ones.

- `virtual int get_my_id()`
  returns a virtual id of the node where the concurrent activity (its `svc` method) is being computed.
- `const int ff_numCores()`3
  returns the number of cores in the target architecture.
- `int ff_mapThreadToCpu(int cpu_id, int priority_level=0)`
  pins the current thread to `cpu_id`. A priority may be set as well, but you need root rights in general, and therefore this should non be specified by normal users.

– void error(const char * str, ...)
is used to print error messages.
– virtual bool ff_send_out(void * task,
unsigned intretry=((unsigned int)-1),
unsigned int ticks=(TICKS2WAIT))
delivers an item onto the output stream, possibly retrying upon failure a given
number of times, after waiting a given number of clock ticks.
– double ffTime()
returns the time spent in the computation of a farm or of pipeline, including
the svc_init and svc_end time. This is a method of both pipeline and farm
classes.
– double ffwTime()
returns the time spent in the computation of a farm or of pipeline, in the svc
method only.
– double ffTime(int tag)
is used to measure time in portions of code. The tag may be: START_TIME,
STOP_TIME or GET_TIME. A ff_ffTime(GET_TIME) returns the time elapsed in
between two consecutive calls to ffTime() with parameter START _TIME and
STOP_TIME, respectively.
– void ffStats(std::ostream & out)
prints the statistics collected while using FastFlow. The program must be
compiled with TRACE_FASTFLOW defined, however.

14   Threads Mapping

FastFlow performance can significantly depend on the mapping of concurrent
activities to existing cores. Which is the best mapping depends on many factors of
the underlying architecture at hand. Here we describe the low-level mechanisms
provided by FastFlow that can be used to devise suitable mapping policies.

In FastFlow there are basically two main ways to pin a ff_node thread to a
core:

– at thread creation time. This feature is supported via a gcc intrinsic operations
that make it possible to create the thread implementing a FastFlow ff_node
directly on a specific core;
– at any time during the run, by using the ff_mapThreadToCpu and ff_getMyCpu
functions.

By default, all threads implementing sequential and parallel nodes of the
skeleton tree are pinned to available cores according to a linear static mapping.
For example, considering a 3-stage pipeline where the first and last stages are
sequential ff_nodes whereas the middle stage of the pipeline is a farm node
having 2 workers that are both pipeline of 2 sequential stages. In this case,
we have in total 8 threads (with ids in the range (0–7)), including the farm
emitter and collector threads. Such threads will be automatically pinned on the
first 8 cores (supposing there are at least 8 cores available) of the underlying

architecture. In particular the first pipeline stage will be pinned to core 0, the emitter of the farm to core 1, the two stages of the first worker to cores 2 and 3, the two stages of the second worker to cores 4 and 5, the collector to core 6 and the last stage to core 7.

To control the initial placement of the threads on the cores the FastFlow programmer may use the class threadMapper. The threadMapper gets in input a string (lets say mapstring) of comma-separated *core-ids*. At thread creation time, the FastFlow run-time will try to pin the thread with id tid in the core id specified in the corresponding position of the mapping string (modulo the number of core-ids in the string). Considering the 3-stage example described above and the following mapping string setup:

```
1    const char worker_mapping[] = "0, 2, 4, 6, 8";
2    threadMapper::instance()->setMappingList(worker_mapping);
3    ....
4    myprogram.run_and_wait_end();
```

The emitter of the farm is placed on core 2, the first sequential stages of the two pipelines in the farm on core 4 and 8, respectively.

In order to re-map threads after they have been created or during the computation, the function ff_mapThreadToCpu may be used. In the following there is an example of the usage of this function in the svc_init method of the ff_node class:

```
1    class myNode: public ff_node {
2        ....
3
4        int svc_init() {
5            printf("Thread currently running on CPU %d\n",ff_getMyCpu());
6            if (ff_mapThreadToCpu(mapThreads(get_my_id)) != 0)
7                printf("Cannot map thread %d (local id %d) on CPU %d\n",
                    getTid(), get_my_id(),
8                        mapThreads(getTid()));
9            return 0;
10       }
11       ...
```

The mapThreads function is a user defined function which gets in input the thread id and returns the core id in which the thread has to be pinned.

FastFlow also provides the possibility of not sticking concurrent activities to a particular core, and leaving instead to the operating system the full responsibility of the thread (dynamic) mapping. This possibility may be exploited by compiling the FastFlow program with the NO_DEFAULT_MAPPING symbol defined:

```
1    ffsrc$ g++ -DNO_DEFAULT_MAPPING -I $FF_ROOT ...
```

Under Linux, this allows threads to be moved between cores by the Linux scheduler. In most cases, this means threads are migrated with a substantial cache migration overhead, however.

15   Advanced Features

The skeletons and features discussed in the previous sections—apart from the C++11 related mechanisms of Sects. 8.7 and 9—are relative to the "core" Fast-Flow implementation, that is to the framework provided since version 1.0.

Skeleton	Modelled parallel pattern
ff_farm	computation of the same function (or of different functions) over all the items of the input stream
ff_pipeline	computation of functions in stages
ff_map	computation of the same function over all the items of a collection (array), reduction of a collection (array) by means of a binary, associative and commutative operator, combination of map and reduce on the same collection (array)
FF_PARFOR	map (possibly with an additional reduce phase) defined through a parallel for
stencil2D	computation of the same function over all the items of a collection (array). The function is computed on the value of the item and of the neighboring items, defined through a proper "stencil"
poolevolution	iteratively evolves a population of individuals (genetic like evolution)
dc	divide and conquer
ff_graphsearch	parallel graph search
ff_mdf	macro data flow (workflow) graph interpreter. The graph may be static or generated dynamically

Fig. 6. Skeletons available in FastFlow (as of December 2013)

More recently, within the activities of the EU FP7 STREP project "Para-Phrase" the FastFlow framework has been extended in several ways to accomplish different necessities from the application programmers. In particular:

- different high level patterns have been added,
- facilities to support coordinated execution of FastFlow program on internetworked multi core machines have been added,
- support for execution of new data parallel patterns on GPUs have been added as well,
- refactoring tools suitable to automatically introduce and refactor FastFlow skeletons in application code have been developed, and
- last but not least, a theoretical framework has been developed showing how the "core" FastFlow customizable components may be used to implement basically any kind of parallel pattern.

In this Section, we briefly outline these features.

15.1   High Level Patterns

FastFlow has been extended with new skeletons modeling general purpose and high level patterns. The table in Fig. 6 summarizes the skeletons provided so far, including the "core" ones. In particular, the following skeletons have been added to the "core" ones:

- The **map** skeleton applies the same computation to all the elements of an input collection (array) producing an output collection. The skeleton may be specialized to target GPU instead of CPU, if present, using either OpenCL or CUDA. The only difference between the instantiation of a map skeleton targeting CPU cores and the same skeleton targeting GPU is in the way used to provide the "worker" code, as in the latter case, OpenCL or CUDA kernels are needed.

- The **reduce** skeleton "sums up" using a commutative and associative binary operator all the elements in a collection (array) producing a single scalar value. As for the map skeleton, two different implementations of the reduce pattern exist targeting CPU or GPU.
- The **divide and conquer** skeleton implements the classical *divide et impera* computations, only targeting CPU, at the moment.
- The **stencil** skeleton applies the same computation to all the elements in an input collection (array) to produce an output collection, as in the map case. However, in case of the stencil, the computation of the single item depends not only on the value of that item in the input collection (as in map skeleton) but also on the values of a set of "neighboring" elements in the input collection. Moreover, the computation is iterative, that is more iterations are performed up to a given "termination condition".
- The **workflow interpreter** skeleton computes a statically or dynamically generated macro data flow graph over input data. It is usually instantiated to compute numerical code—possibly including calls to optimized numerical libraries—with maximum efficiency.
- The **pool evolution** skeleton iteratively computes the evolution of a set of "individuals" in a population by repeatedly (i) selecting a subset of individuals, (ii) "evolving" the selected individuals in new individuals, (iii) selecting a subset of the new individuals to be included in the original population and (iv) checking if the resulting population satisfies a given termination condition.

All these skeletons are provided to application programmers as FastFlow classes that may be instantiated and used in their programs. As an example, a stencil computation expressed by the following sequential code:

```
1  while(k<=maxit && error > tot) {
2    /* copy new solution into old matrix */
3    for(int j=0;j<m;j++)
4      for(int i=0;i<n;++i) uold[i+m*j]=u[i+m*j];
5    /* computes the stencil and residual */
6    for(int j=1;j<(m-1);++j)
7      for(int i=1;i<(n-1);++i) {
8        resid = compute_resid(f,i,j, uold,ax,ay);
9        /* updates solution */
10       u[i + m*j] = uold[i + m*j] - omega * resid;
11       /* accumulates residual error */
12       error =error + resid*resid;
13      }
14   error = sqrt(error) / (n*m);  k++;
15 }
```

may be implemented using a simple stencil skeleton instantiation such as:

```
1    // instantiate stencil pattern
2    stencil2D <double> stencil(u,uold,m,n,n,NUMTHREADS,1,1,false);
3
4    stencil->initInFunc(initU);
```

```
5     stencil ->initOutFunc ( initUold );
6
7     stencil ->computeFunc ( stencilF ,  1,m−1,1,  1,n−1,1);
8     stencil ->reduceFunc ( condF ,  maxit ,  reduceOp ,  0.0);
9
10    stencil ->run_and_wait_end ();
```

where:

- *initU* initializes the single cell of the u matrix. The function is called in a parallel loop in order to execute the initialization phase in parallel;
- *initUold* initializes the single cell of the *uold* matrix as in the previous case;
- *computeFunc* executes the stencil for each pair (i, j) updating the u matrix and reading values from the *uold* matrix;
- *reduceFunc* reduction function used to evaluate the error and for terminating the computation;
- *run_and_wait_end* starts the stencil computation and wait for termination.

More details on the new skeletons provided may be found in [32, 34].

15.2 Targeting Distributed Machines

ff_nodes model the concurrent activities in FastFlow. They are assumed to be independent threads, orchestrated by FastFlow in such a way they have a input channel (stream) providing input tasks to be computed and an output channel (stream) where the results computed out of the input tasks have to be delivered. The whole management of the input and output channels is in charge of the FastFlow run time support, rather than of the application programmer, as evident from the previous sections. These channel are implemented in "core" FastFlow by means of shared memory lock free queues.

Recently, a ff_dnode class has been added supporting the possibility to have one of the input and output channels implemented by means of *transport* layer on top of TCP/IP. The d_node class therefore supports communications between FastFlow threads running on different machines.

ff_dnodes may be used in any place where an ff_node may be used, that is as pipeline stages, farm workers, etc. They still define proper svc methods modeling the local computation of the thread. However, they have additional methods that allow to bind the input or output channel defined as distributed rather than local to an $\langle IP, port \rangle$ pair and to provide proper serialization (marshalling and un-marshalling) procedures for the tasks exchanged with the remote FastFlow node. Default serialization methods are provided in case tasks/results to be transmitted are represented within a single, contiguous memory region. Additional programming effort is required to accomplish non contiguous data serialization. In particular, in order to serialize non contiguous data, the programmer must implement a prepare method such as:

```
1  void prepare ( svector<iovec>& v,  void* ptr,  const int sender=−1) {
2      struct iovec iov={ptr ,taskSize*taskSize*sizeof(double)};
3      v.push_back ( iov );
4  }
```

where a svector<iovec> is filled with struct iovec pairs hosting the pointer and the length of the different memory areas used to represent the complex data structure to be serialized.

The distributed channels implemented on top of the TCP/IP stack[6] support the implementation of different channels, including one-to-one channels as well as one-to-n, n-to-n channels implementing different distribution (scatter, multicast, broadcast) and collection (gather, gatherall) policies. By using d_nodes and the associate channels FastFlow currently supports the implementation of farms with remote workers, pipeline with remote stages targeting both clusters of Linux workstations and cloud nodes [18].

15.3   Targeting GPUs

In the last versions of FastFlow, the execution of FastFlow data parallel patterns such as the ff_map may be directed to GPU cores rather than to CPU cores. A ff_mapCUDA (ff_mapOCL) map skeleton may be used in place of a simple ff_map to use (possibly existing) CUDA (OpenCL) kernels to map the same application onto all the elements of a collection (array). Apart from the specific syntax details needed to pass the CUDA (OpenCL) kernel to the constructor of the ff_mapXXX skeleton, the two skeletons implement all the necessary steps to execute the kernel on the GPU, including all the data transfers needed to move input data to the device memory and results back to the CPU main memory. Additional macros has been defined that simplify the writing of kernel code as well as of the full map skeleton. In particular, the kernel code may be provided through a proper macro taking as arguments the name of the kernel, the type of the input parameter and of the result, the name of the input (formal) parameter and the body of the kernel function. As an example, the code:

```
1 FFMAPFUNC(mapf, float, elem, return (elem+1.0) );
```

defines a kernel named mapf taking a float elem parameter and returning the float elem+1.0 value.

Using this kernel a farm with map workers targeting GPU may be defined as follows:

```
1      ff_farm <> farm;
2      Emitter   E(streamlen, inputsize);
3      Collector C(inputsize);
4      farm.add_emitter(&E);
5      farm.add_collector(&C);
6
7      std::vector<ff_node *> w;
8      for(int i=0;i<nworkers;++i)
9          w.push_back(NEWMAPONSTREAM(oclTask<float>, mapf));
10     farm.add_workers(w);
11     farm.run_and_wait_end();
```

The NEWMAPONSTREAM macro on line 9 defines a map targeting GPU through CUDA or OpenCL—depending on the macro defined in the preamble (ff_CUDA or ff_OCL)—and computing the mapf kernel on float arrays provided through

---

[6] We currently use the zeroMQ library to support the distributed channels ().

a stream[7]. More details on the FastFlow skeletons targeting GPUs may be found in [33]. Reference [38] discusses how a FastFlow module may be implemented automatically splitting map tasks among CPU and GPU cores, such that the overall execution time is optimized.

15.4 Refactoring

Programs using skeletons may be rewritten in such a way the functional semantics is preserved while the non-functional semantics (the aspects relative to performance or power consumption, as an example) is possibly changed.

Different rewriting rules hold, including[8]:

$farm(\Delta, nw) \equiv \Delta$	a farm with nw workers is equivalent to the computation of the worker alone
$pipeline(\Delta_1, \Delta_1) \equiv comp(\Delta_1, \Delta_2)$	a pipeline of two stages is equivalent to the sequential composition of the two stages
$pipe(map(\Delta_1), map(\Delta_2)) \equiv map(pipe(\Delta_1, \Delta_2))$	map promotion: two maps in a pipeline are equivalent to a map with a pipeline worker

These rules have obvious impact on performances. In [6] we have shown that any stream parallel skeleton composition involving farms and pipelines eventually may be substituted by a single farm of sequential workers derived applying the rules listed above and sporting a better or similar—with respect to the original composition—service time. As a further example, a pipeline with two unbalances stages $pipe(Stage1, Stage2)$ may be rewritten with much better performance applying the first rewriting rule in the table above "right-to-left" to obtain a $pipe(Stage1, farm(Stage2, nw))$ in case the second stage has a latency nw times the latency of the first stage.

Therefore, if our original pipeline is implemented through the code:

```
1    ...
2    ff_pipeline pipe;
3    pipe.add_stage(new Stage1());
4    pipe.add_stage(new Stage2());
5    ...
6    pipe.run_and_wait_end();
```

we can easily apply the rewriting rule introducing the farm obtaining a refactored program such as:

```
1    ...
2    ff_pipeline pipe;
3    pipe.add_stage(new Stage1());
4
5    ff_farm<> farm;
```

---

[7] The map itself works on a single input task to produce a single output result, by default.

[8] Δ represents any skeleton composition, in this case.

```
 6    std::vector<ff_node*> w;
 7    for(int i=0;i<nw;i++) w.push_back(new Stage2());
 8    farm.add_workers(w);
 9
10    pipe.add_stage(&farm);
11    ...
12    pipe.run_and_wait_end();
```

It is worth pointing out the negligible programming effort required to refactor the program according to the "logical" rewrite rule listed in the table, especially compared to the effort required when refactoring in the same way programs written with parallel programming frameworks not supporting skeleton/parallel patterns (e.g. MPI). Assuming the latencies of Stage1 and Stage2 were respectively of 100 and 300 ms (per task), and that the program computes 1000 tasks, the completion time of the first version would have been around 300 s, while the one relative to the second version could have been around 100 s, with a 3x speedup.

Within ParaPhrase a refactorer tool supporting rewriting of FastFlow skeletons according to a set of rules including the ones listed above is being developed on top of Eclipse [35].

15.5   RISC-pbb

Last but not least, the FastFlow components used to implement the "core" skeletons, namely the emitter, collector, string of workers, etc. may be considered a sort of "RISC" set of parallel building blocks suitable to be used to build a number of different skeletons implementing a variety of parallel patterns: simple general purpose parallel patterns, domain specific parallel patterns and high level parallel patterns implementing parallel programming models as well. In [23] we define the RISC-pbb set of parallel building blocks corresponding to the base components of FastFlow and in [2] we show:

- how these building blocks may be used to implement high level parallel models (e.g. BSP or Google mapreduce)
- that they are suitable to implement domain specific parallel patterns (e.g. from soft computing/genetic algorithms or from numerical applications)
- that a set of rewriting rules stating equivalences among building block expressions exist, such that they may be used to refactor building block expressions to (i) improve performances and (ii) to target different parallel architectures.

16   Related Work

FastFlow aims at providing programmers of parallel applications with suitable tools enhancing their productivity while designing, developing and tuning parallel applications. In particular, it aims at supporting both the parallelization of existing applications–e.g. exploiting the accelerator facilities of FastFlow–and the development *ex novo* of parallel applications.

In this respect, FastFlow naturally competes with more famous and widely used parallel programming frameworks targeting the same kind of shared memory architectures such as OpenMP or Intel TBB.

OpenMP (http://openmp.org/wp/) naturally and seamlessly supports data parallel patterns, especially those expressed as parallelization of loops. It also supports the implementation of more complex, task parallel patterns, but this requires much more programming effort. In fact, different extensions (e.g. [36,37]) have been developed to increase the possibilities offered to parallelize applications with more complex task parallel patterns in OpenMP. Overall, even if the programming effort may by slightly larger in terms of lines of code, FastFlow still offers more–primitive or composite–patterns than OpenMP, with a comparable efficiency level and with better composition features.

Intel TBB (https://www.threadingbuildingblocks.org/) provides more primitive mechanisms with respect to both OpenMP and FastFlow. These mechanisms may be used to implement different patterns with different amounts of programming effort. However, the lower–with respect to FastFlow–level of abstraction provided to the parallel programmer by Intel TBB has a notable impact on both development and tuning time of parallel applications.

A number of different parallel programming environments from the algorithmic skeleton community have been developed and are currently maintained that directly compete with FastFlow. Muesli [25], Sketo [31], SKEPU [24], OSL [29], Skandium [30], just to mention some of them, all provide a set of parallel patterns as *algorithmic skeletons* suitable to be instantiated–alone or in composition–with business code parameters to implement parallel applications. Some of these frameworks only provide data parallel skeletons (e.g. SKEPU and Sketo). Other use different "host languages" (e.g. Skandium, which is provided as a Java library). In the former case, FastFlow offers a more structured and comprehensive parallel pattern set. In the latter case, the efficiency related to the usage of C++ rather than Java may represent a sensible advantage for Fast-Flow. Some of these programming frameworks also target clusters/networks of workstations (e.g. Muesli) or GPUs (e.g. Meusli and SKEPU). As explained in Sects. 15.2 and 15.3 FastFlow extensions may be used to orchestrate parallel computations on clusters of multi cores [5] and to direct data parallel computation to GPUs (using either CUDA or OpenCL kernels) or to a mix of GPU and CPU cores (using OpenCL) [26,38].

Different research teams participated to the development of FastFlow in different ways. Szügyi and Pataki [39] developed a version of FastFlow fully exploiting the template mechanisms provided by C++ that eventually demonstrates good performances and much better type checking than the original FastFlow. Collins designed advanced tools suitable to automatically configure implementation parameters of FastFlow such that optimal performances may be automatically achieved [21]. Boob et al. [17] developed tools to distribute FastFlow computations on cloud resource exploiting typical virtual machine technologies. Goli and Gonzalèz-Velez demonstrated combined exploitation of CPU and GPU cores with FastFlow [26,27].

Last but not least, different groups are using FastFlow to implement different kinds of parallel applications and frameworks, including business transaction frameworks (http://fix8.org/), deep packet inspection tools (https://github.com/DanieleDeSensi/Peafowl) and rewriting-based calculus for the representation and simulation of biological systems (http://sourceforge.net/projects/cwcsimulator/).

17   Conclusions

We have introduced the basic features of the structured parallel programming framework FastFlow. We discussed this features by illustrating simple sample code and pointing at relevant papers and manuals hosting more detailed description of syntax and usage best practices for FastFlow.

FastFlow has been demonstrated to be very efficient in the execution of structured parallel applications, especially when fine grain parallelism has to be exploited. Different published papers show that the performances achieved with FastFlow applications/kernels on state-of-the-art multi core and distributed architectures are comparable or even better than the performances achieved executing the same applications/kernels using different, more traditional programming frameworks such as OpenMP or the Intel TBB library [10,13,15].

FastFlow is currently being adopted within two FP7 projects, ParaPhrase[9] and Repara[10]. In ParaPhrase, a methodology supporting the development of parallel applications where FastFlow parallel patterns are introduced through semi automatic refactoring of existing code is being developed. Preliminary results on industrial use cases show that the approach is feasible, FastFlow achieves comparable or slightly better performances that OpenMP and, last but not least, that the combined usage of refactoring and FastFlow technology greatly simplifies the development of efficient parallel applications, thus improving the time-to-market of parallel applications. Within Repara (just stared at the moment being), FastFlow is being adopted as the run time system orchestrating the execution of parallel applications on heterogeneous architectures including multicore CPUs, GPUs, FPGAs and DSPs.

FastFlow is an open source framework licensed under LGPL and available at SourceForge[11]. At the moment being the downloads from SourceForge are in the range of thousands. Different researchers and programmers are using it especially in those cases where fine grain parallelism needs to be exploited with the maximum efficiency.

References

1. FastFlow home page (2012). http://mc-fastflow.sourceforge.net
2. Aldinucci, M., Campa, S., Danelutto, M., Kilpatrick, P., Torquati, M.: Design patterns percolating to parallel programming framework implementation. Int. J. Parallel Program. (2013). doi:10.1007/s10766-013-0273-6

---

[9] http://www.paraphrase-ict.eu.
[10] http://www.repara-project.eu/#!.
[11] http://sourceforge.net/projects/mc-fastflow/.

3. Aldinucci, M., Anardu, L., Danelutto, M., Torquati, M., Kilpatrick, P.: Parallel patterns + macro data flow for multi-core programming. In: Proceedings of International Euromicro PDP 2012: Parallel Distributed and network-based Processing, Garching, Germany. IEEE, February 2012
4. Aldinucci, M., Bracciali, A., Liò, P., Sorathiya, A., Torquati, M.: StochKit-FF: efficient systems biology on multicore architectures. In: Guarracino, M.R., et al. (eds.) Euro-Par-Workshop 2010. LNCS, vol. 6586, pp. 167–175. Springer, Heidelberg (2011)
5. Aldinucci, M., Campa, S., Danelutto, M., Kilpatrick, P., Torquati, M.: Targeting distributed systems in FastFlow. In: Caragiannis, I., et al. (eds.) Euro-Par Workshops 2012. LNCS, vol. 7640, pp. 47–56. Springer, Heidelberg (2013)
6. Aldinucci, M., Danelutto, M.: Stream parallel skeleton optimization. In: Proceedings of PDCS: International Conference on Parallel and Distributed Computing and Systems, pp. 955–962. IASTED, ACTA Press, Cambridge, Massachusetts (1999)
7. Aldinucci, M., Danelutto, M., Kilpatrick, P., Meneghin, M., Torquati, M.: Accelerating sequential programs using FastFlow and self-offloading. Technical report TR-10-03, Universitá di Pisa, Dipartimento di Informatica, Italy, February 2010
8. Aldinucci, M., Danelutto, M., Kilpatrick, P., Meneghin, M., Torquati, M.: Accelerating code on multi-cores with FastFlow. In: Jeannot, E., Namyst, R., Roman, J. (eds.) Euro-Par 2011, Part II. LNCS, vol. 6853, pp. 170–181. Springer, Heidelberg (2011)
9. Aldinucci, M., Danelutto, M., Kilpatrick, P., Meneghin, M., Torquati, M.: An efficient unbounded lock-free queue for multi-core systems. In: Kaklamanis, C., Papatheodorou, T., Spirakis, P.G. (eds.) Euro-Par 2012. LNCS, vol. 7484, pp. 662–673. Springer, Heidelberg (2012)
10. Aldinucci, M., Danelutto, M., Kilpatrick, P., Torquati, M.: Targeting heterogeneous architectures via macro data flow. Parallel Process. Lett. 22(2) (2012)
11. Aldinucci, M., Danelutto, M., Kilpatrick, P., Torquati, M.: Fastflow: high-level and efficient streaming on multi-core. In: Pllana, S., Xhafa, F. (eds.) Programming Multi-core and Many-core Computing Systems, Parallel and Distributed Computing, chap. 13. Wiley (2014)
12. Aldinucci, M., Danelutto, M., Meneghin, M., Kilpatrick, P., Torquati, M.: Efficient streaming applications on multi-core with FastFlow: the biosequence alignment test-bed. In: Chapman, B., Desprez, F., Joubert, G.R., Lichnewsky, A., Priol, T., Peters, F.J. (eds.) Parallel Computing: From Multicores and GPU's to Petascale (Proceedings of PARCO 2009, Lyon, France). Advances in Parallel Computing, vol. 19, pp. 273–280, Lyon, France. IOS Press, September 2009
13. Aldinucci, M., Drocco, M., Tordini, F., Coppo, M., Torquati, M.: Parallel stochastic simulators in system biology: the evolution of the species. In: 16th Euromicro Conference on Parallel, Distributed and Network-Based Processing (PDP 2008), pp. 410–419 (2013)
14. Aldinucci, M., Meneghin, M., Torquati, M.: Efficient Smith-Waterman on multi-core with FastFlow. In Danelutto, M., Gross, T., Bourgeois, J. (eds.) Proceedings of International Euromicro PDP 2010: Parallel Distributed and network-based Processing, Pisa, Italy. IEEE, February 2010
15. Aldinucci, M., Ruggieri, S., Torquati, M.: Decision tree building on multi-core using fastflow. Concurr. Comput. Practi. Experien. 26(3), 800–820 (2014)
16. Aldinucci, M., Torquati, M., Meneghin, M.: FastFlow: efficient parallel streaming applications on multi-core. Technical report TR-09-12, Universitá di Pisa, Dipartimento di Informatica, Italy, September 2009

17. Boob, S., González-Vélez, H., Popescu, A.M.: Automated instantiation of hetero-geneous FastFlow CPU/GPU parallel pattern applications in clouds. In: Proceed-ings of International Euromicro PDP 2014: Parallel Distributed and network-based Processing. IEEE Press (2014)
18. Campa, S., Danelutto, M., Torquati, M., González-Vélez, H., Popescu, A.: Towards the deployment of fastflow on distributed virtual architectures. In: Rekdalsbakken, W., Bye, R.T., Zhang, H. (eds.) ECMS, pp. 518–524. European Council for Mod-eling and Simulation (2013)
19. Cole, M.: Algorithmic Skeletons: Structured Management of Parallel Computation. MIT Press, Cambridge (1991)
20. Cole, M.: Bringing skeletons out of the closet: a pragmatic manifesto for skeletal parallel programming. Parallel Comput. 30(3), 389–406 (2004)
21. Collins, A., Fensch, C., Leather, H.: Optimization space exploration of the FastFlow parallel skeleton framework (2012). HLPGPU 2012, http://homepages.inf.ed.ac.uk/s1050857/collins-hlpgpu12.pdf
22. M. Danelutto, L. Deri, and D. De Sensi.: Network Monitoring on Multicores with Algorithmic Skeletons. In Volume 22: Applications, Tools and Techniques on the Road to Exascale Computing, Advances in Parallel Computing, pages 519–526. IOS Press, 2012. 2011, DOI: 10.3233/978-1-61499-041-3-519, Proc. of Intl. Parallel Computing (PARCO)
23. Danelutto, M., Torquati, M.: A RISC building block set for structured parallel pro-gramming. In: 21st Euromicro International Conference on Parallel, Distributed, and Network-Based Processing, PDP 2013, Belfast, United Kingdom, 27 February–1 March, pp. 46–50. IEEE Computer Society (2013)
24. Dastgeer, U., Li, L., Kessler, C.: Adaptive implementation selection in the skepu skeleton programming library. In: Wu, C., Cohen, A. (eds.) APPT 2013. LNCS, vol. 8299, pp. 170–183. Springer, Heidelberg (2013)
25. Ernsting, S., Kuchen, H.: Algorithmic skeletons for multi-core, multi-gpu systems and clusters. IJHPCN 7(2), 129–138 (2012)
26. Goli, M., González-Vélez, H.: Heterogeneous algorithmic skeletons for fast flow with seamless coordination over hybrid architectures. In: 21st Euromicro International Conference on Parallel, Distributed, and Network-Based Processing, PDP 2013, Belfast, United Kingdom, 27 February–1 March, pp. 148–156. IEEE Computer Society (2013)
27. Goli, M., González-Vélez, H.: N-body computations using skeletal frameworks on multicore cpu/graphics processing unit architectures: an empirical performance evaluation. Concurr. Comput. Practi. Experien. 26(4), 972–986 (2014)
28. González-Vélez, H., Leyton, M.: A survey of algorithmic skeleton frameworks: high-level structured parallel programming enablers. Softw. Pract. Exper. 40(12), 1135–1160 (2010)
29. Legaux, J., Loulergue, F., Jubertie, S.: OSL: an algorithmic skeleton library with exceptions. In: Alexandrov, V.N., Lees, M., Krzhizhanovskaya, V.V., Dongarra, J., Sloot, P.M.A. (eds.) ICCS. Procedia Computer Science, vol. 18, pp. 260–269. Elsevier (2013)
30. Leyton, M., Piquer, J.M.: Skandium: multi-core programming with algorithmic skeletons. In: Danelutto, M., Bourgeois, J., Gross, T. (eds.) PDP, pp. 289–296. IEEE Computer Society (2010)
31. Matsuzaki, K., Kakehi, K., Iwasaki, H., Hu, Z., Akashi, Y.: A fusion-embedded skeleton library. In: Danelutto, M., Vanneschi, M., Laforenza, D. (eds.) Euro-Par 2004. LNCS, vol. 3149, pp. 644–653. Springer, Heidelberg (2004)

32. ParaPhrase. Final Pattern Definition Report (2013). http://www.paraphrase-ict.eu/Deliverables
33. ParaPhrase. Heterogeneous Implementation of Initial Generic Patterns (2013). http://www.paraphrase-ict.eu/Deliverables
34. ParaPhrase. Initial Implementation of Application-Specific Patterns (2013). http://www.paraphrase-ict.eu/Deliverables
35. ParaPhrase. Refactoring User Interfaces (2013). http://www.paraphrase-ict.eu/Deliverables
36. Planas, J., Badia, R.M., Ayguadé, E., Labarta, J.: Hierarchical task-based programming with starss. IJHPCA **23**(3), 284–299 (2009)
37. Planas, J., Badia, R.M., Ayguadé, E., Labarta, J.: Self-adaptive ompss tasks in heterogeneous environments. In: IPDPS, pp. 138–149. IEEE Computer Society (2013)
38. Serban, T., Danelutto, M., Kilpatrick, P.: Autonomic scheduling of tasks from data parallel patterns to cpu/gpu core mixes. In: HPCS, pp. 72–79. IEEE (2013)
39. Szűgyi, Z., Pataki, N.: Generative version of the fastflow multicore library. Electr. Notes Theor. Comput. Sci. **279**(3), 73–84 (2011)

DSL in C++ Template Metaprogram

Zoltán Porkoláb[(✉)], Ábel Sinkovics, and István Siroki

Department of Programming Languages and Compilers, Faculty of Informatics,
Eötvös Loránd University, Pázmány Péter Sétány 1/C, 1117 Budapest, Hungary
{gsd,abel,steve}@caesar.elte.hu

Abstract. Domain specific language integration has to provide the right balance between the expressive power of the DSL and the implementation and maintenance cost of the applied integration techniques. In this paper we discuss a DSL integration technique for the C++ programming language. The solution is based on compile-time parsing of the DSL code using the C++ template metaprogramming library called Metaparse. The parser generator is the C++ template metaprogram reimplementation of a runtime Haskell parser generator library. The full parsing phase is executed when the host program is compiled. The library uses only standard C++ language features, thus our solution is highly portable. As a demonstration of the power of this approach, we present a highly efficient and type-safe version of printf and the way it can be constructed using our library. Despite the well known syntactical difficulties of C++ template metaprograms, building embedded languages using Metaparse leads to self-documenting maintainable C++ source code.

1 DSL Integration

Although domain specific languages are indispensable in their domain, the vast majority of the programs execute most of their actions out of that domain. As an example, SQL might be a perfect solution for describing operations related to relational databases, but database servers will create threads, open network connections, communicate with the operating system in the means of a general purpose programming language. The usual solution is that the desired domain-specific language or languages are used together with a general purpose programming language. In most cases the integration of these languages happens by embedding the DSL(s) into the general purpose language with or without some syntactical quotation. However, this integration should add minimal syntactical, semantic and maintenance overhead to the project.

Two fundamental approaches exist when a DSL is about to be integrated into a host language. In one approach some external tool or framework is used to identify, parse, syntactically and semantically check the domain specific language and generate the code integrated into the host language. As an alternative way one can use internal solutions, that do not require other tools than the infrastructure of the host language. Although many of the recent DSL integration approaches focus on the application of external tools [11,16,18,26,29], in modern

V. Zsók et al. (Eds.): CEFP 2013, LNCS 8606, pp. 76–114, 2015.
DOI: 10.1007/978-3-319-15940-9_3

programming languages, like Scala [4] and Haskell [15] there are vital examples for using the internal method. In the case of C++ one of the primary candidates is template metaprogramming [1,3,6,7], in which one can define multi-staged compilation steps using only the C++ compiler.

Regular expression is one of the commonly used domain specific language in modern generic purpose programming languages. They are used for a very special purpose: text manipulation, and have a specific, usually implementation-independent syntax. Regular expressions are mostly implemented as libraries. Classical regular expression libraries, like `stl::regex` from the C++11 standard [17], are powerful and flexible. Patterns are represented as strings which are specified at run-time. In this case a syntax error in the regular expression, such as unbalanced parenthesis, can be detected only at run-time.

The `Boost.Xpressive` is an advanced, object-oriented regular expression library for C++ [30]. The provides two ways for defining a regular expression. Regular expressions in Boost.Xpressive can either be dynamically bound and specified at run-time or statically bound, hard-coded and syntax-checked by the compiler. These regular expressions can refer to each other recursively.

1. **Dynamic Regex.** We can call the `sregex::compile` method in runtime to create a regular expression we specified as a string. This method doesn't provide compile time syntax check for the regex, although it retains the well-known syntax.
2. **Static Regex.** We can build a regex from overloaded `C++` expressions, so called expression templates. Thus Boost.Xpressive library allows an alternative way for embedding regular expressions as DSL: they can be defined using expression templates and thus they are checked at compilation time. Unfortunately, this comes with high syntactical overhead. For example a regular expression in dynamic regex `"(\\w+) (\\w+)!"` looks like this in static regex:

$$(s1= +\_w) >> \text{’ ’} >> (s2= +\_w) >> \text{’!’}$$

Most of the current C++ template metaprogramming development suffers from similar unmaintenable syntax. The syntax of Boost.Xpressive and Boost.Proto [13] as examples, are seriously restricted by the fact that C++ expression templates should conform to the syntax of valid C++ expressions [24,25]. This is in sharp contrast with the flexibility of dynamic regular expressions where the expressions are placed in run-time strings without any restrictions.

Our goal is to combine the best of the two approaches and give a method where we can specify a regex as a string without restrictions but keeping the possibility of compile time syntax checking. This way we could achieve seamless integration without syntactical overhead, thus we don't need to escape the domain of regular expressions when we want to use them in C++.

We will achieve this goal with the help of the `Metaparse` library [22,23]. Metaparse is a C++ template metaprogram library which implements a full-featured parser infrastructure to parse the domain specific code and translate it to native C++ [7]. When implementing the parser we followed L. Andersson's description on the construction of a parser generator in Haskell [2], but leveraged the well known connection between functional programming languages and C++ template metaprogramming. Our parser is executed as a metaprogram during the compilation of the C++ source using no other tool than the standard C++ compiler. Metaparse is the only library the authors are aware of, which supports parsing a string at compile-time and the generation of types as the result of parsing. Further details on Metaparse can be found in [6].

With the help of Metaparse we are able to translate regular expressions in arbitrary syntax to the required input syntax of Boost.Xpressive. We implement these translation by writing simpler parsers and combining them to build a more complex parser. To identify the needed parsers we will write a grammar for regular expressions. These individual parsers are metafunctions with a scope of parsing one element from the grammar. They can process different regex pieces like [abc] or (xyz). We can combine them as described in Sect. 2, thus we can parse ([abc]xyz) too without writing a new parser for this expression. We will show a working library which can parse arbitrary complicated regular expressions and create the respective static Xpressive regular expressions for them using C++ compiler only.

To build a complex parser like this, we need to clearly describe how the possible regular expression pieces can be used together. The parser needs to know the expected order of the pieces, and how they can be embedded within each other. The different expressions need to be categorised and ranked according to their precedence. A grammar can express these relations.

The Xpressive User's guide contains a table which shows line-by-line the Perl regular expression syntax and the corresponding static Xpressive expression. We can use this table as a starting point to determine the elements the parser needs to interpret and convert into static Xpressive objects. Note, the POSIX [5] character classes like [:alnum:] should be written as [[:alnum:]], if we want to comply with the Perl syntax.

It is challenging to identify the main grammatical elements which are based on the precedence of the expressions. We can try to draw syntax trees for concrete expressions to identify what kind of elements we would need in the grammar to build it up.

As we can see on Fig. 1, a regular expression (reg_exp) consists of seq elements. These sequences consist of arbitrary number of unary_item expressions which are items with their possible repetitions. It is necessary to differentiate items and set_items, because the latter has only those expressions of the grammar which can be used within square brackets. Arbitrary number of set_item can be joined with a set element which contains the closing ']' character. A character group like [abc] can be called group in our grammar and its rule can be that it starts with '[' and then it continues with a set or a range expression (range_exp).

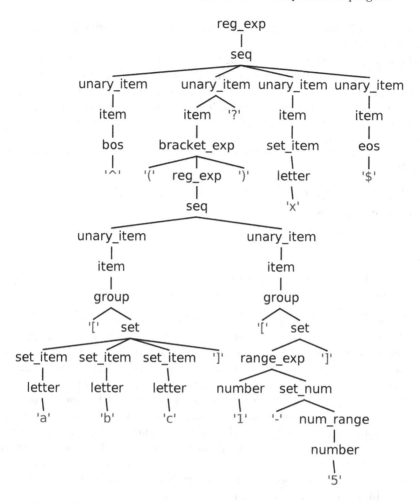

Fig. 1. The syntax tree of the `^([abc][1-5])?x$` regular expression

We can also identify that anything can be put in a bracket expression, so we allow our head element to be used between ' (' and ') '. With different examples we can gradually identify the use-cases of the elements, and deduce the suitable grammar elements. The final version of our grammar can be seen in Appendix A.

2 Parsing Basic Regular Expressions

After we have the grammar, we can commence building up the parsers. Let's start with the less complicated ones, which are at the bottom of our syntax tree. The very first parser we'll build is for the caret character (' ^ '), which has a special meaning in regular expressions. We can put it as the first character of a sequence, which means that the following regular expression elements should match a string from its beginning. The code of this **bos** (beginning of sequence) parser is as follows:

The parser is built using a **typedef**. We can use **lit_c<'^'>** to identify a caret character. The **always** parser can be used to replace this character with our **build_bos** metafunction class. This class has a **type**, as every metafunction class should, and a static **run** method. This method can be used to return the desired static **Xpressive** object, which is in our case a **boost::xpressive::bos** object. The **eos** and **any** elements have been created the same way.

```
struct build_bos
{
  typedef build_bos type;
  static xpressive::sregex run() {
    return xpressive::bos;
  }
};
typedef metaparse::always<
  metaparse::lit_c<'^'>, xlxpressive::build_bos
> bos;
```

So far so good, but how can we use this as a regular expression? We have the '^' character identified by **lit_c**. Our **bos** parser returns the **build_bos** metafunction class, because we use the **always** parser. To get the static **Xpressive** object we can call the **run** method through **type**, since it is **static**.

We have the parser we'd like to test, so we just need to give it the input string from a test case. To do this easily **Metaparse** provides us a **build_parser** metafunction. What it does is exactly what we want: it wraps our parser with a metafunction class which expects an input string, gives it to our parser and returns its result. If our parser fails, a compilation error will be generated. We use the **entire_input** parser around our own parser to ensure that we process the entire input string. So this is how we can use our first simple parser:

```
typedef metaparse::build_parser<
  metaparse::entire_input<xlxpressive::bos>
> regexp_parser;
```

This can be tested with a simple test case like this:

```
[test1]
str=
pat=^
flg=
br0=
[end]
```

The final step is to create an `sregex` object. This can be done by applying our `regexp_parser` on a `boost::mpl::string`, or we can use the `MPLLIBS_STRING` macro, if we can leverage the C++11 standard. For our first simple example here's how we can do this:

```
const sregex re = mpl::apply_wrap1<regexp_parser ,
   MPLLIBS_STRING(" ^ ") >::type::run();
```

To make the whole construct even more usable, we can wrap it with a macro like `REGEX`. This way we can simply create our `Xpressive` regular expression object (`sregex`) using this macro, and then we can use it the normal way:

```
#define REGEX(s) (mpl::apply_wrap1<regexp_parser ,
   MPLLIBS_STRING(s) >::type::run())
const sregex re = REGEX(" ^ ");
```

As we build our solution further we can add new test cases and change the actual parser behind `regexp_parser` to the actual top element we have implemented so far from the grammar. This way we can test the added parser and ensure that we haven't broken anything.

When the parser fails compiler error is generated. Reporting errors in a clear, unambiguous way with the correct information about the place of occurrence is essential for the usability of our approach. The authors investigated the methods of generating valuable diagnostic messages regarding C++ template metaprograms in [9]. In the same paper the authors describe a unit testing framework for C++ template metaprograms that guarantees the execution of all test cases and provides proper summary-report with enhanced and portable error reporting. That method can be used to generate a test framework for the grammar.

3 Combining Regular Expressions

After we have these basic elements we can go up a level on the syntax tree to see how they fit into the upper element, `item` in this case. It looks like this in our grammar:

```
item ::= set_item|bos|eos|any|bracket_exp|group
```

We just simply list the acceptable elements. It is important that these elements are in the order of precedence i.e. if the first clause matches, the others aren't evaluated at all. We can do the same using the `one_of` parser:

```
typedef metaparse::one_of<
   xlxpressive::set_item ,
   xlxpressive::bos ,
   xlxpressive::eos ,
   xlxpressive::any ,
```

```
  xlxpressive :: bracket_exp ,
  xlxpressive :: group
>
item ;
```

We used **typedef** again to create a new element of the grammar. This is a common technique to define our entities in template metaprogramming. As you can see we've listed all the elements we need for a complete item. We will examine some of them in details later on. The very similar **set_item** can be built this way too.

The **item** element with an optional **repetition** behind it construct our next target, the **unary_item**.

```
unary_item ::= item (('*'|'+'|'?'|repeat) '?'?)?
```

This complicated thing after **item** means that it can be followed by a '*', '+', '?' character or a 'repeat{n, m}' construct. This is the **repetition** of **item**. The '?' character is optional, just like this whole **repetition** thing itself. Let's see what we want to identify and what we want that to be transformed into. On the left side we have the regular expressions in their common format, how we use them in **Perl** and on the right side the respective static **Xpressive** form can be seen.

```
a        -> a
a*       -> *a
a+       -> +a
a?       -> !a
a{n,m}   -> repeat<n,m>(a)
a*?      -> -*a
a+?      -> -+a
a??      -> -!a
a{n,m}?  -> -repeat<n,m>(a)
```

The main problem here is this: we can parse an **item** and a **repetition** separately in a **sequence**, but how should we give the result of **item** to the **repetition**? Let me show how we can identify these elements one-by-one, and after that how we can solve this issue. Using a top-to-bottom approach let's write what we want first, break the problem into smaller parts and solve these later on:

```
typedef metaparse :: transform<
  metaparse :: sequence<xlxpressive :: item :: type ,
      xlxpressive :: repetition >,
  xlxpressive :: build_unary_item
>
unary_item ;
```

With **sequence** we can specify an order between the sub-parsers. We accept a **unary_item** only, if it consists of an **item** and then a **repetition**. The **transform** parser will be used many times further on. It is very useful, because it calls the second template parameter with the result of the parser in its first template parameter, which is a **sequence** in our case. The second parameter is a metafunction class responsible for the transformation. We need a metafunction class instead of a simple metafunction, because we need a type here. Metafunction classes are complete types, so we can pass them as metafunction arguments. They are wrappers around their publicly-accessible **apply** metafunction. We have seen how the **item** parser can be built up. Let's create the **repetition** parser, so we're focusing on this part of the grammar now:

```
((’*’|’+’|’?’|repeat) ’?’?)?
repeat ::= ’{’ (number ’,’ number|’,’ number| number ’,’) ’}’
```

The pipe separated list is similar to what we have seen at the **item** element, so we can use the **lit_c** and **one_of** parser combinators [8,10] again. To specify the order between this part and the question mark character, a **sequence** can be used. The numbers can be identified with the **digit_val** parser, if we want the **int** value to be returned. If we want to mark whether we've seen an optional element, like ’?’, or not, we can use the **return_** parser. It simply returns what is its argument without parsing anything. We can use it with **char** and **int** values in our case.

We have the following structure to be parsed: [*+?{] (\d,\d})?’?’?. To handle the optional parts we use the **one_of** parser this way:

```
typedef metaparse :: one_of<
  metaparse :: digit_val ,
  metaparse :: return_< mpl :: int_<−1> >
>
maybe_digit ;
```

It can accept a digit or return −1 otherwise. We should do the same thing for accepting the comma symbol:

```
typedef metaparse :: one_of<
  metaparse :: lit_c <’ , ’>,
  metaparse :: return_< mpl :: char_<’x’> >
>
maybe_comma ;
```

We parse a ’,’ character or return an ’x’. Of course, we can choose any other character instead of ’x’ to express that we've not matched the expected one. We can define **maybe_close_curly_bracket** and **maybe_questionmark** the same way. We should have a return value in case we don't have this repetition part at all. For this we can create a **dont_repeat** type, which can be defined using a **boost::mpl::vector** type sequence the following way:

```
typedef metaparse::return_<
  mpl::vector<
    mpl::char_<'x'>,
    mpl::int_<-1>,
    mpl::char_<'x'>,
    mpl::int_<-1>,
    mpl::char_<'x'>,
    mpl::char_<'x'>
  >
>
dont_repeat;
```

With these structures we can define **repetition** in a self-documenting manner like this:

```
typedef metaparse::transform <
  metaparse::one_of<
    metaparse::sequence<
      metaparse::one_of<
        metaparse::lit_c <'*'>,
        metaparse::lit_c <'+'>,
        metaparse::lit_c <'?'>,
        metaparse::lit_c <'{'>
      >,
      maybe_digit ,
      maybe_comma,
      maybe_digit ,
      maybe_close_curly_bracket ,
      maybe_questionmark
    >,
    dont_repeat
  >,
  xlxpressive::eval_repetition
>
repetition;
```

We've wrapped the whole construct with the **transform** parser combinator again, because we have character and numeric values only and we need to evaluate them and return the corresponding repetition somehow.

With `eval_repetition` we want to give back a "metaprogramming data", which shows what kind of repetition the user has specified. These are the results of our repetition parsing and can be declared as `structs` e.g.:

```
// when we haven't seen repetition
struct no_repeat { typedef no_repeat type; };
// when '*' has been identified
struct any_repeat { typedef any_repeat type; };
// when both '*' and a following '?' have been identified
struct any_may_repeat { typedef any_may_repeat type; };
// etc...
```

Let's just concentrate on `any_repeat`. How can `eval_repetition` return it, while it has the `char` and `int` values only? We can use the template specialization here, because this way like with pattern matching in functional programming, we can uniquely choose and return the needed result. `eval_repetition` is a metafunction class. To do the pattern matching with specialization we can declare a `struct eval_repetition_impl` which has 6 template parameters. We can pass these parameters to the implementation by processing the sequence we've got from the `transform` parser. The `boost::mpl::at_c` metafunction can be used here, since we know the length of the received sequence and we can pass the index as a constant value:

```
struct eval_repetition
{
  template <class Seq>
  struct apply :
    eval_repetition_impl<
      mpl::at_c<Seq, 0>::type::value,
      mpl::at_c<Seq, 1>::type::value,
      mpl::at_c<Seq, 2>::type::value,
      mpl::at_c<Seq, 3>::type::value,
      mpl::at_c<Seq, 4>::type::value,
      mpl::at_c<Seq, 5>::type::value
    > {};
};
```

The implementation for `any_repeat` can be seen below. The listed constants in the template parameters of `eval_repetition_impl` show that we've specialized for the case when the user gave a `'*'` after the `item`. The inheritance can be used here as a technique to return our prepared `any_repeat` type.

```
template <char A, int N, char B, int M, char C, char D>
struct eval_repetition_impl;

template <> struct eval_repetition_impl<'*', -1,'x', -1,'x','x'> : any_repeat {};
```

This is how the `item` and `repetition` elements are recognized. However, to combine them we need to slightly modify the possible results of repetition:

```
//a* -> *a
struct any_repeat
{
  typedef any_repeat type;
  static xpressive::sregex run(xpressive::sregex base) {
    return *base;
  }
};
```

We added an `sregex` parameter to the `run` method, because the `repetition` needs to use the `item` it stands after. In case of `any_repeat` we return the `item`, which is called `base` here, with a '`*`' in front of it.

```
typedef metaparse::transform<
  metaparse::sequence<xlxpressive::item::type,
      xlxpressive::repetition >,
  xlxpressive::build_unary_item
>
unary_item;
```

The `transform` parser of `unary_item` passes the `item` result and then the `repetition` result to `build_unary_item`. These wrapped by Seq type sequence become the template parameter of `apply` metafunction of `build_unary_item`. The first element of Seq is the result of the `item` parser, which is a sub-parser's builder metafunction class e.g. `build_bos`. The second element is the `repetition` data, which has a `run` method now. This method is the key to solve our previously described problem, namely how we can pass the previously used `item` parser as a parameter of `repetition`. The result of parsing a `repetition`, like `any_repeat`, has a `run` method now, after the above modification, which has an `sregex` argument. The `build_unary_item` metafunction class should call the `repetition`'s run method with the identified `sregex` object from `item`.

```
struct build_unary_item
{
  template <class Seq>
  struct apply
  {
    typedef apply type;
    static xpressive::sregex run()
    {
```

```
        return mpl::back<Seq>::type::run(mpl::front<Seq>::
            type::run());
    }
  };
};
```

It can call `item`'s static `run` method through its `type`, so this way within the `repetition`'s `run` method we'll have the actual, preceding `sregex` extracted from the `item` parser.

The idea behind building these separate parsers is that we can call the `run` method of our top element, which calls the lower level element's `run` method and so forth. Through these `run` method call-chains, we can build up more complex regular expressions from the individual parsers.

Let's see how this works through a simple example. Suppose we want to use the ".*" regular expression. We can use the same macro we introduced earlier: `REGEX(".*")`. As you may remember this applies the ".*" `boost::mpl::string` on the top level parser of our library, which can be the `unary_item` parser now.

Here you can see the call-chain of the `run` methods of this example:

```
unary_item::type::run()
-> build_unary_item::apply<Seq>::run()
-> return repetition::type::run(item::type::run());
-> return any_repeat::type::run(build_any::type::run());
-> return any_repeat::type::run(~xpressive::_n);
-> return *~xpressive::_n;
```

Just one thing left here I still owe you, the repeat elements. These differ from the others, since they need two template parameters beside the `item` ('a') argument:

```
a{n,m} -> repeat<n,m>(a)
a{n,m}? -> -repeat<n,m>(a)
```

This is why `eval_repetition_impl` has 6 template parameters instead of just 2. We can pass N and M to the corresponding result type, (`range_repeat` and `may_range_repeat`), using partial template specialization:

```
template <char A, int N, char B, int M, char C, char D>
struct eval_repetition_impl;

template <int N, int M> struct eval_repetition_impl<'{',
    N, ',', M, '}', '?'> : may_range_repeat<N, M> {};
```

With this solution, the `may_range_repeat` result type can directly pass its template parameters to a `boost::xpressive::repeat` instantiation:

```
//a{n, m}? -> -repeat< n, m>(a)
template < int n, int m>
```

```
struct may_range_repeat
{
  typedef may_range_repeat type;
  static xpressive::sregex run(xpressive::sregex base)
  {
    return -xpressive::repeat<n, m>(base);
  }
};
```

We can write **range_repeat** the same way.

qexp has been done in a similar way, but there the **always** parser has been used, because it has simpler sequences like "i:". Another similar parser is **bschar** which processes the non-printable characters we write starting with a backslash like "\ n". We need the metaprogramming result expressions there too, but we don't need to write a complex evaluator like **eval_repetition** and a builder like **build_unary_item**.

Let's summarize what parts we have implemented so far from the grammar:

```
unary_item ::= item (('*'|'+'|'?'|repeat) '?'?)?
repeat ::= '{' (number ',' number|',' number| number ',') '}'
item ::= bos|eos|any
bos ::= '^'
eos ::= '$'
any ::= '.'
```

4   The Top of the Grammar

We continue to climb up the syntax tree, where the only thing left is the **seq** element, before we reach the top element **reg_exp**:

```
seq ::= unary_item*
```

This is the first expression which is built up from an arbitrary number of components. Metaparse gives us an **any** parser combinator which could be used in this case, but we need to build up something from the individually processed **unary_items**. The **foldl** parser combinator suits our needs better in this case. If you're familiar with functional programming, you might already have an idea what this parser could do. It tries to apply repeatedly its first template parameter, a parser. It uses the second parameter as a starting point and executes its third argument, which is a metafunction class by giving the existing result and the next element to that as template parameters. So, we can build something starting from the second argument and building it using the third argument, the metafunction which always has the last parsed element from the first argument, which is our repeated parser.

The parser what we want to apply 0 or more times is the **unary_item**. This is the first parameter, the repeatedly applied parser, which consumes the input string. The "neutral element" of our building process is **empty_seq**. It should give back a kind of regular expression which matches everything, so it doesn't have any effect on the rest of our built expression. Xpressive doesn't really support something like this, but we can use the below solution. It introduces a problem which I'm going to explain in details a bit later.

```cpp
struct empty_seq
{
  typedef empty_seq type;
  static xpressive::sregex run()
  {
    return xpressive::as_xpr("");
  }
};
```

The foldl parser will take this element as its starting state. This means that its "builder" metafunction will append all the parsed elements to this, so that they will look like this: as_xpr("")>>as_xpr('a')>>as_xpr('b')>>.... We use as_xpr to create a static Xpressive object from the empty string. Otherwise, it would be a normal string and we would use the usual right shift operator with it, instead of the overloaded one. When we have an empty input string, our result will be this empty_seq.

Our third parameter is the build_seq metafunction class:

```cpp
struct build_seq
{
  template <class Next, class State>
  struct apply
  {
    typedef apply type;
    static xpressive::sregex run()
    {
      xpressive::sregex s = State::type::run();
      return s >> Next::type::run();
    }
  };
};
```

It gets two template parameters from foldl:

- Next   The next parsed element, which is the apply metafunction of the build_unary_item, so we can call its run method.
- State   The sequence we have built so far. At the beginning, it is the empty_seq. That's why each sequence starts with as_xpr("").

The built simple parser always succeeds, even if unary_item rejects the input string the very first time:

```
typedef metaparse :: foldl <
   xlxpressive :: unary_item ,
   xlxpressive :: empty_seq ,
   xlxpressive :: build_seq
>
seq ;
```

It iterates through our input string with foldl and processes it with theparser unary_item. After each successful parsing, it calls build_seq to assemble the separate unary_items with the "¿¿" operator. We need to use this operator for sequences, because in static Xpressive we must use valid, overloaded C++ language constructs to build up our regular expression, that's the main idea behind it, hence we cannot just put things like characters next to each other i.e. we need to convert our simple ab regular expression into as_xpr(a)>>b. as_xpr is needed to force the compiler to call the overloaded "¿¿" operator and not the one for char types.

By using foldl we've got a short and elegant solution, but with the any parser we'd need to solve where and how to aggregate the sequence, which is simply built by foldl in this case.

We can use the same technique we've seen at seq for our head element, reg_exp.

reg_exp ::= seq ('|' seq)*

I won't go into too much details here, but a few things worth mentioning. For example, we can use foldlp now, because we have at least one element in the arbitrary long sequence. foldlp does exactly what we need here: it executes its second argument first, a parser, and if it succeeds, it applies its first argument repeatedly, which is a parser too, and calls build_reg_exp to assemble the expression:

```
struct reg_exp : metaparse :: transform <
   metaparse :: foldlp <
      metaparse :: last_of < metaparse :: lit_c <'|'>,
         xlxpressive :: seq >,
      xlxpressive :: seq ,
      xlxpressive :: build_reg_exp
   >,
   xlxpressive :: eval_reg_exp
>
{};
```

5   Bracket Expressions

You might have observed that we've declared our top element as a **struct** and not used **typedef**. This is because we need to forward declare **reg_exp**, so that we can use it in the bracket expressions:

```
bracket_exp ::= '(' (reg_exp|qexp) ')'
qexp ::= '?' (no_back_ref|...) reg_exp
```

These expressions can have two forms: (...) and (?...). The difference between them is that the prior is the "simple" bracket expression which saves a back-reference for its wrapped regular expression, while the latter with the starting '?' is for a couple special bracket wrapped constructs like (?i...) which does case-insensitive matching within this bracket expression.

Here are a couple of these question mark prefixed expressions. On the right side of the arrow we've listed what we want to generate for them:

```
(?i:regex) -> icase(regex)
(?>regex)  -> keep(regex)
(?=regex)  -> before(regex)
(?!regex)  -> ~before(regex)
```

To handle these two types, we transform them with separate builder meta-function classes and choose between them with **one_of**. To recognize a bracket expression we need to identify a **qexp** or **reg_exp** between opening and closing brackets. Metaparse gives us a parser called **middle_of** which can be used for sequences with 3 elements to parse all of them, but return the result of the second only.

```
typedef metaparse::transform<
  metaparse::middle_of<
    metaparse::lit_c<'('>,
    metaparse::one_of<
      metaparse::transform< xlxpressive::qexp,
          xlxpressive::build_qexp_based_bracket_exp >,
      metaparse::transform< xlxpressive::reg_exp,
          xlxpressive::build_reg_exp_based_bracket_exp >
    >,
    metaparse::lit_c<')'>
  >,
  xlxpressive::eval_bracket_exp
>
bracket_exp;
```

The **build_qexp_based_bracket_exp** and **eval_bracket_exp** metafunctions simply call the passed type's static **run** method.

However, the `build_reg_exp_based_bracket_exp` metafunction is a bit more interesting one. It does exactly what it says on the tin, but to build a simple bracket expression in static `Xpressive`, where we should give back back-references after each bracketed expression, we need to express this intention explicitly. We cannot simply wrap our `reg_exp` in brackets and return it, because brackets cannot be overloaded this way. To solve this, `Xpressive` uses the `s1...s9` so called sub-match placeholders. So, for example to write a regular expression like (a) in the static `Xpressive` world, we should do this: (s1=a).

Since we're translating "normal" string-based regular expressions into static `Xpressive`, we don't have the actual number of the next sub-match placeholder which we should return. So, we need to count it ourselves.

The easiest way of doing this, if we introduce a global variable; let's call it for example `bracket_counter`. We can increase its value every time when the `run` method is called, before we'd return the bracket-wrapped expression. However, it's not a good idea to use global variables in a library, so we should come up with a solution where our counter has local scope.

We could use the counter as a local variable in the `run` method, if it's passed as a parameter. If we take this idea as a starting-point, we'll find that this can actually solve our problem, if we pass the counter through the `run` method call-chain as a reference. The very first `run` method which we call when we start the evaluation of our regular expression is the one in `eval_reg_exp`. We introduce this counter here as a local variable of the parameterless `run` method which calls the overloaded one. This way we ensure that the counter will be initialized at the start of the evaluation and that `reg_exp` can pass an existing value forward, if we use it in a bracket expression:

```
struct eval_reg_exp
{
  template <class Re>
  struct apply
  {
    typedef apply type;
    static xpressive::sregex run()
    {
      int bracket_counter = 0;

      return Re::type::run(bracket_counter);
    }
    static xpressive::sregex run(int &bracket_counter)
    {
      return Re::type::run(bracket_counter);
    }
  };
};
```

To make it work, we need to modify all the previously created parsers, so that the run method of their build and/or evaluate metafunctions will get the bracket_counter as a reference. The only thing they should do with that is passing it forward to the underlying parser(s), if they have any at all.

For example here's how build_seq can be modified:

```
struct build_seq
{
  template <class Next, class State >
  struct apply
  {
    typedef apply type;
    static xpressive::sregex run(int &bracket_counter)
    {
      xpressive::sregex s=State::type::run(
          bracket_counter);
      return s >> Next::type::run(bracket_counter);
    }
  };
};
```

So every parser will just get and pass the counter without modifying it, except build_reg_exp_based_bracket_exp. We can simply increase it here, evaluate the reg_exp and then choose the right sub-match placeholder with a switch-case construct:

```
struct build_reg_exp_based_bracket_exp
{
  template <class E>
  struct apply
  {
    typedef apply type;
    static xpressive::sregex run(int &bracket_counter)
    {
      ++bracket_counter;
      xpressive::sregex a=E::type::run(bracket_counter);
      xpressive::sregex ret;
      switch(bracket_counter) {
        case 1: ret = (xpressive::s1= a); break;
        case 2: ret = (xpressive::s2= a); break;
        // case 3 .. 9 are similar
      }
      return ret;
    }
  };
};
```

As I mentioned earlier, our solution for seq -where we've used the as_xpr("")
as a neutral element in empty_seq- introduced an issue. This bracket expression
is the parser where we can meet with this. Let me explain it through an example:
let's assume that we want to use the "(foo)" regular expression. We can do it
with our new library this way: const sregex = REGEX("(foo)"). It looks OK,
but when we try it out with our search.hpp test utility, which is used to process
each test cases we generate with gen_test.pl, we get an interesting result:

```
success: 1
matching expected success: 1
size_check: 0 | 1 ~ 2
'foo' VS 'foo'
sub_match: 0
RESULT: 0
```

It shows that our regular expression matched, and that it has the expected
behaviour. However, the sub_match check failed, and this part [0 | 1 ~ 2]
shows that our solution has one less sub-match, than the expected. To find the
root-cause behind this, the best way is to debug the library, level-by-level to see
where it goes wrong. If we do this in our case we can find that at the level of
the seq parser our library doesn't create what we would manually. This isn't a
real problem however, but a speciality, caused by the way how we build up our
regular expressions. We should be aware of this when we use the library.

Let's see what we generate for "(foo)" to understand this:

```
sregex(as_xpr("")) >> sregex(s1= as_xpr('f') >>
                                  as_xpr('o') >>
                                  as_xpr('o'))
```

We have an "empty" regular expression at the front of what the user has
specified. Why this makes a difference can be found in the documentation of
Xpressive [31]. Each sregex need to have its own back-tracking scope. Regarding our solution it means that we cannot iterate through the smatch object after
a regex_search, if we want to see what are the sub-matches. Instead of this, we
should call the nested_results method on the smatch object which we've used
for the search.

Here's an example how we can do it.

```
// If sub_match and size_check failed, try to match with
//    nested results
if (!sub_match && !size_check && w.nested_results().size
      () > 0) {
    sub_match = true;
    nested_result_analyzer nra(m, sub_match);
    nra = std::for_each(
      w.nested_results().begin(),
      w.nested_results().end(),
      nra);
```

```
      size_check = nra.size() == m.size();
   }
}
```

A reference implementation can be found in **xlxpressive**'s source files.

6   Character Groups

In regular expressions we can use character groups like [a-z] or [abc], if we want to exactly list which characters we accept in a character place. However, we can't list any kind of grammar elements between the square brackets e.g. we cannot use a bracket expression there. That's why in the grammar we've allowed char_group, range_exp and set_item only. To make it clear let me give you an example of each, so that we can see the difference between them. On the left side we listed the grammar elements, while in the middle we can see an example for these elements as we would write them in a **Perl** regular expression. The last column shows the static **Xpressive** form of the examples from the second column.

```
char_group      [[:alnum:]]     alnum
range_exp       [0-9]           range('0','9')
set_item        [aB%\w7]        set['a' | 'B' | _w | '7']
```

As you can see, we differentiate them, because they correspond to different kind of **Xpressive** objects. They can be separated by their structure too. Each of them starts with a '[' character, so we first try to parse that. If we succeed, then according to our grammar, we have two choices: char_group or set:

```
group       ::= '[' (char_group|'^'? set)
set         ::= (range_exp|set_item)+ ']'
range_exp   ::= number set_num|letter set_abc|set_item
set_num     ::= '-' num_range|set_item
num_range   ::= number
set_abc     ::= '-' abc_range|set_item
abc_range   ::= letter
```

The **char_group** parser is the easier one. We just need to specify the sequences of the expected letters of the character group names and choose between them with a **one_of** and **always** construct. Here's **alnum** for example. All the others have been done the same way:

```
typedef metaparse::transform<
  metaparse::sequence<
    metaparse::lit_c<'['>,
    metaparse::lit_c<':'>,
    metaparse::one_of<
```

```
    keyword<MPLLIBS_STRING("alnum"), xlxpressive::alnum
        >,
    ...
  >,
  metaparse::lit_c<':'>,
  metaparse::lit_c<']'>,
  metaparse::lit_c<']'>
  >,
  xlxpressive::eval_char_group
>
char_group;
```

As you can see we use a new parser called **keyword** here. A **boost::mpl::string** can be parsed with that, which we specify as its first argument. It returns the optional second argument, if it succeeds. We use **alnum** as this second argument, which is the returned result of our parsing. It looks very much the same as the ones for **unary_item** we have seen previously, but we don't need the extra parameter for the **run** method.

```
// [[: alnum :]] -> alnum
struct alnum
{
  typedef alnum type;
  static xpressive::sregex run()
  {
    return xpressive::alnum;
  }
};
```

The **run** method of the **eval_char_group** metafunction returns whatever the **::type::run()** method of the 3rd element of the passed **Seq** sequence returns, which is the result of the **one_of** parser. In our case, **::type::run()** is called on the **alnum** result, so **eval_char_group** returns **boost::xpressive::alnum**.

```
struct eval_char_group
{
  template <class Seq>
  struct apply
  {
    typedef apply type;
    static xpressive::sregex run(int &bracket_counter)
    {
      return mpl::at_c<Seq, 2>::type::run();
    }
  };
};
```

We get the `bracket_counter` argument in this `run` method, as we introduced them in Sect. 5, but we don't pass it forward. This is because the things like `alnum` are leaf elements in our syntax tree, so they return the needed objects and don't need to do anything with a passed extra argument.

So far so good, let's continue with `set`. This grammar element introduces the most complicated problem we cover in this thesis and needs an advanced technique to solve it. Let me describe the problem with `set` first and then show you what kind of solution we can find in a case like this.

We've named this element of the grammar after the construct of `Xpressive` we want to generate. We can define a `set` in multiple ways in static `Xpressive`:

```
(set= 'a','b','c')
set[ range('0','9') |(set= 'a','b','c') ]
set[ range('0','9') | 'a' | 'b' | 'c' ]
```

The last form suits our needs best, because it can hold characters and `range_exp` elements too. The problem here is that we cannot put the objects of type `boost::xpressive::sregex` returned by our parsers directly into this object. The first thing we might think that, OK, we can try to find out what the exact type of e.g. `range` and return that in its `run` method. Unfortunately, we can't, because it is generated with the help of `Proto` [13]. This means that we should return a type we cannot know, as it's known by the compiler only, when it generates it.

In `C++11` we could use the redefined `auto` keyword [12] to let the constructor automatically deduce the return type from the expression we return. However, we'd like to build a C++98 compliant library as much as possible to foster wider usability.

There is a technique we can use to solve this problem without leaving the frames of `C++98`. It is called Continuation-Passing Style (CPS) [14,20]. When we write functions in CPS we give back the result of the function in its extra "continuation" argument instead of in the return statement. It's like we turn the expression "inside-out", as the innermost part will be evaluated first. This technique is useful in our case, because this extra argument of the function can have a template type, so that we can let the compiler maintain the type of the intermediate temporary elements. These are those types, like the type of the `range` element, which we couldn't know in advance of the compilation, because these are generated by the compiler.

We can build up our `set` expression by passing the already built part as an argument and always just appending that to the newly parsed object. To make it work we always need to have the previous element, so that we can call its `run` method with our newly constructed part. Our current parsers don't have this kind of functionality, so we will amend them. We need to modify only a subset of our parsers however, since not every kind of regular expression is grammatical within `set`. Based on our grammar, we need to write the `range_exp` parser this way and modify `set_item` (its sub-parsers actually):

```
set        ::= (range_exp|set_item)+ ']'
range_exp  ::= number set_num|letter set_abc|set_item
set_num      ::= '-' num_range|set_item
num_range    ::= number
set_abc      ::= '-' abc_range|set_item
abc_range    ::= letter
```

Each parser which can occur in set will have a common extra "interface" called add_set_item and a new run method, which is overloaded with the (T after) argument. These methods make us able to iterate through the parsed elements and call the previous element's overloaded run method.

```
template <class T>
static xpressive::sregex run(T after)
{
  return after;
}

template <class Before>
struct add_set_item {
  typedef add_set_item type;

  template <class T>
  static xpressive::sregex run(T after) {
    return Before::type::run( [current_element] | after);
  }
};
```

add_set_item is a metafunction getting the previous parsed element as its template parameter. In the after parameter its run method gets what has been constructed after our current element. As we have what's before [current_element] and what's after it, we can put it right in the middle of them with the run method call on Before. We'll put these extra methods in the sub-parsers of set_item: bschar, number, letter and non_alphabet. range_exp won't have an argument-less run method, as it cannot be used outside set.

Let's see how the original letter parser looks like and add the modifications one-by-one:

```
struct build_letter
{
  template <class ch> struct apply
  {
    typedef apply type;
    static xpressive::sregex run(int &bracket_counter)
    {
      return xpressive::as_xpr( char_value() );
```

```
    }
    static char char_value ()
    {
      return ch :: value ;
    }
  };
};
typedef metaparse :: transform< metaparse :: letter ,
    xlxpressive :: build_letter
> letter ;
```

We simply return the **char** value wrapped as a static **Xpressive** object. We use a separate method called **char_value()** here, because we'll need it later on for the **range_exp** parser. First we add the overloaded **run** method after our original one.

```
  template <class T>
  static xpressive :: sregex run (T after )
  {
    return after ;
  }
```

After we added this, we should add the **add_set_item** structure, which can call it through the **Before** parameter.

```
  template <class Before>
  struct add_set_item {
    typedef add_set_item type;

    template <class T>
    static xpressive :: sregex run (T after )
    {
      return Before :: type :: run ( char_value () | after ) ;
    }
  };
```

We've used the overloaded **run** method, and the **add_set_item**, just like how we've sketched. We've replaced the placeholder [current_element] with method call **char_value()**, thus we return what the normal **run** method returns, but without wrapping it as an **Xpressive** object. This is how we can add the actually parsed element in the form we want. In the case of **letter** we simply pass the **char** value.

Let's build up **set**. With CPS this is a two way process:

1. We parse the elements left-to-right and creating types which have the previous state and need an **after** parameter.

2. After we've parsed the last set_item or range_exp we have a temporary construct, which can be evaluated backwards by calling its **run** method with a neutral start value. This can be range('4', '2') as it's an empty range.

For the iteration we can use foldl1, because we don't accept an empty set. This part of the parser is similar to the seq and reg_exp parsers in Sect. 4.

```
typedef metaparse :: transform<
  metaparse :: first_of<
    metaparse :: transform<
      metaparse :: foldl1<
        metaparse :: one_of< xlxpressive :: range_exp ,
            xlxpressive :: set_item >,
        xlxpressive :: empty_set ,
        xlxpressive :: build_set
      >,
      xlxpressive :: start_building_set
    >,
    metaparse :: lit_c <'] '>
  >,
  xlxpressive :: eval_set
>
set ;
```

We've seen last_of and middle_of previously, first_of is the one which returns the result of the first parser after accepting a sequence. This way we can get rid of the ']' easily. Let's see what the first phase of parsing does. With foldl1 we parse with one of the range_exp and set_item parsers. We'll specify range_exp later on, so let's just concentrate on set_item now, moreover we can just use letter instead of that.

We start building up the set with the empty_set metafunction class. On the backward way this will construct our final object we return, but in this stage this just has a metafunction which can be called with an after parameter.

```
struct empty_set
{
  typedef empty_set type ;

  template <class T >
  static xpressive :: sregex run(T after )
  {
    return xpressive :: set [ after ];
  }
};
```

The `build_set` metafunction class uses the `add_set_item` interface of the actual `Next` element and passes the current state (`State`) as its template parameter. The `run` method of `add_set_item` is called with the `after` parameter. It's again just a metafunction, like `empty_set`, which has to be evaluated with an `after` parameter. It's like we're unrolling these generated metafunctions as a "wick" after us and when we reach the last element, we'll light it, that is, we work it up backward.

```cpp
struct build_set
{
  template <class Next, class State>
  struct apply
  {
    typedef apply type;
    template <class T>
    static xpressive::sregex run(T after)
    {
      return Next::template add_set_item< State >::type::
        run(after);
    }
  };
};
```

The "lighter" for this string of metafunctions, to close this metaphor, is the `start_building_set` metafunction class. The `transform` parser around `foldl1` calls it with the result of our folding, hence we can open it up. We start the second phase of the parsing with the empty range (e.g. `range(4,2)`). This is where the CPS starts working and the method calls build up our expression in the `after` argument.

```cpp
struct start_building_set
{
  template <class RealSetBuilder>
  struct apply
  {
    typedef apply type;
    static xpressive::sregex run()
    {
      return RealSetBuilder::type::run(xpressive::range(
        '4', '2'));
    }
  };
};
```

The `eval_set` metafunction class is a simple evaluator, which we've seen a couple before. It can call the `run` method of `start_building_set`, because that doesn't need any parameter.

The last element of the second phase is the `empty_set` which wraps the built object and returns our final expression:

```
return boost::xpressive::set[ after ];
```

To see how the backward way works, let's go through the evaluation of a simple character group: [abc]

```
struct eval_set
{
  template <class Set>
  struct apply
  {
    typedef apply type;
    static xpressive::sregex run(int &bracket_counter)
    {
      return Set::type::run();
    }
  };
};
```

On Fig. 2 you can see how `start_building_set` commences the backward build process by calling the `run` method of the last `build_set` with the empty range. In each `build_set` the `State` stores the previously processed `build_set` from the first phase, the `Next` parameter is what the current function can generate, and in the `after` parameter you can see how we build up the full expression. With the `return Next::template add_set_item< State >::type::run(after);` line, we call the `run` method from the `add_set_item` of the current builder e.g. `build_letter`.

In `build_letter`, `Before` is the passed `State` from `build_set`. By calling the `run` method on `Before` (e.g. `return Before::type::run( char_value() | after );`) we jump to the previous `build_set`, but with the extended `after` parameter. In the last `build_letter` we have `empty_set` in `Before`, as we started the folding with that.

We have seen how `char_group` and `set` work and how the sub-parsers of `set_item` should be modified. Let's see how the `range_exp` parser looks like to have everything to build the missing `group` parser.

As mentioned earlier, `range_exp` needs the `add_set_item` interface only to be implemented, because it cannot occur outside `set`. To parse a range we should accept two kind of sequences: `number - number` and `letter - letter`.

With one_of and sequence we can write this easily.

```
typedef metaparse :: transform<
  metaparse :: one_of<
    metaparse :: sequence< xlxpressive :: number, metaparse :: lit_c
      <'-'>, xlxpressive :: number>,
    metaparse :: sequence< xlxpressive :: letter , metaparse :: lit_c
      <'-'>, xlxpressive :: letter >
  >,
  xlxpressive :: build_range
>
range_exp ;
```

What build_range should do is to put together the received results and return the initialized range object. To extract the results from the sequence we can use the boost::mpl::at_c method again, hence we get the elements on the 0 and 2 indices. As we only use range within a set we only define its add_set_item interface.

```
struct build_range
{
  template <class Seq> struct apply {
    typedef apply type;
    template <class T> static sregex run(T after) {
      return after;
    }
```

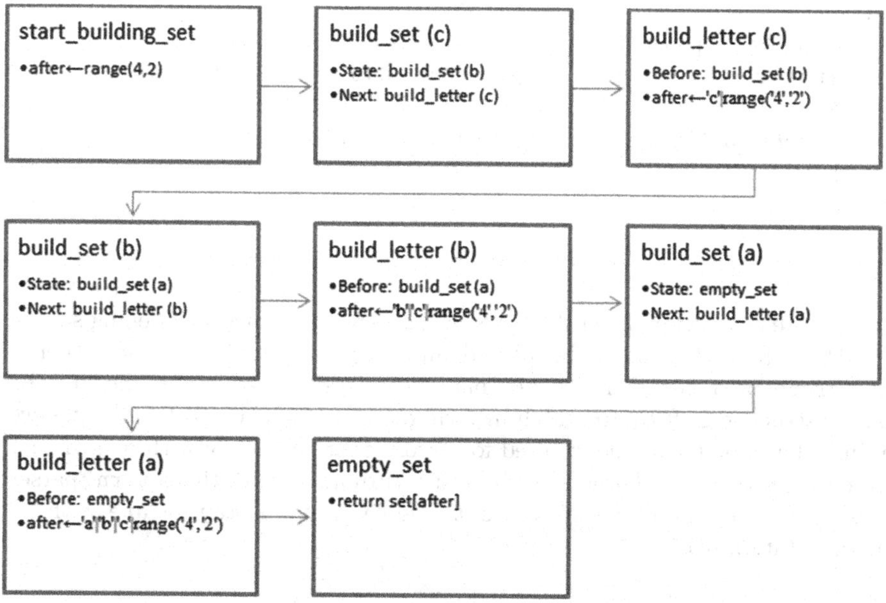

Fig. 2. Continuation-passing style

```
template <class Before> struct add_set_item {
  typedef add_set_item type;
  template <class T> static sregex run(T after) {
    return Before::type::run( range( at_c<Seq, 0>::
      type::char_value(), at_c<Seq, 2>::type::
      char_value() ) | after );
  }
  };
};
};
```

The newly introduced `char_value` method of `build_letter` and `build_number` have been used here. We need to do this, because the `range` Xpressive object needs two `char` arguments.

We have written everything now to be able to parse a `group`. As we did so far we follow the grammar to compose the parser.

```
group ::= '[' (char_group|'^'? set)
```

We'll need a `build_group` metafunction which simply calls the `run` method of its parameter.

```
struct build_group
{
  template <class G >
  struct apply
  {
    typedef apply type;
    static xpressive::sregex run(int &bracket_counter)
    {
      return G::type::run(bracket_counter);
    }
  };
};
```

To write the `group` parser itself we need a `sequence` with the opening square bracket as first element to be parsed and then a `one_of` to parse either a `char_group` or a `set`. The `"'^'?"` part expresses that we might negate the `set` construct, e.g. `[^a]` to match any character except 'a'. To handle this we can use the same technique we used for `unary_item` in Sect. 3: with `one_of` and `lit_c` we parse the '^' character or we just return an 'x' with the `return_` parser to express we shouldn't negate the `set`. We can name it `may_negate` with an implementation like this:

```
typedef metaparse :: one_of<
   metaparse :: lit_c <'^'>,
   metaparse :: return_< mpl :: char_<'x'> >
>
may_negate ;
```

It makes the definition of the **group** parser more readable.

```
typedef metaparse :: transform<
   metaparse :: last_of<
     metaparse :: lit_c <'['>,
     metaparse :: one_of<
       xlxpressive :: char_group ,
       metaparse :: transform<
         metaparse :: sequence<
           may_negate ,
           xlxpressive :: set
         >,
         xlxpressive :: eval_set_sign
       >
     >
   >,
   xlxpressive :: build_group
>
group ;
```

With `eval_set_sign` we can return a positive or a negative **set**. It makes the decision based on the passed character ('^' or 'x'). We can negate a **set** with the '~' operator in **Xpressive**. We only show the implementation of **positive_set**, because **negative_set** can be done the same way with the previously described differences.

```
// [...] -> set [...]
template <class S>
struct positive_set
{
   typedef positive_set type;
   static xpressive :: sregex run(int &bracket_counter)
   {
     return S :: type :: run ( bracket_counter );
   }
};
```

We simply call the `static` `run` method of the received `eval_set` result (S). It can be this simple, because `eval_set_sign` evaluates whether we should return a `set` or a negated `set`.

Let's see how it can be implemented:

```
template <char A, class Set> struct eval_set_sign_impl;
template <class Set> struct eval_set_sign_impl<'x', Set>
   : positive_set<Set> {};

struct eval_set_sign
{
  template <class Seq>
  struct apply :
    eval_set_sign_impl<
      mpl::front<Seq>::type::value,
      mpl::back<Seq>
    > {};
};
```

We've used the same kind of pattern matching with template specialization in the case of `eval_set_sign_impl` what we've seen at `unary_item`. In `eval_set_sign`, we call type::value on the first argument of `eval_set_sign_impl`, because we want to pass the `char` value of `may_negate`.

In this chapter we've seen how we can implement the parsers for all the main elements of our grammar. These parsers have been created gradually following our grammar using a bottom-to-top approach. A few examples have been shown how these parsers can be used to generate static `Xpressive` objects through `run` method call-chains. We've covered some advanced topics too e.g. how the continuous-passing style can be used in template metaprogramming DSL integration to build grammar elements with generated types.

7   Test Case Generation

The test cases play a very important role in template metaprogramming. Without them, after we've written the code and compiled it, we can fix the obvious syntax errors, but apart from that we haven't instantiated any template. To test every newly added element of the grammar we need a test case which makes use of that element.

In [9] the authors describe a unit testing framework for C++ template metaprograms that guarantees the execution of all test cases and provides proper summary-report with enhanced and portable error reporting. The paper also describes how precise diagnostic messages can be generated for template metaprograms.

There are many combinations of regular expressions and we have a restriction on the format of the strings which we can add to our parsers. A `Perl` script can be written to generate these test cases. This way we can ensure that whatever we match with the built **Xpressive** object, it would match in **Perl** too. With the generated test cases, we can use the following template function for verification:

```cpp
template <class Regexp>
bool search(const std::string& s,
            const std::vector<std::string>& m)
{
  const sregex re = apply_wrap1<regexp_parser, Regexp>::
      type::run();
  smatch w;

  const bool success = regex_search(s, w, re);
  if ( (success && m.size() == 0) ||
       (!success && m.size() != 0) ) {
    return false;
  }
  if (w.size() != m.size()) { return false; }
  for (int i = 0; i < m.size(); ++i) {
    if (i >= w.size() || w[i].str() != m[i]) {
      return false;
    }
  }
  return true;
}
```

A reference implementation can be found in **xlxpressive**'s source files [28].

We can adapt the format of the **libs/xpressive/test/regress.txt** file, which contains **Xpressive**'s regression tests. Here is an example to show the structure of a test case:

```
[test37]
str=2001    foobar
pat=[1-9][0-9]+\\s*[abfor]+$
flg=
br0=2001    foobar
[end]
```

Each test case starts with its name in square brackets, then it has key-value pairs and is closed with the **[end]** tag. The key-value pairs have the below meaning:

- **str** The input string.
- **pat** The regular expression we're testing.
- **flg** The behaviour of the **Xpressive** regular expression algorithm can be modified with a couple of flags e.g. 'i' for case insensitive search.

– br0-n   br0 contains the whole matched string. Every other one comes from the back-referencing of bracket expressions. If a test case doesn't contain any br element it means that we expect that the test case will fail.

8   Conclusion

Our goal was to demonstrate how we can use template metaprogramming to provide smooth DSL embedding. The DSL we've chosen was Boost.Xpressive whom domain is regular expression. It provides an approach called "static regex" where we can write our regular expressions in the form of C++ expressions. However, the syntax of static regex is very different than the original regular expression syntax. Our aim was to provide a new interface for Xpressive which enables us to write the regular expressions in flexible string format but still enable compile-time checking.

First, we've written a grammar for these regular expressions. Then we've used this grammar to walk through the process how we can build compile time parsers with the help of the Metaparse library. We've successfully built all the parsers while we've encountered and solved more and more advanced problems. The parsers created following this approach can parse separate grammar elements. We've shown how the run method chain can construct a static Xpressive object.

We have created a working implementation of this library as an open source project available on github [28]. It contains more than 40 generated test cases showing what our solution can do at this stage.

As we've introduced the REGEX macro earlier, we can do a comparison to demonstrate what our approach is capable for. The below lines show grammatically equivalent regular expressions. The first line is the static Xpressive example built by hand and the second line shows how it looks like as an input of our new interface. The \\ characters show extra line-breaks.

```
(s1= +_w) >> '' >> (s2= +_w) >>'!';
REGEX("(\\w+) (\\w+)!");

'$' >> +_d >> '.' >> _d >> _d;
REGEX("\\$\\d+\\.\\d\\d")));

bos >> set[as_xpr('a')|'b'|'c'|'d'] >> range('3','8') >> \\
  '.' >> 'f' >> 'o' >> 'o'  >> eos;
REGEX("^[abcd][3-8]\\.foo$");

bos>>(s1=+range('0','9')>>!(s2='.'>>*range('0','9')))>> \\
  (s3=set[as_xpr('C')|'F'])>>eos;
REGEX("^([0-9]+(\\.[0-9]*)?)([CF])$");
```

Our new interface is more readable and natural, while it still ensures compile time validation. Someone who understands regular expressions should be able to use our solution easily at the very first time, while the original interface needs to be studied much longer.

A similar approach to the one presented in this paper can be used to provide a human readable syntax for template metaprograms where the metafunctions written in the DSL can interact with metafunctions defined in a regular way [22]. While the approach used to provide a DSL for template metaprograms focuses on providing a language for a compile-time domain, the one presented in this paper focuses on providing a language for a runtime domain.

This paper addresses expressing regular expressions in their orignal syntax as part of standard C++ code. The usability of the solution presented depends on being able to provide understandable and readable error messages. Our future plan is to investigate how to achieve generating useful error messages when the regular expressions are not valid.

The construction of the parsers preserve the structure of the grammar. Another interesting area for future research is extracting the grammar from the parsers and making use of it for automatic test case generation.

As a summary we can say that using C++ template metaprogrammimg is a good approach for embedding domain specific languages, if we construct our own parsers with the help of the **Metaparse** parser combinators. These have been created in such a way that we can easily combine them to parse our grammar elements. With their combinations we can tackle complex problems, like the smooth integration of regular expressions. We've also seen that a grammar should be created first, if we start embedding a DSL and that how important the test cases are, when we work on template metaprograms.

It can be subject of future works how this approach can be used for embedding other DSLs like **SQL** expressions or **Boost.Spirit** parsers.

A The Grammar

```
reg_exp ::= seq ('|' seq)*
seq ::= unary_item*
unary_item ::= item (('*'|'+'|'?'|repeat) '?'?)?
repeat ::= '{' (number ',' number|',' number| number ',') '}'
item ::= bos|eos|any|bracket_exp|group|set_item
set_item ::= bschar|number|letter|non_alphabet
non_alphabet ::= space|','|';'|':'|'='|'~'|'<'|'>'|
                 '-'|'_'|'!'|'@'|'#'|'%'|'&'|'/'
letter ::= 'A'-'Z'|'a'-'z'
number ::= '0'-'9'
bos ::= '^'
eos ::= '$'
any ::= '.'
bracket_exp ::= '(' (reg_exp|qexp) ')'
qexp ::= '?' (no_back_ref|icase|keep|before|not_before|
             after|not_after|mark_tag_create|mark_tag_use) reg_exp
no_back_ref     ::= ":"
icase           ::= "i:"
```

```
keep                ::= '>'
before              ::= '='
not_before          ::= '!'
after               ::= "<="
not_after           ::= "<!"
mark_tag_create     ::= "P<" name '>'
mark_tag_use        ::= "P=" name
name                ::= letter+
bschar ::= '\' (bs_backslash|bs_back_ref|bs_boundary|
               bs_digit|bs_word|bs_space|bs_new_line|
               bs_caret|bs_dollar|bs_full_stop|bs_plus)
bs_backslash ::= '\'
bs_back_ref  ::= number
bs_boundary  ::= 'b'|not_bs_boundary
not_bs_boundary ::= 'B'
bs_digit     ::= 'd'|not_bs_digit
not_bs_digit ::= 'D'
bs_word      ::= 'w'|not_bs_word
not_bs_word  ::= 'W'
bs_space     ::= 's'|not_bs_space
not_bs_space ::= 'S'
bs_new_line  ::= "r\n"|'n'
bs_caret     ::= '^'
bs_dollar    ::= '$'
bs_full_stop ::= '.'
bs_plus      ::= '+'
group ::= '[' (char_group|'^'? set)
set ::= (range_exp|set_item)+ ']'
range_exp ::= number set_num|letter set_abc|set_item
set_num      ::= '-' num_range|set_item
num_range    ::= number
set_abc      ::= '-' abc_range|set_item
abc_range    ::= letter
spaces ::= space*
space ::= ' '|'\n'|'\t'|'\r'
char_group   ::= "[:" ('a' set_a|'b' set_b|'c' set_c|'d' set_d|
                     'g' set_g|'l' set_l|'p' set_p|'s' set_s|
                     'u' set_u|'x' set_x|set)
set_a        ::= 'l' set_al|set
set_al       ::= 'n' set_aln|'p' set_alp|set
set_aln      ::= 'u' set_alnu|set
set_alnu     ::= 'm' set_alnum|set
set_alnum    ::= ':' set_alnumT|set
set_alnumT   ::= ']' set_alnumX|set
set_alnumX   ::= ']'
set_alp      ::= 'h' set_alph|set
set_alph     ::= 'a' set_alpha|set
set_alpha    ::= ':' set_alphaT|set
set_alphaT   ::= ']' set_alphaX|set
set_alphaX   ::= ']'
```

```
set_b         ::= 'l' set_bl|set
set_bl        ::= 'a' set_bla|set
set_bla       ::= 'n' set_blan|set
set_blan      ::= 'k' set_blank|set
set_blank     ::= ':' set_blankT|set
set_blankT    ::= ']' set_blankX|set
set_blankX    ::= ']'
set_c         ::= 'n' set_cn|set
set_cn        ::= 't' set_cnt|set
set_cnt       ::= 'r' set_cntr|set
set_cntr      ::= 'l' set_cntrl|set
set_cntrl     ::= ':' set_cntrlT|set
set_cntrlT    ::= ']' set_cntrlX|set
set_cntrlX    ::= ']'
set_d         ::= 'i' set_di|set
set_di        ::= 'g' set_dig|set
set_dig       ::= 'i' set_digi|set
set_digi      ::= 't' set_digit|set
set_digit     ::= ':' set_digitT|set
set_digitT    ::= ']' set_digitX|set
set_digitX    ::= ']'
set_g         ::= 'r' set_gr|set
set_gr        ::= 'a' set_gra|set
set_gra       ::= 'p' set_grap|set
set_grap      ::= 'h' set_graph|set
set_graph     ::= ':' set_graphT|set
set_graphT    ::= ']' set_graphX|set
set_graphX    ::= ']'
set_l         ::= 'o' set_lo|set
set_lo        ::= 'w' set_low|set
set_low       ::= 'e' set_lowe|set
set_lowe      ::= 'r' set_lower|set
set_lower     ::= ':' set_lowerT|set
set_lowerT    ::= ']' set_lowerX|set
set_lowerX    ::= ']'
set_p         ::= 'r' set_pr|'u' set_pu|set
set_pr        ::= 'i' set_pri|set
set_pri       ::= 'n' set_prin|set
set_prin      ::= 't' set_print|set
set_print     ::= ':' set_printT|set
set_printT    ::= ']' set_printX|set
set_printX    ::= ']'
set_pu        ::= 'n' set_pun|set
set_pun       ::= 'c' set_punc|set
set_punc      ::= 't' set_punct|set
set_punct     ::= ':' set_punctT|set
set_punctT    ::= ']' set_punctX|set
set_punctX    ::= ']'
set_s         ::= 'p' set_sp|set
set_sp        ::= 'a' set_spa|set
```

```
set_spa      ::= 'c' set_spac|set
set_spac     ::= 'e' set_space|set
set_space    ::= ':' set_spaceT|set
set_spaceT   ::= ']' set_spaceX|set
set_spaceX   ::= ']'
set_u        ::= 'p' set_up|set
set_up       ::= 'p' set_upp|set
set_upp      ::= 'e' set_uppe|set
set_uppe     ::= 'r' set_upper|set
set_upper    ::= ':' set_upperT|set
set_upperT   ::= ']' set_upperX|set
set_upperX   ::= ']'
set_x        ::= 'x' set_xd|set
set_xd       ::= 'd' set_xdi|set
set_xdi      ::= 'i' set_xdig|set
set_xdig     ::= 'g' set_xdigi|set
set_xdigi    ::= 'i' set_xdigit|set
set_xdigit   ::= ':' set_xdigitT|set
set_xdigitT  ::= ']' set_xdigitX|set
set_xdigitX  ::= ']'
```

References

1. Abrahams, D., Gurtovoy, A.: C++ Template Metaprogramming, Concepts, Tools, and Techniques from Boost and Beyond. Addison-Wesley, Boston (2004). p. 400. ISBN-0321-22725-6
2. Andersson, L.: Parsing with Haskell, 28 October 2001. http://www.cs.lth.se/eda120/assignment4/parser.pdf
3. Gil, Y., Lenz, K.: Simple and safe SQL queries with C++ templates. In: Consela, C., Lawall, J.L. (eds) 6th International Conference on Generative Programming and Component Engineering, GPCE 2007, Salzburg, Austria, pp. 13–24, 1–3 October 2007
4. Odersky, M., Spoon, L., Venners, B.: Programming in Scala, 2nd edn. Artima (2010). ISBN-10: 0981531644
5. The POSIX standard, 1003.1-2008 - IEEE Standard for Information Technology - Portable Operating System Interface (POSIX(R)). http://standards.ieee.org/findstds/standard/1003.1-2008.html
6. Porkoláb, Z., Sinkovics, Á.: Domain-specific language integration with compile-time parser generator library. In: Visser, E., Järvi, J. (eds) Proceedings of the Ninth International Conference on Generative Programming and Component Engineering, GPCE 2010, Eindhoven, The Netherlands, 10–13 October 2010
7. Sinkovics, Á., Porkoláb, Z.: Domain-specific language Integration with C++ template metaprogramming. In: Mernik, M. (ed) Formal and Practical Aspects of Domain-Specific Languages: Recent Developments, pp. 33–56. Published by Information Science Reference (an imprint of IGI Global), Hershey. ISBN 978-1-4666-2092-6 (hardcover) - ISBN 978-1-4666-2093-3 (ebook) - ISBN 978-1-4666-2094-0 pp. 33-56

8. Sinkovics, Á., Porkoláb, Z.: Implementing monads for C++ template metaprograms. In: Science of Computer Programming, Available online 23 January 2013. ISSN 0167–6423, doi:10.1016/j.scico.2013.01.002. (http://www.sciencedirect.com/science/article/pii/S0167642313000051)
9. Sinkovics, Á., Sajó, E., Porkoláb, Z.: Towards more reliable C++ template metaprograms. In: Penjam, J. (ed.) 12th Symposium on Programming Languages and Software Tools (SPLST 2011), Tallinn, Estonia, pp. 260–271, 5–7 October 2011
10. Sinkovics, Á., Porkoláb, Z.: Expressing C++ template metaprograms as lambda expressions. In: Horváth, Z., Zsók, V., Achten, P., Koopman, P. (eds.) Proceedings of Tenth Symposium on Trends in Functional Programming, Komrno, Slovakia, pp. 97–111, 2–4 June 2009
11. Visser, E.: Program transformation with Stratego/XT. In: Lengauer, C., Batory, D., Blum, A., Odersky, M. (eds.) Domain-Specific Program Generation. LNCS, vol. 3016, pp. 216–238. Springer, Heidelberg (2004)
12. The auto specified in C++11. http://en.cppreference.com/w/cpp/language/auto
13. The Boost. Proto library. http://www.boost.org/doc/libs/1_53_0/doc/html/proto.html
14. Continuation-passing style on Wikipedia. http://en.wikipedia.org/wiki/Continuation-passing_style
15. Marlow, S. (ed.): Haskell 2010 Language report (2010). http://www.haskell.org/haskellwiki/Language_and_library_specification
16. Icon, The Icon Programming Language. http://www.cs.arizona.edu/icon
17. The ISO C++11 standard, ISO/IEC 14882:2011(E) Information technology - Programming languages - C++. http://www.iso.org/iso/catalogue_detail.htm?csnumber=50372
18. Katahdin. http://www.chrisseaton.com/katahdin
19. Milewski, B.: Haskell and C++ template metaprogramming. http://bartoszmilewski.wordpress.com/2009/10/26/haskellc-video-and-slides
20. Milewski, B., Niebler, E.: Compile-Time/Run-Time Functional Programming in C++. http://2012.cppnow.org/session/variadic-template-metaprogramming-using-monads
21. The MPL Reference Manual. http://www.boost.org/doc/libs/1_53_0/libs/mpl/doc/refmanual.html
22. Sinkovics, Á., Porkoláb, Z.: Metaparse - Compile-time parsing with template metaprogramming. http://2012.cppnow.org/session/metaparse-compile-time-parsing-with-template-metaprogramming
23. The User Manual of mpllibs metaparse. http://abel.web.elte.hu/mpllibs/metaparse/manual.html
24. Veldhuizen, T., Gannon, D.: Active libraries: rethinking the roles of compilers and libraries. In: Proceedings of the SIAM Workshop on Object Oriented Methods for Inter-Operable Scientific and Engineering Computing OO 1998 (1998)
25. Veldhuizen, T.: Expression templates. C++ Report 7, 26–31 (1995)
26. The Stratego Program Transformation Language. http://strategoxt.org/
27. The Template Haskell programming language. http://www.haskell.org/haskellwiki/Template_Haskell
28. The xlxpressive library. https://github.com/istvans/mpllibs/tree/master/mpllibs/xlxpressive

29. The XMF programming language. http://itcentre.tvu.ac.uk/clark/xmf.html
30. The Boost Xpressive library. http://www.boost.org/doc/libs/1_55_0/doc/html/xpressive.html
31. Xpressive - "Nested Regexes and Sub-Match Scoping" and "Nested Results". http://www.boost.org/doc/libs/1_53_0/doc/html/xpressive/user_s_guide.html#boost_xpressive.user_s_guide.grammars_and_nested_matches.nested_regexes_and_sub_match_scoping

The IDRIS Programming Language
Implementing Embedded Domain Specific Languages with Dependent Types

Edwin Brady[✉]

University of St Andrews, Fife KY16 9SX, UK
ecb10@st-andrews.ac.uk

Abstract. Types describe a program's meaning. Dependent types, which allow types to be predicated on values, allow a program to be given a more precise type, and thus a more precise meaning. Typechecking amounts to verifying that the implementation of a program matches its intended meaning. In this tutorial, I will describe IDRIS, a pure functional programming language with dependent types, and show how it may be used to develop *verified* embedded domain specific languages (EDSLs). IDRIS has several features intended to support EDSL development, including syntax extensions, overloadable binders and implicit conversions. I will describe how these features, along with dependent types, can be used to capture important functional and extra-functional properties of programs, how resources such as file handles and network protocols may be managed through EDSLs, and finally describe a general framework for programming and reasoning about side-effects, implemented as an embedded DSL.

1 Introduction

In conventional programming languages, there is a clear distinction between *types* and *values*. For example, in Haskell [13], the following are types, representing integers, characters, lists of characters, and lists of any value respectively:

– Int, Char, [Char], [a]

Correspondingly, the following values are examples of inhabitants of those types:

– 42, 'a', "Hello world!", [2,3,4,5,6]

In a language with *dependent types*, however, the distinction is less clear. Dependent types allow types to "depend" on values — in other words, types are a *first class* language construct and can be manipulated like any other value. A canonical first example is the type of lists of a specific length[1], Vect n a, where a is the element type and n is the length of the list and can be an arbitrary term.

---

[1] Typically, and perhaps confusingly, referred to in the dependently typed programming literature as "vectors".

© Springer International Publishing Switzerland 2015
V. Zsók et al. (Eds.): CEFP 2013, LNCS 8606, pp. 115–186, 2015.
DOI: 10.1007/978-3-319-15940-9_4

When types can contain values, and where those values describe properties (e.g. the length of a list) the type of a function can describe some of its own properties. For example, concatenating two lists has the property that the resulting list's length is the sum of the lengths of the two input lists. We can therefore give the following type to the app function, which concatenates vectors:

```
app : Vect n a -> Vect m a -> Vect (n + m) a
```

This tutorial introduces IDRIS, a general purpose functional programming language with dependent types, and in particular how to use IDRIS to implement Embedded Domain Specific Languages (EDSLs). It includes a brief introduction to the most important features of the language for EDSL development, and is aimed at readers already familiar with a functional language such as Haskell or OCaml. In particular, a certain amount of familiarity with Haskell syntax is assumed, although most concepts will at least be explained briefly.

1.1   Outline

The tutorial is organised as follows:

- This Section describes how to download and install IDRIS and build an introductory program.
- Section 2 introduces the fundamental features of the language: primitive types, and how to define types and functions.
- Section 3 describes type classes in IDRIS and gives two specific examples, Monad and Applicative.
- Section 4 describes dependent pattern matching, in particular *views*, which give a means of abstracting over pattern matching.
- Section 5 introduces proofs and theorem proving in IDRIS, and introduces *provisional* definitions, which are pattern definitions which require additional proof obligations.
- Section 6 gives a first example of EDSL implementation, a well-typed interpreter
- Section 7 describes how IDRIS provides support for interactive program development, and in particular how this is incorporated into text editors.
- Section 8 introduces syntactic support for EDSL implementation.
- Section 9 gives an extending example of an EDSL, which supports *resource aware* programming.
- Section 10 describes how IDRIS supports side-effecting and stateful programs with system interaction, by using an EDSL.
- Finally, Sect. 11 concludes and provides references to further reading.

Many of these sections (Sects. 2, 4, 5, 7, 8 and 10) end with exercises to reinforce your understanding. The tutorial includes several examples, which have been tested with IDRIS version 0.9.14. The files are available in the IDRIS distribution, so that you can try them out easily[2]. However, it is strongly recommended that you type them in yourself, rather than simply loading and reading them.

---

[2] https://github.com/idris-lang/Idris-dev/tree/master/examples.

1.2   Downloading and Installing

IDRIS requires an up to date Haskell Platform[3]. Once this is installed, IDRIS can be installed with the following commands:

```
cabal update
cabal install idris
```

This will install the latest version released on Hackage, along with any dependencies. If, however, you would like the most up to date development version, you can find it on GitHub at https://github.com/idris-lang/Idris-dev. You can also find up to date download instructions at http://idris-lang.org/download.

To check that installation has succeeded, and to write your first IDRIS program, create a file called "hello.idr" containing the following text:

```
module Main

main : IO ()
main = putStrLn "Hello world"
```

We will explain the details of how this program works later. For the moment, you can compile the program to an executable by entering `idris hello.idr -o hello` at the shell prompt. This will create an executable called `hello`, which you can run:

```
$ idris hello.idr -o hello
$ ./hello
Hello world
```

Note that the $ indicates the shell prompt! Some useful options to the `idris` command are:

- `-o prog` to compile to an executable called `prog`.
- `--check` type check the file and its dependencies without starting the interactive environment.
- `--help` display usage summary and command line options.

1.3   The Interactive Environment

Entering `idris` at the shell prompt starts up the interactive environment. You should see something like Listing 1.

This gives a `ghci`-style interface which allows evaluation of expressions, as well as type checking expressions, theorem proving, compilation, editing and various other operations. `:?` gives a list of supported commands. Listing 2 shows an example run in which `hello.idr` is loaded, the type of `main` is checked and then the program is compiled to the executable `hello`.

---

[3] http://haskell.org/platform.

Listing 1. Idris prompt

```
$ idris
```

```
     ____    __    _
    /  _/___/ /____(_)____
    / // __  / __/ / ___/      Version 1.0
  _/ // /_/ / /  / (__  )      http://www.idris-lang.org/
 /___/\__,_/_/  /_/____/       Type :? for help

Idris>
```

Listing 2. Sample Interactive Run

```
$ idris hello.idr
```

```
     ____    __    _
    /  _/___/ /____(_)____
    / // __  / __/ / ___/      Version 1.0
  _/ // /_/ / /  / (__  )      http://www.idris-lang.org/
 /___/\__,_/_/  /_/____/       Type :? for help

Type checking ./hello.idr
*hello> :t main
Main.main : IO ()
*hello> :c hello
*hello> :q
Bye bye
$ ./hello
Hello world
```

Type checking a file, if successful, creates a bytecode version of the file (in this case hello.ibc) to speed up loading in future. The bytecode is regenerated on reloading if the source file changes.

2   Types and Functions

2.1   Primitive Types

IDRIS defines several primitive types: Int, Integer and Float for numeric operations, Char and String for text manipulation, and Ptr which represents foreign pointers. There are also several data types declared in the library, including Bool, with values True and False. We can declare some constants with these types. Enter the following into a file prims.idr and load it into the IDRIS interactive environment by typing idris prims.idr:

```
module prims

x : Int
x = 42
```

```
foo : String
foo = "Sausage machine"

bar : Char
bar = 'Z'

quux : Bool
quux = False
```

An IDRIS file consists of a module declaration (here `module prims`) followed by an optional list of imports (none here, however IDRIS programs can consist of several modules, each of which has its own namespace) and a collection of declarations and definitions. The order of definitions is significant — functions and data types must be defined before use. Each definition must have a type declaration (here, `x : Int, foo : String`, etc.). Indentation is significant — a new declaration begins at the same level of indentation as the preceding declaration. Alternatively, declarations may be terminated with a semicolon.

A library module `prelude` is automatically imported by every IDRIS program, including facilities for IO, arithmetic, data structures and various common functions. The prelude defines several arithmetic and comparison operators, which we can use at the prompt. Evaluating things at the prompt gives an answer, and the type of the answer. For example:

```
*prims> 6*6+6
42 : Integer
*prims> x == 6*6+6
True : Bool
```

All of the usual arithmetic and comparison operators are defined for the primitive types (e.g. `==` above checks for equality). They are overloaded using type classes, as we will discuss in Sect. 3 and can be extended to work on user defined types. Boolean expressions can be tested with the `if...then...else` construct:

```
*prims> if x == 6 * 6 + 6 then "The answer!"
                          else "Not the answer"
"The answer!" : String
```

2.2 Data Types

Data types are defined in a similar way to Haskell data types, with a similar syntax. Natural numbers and lists, for example, can be declared as follows:

```
data Nat    = Z   | S Nat          -- Natural numbers
                                   -- (zero, successor)
data List a = Nil | (::) a (List a) -- Polymorphic lists
```

The above declarations are taken from the standard library. Unary natural numbers can be either zero (`Z`), or the successor of another natural number (`S k`). Lists can either be empty (`Nil`) or a value added to the front of another list

(x :: xs). In the declaration for List, we used an infix operator :: . New
operators such as this can be added using a fixity declaration, as follows:

infixr 10 ::

Functions, data constructors and type constructors may all be given infix operators as names. They may be used in prefix form if enclosed in brackets, e.g.
(::). Infix operators can use any of the symbols:

:+-*/=_.?|&><!@$%^~ .

2.3   Functions

Functions are implemented by pattern matching, again using a similar syntax
to Haskell. The main difference is that IDRIS requires type declarations for all
functions, and that IDRIS uses a single colon : (rather than Haskell's double
colon ::). Some natural number arithmetic functions can be defined as follows,
again taken from the standard library:

```
-- Unary addition
plus : Nat -> Nat -> Nat
plus Z     y = y
plus (S k) y = S (plus k y)

-- Unary multiplication
mult : Nat -> Nat -> Nat
mult Z     y = Z
mult (S k) y = plus y (mult k y)
```

The standard arithmetic operators + and * are also overloaded for use by Nat,
and are implemented using the above functions. Unlike Haskell, there is no
restriction on whether types and function names must begin with a capital letter or not. Function names (plus and mult above), data constructors (Z, S,
Nil and ::) and type constructors (Nat and List) are all part of the same
namespace. As a result, it is not possible to use the same name for a type and
data constructor.

Like arithmetic operations, integer literals are also overloaded using type
classes, meaning that we can test these functions as follows:

```
Idris> plus 2 2
4 : Nat
Idris> mult 3 (plus 2 2)
12 : Nat
```

Aside: It is natural to ask why we have unary natural numbers when our computers have integer arithmetic built in to their CPU. The reason is primarily that
unary numbers have a convenient structure which is easy to reason about, and
easy to relate to other data structures, as we will see later. Nevertheless, we do
not want this convenience to be at the expense of efficiency. IDRIS knows about
the relationship between Nat (and similarly structured types) and numbers, so
optimises the representation and functions such as plus and mult.

where Clauses. Functions can also be defined *locally* using where clauses. For example, to define a function which reverses a list, we can use an auxiliary function which accumulates the new, reversed list, and which does not need to be visible globally:

```
reverse : List a -> List a
reverse xs = revAcc [] xs where
  revAcc : List a -> List a -> List a
  revAcc acc [] = acc
  revAcc acc (x :: xs) = revAcc (x :: acc) xs
```

Indentation is significant — functions in the where block must be indented further than the outer function.

Scope. Any names which are visible in the outer scope are also visible in the where clause (unless they have been redefined, such as xs here). A name which appears only in the type will be in scope in the where clause if it is a *parameter* to one of the types, i.e. it is fixed across the entire structure.

As well as functions, where blocks can include local data declarations, such as the following where MyLT is not accessible outside the definition of foo:

```
foo : Int -> Int
foo x = case isLT of
             Yes => x*2
             No => x*4
    where
        data MyLT = Yes | No

        isLT : MyLT
        isLT = if x < 20 then Yes else No
```

In general, functions defined in a where clause need a type declaration just like any top level function. However, the type declaration for a function f *can* be omitted if:

– f appears in the right hand side of the top level definition
– The type of f can be completely determined from its first application

So, for example, the following definitions are legal:

```
even : Nat -> Bool
even Z = True
even (S k) = odd k where
  odd Z = False
  odd (S k) = even k

test : List Nat
test = [c (S 1), c Z, d (S Z)]
  where c x = 42 + x
        d y = c (y + 1 + z y)
              where z w = y + w
```

2.4 Dependent Types

Vectors. A standard example of a dependent type is the type of "lists with length", conventionally called vectors in the dependent type literature. In the IDRIS library, vectors are declared as follows:

```
data Vect : Nat -> Type -> Type where
     Nil  : Vect Z a
     (::) : a -> Vect k a -> Vect (S k) a
```

Note that we have used the same constructor names as for List. Ad-hoc name overloading such as this is accepted by IDRIS, provided that the names are declared in different namespaces (in practice, normally in different modules). Ambiguous constructor names can normally be resolved from context.

This declares a family of types, and so the form of the declaration is rather different from the simple type declarations earlier. We explicitly state the type of the type constructor Vect—it takes a Nat and a type as an argument, where Type stands for the type of types. We say that Vect is *indexed* over Nat and *parameterised* by Type. Each constructor targets a different part of the family of types. Nil can only be used to construct vectors with zero length, and :: to construct vectors with non-zero length. In the type of ::, we state explicitly that an element of type a and a tail of type Vect k a (i.e., a vector of length k) combine to make a vector of length S k.

We can define functions on dependent types such as Vect in the same way as on simple types such as List and Nat above, by pattern matching. The type of a function over Vect will describe what happens to the lengths of the vectors involved. For example, ++, defined in the library, appends two Vects:

```
(++) : Vect n a -> Vect m a -> Vect (n + m) a
(++) Nil        ys = ys
(++) (x :: xs) ys = x :: xs ++ ys
```

The type of (++) states that the resulting vector's length will be the sum of the input lengths. If we get the definition wrong in such a way that this does not hold, IDRIS will not accept the definition. For example:

```
(++) : Vect n a -> Vect m a -> Vect (n + m) a
(++) Nil        ys = ys
(++) (x :: xs) ys = x :: xs ++ xs -- BROKEN
```

```
$ idris vbroken.idr --check
vbroken.idr:3:Can't unify Vect n a with Vect m a

Specifically:
     Can't unify n with m
```

This error message suggests that there is a length mismatch between two vectors — we needed a vector of length m, but provided a vector of length n.

Finite Sets. Finite sets, as the name suggests, are sets with a finite number of elements. They are declared as follows (again, in the prelude):

```
data Fin : Nat -> Type where
   fZ : Fin (S k)
   fS : Fin k -> Fin (S k)
```

For all n : Nat, Fin n is a type containing exactly n possible values: fZ is the first element of a finite set with S k elements, indexed by zero; fS n is the n+1th element of a finite set with S k elements. Fin is indexed by a Nat, which represents the number of elements in the set. Obviously we can't construct an element of an empty set, so neither constructor targets Fin Z.

A useful application of the Fin family is to represent bounded natural numbers. Since the first n natural numbers form a finite set of n elements, we can treat Fin n as the set of natural numbers bounded by n.

For example, the following function which looks up an element in a Vect, by a bounded index given as a Fin n, is defined in the prelude:

```
index : Fin n -> Vect n a -> a
index fZ     (x :: xs) = x
index (fS k) (x :: xs) = index k xs
```

This function looks up a value at a given location in a vector. The location is bounded by the length of the vector (n in each case), so there is no need for a run-time bounds check. The type checker guarantees that the location is no larger than the length of the vector.

Note also that there is no case for Nil here. This is because it is impossible. Since there is no element of Fin Z, and the location is a Fin n, then n can not be Z. As a result, attempting to look up an element in an empty vector would give a compile time type error, since it would force n to be Z.

Implicit Arguments. Let us take a closer look at the type of index:

```
index : Fin n -> Vect n a -> a
```

It takes two arguments, an element of the finite set of n elements, and a vector with n elements of type a. But there are also two names, n and a, which are not declared explicitly. These are *implicit* arguments to index. We could also write the type of index as:

```
index : {a:Type} -> {n:Nat} -> Fin n -> Vect n a -> a
```

Implicit arguments, given in braces {} in the type declaration, are not given in applications of index; their values can be inferred from the types of the Fin n and Vect n a arguments. Any name with a *lower case initial letter* which appears as a parameter or index in a type declaration, but which is otherwise free, will be automatically bound as an implicit argument. Implicit arguments can still be given explicitly in applications, using {a=value} and {n=value}, for example:

```
index {a=Int} {n=2} fZ (2 :: 3 :: Nil)
```

In fact, any argument, implicit or explicit, may be given a name. We could have declared the type of index as:

```
index : (i:Fin n) -> (xs:Vect n a) -> a
```

It is a matter of taste whether you want to do this — sometimes it can help document a function by making the purpose of an argument more clear.

"using" Notation. Sometimes it is useful to provide types of implicit arguments, particularly where there is a dependency ordering, or where the implicit arguments themselves have dependencies. For example, we may wish to state the types of the implicit arguments in the following definition, which defines a predicate on vectors:

```
data Elem : a -> List a -> Type where
    Here :  {x:a} -> {xs:List a} ->
            Elem x (x :: xs)
    There : {x,y:a} -> {xs:List a} ->
            Elem x xs -> Elem x (y :: xs)
```

An instance of Elem x xs states that x is an element of xs. We can construct such a predicate if the required element is Here, at the head of the list, or There, in the tail of the list. For example:

```
testList : List Int
testList = 3 :: 4 :: 5 :: 6 :: Nil

inList : Elem 5 testList
inList = There (There Here)
```

If the same implicit arguments are being used several times, it can make a definition difficult to read. To avoid this problem, a using block gives the types and ordering of any implicit arguments which can appear within the block:

```
using (x:a, y:a, xs:List a)
    data Elem : a -> List a -> Type where
        Here  : Elem x (x :: xs)
        There : Elem x xs -> Elem x (y :: xs)
```

Note: Declaration Order and mutual Blocks. In general, functions and data types must be declared before use, since dependent types allow functions to appear as part of types, and their reduction behaviour to affect type checking. However, this restriction can be relaxed by using a mutual block, which allows data types and functions to be defined simultaneously:

```
mutual
    even : Nat -> Bool
    even Z = True
    even (S k) = odd k
```

```
odd : Nat -> Bool
odd Z = False
odd (S k) = even k
```

In a mutual block, the IDRIS type checker will first check all of the type declarations in the block, then the function bodies. As a result, none of the function types can depend on the reduction behaviour of any of the functions in the block.

2.5 I/O

Computer programs are of little use if they do not interact with the user or the system in some way. The difficulty in a pure language such as IDRIS — that is, a language where expressions do not have side-effects — is that I/O is inherently side-effecting. Therefore in IDRIS, such interactions are encapsulated in the type IO:

```
data IO a -- IO operation returning a value of type a
```

We'll leave the definition of IO abstract, but effectively it describes what the I/O operations to be executed are, rather than how to execute them. The resulting operations are executed externally, by the run-time system. We've already seen one IO program:

```
main : IO ()
main = putStrLn "Hello world"
```

The type of putStrLn explains that it takes a string, and returns an element of the unit type () via an I/O action. There is a variant putStr which outputs a string without a newline:

```
putStrLn : String -> IO ()
putStr   : String -> IO ()
```

We can also read strings from user input:

```
getLine : IO String
```

A number of other I/O operations are defined in the prelude, for example for reading and writing files, including:

```
data File -- abstract
data Mode = Read | Write | ReadWrite

openFile  : String -> Mode -> IO File
closeFile : File -> IO ()

fread   : File -> IO String
fwrite  : File -> String -> IO ()
feof    : File -> IO Bool

readFile : String -> IO String
```

2.6 "do" Notation

I/O programs will typically need to sequence actions, feeding the output of one computation into the input of the next. IO is an abstract type, however, so we can't access the result of a computation directly. Instead, we sequence operations with do notation:

```
greet : IO ()
greet = do putStr "What is your name? "
           name <- getLine
           putStrLn ("Hello " ++ name)
```

The syntax x <- iovalue executes the I/O operation iovalue, of type IO a, and puts the result, of type a, into the variable x. In this case, getLine returns an IO String, so name has type String. Indentation is significant — each statement in the do block must begin in the same column. The return operation allows us to inject a value directly into an IO operation:

```
return : a -> IO a
```

As we will see later, do notation is more general than this, and can be overloaded.

2.7 Laziness

Normally, arguments to functions are evaluated before the function itself (that is, IDRIS uses *eager* evaluation). However, consider the following function:

```
boolCase : Bool -> a -> a -> a
boolCase True  t e = t
boolCase False t e = e
```

This function uses one of the t or e arguments, but not both (in fact, this is used to implement the if...then...else construct as we will see later. We would prefer if *only* the argument which was used was evaluated. To achieve this, IDRIS provides a Lazy data type, which allows evaluation to be suspended:

```
data Lazy : Type -> Type where
     Delay : (val : a) -> Lazy a

Force : Lazy a -> a
```

A value of type Lazy a is unevaluated until it is forced by Force. The IDRIS type checker knows about the Lazy type, and inserts conversions where necessary between Lazy a and a, and vice versa. We can therefore write boolCase as follows, without any explicit use of Force or Delay:

```
boolCase : Bool -> Lazy a -> Lazy a -> a
boolCase True  t e = t
boolCase False t e = e
```

2.8   Useful Data Types

The IDRIS prelude includes a number of useful data types and library functions (see the `lib/` directory in the distribution). The functions described here are imported automatically by every IDRIS program, as part of `Prelude.idr` in the prelude package.

List and Vect. We have already seen the `List` and `Vect` data types:

```
data List a = Nil | (::) a (List a)

data Vect : Nat -> Type -> Type where
   Nil  : Vect Z a
   (::) : a -> Vect k a -> Vect (S k) a
```

Note that the constructor names are the same for each — constructor names (in fact, names in general) can be overloaded, provided that they are declared in different namespaces (in practice, typically different modules), and will be resolved according to their type. As syntactic sugar, any type with the constructor names `Nil` and `::` can be written in list form. For example:

- `[]` means `Nil`
- `[1,2,3]` means `1 :: 2 :: 3 :: Nil`

The library also defines a number of functions for manipulating these types. `map` is overloaded both for `List` and `Vect` and applies a function to every element of the list or vector.

```
map : (a -> b) -> List a -> List b
map f []       = []
map f (x :: xs) = f x :: map f xs

map : (a -> b) -> Vect n a -> Vect n b
map f []       = []
map f (x :: xs) = f x :: map f xs
```

For example, to double every element in a vector of integers, we can define the following:

```
intVec : Vect 5 Int
intVec = [1, 2, 3, 4, 5]

double : Int -> Int
double x = x * 2
```

Then we can use `map` at the IDRIS prompt:

```
map> map double intVec
[2, 4, 6, 8, 10] : Vect 5 Int
```

For more details of the functions available on `List` and `Vect`, look in the library, in `Prelude/List.idr` and `Prelude/Vect.idr` respectively. Functions include filtering, appending, reversing, etc.

Maybe. Maybe describes an optional value. Either there is a value of the given type, or there isn't:

```
data Maybe a = Just a | Nothing
```

Maybe is one way of giving a type to an operation that may fail. For example, indexing a List (rather than a vector) may result in an out of bounds error:

```
list_lookup : Nat -> List a -> Maybe a
list_lookup _      Nil        = Nothing
list_lookup Z      (x :: xs) = Just x
list_lookup (S k) (x :: xs) = list_lookup k xs
```

The maybe function is used to process values of type Maybe, either by applying a function to the value, if there is one, or by providing a default value:

```
maybe : Maybe a -> | (def:b) -> (a -> b) -> b
```

The vertical bar | before the default value is a *laziness* annotation. Normally expressions are evaluated eagerly, before being passed to a function. However, in this case, the default value might not be used and if it is a large expression, evaluating it will be wasteful. The | annotation tells the compiler not to evaluate the argument until it is needed.

Tuples. Values can be paired with the following built-in data type:

```
data Pair a b = MkPair a b
```

As syntactic sugar, we can write (a, b) which, according to context, means either Pair a b or MkPair a b. Tuples can contain an arbitrary number of values, represented as nested pairs:

```
fred : (String, Int)
fred = ("Fred", 42)

jim : (String, Int, String)
jim = ("Jim", 25, "Cambridge")
```

Dependent Pairs. Dependent pairs allow the type of the second element of a pair to depend on the value of the first element:

```
data Sigma : (A : Type) -> (P : A -> Type) -> Type where
     Sg_intro : {P : A -> Type} ->
                (a : A) -> P a -> Sigma A P
```

Again, there is syntactic sugar for this. (a : A ** P) is the type of a dependent pair of A and P, where the name a can occur inside P. (a ** p) constructs a value of this type. For example, we can pair a number with a Vect of a particular length.

```
vec : (n : Nat ** Vect n Int)
vec = (2 ** [3, 4])
```

The type checker can infer the value of the first element from the length of the vector; we can write an underscore _ in place of values which we expect the type checker to fill in, so the above definition could also be written as:

```
vec : (n : Nat ** Vect n Int)
vec = (_ ** [3, 4])
```

We might also prefer to omit the type of the first element of the pair, since, again, it can be inferred:

```
vec : (n ** Vect n Int)
vec = (_ ** [3, 4])
```

Without the syntactic sugar, this would be written in full as follows:

```
vec : Sigma Nat (\n => Vect n Int)
vec = Sg_intro 2 [3,4]
```

One use for dependent pairs is to return values of dependent types where the index is not necessarily known in advance. For example, if we filter elements out of a Vect according to some predicate, we will not know in advance what the length of the resulting vector will be:

```
filter : (a -> Bool) -> Vect n a -> (p ** Vect p a)
```

If the Vect is empty, the result is easy:

```
filter p Nil = (_ ** [])
```

In the : : case, we need to inspect the result of a recursive call to filter to extract the length and the vector from the result. We use a case expression to inspect the intermediate value:

```
filter p (x :: xs)
    = case filter p xs of
         (_ ** xs') => if p x then (_ ** x :: xs')
                              else (_ ** xs')
```

so. The so data type is a predicate on Bool which guarantees that the value is true:

```
data so : Bool -> Type where
     oh : so True
```

This is most useful for providing a static guarantee that a dynamic check has been made. For example, we might provide a safe interface to a function which draws a pixel on a graphical display as follows, where so (inBounds x y) guarantees that the point (x,y) is within the bounds of a 640x480 window:

```
inBounds : Int -> Int -> Bool
inBounds x y = x >= 0 && x < 640 && y >= 0 && y < 480

drawPoint : (x : Int) -> (y : Int) ->
            so (inBounds x y) -> IO ()
drawPoint x y p = unsafeDrawPoint x y
```

2.9   More Expressions

let Bindings. Intermediate values can be calculated using `let` bindings:

```
mirror : List a -> List a
mirror xs = let xs' = rev xs in
            xs ++ xs'
```

We can do simple pattern matching in `let` bindings too. For example, we can extract fields from a record as follows, as well as by pattern matching at the top level:

```
data Person = MkPerson String Int

showPerson : Person -> String
showPerson p = let MkPerson name age = p in
               name ++ " is " ++ show age ++
               " years old"
```

List Comprehensions. IDRIS provides *comprehension* notation as a convenient shorthand for building lists. The general form is:

```
[ expression | qualifiers ]
```

This generates the list of values produced by evaluating the `expression`, according to the conditions given by the comma separated `qualifiers`. For example, we can build a list of Pythagorean triples as follows:

```
pythag : Int -> List (Int, Int, Int)
pythag n = [ (x, y, z) | z <- [1..n], y <- [1..z],
                         x <- [1..y],
                         x * x + y * y == z * z ]
```

The `[a..b]` notation is another shorthand which builds a list of numbers between a and b. Alternatively `[a,b..c]` builds a list of numbers between a and c with the increment specified by the difference between a and b. This works for any enumerable type.

case Expressions. Another way of inspecting intermediate values of *simple* types, as we saw with `filter` on vectors, is to use a `case` expression. The following function, for example, splits a string into two at a given character:

```
splitAt : Char -> String -> (String, String)
splitAt c x = case break (== c) x of
                  (x, y) => (x, strTail y)
```

break is a library function which breaks a string into a pair of strings at the point where the given function returns true. We then deconstruct the pair it returns, and remove the first character of the second string.

Restrictions: The case construct is intended for simple analysis of intermediate expressions to avoid the need to write auxiliary functions, and is also used internally to implement pattern matching let and lambda bindings. It will *only* work if:

– Each branch *matches* a value of the same type, and *returns* a value of the same type.
– The type of the expression as a whole can be determined without checking the branches of the case-expression itself. This is because case expressions are lifted to top level functions by the IDRIS type checker, and type checking is type-directed.

2.10   Dependent Records

Records are data types which collect several values (the record's *fields*) together. IDRIS provides syntax for defining records and automatically generating field access and update functions. For example, we can represent a person's name and age in a record:

```
record Person : Type where
    MkPerson : (name : String) ->
               (age : Int) -> Person

fred : Person
fred = MkPerson "Fred" 30
```

Record declarations are like data declarations, except that they are introduced by the record keyword, and can only have one constructor. The names of the binders in the constructor type (name and age) here are the field names, which we can use to access the field values:

```
*record> name fred
"Fred" : String
*record> age fred
30 : Int
*record> :t name
name : Person -> String
```

We can also use the field names to update a record (or, more precisely, produce a new record with the given fields updated).

```
*record> record { name = "Jim" } fred
MkPerson "Jim" 30 : Person
*record> record { name = "Jim", age = 20 } fred
MkPerson "Jim" 20 : Person
```

The syntax record { field = val, ... } generates a function which updates the given fields in a record.

Records, and fields within records, can have dependent types. Updates are allowed to change the type of a field, provided that the result is well-typed, and the result does not affect the type of the record as a whole. For example:

```
record Class : Type where
     ClassInfo : (students : Vect n Person) ->
                 (className : String) ->
                 Class
```

It is safe to update the students field to a vector of a different length because it will not affect the type of the record:

```
addStudent : Person -> Class -> Class
addStudent p c = record { students = p :: students c } c

*record> addStudent fred (ClassInfo [] "CS")
ClassInfo [(MkPerson "Fred" 30)] "CS" : Class
```

Exercises

1. Write a function repeat : (n : Nat) -> a -> Vect n a which constructs a vector of n copies of an item.
2. Consider the following function types:

   ```
   vtake : (n : Nat) -> Vect (n + m) a -> Vect n a
   vdrop : (n : Nat) -> Vect (n + m) a -> Vect m a
   ```

   Implement these functions. Do the types tell you enough to suggest what they should do?
3. A matrix is a 2-dimensional vector, and could be defined as follows:

   ```
   Matrix : Type -> Nat -> Nat -> Type
   Matrix a n m = Vect (Vect a m) n
   ```

   (a) Using repeat, above, and Vect.zipWith, write a function which transposes a matrix.

   Hints: Remember to think carefully about its type first! zipWith for vectors is defined as follows:

   ```
   zipWith : (a -> b -> c) ->
             Vect a n -> Vect b n -> Vect c n
   zipWith f []      []      = []
   zipWith f (x::xs) (y::ys) = f x y :: zipWith f xs ys
   ```

   (b) Write a function to multiply two matrices.

3   Type Classes

We often want to define functions which work across several different data types. For example, we would like arithmetic operators to work on Int, Integer and Float at the very least. We would like == to work on the majority of data types. We would like to be able to display different types in a uniform way.

To achieve this, we use a feature which has proved to be effective in Haskell, namely *type classes*. To define a type class, we provide a collection of overloaded operations which describe the interface for *instances* of that class. A simple example is the Show type class, which is defined in the prelude and provides an interface for converting values to Strings:

```
class Show a where
    show : a -> String
```

This generates a function of the following type (which we call a *method* of the Show class):

```
show : Show a => a -> String
```

We can read this as "under the constraint that a is an instance of Show, take an a as input and return a String." An instance of a class is defined with an instance declaration, which provides implementations of the function for a specific type. For example, the Show instance for Nat could be defined as:

```
instance Show Nat where
    show Z = "Z"
    show (S k) = "s" ++ show k

Idris> show (S (S (S Z)))
"sssZ" : String
```

Like Haskell, by default only one instance of a class can be given for a type—instances may not overlap[4]. Also, type classes and instances may themselves have constraints, for example:

```
class Eq a => Ord a where ...
instance Show a => Show (List a) where ...
```

3.1   Monads and do-Notation

In general, type classes can have any number (greater than 0) of parameters, and the parameters can have *any* type. If the type of the parameter is not Type, we need to give an explicit type declaration. For example:

```
class Monad (m : Type -> Type) where
    return : a -> m a
    (>>=)  : m a -> (a -> m b) -> m b
```

---

[4] *Named* instances are also available, but beyond the scope of this tutorial.

The Monad class allows us to encapsulate binding and computation, and is the basis of do-notation introduced in Sect. 2.6. Inside a do block, the following syntactic transformations are applied:

– x < − v; e becomes v >>= (\x => e)
– v; e becomes v >>= (_ => e)
– let x = v; e becomes let x = v in e

IO is an instance of Monad, defined using primitive functions. We can also define an instance for Maybe, as follows:

```
instance Monad Maybe where
    return = Just

    Nothing  >>= k = Nothing
    (Just x) >>= k = k x
```

Using this we can, for example, define a function which adds two Maybe Ints, using the monad to encapsulate the error handling:

```
m_add : Maybe Int -> Maybe Int -> Maybe Int
m_add x y = do x' <- x -- Extract value from x
               y' <- y -- Extract value from y
               return (x' + y') -- Add them
```

This function will extract the values from x and y, if they are available, or return Nothing if they are not. Managing the Nothing cases is achieved by the >>= operator, hidden by the do notation.

```
*classes> m_add (Just 20) (Just 22)
Just 42 : Maybe Int
*classes> m_add (Just 20) Nothing
Nothing : Maybe Int
```

3.2   Idiom Brackets

While do notation gives an alternative meaning to sequencing, idioms give an alternative meaning to *application*. The notation and larger example in this section is inspired by Conor McBride and Ross Paterson's paper "Applicative Programming with Effects" [12].

First, let us revisit m_add above. All it is really doing is applying an operator to two values extracted from Maybe Ints. We could abstract out the application:

```
m_app : Maybe (a -> b) -> Maybe a -> Maybe b
m_app (Just f) (Just a) = Just (f a)
m_app _         _        = Nothing
```

Using this, we can write an alternative m_add which uses this alternative notion of function application, with explicit calls to m_app:

```
m_add' : Maybe Int -> Maybe Int -> Maybe Int
m_add' x y = m_app (m_app (Just (+)) x) y
```

Rather than having to insert m_app everywhere there is an application, we can use *idiom brackets* to do the job for us. To do this, we use the Applicative class, which captures the notion of application for a data type:

```
infixl 2 <$>
```

```
class Applicative (f : Type -> Type) where
    pure  : a -> f a
    (<$>) : f (a -> b) -> f a -> f b
```

Maybe is made an instance of Applicative as follows, where $<\$>$ is defined in the same way as m_app above:

```
instance Applicative Maybe where
    pure = Just
    (Just f) <$> (Just a) = Just (f a)
    _        <$> _        = Nothing
```

Using *idiom brackets* we can use this instance as follows, where a function application [| f a1 ... an |] is translated into pure f <$> a1 <$> ... <$> an:

```
m_add' : Maybe Int -> Maybe Int -> Maybe Int
m_add' x y = [| x + y |]
```

An Error-Handling Interpreter. Idiom brackets are often useful when defining evaluators for embedded domain specific languages. McBride and Paterson describe such an evaluator [12], for a small language similar to the following:

```
data Expr = Var String      -- variables
          | Val Int         -- values
          | Add Expr Expr   -- addition
```

Evaluation will take place relative to a context mapping variables (represented as Strings) to integer values, and can possibly fail. We define a data type Eval to wrap an evaluation function:

```
data Eval : Type -> Type where
    MkEval : (List (String, Int) -> Maybe a) -> Eval a
```

We begin by defining a function to retrieve values from the context during evaluation:

```
fetch : String -> Eval Int
fetch x = MkEval fetchVal where
    fetchVal : List (String, Int) -> Maybe Int
    fetchVal [] = Nothing
    fetchVal ((v, val) :: xs)
            = if (x == v) then Just val
                          else fetchVal xs
```

When defining an evaluator for the language, we will be applying functions in the context of an Eval, so it is natural to make Eval an instance of Applicative. Before Eval can be an instance of Applicative it is necessary to make Eval an instance of Functor:

```
instance Functor Eval where
    fmap f (MkEval g) = MkEval (\e => fmap f (g e))

instance Applicative Eval where
    pure x = MkEval (\e => Just x)
    (<$>) (MkEval f) (MkEval g)
        = MkEval (\x => app (f x) (g x)) where
      app : Maybe (a -> b) -> Maybe a -> Maybe b
      app (Just fx) (Just gx) = Just (fx gx)
      app _         _         = Nothing
```

Evaluating an expression can now make use of the idiomatic application to handle errors:

```
eval : Expr -> Eval Int
eval (Var x)   = fetch x
eval (Val x)   = [| x |]
eval (Add x y) = [| eval x + eval y |]


runEval : List (String, Int) -> Expr -> Maybe Int
runEval env e = case eval e of
    MkEval envFn => envFn env
```

By defining appropriate Monad and Applicative instances, we can overload notions of binding and application for specific data types, which can give more flexibility when implementing EDSLs. ......

4   Views and the "with" Rule

4.1   Dependent Pattern Matching

Since types can depend on values, the form of some arguments can be determined by the value of others. For example, if we were to write down the implicit length arguments to (++), we'd see that the form of the length argument was determined by whether the vector was empty or not:

```
(++) : Vect n a -> Vect m a -> Vect (n + m) a
(++) {n=Z}   []        ys = ys
(++) {n=S k} (x :: xs) ys = x :: xs ++ ys
```

If n was a successor in the [] case, or zero in the :: case, the definition would not be well typed.

4.2   The **with** Rule — Matching Intermediate Values

Very often, we need to match on the result of an intermediate computation. IDRIS provides a construct for this, the with rule, inspired by views in EPIGRAM [11], which takes account of the fact that matching on a value in a dependently typed language can affect what we know about the forms of other values —we can learn the form of one value by testing another. For example, a Nat is either even or odd. If it's even it will be the sum of two equal Nats. Otherwise, it is the sum of two equal Nats plus one:

```
data Parity : Nat -> Type where
     even : Parity (n + n)
     odd  : Parity (S (n + n))
```

We say Parity is a *view* of Nat. It has a *covering function* which tests whether it is even or odd and constructs the predicate accordingly.

```
parity : (n:Nat) -> Parity n
```

We will return to this function in Sect. 5.5 to complete the definition of parity. For now, we can use it to write a function which converts a natural number to a list of binary digits (least significant first) as follows, using the with rule:

```
natToBin : Nat -> List Bool
natToBin Z = Nil
natToBin k with (parity k)
   natToBin (j + j)     | even = False :: natToBin j
   natToBin (S (j + j)) | odd  = True  :: natToBin j
```

The value of the result of parity k affects the form of k, because the result of parity k depends on k. So, as well as the patterns for the result of the intermediate computation (even and odd) right of the |, we also write how the results affect the other patterns left of the |. Note that there is a function in the patterns (+) and repeated occurrences of j — this is allowed because another argument has determined the form of these patterns.

4.3   Membership Predicates

We have already seen (in Sect. 2.4) the Elem x xs type, an element of which is a proof that x is an element of the list xs:

```
using (x:a, y:a, xs:List a)
   data Elem : a -> List a -> Type where
      Here : Elem x (x :: xs)
      There : Elem x xs -> Elem x (y :: xs)
```

We have also seen how to construct proofs of this at compile time. However, data is not often available at compile-time — proofs of list membership may arise due to user data, which may be invalid and therefore needs to be checked. What we need, therefore, is a function which constructs such a predicate, taking into account possible failure. In order to do so, we need to be able to construct *equality* proofs.

Propositional Equality. IDRIS allows propositional equalities to be declared, allowing theorems about programs to be stated and proved. Equality is built in, but conceptually has the following definition:

```
data (=) : a -> b -> Type where
     refl : x = x
```

Equalities can be proposed between any values of any types, but the only way to construct a proof of equality is if values actually are equal. For example:

```
fiveIsFive : 5 = 5
fiveIsFive = refl

twoPlusTwo : 2 + 2 = 4
twoPlusTwo = refl
```

Decidable Equality. The library provides a Dec type, with two constructors, Yes and No. Dec represents *decidable* propositions, either containing a proof that a type is inhabited, or a proof that it is not. Here, _|_ represents the empty type, which we will discuss further in Sect. 5.1:

```
data Dec : Type -> Type where
     Yes : a                -> Dec a
     No  : (a -> _|_) -> Dec a
```

We can think of this as an informative version of Bool — not only do we know the truth of a value, we also have an explanation for it. Using this, we can write a type class capturing types which can not only be compared for equality, but which also provide a *proof* of that equality:

```
class DecEq t where
      decEq : (x1 : t) -> (x2 : t) -> Dec (x1 = x2)
```

Using DecEq, we can construct equality proofs where necessary at run-time. There are instances defined in the prelude for primitive types, as well as many of the types defined in the prelude such as Bool, Maybe a, List a, etc.

Now that we can construct equality proofs dynamically, we can implement the following function, which dynamically constructs a proof that x is contained in a list xs, if possible:

```
isElem : DecEq a =>
            (x : a) -> (xs : List a) -> Maybe (Elem x xs)
isElem x [] = Nothing
isElem x (y :: xs) with (decEq x y)
   isElem x (x :: xs) | (Yes refl) = return Here
   isElem x (y :: xs) | (No f) = do p <- isElem x xs
                                    return (There p)
```

This function works first by checking whether the list is empty. If so, the value cannot be contained in the list, so it returns Nothing. Otherwise, it uses decEq to try to construct a proof that the element is at the head of the list. If it succeeds, dependent pattern matching on that proof means that x must be at the head of the list. Otherwise, it searches in the tail of the list.

Exercises

1. The following view describes a pair of numbers as a difference:

```
data Cmp : Nat -> Nat -> Type where
     cmpLT : (y : _) -> Cmp x (x + S y)
     cmpEQ : Cmp x x
     cmpGT : (x : _) -> Cmp (y + S x) y
```

(a) Write the function cmp : (n : Nat) -> (m : Nat) -> Cmp n m which proves that every pair of numbers can be expressed in this way.

(b) Assume you have a vector xs : Vect a n, where n is unknown. How could you use cmp to construct a suitable input to vtake and vdrop from xs?

2. You are given the following definition of binary trees:

```
data Tree a = Leaf | Node (Tree a) a (Tree a)
```

Define a membership predicate ElemTree and a function elemInTree which calculates whether a value is in the tree, and a corresponding proof.

```
data ElemTree : a -> Tree a -> Type where ...

elemInTree : DecEq a =>
        (x : a) -> (t : Tree a) -> Maybe (ElemTree x t)
```

5   Theorem Proving

As we have seen in Sect. 4.3, IDRIS supports *propositional* equality:

```
data (=) : a -> b -> Type where
     refl : x = x
```

We have used this to build membership proofs of Lists, but it is more generally applicable. In particular, we can *reason* about equality. The library function replace uses an equality proof to transform a predicate on one value into a predicate on another, equal, value:

```
replace : {P : a -> Type} -> x = y -> P x -> P y
replace refl prf = prf
```

The library function cong is a function defined in the library which states that equality respects function application:

```
cong : {f : t -> u} -> a = b -> f a = f b
cong refl = refl
```

Using the equality type, `replace`, `cong` and the properties of the type system, we can write proofs of theorems such as the following, which states that addition of natural numbers is commutative:

```
plus_commutes : (n, m : Nat) -> plus n m = plus m n
```

In this section, we will see how to develop such proofs.

5.1 The Empty Type

There is an empty type, $\bot$, which has no constructors. It is therefore impossible to construct an element of the empty type, at least without using a partially defined or general recursive function (which will be explained in more detail in Sect. 5.4). We can therefore use the empty type to prove that something is impossible, for example zero is never equal to a successor:

```
disjoint : (n : Nat) -> Z = S n -> _|_
disjoint n p = replace {P = disjointTy} p ()
  where
    disjointTy : Nat -> Type
    disjointTy Z = ()
    disjointTy (S k) = _|_
```

Here we use `replace` to transform a value of a type which can exist, the empty tuple, to a value of a type which can't, by using a proof of something which can't exist. Once we have an element of the empty type, we can prove anything. `FalseElim` is defined in the library, to assist with proofs by contradiction.

```
FalseElim : _|_ -> a
```

5.2 Simple Theorems

When type checking dependent types, the type itself gets *normalised*. So imagine we want to prove the following theorem about the reduction behaviour of `plus`:

```
plusReduces : (n:Nat) -> plus Z n = n
```

We've written down the statement of the theorem as a type, in just the same way as we would write the type of a program. In fact there is no real distinction between proofs and programs. A proof, as far as we are concerned here, is merely a program with a precise enough type to guarantee a particular property of interest.

We won't go into details here, but the Curry-Howard correspondence [10] explains this relationship. The proof itself is trivial, because `plus Z n` normalises to n by the definition of `plus`:

```
plusReduces n = refl
```

It is slightly harder if we try the arguments the other way, because plus is defined by recursion on its first argument. The proof also works by recursion on the first argument to `plus`, namely n.

```
plusReducesZ : (n:Nat) -> n = plus n Z
plusReducesZ Z = refl
plusReducesZ (S k) = cong (plusReducesZ k)
```

We can do the same for the reduction behaviour of plus on successors:

```
plusReducesS : (n:Nat) -> (m:Nat) ->
                     S (plus n m) = plus n (S m)
plusReducesS Z m = refl
plusReducesS (S k) m = cong (plusReducesS k m)
```

Even for simple theorems like these, the proofs are a little tricky to construct directly. When things get even slightly more complicated, it becomes too much to think about to construct proofs in this 'batch mode'. IDRIS therefore provides an interactive proof mode.

5.3   Interactive Theorem Proving

Instead of writing the proof in one go, we can use IDRIS's interactive proof mode. To do this, we write the general *structure* of the proof, and use the interactive mode to complete the details. We'll be constructing the proof by *induction*, so we write the cases for Z and S, with a recursive call in the S case giving the inductive hypothesis, and insert *metavariables* for the rest of the definition:

```
plusReducesZ' : (n:Nat) -> n = plus n Z
plusReducesZ' Z       = ?plusredZ_Z
plusReducesZ' (S k) = let ih = plusReducesZ' k in
                           ?plusredZ_S
```

On running IDRIS, two global names are created, plusredZ_Z and plusredZ_S, with no definition. We can use the :m command at the prompt to find out which metavariables are still to be solved (or, more precisely, which functions exist but have no definitions), then the :t command to see their types and contexts:

```
*theorems> :m
Global metavariables:
        [plusredZ_S,plusredZ_Z]

*theorems> :t plusredZ_Z
------------------------------------
plusredZ_Z : 0 = 0

*theorems> :t plusredZ_S
  k : Nat
  ih : k = plus k 0
------------------------------------
plusredZ_S : S k = S (plus k 0)
```

The :p command enters interactive proof mode, which can be used to complete the missing definitions. This gives us a list of premises (above the line; there are none here) and the current goal (below the line; named {hole0} here). At the prompt we can enter tactics to direct the construction of the proof. In this case, we can normalise the goal with the compute tactic:

```
-plusredZ_Z> compute

---------------------------- (plusredZ_Z) --------
{hole0} : Z = Z
```

Now we have to prove that Z equals Z, which is easy to prove by refl. To apply a function, such as refl, we use refine which introduces subgoals for each of the function's explicit arguments (refl has none):

```
-plusredZ_Z> refine refl
plusredZ_Z: no more goals
```

Here, we could also have used the trivial tactic, which tries to refine by refl, and if that fails, tries to refine by each name in the local context. When a proof is complete, we use the qed tactic to add the proof to the global context, and remove the metavariable from the unsolved metavariables list. This also outputs a log of the proof:

```
-plusredZ_Z> qed
plusredZ_Z = proof
    compute
    refine refl

*theorems> :m
Global metavariables:
        [plusredZ_S]
```

The :addproof command, at the interactive prompt, will add the proof to the source file (effectively in an appendix). Let us now prove the other required lemma, plusredZ_S:

```
*theorems> :p plusredZ_S

---------------------------- (plusredZ_S) --------
{hole0} : (k : Nat) -> (k = plus k 0) -> S k = plus (S k) 0
```

In this case, the goal is a function type, using k (the argument accessible by pattern matching) and ih — the local variable containing the result of the recursive call. We can introduce these as premises using the intro tactic twice (or intros, which introduces all arguments as premises). This gives:

```
k : Nat
ih : k = plus k Z
---------------------------- (plusredZ_S) --------
{hole2} : S k = plus (S k) 0
```

Since plus is defined is defined by recursion on its first argument, the term plus (S k) 0 in the goal can be simplified using compute:

```
k : Nat
ih : k = plus k Z
---------------------------- (plusredZ_S) --------
{hole2} : S k = S (plus k 0)
```

We know, from the type of ih, that k = plus k 0, so we would like to use this knowledge to replace plus k 0 in the goal with k. We can achieve this with the rewrite tactic:

```
-plusredZ_S> rewrite ih

k : Nat
ih : k = plus k 0
---------------------------- (plusredZ_S)   --------
{hole3} : S k = S k

-plusredZ_S>
```

The rewrite tactic takes an equality proof as an argument, and tries to rewrite the goal using that proof. Here, it results in an equality which is trivially provable:

```
-plusredZ_S> trivial
plusredZ_S: no more goals
-plusredZ_S> qed
plusredZ_S = proof
    intros
    rewrite ih
    trivial
```

Again, we can add this proof to the end of our source file using the :addproof command at the interactive prompt.

5.4   Totality Checking

If we really want to trust our proofs, it is important that they are defined by *total* functions. A total function is a function which is defined for all possible inputs and is guaranteed to terminate. Otherwise we could construct an element of the empty type, from which we could prove anything:

```
-- making use of 'hd' being partially defined
empty1 : _|_
empty1 = hd [] where
    hd : List a -> a
    hd (x :: xs) = x
```

```
-- not terminating
empty2 : _|_
empty2 = empty2
```

Internally, IDRIS checks every definition for totality, and we can check at the prompt with the :total command. We see that neither of the above definitions is total:

```
*theorems> :total empty1
possibly not total due to: empty1, hd
    not total as there are missing cases
*theorems> :total empty2
possibly not total due to recursive path empty2
```

Note the use of the word "possibly" — a totality check can, of course, never be certain due to the undecidability of the halting problem. The check is, therefore, conservative. It is also possible (and indeed advisable, in the case of proofs) to mark functions as total so that it will be a compile time error for the totality check to fail:

```
total empty2 : _|_
empty2 = empty2

Type checking ./theorems.idr
theorems.idr:25:empty2 is possibly not total due to
recursive path empty2
```

Reassuringly, our proof in Sect. 5.1 that the zero and successor constructors are disjoint is total:

```
*theorems> :total disjoint
Total
```

The totality check is, necessarily, conservative. To be recorded as total, a function f must:

- Cover all possible inputs.
- Be *well-founded* — i.e. by the time a sequence of (possibly mutually) recursive calls reaches f again, it must be possible to show that one of its arguments has decreased.
- Not use any data types which are not *strictly positive*.
- Not call any non-total functions.

Directives and Compiler Flags for Totality. By default, IDRIS allows all definitions, whether total or not. However, it is desirable for functions to be total as far as possible, as this provides a guarantee that they provide a result for all possible inputs, in finite time. It is possible to make total functions a requirement, either:

- By using the `--total` compiler flag.
- By adding a `%default total` directive to a source file. All definitions after this will be required to be total, unless explicitly flagged as `partial`.

All functions *after* a `%default total` declaration are required to be total. Correspondingly, after a `%default partial` declaration, the requirement is relaxed.

5.5   Provisional Definitions

Sometimes when programming with dependent types, the type required by the type checker and the type of the program we have written will be different (in that they do not have the same normal form), but nevertheless provably equal. For example, recall the `parity` function:

```
data Parity : Nat -> Type where
    even : Parity (n + n)
    odd  : Parity (S (n + n))

parity : (n:Nat) -> Parity n
```

We would like to implement this as follows:

```
parity : (n:Nat) -> Parity n
parity Z       = even {n=Z}
parity (S Z) = odd {n=Z}
parity (S (S k)) with (parity k)
    parity (S (S (j + j)))       | even = even {n=S j}
    parity (S (S (S (j + j))))   | odd  = odd {n=S j}
```

This simply states that zero is even, one is odd, and recursively, the parity of k+2 is the same as the parity of k. Explicitly marking the value of n in even and odd is necessary to help type inference. Unfortunately, the type checker rejects this:

```
views.idr:12:Can't unify Parity (plus (S j) (S j)) with
Parity (S (S (plus j j)))
```

The type checker is telling us that `(j+1)+(j+1)` and `2+j+j` do not normalise to the same value. This is because `plus` is defined by recursion on its first argument, and in the second value, there is a successor symbol on the second argument, so this will not help with reduction. These values are obviously equal—how can we rewrite the program to fix this problem?

Provisional definitions help with this problem by allowing us to defer the proof details until a later point. There are two main motivations for supporting provisional definitions:

- When *prototyping*, it is useful to be able to *test* programs before finishing all the details of proofs. This is particularly useful if testing reveals that we would need to prove something which is untrue!
- When *reading* a program, it is often much clearer to defer the proof details so that they do not distract the reader from the underlying algorithm.

Provisional definitions are written in the same way as ordinary definitions, except that they introduce the right hand side with a ?= rather than =. We define `parity` as follows:

```
parity : (n:Nat) -> Parity n
parity Z     = even {n=Z}
parity (S Z) = odd {n=Z}
parity (S (S k)) with (parity k)
  parity (S (S (j + j)))      | even ?= even {n=S j}
  parity (S (S (S (j + j))))  | odd  ?= odd {n=S j}
```

When written in this form, instead of reporting a type error, IDRIS will insert a metavariable standing for a theorem which will correct the type error. IDRIS tells us we have two proof obligations, with names generated from the module and function names:

```
*views> :m
Global metavariables:
        [views.parity_lemma_2,views.parity_lemma_1]
```

The first of these has the following type and context:

```
*views> :t views.parity_lemma_1
  j : Nat
  value : Parity (plus (S j) (S j))
--------------------------------------
parity_lemma_1 : Parity (S (S (plus j j)))
```

The two arguments are `j`, the variable in scope from the pattern match, and `value`, which is the value we gave in the right hand side of the provisional definition. Our aim is to rewrite the type so that we can use this value. We can achieve this using the following theorem from the prelude:

```
plusSuccRightSucc : (left : Nat) -> (right : Nat) ->
    S (left + right) = left + (S right)
```

After starting the theorem prover with :p `parity_lemma_1` and applying `intro` twice, we have:

```
 j : Nat
 value : Parity (S (plus j (S j)))
-------------------------- (views.parity_lemma_1) --------
{hole2} : Parity (S (S (j + j)))
```

We need to use `compute` to unfold the definition of (+).

```
-views.parity_lemma_1> compute

 j : Nat
 value : Parity (S (plus j (S j)))
-------------------------- (views.parity_lemma_1) --------
{hole2} : Parity (S (S (plus j j)))
```

Then we apply the `plusSuccRightSucc` rewrite rule, symmetrically, to `j` and `j`, giving:

```
-views.parity_lemma_1> rewrite sym (plusSuccRightSucc j j)

  j : Nat
  value : Parity (S (plus j (S j)))
  -------------------------- (views.parity_lemma_1) --------
  {hole3} : Parity (S (plus j (S j)))
```

`sym` is a function, defined in the library, which reverses the order of the rewrite:

```
sym : l = r -> r = l
sym refl = refl
```

We can complete this proof using the `trivial` tactic, which finds `value` in the premises. The proof of the second lemma proceeds in exactly the same way.

We can now test the `natToBin` function from Sect. 4.2 at the prompt. The number 42 is 101010 in binary. The binary digits are reversed:

```
*views> show (natToBin 42)
"[False, True, False, True, False, True]" : String
```

5.6 Suspension of Disbelief

IDRIS requires that proofs be complete before compiling programs (although evaluation at the prompt is possible without proof details). Sometimes, especially when prototyping, it is easier not to have to do this. It might even be beneficial to test programs before attempting to prove things about them — if testing finds an error, you know you should not waste your time proving something!

Therefore, IDRIS provides a built-in coercion function, which allows you to use a value of the incorrect types:

```
believe_me : a -> b
```

Obviously, this should be used with caution. It is useful when prototyping, and can also be appropriate when asserting properties of external code (perhaps in an external C library). The "proof" of `views.parity_lemma_1` using this is:

```
views.parity_lemma_2 = proof
    intro
    intro
    exact believe_me value
```

The `exact` tactic allows us to provide an exact value for the proof. In this case, we assert that the value we gave was correct.

5.7 Example: Binary Numbers

Previously, we implemented conversion to binary numbers using the `Parity` view. Here, we show how to use the same view to implement a verified conversion to binary. We begin by indexing binary numbers over their Nat equivalent. This is a common pattern, linking a representation (in this case Binary) with a meaning (in this case Nat):

```
data Binary : Nat -> Type where
     bEnd : Binary Z
     bO : Binary n -> Binary (n + n)
     bI : Binary n -> Binary (S (n + n))
```

bO and bI take a binary number as an argument and effectively shift it one bit left, adding either a zero or one as the new least significant bit. The index, n + n or S (n + n) states the result that this left shift then add will have to the meaning of the number. This will result in a representation with the least significant bit at the front.

Now a function which converts a Nat to binary will state, in the type, that the resulting binary number is a faithful representation of the original Nat:

```
natToBin : (n:Nat) -> Binary n
```

The Parity view makes the definition fairly simple — halving the number is effectively a right shift after all — although we need to use a provisional definition in the odd case:

```
natToBin : (n:Nat) -> Binary n
natToBin Z = bEnd
natToBin (S k) with (parity k)
   natToBin (S (j + j))     | even  = bI (natToBin j)
   natToBin (S (S (j + j))) | odd  ?= bO (natToBin (S j))
```

The problem with the odd case is the same as in the definition of parity, and the proof proceeds in the same way:

```
natToBin_lemma_1 = proof
     intro
     intro
     rewrite sym (plusSuccRightSucc j j)
     trivial
```

To finish, we'll implement a main program which reads an integer from the user and outputs it in binary.

```
main : IO ()
main = do putStr "Enter a number: "
          x <- getLine
          print (natToBin (fromInteger (cast x)))
```

For this to work, of course, we need a Show instance for Binary n:

```
instance Show (Binary n) where
     show (bO x) = show x ++ "0"
     show (bI x) = show x ++ "1"
     show bEnd = ""
```

Exercises

1. Implement the following functions, which verify some properties of natural number addition:

```
plus_nSm : (n : Nat) -> (m : Nat) -> n + S m = S (n + m)
plus_commutes : (n : Nat) -> (m : Nat) -> n + m = m + n
plus_assoc : (n : Nat) -> (m : Nat) -> (p : Nat) ->
             n + (m + p) = (n + m) + p
```

2. One way we have seen to define a reverse function for lists is as follows:

```
reverse : List a -> List a
reverse xs = revAcc [] xs where
  revAcc : List a -> List a -> List a
  revAcc acc [] = acc
  revAcc acc (x :: xs) = revAcc (x :: acc) xs
```

Write the equivalent function for vectors,

```
vect_reverse : Vect n a -> Vect n a
```

Hint: You can use the same structure as the definition for `List`, but you will need to think carefully about the type for `revAcc`, and may need to do some theorem proving.

6 EDSL Example 1: The Well-Typed Interpreter

In this section, we will use the features we have seen so far to write a larger example, an interpreter for a simple functional programming language, implemented as an Embedded Domain Specific Language. The *object language* (i.e., the language we are implementing) has variables, function application, binary operators and an `if...then...else` construct. We will use the type system from the *host language* (i.e. IDRIS) to ensure that any programs which can be represented are well-typed.

First, let us define the types in the language. We have integers, booleans, and functions, represented by `Ty`:

```
data Ty = TyInt | TyBool | TyFun Ty Ty
```

We can write a function to translate these representations to a concrete IDRIS type — remember that types are first class, so can be calculated just like any other value:

```
interpTy : Ty -> Type
interpTy TyInt       = Int
interpTy TyBool      = Bool
interpTy (TyFun A T) = interpTy A -> interpTy T
```

We will define a representation of our language in such a way that only well-typed programs can be represented. We index the representations of expressions by their type and the types of local variables (the context), which we'll be using regularly as an implicit argument, so we define everything in a using block:

```
using (G:Vect n Ty)
```

The full representation of expressions is given in Listing 3. They are indexed by the types of the local variables, and the type of the expression itself:

```
data Expr : Vect n Ty -> Ty -> Type
```

Since expressions are indexed by their type, we can read the typing rules of the language from the definitions of the constructors. Let us look at each constructor in turn.

Listing 3. Expression representation

```
data Expr : Vect n Ty -> Ty -> Type where
    Var : HasType i G t -> Expr G t
    Val : (x : Int) -> Expr G TyInt
    Lam : Expr (a :: G) t -> Expr G (TyFun a t)
    App : Expr G (TyFun a t) -> Expr G a -> Expr G t
    Op  : (interpTy a -> interpTy b -> interpTy c) ->
          Expr G a -> Expr G b -> Expr G c
    If  : Expr G TyBool ->
          Lazy (Expr G a) -> Lazy (Expr G a) -> Expr G a
```

We use a nameless representation for variables — they are *de Bruijn indexed*. Variables are represented by a proof of their membership in the context, HasType i G T, which is a proof that variable i in context G has type T. This is defined as follows:

```
data HasType : Fin n -> Vect n Ty -> Ty -> Type where
    stop : HasType fZ (t :: G) t
    pop  : HasType k G t -> HasType (fS k) (u :: G) t
```

We can treat *stop* as a proof that the most recently defined variable is well-typed, and *pop n* as a proof that, if the nth most recently defined variable is well-typed, so is the n+1th. In practice, this means we use stop to refer to the most recently defined variable, pop stop to refer to the next, and so on, via the Var constructor:

```
Var : HasType i G t -> Expr G t
```

So, in an expression \x. \y. x y, the variable x would have a de Bruijn index of 1, represented as pop stop, and y 0, represented as stop. We find these by counting the number of lambdas between the definition and the use.

A value carries a concrete representation of an integer:

```
Val : (x : Int) -> Expr G TyInt
```

A lambda creates a function. In the scope of a function of type a -> t, there is a new local variable of type a, which is expressed by the context index:

Listing 4. Intepreter definition

```
interp : Env G -> Expr G t -> interpTy t
interp env (Var i)     = lookup i env
interp env (Val x)     = x
interp env (Lam body)  = \x => interp (x :: env) body
interp env (App f s)   = (interp env f) (interp env s)
interp env (Op op x y) = op (interp env x) (interp env y)
interp env (If x t e)  = if interp env x
                            then interp env t
                            else interp env e
```

```
Lam : Expr (a :: G) t -> Expr G (TyFun a t)
```

Function application produces a value of type t given a function from a to t and a value of type a:

```
App : Expr G (TyFun a t) -> Expr G a -> Expr G t
```

Given these constructors, the expression \x. \y. x y above would be represented as Lam (Lam (App (Var (pop stop)) (Var stop))).

We also allow arbitrary binary operators, where the type of the operator informs what the types of the arguments must be:

```
Op  : (interpTy a -> interpTy b -> interpTy c) ->
      Expr G a -> Expr G b -> Expr G c
```

Finally, If expressions make a choice given a boolean. Each branch must have the same type, and we will evaluate the branches lazily so that only the branch which is taken need be evaluated:

```
If  : Expr G TyBool ->
      Lazy (Expr G a) -> Lazy (Expr G a) -> Expr G a
```

When we evaluate an Expr, we'll need to know the values in scope, as well as their types. Env is an environment, indexed over the types in scope. Since an environment is just another form of list, albeit with a strongly specified connection to the vector of local variable types, we use the usual :: and Nil constructors so that we can use the usual list syntax. Given a proof that a variable is defined in the context, we can then produce a value from the environment:

```
data Env : Vect n Ty -> Type where
    Nil : Env Nil
    (::) : interpTy a -> Env G -> Env (a :: G)

lookup : HasType i G t -> Env G -> interpTy t
lookup stop    (x :: xs) = x
lookup (pop k) (x :: xs) = lookup k xs
```

Given this, an interpreter (Listing 4) is a function which translates an Expr into a concrete IDRIS value with respect to a specific environment:

```
interp : Env G -> Expr G t -> interpTy t
```

To translate a variable, we simply look it up in the environment:

```
interp env (Var i) = lookup i env
```

To translate a value, we just return the concrete representation of the value:

```
interp env (Val x) = x
```

Lambdas are more interesting. In this case, we construct a function which interprets the scope of the lambda with a new value in the environment. So, a function in the object language is translated to an IDRIS function:

```
interp env (Lam body) = \x => interp (x :: env) body
```

For an application, we interpret the function and its argument and apply it directly. We know that interpreting f must produce a function, because of its type:

```
interp env (App f s) = (interp env f) (interp env s)
```

Operators and If expressions are, again, direct translations into the equivalent IDRIS constructs. For operators, we apply the function to its operands directly, and for If, we apply the IDRIS if...then...else construct directly.

```
interp env (Op op x y) = op (interp env x) (interp env y)
interp env (If x t e)  = if interp env x
                            then interp env t
                            else interp env e
```

We can make some simple test functions. Firstly, adding two inputs \x. \y. y + x is written as follows:

```
add : Expr G (TyFun TyInt (TyFun TyInt TyInt))
add = Lam (Lam (Op (+) (Var stop) (Var (pop stop))))
```

More interestingly, we can write a factorial function (i.e. \x. if (x == 0) then 1 else (fact (x-1) * x)) which is written as follows:

```
fact : Expr G (TyFun TyInt TyInt)
fact = Lam (If (Op (==) (Var stop) (Val 0))
               (Val 1)
               (Op (*)
                   (App fact (Op (-) (Var stop) (Val 1)))
                   (Var stop)))
```

To finish, we write a main program which interprets the factorial function on user input:

```
main : IO ()
main = do putStr "Enter a number: "
          x <- getLine
          print (interp [] fact (cast x))
```

Here, cast is an overloaded function which converts a value from one type to another if possible. Here, it converts a string to an integer, giving 0 if the input is invalid. An example run of this program at the IDRIS interactive environment is shown in Listing 5.

Aside: cast. The prelude defines a type class Cast which allows conversion between types:

```
class Cast from to where
    cast : from -> to
```

It is a *multi-parameter* type class, defining the source type and object type of the cast. It must be possible for the type checker to infer *both* parameters at the point where the cast is applied. There are casts defined between all of the primitive types, as far as they make sense.

Listing 5. Running the well-typed interpreter

```
$ idris interp.idr

     /   _/___/ /____(_)____
    / //  _  / ___/ / ___/      Version 0.9.14.
  _/ // /_/ / /  / / (__  )      http://www.idris-lang.org/
 /___/\__,_/_/  /_/____/         Type :? for help

Type checking ./interp.idr
*interp> :exec
Enter a number: 6
720
*interp>
```

7   Interactive Editing

By now, we have seen several examples of how IDRIS' dependent type system can give extra confidence in a function's correctness by giving a more precise description of its intended behaviour in its *type*. We have also seen an example of how the type system can help with EDSL development by allowing a programmer to describe the type system of an object language. However, precise types give us more than verification of programs — we can also exploit types to help write programs which are *correct by construction*.

The IDRIS REPL provides several commands for inspecting and modifying parts of programs, based on their types, such as case splitting on a pattern variable, inspecting the type of a metavariable, and even a basic proof search mechanism. In this section, we explain how these features can be exploited by a text editor, and specifically how to do so in Vim[5]. An interactive mode for Emacs[6] is also available.

---

[5] https://github.com/idris-hackers/idris-vim.
[6] https://github.com/idris-hackers/idris-emacs.

7.1 Editing at the REPL

The REPL provides a number of commands, which we will describe shortly, which generate new program fragments based on the currently loaded module. These take the general form

```
:command [line number] [name]
```

That is, each command acts on a specific source line, at a specific name, and outputs a new program fragment. Each command has an alternative form, which *updates* the source file in-place:

```
:command! [line number] [name]
```

When the REPL is loaded, it also starts a background process which accepts and responds to REPL commands, using idris --client. For example, if we have a REPL running elsewhere, we can execute commands such as:

```
$ idris --client ':t plus'
Prelude.Nat.plus : Nat -> Nat -> Nat
$ idris --client '2+2'
4 : Integer
```

A text editor can take advantage of this, along with the editing commands, in order to provide interactive editing support.

7.2 Editing Commands

:addclause. The :addclause n f command (abbreviated :ac n f) creates a template definition for the function named f declared on line n.

For example, if the code beginning on line 94 contains...

```
vzipWith : (a -> b -> c) ->
           Vect n a -> Vect n b -> Vect n c
```

... then :ac 94 vzipWith will give:

```
vzipWith f xs ys = ?vzipWith_rhs
```

The names are chosen according to hints which may be given by a programmer, and then made unique by the machine by adding a digit if necessary. Hints can be given as follows:

```
%name Vect xs, ys, zs, ws
```

This declares that any names generated for types in the Vect family should be chosen in the order xs, ys, zs, ws.

:casesplit. The :casesplit n x command, abbreviated :cs n x, splits the pattern variable x on line n into the various pattern forms it may take, removing any cases which are impossible due to unification errors. For example, if the code beginning on line 94 is...

```
vzipWith : (a -> b -> c) ->
           Vect n a -> Vect n b -> Vect n c
vzipWith f xs ys = ?vzipWith_rhs
```

... then :cs 96 xs will give:

```
vzipWith f [] ys = ?vzipWith_rhs_1
vzipWith f (x :: xs) ys = ?vzipWith_rhs_2
```

That is, the pattern variable xs has been split into the two possible cases []
and x :: xs. Again, the names are chosen according to the same heuristic. If
we update the file (using :cs!) then case split on ys on the same line, we get:

```
vzipWith f [] [] = ?vzipWith_rhs_3
```

That is, the pattern variable ys has been split into one case [], IDRIS having
noticed that the other possible case y :: ys would lead to a unification error.

:addmissing. The :addmissing n f command, abbreviated :am n f, adds
the clauses which are required to make the function f on line n cover all inputs.
For example, if the code beginning on line 94 is...

```
vzipWith : (a -> b -> c) ->
           Vect n a -> Vect n b -> Vect n c
vzipWith f [] [] = ?vzipWith_rhs_1
```

... then :am 96 vzipWith gives:

```
vzipWith f (x :: xs) (y :: ys) = ?vzipWith_rhs_2
```

That is, it notices that there are no cases for non-empty vectors, generates
the required clauses, and eliminates the clauses which would lead to unification
errors.

:proofsearch. The :proofsearch n f command, abbreviated :ps n f, attempts
to find a value for the metavariable f on line n by proof search, trying values of
local variables, recursive calls and constructors of the required family. Option-
ally, it can take a list of *hints*, which are functions it can try applying to solve
the metavariable. For example, if the code beginning on line 94 is...

```
vzipWith : (a -> b -> c) ->
           Vect n a -> Vect n b -> Vect n c
vzipWith f [] [] = ?vzipWith_rhs_1
vzipWith f (x :: xs) (y :: ys) = ?vzipWith_rhs_2
```

... then :ps 96 vzipWith_rhs_1 will give

```
[]
```

This works because it is searching for a Vect of length 0, of which the empty
vector is the only possibility. Similarly, and perhaps surprisingly, there is only
one possibility if we try to solve :ps 97 vzipWith_rhs_2:

```
f x y :: (vzipWith f xs ys)
```

This works because `vzipWith` has a precise enough type: The resulting vector has to be non-empty (`::`); the first element must have type c and the only way to get this is to apply f to x and y; finally, the tail of the vector can only be built recursively.

:makewith. The `:makewith n f` command, abbreviated `:mw n f`, adds a with to a pattern clause. For example, recall `parity`. If line 10 is...

```
parity (S k) = ?parity_rhs
```

... then `:mw 10 parity` will give:

```
parity (S k) with (_)
    parity (S k) | with_pat = ?parity_rhs
```

If we then fill in the placeholder _ with `parity` k and case split on `with_pat` using `:cs 11 with_pat` we get the following patterns:

```
parity (S (plus n n)) | even = ?parity_rhs_1
parity (S (S (plus n n))) | odd = ?parity_rhs_2
```

Note that case splitting has normalised the patterns here (giving plus rather than +). In any case, we see that using interactive editing significantly simplifies the implementation of dependent pattern matching by showing a programmer exactly what the valid patterns are.

7.3 Interactive Editing in Vim

The editor mode for Vim provides syntax highlighting, indentation and interactive editing support using the commands described above. Interactive editing is achieved using the following editor commands, each of which update the buffer directly:

- \d adds a template definition for the name declared on the current line (using `:addclause`.)
- \c case splits the variable at the cursor (using `:casesplit`.)
- \m adds the missing cases for the name at the cursor (using `:addmissing`.)
- \w adds a with clause (using `:makewith`.)
- \o invokes a proof search to solve the metavariable under the cursor (using `:proofsearch`.)
- \p invokes a proof search with additional hints to solve the metavariable under the cursor (using `:proofsearch`.)

There are also commands to invoke the type checker and evaluator:

- \t displays the type of the (globally visible) name under the cursor. In the case of a metavariable, this displays the context and the expected type.
- \e prompts for an expression to evaluate.
- \r reloads and type checks the buffer.

Corresponding commands are also available in the Emacs mode. Support for other editors can be added in a relatively straighforward manner by using `idris --client`.

Exercises

Re-implement the following functions using interactive editing mode as far as possible:

```
append    : Vect n a -> Vect m a -> Vect (n + m) a
vzipWith  : (a -> b -> c) ->
            Vect n a -> Vect n b -> Vect n b
isElem    : DecEq a =>
            (x : a) -> (xs : List a) -> Maybe (Elem x xs)
cmp       : (n : Nat) -> (m : Nat) -> Cmp n m
```

When does :proofsearch succeed and when does it fail? How often does it provide the definition you would expect?

8 Support for EDSL Implementation

IDRIS supports the implementation of EDSLs in several ways. For example, as we have already seen, it is possible to extend do notation and idiom brackets. Another important way is to allow extension of the core syntax. In this section I describe further support for EDSL development. I introduce syntax rules and dsl notation [8], and describe how to make programs more concise with *implicit* conversions.

8.1 syntax Rules

We have seen if...then...else expressions, but these are not built in — instead, we define a function in the prelude, using laziness annotations to ensure that the branches are only evaluated if required...

```
boolElim : (x:Bool) -> |(t : a) -> |(f : a) -> a
boolElim True  t e = t
boolElim False t e = e
```

... and extend the core syntax with a syntax declaration:

syntax if [test] **then** [t] **else** [e] = boolElim test t e

The left hand side of a syntax declaration describes the syntax rule, and the right hand side describes its expansion. The syntax rule itself consists of:

- **Keywords** — here, if, then and else, which must be valid identifiers.
- **Non-terminals** — included in square brackets, [test], [t] and [e] here, which stand for arbitrary expressions. To avoid parsing ambiguities, these expressions cannot use syntax extensions at the top level (though they can be used in parentheses.)
- **Names** — included in braces, which stand for names which may be bound on the right hand side.
- **Symbols** — included in quotations marks, e.g. ":=". This can also be used to include reserved words in syntax rules, such as "let" or "in".

The limitations on the form of a syntax rule are that it must include at least one symbol or keyword, and there must be no repeated variables standing for non-terminals. Any expression can be used, but if there are two non-terminals in a row in a rule, only simple expressions may be used (that is, variables, constants, or bracketed expressions). Rules can use previously defined rules, but may not be recursive. The following syntax extensions would therefore be valid:

```
syntax [var] ":=" [val]              = Assign var val
syntax [test] "?" [t] ":" [e]        = if test then t
                                            else e
syntax select [x] from [t] where [w] = SelectWhere x t w
syntax select [x] from [t]           = Select x t
```

Syntax rules may also be used to introduce alternative binding forms. For example, a for loop binds a variable on each iteration:

```
forLoop : List a -> (a -> IO ()) -> IO ()
forLoop [] f = return ()
forLoop (x :: xs) f = do f x; forLoop xs f

syntax for {x} "in" [xs] ":" [body]
            = forLoop xs (\x => body)

main : IO ()
main = do for x in [1..10]:
              putStrLn ("Number " ++ show x)
          putStrLn "Done!"
```

Note that we have used the {x} form to state that x represents a bound variable, substituted on the right hand side. We have also put "in" in quotation marks since it is already a reserved word.

8.2 dsl Notation

The well-typed interpreter in Sect. 6 is a simple example of a common programming pattern with dependent types, namely: describe an *object language* and its type system with dependent types to guarantee that only well-typed programs can be represented, then program using that representation. Using this approach we can, for example, write programs for serialising binary data [2] or running concurrent processes safely [6].

Unfortunately, the form of object language programs makes it rather hard to program this way in practice. Recall the factorial program in Expr for example:

```
fact : Expr G (TyFun TyInt TyInt)
fact = Lam (If (Op (==) (Var stop) (Val 0))
               (Val 1)
               (Op (*)
                  (app fact (Op (-) (Var stop) (Val 1)))
                  (Var stop)))
```

It is hard to expect EDSL users to program in this style! Therefore, IDRIS provides syntax overloading [8] to make it easier to program in such object languages:

```
dsl expr
    lambda        = Lam
    variable      = Var
    index_first   = stop
    index_next    = pop
```

A dsl block describes how each syntactic construct is represented in an object language. Here, in the expr language, any IDRIS lambda is translated to a Lam constructor; any variable is translated to the Var constructor, using pop and stop to construct the de Bruijn index (i.e., to count how many bindings since the variable itself was bound). It is also possible to overload let in this way. We can now write fact as follows:

```
fact : Expr G (TyFun TyInt TyInt)
fact = expr (\x => If (Op (==) x (Val 0))
            (Val 1)
            (Op (*) (app fact (Op (-) x (Val 1))) x))
```

In this new version, expr declares that the next expression will be overloaded. We can take this further, using idiom brackets, by declaring:

```
(<$>) : (f : Expr G (TyFun a t)) -> Expr G a -> Expr G t
(<$>) = App

pure : Expr G a -> Expr G a
pure = id
```

Note that there is no need for these to be part of an instance of Applicative, since idiom bracket notation translates directly to the names <$> and pure, and ad-hoc type-directed overloading is allowed. We can now say:

```
fact : Expr G (TyFun TyInt TyInt)
fact = expr (\x => If (Op (==) x (Val 0))
            (Val 1)
            (Op (*) [| fact (Op (-) x (Val 1)) |] x))
```

With some more ad-hoc overloading and type class instances, and a new syntax rule, we can even go as far as:

```
syntax IF [x] THEN [t] ELSE [e] = If x t e

fact : Expr G (TyFun TyInt TyInt)
fact = expr (\x => IF x == 0
                THEN 1
                ELSE [| fact (x - 1) |] * x)
```

8.3   Auto Implicit Arguments

We have already seen implicit arguments, which allows arguments to be omitted when they can be inferred by the type checker, e.g.

```
index : {a:Type} -> {n:Nat} -> Fin n -> Vect n a -> a
```

In other situations, it may be possible to infer arguments not by type checking but by searching the context for an appropriate value, or constructing a proof. For example, the following definition of head which requires a proof that the list is non-empty:

```
isCons : List a -> Bool
isCons [] = False
isCons (x :: xs) = True

head : (xs : List a) -> (isCons xs = True) -> a
head (x :: xs) _ = x
```

If the list is statically known to be non-empty, either because its value is known or because a proof already exists in the context, the proof can be constructed automatically. Auto implicit arguments allow this to happen silently. We define head as follows:

```
head : (xs : List a) -> {auto p : isCons xs = True} -> a
head (x :: xs) = x
```

The auto annotation on the implicit argument means that IDRIS will attempt to fill in the implicit argument using the trivial tactic, which searches through the context for a proof, and tries to solve with refl if a proof is not found. Now when head is applied, the proof can be omitted. In the case that a proof is not found, it can be provided explicitly as normal:

```
head xs {p = ?headProof}
```

More generally, we can fill in implicit arguments with a default value by annotating them with default. The definition above is equivalent to:

```
head : (xs : List a) ->
        {default proof { trivial; }
             p : isCons xs = True} -> a
head (x :: xs) = x
```

8.4   Implicit Conversions

IDRIS supports the creation of *implicit conversions*, which allow automatic conversion of values from one type to another when required to make a term type correct. This is intended to increase convenience and reduce verbosity. A contrived but simple example is the following:

```
implicit intString : Int -> String
intString = show

test : Int -> String
test x = "Number " ++ x
```

In general, we cannot append an `Int` to a `String`, but the implicit conversion function `intString` can convert x to a `String`, so the definition of `test` is type correct. An implicit conversion is implemented just like any other function, but given the `implicit` modifier, and restricted to one explicit argument.

Only one implicit conversion will be applied at a time. That is, implicit conversions cannot be chained. Implicit conversions of simple types, as above, are however discouraged! More commonly, an implicit conversion would be used to reduce verbosity in an embedded domain specific language, or to hide details of a proof. We will see an example of this in the next section.

Exercises

1. Add a `let` binding construct to the `Expr` language from Sect. 6, and extend the `interp` function and `dsl` notation to handle it.
2. Define the following function, which updates the value in a variable:

   ```
   update : HasType i G t -> Env G -> interpTy t -> Env G
   ```

3. Using `update` and `let`, you can extend `Expr` with imperative features. Add the following constructs:
   (a) Sequencing actions
   (b) Input and output operations
   (c) `for` loops
   Note that you will need to change the type of `interp` so that it supports `IO` and returns an updated environment:

   ```
   interp : Env G -> Imp G t -> IO (interpTy t, Env G)
   ```

   For each of these features, how could you use `syntax` macros, `dsl` notation, or any other feature to improve the readability of programs in your language?

9   EDSL Example 2: A Resource Aware Interpreter

In a typical file management API, such as that in Haskell, we might find the following typed operations:

```
open  : String -> Purpose -> IO File
read  : File              -> IO String
close : File              -> IO ()
```

Unfortunately, it is easy to construct programs which are well-typed, but nevertheless fail at run-time, for example, if we read from a file opened for writing:

```
fprog filename = do h <- open filename Writing
                    content <- read h
                    close h
```

If we make the types more precise, parameterising open files by purpose, fprog is no longer well-typed, and will therefore be rejected at compile-time.

```
data Purpose = Reading | Writing

open  : String -> (p:Purpose) -> IO (File p)
read  : File Reading           -> IO String
close : File p                 -> IO ()
```

However, there is still a problem. The following program is well-typed, but fails at run-time — although the file has been closed, the handle h is still in scope:

```
fprog filename = do h <- open filename Reading
                    content <- read h
                    close h
                    read h
```

Furthermore, we did not check whether the handle h was created successfully. Resource management problems such as this are common in systems programming — we need to deal with files, memory, network handles, etc., ensuring that operations are executed only when valid and errors are handled appropriately.

9.1   Resource Correctness as an EDSL

To tackle this problem, we can implement an EDSL which tracks the *state* of resources at any point during program execution in its *type*, and ensures that any resource protocol is correctly executed. We begin by categorising resource operations into creation, update and usage operations, by lifting them from IO. We illustrate this using Creator; Updater and Reader can be defined similarly.

```
data Creator a = MkCreator (IO a)

ioc : IO a -> Creator a
ioc = MkCreator
```

The MkCreator constructor is left abstract, so that a programmer can lift an operation into Creator using ioc, but cannot run it directly. IO operations can be converted into resource operations, tagging them appropriately:

```
open  : String -> (p:Purpose)
                        -> Creator (Either () (File p))
close : File p          -> Updater ()
read  : File Reading -> Reader String
```

Here: open creates a resource, which may be either an error (represented by ()) or a file handle that has been opened for the appropriate purpose; close updates a

Listing 6. Resource constructs

```
data Res : Vect n Ty -> Vect n Ty -> Ty -> Type where

    Let    : Creator (interpTy a) ->
             Res (a :: G) (Val () :: G') (R t) ->
             Res G G' (R t)
    Update : (a -> Updater b) ->
             (p : HasType i G (Val a)) ->
             Res G (update G p (Val b)) (R ())
    Use    : (a -> Reader b) -> HasType i G (Val a) ->
             Res G G (R b)
    ...
```

Listing 7. Control constructs

```
data Res : Vect Ty n -> Vect Ty n -> Ty -> Type where
    ...
    Lift   : IO a -> Res G G (R a)
    Check  : (p:HasType i G
                (Choice (interpTy a) (interpTy b))) ->
             Res (update G p a) (update G p c) t ->
             Res (update G p b) (update G p c) t ->
             Res G (update G p c) t
    While  : Res G G (R Bool) ->
             Res G G (R ()) -> Res G G (R ())
    Return : a -> Res G G (R a)
    (>>=)  : Res G G' (R a) ->
             (a -> Res G' G'' (R t)) ->
             Res G G'' (R t)
```

resource from a File p to a () (i.e., it makes the resource unavailable); and read accesses a resource (i.e., it reads from it, and the resource remains available). They are implemented using the relevant (unsafe) IO functions from the IDRIS library. Resource operations are executed via a resource management EDSL, Res, with resource constructs (Listing 6), and control constructs (Listing 7).

As we did with Expr in Sect. 6, we index Res over the variables in scope (which represent resources), and the type of the expression. This means that firstly we can refer to resources by *de Bruijn* indices, and secondly we can express precisely how operations may be combined. Unlike Expr, however, we allow types of variables to be updated. Therefore, we index over the input set of resource states, and the output set:

```
data Res : Vect Ty n -> Vect Ty n -> Ty -> Type
```

We can read `Res G G' T` as, "an expression of type T, with input resource states G and output resource states G'". Expression types can be resources, values, or a choice type:

data Ty = R Type | Val Type | Choice Type Type

The distinction between *resource* types, R a, and *value* types, Val a, is that resource types arise from IO operations. A choice type corresponds to Either — we use Either rather than Maybe as this leaves open the possibility of returning informative error codes:

```
interpTy : Ty -> Type
interpTy (R t) = IO t
interpTy (Val t) = t
interpTy (Choice x y) = Either x y
```

As with the interpreter in Sect. 6, we represent variables by proofs of context membership:

```
data HasType : Fin n -> Vect n Ty -> Ty -> Type where
     stop : HasType fZ (t :: G) t
     pop  : HasType k G t -> HasType (fS k) (u :: G) t
```

As well as a `lookup` function for retrieving values in an environment corresponding to a context, we also implement an `update` function:

```
data Env  : Vect n Ty -> Type where
     Nil  : Env Nil
     (::) : interpTy a -> Env G -> Env (a :: G)

lookup : HasType G i a -> Env G -> interpTy a
lookup stop     (x :: xs) = x
lookup (pop k)  (x :: xs) = lookup k xs

update : (G : Vect n Ty) ->
         HasType G i b -> Ty -> Vect n Ty
update (x :: xs) stop    y = y :: xs
update (x :: xs) (pop k) y = x :: update xs k y
```

The type of the `Let` construct explicitly shows that, in the scope of the `Let` expression, a new resource of type a is added to the set, having been made by a `Creator` operation. Furthermore, by the end of the scope, this resource must have been consumed (i.e. its type must have been updated to Val ()):

```
Let : Creator (interpTy a) ->
      Res (a :: G) (Val () :: G') (R t) ->
      Res G G' (R t)
```

The `Update` construct applies an `Updater` operation, changing the type of a resource in the context. Here, using `HasType` to represent resource variables allows us to write the required type of the update operation simply as a -> `Updater` b, and put the operation first, rather than the variable.

```
Update : (a -> Updater b) ->
         (p : HasType G i (Val a)) ->
         Res G (update G p (Val b)) (R ())
```

The Use construct simply executes an operation without updating the context, provided that the operation is well-typed:

```
Use : (a -> Reader b) -> HasType G i (Val a) ->
      Res G G (R b)
```

Finally, we provide a small set of control structures: Check, a branching construct that guarantees that resources are correctly defined in each branch; While, a loop construct that guarantees that there are no state changes during the loop; Lift, a lifting operator for IO functions, Return to inject pure values into a Res program, and (>>=) to support do-notation using ad-hoc name overloading. Note that we cannot make Res an instance of the Monad type class to support do-notation, since the type of >>= here captures updates in the resource set.

We use dsl-notation to overload the IDRIS syntax, in particular providing a let-binding to bind a resource and give it a human-readable name:

```
dsl res
    variable = id
    let = Let
    index_first = stop
    index_next = pop
```

To further reduce notational overhead, we can make Lifting an IO operation implicit, using an implicit conversion as described in Sect. 8.4:

```
implicit ioLift : IO a -> Res G G a
ioLift = Lift
```

The interpreter for Res is written in continuation-passing style, where each operation passes on a result and an updated environment (containing resources):

```
interp : Env G -> Res G G' t ->
         (Env G' -> interpTy t -> IO u) -> IO u

syntax RES [x] = {G:Vect n Ty} -> Res G G (R x)
syntax run [prog] = interp [] prog (\env, res => res)
```

The syntax rules provides convenient notations for declaring the type of a resource aware program, and for running a program in any context. For reference, the full interpreter is presented in Listing 8.

Listing 8. Resource EDSL Interpreter

```
interp : Env G -> Res G G' t ->
         (Env G' -> interpTy t -> IO u) -> IO u
interp env (Let val scope) k =
```

```
        do x <- getCreator val
           interp (x :: env) scope
                   (\env', scope' => k (envTail env') scope')
    interp env (Update method x) k =
           do x' <- getUpdater (method (envLookup x env))
              k (envUpdateVal x x' env) (return ())
    interp env (Use method x) k =
           do x' <- getReader (method (envLookup x env))
              k env (return x')
    interp env (Lift io) k =
        k env io
    interp env (Check x left right) k =
        either (envLookup x env)
                  (\a => interp (envUpdate x a env) left k)
                  (\b => interp (envUpdate x b env) right k)
    interp env (While test body) k
        = interp env test (\env', result =>
             do r <- result
                if (not r)
                   then (k env' (return ()))
                   else (interp env' body (\env'', body' =>
                            do v <- body'
                               interp env'' (While test body) k ))
    interp env (Return v) k = k env (return v)
    interp env (v >>= f) k
      = interp env v (\env', v' => do n <- v'
                                      interp env' (f n) k)
```

9.2   Example: File Management

We can use Res to implement a safe file-management protocol, where each file
must be opened before use, opening a file must be checked, and files must be
closed on exit. We define the following operations for opening, closing, reading
a line[7], and testing for the end of file.

```
open  : String -> (p:Purpose)
                       -> Creator (Either () (File p))
close : File p         -> Updater ()
read  : File Reading -> Reader String
eof   : File Reading -> Reader Bool
```

Since these operations are now managed by the Res EDSL rather than directly
as IO operations, we should ensure that the programmer cannot use the original
IO operations. Names can be *hidden* using the %hide directive as follows:

---

[7] Reading a line may fail, but for the purposes of this example, we consider this
harmless and return an empty string.

```
%hide openFile
%hide closeFile
...
```

Returning to our simple example from the beginning of this Section, we now write the file-reading program as follows:

```
fprog : String -> RES String
fprog filename =
    res do let h = open filename Reading
           Check h
                 putStrLn "File error"
              do content <- Use read h
                 Update close h
```

This is well-typed because the file is opened for reading, and by the end of the scope, the file has been closed. Syntax overloading allows us to name the resource h rather than using a *de Bruijn* index or context membership proof.

10   An EDSL for Managing Side Effects

The resource aware EDSL presented in the previous section handles an instance of a more general problem, namely how to deal with side-effects and state in a pure functional language.

In this section, I describe how to implement effectful programs in IDRIS using an EDSL Effects for capturing *algebraic effects* [1], in such a way that they are easily composable, and translatable to a variety of underlying contexts using *effect handlers*. I will give a collection of example effects (State, Exceptions, File and Console I/O, random number generation and non-determinism) and their handlers, and some example programs which combine effects.

The Effects EDSL makes essential use of dependent types, firstly to verify that a specific effect is available to an effectful program using simple automated theorem proving, and secondly to track the state of a resource by updating its type during program execution. In this way, we can use the Effects DSL to verify implementations of resource usage protocols.

The framework consists of a DSL representation Eff for combining mutable effects and implementations of several predefined effects. We refer to the whole framework with the name Effects. Here, we describe how to *use* Effects; implementation details are described elsewhere [4].

The Effects library is included as part of the main IDRIS distribution, but is not imported by default. In order to use it, you must invoke IDRIS with the -p effects flag, and use the following in your programs:

```
import Effects
```

10.1 Programming with **Effects**

An effectful program f has a type of the following form:

```
f : (x1 : a1) -> (x2 : a2) -> ... ->
      { eff ==> {result} effs' } Eff t
```

That is, the return type gives the effects that f supports (effs, of type List EFFECT), the effects available *after* running f (effs') which may be calculated using the result of the operation result of type t.

A function which does not update its available effects has a type of the following form:

```
f : (x1 : a1) -> (x2 : a2) -> ... -> { eff } Eff t
```

In fact, the notation { eff } is itself syntactic sugar, in order to make Eff types more readable. In full, the type of Eff is:

```
Eff : (x : Type) ->
        List EFFECT -> (x -> List EFFECT) -> Type
```

That is, it is indexed over the type of the computation, the list of input effects and a function which computes the output effects from the result. With syntax overloading, we can create syntactic sugar which allows us to write Eff types as described above:

```
syntax "{" [inst] "}" [eff] = eff inst (\result => inst)
syntax "{" [inst] "==>" "{" {b} "}" [outst] "}" [eff]
       = eff inst (\b => outst)
syntax "{" [inst] "==>" [outst] "}" [eff]
       = eff inst (\result => outst)
```

Side effects are described using the EFFECT type; we will refer to these as *concrete* effects. For example:

```
STATE       : Type -> EFFECT
EXCEPTION : Type -> EFFECT
FILE_IO     : Type -> EFFECT
STDIO       : EFFECT
RND         : EFFECT
```

States are parameterised by the type of the state being carried, and exceptions are parameterised by a type representing errors. File I/O allows a single file to be processed, with the type giving the current state of the file (i.e. closed, open for reading, or open for writing). Finally, STDIO and RND permit console I/O and random number generation respectively. For example, a program with some integer state, which performs console I/O and which could throw an exception carrying some error type Err would have the following type:

```
example : { [EXCEPTION Err, STDIO, STATE Int] } Eff ()
```

First Example: State. In general, an effectful program implemented in the Eff structure has the look and feel of a monadic program written with do-notation. To illustrate basic usage, let us implement a stateful function, which tags each node in a binary tree with a unique integer, depth first, left to right. We declare trees as follows:

```
data Tree a = Leaf
            | Node (Tree a) a (Tree a)
```

To tag each node in the tree, we write an effectful program which, for each node, tags the left subtree, reads and updates the state, tags the right subtree, then returns a new node with its value tagged. The type expresses that the program requires an integer state:

```
tag : Tree a -> { [STATE Int] } Eff (Tree (Int, a))
```

The implementation traverses the tree, using get and put to manipulate state:

```
tag Leaf = return Leaf
tag (Node l x r)
    = do l' <- tag l
         lbl <- get; put (lbl + 1)
         r' <- tag r
         return (Node l' (lbl, x) r')
```

The Effects system ensures, statically, that any effectful functions which are called (get and put here) require no more effects than are available. The types of these functions are:

```
get : { [STATE x] } Eff x
put : x -> { [STATE x] } Eff ()
```

A program in Eff can call any other function in Eff provided that the calling function supports at least the effects required by the called function. In this case, it is valid for tag to call both get and put because all three functions support the STATE Int effect.

To run a program in Eff, it is evaluated in an appropriate *computation context*, using the run or runPure function. The computation context explains how each effectful operation, such as get and put here, are to be executed in that context. Using runPure, which runs an effectful program in the identity context, we can write a runTag function as follows, using put to initialise the state:

```
runTag : (i : Int) -> Tree a -> Tree (Int, a)
runTag i x = runPure (do put i
                         tag x)
```

Effects and Resources. Each effect is associate with a *resource*, which is initialised before an effectful program can be run. For example, in the case of STATE Int the corresponding resource is the integer state itself. The types of runPure and run show this (slightly simplified here for illustrative purposes):

```
runPure : {env : Env id xs} -> { xs } Eff a -> a
run : Applicative m =>
        {env : Env m xs} -> { xs } Eff a -> m a
```

The env argument is implicit, and initialised automatically where possible using default values given by instances of the following type class:

```
class Default a where
    default : a
```

Instances of Default are defined for all primitive types, and many library types such as List, Vect, Maybe, pairs, etc. However, where no default value exists for a resource type (for example, you may want a STATE type for which there is no Default instance) the resource environment can be given explicitly using one of the following functions:

```
runPureInit : Env id xs -> { xs } Eff a -> a
runInit : Applicative m =>
            Env m xs -> { xs } Eff a -> a
```

To be well-typed, the environment must contain resources corresponding exactly to the effects in xs. For example, we could also have implemented runTag by initialising the state as follows:

```
runTag : (i : Int) -> Tree a -> Tree (Int, a)
runTag i x = runPureInit [i] (tag x)
```

As we will see, the particular choice of computation context can be important. Programs with exceptions, for example, can be run in the context of IO, Maybe or Either.

Labelled Effects. What if we have more than one state, especially more than one state of the same type? How would get and put know which state they should be referring to? For example, how could we extend the tree tagging example such that it additionally counts the number of leaves in the tree? One possibility would be to change the state so that it captured both of these values, e.g.:

```
tag : Tree a ->
        { [STATE (Int, Int)] } Eff (Tree (Int, a))
```

Doing this, however, ties the two states together throughout (as well as not indicating which integer is which). It would be nice to be able to call effectful programs which guaranteed only to access one of the states, for example. In a larger application, this becomes particularly important.

The Effects library therefore allows effects in general to be *labelled* so that they can be referred to explicitly by a particular name. This allows multiple effects of the same type to be included. We can count leaves and update the tag separately, by labelling them as follows:

```
tag : Tree a -> { ['Tag ::: STATE Int,
                  'Leaves ::: STATE Int] }
        Eff (Tree (Int, a))
```

The : : : operator allows an arbitrary label to be given to an effect. This label can be any type—it is simply used to identify an effect uniquely. Here, we have used a symbol type. In general 'name introduces a new symbol, the only purpose of which is to disambiguate values[8].

When an effect is labelled, its operations are also labelled using the : - operator. In this way, we can say explicitly which state we mean when using get and put. The tree tagging program which also counts leaves can be written as follows:

```
tag Leaf = do 'Leaves :- update (+1)
               pure Leaf
tag (Node l x r)
   = do l' <- tag l
        i <- 'Tag :- get
        'Tag :- put (i + 1)
        r' <- tag r
        pure (Node l' (i, x) r')
```

The update function here is a combination of get and put, applying a function to the current state.

```
update : (x -> x) -> { [STATE x] } Eff ()
```

Finally, our top level runTag function now returns a pair of the number of leaves, and the new tree. Resources for labelled effects are intialised using the : = operator (reminiscent of assignment in an imperative language):

```
runTag : (i : Int) -> Tree a -> (Int, Tree (Int, a))
runTag i x = runPureInit ['Tag := i, 'Leaves := 0]
                   (do x' <- treeTagAux x
                       leaves <- 'Leaves :- get
                       pure (leaves, x'))
```

To summarise, we have:

- : : : to convert an effect to a labelled effect.
- : - to convert an effectful operation to a labelled effectful operation.
- : = to initialise a resource for a labelled effect.

Or, more formally with their types (slightly simplified to account only for the situation where available effects are not updated):

```
(:::)  : lbl -> EFFECT -> EFFECT
(:-)   : (l : lbl) ->
             { [x] } Eff a -> { [l ::: x] } Eff a
(:=)   : (l : lbl) -> res -> LRes l res
```

---

[8] In practice, 'name simply introduces a new empty type.

Here, LRes is simply the resource type associated with a labelled effect. Note that labels are polymorphic in the label type lbl. Hence, a label can be anything— a string, an integer, a type, etc.

! -Notation. In many cases, using do-notation can make programs unnecessarily verbose, particularly in cases where the value bound is used once, immediately. The following program returns the length of the String stored in the state, for example:

```
stateLength : { [STATE String] } Eff Nat
stateLength = do x <- get
                 pure (length x)
```

This seems unnecessarily verbose, and it would be nice to program in a more direct style in these cases. IDRIS provides !-notation to help with this. The above program can be written instead as:

```
stateLength : { [STATE String] } Eff Nat
stateLength = pure (length !get)
```

The notation !expr means that the expression expr should be evaluated and then implicitly bound. Conceptually, we can think of ! as being a prefix function with the following type:

```
(!) : { xs } Eff a -> a
```

Note, however, that it is not really a function, merely syntax! In practice, a subexpression !expr will lift expr as high as possible within its current scope, bind it to a fresh name x, and replace !expr with x. Expressions are lifted depth first, left to right. In practice, !-notation allows us to program in a more direct style, while still giving a notational clue as to which expressions are effectful.

For example, the expression...

```
let y = 42 in f !(g !(print y) !x)
```

... is lifted to:

```
let y = 42 in do y' <- print y
                 x' <- x
                 g' <- g y' x'
                 f g'
```

10.2   An Effectful Evaluator

Consider an evaluator for a simple expression language, supporting variables, integers, addition and random number generation, declared as follows:

```
data Expr = Var String   | Val Integer
          | Add Expr Expr | Random Integer
```

In order to implement an evaluator for this language, we will need to carry a state, holding mappings from variables to values, and support exceptions (to handle variable lookup failure) and random numbers. The environment is simply a mapping from `Strings` representing variable names to `Integers`:

```
Vars : Type
Vars = List (String, Int)
```

The evaluator invokes supported effects where needed. We use the following effectful functions:

```
get    : { [STATE x] } Eff x
raise  : a -> { [EXCEPTION a] } Eff b
rndInt : Int -> Int -> { [RND] } Eff Int
```

The evaluator itself (Listing 9) is written as an instance of `Eff`, invoking the required effectful functions with the `Effects` framework checking that they are available.

Listing 9. Effectful evaluator

```
eval : Expr -> { [EXCEPTION String, RND, STATE Vars] } Eff t
eval (Val x) = return x
eval (Var x) = do vs <- get
                  case lookup x vs of
                      Nothing => raise ("Error " ++ x)
                      Just val => return val
eval (Add l r) = [| eval l + eval r |]
eval (Random upper) = rndInt 0 upper
```

In order to run the evaluator, we must provide initial values for the resources associated with each effect. Exceptions require the unit resource, random number generation requires an initial seed, and the state requires an initial environment. We use `Maybe` as the computation context to be able to handle exceptions:

```
runEval : List (String, Int) -> Expr -> Maybe Int
runEval env expr = runInit [(), 123456, env] (eval expr)
```

Extending the evaluator with a new effect, such as STDIO is a matter of extending the list of available effects in its type. We could use this, for example, to print out the generated random numbers:

```
eval : Expr ->
       { [EXCEPTION String, STDIO,
              RND, STATE Vars] } Eff t
...
eval (Random upper) = do num <- rndInt 0 upper
                         putStrLn (show num)
                         return num
```

We can insert the STDIO effect anywhere in the list without difficulty. The only requirements are that its initial resource is in the corresponding position in the call to `runInit`, and that `runInit` instantiates a context which supports STDIO, such as IO:

```
runEval : List (String, Int) -> Expr -> IO Int
runEval env expr
    = runInit [(), (), 123456, env] (eval expr)
```

10.3 Implementing Effects

In order to implement a new effect, we define a new type (of kind `Effect`) and explain how that effect is interpreted in some underlying context `m`. An `Effect` describes an effectful computation, parameterised by the type of the computation `t`, an input resource `res`, and an output resource `res'` computed from the result of the operation.

```
Effect : Type
Effect = (t : Type) ->
         (res : Type) -> (res' : t -> Type) ->
         Type
```

We describe effects as algebraic data types. To *run* an effect, we require an interpretation in a computation context `m`. To achieve this, we make effects and contexts instances of a type class, `Handler`, which has a method `handle` explaining this interpretation:

```
class Handler (e : Effect) (m : Type -> Type) where
    handle : (r : res) -> (eff : e t res resk) ->
             (k : ((x : t) -> resk x -> m a)) -> m a
```

Handlers are parameterised by the effect they handle, and the context in which they handle the effect. This allows several different context-dependent handlers to be written, e.g. exceptions could be handled differently in an `IO` setting than in a `Maybe` setting. When effects are combined, as in the evaluator example, all effects must be handled in the context in which the program is run.

An effect `e t res res'` updates a resource type `res` to a resource type `res'`, returning a value `t`. The handler, therefore, implements this update in a context `m` which may support side effects. The handler is written in continuation passing style. This is for two reasons: firstly, it returns two values, a new resource and the result of the computation, which is more cleanly managed in a continuation than by returning a tuple; secondly, and more importantly, it gives the handler the flexibility to invoke the continuation any number of times (zero or more).

An `Effect`, which is the internal algebraic description of an effect, is promoted into a concrete `EFFECT`, which is expected by the `Eff` structure, with the `MkEff` constructor:

```
data EFFECT : Type where
     MkEff : Type -> Effect -> EFFECT
```

`MkEff` additionally records the resource state of an effect. In the remainder of this section, we describe how several effects can be implemented in this way: mutable state; console I/O; exceptions; files; random numbers; and non-determinism.

State. In general, effects are described algebraically in terms of the operations they support. In the case of `State`, the supported effects are reading the state (`Get`) and writing the state (`Put`).

```
data State : Effect where
     Get :        { a }         State a
     Put : b -> { a ==> b } State ()
```

The resource associated with a state corresponds to the state itself. So, the `Get` operation leaves this state intact (with a resource type a on entry and exit) but the `Put` operation may update this state (with a resource type a on entry and b on exit). That is, a `Put` may update the type of the stored value. Note that we are using the same syntactic sugar for updating the resource type as we used earlier for giving lists of effects. In full, `State` would be written as:

```
data State : Effect where
     Get :        State a   a  (\x => a)
     Put : b -> State ()  a  (\x => b)
```

We can implement a handler for this effect, for all contexts m, as follows:

```
instance Handler State m where
         handle st Get        k = k st st
         handle st (Put n) k = k n ()
```

When running `Get`, the handler passes the current state to the continuation as both the return value (the second argument of the continuation k) and the new resource value (the first argument of the continuation). When running `Put`, the new state is passed to the continuation as the new resource value.

We then convert the algebraic effect `State` to a concrete effect usable in an `Effects` program using the `STATE` function, to which we provide the initial state type as follows:

```
STATE : Type -> EFFECT
STATE t = MkEff t State
```

As a convention, algebraic effects, of type `Effect`, have an initial upper case letter. Concrete effects, of type `EFFECT`, are correspondingly in all upper case.

Algebraic effects are promoted to `Effects` programs with concrete effects by using a coercion with an implicit, automatically constructed, proof argument:

```
call : {e : Effect} ->
       (eff : e t a b) -> {auto prf : EffElem e a xs} ->
       Eff t xs (\v => updateResTy v xs prf eff)
```

How this function works and how the proof is calculated are beyond the scope of this tutorial. However, its purpose is to allow a programmer to use an algebraic effect in an `Effects` program *without* any explicit syntax. We can therefore define get and put as follows:

```
get : { [STATE x] } Eff x
get = call Get
```

```
put : x -> { [STATE x] } Eff ()
put val = call (Put val)
```

We may also find it useful to mutate the *type* of a state, considering that states may themselves have dependent types (we may, for example, add an element to a vector in a state). The Put constructor supports this, so we can implement putM to update the state's type:

```
putM : y -> { [STATE x] ==> [STATE y] } Eff ()
putM val = call (Put val)
```

Finally, it may be useful to combine get and put in a single update:

```
update : (x -> x) -> { [STATE x] } Eff ()
update f = do val <- get; put (f val)

updateM : (x -> y) -> { [STATE x] ==> [STATE y] } Eff ()
updateM f = do val <- get; putM (f val)
```

Console I/O. Consider a simplified version of console I/O which supports reading and writing strings. There is no associated resource, although in an alternative implementation we may associate it with an abstract world state, or a pair of handles for stdin/stdout. Algebraically we describe console I/O as follows:

```
data StdIO : Effect where
     PutStr : String -> { () } StdIO ()
     GetStr : { () } StdIO String
     PutCh : Char -> { () } StdIO ()
     GetCh : { () } StdIO Char

STDIO : EFFECT
STDIO = MkEff () StdIO
```

The obvious way to handle StdIO is via the IO monad:

```
instance Handler StdIO IO where
     handle () (PutStr s) k = do putStr s; k () ()
     handle () GetStr     k = do x <- getLine; k x ()
     handle () (PutCh c)  k = do putChar c; k () ()
     handle () GetCh      k = do x <- getChar; k x ()
```

Unlike the State effect, for which the handler worked in *all* contexts, this handler only applies to effectful programs run in an IO context. We can implement alternative handlers, and indeed there is no reason that effectful programs in StdIO must be evaluated in a monadic context. For example, we can define I/O stream functions:

```
data IOStream a
    = MkStream (List String -> (a, List String))
```

```
instance Handler StdIO IOStream where
    ...
```

A handler for StdIO in IOStream context generates a function from a list of strings (the input text) to a value and the output text. We can build a pure function which simulates real console I/O:

```
mkStrFn : Env IOStream xs -> Eff IOStream xs a ->
            List String -> (a, List String)

mkStrFn {a} env p input = case mkStrFn' of
                                MkStream f => f input
    where injStream : a -> IOStream a
          injStream v = MkStream (\x => (v, []))
          mkStrFn' : IOStream a
          mkStrFn' = runWith injStream env p
```

This requires an alternative means of running effectful programs, runWith, which takes an additional argument explaining how to inject the result of a computation into the appropriate computation context:

```
runWith : (a -> m a) ->
            Env m xs -> Eff a xs xs' -> m a
```

To illustrate this, we write a simple console I/O program:

```
name : { [STDIO] } Eff ()
name = do putStr "Name? "
          n <- getStr
          putStrLn ("Hello " ++ show n)
```

Using mkStrFn, we can run this as a pure function which uses a list of strings as its input, and gives a list of strings as its output. We can evaluate this at the IDRIS prompt:

```
*name> show $ mkStrFn [()] name ["Edwin"]
((), ["Name?" , "Hello Edwin\n"])
```

This suggests that alternative, pure, handlers for console I/O, or any I/O effect, can be used for unit testing and reasoning about I/O programs without executing any real I/O.

Exceptions. The exception effect supports only one operation, Raise. Exceptions are parameterised over an error type e, so Raise takes a single argument to represent the error. The associated resource is of unit type, and since raising an exception causes computation to abort, raising an exception can return a value of any type.

```
data Exception : Type -> Effect where
     Raise : a -> { () } Exception a b

EXCEPTION : Type -> EFFECT
EXCEPTION e = MkEff () (Exception e)
```

The semantics of Raise is to abort computation, therefore handlers of exception effects do not call the continuation k. In any case, this should be impossible since passing the result to the continuation would require the ability to invent a value in any arbitrary type b! The simplest handler runs in a Maybe context:

```
instance Handler (Exception a) Maybe where
     handle _ (Raise e) k = Nothing
```

Exceptions can be handled in any context which supports some representation of failed computations. In an Either e context, for example, we can use Left to represent the error case:

```
instance Handler (Exception e) (Either e) where
     handle _ (Raise e) k = Left err
```

Random Numbers. Random number generation can be implemented as an effect, with the resource tracking the *seed* from which the next number will be generated. The Random effect supports one operation, getRandom, which requires an Int resource and returns the next number:

```
data Random : Type -> Type -> Type -> Type where
     GetRandom : { Int } Random Int
     SetSeed   : Int -> { Int } Random ()

RND : EFFECT
RND = MkEff Integer Random
```

Handling random number generation shows that it is a state effect in disguise, where the effect updates the seed. This is a simple linear congruential pseudo-random number generator:

```
instance Handler Random m where
     handle seed GetRandom k
          = let seed' = 1664525 * seed + 1013904223 in
                 k seed' seed'
     handle seed (SetSeed n) k = k () n
```

Alternative handlers could use a different, possibly more secure approach. In any case, we can implement a function which returns a random number between a lower and upper bound as follows:

```
rndInt : Int -> Int -> Eff [RND] Int
rndInt lower upper
     = do v <- GetRandom
          return (v `mod` (upper - lower) + lower)
```

Non-determinism. Non-determinism can be implemented as an effect
Selection, in which a Select operation chooses one value non-
deterministically from a list of possible values:

```
data Selection : Effect where
     Select : List a -> { () } Selection a
```

We can handle this effect in a Maybe context, trying every choice in a list given
to Select until the computation succeeds:

```
instance Handler Selection Maybe where
     handle _ (Select xs) k = tryAll xs where
          tryAll [] = Nothing
          tryAll (x :: xs) = case k x () of
                                  Nothing => tryAll xs
                                  Just v => Just v
```

The handler for Maybe produces at most one result, effectively performing a
depth first search of the values passed to Select. The handler runs the continuation for every element of the list until the result of running the continuation
succeeds.

Alternatively, we can find *every* possible result by handling selection in a
List context:

```
instance Handler Selection List where
     handle r (Select xs) k = concatMap (\x => k x r) xs
```

We can use the Selection effect to implement search problems by non-
deterministically choosing from a list of candidate solutions. For example, a
solution to the n-queens problem can be implemented as follows. First, we write
a function which checks whether a point on a chess board attacks another if
occupied by a queen:

```
no_attack : (Int, Int) -> (Int, Int) -> Bool
no_attack (x, y) (x', y')
    = x /= x' && y /= y' && abs (x - x') /= abs (y - y')
```

Then, given a column and a list of queen positions, we find the rows on which a
queen may safely be placed in that column:

```
rowsIn : Int -> List (Int, Int) -> List Int
rowsIn col qs
     = [ x | x <- [1..8], all (no_attack (x, col)) qs ]
```

Finally, we compute a solution by accumulating a set of queen positions, column
by column, non-deterministically choosing a position for a queen in each column.

```
addQueens : Int -> List (Int, Int) ->
                  { [SELECT] } Eff (List (Int, Int))
addQueens 0   qs = return qs
addQueens col qs
     = do row <- select (rowsIn col qs)
          addQueens (col - 1) ((row, col) :: qs)
```

We can run this in Maybe context, to retrieve one solution, or in List context, to retrieve all solutions. In a Maybe context, for example, we can define:

```
getQueens : Maybe (List (Int, Int))
getQueens = run [()] (addQueens 8 [])
```

Then to find the first solution, we run getQueens at the REPL:

```
*Queens> show getQueens
"Just [(4, 1), (2, 2), (7, 3), (3, 4),
       (6, 5), (8, 6), (5, 7), (1, 8)]" : String
```

10.4   Dependent Effects

In the programs we have seen so far, the available effects have remained constant. Sometimes, however, an operation can *change* the available effects. The simplest example occurs when we have a state with a dependent type—adding an element to a vector also changes its type, for example, since its length is explicit in the type. In this section, we will see how Effects supports this. Firstly, we will see how states with dependent types can be implemented. Secondly, we will see how the effects can depend on the *result* of an effectful operation. Finally, we will see how this can be used to implement a type-safe and resource-safe protocol for file management.

Dependent States. Suppose we have a function which reads input from the console, converts it to an integer, and adds it to a list which is stored in a STATE. It might look something like the following:

```
readInt : { [STATE (List Int), STDIO] } Eff ()
readInt = do let x = trim !getStr
             put (cast x :: !get)
```

But what if, instead of a list of integers, we would like to store a Vect, maintaining the length in the type?

```
readInt : { [STATE (Vect n Int), STDIO] } Eff ()
readInt = do let x = trim !getStr
             put (cast x :: !get)
```

This will not type check! Although the vector has length n on entry to readInt, it has length S n on exit. The Effects DSL allows us to express this as follows:

```
readInt : { [STATE (Vect n Int), STDIO] ==>
             [STATE (Vect (S n) Int), STDIO] } Eff ()
readInt = do let x = trim !getStr
             putM (cast x :: !get)
```

The notation { xs ==> xs' } Eff a in a type means that the operation begins with effects xs available, and ends with effects xs' available. Since the type is updated, we have used putM to update the state.

Result-Dependent Effects. Often, whether a state is updated could depend on the success or otherwise of an operation. In the readInt example, we might wish to update the vector only if the input is a valid integer (i.e. all digits). As a first attempt, we could try the following, returning a Bool which indicates success:

```
readInt : { [STATE (Vect n Int), STDIO] ==>
            [STATE (Vect (S n) Int), STDIO] } Eff Bool
readInt = do let x = trim !getStr
             case all isDigit (unpack x) of
                  False => pure False
                  True => do putM (cast x :: !get)
                             pure True
```

Unfortunately, this will not type check because the vector does not get extended in both branches of the case!

```
MutState.idr:18:19:When elaborating right hand side
of Main.case block in readInt:
Unifying n and S n would lead to infinite value
```

Clearly, the size of the resulting vector depends on whether or not the value read from the user was valid. We can express this in the type:

```
readInt : { [STATE (Vect n Int), STDIO] ==>
            {ok} if ok
                    then [STATE (Vect (S n) Int), STDIO]
                    else [STATE (Vect n Int), STDIO] }
          Eff Bool
readInt = do let x = trim !getStr
             case all isDigit (unpack x) of
                  False => with_val False (pure ())
                  True => do putM (cast x :: !get)
                             with_val True (pure ())
```

The notation { xs ==> {res} xs' } Eff a in a type means that the effects available are updated from xs to xs', *and* the resulting effects xs' may depend on the result of the operation res, of type a. Here, the resulting effects are computed from the result ok—if True, the vector is extended, otherwise it remains the same. We also use with_val to return a result:

```
with_val : (val : a) ->
           ({ xs ==> xs' val } Eff ()) ->
           { xs ==> xs' } Eff a
```

We cannot use pure here, as before, since pure does not allow the returned value to update the effects list. The purpose of with_val is to update the effects before returning. As a shorthand, we can write

```
pureM val
```

... instead of...

```
with_val val (pure ())
```

... so our program is:

```
readInt : { [STATE (Vect n Int), STDIO] ==>
              {ok} if ok
                    then [STATE (Vect (S n) Int), STDIO]
                    else [STATE (Vect n Int), STDIO] }
            Eff Bool
readInt = do let x = trim !getStr
             case all isDigit (unpack x) of
                  False => pureM False
                  True => do putM (cast x :: !get)
                             pureM True
```

When using the function, we will naturally have to check its return value in order to know what the new set of effects is. For example, to read a set number of values into a vector, we could write the following:

```
readN : (n : Nat) ->
         { [STATE (Vect m Int), STDIO] ==>
           [STATE (Vect (n + m) Int), STDIO] } Eff IO ()
readN Z = pure ()
readN {m} (S k)
    = case !readInt of
           True => rewrite plusSuccRightSucc k m in
                      readN k
           False => readN (S k)
```

The case analysis on the result of readInt means that we know in each branch whether reading the integer succeeded, and therefore how many values still need to be read into the vector. What this means in practice is that the type system has verified that a necessary dynamic check (i.e. whether reading a value succeeded) has indeed been done.

Aside: Only case will work here. We cannot use if/then/else because the then and else branches must have the same type. The case construct, however, abstracts over the value being inspected in the type of each branch.

File Management. A practical use for dependent effects is in specifying resource usage protocols and verifying that they are executed correctly. For example, file management follows a resource usage protocol with the following (informally specified) requirements:

- It is necessary to open a file for reading before reading it
- Opening may fail, so the programmer should check whether opening was successful
- A file which is open for reading must not be written to, and vice versa
- When finished, an open file handle should be closed
- When a file is closed, its handle should no longer be used

These requirements can be expressed formally in `Effects`, by creating a `FILE_IO` effect parameterised over a file handle state, which is either empty, open for reading, or open for writing. The `FILE_IO` effect's definition is given in Listing 10. Note that this effect is mainly for illustrative purposes—typically we would also like to support random access files and better reporting of error conditions.

Listing 10. File I/O Effect

```
FILE_IO : Type -> EFFECT

data OpenFile : Mode -> Type

open   : String -> (m : Mode) ->
         { [FILE_IO ()] ==>
           {ok} [FILE_IO (if ok then OpenFile m else ())] }
         Eff Bool
close : { [FILE_IO (OpenFile m)] ==> [FILE_IO ()] }
         Eff ()

readLine  : { [FILE_IO (OpenFile Read)] } Eff String
writeLine : { [FILE_IO (OpenFile Write)] } Eff ()
eof       : { [FILE_IO (OpenFile Read)] } Eff Bool

instance Handler FileIO IO
```

In particular, consider the type of `open`:

```
open   : String -> (m : Mode) ->
  { [FILE_IO ()] ==>
    {ok} [FILE_IO (if ok then OpenFile m else ())] }
  Eff Bool
```

This returns a `Bool` which indicates whether opening the file was successful. The resulting state depends on whether the operation was successful; if so, we have a file handle open for the stated purpose, and if not, we have no file handle. By `case` analysis on the result, we continue the protocol accordingly.

Listing 11. Reading a File

```
readFile : { [FILE_IO (OpenFile Read)] } Eff (List String)
readFile = readAcc [] where
    readAcc : List String -> { [FILE_IO (OpenFile Read)] }
              Eff (List String)
    readAcc acc = if (not !eof)
                  then readAcc (!readLine :: acc)
                  else pure (reverse acc)
```

Given a function `readFile` (Listing 11) which reads from an open file until reaching the end, we can write a program which opens a file, reads it, then displays the contents and closes it, as follows, correctly following the protocol:

```
dumpFile : String -> { [FILE_IO (), STDIO] } Eff ()
dumpFile name = case !(open name Read) of
                    True => do putStrLn (show !readFile)
                               close
                    False => putStrLn ("Error!")
```

The type of dumpFile, with FILE_IO () in its effect list, indicates that any use of the file resource will follow the protocol correctly (i.e. it both begins and ends with an empty resource). If we fail to follow the protocol correctly (perhaps by forgetting to close the file, failing to check that open succeeded, or opening the file for writing) then we will get a compile-time error. For example, changing open name Read to open name Write yields a compile-time error of the following form:

```
FileTest.idr:16:18:When elaborating right hand side
of Main.case block in testFile:
Can't solve goal
        SubList [(FILE_IO (OpenFile Read))]
                [(FILE_IO (OpenFile Write)), STDIO]
```

In other words: when reading a file, we need a file which is open for reading, but the effect list contains a FILE_IO effect carrying a file open for writing.

Exercise

Consider the interpreter you implemented in the Sect. 8 exercises. How could you use Effects to improve this? For example:

1. What should be the type of interp?
2. Can you separate the *imperative* parts from the *evaluation*? What are the effects required by each?

11   Conclusion

In this tutorial, we have covered the fundamentals of dependently typed programming in IDRIS, and particularly those features which support embedded domain specific language implementation (EDSL). We have seen several examples of EDSLs in IDRIS:

- A well-typed interpreter for the simply typed λ-calculus, which shows how to implement an EDSL where the type-correctness of programs in the *object* language is verified by the *host* language's type system.
- An interpreter for a *resource-safe* EDSL, capturing the state of resources such as file handles at particular points during program execution, ensuring, at compile time, that a program can only execute operations which are valid at those points.
- An EDSL for managing side-effecting programs, which generalises the resource-safe EDSL and allows several effects and resource to be managed simultaneously.

11.1 Further Reading

Further information about IDRIS programming, and programming with dependent types in general, can be obtained from various sources:

- The IDRIS web site (http://idris-lang.org/), which includes links to tutorials, some lectures and the mailing list. In particular, the IDRIS tutorial [5] describes the language in full, including many features not discussed here such as type providers [9], the foreign function interface, and compiling via Javascript.
- The IRC channel # idris, on chat.freenode.net.
- Examining the prelude and exploring the samples in the distribution.
- Various papers (e.g. [2,3,7,8]), which describe implementation techniques and programming idioms.

Acknowledgements. I am grateful to the Scottish Informatics and Computer Science Alliance (SICSA) for funding this research. I would also like to thank the many contributors to the IDRIS system and libraries, as well as the reviewers for their helpful and constructive suggestions.

References

1. Bauer, A., Pretnar, M.: Programming with Algebraic Effects and Handlers (2012). http://arxiv.org/abs/1203.1539
2. Brady, E.: Idris - systems programming meets full dependent types. In: Programming Languages Meets Program Verification (PLPV 2011), pp. 43–54 (2011)
3. Brady, E.: Idris, a general-purpose dependently typed programming language: design and implementation. J. Funct. Program. **23**, 552–593 (2013)
4. Brady, E.: Programming and reasoning with algebraic effects and dependent types. In: ICFP 2013: Proceedings of the 18th ACM SIGPLAN International Conference on Functional Programming. ACM (2013)
5. Brady, E.: Programming in Idris : a tutorial (2013)
6. Brady, E., Hammond, K.: Correct-by-construction concurrency: using dependent types to verify implementations of effectful resource usage protocols. Fundamenta Informaticae **102**(2), 145–176 (2010)
7. Brady, E., Hammond, K.: Scrapping your inefficient engine: using partial evaluation to improve domain-specific language implementation. In: ICFP 2010: Proceedings of the 15th ACM SIGPLAN International Conference on Functional Programming, pp. 297–308. ACM, New York (2010)
8. Brady, E., Hammond, K.: Resource-safe systems programming with embedded domain specific languages. In: Russo, C., Zhou, N.-F. (eds.) PADL 2012. LNCS, vol. 7149, pp. 242–257. Springer, Heidelberg (2012)
9. Christiansen, D.: Dependent type providers. In: WGP 2013: Proceedings of the 9th ACM SIGPLAN Workshop on Generic Programming. ACM (2013)
10. Howard, W.A.: The formulae-as-types notion of construction. In: Seldin, J.P., Hindley, J.R. (eds.) To H.B.Curry: Essays on Combinatory Logic, Lambda Calculus and Formalism. Academic Press, New York (1980). A reprint of an unpublished manuscript from 1969

11. McBride, C., McKinna, J.: The view from the left. J. Funct. Program. **14**(1), 69–111 (2004)
12. McBride, C., Paterson, R.: Applicative programming with effects. J. Funct. Program. **18**, 1–13 (2008)
13. Peyton Jones, S., et al.: Haskell 98 language and libraries - the revised report (2002). http://www.haskell.org/

An Introduction to Task Oriented Programming

Peter Achten, Pieter Koopman, and Rinus Plasmeijer[✉]

Institute for Computing and Information Sciences (iCIS),
Radboud University Nijmegen, Nijmegen, The Netherlands
{p.achten,pieter,rinus}@cs.ru.nl

Abstract. Task Oriented Programming (or shortly TOP) is a new programming paradigm. It is used for developing applications where human beings closely collaborate on the internet to accomplish a common goal. The tasks that need to be done to achieve this goal are described on a very high level of abstraction. This means that one does need to worry about the technical realization to make the collaboration possible. The technical realization is generated fully automatically from the abstract description. TOP can therefore be seen as a model driven approach. The tasks described form a model from which the technical realization is generated.

This paper describes the *iTask* system which supports TOP as an Embedded Domain Specific Language (EDSL). The host language is the pure and lazy functional language *Clean*.

Based on the high level description of the tasks to do, the *iTask* system generates a web-service. This web-service offers a web interface to the end-users for doing their work, it coordinates the tasks being described, and it provides the end-users with up-to-date information about the status of the tasks being performed by others.

Tasks are typed, every task processes a value of a particular type. Tasks can be calculated dynamically. Tasks can be higher order: the result of a task may be a newly generated task which can be passed around and be assigned to some other worker later on. Tasks can be anything. Also the management of tasks can be expressed as a task. For example, commonly there will be many tasks assigned to someone. A task, predefined in the library for convenience, offers the tasks to do to the end-user much like an email application offers an interface to handle emails. This enables the end-user to freely choose which tasks to work on. However, one can define other ways for managing tasks.

A new aspect of the system is that tasks have become reactive: a task does not deliver one value when the task is done, but, while the work takes place, it constantly produces updated versions of the task value reflecting the progress of the work taken place. This current task value can be observed by others and may influence the things others can see or do.

© Springer International Publishing Switzerland 2015
V. Zsók et al. (Eds.): CEFP 2013, LNCS 8606, pp. 187–245, 2015.
DOI: 10.1007/978-3-319-15940-9_5

1   The Task-Oriented Programming Paradigm

1.1   Introduction

These lecture notes are about *Task-Oriented Programming (TOP)*. TOP is a
programming paradigm that has been developed to address the challenges software developers face when creating *interactive, distributed, multi-user* applications. *Interactive* applications provide their users with an optimal experience and
usage of the application. Programming interactive components in an application
is challenging because it requires deep understanding of GUI toolkits. Additionally, the program structure (for instance widget-based event handling with
callback functions and state management) makes it hard to figure out what the
application is doing. *Distributed* applications spread their computational activities on arbitrarily many computing devices, such as desktop computers, notebooks, tablets, smart phones, each running one operating system or another.
The challenges that you face concern programming the operating systems of
each device, keeping track of the distributed computations in order to coordinate these tasks correctly and effectively, and executing the required communication protocols. *Multi-user* applications serve users who work together in order
to achieve common goals. A simple example of a common goal could be to write,
or design something together. In this area the challenges concern keeping track
of users, aiding them with their work, and making sure that they do not get in
each other's way. More challenging examples are modern health care institutes,
multi-national companies, command and control systems, where thousands of
people do a job in collaboration with many others, and ICT plays an important
role to connect the activities. We have written these lecture notes to show how
contemporary, state-of-art programming language concepts can be used to rise
to the challenge of creating applications in a structured way, using a carefully
balanced mixture of the novel concept of *tasks* with the proven concepts of types,
type systems, functional and type-indexed programming.

The Internet forms a natural habitat for the kind of applications that TOP
has been designed for (Fig. 1) because its architecture makes TOP applications
available on a wide range of equipment, such as desktop computers, notebooks,
smart phones, and tablets. In addition, it is very natural for a TOP application
to serve more than a single user. TOP applications can deploy web services, or
provide these themselves. Under the hood the application uses a clients-server
architecture. The client sides implement the front-end components of the application, running in web browsers or as apps on smart phones and tablets. The server
side runs as a web service and basically implements the back-end coarse grain
coordination and synchronization of the front-end components. During the operations, it can use other web services, rely on sensor data, use remote procedure
calls, and synchronize data 'in the cloud' or back-end database systems.

Unless one can manage to separate the concerns in a well organized manner,
programming this kind of applications is a white-water canoeing experience in
which there is a myriad of rapids to be taken in the form of design issues, implementation details, operating system limitations, and environment requirements.

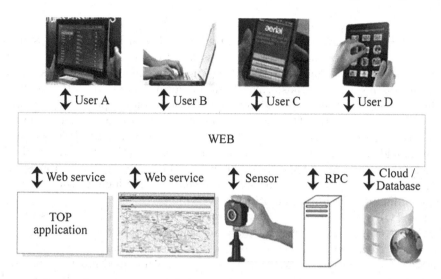

Fig. 1. The Internet habitat of TOP applications

TOP steers the programmer away from these rapids and guides to placid waters. It forces the programmer to think of the work that the intended processors (humans and computers) of your applications are required to do, as well as the structure of the information that is required to coordinate this work properly. TOP offers a *declarative* style of programming in which *what* takes precedence over *how*. A TOP program relates to work in a similar way as René Magritte's well known painting of a pipe relates to a real pipe (Fig. 2). In a TOP program *tasks* are specifications of *what* work must be performed by the users and computing machinery of an application. *How* the specification is executed is the concern of the TOP language implementation, taking the rapids. For instance, the task of obtaining information from users should require only a data model of the

Fig. 2. *La Trahison des Images* (*The Treachery of Images*), 1928–1929, by René Magritte – "This is not a pipe"

information; the TOP language implementation of this task handles the entire user interface management. Similarly, the task of coordinating tasks should require only the data model of the processed data; the TOP language implementation of this task handles all coordination and communication issues. Often data models need to be transformed from one format to another. It should be sufficient to specify the computation that is restricted on the proper domain and range and trust that the TOP language implementation knows when to invoke these computations on the proper data values without unexpected side-effects.

It should be clear that *types* play a pivotal role in TOP: they are used for modeling information and specify the domains and ranges of computations; the TOP language implementation uses them to generate and handle user interfaces and coordinate work implementations.

The TOP language that we have developed and use in this paper is *iTask*. Figure 3 gives a bird's-eye view of the main components of the *iTask* language. *iTask* is a *combinator language*. Combinator languages emphasize the use of *combinators* to construct programs. A combinator is a named *programming pattern* that in a very precise way states how a new piece of program is assembled from smaller pieces of programs. *iTask* is also an example of an *embedded language*. Embedded languages borrow key language aspects from an existing language, the *host language*. In this way they receive the benefits of known language constructs and, more importantly, do not have to re-invent the wheel. In the case of *iTask* the host language is the purely functional programming language *Clean*. Consequently, the combinators are expressed as functions, and the model types can be expressed with the rich type language of *Clean*. *iTask* extends its host language with a library that implements all type-indexed algorithms, web client handling, server side handling, and much more.

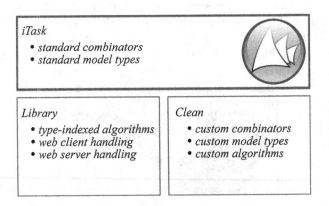

Fig. 3. The *iTask* language is embedded in the functional language *Clean*

TOP applications developed in *iTask* appear as a web service to the rest of the world and the *iTask* clients that connect with your application. Figure 4 shows how *iTask* applications fit in the Internet habitat. An *iTask* application acts as a

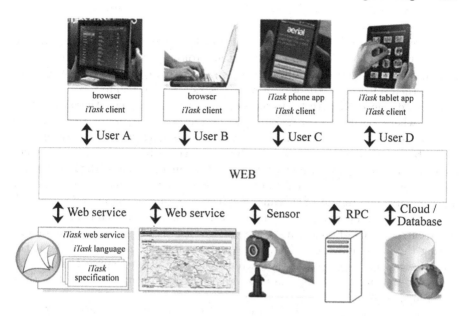

Fig. 4. *iTask* applications are Internet species

web service that can be used by other Internet applications. Users connect with the application via a standard web browser on a personal computer, or an app on a smart phone or tablet.

2 TOP Programming with iTasks

In this section we briefly explain how tasks and their signatures are denoted (Sect. 2.1), and how to set up the code examples in the *iTask* system (Sect. 2.2). The syntax of the host language *Clean* is very similar to *Haskell*. In Appendix A we give a brief overview of some *Clean* specific parts that we use in these lecture notes. Both the *Clean* programming environment and the *iTask* toolkit can be obtained at wiki.clean.cs.ru.nl.

2.1 Task Signatures

A task has two components: a description of the *work* that has to be performed, and the typed interface that determines the *type* of the task values that are communicated to the environment in which the work is performed.

Tasks abstract from activities within software systems, regardless whether these are executed by computer systems or humans, how long they will take, and what resources are consumed. For instance, a task can describe the job to interview a particular person without predetermining whether this must be done with a human interviewer or via an online questionnaire. As another example, a task can describe the job that pieces of music must be played without predetermining whether a user starts to play guitar or let some music player application randomly pick and play a digitized music file from a play list. Work abstraction is a good thing, because it allows the context in which tasks operate not to trouble themselves with the way in which tasks are implemented.

Tasks do need to have up-to-date knowledge about each other's progress. This is where the type of a task enters the picture. Commonly, tasks process information, and often the environment would like to know what the current state is of a task. Other tasks can see how things are going by inspecting the current value of a task which may change over time. The current value of the information that is processed by a task is called its *task value*. The task value may change over time, but its type remains the same. For instance, during the interviewing task above, the task value might be the notes that are made by the human interviewer or the current state of the online questionnaire that is filled in by the interviewee. During the music playing task, the task value might be information about the current song that is played or the current recording of the digitized music that is played. In both examples, the task values change during the task, but their type remains constant.

Tasks are typed in the following way: if the type of the task value is T, then the corresponding task has type (Task T). So, a task with name t and task value type T has signature t :: Task T (see signatures, page 240).

To describe what a task is about you need additional information. In these lecture notes we describe this in a functional style. A task is represented by a function which obtains the additional information via the function arguments. If we require n arguments of consecutive types $A_1 \ldots A_n$ to describe a named task t of type (Task T), then this is specified by a *task function* with signature t :: $A_1 \ldots A_n$ -> Task T. Note that if $n = 0$, then t is the constant function that defines a task right away. Such a function has signature t :: Task T.

To give you a feeling how to read and write signatures of tasks, we show a few examples.

- A user who is writing a piece of text is performing a task with a task value that reflects the current content of that text. Let's name this task write_text. The text content can be modeled in different ways. As an example, you can choose a basic string representation, or a structure representation of the text that includes mark-up information, or a *pdf* document that tells exactly how the document should be rendered. Let us defer the decision how to represent the text exactly, and introduce some opaque type Text. We can define the signature of the task to write a piece of text as follows:

```
write_text :: Task Text
```

Observe that this task requires no further arguments.

- A task to interview a certain person, identified by a value of type User, may result in a Questionnaire document. Let's name this task interview. If we ignore the details of the user identification and questionnaire, then the signature of this task is:

```
interview :: User -> Task Questionnaire
```

This is an example of a task function with one argument, `User`.

– A computer that sorts a list of data is performing a computational task that ultimately returns a list with the sorted data. Let us name this task `sort_data`. This task requires as argument the list of data that must be sorted. For sorting, it suffices to know that the list elements possess an ordering relation, so this task should work for any element type, indicated with a type *variable* `a`, provided that an instance of the type class `Ord` for `a` is present. The signature of the sorting task function is specified by (see overloading, page 240):

```
sort_data :: [a] -> Task [a] | Ord, iTask a
```

In a signature, the occurring type class restrictions are enumerated after the `|` separator. The type of the task value must always be an instance of the `iTask` type class. For this reason, the type class restriction `iTask` is also included for values of type `a`.

– Assume that the task would be to start some given task argument at a given point in time. Hence, when performing such a task one first needs to wait until the given moment in time has passed, and then perform the given task argument. Let us name this task `wait_to_do`.

```
wait_to_do :: Time (Task a) -> Task a | iTask a
```

`Time` is a data type that models clock time. Note that `wait_to_do` is an example of a *higher-order* task function. A higher-order task function is a task function that has at least one argument that is itself a task(function).

These examples illustrate that the functional style of programming carries over to tasks in a natural way.

2.2   Modules and Kick-Start Wrapper Functions

We set up an infrastructure for the TOP examples that are presented in these lecture notes.

The host language *Clean* is a modular language. Modules collect task definitions, data types, and functions that are logically related (see modules, page 235).

We have assembled a couple of *kickstart* wrapper functions and put them in the module `TOPKickstart` that can be imported by a TOP main module. The kickstart wrapper functions are enumerated in Fig. 5. The `one–` wrapper functions are intended for a single user and the `multi–` wrapper functions assume the existence of a set of registered users. The `–App` wrapper functions support a single application only and the `–Apps` wrapper functions provide infrastructure to manage several applications.

The corresponding `TopKickstart.dcl` module is given in Fig. 6. Note that line 2 makes the entire iTasks *api* available to your TOP programs if you import `TopKickstart` yourself. The signatures of the four kickstart wrapper functions

	one user	multi-user
single application	oneTOPApp	multiTOPApp
multiple applications	oneTOPApps	multiTOPApps

Fig. 5. The four possible kickstart wrapper functions for *iTask* examples.

```
definition module TOPKickstart                                      1
import iTasks                                                       2
                                                                   3
oneTOPApp    :: (Task a)     !*World -> *World | iTask a           4
multiTOPApp  :: (Task a)     !*World -> *World | iTask a           5
oneTOPApps   :: [BoxedTask]  !*World -> *World                     6
multiTOPApps :: [BoxedTask]  !*World -> *World                     7
                                                                   8
:: BoxedTask = E.a: BoxedTask String String (Task a) & iTask a    9
```

Fig. 6. The kickstart module with four wrapper functions.

are given at lines 4–7. The –App wrapper functions expect a single task definition as argument. The type of this task, (Task a), can be anything provided that it is an instance of the iTask type class. The –Apps wrapper functions are provided with arbitrarily many tasks. In order to properly model the fact that these tasks need not have to have identical types, these are encapsulated within the BoxedTask type. An explanation of this type can be found in Example 2 (see algebraic types, page 241).

When developing an application in these notes, we always tell which type of applications of Fig. 5 we are creating, and thus which kickstart wrapper function of Fig. 6 is required.

3   User Interaction

Having warmed up, we start our introduction on TOP with the means to interact with the user. The *type-indexed programming* foundation of TOP plays a crucial role. The information that must be displayed or received is *modeled* using the rich type language of *Clean*. The proper interactive tasks are created by *instantiating* the existing type-indexed task functions.

3.1   Displaying Information to the User

Many text books on programming languages start with a *"Hello, world"* program, a tradition initiated in the well known C programming book by Kernighan and Ritchie [1]. We follow this tradition.

EXAMPLE 1. *'Hello, world' as single application for a single user*
We create a main module with the name `MyHelloWorldApp`:

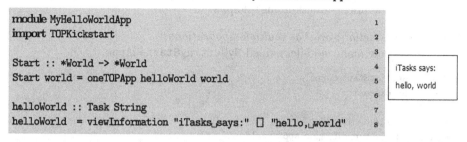

```
module MyHelloWorldApp                                              1
import TOPKickstart                                                 2
                                                                   3
Start :: *World -> *World                                          4
Start world = oneTOPApp helloWorld world                           5
                                                                   6
helloWorld :: Task String                                          7
helloWorld = viewInformation "iTasks_says:" [] "hello,_world"      8
```

iTasks says:
hello, world

Just like its host language *Clean*, for an *iTask* program the main entry point is the `Start` function. Tasks, no matter how small, change the world. This is reflected in the type of the `Start` function (line 4). We use the `oneTOPApp` kickstart wrapper function (line 5) to create a single TOP application for a single user. The single TOP application is the task named `helloWorld`. The sole purpose of this task is to display the text `"hello,_world"`. Because that is a value of type `String`, the type of the `helloWorld` task is `Task String` (line 7). At execution, an output similar to the one displayed to the right of the program should be produced (see side-effects, page 239).

The `hello, world` text in Example 1 is displayed with the task function `viewInformation`. Its signature is:

```
viewInformation :: d [ViewOption m] m -> Task m | descr d & iTask m
```

It is an overloaded function due to the type class restrictions (`| descr d & iTask m`). This task function has three arguments:

- The first argument has type `d` and is a descriptor to inform the user what she is looking at. The `descr` type class supports several data types as instances, of which in this section we use only two: the basic type `String` and the *iTask* type `Title`, which is defined as:

  ```
  :: Title = Title String
  ```

  In both cases, a (typically short) text is displayed to give guidance to the user. They only differ in the way they are rendered. In case of a `String` value, the text is presented along the task rendering. In case of a `Title` value, the text is displayed more prominently in a small title bar above the task rendering.
- The second argument has type `[ViewOption m]` and can be used to fine-tune the visualization of the information. However, that does not concern us right now, so we use an empty list, denoted by `[ ]`.
- The third argument has type `m` and is the value that must be displayed. The `iTask` type class implements the type-indexed generation of tasks from types. Of course, this is only possible if the concrete type on which you apply this function is (made) available. How this is done, is explained in Sect. 3.3. For now you can assume that you can provide `viewInformation` with values of almost any conceivable data type.

Up until Sect. 6 we develop a number of very small tasks (in Sect. 6 we introduce multi-user applications). It is convenient to collect the small tasks using the kick start wrapper function oneTOPApps.

EXAMPLE 2. *'Hello, world' as multiple applications*
We create a new main module, named MyGettingStartedApps.

```
module MyGettingStartedApps                                          1
import TOPKickstart                                                  2
                                                                    3
Start :: *World -> *World                                           4
Start world    = oneTOPApps apps world                              5
                                                                    6
apps           = [ BoxedTask (get_started +++ "Hello world")        7
                             "Hello, world in TOP"                   8
                             helloWorld                              9
                   ]                                                10
where                                                              11
    top        = "TOP/"                                            12
    get_started = top +++ "Getting Started/"                       13
                                                                   14
helloWorld :: Task String                                          15
helloWorld = viewInformation "iTasks says:" [] "hello, world"      16
```

Within any (task) function definition, local definitions can be introduced after the keyword where. The scope of these definitions extends to the entire right hand side of the function body (apps in this example). Here, this facility is used to prepare for future extensions of this example, in which the text fragments top and get_started are shared.

We use the single user, multiple application kickstart wrapper function oneTOPApps, and provide it with only one boxed task, helloWorld, in lines 7–10. Figure 7 shows how this application is rendered within a browser. The first argument of this boxed task, the text "TOP/Getting Started/Hello world", is used to generate the task hierarchy that is depicted in the left-top area **1** in Fig. 7 (the function +++ concatenates its two String arguments). The second argument, the text "Hello, world in TOP", is depicted in the description area at the left bottom **2** when the task is selected by the user. If it is started, then it appears in the task list of the user which is the right top area **3**. In order to actually work on it, it can be opened, in which case its current state is rendered in the right bottom work area **4**. In the work area it can be closed and reopened at any later time without harm. Deleting it in the task list area removes it permanently.

3.2   Getting Information from the User

The viewInformation task function displays information to the user. The dual task is getting information from the user. This task is called updateInformation.

Fig. 7. 'Hello, world' as one task in a multi-application context.

```
updateInformation :: d [UpdateOption m m] m -> Task m | descr d & iTask m
```

The first argument of this function has exactly the same purpose as the first argument of `viewInformation` and informs the user what she is supposed to do. The second argument is used for fine-tuning purposes, and we ignore it for the time being, and use the empty list [ ]. The third argument is the initial value that is rendered to the user in such a way that she can alter its content.

EXAMPLE 3. *What's your name?*
We extend Example 2 with a task to ask for a user's name.

```
module MyGettingStartedApps                                    1
import TOPKickstart                                            2
                                                              3
Start :: *World -> *World                                     4
Start world    = oneTOPApps apps world                        5
                                                              6
apps           = [ BoxedTask (get_started +++ "Hello world")  7
                            "Hello, world in TOP"             8
                            helloWorld                         9
                 , BoxedTask (get_started +++ "Your name?")   10
                            "Please give your name"           11
                            giveName                           12
                 ]                                             13
where                                                         14
   top        = "TOP/"                                        15
   get_started = top +++ "Getting Started/"                   16
                                                              17
helloWorld :: Task String                                     18
helloWorld = viewInformation "iTasks says:" [] "hello, world" 19
```

```
                                                                              20
giveName :: Task String                                                       21
giveName = updateInformation "iTasks_asks:" [] "Dr._Livingstone?"             22
```

The only modifications are lines 10–12 in which a new boxed task is included in the apps list, and lines 21–22 in which the new task giveName is defined. Figure 8 shows where the new boxed task can be selected by the user in the task hierarchy, and how the giveName task is rendered in the work area.

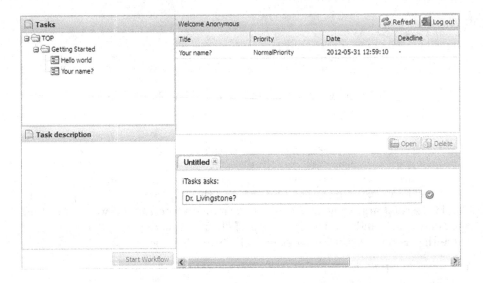

Fig. 8. Two tasks in a multi-application context.

Example 3 shows how to add a (boxed) task to the multi-application infrastructure that is created by the wrapper kickstart function oneTOPApps. In the remainder of these notes we restrict ourselves to discussing only the task functions that are added as boxed tasks.

3.3   Working with Data Models

Rendering and updating information by means of the functions viewInformation and updateInformation tasks works for the primitive types (booleans, integers, reals, characters, strings). Although this is useful, it is not very exciting either. Fortunately, the rendering mechanism also works for any custom defined type. The point of type-indexed programming is to encourage you to think in terms of data models and use generic functions instead of re-implementing similar tasks over and over again.

EXAMPLE 4. *Editing music tracks*

Suppose we own a collection of legally acquired digitized music and want to keep track of them in. For each piece of music we store the music storage medium (for instance *cd, dvd, blue ray*), the name of the album, name of performing artist, year of appearance, track number on album, track title, track duration, and tags. One way to model this is with the following types:

```
:: Track     = { medium :: Medium                                          1
             , album  :: Name                                              2
             , artist :: Name                                              3
             , year   :: Year                                              4
             , track  :: TrackNr                                           5
             , title  :: Name                                              6
             , time   :: Time                                              7
             , tags   :: [Tag]                                             8
             }                                                             9
:: Medium    = BlueRay | DVD | CD | MP3 | Cassette | LP | Single | Other String 10
:: Name      :== String                                                  11
:: Year      :== Int                                                     12
:: TrackNr   :== Int                                                     13
:: Tag       :== String                                                 14
```

In this definition, Track and Medium are *new* types. Track is a *record* type, which is a collection of *field names* (medium, album, and so on) that have types themselves (Medium, Name, and so on) (see record types, page 242). Medium is an example of an algebraic type which enumerates alternative data constructors (BlueRay, DVD, ..., Other) that may be parameterized (Other is parameterized with a String) (see algebraic types, page 241). Name, Year, TrackNr, and Tag merely introduces a *synonym type name* for another type (see synonym types, page 243). Although the type Time (line 7) is not a primitive type in the host language, it happens to be predefined in the *iTask* toolkit. Just like Track, it is a record type:

```
:: Time = { hour :: Int
         , min  :: Int
         , sec  :: Int
         }
```

but unlike Track, its rendering differs from the default scheme that the toolkit provides you with.

When defining a record value you need to enumerate each and every record field and provide it with a value. The order of record fields is irrelevant. Record fields are separated by a comma, and the entire enumeration is delimited by { and }. Similarly, when defining a list value you enumerate each and every element, separated by a comma and delimited by [and]. As an example, we define a value of type Track:

```
track = { medium = CD
        , album  = "Professor␣Satchafunkilus␣and␣the␣musterion␣of␣rock"
```

```
      , artist = "Joe Satriani"
      , year   = 2008
      , track  = 4
      , title  = "Professor Satchafunkilus"
      , time   = {hour=0, min=4, sec=47}
      , tags   = ["metal", "guitar", "rock", "instrumental", "guitar hero"]
      }
```

In order to make the TOP infrastructure available for a custom type t requires the declaration derive class iTask t in the specification. In our example, this concerns the new types Track and Medium:

```
derive class iTask Track, Medium
```

With the derived generic machinery available, Track values can be displayed in exactly the same way as done earlier with String values:

```
viewTrack :: Track -> Task Track
viewTrack x = viewInformation (Title "iTasks says:") [] x
```

The viewTrack task function displays any track value that it is provided with. We can add (viewTrack track) to the list of boxed tasks in Example 2. Selecting this task gives the output as displayed in Fig. 9. The type-indexed algorithm recursively analyzes the structure of the value, guided by its type, and transforms the found components of its argument value into displays of those values and assembles them into one large form displaying the entire record value. Observe how the structure of the record type Track and the structure of the algebraic type Medium is rendered by the generic algorithm. Because viewInformation is a task that only displays its argument value, but does not alter it, the task value of (viewTrack track) is continuously the value track.

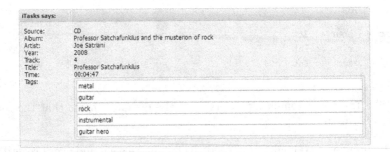

Fig. 9. The generated view of an example track.

The same principle of recursively analyzing the structure of a value is applied by updateInformation. In order to demonstrate this, we define this task function:

```
editTrack :: Track -> Task Track
editTrack x = updateInformation (Title "iTasks_says:") [] x
```

and add (editTrack track) to the collection of boxed tasks. The output is quite a different interactive element, as witnessed by Fig. 10. Instead of generating displays of component values, the algorithm now transforms them into interactive elements that can be viewed and edited by the user. The data constructors of the algebraic data type Medium can be selected with a menu, text entries are rendered as text input fields, numbers appear with increment and decrement facilities, and list elements can be edited, moved around in the list, deleted, and new list elements can be added. Initially, the task value of this editor task is track. With each user interaction, the task value is altered according to the input. It should be noted that the generated interactive elements are *type-safe*. An end-user can only type in values of appropriate type. For instance, entering the text "four" in the track field is rejected. In most cases it is not possible to enter illegal values. In other cases, illegal input is rejected, and replaced by the previous (legal) value.

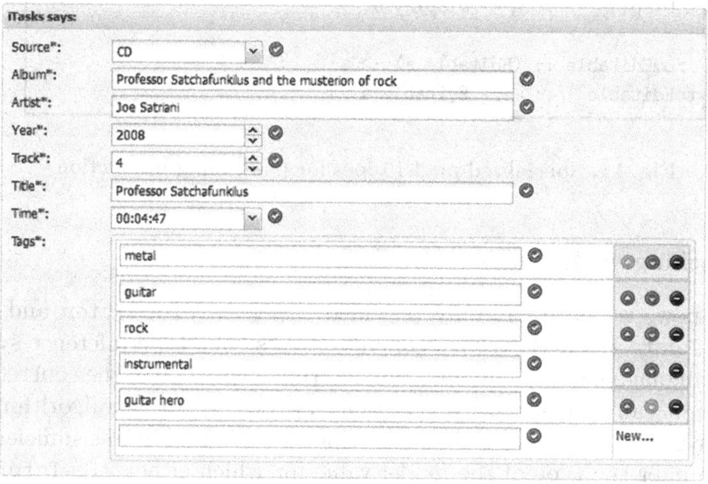

Fig. 10. The generated editor of an example track.

3.4 Working with Specialization

As mentioned in Example 4, the type Time is predefined in the *iTask* toolkit. Figures 9 and 10 illustrate that definitions have been provided to instruct the generic algorithm how to display and edit values of this type in a way that is *different from the default generic case*. This mechanism is called *specialization* and plays a significant role in the generic machinery that underlies task oriented programming because it allows to deviate from the general behavior.

There are many examples to be found within the *iTask* toolkit of specialized data model types. We do not wish to enumerate them all. For now we turn our attention to two dual types, `Display` and `Editable` (Fig. 11), that interact nicely with the `viewInformation` and `updateInformation` tasks. If x is a model value of type t, then (`Display` x) is a model value of type (`Display` t) but it is rendered as a *display* of value x (hence, a user cannot alter its content). Basically, this is the same rendering as is normally provided by `viewInformation`. If x is a model value of type t, then (`Editable` x) is a model value of type (`Editable` t) but it is rendered as an *editor* of value x (hence, a user can alter its content). Basically, this is the same rendering as is normally provided by `updateInformation`. Using these values within data models allows one to specify very precisely what subcomponents can only be viewed by the user, and what subcomponents can be edited.

```
:: Display  a = Display  a
:: Editable a = Editable a

fromDisplay  :: (Display a) -> a
toDisplay    :: a -> Display a

fromEditable :: (Editable a) -> a
toEditable   :: a -> Editable a
```

Fig. 11. Specialized model types for fine-tuning interaction.

3.5   Working with Types

Up until now, we have carefully provided the `viewInformation` and `update Information` task functions with concrete values. The type inference system of the host language *Clean* commonly can determine the type of the concrete value, and hence, it can be decided what instance of the type-driven algorithm should be used or generated. Commonly, a description of a task obtains sufficient information to infer the type of the model value for which either `viewInformation` or `updateInformation` need to be called.

Sometimes this is not possible, and one has to explicitly has to define the wanted type in the context such that the compiler can deduce the types for the tasks involved. Given a type, the proper instance can be determined. This is very useful in situations where it is not possible to conjure up a meaningful value of the desired type. In the case of interactive tasks, one sometimes does not want to specify an initial value but instead want to resort to a *blank* editor for values of that type, and let the user enter the proper information. This can be done with the following variant of `updateInformation` that omits the value to be altered:

```
enterInformation :: d [EnterOption m] -> Task m | descr d & iTask m
```

Just like before, the first argument is the descriptor to tell the user what is expected of her, and again we ignore the list of rendering options. The signature of this task function is actually quite odd: the `enterInformation` task function can generate a user-interface to produce a value of type m. This can only be done if it can be statically determined what concrete type m has. In this situation it becomes paramount to specify the type of the task value that is processed.

Earlier on, we used (`editTrack track`) to create an interactive task with the specific initial value `track` to allow users to alter this value. Alternatively, and more sensibly, we can specify the following interactive task:

```
inventTrack :: Task Track
inventTrack = enterInformation (Title "Invent␣a␣track") []
```

The generic algorithm, using the type information that a `Track` value needs to be analyzed, generates a blank interactive component (Fig. 12).

Fig. 12. The generated editor of a blank track.

The generic algorithm knows how to deal with lists, as is witnessed by creating views for *list-of-tags* in the examples. In exactly the same spirit, we can create viewers, editors, and inventors for *list-of-tracks* almost effortlessly:

```
viewTracks :: [Track] -> Task [Track]
viewTracks xs = viewInformation (Title "View␣Tracks") [] xs

editTracks :: [Track] -> Task [Track]
editTracks xs = updateInformation (Title "Edit␣Tracks") [] xs

inventTracks :: Task [Track]
inventTracks = enterInformation (Title "Invent␣Tracks") []
```

The only thing that has changed is that the function signatures mention `[Track]` instead of `Track`. More interestingly, in case of `inventTracks`, the specified type dictates that an interactive element must be generated that handles a list of track values.

EXERCISE 1. *"Hello, world"*
Compile and run Example 1. Experiment with type class instances of the `descr`
type class other than `String` and `Title`. Recompile and run to see the effect.

EXERCISE 2. *"Hello, worlds"*
Compile and run Example 2. Experiment with the arguments of the `BoxedTask`
container by adding a few other tasks that display messages.

EXERCISE 3. *Entering text*
Add the following task to the collection of tasks of Example 2:

```
helloWorld2 :: Task String
helloWorld2 = updateInformation"iTasks_says:" [] "hello,_world"
```

Recompile and run to see what the effect is.

EXERCISE 4. *Your favorite collection*
Design a data model for your favorite collection (for instance books, movies,
friends, recipes) in a similar way as done in Example 4. Check what it looks like
using `viewInformation`, `updateInformation`, and `enterInformation`.

EXERCISE 5. *Editing your favorite collection*
Create tasks to view and edit your favorite collection in the same way as explained
on page 203 for collections of `Task` values with the functions `viewTracks`, `edit`
`Tracks`, and `inventTracks`. Recompile and run to see the effect.   □

4   Composition

In the previous section we have shown how a program exchanges information
with the user using interactive tasks. The information is put away in the corresponding task value. Other tasks may need that information to proceed correctly.
In TOP the composition of tasks is specified by means of task combinators. Combinators are functions that define how its argument tasks are combined into a
new task. For reasons of readability, they are often specified as operators to allow
an infix style of writing in the way we are used to when dealing with arithmetic
expressions such as +, -, *, and /. In this section we introduce combinators
for sequential and parallel composition, and show that this can be combined
seamlessly with host language features such as choice and recursion.

4.1   Basic Tasks

The interactive task functions to view, update and enter information that are
presented in Sect. 3 (`viewInformation`, `updateInformation`, and `enter`
`Information`) are all examples of *basic tasks*. A task(function) is *basic* if it
cannot be dissected into other task(function)s. An example of a non-interactive
basic task is the `return` task function (see strictness, page 244):

```
return :: !a -> Task a | iTask a
```

The sole purpose of (return e) is to evaluate expression e to a value x and stick to that value. It is a task which task value is always x. Despite its apparent simplistic form, the return task function is actually quite powerful: it allows one to introduce arbitrary computations in e to calculate a value for further processing.

EXAMPLE 5. *Sort track tags*
We can use return to define a task that makes sure that the tag list of a track is sorted (see record updates, page 243):

```
sortTagsOfTrack :: Track -> Task Track
sortTagsOfTrack x = return {x & tags = sort x.tags}
```

The function sort :: [a] -> [a] | Ord a is a library function of the host language that sorts a list of values, provided that the ordering operator < (which is part of the Ord type class) is available for the element types. For tags, which are of primitive type String, the ordering operator has been defined.

4.2   Sequential Composition

Naïve sequential composition of tasks simply puts them in succession (see operators, page 236):

```
(>>|) infixl 1 :: (Task a) (Task b) -> Task b | iTask a & iTask b
```

The combinator >>|, pronounced as *then*, is defined as a left-associative (infixl) operator of very low priority (1). In (ta >>| tb), first task ta is evaluated. As soon as it is finished, evaluation proceeds with task tb. The types of the task values of ta and tb need not be identical. In addition, the type of the task value of the composite task is the same as tb's task value type. Indeed, the task value of the composite task is the task value of tb.

As an example, we first ask the user to provide her name, and then greet her:

```
greet :: Task String
greet =   giveName
      >>| helloWorld
```

We adopt the notational convention to write down the task function names below each other, as well as the task combinator functions.

The greet task is unsatisfactory, as it does bother the user to enter her name, but does not use that input to greet her properly. If we inspect the type of the naïve task combinator >>|, then we can tell that it is impossible for the second task argument to have access to the result value of the first task argument.

In most cases, follow-up tasks depend on task values produced by preceding tasks. If we express this dependency by means of a function, we obtain a non-naïve sequential combinator function, >>=, which is pronounced as *bind*.

```
(>>=) infixl 1 :: (Task a) (a -> Task b) -> Task b | iTask a & iTask b
```

In (ta >>= tb), first task ta is evaluated. As soon as it is finished, its task value, x say, is applied to the second argument of bind, *which is now a task function instead of a simple task*, thus resulting in the computation (tb x). The computation can use this value to decide what to do next, which is expressed by means of a task expression of type (Task b). We can now create an improved version of the greet task (see lambda-abstractions, page 239):

```
greet :: Task String
greet =             giveName
       >>= \name -> viewInformation "iTask_says:" [] ("Hello,_" +++ name)
```

We extend the notational convention by putting also the task value names below each other, in the *lambda*-abstraction after the >>= task combinator. The example shows that the second argument of the bind combinator is a (very simple) computation that prefixes the String value "Hello,_" to the given input of the user of the first task.

EXAMPLE 6. *Binding two tasks*
We bind editTrack and viewTrack and obtain a task that first allows the user to edit a track value, and when she confirms she is ready, displays the edited value.

```
editTask2 :: Track -> Task Track
editTask2 x =              editTrack x
             >>= \new -> viewTrack new
```

Note that the editTask2 task function can also be written down slightly shorter because viewTrack is already a task function of a type that matches with the second argument of >>=:

```
// Alternative definition of editTask2:
editTask2 :: Track -> Task Track
editTask2 x =   editTrack x
             >>= viewTrack
```

The bind combinator >>= profits optimally of the fact that its second argument is a function that is applied to the information that is transferred from the first argument task to whatever task is computed by the function. This has the following advantages: (*a*) the information is available to all tasks that are created, and (*b*) we can compute what follow-up tasks to create, using the information and the full expressive power of the host language. We illustrate this with a number of examples.

EXAMPLE 7. *Availability of information*
Here is an alternative way of entering a track, by entering the fields in succession.

```
enterTrack :: Task Track                                        1
enterTrack                                                      2
```

```
    =                    enterInformation "Select medium:" []        3
    >>= \medium -> enterInformation "Enter album:"   []             4
    >>= \album  -> enterInformation "Enter artist:"  []             5
    >>= \artist -> enterInformation "Enter year:"    []             6
    >>= \year   -> enterInformation "Enter track:"   []             7
    >>= \track  -> enterInformation "Enter title:"   []             8
    >>= \title  -> enterInformation "Enter time:"    []             9
    >>= \time   -> enterInformation "Enter tags:"    []            10
    >>= \tags   -> return                                          11
                  (newTrack medium album artist year track title time tags)   12
                                                                    13
newTrack :: Medium Name Name Year TrackNr Name Time [Tag] -> Track  14
newTrack medium album artist year track title time tags            15
    = { medium = medium, album = album, artist = artist, year = year   16
      , track = track, title = title, time = time, tags = tags}    17
```

This example demonstrates two important aspects:

– the individual task values (medium, album, ...) that are retrieved during the execution can be used later in the sequence of tasks;
– the type-indexed character of the enterInformation task function is driven by the type of the newTrack function, which in turn is enforced by the type model of the Track record fields. In the first call of enterInformation it must yield a task value of type Medium, in the calls on lines 4, 5, and 8 the task value has type String, in the calls on lines 6 and 7 it is an Int, in line 9 it results in a Time task value, and finally, in line 10 it creates a task value of type [String].

EXAMPLE 8. *Dependency of information*
In Example 7 the user can enter any number for the year field. It is much nicer to check for the earliest possible year depending on the value of the medium field of the track that is about to be entered. Suppose that we know of each music storage medium (except, of course, the Other case) when the first commercially available products were approximately available (see pattern matching, page 237):

```
firstYearPossible :: Medium -> Year
firstYearPossible BlueRay       = 2006
firstYearPossible DVD           = 1996
firstYearPossible MP3           = 1993
firstYearPossible CD            = 1981
firstYearPossible Musicassette = 1964
firstYearPossible Single        = 1949
firstYearPossible LP            = 1948
firstYearPossible other         = 0
```

Using this information, we construct a task that repeatedly asks the user to enter correct year values. The repetition is expressed recursively. Any entered value that appears earlier than deemed possible on that particular music storage medium is rejected.

```
enterYear :: Medium -> Task Year                                            1
enterYear medium                                                            2
    =            updateInformation "Enter_year:" [] first                   3
    >>= \year -> if (year >= first)                                         4
                    (return year)                                           5
                    (    viewInformation "Incorrect_year:" []               6
                            ( medium +++> "s_were_not_available_before_" +++ 7
                                year  +++> "._Please_enter_another_year."   8
                            )                                               9
                        >>| enterYear medium                                10
                    )                                                       11
    where first = firstYearPossible medium                                  12
```

The predefined operator +++> (line 7 and 8) converts its first argument to a
String value and concatenates it with the second argument. A similar operator
<+++ is available in which the arguments are flipped. They can be used for any
type of argument for which the generic iTask system has been generated. Also
note the use of the naïve then combinator >>| on line 10: the task value of the
messaging task is not relevant for asking the user again.

4.3   Intermezzo: Task Values

Now that we are getting in the business of composing tasks, we need to be
more precise about tasks and task values. During execution, task values can
change. A task can have no task value, e.g. which is initially the case for every
enterInformation task function. A task value can be stable, e.g. which is the
case with the return task. A task value may be unstable and varies over time, e.g.
when the end-user changes information in response to an updateInformation
function. It is entirely well possible that further processing of an unstable value
eliminates the task value, for instance, when the end-user creates blank fields
within the updateInformation task. Stable values, however, remain stable. The
diagram below displays these possible transitions of task values.

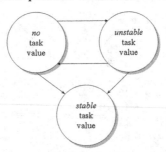

Precisely these task values are available by means of the following two algebraic data types:

```
:: TaskValue a = NoValue  | Value a Stability
:: Stability   = Unstable | Stable
```

Task combinator functions can inspect these task values and decide how they influence the composite behavior of tasks. This is also done by the >>| and >>= combinators. Both task combinator functions inspect the 'stability' of their first task argument's task value during execution. As soon as that task produces a *stable* task value, the combinators make sure that the second task argument gets executed. If the first argument task has an unstable task value, then it is left to the user of the application to decide whether she is happy with that value. Hence, infrastructure is created to allow her to confirm that the current, unstable, value is fine to proceed with.

4.4   Parallel Composition

Alongside sequential composition is *parallel composition*, with which you express that tasks are available at the same time. We discuss two parallel task combinator functions that are often very useful. Because of their resemblance with the logical operators && and ||, their names are written as -&&- and -||- (pronounce as *and*, *or* respectively). Their signatures are:

```
(-&&-) infixr 4 :: (Task a) (Task b) -> Task (a, b) | iTask a & iTask b
(-||-) infixr 3 :: (Task a) (Task a) -> Task  a      | iTask a
```

The purpose of -&&- is to execute its argument tasks in parallel and assemble their individual task values into a pair. The types of the task values need not be of the same type, but this is of course allowed. The composite task only has a stable task value if both argument tasks have a stable task value. If either one of the argument tasks has no task value, then the composite task also does not possess one. In the other cases, the composite task has an unstable task value.

The purpose of -||- is to offer the user two alternative ways to produce a task value. For this reason, the types of its task arguments must be identical. The only situation in which the composite task does not have a task value is when both argument tasks have no task value. In any other case, the task value of the composite task is the task value of *the most recently changed* or *stable* task value.

EXAMPLE 9. *Entering an album with 'and'*
Entering tracks individually is fine for albums with a small number of tracks, or for single purchases, but it is an inconvenient way of entering albums that have more than four tracks. We wish to enter the album information (with a task called enterAlbumInfo) separately from entering the track list (with a task called enterTracklist). We define the composite task enterAlbum that performs these tasks in parallel and combines their result with the pure computation newAlbum:

```
enterAlbum :: Task [Track]
enterAlbum
    =                       enterAlbumInfo -&&- enterTracklist
    >>= \(info, tracks) -> return (newAlbum info tracks)
```

The distinct task value results of `enterAlbumInfo` and `enterTracklist` are called `info` and `tracks` respectively. The function `newAlbum` is a pure computation that creates a list of `Track` values (see list comprehensions, page 238):

```
newAlbum :: (Medium, Name, Name, Year) [(Name, Time, [Tag])] -> [Track]
newAlbum (medium, album, artist, year) tracks
    = [ newTrack medium album artist year nr song t tags
      \\ (song, t, tags) <- tracks & nr <- [1.]
      ]
```

The two tasks to enter the album information and the track list can proceed as described earlier. We choose sequential input for the album information, to allow the input of year values to be checked against the chosen medium value. The track list is entered as a list of track fields.

```
enterAlbumInfo :: Task (Medium, Name, Name, Year)
enterAlbumInfo
    =             enterInformation "Select medium:" []
    >>= \medium -> enterInformation "Enter album:"  []
    >>= \album  -> enterInformation "Enter artist:" []
    >>= \artist -> enterYear medium
    >>= \year   -> return (medium, album, artist, year)

enterTracklist :: Task [(Name, Time, [Tag])]
enterTracklist
    = enterInformation "Enter tracks:" []
```

EXERCISE 6. *Edit and view a track*
Add (`editTask2 track`) of Example 6 to your collection of top level tasks and compile and run your extended application. Manipulate the fields in the `editTrack` task and see when the bind combinator `>>=` allows you to enter the `viewTrack` task and when it prohibits you from doing that.

EXERCISE 7. *Edit and sort track tags*
Alter the `editTask2` task in such a way that before viewing the new track, the task first sorts the tag list of the new track using `sortTagsOfTrack` of Example 5. Hence, after editing a track, the user always sees a tag list in alphabetic order.

EXERCISE 8. *Edit and view a track list*
Create a recursive task of signature `enterTracks :: [Track] -> Task [Track]` that allows the user to enter tracks in succession. It displays the argument list of tracks, and appends new tracks to this list until the user decides that the list is complete. In that case, the accumulated track list is returned.

EXERCISE 9. *Compare 'and' with 'or'*
Add the tasks `and` and `or` to your collection of top level tasks.

```
and =           updateInformation "A:" [] 42
         -&&- updateInformation "B:" [] 58
    >>= \x -> viewInformation   "C:" [] x

or  =           updateInformation "A:" [] 42
         -||- updateInformation "B:" [] 58
    >>= \x -> viewInformation   "C:" [] x
```

Compile and run your extended application. Explain the difference in behavior and return values.

5   Environment Interaction

In the previous section we have shown a number of ways to compose tasks. With these forms of composition communication between co-tasks is organized in a structured way. However, programs sometimes exhibit ad hoc communication patterns. This is often the case when interacting with the 'external world' and external tools need to be called, or persistent information is shared using the file system or databases.

In TOP, ad hoc communication between internal tasks and the external world is provided by means of *shared data sources*. A shared data source contains information which can be shared between different tasks or with the outside world, and can be read and written via a typed, abstract interface. *Shared data sources abstract over the way their content is accessed* in an analogous manner that tasks abstract over the way work is performed. We depict this in the following way:

The content $\square$ of a shared data source can be (part of) the file system, a shared memory, a clock, a random stream, and so on. A shared data source can be read from via a typed interface $\triangle$ and written to via another typed interface $\triangledown$. The read and write data types need not be the same. For instance, if the shared data source is a stopwatch, then the write type can represent stopwatch actions such as resetting, pausing, continuing, and so on, whereas its read type can represent elapsed time.

We explain how to get access to external resources in Sect. 5.1, and how to create local shared data sources in Sect. 5.2. Interactive tasks turn out to interact seamlessly with shared data sources. We integrate them in Sect. 5.3. Finally, we discuss two subjects that are concerned with the environment: basic file handling in Sect. 5.4 and basic time handling in Sect. 5.5.

5.1   Basic Environment Interaction

In this section we introduce the basic means to interact with external resources. We start with an example.

EXAMPLE 10. *Limiting year input values*

Time is an obvious external resource. Let us enhance the `enterYear` task of Example 8 (page 207) to also disallow inputs that exceed the current year. To obtain the current date we use the expression (`get currentDate`), which is a task of type (`Task Date`). `Date` is a predefined type:

```
:: Date = { day  :: Int // 1..31
          , mon  :: Int // 1..12
          , year :: Int }
```

We adopt the `enterYear` task to obtain the current date and use it to compare it with the user's input (see disambiguating records, page 242); (see guards, page 236):

```
enterYear :: Medium -> Task Year                                              1
enterYear medium                                                             2
    =            get currentDate                                            3
    >>= \today -> updateInformation "Enter year:" [] first                  4
    >>= \year  -> if (year >= first && year <= today.Date.year)            5
                    (return year)                                           6
                    (   viewInformation "Incorrect year:" []               7
                        (   message year +++ ". Please enter another year." )  8
                    >>| enterYear medium                                    9
                    )                                                      10
where                                                                      11
    first   = firstYearPossible medium                                     12
    message year                                                           13
    | year < first = medium +++> ("s were not available before" <+++ year)  14
    | otherwise    = "It is not yet" <+++ year                             15
```

In line 3 the current date is obtained from the environment. If the user input, provided in line 4, lies nicely between the two bounds, checked in line 5, then the input is returned. In the other case we provide the user with a matching message, defined by the function `message`, and start over again.

A shared data source that allows reading values of type r and writing values of type w is of type `ReadWriteShared r w`. For the time being, we consider this to be an opaque type with three access functions:

```
get    ::            (ReadWriteShared r w) -> Task r | iTask r
set    ::         w  (ReadWriteShared r w) -> Task w | iTask w
update :: (r->w) (ReadWriteShared r w) -> Task w | iTask r & iTask w
```

The `get` and `set` access functions are task functions that read and write the shared data source. A frequently occurring pattern is to `get` a value x from a shared data source and immediately `set` it to ($f\ x$). This can be shorthanded to (`update f`).

In Example 10, `currentDate` is a shared data source that allows reading values of type `Date`, but it does not allow writing. This is expressed by using the trivial `Void` type (`:: Void = Void`) for its write interface type. Hence, `currentDate` has type ReadWriteShared Date Void. For such *read only* shared data sources, a synonym type ReadOnlyShared, is introduced to express more clearly that you can only read values from such an entity. Analogously, for *write only* shared data source, the type synonym WriteOnlyShared is introduced. Finally, because often the read and write type interface is identical, the shorter type synonym Shared can be used.

```
:: Shared         rw  :== ReadWriteShared rw  rw
:: ReadOnlyShared  r  :== ReadWriteShared r Void
:: WriteOnlyShared w  :== ReadWriteShared Void w
```

The currentDate shared data source is an example of a globally available shared data source. One can imagine many such shared data sources, and in these lecture notes we encounter a few more. For now, we limit ourselves to three shared data sources that are concerned with time:

```
currentDate     :: ReadOnlyShared Date
currentTime     :: ReadOnlyShared Time
currentDateTime :: ReadOnlyShared DateTime

:: DateTime     = DateTime Date Time
```

Unsurprisingly, currentTime allows you to access the current time. currentDate Time is just a convenient way to get both the date and time in one go.

5.2 Ad Hoc Data Sharing

As explained above, the *iTask* toolkit provides you with a number of predefined shared data sources to 'connect' with the external world. You can also create shared data sources for internal purposes.

```
sharedStore :: !String !a -> Shared a | JSONEncode{|*|}, JSONDecode{|*|}, TC a
```

With (sharedStore e_n e_v), a shared data source is created which name is the result of evaluating e_n, and which initial content is the result of evaluating e_v. The details of the classes JSONEncode, JSONDecode, and TC do not concern us right now: basically, they are available whenever you include **derive class** iTask ... for your model data types. The shared data source that you create with this function can be accessed with the get, set, and update functions of page 212.

EXAMPLE 11. *A shared* Track *data source*
We define a shared data source that can be used to manipulate a Track value:

```
trackStore :: Shared Track
trackStore = sharedStore "StoreTrack" track
```

This creates a shared data source that is identified with the name "StoreTrack" and that has initial value track (page 199).

5.3   Interactive Tasks and Data Sharing

The interactive tasks `viewInformation` and `updateInformation` manipulate a model value. For your convenience, we repeat their signatures:

```
viewInformation   :: d [ViewOption   m ] m -> Task m | descr d & iTask m
updateInformation :: d [UpdateOption m m] m -> Task m | descr d & iTask m
```

These interactive tasks work *in isolation* on their task value, which is fine for many situations. However, work situations in which several interactive tasks view and update the *same information* require a more general version of these interactive tasks. Instead of editing the *current value* of the shared data source, they manipulate the *shared data source* directly.

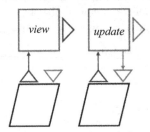

In case of *viewing* the current value of a shared data source, its current value is *read* and *displayed*. In case of *updating* the current value of a shared data source, its current value is also read and displayed, but also *written* at each update.

Basically, this means that in the signatures above, the value type m must be replaced by an appropriate shared data source type. When doing this, we obtain the following, more general, interactive tasks:

```
viewSharedInformation   :: d [ViewOption   r ] (ReadWriteShared r w) -> Task r
                                                                     | descr d
                                                                     & iTask r
updateSharedInformation :: d [UpdateOption r w] (ReadWriteShared r w) -> Task w
                                                                     | descr d
                                                                     & iTask r
                                                                     & iTask w
```

These signatures show that the interactive tasks get 'connected' with a shared data source. For `viewSharedInformation`, this means that a task is created that displays the *current* value of the argument shared data source. Hence, whenever the shared data source obtains a new value, then this is displayed by the `viewSharedInformation` task. Because it *views* a value, its task value type corresponds with the *read* value type of the shared data source. The task always tries to show the current value of that can be read from the shared data source. Of course, when the shared data source is changed by someone, it may take some time before a task is informed that a change has happened.

The `updateSharedInformation` task also gets connected with a shared data source, but in addition to displaying the current value of the shared data source, it also allows updating its value. Every time this is done, all other 'connected' tasks refresh their displayed value as well. Because `updateSharedInformation` *writes* a value, its task value type corresponds with the *write* value type of the shared data source. Its task value is always the currently written value to the shared data source.

Viewing and updating tasks that are connected with shared data sources allows us to create intricate networks of interactive tasks (see Fig. 13).

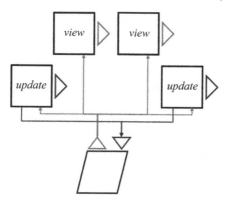

Fig. 13. Creating networks of interactive tasks via shared data sources

EXAMPLE 12. *Update and view a shared data source*
In this example we wish to create two tasks: one that allows the user to view and alter a `Track` value, and one that displays the result of these actions. This value is stored in the shared data source `trackStore` that was created in Example 11. Hence we need to combine two interactive tasks, one for viewing and one for updating a shared data source. We combine them with the 'and' operator `-&&-`:

```
editAndView :: Task (Track, Track)
editAndView
    = viewSharedInformation   (Title "View a Track")  [] trackStore
        -&&-
      updateSharedInformation (Title "Edit a Track")  [] trackStore
```

The resulting task is depicted in Fig. 14. Any user action that is performed in the editing task is displayed in the viewing task.

Admittedly, in its current form Example 12 seems silly because the editing task already allows the user to view the current task value. However, if you imagine that the viewing task is performed by *another user*, then this is a sensible way of arranging work. In Sect. 6 we show how to distribute tasks to users. Nevertheless, also for a single user this pattern can make sense if only the viewing task processes the value of the shared data source to a more useful format and renders it accordingly. Up until now we have ignored the option list arguments of the interactive tasks. It is time to throw some light on this matter.

Viewing and updating tasks that are connected with a shared data source that reads its values as type `r` should be allowed to transform them to another

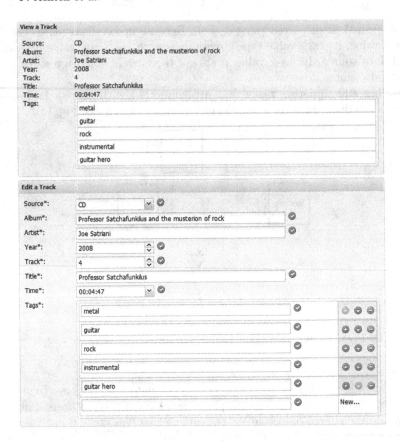

Fig. 14. Edit and view a shared track value.

domain of some type v using a function $f :: r \rightarrow v$. The tasks then display and update values of the new domain. Hence, in case of updating tasks, the user creates a new value of type v that must be placed back into the shared data store that writes its values as some type w. In general, you need both the new value of type v *and* the current read value of the shared data source of type r. Hence, the new value to be stored in the shared data source is computed by a function $g :: r \, v \rightarrow w$.

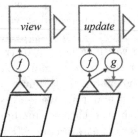

We want to associate f with the viewing task by means of a data constructor (ViewWith f) and the functions f and g with the updating task with data constructor (UpdateWith f g). The type definitions of these data constructors are:

```
:: ViewOption   r  = E.v: ViewWith   (r -> v)              & iTask v
:: UpdateOption r w = E.v: UpdateWith (r -> v) (r v -> w) & iTask v
```

Views need to be created of type v, so generic machinery for them has to be in place. This is enforced by the iTask v class constraint. The existential encapsulation E.v provides us with full freedom to choose any domain of our liking.

EXAMPLE 13. *Update and view a shared data source, revised*
We improve Example 12 by letting the viewing task only display a text message that informs the viewer what *album* of which *artist* is being edited. For this purpose, we add a viewing option to the viewing task (the rest of Example 12 remains unaltered):

```
editAndView :: Task (Track, Track)
editAndView
    = viewSharedInformation   (Title "View_a_Track") [ViewWith view] trackStore
        -&&-
      updateSharedInformation (Title "Edit_a_Track") [] trackStore
where
    view :: Track -> String
    view track
      = "You_are_editing_album" +++ track.album +++ "_by_" +++ track.artist
```

The resulting view task is shown in Fig. 15.

5.4 File Interaction

Every so often, an application is required to access data that is stored in a format dictated externally. The application must read and write this data. Suppose that a file is stored at a location identified by the string value *filepath*. The task function (importTextFile *filepath*) obtains the entire content of that file as a string value, and (exportTextFile *filepath str*) replaces the entire current content of that file with *str*. The signatures of these task functions are:

```
:: FilePath :== String

importTextFile :: FilePath        -> Task String
exportTextFile :: FilePath String -> Task String
```

EXAMPLE 14. *Retrieving and storing tracks to file*
In this example we create two tasks: (*a*) a named task importTracks that imports tracks from a text file; and (*b*) a named task exportTracks that exports tracks to a text file. The format of the text file uses the *newline* character to

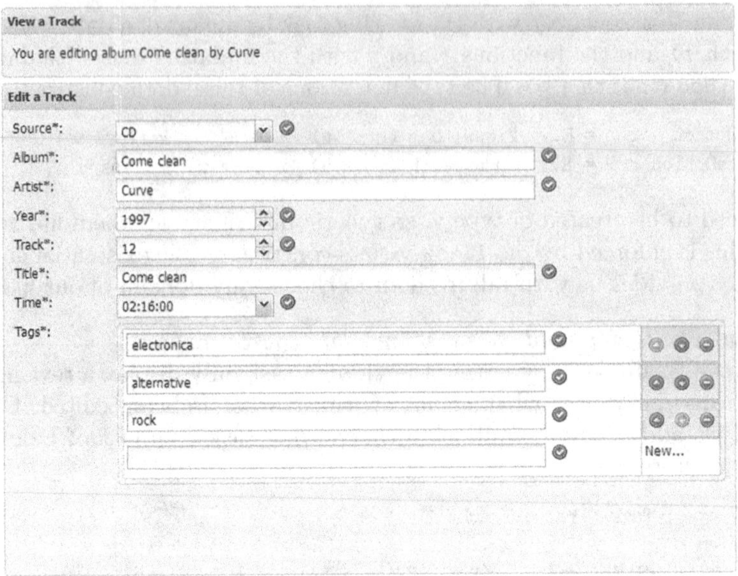

Fig. 15. Edit and view a shared track value, revised version.

separate entire entries, and uses the *tab* character to separate the fields within an entry. This is a fairly common format for simple databases.

We start with the *importing* task, naming it `importTracks`. Given a file location, it reads the file content and returns a list of `Track` values. It has signature:

```
importTracks :: FilePath -> Task [Track]
```

The function uses the `importTextFile` function to read in the entire contents of the text file. This provides us with a `String` value. We split the conversion of this value to a list of `Track` values into two steps: first, the entries and their fields are parsed (`tabSeparatedEntries`), and second, this list of fields is transformed to a list of track values (`toTrackList`). The signatures of these two functions are:

```
tabSeparatedEntries ::   String  -> [[String]]
toTrackList         :: [[String]] ->  [Track]
```

With these two functions, `importTracks` can be defined:

```
importTracks :: FilePath -> Task [Track]
importTracks filepath
    =              importTextFile filepath
   >>= \content -> return (toTrackList (tabSeparatedEntries content))
```

The two functions that still need to be implemented are pure computations:

```
tabSeparatedEntries :: String -> [[String]]                                    1
tabSeparatedEntries str                                                        2
    = map (split "\t") (split "\n" str)                                        3
                                                                               4
toTrackList :: [[String]] -> [Track]                                           5
toTrackList entries                                                            6
    = [ newTrack (fromString mdm) alb art (fromString yr) (fromString nr) title 7
                  (fromString t)                                               8
                  (split "," tags)                                             9
        \\ [mdm, alb, art, yr, nr, title, t, tags: _] <- entries             10
      ]                                                                       11
```

The `split` function takes a separator string and source string and yields all source fragments that are separated by the separator string. The track tags are separated by a *comma* character, and hence, `split` can be used to create the list of tags (line 9). The `split` function is part of the `Text` module that needs to be imported explicitly. For converting textual representations of values to the values themselves, the host language *Clean* provides a type class `fromString`:

```
class fromString a :: !String -> a
```

For `Time` values, an instance is already provided in *iTask*. This is not the case for `Medium` values and `Int` values. Let us start with parsing `Medium` values:

```
fromString "BlueRay"          = BlueRay                                         1
fromString "DVD"              = DVD                                             2
fromString "MP3"              = MP3                                             3
fromString "CD"               = CD                                             4
fromString "Musicassette"     = Musicassette                                   5
fromString "Single"          = Single                                          6
fromString "LP"              = LP                                              7
fromString other                                                               8
| startsWith prefix other = Other postfix                                      9
where prefix                 = "Other "                                       10
      postfix                = other                                          11
fromString wrong             = abort ("unexpected input in fromString: " +++ wrong)12
```

This is fairly straightforward: the only challenging bit concerns parsing `Other` values. The `startsWith` function from the `Text` module can be used to check whether the text starts with the "`Other `" text (line 9), and, if this is the case, it can produce the correct value. In any other case, the text cannot be parsed, and a runtime error is generated (line 12).

For `Int` values, the situation is less complicated because the desired functionality is already available as the `String` instance of the `toInt` type class, which converts a `String` value to an `Int` value. Hence, the implementation of the `Int` instance of the `fromString` type class is trivial:

```
instance fromString Int where fromString str = toInt str
```

The *exporting* task basically needs to perform the inverse operations of the parts introduced above for the importing task. For that reason, we build this task in inverse order as well. Converting values to descriptions of these values is supported by the host language *Clean* with the type class toString:

```
class toString a :: !a -> String
```

For Time and Int values, instances are already available, but this is not the case for Medium values. However, because Medium is an instance of the iTask class, and hence can be serialized, its implementation is easy enough:

```
instance toString Medium where toString m = "" <+++ m
```

We proceed by defining the inverse operations of the functions toTrackList and call it fromTrackList, and tabSeparatedEntries and call it tabSeparated String. Both functions use the inverse operation of split, which is called join. The join function takes a glue string and list of strings and concatenates the list elements, using the glue string between each element.

```
fromTrackList :: [Track] -> [[String]]                                      1
fromTrackList tracks                                                        2
    = [ [ toString medium, album, artist, toString year, toString track, title  3
        , toString time, join "," tags]                                     4
      \\ {medium, album, artist, year, track, title, time, tags} <- tracks  5
      ]                                                                      6
                                                                            7
tabSeparatedString :: [[String]] -> String                                  8
tabSeparatedString entries                                                  9
    = join "\n" (map (join "\t") entries)                                   10
```

The tag list is joined with the *comma* character (line 4), and the fields and entries with the *tab* and *newline* character respectively (line 10). With these functions, we can define the exporting tracks task as follows:

```
exportTracks :: FilePath [Track] -> Task Void
exportTracks filepath tracks
    =   exportTextFile filepath (tabSeparatedString (fromTrackList tracks))
    >>| return Void
```

5.5   Time Interaction

In Sect. 5.1 we have shown how to obtain the current date and time. In many work situations it is important that tasks start at the right time, or are guaranteed to terminate within some specified time limit. For this purpose *iTask* offers a number of time related task functions:

```
waitForTime     :: !Time     -> Task Time
waitForDate     :: !Date     -> Task Date
waitForDateTime :: !DateTime -> Task DateTime
waitForTimer    :: !Time     -> Task Time
```

The first three task functions wait until the specified time, date, or both has elapsed. Their task value result is identical to the argument value. The last task function waits the specified amount of time from the moment this task function is called. Its return value is the time when the timer went off.

EXAMPLE 15. *Extending tasks with a deadline*
In this example we create a new task combinator function that extends any given task t with a time limit d. The intended signature of this task combinator is:

```
deadline :: !(Task a) !Time -> Task (Maybe a)
```

The Maybe type represents an optional value and is defined as:

```
:: Maybe a = Nothing | Just a
```

Hence, no value is encoded as Nothing, and a value x as (Just x).

The function (deadline t d) should execute task t. If t returns within time limit d with a result value x, then the combined task returns (Just x). However, if t does not terminate within time limit d, then the combined task returns Nothing. Besides executing t this combinator executes a *timing task*. The first task that completes terminates the combined task. Hence, it makes sense to use the -||- task combinator (Sect. 4.4) for this purpose. It demands that its two task arguments have task values of the same type. If we let the timing task return Nothing, then all we need to do is make sure that the original task t returns (Just x) instead of just x. We create two wrapper functions for that purpose:

```
just :: !(Task a) -> Task (Maybe a) | iTask a
just    t = t >>= \x -> return (Just x)

nothing :: !(Task a) -> Task (Maybe b) | iTask a & iTask b
nothing t = t >>| return Nothing
```

(just t) executes t, and if it produces a stable task value x, it produces (Just x). Similarly, (nothing t) also executes t, but after that produces a stable task value it is ignored, and instead only Nothing is returned.

The timing task can use waitForTimer task function:

```
timer :: !Time -> Task (Maybe a) | iTask a
timer d = nothing (waitForTimer d)
```

Hence, this is a task that waits the specified amount of time and then returns with Nothing. We can now implement the deadline task:

```
deadline :: !(Task a) !Time -> Task (Maybe a) | iTask a
deadline t d = (just t) -||- (timer d)
```

The argument task is executed, as well as the timer task. The first task that terminates determines the result of the combined task.

EXERCISE 10. *Limiting year input values*
In Example 10, the task function `enterYear` repeatedly asks the user for a year value until it lies within a given lower and upper bound value. It so happens that the *iTask* toolkit provides a data model for such kind of bounded values:

```
:: BoundedInt = { min :: Int    // the lower bound
                , cur :: Int    // the current value (min ≤ cur ≤ max)
                , max :: Int    // the upper bound
                }
```

Use this type to define `enterYear` in such a way that it asks the user only once for a proper year value.

EXERCISE 11. *Edit a track list and view information*
In Exercise 8 you have created a task that allows the user to successively enter tracks. Enhance this task in a similar way as shown in Example 13. Display the *number of artists, number of albums, number of tracks*, and *total playing time.*

6   Collaboration

Up until this point we have discussed applications that serve a single user. We now extend this to serve arbitrarily many registered users. For this purpose we switch to the `multiTOPApp` or `multiTOPApps` kickstart wrapper functions (see Figs. 5 and 6). These wrapper functions add infrastructure to handle an arbitrary number of users. They use a custom defined module, `UserAdmin`. It is based on the core concept of a user. In this section, we use the functionality provided by the `UserAdmin` module.

When executing an application created by means of `multiTOPApp(s)`, the user is first asked to provide account information (see Fig. 16). This is used by the application to establish who it is serving. The infrastructure allows users to enter the application anonymously. It is up to the application whether or not this flaws the user experience. All applications maintain a shared data source containing information about the accounts and users that can be served by the application. The first thing to do is set up a collection of users (Sect. 6.1). As soon as a user base is available, an application can distribute its activities amongst the members of its user base (Sect. 6.2).

6.1   Employing Users

Employing users is actually not very different from adding tracks to a track list that is stored in a shared data source. Each application has a shared data source available that is called `userAccounts`. The involved type definitions are given in Fig. 17. Because `userAccounts` is a shared data source, it can be read with the task (`get userAccounts`) and written with the task (`set accounts userAccounts`) where `accounts` is a list of user account values. The

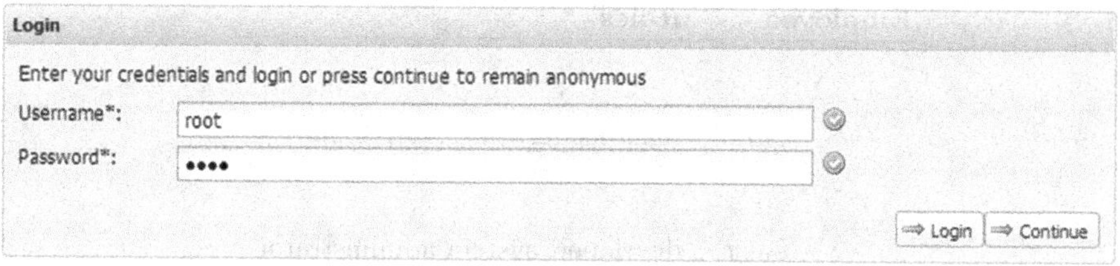

Fig. 16. Entering a multi-user application.

`credentials` consist of a user name and password. Note that the `Password` type
is specialized within the *iTask* toolkit: when an editor is created for it it displays
an edit box in which the user input is cloaked, as shown in Fig. 16. If a `title` is
provided, then this is used by the application to address the user instead of her
user name. Users can have different `roles` within an organization. Work can be
assigned to users that have particular roles.

```
userAccounts :: Shared [UserAccount]

:: UserAccount = { credentials :: Credentials
                 , title       :: Maybe UserTitle
                 , roles       :: [Role]
                 }
:: Credentials = { username    :: Username
                 , password    :: Password
                 }
:: Password   = Password String
:: Username   = Username UserId
:: UserId     :== String
:: UserTitle  :== String
:: Role       :== String
```

Fig. 17. Fragment of module `UserAdmin` concerning user accounts.

EXAMPLE 16. *The* CLEAN *company*
For illustration purposes, we introduce the fictitious CLEAN company. Its employees and their roles are displayed in Fig. 18.

EXERCISE 12. *Employ your users*
Create a main module that uses the kickstart wrapper function `multiTOPApps`
to manage several top level tasks for multiple users. Fill its boxed task list with
a task called `employ` that adds user accounts to the `userAccounts` shared data
source. You can use any technique that has been discussed in the preceding
sections or use the dedicated tasks in the `UserAdmin` module. Compile and run

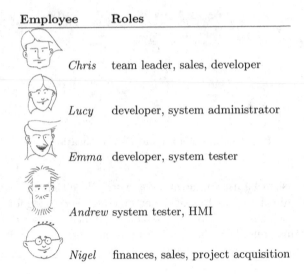

Fig. 18. The CLEAN company employees and their roles.

to sign up all employees of the CLEAN company who are enumerated in Fig. 18. Choose passwords of your liking. Their user names are identical to their first names, so they do not require an additional title.

6.2 Distributing Work

Having a user base available, it is time to assign work to them. Before we explain how to do this, we first discuss the model types that are related with users and their properties. They are displayed in Fig. 19.

```
:: User            = AnonymousUser      SessionId
                   | AuthenticatedUser UserId [Role] (Maybe UserTitle)
:: UserConstraint = AnyUser
                   | UserWithId    UserId
                   | UserWithRole Role
```

Fig. 19. The user model types.

To an application, a user is either anonymous or belongs to the registered set of users. In the first case, a user is identified by means of the application's session which, for now, we consider to be opaque. Authenticated users are confirmed to be part of the collection of users that the application is allowed to serve. Their attributes originate from the user account details (Fig. 17). The UserConstraint model is used to define a subset of the authenticated users.

AnyUser imposes no constraint on this set, and hence, all users are eligible. In case of (UserWithId *uid*), the user with username (Username *uid*) is selected. In case of (UserWithRole *role*), any user that has *role* associated with her can be chosen.

User, UserId, and UserConstraint values can be used to indicate users to assign work to. If value *u* is of either of these types, then the task (*u* @: *t*) makes task *t* available to all users who belong to *u*. As soon as one of them decides to perform task *t*, it becomes unavailable to the other users. They receive some notification that task *t* is being executed by that user. The signature of operator @: is:

```
(@:) infix 3 :: user (Task a) -> Task a | iTask a & toUserConstraint user
instance toUserConstraint User
instance toUserConstraint UserId
instance toUserConstraint UserConstraint
```

EXAMPLE 17. *Addressing the* CLEAN *company users*
In the CLEAN company case, AnyUser refers to all employees. (UserWithId "Lucy") addresses Lucy. All sales persons, Chris and Nigel, are addressed with the value (UserWithRole "sales"). Hence, (UserWithRole "sales") @: *t* makes task *t* available to Chris and Nigel. The one who is the first to start on that task can finish it, and the other is informed that the job is being processed.

The user model types are ordinary types and therefore can also be used as values that are manipulated by the *iTask* type-driven functions. The task (get currentUser) can be used to find out which current User a task is serving.

EXAMPLE 18. *Update and view a shared data source, distributed*
We turn Example 12 into a distributed application. First, we assign the two sub tasks to two users:

```
editAndViewDistributed :: (user1, user2) -> Task (Track, Track)
                        | toUserConstraint user1 & toUserConstraint user2
editAndViewDistributed (user1, user2)
    = (user1 @: updateSharedInformation (Title "Edit␣a␣Track") [] trackStore)
      -&&-
      (user2 @: viewSharedInformation   (Title "View␣a␣Track") [] trackStore)
```

Second, we determine who the current user is, and ask who is supposed to perform the view task while editing a track.

```
editAndViewTrack :: Task Track
editAndViewTrack
    =                 get currentUser
    >>= \me        -> updateInformation (Title "Enter␣a␣user␣name") [] "user"
    >>= \you       -> editAndViewDistributed (me, you)
    >>= \(track, _) -> return track
```

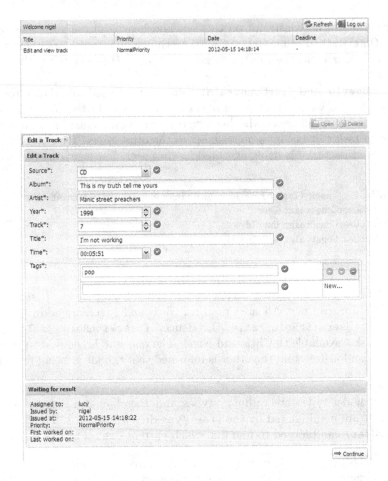

Fig. 20. Nigel, editing a track.

Suppose Nigel started the application and indicated Lucy to view his editing actions. Nigel can edit a track to his liking and tell that the sub task has been delegated to Lucy (Fig. 20). Lucy has received an extra task in her task list to follow Nigel's progress (Fig. 21).

EXAMPLE 19. *Making an appointment*
In this example, we create a task to make an appointment with a registered user.

```
appointment :: Task (Date, Time)                                               1
appointment                                                                    2
    =               get currentDate                                            3
    >>= \today   -> get currentTime                                            4
    >>= \now     -> enterInformation  (Title "Who do you wish to meet?") []     5
    >>= \user    -> updateInformation (Title "When to meet?") [] [(today, now)] 6
```

```
>>= \options -> UserWithId user                                            7
            @:                                                             8
            (updateInformation (Title "Select_appropriate_date-time_pairs")  9
                            [] (map toDisplay options)                   10
            >>= return                                                   11
            )                                                            12
>>= \selected -> if (isEmpty selected)                                   13
            appointment                                                  14
            (return (fromDisplay (hd selected)))                         15
```

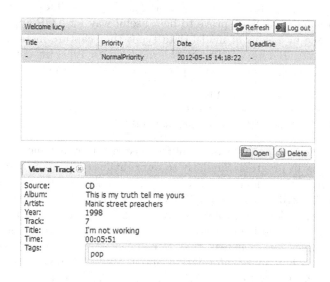

Fig. 21. Lucy, viewing Nigel's progress.

We obtain the current date and time (lines 3 and 4), ask the current user to choose a registered user (line 5) and create a number of possible date-time pairs (line 6). Hence, `user` and `options` are values of type `UserId` and `[(Date, Time)]` respectively. We ask `user` to select date-time pairs. Because we do not want her to alter these values, they are rendered as displays. She can only alter the *order* of suggested date-time pairs, and remove pairs. When done, the original user receives the selection as value `selected` (line 13). In case all options were inappropriate, the task starts all over again (line 14), otherwise the first pair is returned after stripping the `Display` data constructor of its model value.

EXERCISE 13. *Making an appointment*
Example 19 defines a task that never terminates in case the requested user consistently removes all suggested date-time pairs, or simply is inactive. Alter the example in such a way that the original user can decide to abandon this task.

7 Managing Work

Within an application, the various tasks need to keep track of each other's progress, and be able to change their course of action if necessary. In order to achieve this, an application needs to have means to detect and signal that its intended progress is hampered (Sects. 7.1 and 7.2) *and* it needs to adapt its behavior to handle new situations (Sect. 7.3).

7.1 Monitoring Work

In Sect. 6.2, we have introduced the task (get currentUser). Shared data sources such as currentUser prove to be a useful way for TOP applications to leave their trace by means of model data types that capture meta-information about their tasks. Before we discuss the model data types in detail, we first present the shared data sources that play a role in this context:

```
currentUser    :: ReadOnlyShared User
currentTopTask :: ReadOnlyShared TaskId
topLevelTasks  :: ReadOnlyShared (TaskList Void)
```

They are all *read-only* shared data sources because they are merely a shadow of the real tasks in progress. Similarly to currentUser, the named shared data source currentTopTask identifies *which task* is currently evaluated via an opaque value of type TaskId. For now, it suffices to know that a TaskId value uniquely identifies a task. The shared data source topLevelTasks gives access to all top level tasks that are being worked on. It basically gives you a list of meta-information values for each task that is being worked on. The TaskId value serves as key to find more information about a specific task. The meta-task information is fairly extensive, as displayed in Fig. 22. Right now, we are only interested in the items field that describes each and every top level task with a (TaskListItem Void) record value. It gives you its TaskId identification value and the current task value. The current task value may not seem very interesting for tasks of type (Task Void), because it can only deliver Void. Still, one can tell whether or not this value is present, and, if so, whether or not it is stable. In the *iTask* system we can obtain a task list for parallel collections of tasks. The TaskMeta information is a list of key-value pairs that is used for layout purposes. This does not concern us right now. More interesting for keeping track of progress are the ManagementMeta and ProgressMeta model types. With this information, we can learn of a task's starting time, possible deadline, when it was last worked on, by whom it was issued, and so on.

EXAMPLE 20. *Monitoring tasks*
The easiest way to monitor the current tasks is by adding the following task to your application:

```
monitorTaskList :: Task Void
monitorTaskList
    = viewSharedInformation (Title "Task_list:") [] topLevelTasks
```

```
    >>| return Void

derive class iTask TaskList, TaskListId
```

```
:: TaskList      a = { listId          ::  TaskListId a
                     , items           ::  [TaskListItem a]
                     }
:: TaskListItem a = { taskId           ::  TaskId
                     , value           ::  TaskValue a         // SECTION 4.3
                     , taskMeta        ::  TaskMeta
                     , managementMeta  ::  Maybe ManagementMeta
                     , progressMeta    ::  Maybe ProgressMeta
                     }
:: TaskMeta       :== [TaskAttribute]
:: TaskAttribute :== (String, String)
:: ManagementMeta  = { title           ::  Maybe String
                     , worker          ::  UserConstraint      // SECTION 6.2
                     , role            ::  Maybe Role          // SECTION 6.1
                     , startAt         ::  Maybe DateTime      // SECTION 5.1
                     , completeBefore  ::  Maybe DateTime
                     , notifyAt        ::  Maybe DateTime
                     , priority        ::  TaskPriority
                     }
:: ProgressMeta    = { issuedAt        ::  DateTime
                     , issuedBy        ::  User                // SECTION 6.2
                     , status          ::  Stability           // SECTION 4.3
                     , firstEvent      ::  Maybe DateTime
                     , latestEvent     ::  Maybe DateTime
                     }
:: TaskPriority    = HighPriority
                   | NormalPriority
                   | LowPriority
```

Fig. 22. The model types that provide task meta-information.

Using the technique described in Sect. 5.3, it connects a display to the topLevel
Tasks shared data source, thus allowing the end user to keep an up-to-date
view of the set of top level tasks. As soon as the user chooses to continue,
monitorTaskList terminates.

7.2 Monitoring Data

Interactive tasks can be connected with a shared data source. This is useful, as
demonstrated by Example 20, because it keeps us up-to-date with the *current*
value of the shared data source. However, sometimes we need to know *when* a
shared data source is altered. In general, we want to impose a condition on the
read value of a shared data source that acts as a trigger to continue evaluation.
This can be done with the task function wait:

```
wait :: d (r -> Bool) (ReadWriteShared r w) -> Task r | descr d & iTask r
```

Just like interactive tasks, `wait` receives a description of its purpose that is displayed to the user. The predicate p of type $(r \text{ -> } Bool)$ is a condition on the current read value of the shared data source of type $(ReadWriteShared\ r\ w)$. As soon as the shared data source has a read value x for which $(p\ x)$ evaluates to `True`, then this also results in a stable task value x for the `wait` task.

EXAMPLE 21. *Monitoring data*
Consider this application of the `wait` task function:

```
waitForChange :: (ReadWriteShared r w) -> Task r | iTask r
waitForChange rws
  =             get rws
  >>= \current -> wait (Title "Waiting for new value:") ((=!=) current) rws
```

The task first reads the current value of the shared data source, and then monitors the shared data source until it has a different value. This difference is determined by the generic unequality operator `=!=` that is part of the `iTask` class. (This is also true for the generic equality operator `===`.)

7.3   Change Course of Action

In the previous two sub sections we have discussed how to monitor tasks and shared data sources. This can be used to *signal* deviating or unexpected behavior, and try to *respond* to these situations.

For *signalling*, TOP supports *exception handling* in a common *try-catch* style. We can use the following two task functions for this purpose:

```
throw ::            !e            -> Task a | iTask a & iTask e
try   :: (Task a) (e -> Task a) -> Task a | iTask a & iTask e
```

When a task encounters a situation that cannot be handled locally or sufficiently gracefully, it can *throw an exception value*, using the task function $(throw\ e)$, where e is an arbitrary expression that is completely reduced to a value. The expression can use the available local information to create some useful model value. As always, any type is valid, provided that the generic machinery has been made available for it. In $(try\ t\ r)$, task t is evaluated. If it throws no exceptional value then the task value of t is also the task value of $(try\ t\ r)$. However, if at some point within evaluation of t an exceptional value v is thrown, then evaluation of t is abandoned. If the type of the exceptional value v can be unified at run-time with the statically known type e of the exception handler r, then evaluation continues with $(r\ v)$. In that case this is also the result of $(try\ t\ r)$. If the two types cannot be unified (typically when an exception is raised for which this exception handler has not been designed) then $(try\ t\ r)$ itself re-throws the very same exceptional value v, hoping that its context can handle the exception. Uncaught exceptions that escape all exception handlers are finally caught at the top-level, and only reported to the user.

EXAMPLE 22. *File import and export exceptions*

In Sect. 5.4 we have introduced the basic file import and export task functions `importTextFile` and `exportTextFile`. Both functions might throw an exception of type `FileException`:

```
:: FileException = FileException !FilePath !FileError
:: FileError    = CannotOpen | CannotClose | IOError
```

Here, `FilePath` has the same role as in the argument of the two task functions and is supposed to point to a valid text file. The `FileError` values provide more detail about the nature of the exception. In case of `CannotOpen`, the indicated file could not be opened, either because it did not exist or because it was locked, perhaps by another task or application. In case of `CannotClose`, the indicated file could not be closed after reading the content. Other errors are report by means of `IOError`.

With these exceptions, we can enhance the tasks that were defined in Example 14, viz. `importTracks` and `exportTracks` that both assumed that everything is executed flawlessly. For `importTracks`, it makes sense to alter the task result type to a `Maybe` value that signals that the file was not read properly:

```
importTracks :: FilePath -> Task (Maybe [Track])
importTracks filepath
    = try (               importTextFile filepath
        >>= \content -> return (Just (toTrackList (tabSeparatedEntries content)))
      ) handleFileError
where
    handleFileError :: FileException -> Task (Maybe [Track])
    handleFileError _ = return Nothing
```

For `exportTracks`, we alter the task value type to a `Bool` to properly report success or failure:

```
exportTracks :: FilePath [Track] -> Task Bool
exportTracks filepath tracks
    = try (   exportTextFile filepath (tabSeparatedString (fromTrackList tracks))
          >>| return True
      ) handleFileError
where
    handleFileError :: FileException -> Task Bool
    handleFileError _ = return False
```

Note how both task functions introduce an exception handler with an explicit type. This is required by the signature of `try`, which needs to know for which type the event handler is defined.

For *responding*, TOP allows you to *terminate* currently running tasks as well as dynamically *create* new tasks.

```
removeTask               :: !TaskId !(ReadOnlyShared (TaskList a))
                            -> Task Void  | iTask a
appendTopLevelTaskFor :: !user !(Task a) -> Task TaskId | iTask a
                                              & toUserConstraint user
```

(removeTask *tid sds*) locates the task that is identified by *tid* within the given shared data source task list administration *sds* and stops and removes that task if found. Note that for argument *sds*, you can use the shared data source topLevelTasks that was defined in Sect. 7.1. (appendTopLevelTaskFor *u t*) dynamically creates a new task *t* for (any of the) user(s) *u*, in a similar way to the task assignment operator @: (Sect. 6.2). The difference is that appendTopLevel TaskFor only *spawns t* and returns with the stable task value that identifies the spawned task. In contrast, (*u* @: *t*) creates a *stub* in the current task that tells the current user that task *t* has been spawned for (any of the) user(s) *u*, and that you need to wait for its result task value.

EXAMPLE 23. *Birthday cake at the* CLEAN *company*
In the CLEAN company, it is a good habit to celebrate one's birthday with cake. We develop a task to select a time of day and invite everybody else for cake. We get to know our colleagues via the task (get userAccounts) (Fig. 17). From this list it is easy to obtain all names:

```
names :: [UserAccount] -> [UserId]
names accounts
    = [uid \\ {credentials={username=Username uid}} <- accounts]
```

To invite everybody (except yourself) and announce your birthday, we need to obtain our identity with (get currentUser) (Sect. 7.1) and our name.

```
name :: User -> UserId
name (AuthenticatedUser id _ _) = id name
anonymous                       = "somebody"
```

The invitation displays the occasion and time.

```
cake :: UserId Time -> Task String
cake person time
    = viewInformation "Birthday cake" [] ("To celebrate " <+++ person <+++
                          "'s birthday, we have cake at " <+++ time
                          )
```

All that remains to be done is to put these parts in the right order:

```
birthdaycake :: Task [TaskId]                                             1
birthdaycake                                                              2
    =                    get userAccounts                                3
    >>= \accounts -> get currentUser                                     4
    >>= \me       -> get currentTime                                     5
    >>= \now      -> updateInformation (Title "When to eat cake?") [] now 6
    >>= \time     -> let colleagues = removeMembers (names accounts) [name me] 7
```

```
invite    = cake (name me) time in                           8
all (map (flip appendTopLevelTaskFor invite) colleagues)    9
```

The user accounts are obtained (line 3), the current user is determined (line 4), as well as the current time (line 5). We think of a suitable time to treat to cake (line 6) and exclude ourselves from the list of colleagues (line 7). The invitation task (line 8) is finally sent to every colleague (line 9). The `all` function is a task combinator function defined for the occasion: it receives a list of tasks, executes them all, and collects their resulting task values for further processing:

```
all :: [Task a] -> Task [a] | iTask a
all []     = return []
all [t:ts] =          t
             >>= \v  -> all ts
             >>= \vs -> return [v:vs]
```

EXERCISE 14. *Improved user feedback*
In Example 22, the exception handlers do not attempt to inform the user that anything has gone wrong. Define for both task functions better exception handlers that tell the user what exception has occurred, and remind her of the file path that was used.

EXERCISE 15. *Remove birthday cake invitations*
In Example 23, all users except the initiator receive an extra task. Of course it is polite to remove these tasks for these users after the event. Extend the `birthdaycake` task in such a way that the extra tasks are removed, using the `removeTask` function that has been presented in this section.

8   Related Work

The TOP paradigm emerged during continued work on the iTask system. In its first incarnation [2], *iTask*1, the notion of tasks was introduced for the specification of dedicated workflow management systems. In *iTask*1 and its successor *iTask*2 [3], a task is an opaque unit of work that, once completed, yields a result from which subsequent tasks can be computed. When deploying these systems for real-world applications, viz. in telecare [4] and modeling the dynamic task of coordinating Coast Guard Search and Rescue operations [5,6] it was observed that this concept of task is not adequate to express the coordination of tasks where teams constantly need to be informed about the progress made by others. The search for better abstraction has resulted in the TOP approach and task concept as introduced in these lecture notes.

Task-Oriented programming touches on two broad areas of research. First the programming of interactive multi-user (web) applications, and second the specification of tasks.

There are many languages, libraries and frameworks for programming multi-user web applications. Some of them are academic, and many more are in the open-source and proprietary commercial software markets. Examples from the academic functional programming community include: the Haskell cgi library [7]; the Curry approach [8]; writing xml applications [9] in *SMLserver* [10]; WashCGI [11]; the Hop [12,13] web programming language; Links [14] and formlets [15]. All these solutions address the technical challenges of creating multi-user web applications. Naturally, these challenges also need to be addressed within the TOP approach. The principal difference between TOP and these web technologies is the emphasis on using tasks both as modeling and programming unit to abstract from these issues, including coordination of tasks that may or may not have a value.

Tasks are an ambiguous notion used in different fields, such as Workflow Management Systems (WFMS), human-computer interaction, and ergonomics. Although the *iTask*1 system was influenced and partially motivated by the use of tasks in WFMSs [16], *iTask*3 has evolved to the more general TOP approach of structuring software systems. As such, it is more similar in spirit to the WebWorkFlow project [17], which is an object oriented approach that breaks down the logic into separate clauses instead of functions. Cognitive Task Analysis methods [18] seek to understand how people accomplish tasks. Their results are useful in the design of software systems, but they are not software development methods. In Robotics the notion of task and even the "Task-Oriented Programming" moniker are also used. In this field it is used to indicate a level of autonomy at which robots are programmed. To the best of our knowledge, TOP as a paradigm for interactive multi-user systems, rooted in functional programming is a novel approach, distinct from other uses of the notion of tasks in the fields mentioned above.

9   Conclusions and Future Work

In this paper we introduced Task-Oriented Programming, a paradigm for programming interactive web-based multi-user applications in a domain specific language, embedded in a pure functional language.

The distinguishing feature of TOP is the ability to concisely describe and implement collaboration and complex interaction of tasks. This is achieved by four core concepts: (1) *Tasks observe intermediate values of other tasks* and react on these values before the other tasks are completely finished. (2) *Tasks running in parallel communicate via shared data sources*. Shared data sources enable useful lightweight communication between related tasks. By restricting the use of shared data sources we avoid an overly complex semantics. (3) *Tasks interact with users based on arbitrary typed data*, the interface required for this type is derived by type driven generic programming. (4) *Tasks are composed* to more complex tasks *using a small set of combinators*.

Commonly, web applications are *heterogeneous*, i.e.: they are constructed out of components that have been developed using different programming languages and programming tools. An advantage of the TOP approach is that even complex applications can be defined in one formalism.

TOP is embedded in Clean by offering a newly developed *iTask3* library. We have used TOP successfully for the development of a prototype implementation of a Search and Rescue decision support system for the Dutch Coast Guard. The coordination of such operations requires up-to-date information of subtasks, which is precisely suited for TOP. The *iTask* system has also successfully been used to investigate more efficient ways of working on Navy Vessels. The goal here is to get a significant reduction of crew members and systems. There are many application areas where the TOP approach can be of use. With industrial partners we want to investigate and validate the suitability of the TOP paradigm to handle complex real world distributed application areas in several domains.

Acknowledgements. The authors wish to thank the reviewers for their constructive feedback.

A   Functional Programming in Clean

This section gives a brief overview of functional programming in *Clean* [19]. *Clean* is a pure lazy functional programming language. It has many similarities with *Haskell*.

A.1   Clean Nutshells

This section contains a set of brief overviews of topics in *Clean*. These overviews should be short enough to read while studying other parts of this paper without loosing the flow of those parts. The somewhat experienced functional programmer is introduced to particular syntax or language constructs in *Clean*.

Modules. A module with name M is represented physically by two text files that reside in the same directory: one with file name M.dcl and one with file name M.icl.

The M.icl file is the *implementation* module. It contains the (task) functions and data type definitions of the module. Its first line repeats its name:

implementation module M

An implementation module can always use its own definitions. By importing other modules, it can use the definitions that are made visible by those modules as well:

import M_1, M_2, ..., M_n

The M.dcl file is the *definition* module. It contains M's interface to other modules. The first line of a definition module also gives its name:

definition module M

A definition module basically serves two purposes.

- It exports identifiers of its own implementation module by repeating their signature. Hence, identifiers which signatures are not repeated are *cloaked* for other modules.
- It acts as a serving-hatch for identifiers that are exported by other modules by importing their module names. In this way you can create libraries of large collections of related identifiers.

Operators. *Operators* are binary (two arguments) functions that can be written in *infix* style (between its arguments) instead of the normal *prefix* style (before its arguments). Operators are used to increase readability of your programs. With an operator declaration you associate two other attributes as well. The first attribute is the *fixity* which indicates in which direction the binding power works in case of operators with the same precedence. It is expressed by one of the keywords `infixl`, `infix`, and `infixr`. The second attribute is its *precedence* which indicates the binding power of the operator. It is expressed as an integer value between 0 and 9, in which a higher value indicates a stronger binding power.

The snapshot below of common operators as defined in the host language *Clean* illustrates this.

```
class (==) infix  4 a :: !a !a -> Bool
class (+)  infixl 6 a :: !a !a -> a
class (-)  infixl 6 a :: !a !a -> a
class (*)  infixl 7 a :: !a !a -> a
class (/)  infixl 7 a :: !a !a -> a
class (^)  infixr 8 a :: !a !a -> a
```

(These operators are *overloaded* to allow you to instantiate them for your own types.) Due to the lower precedence of ==, the expression $x + y == y + x$ must be read as $(x + y) == (y + x)$. Due to the fixities, the expression $x - y - z$ must be read as $(x - y) - z$, and $x \hat{\ } y \hat{\ } z$ as $x \hat{\ } (y \hat{\ } z)$. In case of expressions that use operators of the same precedence but with conflicting fixities you must work out the correct order yourself using brackets ( ).

Guards. Pattern matching is an expressive way to perform case distinction in function alternatives, but it is limited to investigating the structure of function arguments. *Guards* extend this with conditional expressions. Here are two examples.

`sign :: !Int -> Int`
`sign 0  = 0`
`sign x`
`| x < 0 = -1`
`sign x  = 1`
	`instance < Date where` 1
	  `< x y` 2
	  `| x.year <  y.year    = True` 3
	  `| x.year == y.year` 4
	    `| x.mon <  y.mon = True` 5
	    `| x.mon == y.mon = x.day < y.day` 6
	    `| otherwise     = False` 7
	  `| otherwise       = False` 8

In **sign**, the first alternative matches only if the argument evaluates to the value 0. In that case, **sign** results in the value 0. The second alternative imposes no pattern restrictions, but it does have a guard (| x < 0). Even though the pattern always matches, evaluation of the guard must result in **True** if the second alternative of **sign** is to be chosen. Therefor, the value **-1** is returned only if the argument is a negative number. Finally, the last alternative has neither a pattern restriction nor a guarded restriction, and therefor matches all remaining cases, which concern the positive numbers. In those cases, the result is 1.

The implementation of < for **Date** values illustrates *nested* guards. In contrast with top-level guards, nested guards must be completed with **otherwise** to catch any remaining cases. The **otherwise** keyword can also be used in top-level guards, as is shown on the last line of the < function. The < function first checks the guard on line 3 and returns **True** if the first **year** field is smaller than the second **year** field. If the guard evaluates to **False**, then the second guard on line 4 is tested. In case of equal **year** field values, evaluation continues with the nested guards on lines 5–7 that inspect the **month** fields. If the first nested guard on line 5 evaluates to **True**, then the comparison also yields **True**. In case of a **False** result, the second nested guard on line 6 is tested. In case of equal **month** field values, the comparison of the **day** values provides the final answer. Finally, to complete the nested guards, the last case on line 7 concludes that the first argument is not smaller than the second, a conclusion that is shared by the last top-level guard on line 8.

Choice and Pattern Matching. In Example 8 the function **firstYearPossible** uses *pattern matching* to relate values of type **Medium** with year values. The **enterYear** function uses **if** to determine whether or not the user's input is valid. Unlike most programming languages, in which an *if-then-else* construct is supported in the language, it can be straightforwardly incorporated as a function in a lazy functional language, using pattern matching as well. Let's examine the type and implementation of **if**:

```
if :: !Bool a a -> a
if True then else = then
if _    _    else = else
```

The *type* tells you that the **Bool** argument is strict in **if**: it must always be evaluated in order to know whether its result is **True** or **False**. The *implementation* uses the evaluation strategy of the host language to make the choice effective. The **if** function has two alternatives, each indicated by repeating the function name and its arguments. Alternatives are examined in textual order, from top to bottom. Up until now the arguments of functions were only variables, but in fact they are *patterns*. A pattern *p* is one of the following.

– A *variable*, expressed by means of an identifier that starts with a lowercase character or simply the _ wildcard symbol in case the variable is not used at all. A variable identifies and matches any computation without forcing evaluation. Within the same alternative, the variable identifiers must be different.

- A *constant* in the language, such as 0, False, 3.14, '$', and "hello,␣world". To match successfully, the argument is evaluated fully to determine whether it has exactly the same constant value.
- A *composite* pattern, which is either a *tuple* $(p_1, \ldots, p_n)$, a *data constructor* $(d \; p_1 \ldots p_n)$ where n is the arity of d, a *record* $\{f_1=p_1, \ldots, f_n=p_n\}$, or a *list* $[p_1, \ldots, p_n]$ or $[p_1, \ldots, p_n : p_{n+1}]$. Matching proceeds recursively to each part that is specified in the pattern. In case of records, only the mentioned record fields are matched. In case of lists, p_1 upto p_n are matched with the first n elements of the list, if present, and p_{n+1} with the remainder of the list.

Patterns control evaluation of arguments *until it is discovered that it either matches or not*. Only if all patterns in the same alternative match, computation proceeds with the corresponding right-hand side of that alternative; otherwise computation proceeds with the next alternative.

Hence, in the case of if its second argument is returned if the evaluation of the first argument results in True. If it results in False the second alternative is tried. Because it does not impose any restriction, and hence also causes no further evaluation, it matches, and the third argument is returned.

In firstYearPossible the data constructors are also matched from top to bottom. The last case always matches, and returns the value 0.

List Comprehensions. Lists are the workhorse of functional programming. *List comprehensions* allow you to concisely express list manipulations. Their simplest form is:

> [e \\ p <- g]

Generator g is an expression that is or yields a list. (Note that g can also evaluate to an array. In that case you need to use <-: instead of <- to extract array elements.) From the generator, values are extracted from the front to the back. Each value is matched with the pattern p. If this succeeds, then the pattern variables in p are bound to the corresponding parts of the extracted value, and expression e, that typically uses these bound pattern variables, yields an element of the result list. If matching fails, then the next element of the generator is tried.

Besides the pattern p, elements can also be selected using a *guarded condition*:

> [e \\ p <- g | c]

Here, c is a boolean expression that can use any of the pattern variables that are introduced at generator patterns to its left. For each extracted value from the sequence for which the pattern match succeeds, the guarded condition is evaluated. Only if the condition also evaluates to True, a list element is added.

It is possible to use several pattern-generator pairs p <- g in one list comprehension. They are combined either in *parallel* with the & symbol or as a *cartesian product* with the , symbol.

- In p_1 <- g_1 & p_2 <- g_2, values are extracted from g_1 and g_2 at the same index positions and matched against p_1 and p_2 respectively. The shortest generator determines termination of this value-extraction process.

– In p_1 <- g_1 , p_2 <- g_2, for each extracted value from g_1 that matches p_1 *all* values from g_2 are extracted and matched against p_2.

Each and every one of the above ways to manipulate lists is already very expressive. However, they can be combined in arbitrary ways. This can be daunting at times, but once you get used to the expressive power, list comprehensions often prove to be the best tool for list processing tasks.

λ-Abstractions. *Lambda*-abstractions \x -> e allow you to introduce *anonymous* functions 'on the spot'. They typically occur in situations where an ad hoc function is required, for which it does not make much sense to come up with a separate function definition. This frees you from thinking of a proper identifier and perhaps a type signature as well. The bind combinator >>= is an excellent example of such a situation because in general you need to give a name x to the task value of the first task, and want to give an expression e that uses x. If you weren't interested in x, you would have used the naïve then combinator >>| instead.

Modelling Side-Effects. In a pure functional programming language all results must be explicit function results. This implies that a changed state should also be a function result. The type of the Start function in Example 1 is *World -> *World, this indicates that it changes the world. There are two things worth noting at this moment:

– The basic type World is *annotated* with the *uniqueness attribute* *. In a function type any argument can be annotated with this attribute. This enforces the property that whenever the function is evaluated, it has the *sole reference* to the corresponding argument value. This is useful because it allows the function implementation to *destructively update* that value without compromising the semantics of the functional programming language. This can only be done if the function body itself does not violate this uniqueness property. This is checked statically.
– The basic type World represents the 'external' environment of a program. If the Start function has an argument, the language assumes that it is of type World. The language provides no other means to create a value of type World, so if an application is to do any interaction with the external environment, it must have a Start function with a uniquely attributed World argument.

Incorporating side-effects safely in a functional language has received a lot of attention in the functional language research community. For lazy functional languages a host of techniques has been proposed. Well-known examples are *monads*, *continuations*, and *streams*. For eager functional languages, the situation is less complicated because in these languages programs exhibit an execution order that is more predictable.

Signatures. A signature $x :: t$ declares that identifier x has type t. An identifier x starts with a lowercase or uppercase letter and has no whitespace characters. The type t can be either of the following forms.

- It is one of the basic types, which are: `Bool`, `Int`, `Real`, `Char`, `String`, `File`, and `World`.
- It is a type variable. Their identifiers start with a lowercase character.
- It is a composite type, using one of the language type constructors `[ ]`, `{ }`, `(,)`, and `->`.
    - If t is a type, then `[t]` is the *list-of-t* type.
    - If t is a type, then `{t}` is the *array-of-t* type.
    - If t_1 and t_2 are types, then (t_1,t_2) is the *tuple-of-t_1-and-t_2* type. This generalizes to t_1 upto t_n with $2 \leq n \leq 32$, separating each type by `,`. Hence, (t_1,t_2,t_3), (t_1,t_2,t_3,t_4) and so on are also tuple types.
    - If t_1 and t_2 are types, then t_1 `->` t_2 is the *function-of-t_1-to-t_2* type. This generalizes to $t_1 \ldots t_n$ `->` t_{n+1}, where $t_1 \ldots t_n$ are the argument types, and t_{n+1} is the result type. The function argument types are separated by whitespace characters. So, t_1 t_2 `->` t_3, t_1 t_2 t_3 `->` t_4 and so on are also function types.
- It is a custom defined type, using either an algebraic type or a record type. Their type names are easily recognized because they always start with an uppercase character. Examples of algebraic and record types can be found in Sect. 3.3.

Signatures can be *overloaded*, in which case they are extended with one or more *overloading constraints*, resulting in $x :: t \mid tc_1\ a_1\ \&\ \ldots\&\ tc_n\ a_n$. A constraint $tc_i\ a_i$ is a pair of a type class tc_i and a type variable a_i that must occur in t. Note that $tc_1\ a\ \&\ tc_2\ a\ \&\ \ldots\&\ tc_n\ a$ can be shorthanded to tc_1, tc_2, $\ldots, tc_n\ a$.

Overloading. *Overloading* is a common and useful concept in programming languages that allows you to use the same identifier for different, yet related, values or computations. In the host language *Clean* overloading is introduced in an explicit way: if you wish to reuse a certain identifier x, then you declare it via a *type class*:

class $x\ a_1\ \ldots\ a_n :: t$

with the following properties:

- the *type variables* $a_1\ \ldots\ a_n$ $(n > 0)$ must be different and start with a lowercase character;
- the *type scheme* t can be any type that uses the type variables a_i.

This declaration introduces the type class x with the single *type class member* x. It is possible to declare a type class x with several type class members $x_1 \ldots x_k$:

```
class x a₁ ... aₙ
  where x₁ :: t₁

          ⋮

    xₖ :: tₖ
```

It is customary, but not required, that in this case identifier x starts with an uppercase character. The identifiers x_i need to be different, and their types t_i can use any of the type variables a_i.

Type classes can be *instantiated* with concrete types. This must always be done for all of its type variables and all type class members. The general form of such an instantiation is:

instance x t_1' ... t_n' | tc_1 b_1 & ... & tc_m b_m
  where ...

with the following properties:

- the types t_1' ... t_n' are substituted for the type variables a_1 ... a_n of the type class x. They are not required to be different but they are not allowed to share type variables;
- the types t_i' can be overloaded themselves, in which case their type class constraints tc_i b_i are enumerated after | (which is absent in case of no constraints). The type variable b_i must occur in one of the types t_i';
- the **where** keyword is followed by implementations of all class member functions. Of course, these implementations must adhere to the types that result after substitution of the corresponding type schemes t_i.

Algebraic and ∃-Types. The BoxedTask type in Fig. 6 is an example of an *algebraic type* that is *existentially quantified*. Algebraic types allow you to introduce new constants in your program, and give them a type at the same time. The general format of an algebraic type declaration is:

:: t a_1 ... a_m = d_1 t_{11} ... t_{1c_1} | ... | d_n t_{n1} ... t_{nc_n}

with the following properties:

- the type constructor t is an identifier that starts with an uppercase character;
- the type variables a_i $(0 \leq i \leq m)$ must be different and start with a lowercase character;
- the data constructors d_i $(1 \leq i \leq n)$ must be different and start with an uppercase character;
- the data constructors can have zero or more arguments. An argument is either one of the type variables a_i or a type that may use the type variables a_i.

From these properties it follows that all occurrences of type variables in data constructors (all right hand side declarations) must be accounted for in the type constructor (on the left hand side). With *existential quantification* it is possible to circumvent this: for each data constructor one can introduce type variables that are known only locally to the data constructor. A data constructor can be enhanced with such local type variables in the following way:

E. $b_1 \ldots b_k : d_i\ t_{i1} \ldots t_{ic_i}\ \&\ tc_1\ x_1\ \&\ \ldots \&\ tc_l\ x_l$

with the following properties:

- the type variables b_j $(0 \le j \le k)$ must be different and start with a lowercase character;
- the arguments of the data constructor d_i can now also use any of the existentially quantified type variables b_i;
- the pairs $tc\ x$ are type class constraints, in which tc indicates a type class and x is one of the existentially quantified type variables b_i.

From these properties it follows that it does not make sense to introduce an existentially quantified type variable in a data constructor without adding information how values of that type can be *used*. There are basically two ways of doing this. The first is to add functions of the same type that handle these encapsulated values (in a very similar way to methods in classes in object oriented programming). The second is to constrain the encapsulated type variables to type classes.

Record Types. Record types are useful to create named collections of data. The parts of such a collection can be referred to by means of a field name. The general format of a record type declaration is:

$$:: t\ a_1 \ldots a_m = \{ r_1 :: t_1, \ldots, r_n :: t_n \}$$

with the following properties:

- the type constructor t is an identifier that starts with an uppercase character;
- the type variables a_i $(0 \le i \le m)$ must be different and start with a lowercase character;
- the pairs $r_i :: t_i$ $(1 \le i \le n)$ determine the components of the record type. The field names r_i must be different and start with a lowercase character. The types t_i can use the type variables a_i.

Just like algebraic types, record types can also introduce existentially quantified type variables on the right-hand side of the record type. However, unlike algebraic types, their use can not be constrained by means of type classes. Hence, if you need to access these encapsulated values afterwards, you need to include function components within the record type definition.

Disambiguating Records. Within a program record field *names* are allowed to occur in several record types (the corresponding field *types* are allowed to be different). This helps you to choose proper field names, without worrying too much about their existence in other records. The consequence of this useful feature is that once in a while you need to explicit about the record value that is created (in case of records with exactly the same set of record field names) and when using record field selectors (either in a pattern match or with the .*field* notation). Type constructor names are required to be unique within a program, hence they are used to disambiguate these cases.

- When creating a record value, you are obliged to give a value to each and every record field of that type. If a record has a field with a unique name, then it is clear which record type is intended. Only if two records have the same set of field names, you need to include the type constructor name t within the record value definition.

  $$\ldots \; \{ \, t \mid f_1 = e_1 \, , \; \ldots, \; f_n = e_n \} \; \ldots$$

- If a record pattern has at least one field with a unique name, then it is clear which record type is intended. The record pattern is disambiguated by including the type constructor name t in the pattern in an analogous way as described above when creating a record value, except that you do not need to mention all record fields and that the right hand sides of the fields are patterns rather than expressions:

  $$\ldots \; \{ \, t \mid f_1 = p_1 \, , \; \ldots, \; f_n = p_n \} \; \ldots$$

- If a record field selection $e.f$ uses a unique field name f, then it is clear which record type is intended. A record field selection can be disambiguated by including the type constructor name t as a field selector. Hence, $e.t.f$ states that field f of record type t must be used.

Record Updates. Record values are defined by enumerating each and every record field, along with a value. Example 5 shows that new record values can also be constructed from old record values. If r is a record (or an expression that yields a record value), then a new record value can be created by specifying only what record fields are different. The general format of such a *record update* is:

$$\{ \, r \, \& \, f_1 = e_1 \, , \; \ldots, \; f_n = e_n \}$$

This expression creates a new record value that is identical to r, except for the fields f_i that have values e_i $(0 < i \le n)$ respectively. A record field should occur at most once in this expression.

Synonym Types. Synonym types only introduce a new type constructor name for another type. The general formal of a type synonym declaration is:

$$:: \; t' \, a_1 \, \ldots \, a_n \; :== \; t$$

with the following properties:

- the type constructor t' is an identifier that starts with an uppercase character;
- the type variables a_i $(0 \le i \le n)$ must be different and start with a lowercase character;
- the type t can be any type that uses the type variables a_i. However, a synonym type is not allowed to be recursive, either directly or indirectly.

Synonym types are useful for documentation purposes of your model types, as illustrated in Example 4. Although the name t' must be new, t' does not introduce a new type: it is completely exchangeable with any occurrence of t.

Strictness. In the signature of the basic task function `return` the first argument is provided with a *strictness annotation*, `!`. Recall that *iTask* is embedded in *Clean*, which is a *lazy* language. In a lazy language, computation is driven by *the need to produce a result*. As a simple example, consider the function `const` that does nothing but return its first argument:

```
const x y = x
```

There is absolutely no need for `const` to evaluate argument y to a value. However, argument x is returned by `const`, so its evaluation better produces a result or otherwise `const x y` won't produce a result either.

The more general, and more technical, way of phrasing this is the following. Suppose we have a function f that has a formal argument x. Let e be a diverging computation (it either takes infinitely long or aborts without producing a result). If $(f\ e)$ also diverges, then argument x is said to be strict in f. Note that this is a property of the function, and not of the argument. In case of `const`, it is no problem that argument y might be a diverging computation because it is not needed by `const` to compute its result. The consequence is that with respect to termination properties, it does not matter if strict function arguments are evaluated *before* the function is called. In many cases, this increases the performance of the application because you do not need to maintain suspended computations (due to lazy evaluation), but instead can evaluate them to a result and use that instead.

The strictness property of function arguments is expressed in the function signature by prefixing the argument that is strict in that function with the `!` annotation. In case of `const`, its signature is:

```
const :: !a b -> a
```

References

1. Kernighan, B., Ritchie, D.: The C Programming Language, 2nd edn. Prentice Hall, Englewood Cliffs (1988)
2. Plasmeijer, R., Achten, P., Koopman, P.: iTasks: executable specifications of interactive work flow systems for the web. In: Hinze, R., Ramsey, N. (eds.) Proceedings of the International Conference on Functional Programming, ICFP 2007, Freiburg, Germany, pp. 141–152. ACM Press (2007)
3. Lijnse, B., Plasmeijer, R.: iTasks 2: iTasks for end-users. In: Morazán, M.T., Scholz, S.-B. (eds.) IFL 2009. LNCS, vol. 6041, pp. 36–54. Springer, Heidelberg (2010)
4. van der Heijden, M., Lijnse, B., Lucas, P.J.F., Heijdra, Y.F., Schermer, T.R.J.: Managing COPD exacerbations with telemedicine. In: Peleg, M., Lavrač, N., Combi, C. (eds.) AIME 2011. LNCS, vol. 6747, pp. 169–178. Springer, Heidelberg (2011)
5. Jansen, J., Lijnse, B., Plasmeijer, R.: Towards dynamic workflows for crisis management. In: French, S., Tomaszewski, B., Zobel, C. (eds.) Proceedings of the 7th International Conference on Information Systems for Crisis Response and Management, ISCRAM 2010, Seattle, WA, USA, May 2010

6. Lijnse, B., Jansen, J., Nanne, R., Plasmeijer, R.: Capturing the Netherlands coast guard's SAR workflow with iTasks. In: Mendonca, D., Dugdale, J. (eds.) Proceedings of the 8th International Conference on Information Systems for Crisis Response and Management, ISCRAM 2011, Lisbon, Portugal. ISCRAM Association, May 2011

7. Meijer, E.: Server side web scripting in Haskell. J. Funct. Program **10**(1), 1–18 (2000)

8. Hanus, M.: High-level server side web scripting in Curry. In: Ramakrishnan, I.V. (ed.) PADL 2001. LNCS, vol. 1990, pp. 76–92. Springer, Heidelberg (2001)

9. Elsman, M., Larsen, K.F.: Typing XHTML web applications in ML. In: Jayaraman, B. (ed.) PADL 2004. LNCS, vol. 3057, pp. 224–238. Springer, Heidelberg (2004)

10. Elsman, M., Hallenberg, N.: Web programming with SMLserver. In: Dahl, V. (ed.) PADL 2003. LNCS, vol. 2562, pp. 74–91. Springer, Heidelberg (2002)

11. Thiemann, P.: WASH/CGI: server-side web scripting with sessions and typed, compositional forms. In: Adsul, B., Ramakrishnan, C.R. (eds.) PADL 2002. LNCS, vol. 2257, p. 192. Springer, Heidelberg (2002)

12. Serrano, M., Gallesio, E., Loitsch, F.: Hop, a language for programming the web 2.0. In: Proceedings of the 11th International Conference on Object-Oriented Programming, Systems, Languages, and Applications, OOPSLA 2006, Portland, Oregon, USA, 22–26 October 2006, pp. 975–985 (2006)

13. Loitsch, F., Serrano, M.: Hop client-side compilation. In: Proceedings of the 7th Symposium on Trends in Functional Programming, TFP 2007, New York, NY, USA, Interact, 2–4 April 2007, pp. 141–158 (2007)

14. Cooper, E., Lindley, S., Yallop, J.: Links: web programming without tiers. In: de Boer, F.S., Bonsangue, M.M., Graf, S., de Roever, W.-P. (eds.) FMCO 2006. LNCS, vol. 4709, pp. 266–296. Springer, Heidelberg (2007)

15. Cooper, E., Lindley, S., Wadler, P., Yallop, J.: An idiom's guide to formlets. Technical report, The University of Edinburgh, UK (2007). http://groups.inf.ed.ac.uk/links/papers/formlets-draft2007.pdf

16. van der Aalst, W., ter Hofstede, A., Kiepuszewski, B., Barros, A.: Workflow patterns. Technical Report FIT-TR-2002-02, Queensland University of Technology (2002)

17. Hemel, Z., Verhaaf, R., Visser, E.: WebWorkFlow: an object-oriented workflow modeling language for web applications. In: Czarnecki, K., Ober, I., Bruel, J.-M., Uhl, A., Völter, M. (eds.) MODELS 2008. LNCS, vol. 5301, pp. 113–127. Springer, Heidelberg (2008)

18. Crandall, B., Klein, G., Hoffman, R.R.: Working Minds: A Practitioner's Guide to Cognitive Task Analysis. MIT Press, Cambridge (2006)

19. Plasmeijer, R., van Eekelen, M.: Clean language report (version 2.1) (2002). http://clean.cs.ru.nl

Spreadsheet Engineering

Jácome Cunha[1,2], João Paulo Fernandes[1,3], Jorge Mendes[1,2],
and João Saraiva[1(✉)]

[1] HASLab/INESC TEC, Universidade do Minho, Braga, Portugal
{jacome,jpaulo,jorgemendes,jas}@di.uminho.pt
[2] CIICESI, ESTGF, Instituto Politécnico do Porto, Porto, Portugal
{jmc,jcmendes}@estgf.ipp.pt
[3] Reliable and Secure Computation Group ((rel)ease),
Universidade da Beira Interior, Covilhã, Portugal
jpf@di.ubi.pt

Abstract. These tutorial notes present a methodology for spreadsheet engineering. First, we present data mining and database techniques to reason about spreadsheet data. These techniques are used to compute relationships between spreadsheet elements (cells/columns/rows), which are later used to infer a model defining the business logic of the spreadsheet. Such a model of a spreadsheet data is a visual domain specific language that we embed in a well-known spreadsheet system.

The embedded model is the building block to define techniques for model-driven spreadsheet development, where advanced techniques are used to guarantee the model-instance synchronization. In this model-driven environment, any user data update has to follow the model-instance conformance relation, thus, guiding spreadsheet users to introduce correct data. Data refinement techniques are used to synchronize models and instances after users update/evolve the model.

These notes briefly describe our model-driven spreadsheet environment, the MDSheet environment, that implements the presented methodology. To evaluate both proposed techniques and the MDSheet tool, we have conducted, in laboratory sessions, an empirical study with the summer school participants. The results of this study are presented in these notes.

1   Introduction

Spreadsheets are one of the most used software systems. Indeed, for a non-professional programmer, like for example, an accountant, an engineer, a manager, etc., the programming language of choice is a spreadsheet. These *programmers* are often referred to as *end-user programmers* [53] and their numbers are increasing

This work is part funded by ERDF - European Regional Development Fund through the COMPETE Programme (operational programme for competitiveness) and by National Funds through the FCT - Fundação para a Ciência e a Tecnologia (Portuguese Foundation for Science and Technology) within projects FCOMP-01-0124-FEDER-010048, and FCOMP-01-0124-FEDER-020532. The first author was funded by FCT grant SFRH/BPD/73358/2010.

© Springer International Publishing Switzerland 2015
V. Zsók et al. (Eds.): CEFP 2013, LNCS 8606, pp. 246–299, 2015.
DOI: 10.1007/978-3-319-15940-9_6

rapidly. In fact, they already outnumber professional programmers [68]! The reasons for the tremendous commercial success that spreadsheets experience undergoes continuous debate, but it is almost unanimous that two key aspects are recognized. Firstly, spreadsheets are highly flexible, which inherently guarantees that they are intensively multi-purpose. Secondly, the initial learning effort associated with the use of spreadsheets is objectively low. These facts suggest that the spreadsheet is also a significant target for the application of the principles of programming languages.

As a programming language, and as noticed by Peyton-Jones et al. [45], spreadsheets can be seen as simple functional programs. For example, the following (spreadsheet) data:

```
A1 = 44
A2 = (A1-20)* 3/4
A3 = SUM(A1,A2)
```

is a functional program! If we see spreadsheets as a functional program, then it is a very simple and flat one, where there are no functions apart from the built-in ones (for example, the SUM function is a predefined one). A program is a single collection of equations of the form "variable = formula", with no mechanisms (like functions) to structure our code. When compared to modern (functional) programming languages, spreadsheets lack support for abstraction, testing, encapsulation, or structured programming. As a result, they are error-prone: numerous studies have shown that existing spreadsheets contain too many errors [57,58,62,63].

To overcome the lack of advanced principles of programming languages, and, consequently the alarming rate of errors in spreadsheets, several researchers proposed the use of abstraction and structuring mechanisms in spreadsheets: Peyton-Jones et al. [45] proposed the use of user-defined functions in spreadsheets. Erwig et al. [29], Hermans et al. [39], and Cunha et al. [19] introduced and advocate the use of models to abstractly represent the business logic of the spreadsheet data.

In this tutorial notes, we build upon these results and we present in detail a Model-Driven Engineering (MDE) approach for spreadsheets. First, we present the design of a Visual, Domain Specific Language (VDSL). In [29] a domain specific modeling language, named ClassSheet, was introduced in order to allow end users to reason about their spreadsheets by looking at a concise, abstract and simple model, instead of looking into large and complex spreadsheet data. In fact, ClassSheets offer to end users what API definitions offer to programmers and database schemas offer to database experts: an abstract mechanism to understand and reason about their programs/databases without having to look into large and complex implementations/data. ClassSheets have both a textual and visual representation, being the later very much like a spreadsheet! In the design of the ClassSheet language we follow a well-know approach in a functional setting: the embedding of a domain specific language in a host functional language [44,70]. To be more precise, we define the embedding of a visual, domain specific modeling language in a host spreadsheet system.

Secondly, we present the implementation of this VDSL. To provide a full MDE environment to end users we use data refinement techniques to express the type-safe evolution of a model (after an end-user update) and the automatic co-evolution of the spreadsheet data (that is, the instance) [28]. This novel implementation of the VDSL guarantees the model/instance conformance after the model evolves. Moreover, we also use principles from syntax-based editors [27,30,47] where an initial spreadsheet instance is generated from the model, that has some knowledge about the business logic off the data. Using such knowledge the spreadsheet instance guides end users introducing correct data. In fact, in these generated spreadsheets only updates that conform to the model are allowed.

Finally, we present the results of the empirical study we conducted with the school participants in order to realize whether the use of MDE approach is useful for end users, or not. In the laboratory sessions of this tutorial, we taught participants to use our model-driven spreadsheet environment. Then, the students were asked to perform a set of model-driven spreadsheet tasks, and to write small reports about the advantages/disadvantages of our approach when compared to a regular spreadsheet system.

The remaining of this paper is organized as follows. In Sect. 2 we give a brief overview of the history of spreadsheets. We also present some horror stories that recently had social and financial impact. In Sect. 3 we present data mining and database techniques that are the building blocks of our approach to build models for spreadsheets. Section 4 presents models for defining the business logic of a spreadsheet. First, we present in detail ClassSheet models. After that, we present techniques to automatically infer such a model from (legacy) spreadsheet data. Next, we show the embedding of the ClassSheet models in a widely used spreadsheet system. Section 5 presents a framework for the evolution of model-driven spreadsheets in Haskell. This framework is expressed using data refinements where by defining a model-to-model transformation we get for free the forward and backward transformations that map the data (i.e., the instance). In Sect. 6 we present MDSheet: a MDE environment for spreadsheets. Finally, in Sect. 7 we present the results of the empirical study with the school participants where we validate the use of a MDE approach in spreadsheet development. Section 8 presents the conclusions of the tutorial paper.

2   Spreadsheets: A History of Success?

The use of a tabular-like structure to organize data has been used for many years. A good example of structuring data in this way is the Plimpton 322 tablet (Fig. 1), dated from around 1800 BC [65]. The Plimpton 322 tablet is an example of a table containing four columns and fifteen rows with numerical data. For each column there is a descriptive header, and the fourth column contains a numbering of the rows from one to fifteen, written in the Babylonian number system. This tablet contains Pythagorean triples [14], but was more likely built as a list of regular reciprocal pairs [65].

A tabular layout allows a systematic analysis of the information displayed and it helps to structure values in order to perform calculations.

Fig. 1. Plimpton 322 – a tablet from around 1800 BC (A good explanation of the Plimpton 322 tablet is available at Bill Casselman's webpage http://www.math.ubc. ca/~cass/courses/m446-03/pl322/pl322.html).

The terms *spreadsheet* and *worksheet* originated in accounting even before electronic spreadsheets existed. Both had the same meaning, but the term worksheet was mostly used until 1970 [16]. Accountants used a spreadsheet or worksheet to prepare their budgets and other tasks. They would use a pencil and paper with columns and rows. They would place the accounts in one column, the corresponding amount in the next column, etc. Then they would manually total the columns and rows, as in the example shown in Fig. 2. After 1970 the term spreadsheet became more widely used [16].

This worked fine, except when the accountant needed to make a change to one of the numbers. This change would result in having to recalculate, by hand, several totals!

The benefits make (paper) tables applicable to a great variety of domains, like for example on student inquiries or exams, taxes submission, gathering and

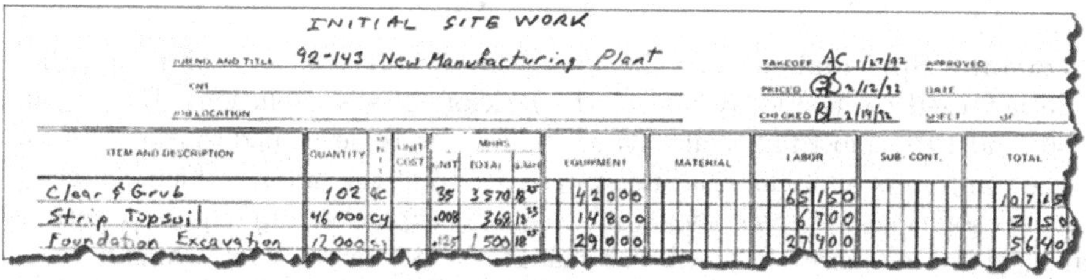

Fig. 2. A hand-written budget spreadsheet.

MULTIPLICATION TABLE

	1	2	3	4	5	6	7	8	9	10
1	1	2	3	4	5	6	7	8	9	10
2	2	4	6	8	10	12	14	16	18	20
3	3	6	9	12	15	18	21	24	27	30
4	4	8	12	16	20	24	28	32	36	40
5	5	10	15	20	25	30	35	40	45	50
6	6	12	18	24	30	36	42	48	54	60
7	7	14	21	28	35	42	49	56	63	70
8	8	16	24	32	40	48	56	64	72	80
9	9	18	27	36	45	54	63	72	81	90
10	10	20	30	40	50	60	70	80	90	100

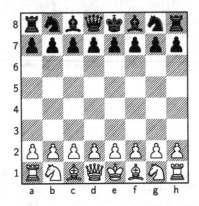

Fig. 3. Paper spreadsheet for a multiplication table.

Fig. 4. Chess boards have a tabular layout, with letters identifying columns and numbers identifying rows.

analysis of sport statistics, or any purpose that requires input of data and/or performing calculations. An example of such a table used by students is the multiplication table as displayed in Fig. 3.

This spreadsheet has eleven columns and eleven rows, where the first row and column work as a header to identify the information, and the actual results of the multiplication table are shown in the other cells of the table.

Tabular layouts are also common in games. The chess game is a good example of a tabular layout game as displayed in Fig. 4.

Electronic Spreadsheets. While spreadsheets were very used on paper, they were not used electronically due to the lack of software solutions. During the 1960s and 1970s most financial software bundles were developed to run on mainframe computers and time-sharing systems. Two of the main problems of these software solutions were that they were extremely expensive and required a technical expertise to operate [16]. All that changed in 1979 when VisiCal was released for the Apple II system [13]. The affordable price and the easy to use tabular interface made it a tremendous success, mainly because it did not need any programming knowledge to be operated. VisiCal was the first spreadsheet software to include a textual interface composed by cells and established how the graphical interface of every other spreadsheet software that came after it would be like. It consisted of a column/row tabulation program with an WYSI-WYG interface, providing cell references (format A1, A3..A6). Other important aspect included the fast recalculation of values every time a cell was changed, as opposed to previous solutions that took hours to compute results under the same circumstances [16]. VisiCal not only made spreadsheets available to a wider audience, but also led to make personal computers more popular by introducing them to the financial and business communities and others.

In 1984, Lotus 1-2-3 was released for MS-DOS with major improvements, which included graphics generation, better performance, and user friendly interface, which led it to dethrone VisiCal as the number one spreadsheet system. It was only in 1990, when Microsoft Windows gained significant market share, that Lotus 1-2-3 lost the position as the most sold spreadsheet software. At that time only Microsoft Excel[1] was compatible with Windows, which raised sales by a huge amount making it the market leading spreadsheet system [16].

In the mid eighties the free software movement started and soon free open source alternatives can be used, namely Gnumeric[2], OpenOffice Calc[3] and derivatives like LibreOffice Calc[4].

More recently, web/cloud-based spreadsheet host systems have been developed, e.g., Google Drive[5], *Microsoft* Office 365[6], and ZoHo Sheet[7] which are making spreadsheets available in different type of mobile devices (from laptops, to tablets and mobile phones!). These systems are not dependent on any particular operating system, allow to create and edit spreadsheets in an online collaborative environment, and provide import/export of spreadsheet files for offline use.

In fact, spreadsheet systems have evolved into powerful systems. However, the basic features provided by spreadsheet host systems remain roughly the same:

- a spreadsheet is a tabular structure composed by cells, where the columns are referenced by letters and the rows by numbers;
- cells can contain either values or formulas;
- formulas can have references for other cells (e.g., A1 for the individual cell in column A and row 1 or A3:B5 for the range of cells starting in cell A3 and ending in cell B5);
- instant automatic recalculation of formulas when cells are modified;
- ease to copy/paste values, with references being updated automatically.

---

[1] Microsoft Excel: http://office.microsoft.com/en-us/excel.

[2] Gnumeric: http://projects.gnome.org/gnumeric.

[3] OpenOffice: http://www.openoffice.org.

[4] LibreOffice: http://www.libreoffice.org.

[5] Google Drive: http://drive.google.com.

[6] Microsoft Office 365: http://www.microsoft.com/en-us/office365/online-software.aspx.

[7] ZoHo Sheet: http://sheet.zoho.com.

Spreadsheets are a relevant research topic, as they play a pivotal role in modern society. Indeed, they are inherently multi-purpose and widely used both by individuals to cope with simple needs as well as by large companies as integrators of complex systems and as support for business decisions [40]. Also, their popularity is still growing, with an almost impossible to estimate but staggering number of spreadsheets created every year. Spreadsheet popularity is due to characteristics such as their low entry barrier, their availability on almost any computer and their simple visual interface. In fact, being a conventional language that is understood by both professional programmers and end users [53], spreadsheets are many times used as bridges between these two communities which often face communication problems. Ultimately, spreadsheets seem to hit the sweet spot between flexibility and expressiveness.

Spreadsheets have probably passed the point of no return in terms of importance. There are several studies that show the success of spreadsheets:

- it is estimated that 95 % of all U.S. firms use them for financial reporting [60];
- it is also known that 90 % of all analysts in industry perform calculations in spreadsheets [60];
- finally, studies show that 50 % of all spreadsheets are the basis for decisions [40].

This importance, however, has not been achieved together with effective mechanisms for error prevention, as shown by several studies [57,58]. Indeed, spreadsheets are known to be error-prone, a claim that is supported by the long list of real problems that were blamed on spreadsheets, which is compiled, available and frequently updated at the *European Spreadsheet Risk Interest Group (EuSpRIG)* web site[8].

One particularly sad example in this list involves our country (and other European countries), which currently undergoes a financial rescue plan based on intense austerity whose merit was co-justified upon [64]. The authors of that paper present evidence that GDP growth slows to a snail's pace once the sovereign debt of a nation exceeds 90 % of GDP, and it was precisely this evidence that was several times politically used to argue for austerity measures.

Unfortunately, the fact is that the general conclusion of [64] has been publicly questioned given that a formula range error was found in the spreadsheet supporting the authors' calculations. While the authors have later re-affirmed their original conclusions, the public pressure was so intense that a few weeks later they felt the need to publish an errata of their 2010 paper. It is furthermore unlikely that the concrete social and economical impacts of that particular spreadsheet error will ever be determined.

Given the massive use of spreadsheets and the their alarming number of errors, many researcher have been working on this topic. Burnett et al. studied the use of end-users programming principles to spreadsheets [15,36,66,67], as well as the use of software engineering techniques [35,37]. Erwig et al. applied

---

[8] This list of horror stories is available at: http://www.eusprig.org/horror-stories.htm.

several techniques from software engineering to spreadsheets, such as testing and debugging [3,4,7,8], model-driven approaches [5,9,29,32,33,50]. Erwig also studied the use in spreadsheets of programming languages techniques such as type systems [1,2,6,34]. Hermans et al. studied how to help users better understand the spreadsheets they use [40–42]. In this context, Cunha et al. proposed a catalog of smells for spreadsheets [21] and a tool to detect them [22]. Panko et al. have been developing very interesting work to understand the errors found in spreadsheets [56–59].

3 Spreadsheet Analysis

Spreadsheets, like other software systems, usually start as simple, single user software systems and rapidly evolve into complex and large systems developed by several users [40]. Such spreadsheets become hard to maintain and evolve because of the large amount of data they contain, the complex dependencies and formulas used (that very often are poor documented [41]), and finally because the developers of those spreadsheets may not be available (because they may have left the company/project). In these cases to understand the business logic defined in such legacy spreadsheets is a hard and time consuming task [40].

In this section we study techniques to analyze spreadsheet data using technology from both the data mining and the database realms. This technology is used to mine the spreadsheet data in order to automatically compute a model describing the business logic of the underlying spreadsheet data.

3.1 Spreadsheet Data Mining

Before we present these techniques, let us consider the example spreadsheet modeling an airline scheduling system which we adapted from [51] and illustrated in Fig. 5.

The labels in the first row have the following meaning: **PilotId** represents a unique identification code for each pilot, **Pilot-Name** is the name of the pilot, and column labeled **Phone** contains his phone number. Columns labeled **Depart** and **Destination** contain the departure and destination airports, respectively. The column **Date** contains the date of the flight and **Hours** defines the number of hours of the flight. Next columns define the plain used in the flight: **N-Number** is a unique number of the plain, **Model** is the model of the plane, and **Plane-Name** is the name of the plane.

	A	B	C	D	E	F	G	H	I	J
1	Pilot-Id	Pilot-Name	Phone	Depart	Destination	Date	Hours	N-Number	Model	Plane-Name
2	pl1	John	321654987	OPO	NAT	12/12/2010 – 14:00	07:00	N2342	B 747	Magalhães
3	pl2	Mike	147258369	OPO	NAT	01/01/2011 – 16:00	07:00	N2342	B 747	Magalhães
4	pl1	John	321654987	LIS	AMS	16/12/2010 – 10:00	02:45	N341	B 777	Cabral
5	pl3	John	469184201	OPO	CLJ	13/07/2013 – 10:00	05:45	N101	A 380	DSL
6										

Fig. 5. A spreadsheet representing pilots, planes and flights.

This spreadsheet defines a valid model to represent the information for scheduling flights. However, it contains *redundant information*. For example, the displayed data specifies the name of the plane *Magalhães* twice. This kind of redundancy makes the maintenance and update of the spreadsheet complex and error-prone. In fact, two well-known database problems occur when organizing our data in a non-normalized way [71]:

- Update Anomalies: this problem occurs when we change information in one tuple but leave the same information unchanged in the others. In our example, this may happen if we change the name of the plane *Magalhães* on row 2, but not on row 3. As a result the data will become inconsistent!
- Deletion Anomalies: problem happens when we delete some tuple and we lose other information as a side effect. For example, if we delete row 3 in the spreadsheet all the information concerning the pilot *Mike* is eliminated.

As a result, a mistake is easily made, for example, by mistyping a name and thus corrupting the data. The same information can be stored without redundancy. In fact, in the database community, techniques for database normalization are commonly used to minimize duplication of information and improve data integrity. Database normalization is based on the detection and exploitation of *functional dependencies* inherent in the data [51,72].

Exercise 1. *Consider the data in the following table and answer the questions.*

movieID	title	language	renterNr	renterNm	rentStart	rentFinished	rent	totalToPay
mv23	Little Man	English	c33	Paul	01-04-2010	26-04-2010	0.5	12.50
mv1	The Ohio	English	c33	Paul	30-03-2010	23-04-2010	0.5	12.00
mv21	Edmond	English	c26	Smith	02-04-2010	04-04-2010	0.5	1.00
mv102	You, Me, D	English	c3	Michael	22-03-2010	03-04-2010	0.3	3.60
mv23	Little Man	English	c26	Smith	02-12-2009	04-04-2010	0.5	61.50
mv23	Little Man	English	c14	John	12-04-2010	16-04-2010	0.5	2.00

1. *Which row(s) can be deleted without causing a deletion anomaly?*
2. *Identify two attributes that can cause update anomalies when editing the corresponding data.*

3.2 Databases Technology

In order to infer a model representing the business logic of a spreadsheet data, we need to analyze the data and define relationships between data entities. Objects that are contained in a spreadsheet and the relationships between them are reflected by the presence of *functional dependencies* between spreadsheet columns. Informally, a functional dependency between a column C and another column C' means that the values in column C determine the values in column

C', that is, there are no two rows in the spreadsheet that have the same value in column C but differ in their values in column C'.

For instance, in our running example the functional dependency between column A (**Pilot-Id**) and column B (**Pilot-Name**) exists, meaning that the identification number of a pilot determines its name. That is to say that, there are no two rows with the same id number (column A), but differ in their names (column B). A similar functional dependency occurs between identifier (i.e., number) of a plane **N-Number** and its name **Plane-Name**.

This idea can be extended to multiple columns, that is, when any two rows that agree in the values of columns $C_1, \ldots, C_n$ also agree in their value in columns $C'_1, \ldots, C'_m$, then $C'_1, \ldots, C'_m$ are said to be *functionally dependent* on $C_1, \ldots, C_n$.

In our running example, the following functional dependencies hold:

$$Depart, Destination \rightharpoonup Hours$$

stating that the departure and destination airports determines the number of hours of the flight.

Definition 1. *A functional dependency between two sets of attributes A and B, written $A \rightharpoonup B$, holds in a table if for any two tuples t and t' in that table $t[A] = t'[A] \implies t[B] = t'[B]$ where $t[A]$ yields the (sub)tuple of values for the attributes in A. In other words, if the tuples agree in the values for attribute set A, they agree in the values for attribute set B. The attribute set A is also called antecedent, and the attribute set B consequent.*

Our goal is to use the data in a spreadsheet to identify functional dependencies. Although we use all the data available in the spreadsheet, we consider a particular instance of the spreadsheet domain only. However, there may exist counter examples to the dependencies found, but these just happen not to be included in the spreadsheet. Thus, the dependencies we discover are always an approximation. On the other hand, depending on the data, it can happen that many "accidental" functional dependencies are detected, that is, functional dependencies that do not reflect the underlying model.

For instance, in our example we can identify the following dependency that just happens to be fulfilled for this particular data set, but that does certainly *not* reflect a constraint that should hold in general: *Model $\rightharpoonup$ Plane_Name*, that is to say that the model of a plane determines its name! In fact, the data contained in the spreadsheet example supports over 30 functional dependencies. Next we list a few more that hold for our example.

Pilot-ID $\rightharpoonup$ Pilot-Name
Pilot-ID $\rightharpoonup$ Phone
Pilot-ID $\rightharpoonup$ Pilot-Name, Phone
Depart, Destination $\rightharpoonup$ Hours
Hours $\rightharpoonup$ Model

Exercise 2. *Consider the data in the following table.*

proj1	John	New York	30-03-2010	50000	Long Island	Richy	34	USA	Mike	inst3	36	6
proj1	John	New York	30-03-2010	50000	Long Island	Tim	33	JP	Anthony	inst1	24	4
proj1	John	New York	30-03-2010	50000	Long Island	Mark	30	UK	Alfred	inst3	36	6
proj2	John	Los Angels	02-04-2010	3000	Los Angels	Richy	34	USA	Mike	inst2	30	5
proj3	Paul	Chicago	01-01-2009	12000	Chicago	Tim	33	JP	Anthony	inst1	24	4
proj3	Paul	Chicago	01-01-2009	12000	Chicago	Mark	30	UK	Alfred	inst1	24	4

Which are the functional dependencies that hold in this case?

Because spreadsheet data may induce too many functional dependencies, the next step is therefore to filter out as many of the accidental dependencies as possible and keep the ones that are indicative of the underlying model. The process of identifying the "valid" functional dependencies is, of course, ambiguous in general. Therefore, we employ a series of heuristics for evaluating dependencies.

Note that several of these heuristics are possible only in the context of spreadsheets. This observation supports the contention that end-user software engineering can benefit greatly from the context information that is available in a specific end-user programming domain. In the spreadsheet domain rich context is provided, in particular, through the spatial arrangement of cells and through labels [31].

Next, we describe five heuristics we use to discard accidental functional dependencies. Each of these heuristics can add support to a functional dependency.

Label semantics. This heuristic is used to classify antecedents in functional dependencies. Most antecedents (recall that antecedents determine the values of consequents) are labeled as "code", "id", "nr", "no", "number", or are a combination of these labels with a label more related to the subject. functional dependency with an antecedent of this kind receives high support.

For example, in our property renting spreadsheet, we give high support to the functional dependency *N-Number* $\rightarrow$ *Plane-Name* than to the *Plane-Name* $\rightarrow$ *N-Number* one.

Label arrangement. If the functional dependency respects the original order of the attributes, this counts in favor of this dependency since very often key attributes appear to the left of non-key attributes.

In our running example, there are two functional dependencies induced by columns *N-Number* and *Plane-Name*, namely *N-Number* $\rightarrow$ *Plane-Name* and *Plane-Name* $\rightarrow$ *N-Number*. Using this heuristic we prefer the former dependency to the latter.

Antecedent size. Good primary keys often consist of a small number of attributes, that is, they are based on small antecedent sets. Therefore, the smaller the number of antecedent attributes, the higher the support for the functional dependency.

Ratio between antecedent and consequent sizes. In general, functional dependencies with smaller antecedents and larger consequents are stronger and thus more likely to be a reflection of the underlying data model. Therefore, a functional dependency receives the more support, the smaller the ratio of the number of consequent attributes is compared to the number of antecedent attributes.

Single value columns. It sometimes happens that spreadsheets have columns that contain just one and the same value. In our example, the column labeled *country* is like this. Such columns tend to appear in almost every functional dependency's consequent, which causes them to be repeated in many relations. Since in almost all cases, such dependencies are simply a consequence of the limited data (or represent redundant data entries), they are most likely not part of the underlying data model and will thus be ignored.

After having gathered support through these heuristics, we aggregate the support for each functional dependency and sort them from most to least support. We then select functional dependencies from that list in the order of their support until all the attributes of the schema are covered.

Based on these heuristics, our algorithm produces the following dependencies for the flights spreadsheet data:

$$Pilot\text{-}ID \rightarrow Pilot\text{-}Name, Phone$$
$$N\text{-}Number \rightarrow Model, Plane\text{-}Name$$
$$Pilot\text{-}ID, N\text{-}Number, Depart, Destination, Date, Hours \rightarrow \emptyset$$

Exercise 3. *Consider the data in the following table and answer the next questions.*

project_nr	manager	location	delivery_date	budget	employee_name	age	nationality
proj1	John	New York	30-03-2010	50000	Richy	34	USA
proj1	John	New York	30-03-2010	50000	Tim	33	JP
proj1	John	New York	30-03-2010	50000	Mark	30	UK
proj2	John	Los Angels	02-04-2010	3000	Richy	34	USA
proj3	Paul	Chicago	01-01-2009	12000	Tim	33	JP
proj3	Paul	Chicago	01-01-2009	12000	Mark	30	UK

1. *Which are the functional dependencies that hold in this case?*
2. *Was this exercise easier to complete than Exercise 2? Why do you think this happened?*

Relational Model. Knowledge about the functional dependencies in a spreadsheet provides the basis for identifying tables and their relationships in the data, which form the basis for defining models for spreadsheet. The more accurate we can make this inference step, the better the inferred models will reflect the actual business models.

It is possible to construct a relational model from a set of observed functional dependencies. Such a model consists of a set of relation schemas (each given by a set of column names) and expresses the basic business model present in the spreadsheet. Each relation schema of such a model basically results from grouping functional dependencies together.

For example, for the spreadsheet in Fig. 5 we could infer the following relational model (underlined column names indicate those columns on which the other columns are functionally dependent).

Pilots (*Pilot-Id*, Pilot-Name, Phone)
Planes (*N-Number*, Model, Plane-Name
Flights (*Pilot-ID, N-Number, Depart, Destination, Date, Hours*)

The model has three relations: *Pilots* stores information about pilots; *Planes* contains all the information about planes, and *Flights* stores the information on flights, that is, for a particular pilot, a specific number of a plane, it stores the depart and destination airports and the data ans number of hours of the flights.

Note that several models could be created to represent this system. We have shown that the models our tool automatically generates are comparable in quality to the ones designed by database experts [19].

Although a relational model is very expressive, it is not quite suitable for spreadsheets since spreadsheets need to have a layout specification.

In contrast, the *ClassSheet* modeling framework offers high-level, object-oriented formal models to specify spreadsheets and thus present a promising alternative [29].

ClassSheets allow users to express business object structures within a spreadsheet using concepts from the Unified Modeling Language (UML). A spreadsheet application consistent with the model can be automatically generated, and thus a large variety of errors can be prevented.

We therefore employ ClassSheet as the underlying modeling approach for spreadsheets and transform the inferred relational model into a ClassSheet model.

Exercise 4. *Use the HaExcel libraries to infer the functional dependencies from the data given in Exercise 3.[9] For the functional dependencies computed, create the corresponding relational schema.*

4   Model-Driven Spreadsheet Engineering

The use of abstract models to reason about concrete artifacts has successfully and widespreadly been employed in science and in engineering. In fact, there are many fields for which model-driven engineering is the default, uncontested approach to follow: it is a reasonable assumption that, excluding financial or cultural limitations, no private house, let alone a bridge or a skyscraper, should be built before a model for it has been created and has been thoroughly analyzed and evolved.

---

[9] HaExcel can be found at http://ssaapp.di.uminho.pt.

Being itself a considerably more recent scientific field, not many decades have passed since software engineering has seriously considered the use of models. In this section, we study model-driven approaches to spreadsheet software engineering.

4.1 Spreadsheet Models

In an attempt to overcome the issue of spreadsheet errors using model-driven approaches, several techniques have been proposed, namely the creation of spreadsheet templates [9], the definition of ClassSheet [29] models and the use of class diagrams to specify spreadsheets [39]. These proposals guarantee that users may safely perform particular editing steps on their spreadsheets and they introduce a form of model-driven software development: a spreadsheet business model is defined from which a customized spreadsheet application is generated guaranteeing the consistency of the spreadsheet with the underlying model.

Despite of its huge benefits, model-driven software development is sometimes difficult to realize in practice. In the context of spreadsheets, for example, the use of model-driven software development requires that the developer is familiar both with the spreadsheet domain (business logic) and with model-driven software development. In the particular case of the use of templates, a new tool is necessary to be learned, namely ViTSL [9]. By using this tool, it is possible to generate a new spreadsheet respecting the corresponding model. This approach, however, has several drawbacks: first, in order to define a model, spreadsheet model developers will have to become familiar with a new programming environment. Second, and most important, there is no connection between the stand alone model development environment and the spreadsheet system. As a result, it is not possible to (automatically) synchronize the model and the spreadsheet data, that is, the co-evolution of the model and its instance is not possible.

The first contribution of our work is the embedding of ClassSheet spreadsheet models in spreadsheets themselves. Our approach closes the gap between creating and using a domain specific language for spreadsheet models and a totally different framework for actually editing spreadsheet data. Instead, we unify these operations within spreadsheets: in one worksheet we define the underlying model while another worksheet holds the actual data, such that the model and the data are kept synchronized by our framework. A summarized description of this work has been presented in [23,26], a description that we revise and extend in this paper, in Sect. 4.5.

ClassSheet Models. ClassSheets are a high-level, object-oriented formalism to specify the business logic of spreadsheets [29]. This formalism allows users to express business object structures within a spreadsheet using concepts from the UML [69].

ClassSheets define (work)sheets (s) containing classes (c) formed by blocks (b). Both sheets and classes can be expandable, i.e., their instances can be repeated either horizontally ($c^{\rightarrow}$) or vertically ($b^{\downarrow}$). Classes are identified by labels (l). A block can represent in its basic form a spreadsheet cell, or it can be a composition of other blocks. When representing a cell, a block can contain a basic value (φ, e.g., a string or an integer) or an attribute ($a = f$), which is composed by an attribute name (a) and a value (f). Attributes can define three types of cells: '(1), an input value, where a default value gives that indication, (2), a named reference to another attribute ($n.a$, where n is the name of the class and a the name of the attribute) or (3), an expression built by applying functions to a varying number of arguments given by a formula ($\varphi(f,\ldots,f)$).

ClassSheets can be represented textually, according to the grammar presented in Fig. 6 and taken directly from [29], or visually as described further below.

$$
\begin{array}{llll}
f \in Fml & ::= \varphi \mid n.a \mid \varphi(f,\ldots,f) & (formulas) \\
b \in Block & ::= \varphi \mid a = f \mid b|b \mid b\,\widehat{}\,b & (blocks) \\
l \in Lab & ::= h \mid v \mid .n & (class\ labels) \\
h \in Hor & ::= \underline{n} \mid |\underline{n} & (horizontal) \\
v \in Ver & ::= |n \mid |\underline{n} & (vertical) \\
c \in Class & ::= l : b \mid l : b^{\downarrow} \mid c\,\widehat{}\,c & (classes) \\
s \in Sheet & ::= c \mid c^{\rightarrow} \mid s|s & (sheets)
\end{array}
$$

Fig. 6. Syntax of the textual representation of ClassSheets.

Vertically Expandable Tables. In order to illustrate how ClassSheets can be used in practice we shall consider the example spreadsheet defining a airline scheduling system as introduced in Sect. 3. In Fig. 7a we present a spreadsheet containing the pilot's information only. This table has a title, **Pilots**, and a row with labels, one for each of the table's column: **ID** represents a unique pilot identifier, **Name** represents the pilot's name and **Phone** represents the pilot's phone contact. Each of the subsequent rows represents a concrete pilot.

	A	B	C
1	**Pilots**		
2	**ID**	**Name**	**Phone**
3	pl1	John	321654987
4	pl2	Mike	147258369
5	pl3	Anne	369248136

(a) Pilots' table.

	A	B	C
1	**Pilots**		
2	**ID**	**Name**	**Phone**
3	id=""	name=""	phone=0
⋮			

(b) Pilots' visual ClassSheet model.

Pilots : Pilots ⌙   ⌙   ^
Pilots : ID   ⌐ Name   ⌐ Phone   ^
Pilots : (id= "" ⌐ name= "" ⌐ phone= 0)$^{\downarrow}$

(c) Pilots' textual ClassSheet model.

Fig. 7. Pilots' example.

Tables such as the one presented in Fig. 7a are frequently used within spreadsheets, and it is fairly simple to create a model specifying them. In fact, Fig. 7b represents a visual ClassSheet model for this pilot's table, whilst Fig. 7c shows the textual ClassSheet representation. In the next paragraphs we explain such a model. To model the labels we use a textual representation and the exact same names as in the data sheet (**Pilots**, **ID**, **Name** and **Phone**). To model the actual data we abstract concrete column cell values by using a single identifier: we use the one-worded, lower-case equivalent of the corresponding column label (*id*, *name*, and *phone*). Next, a default value is associated with each column: columns **A** and **B** hold strings (denoted in the model by the empty string "" following the = sign), and column **C** holds integer values (denoted by 0 following =). Note that the last row of the model is labeled on the left hand-side with vertical ellipses. This means that it is possible for the previous block of rows to expand vertically, that is, the tables that conform to this model can have as many rows/pilots as needed. The scope of the expansion is between the ellipsis and the black line (between labels 2 and 3). Note that, by definition, ClassSheets do not allow for nested expansion blocks, and thus, there is no possible ambiguity associated with this feature. The instance shown in Fig. 7a has three pilots.

Horizontally Expandable Tables. In the lines of what we described in the previous section, airline companies must also store information on their airplanes. This is the purpose of table **Planes** in the spreadsheet illustrated in Fig. 8a, which is organized as follows: the first column holds labels that identify each row, namely, **Planes** (labeling the table itself), **N-Number**, **Model** and **Name**; cells in row **N-Number** (respectively **Model** and **Name**) contain the unique n-number identifier of a plane, (respectively the model of the plane and the name of the plane). Each of the subsequent columns contains information about one particular aircraft.

The **Planes** table can be visually modeled by the illustration in Fig. 8b and textually by the definition in Fig. 8c. This model may be constructed following the same strategy as in the previous section, but now swapping columns and

	A	B	C	D
1	Planes			
2	N-Number	N2342	N341	N1343
3	Model	B 747	B 777	A 380
4	Name	Magalhães	Cabral	Nunes

(a) Planes' table.

	A	B	...
1	Planes		
2	N-Number	n-number=""	
3	Model	model=""	
4	Name	name=""	

(b) Planes' visual ClassSheet model.

$$\left(\begin{array}{ll} \textbf{|Planes:} & \text{Planes} \\ \textbf{N-Number:} & \text{N-Number} \\ \textbf{Model:} & \text{Model} \\ \textbf{Name:} & \text{Name} \end{array} \right) \rightarrow \left(\begin{array}{ll} \textbf{|Planes:} & \sqcup \\ \textbf{N-Number} & \text{n-number= ""} \\ \textbf{Model:} & \text{model= ""} \\ \textbf{Name:} & \text{name= ""} \end{array} \right) \rightarrow$$

(c) Planes' textual ClassSheet model.

Fig. 8. Planes' example.

rows: the first column contains the label information and the second one the names abstracting concrete data values: again, each cell has a name and the default value of the elements in that row (in this example, all the cells have as default values empty strings); the third column is labeled not as C but with ellipses meaning that the immediately previous column is horizontally expandable. Note that the instance table has information about three planes.

Relationship Tables. The examples used so far (the tables for pilots and planes) are useful to store the data, but another kind of table exists and can be used to relate information, being of more practical interest.

Having pilots and planes, we can set up a new table to store information from the flights that the pilots make with the planes. This new table is called a *relationship* table since it relates two entities, which are the pilots and the planes. A possible model for this example is presented in Fig. 9, which also depicts an instance of that model.

	A	B	C	D	E	...	F
1	Flights	PlanesKey					
2		plane_key=**Planes**.n-number					
3	PilotsKey	Depart	Destination	Date	Hours		Total Pilot Hours
4	pilot_key=**Pilots**.ID	depart=""	destination=""	date=d	hours=0		total=SUM(hours)
5							total=SUM(**PilotsKey**.total)

(a) Flights' visual ClassSheet model.

	A	B	C	D	E	F	G	H	I	J
1	Flights	PlanesKey				PlanesKey				
2		N2342				N341				
3	PilotsKey	Depart	Destination	Date	Hours	Depart	Destination	Date	Hours	Total Pilot Hours
4	pl1	OPO	NAT	12/12/2010 – 14:00	07:00	LIS	AMS	16/12/2010 – 10:00	02:45	09:45
5	pl2	OPO	NAT	01/01/2011 – 16:00	07:00					07:00
6										16:45

(b) Flights' table.

Fig. 9. Flights' table, relating pilots and planes.

The flights' table contains information from distinct entities. In the model (Fig. 9a), there is the class **Flights** that contains all the information, including:

- information about planes (class **PlanesKey**, columns B to E), namely a reference to the planes table (cell B2);
- information about pilots (class **PilotsKey**, rows 3 and 4), namely a reference to the pilots table (cell A4);
- information about the flights (in the range B3:E4), namely the depart location (cell B4), the destination (cell C4), the time of departure (cell D4) and the duration of the flight (cell E4);
- the total hours flown by each pilot (cell F4), and also a grand total (cell F5). We assume that the same pilot does not appear in two different rows. In fact, we could use ClassSheet extensions to ensure this [23,25].

For the first flight stored in the data (Fig. 9b), we know that the pilot has the identifier *pl1*, the plane has the n-number *N2342*, it departed from *OPO* in direction to *NAT* at 14:00 on December 12, 2010, with a duration of 7 h.

Note that we do not show the textual representation of this part of the model because of its complexity and because it would not improve the understandability of this document.

Exercise 5. *Consider we would like to construct a spreadsheet to handle a school budget. This budget should consider different categories of expenses such as personnel, books, maintenance, etc. These different items should be laid along the rows of the spreadsheet. The budget must also consider the expenses for different years. Each year must have information about the number of items bought, the price per unit, and the total amount of money spent. Each year should be created after the previous one in an horizontal displacement.*

1. *Define a standard spreadsheet that contains data at least for two years and several expenses.*
2. *Define now a ClassSheet defining the business logic of the school budget. Please note that the spreadsheet data defined in the previous item should be an instance of this model.*

Exercise 6. *Consider the spreadsheets given in all previous exercises. Define a ClassSheet that implements the business logic of the spreadsheet data.*

4.2   Inferring Spreadsheet Models

In this section we explain in detail the steps to automatically extract a ClassSheet model from a spreadsheet [19]. Essentially, our method involves the following steps:

1. Detect all functional dependencies and identify model-relevant functional dependencies;
2. Determine relational schemas with candidate, foreign, and primary keys;
3. Generate and refactor a relational graph;
4. Translate the relational graph into a ClassSheet.

We have already introduced steps 1 and 2 in Sect. 3. In the following subsections we will explain the steps 3 and 4.

The Relational Intermediate Directed Graph. In this sub-section we explain how to produce a *Relational Intermediate Directed (RID) Graph* [11]. This graph includes all the relationships between a given set of schemas. Nodes in the graph represent schemas and directed edges represent foreign keys between those schemas. For each schema, a node in the graph is created, and for each foreign key, an edge with cardinality "*" at both ends is added to the graph.

Figure 10 represents the RID graph for the flights scheduling. This graph can generally be improved in several ways. For example, the information about foreign

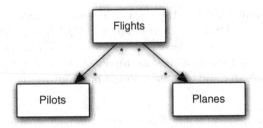

Fig. 10. RID graph for our running example.

keys may lead to additional links in the RID graph. If two relations reference each other, their relationship is said to be *symmetric* [11]. One of the foreign keys can then be removed. In our example there are no symmetric references.

Another improvement to the RID graph is the detection of relationships, that is, whether a schema is a relationship connecting other schemas. In such cases, the schema is transformed into a relationship. The details of this algorithm are not so important and left out for brevity.

Since the only candidate key of the schema *Flights* is the combination of all the other schemas' primary keys, it is a relationship between all the other schemas and is therefore transformed into a relationship. The improved RID graph can be seen in Fig. 11.

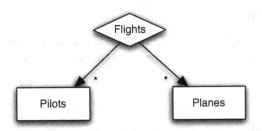

Fig. 11. Refactored RID graph.

Generating ClassSheets. The RID graph generated in Sect. 4.2 can be directly translated into a ClassSheet diagram. By default, each node is translated into a class with the same name as the relation and a vertically expanding block. In general, for a relation of the form

$$\underline{A_1}, \ldots, \underline{A_n}, A_{n+1}, \ldots, A_m$$

and default values $da_1, \ldots, da_n, d_{n+1}, \ldots, d_m$, a ClassSheet class/table is generated as shown in Fig. 12[10]. From now on this rule is termed *rule 1.*

---

[10] We omit here the column labels, whose names depend on the number of columns in the generated table.

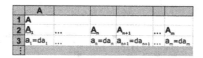

Fig. 12. Generated class for a relation A.

This ClassSheet represents a spreadsheet "table" with name **A**. For each attribute, a column is created and is labeled with the attribute's name. The default values depend on the attribute's domain. This table expands vertically, as indicated by the ellipses. The key attributes become underlined labels.

A special case occurs when there is a foreign key from one relation to another. The two relations are created basically as described above but the attributes that compose the foreign key do not have default values, but references to the corresponding attributes in the other class. Let us use the following generic relations:

$$M(M_1, \ldots, M_r, M_{r+1}, \ldots, M_s)$$
$$N(\underline{N_1, \ldots, N_t, M_m, \ldots, M_n}, M_o, \ldots, M_p, N_{t+1}, \ldots, N_u)$$

Note that $M_n, \ldots, M_m, M_o, \ldots, M_p$ are foreign keys from the relation N to the relation M, where $1 \leqslant n, m, o, p \leqslant r$, $n \leqslant m$, and $o \leqslant p$. This means that the foreign key attributes in N can only reference key attributes in the M. The corresponding ClassSheet is illustrated in Fig. 13. This rule is termed *rule 2*.

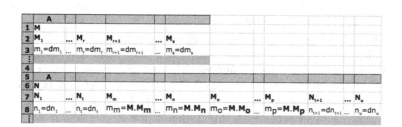

Fig. 13. Generated ClassSheet for relations with foreign keys.

Relationships are treated differently and will be translated into cell classes. We distinguish between two cases: *(A)* relationships between two schemas, and *(B)* relationships between more than two schemas.

For case *(A)*, let us consider the following set of schemas:

$$M(\underline{M_1, \ldots, M_r}, M_{r+1}, \ldots, M_s)$$
$$N(\underline{N_1, \ldots, N_t}, N_{t+1}, \ldots, N_u)$$
$$R(\underline{M_1, \ldots, M_r, N_1, \ldots, N_t, R_1, \ldots, R_x}, R_{x+1}, \ldots, R_y)$$

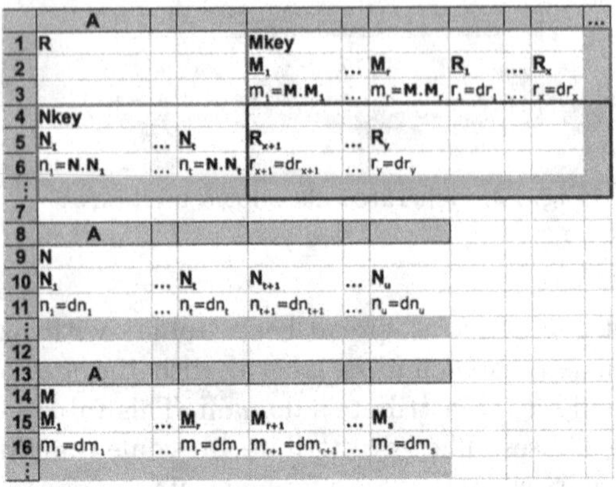

Fig. 14. ClassSheet of a relationship connecting two relations.

The ClassSheet that is produced by this translation is shown in Fig. 14 and explained next.

For both nodes M and N a class is created as explained before (lower part of the ClassSheet). The top part of the ClassSheet is divided in two classes and one cell class. The first class, **NKey**, is created using the key attributes from the **N** class. All its values are references to **N**. For example, $n1 = \mathbf{N}.\mathbf{N1}$ references the values in column A in class **N**. This makes the spreadsheet easier to maintain while avoiding insertion, modification and deletion anomalies [17]. Class **Mkey** is created using the key attributes of the class **M** and the rest of the key attributes of the relationship R. The cell class (with blue border) is created using the rest of the attributes of the relationship R.

In principle, the positions of **M** and **N** are interchangeable and we have to choose which one expands vertically and which one expands horizontally. We choose whichever combination minimizes the number of empty cells created by the cell class, that is, the number of key attributes from **M** and **R** should be similar to the number of non-key attributes of **R**. This rule is named *rule A*. Three special cases can occur with this configuration.

Case 1. The first case occurs when one of the relations **M** or **N** might have only key attributes. Let us assume that **M** is in this situation:

$$M(\underline{M_1, \ldots, M_r})$$
$$N(\underline{N_1, \ldots, N_t}, N_{t+1}, \ldots, N_u)$$
$$R(\underline{M_1, \ldots, M_r, N_1, \ldots, N_t}, R_1, \ldots, R_x, R_{x+1}, \ldots, R_y)$$

In this case, and since all the attributes of that class are already included in the class **MKey** or **NKey**, no separated class is created for it. The resultant ClassSheet would be similar to the one presented in Fig. 14, but a separated class would not be created for **M** or for **N** or for both. Figure 15 illustrates this situation. This rule is from now on termed *rule A1*.

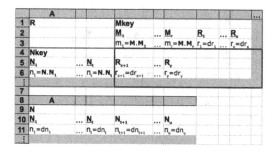

Fig. 15. ClassSheet where one entity has only key attributes.

Case 2. The second case occurs when the key of the relationship R is only composed by the keys of M and N (defined as before), that is, R is defined as follows:

$$M(\underline{M_1, \ldots, M_r}, M_{r+1}, \ldots, M_s)$$
$$N(\underline{N_1, \ldots, N_t}, N_{t+1}, \ldots, N_u)$$
$$R(\underline{M_1, \ldots, M_r, N_1, \ldots, N_t}, R_1, \ldots, R_x)$$

The resultant ClassSheet is shown in Fig. 16.

The difference between this ClassSheet model and the general one is that the **MKey** class on the top does not contain any attribute from R: all its attributes are contained in the cell class. This rule is from now on named *rule A2*.

Case 3. Finally, the third case occurs when the relationship is composed only by key attributes as illustrated next:

$$M(\underline{M_1, \ldots, M_r}, M_{r+1}, \ldots, M_s)$$
$$N(\underline{N_1, \ldots, N_t}, N_{t+1}, \ldots, N_u)$$
$$R(\underline{M_1, \ldots, M_r, N_1, \ldots, N_t})$$

In this situation, the attributes that appear in the cell class are the non-key attributes of **N** and no class is created for **N**. Figure 17 illustrates this case. From now on this rule is named *rule A3*.

For case *(B)*, that is, for relationships between more than two tables, we choose between the candidates to span the cell class using the following criteria:

1. **M** and **N** should have small keys;
2. the number of empty cells created by the cell class should be minimal.

This rule is from now on named *rule B*.

After having chosen the two relations (and the relationship), the generation proceeds as described above. The remaining relations are created as explained in the beginning of this section.

	A			Mkey		
1	R			Mkey		
2				M_1	...	M_r
3				$m_1 = M.M_1$	...	$m_r = M.M_r$
4	Nkey					
5	N_1	...	N_k	R_1	...	R_x
6	$n_1 = N.N_1$	...	$n_k = N.N_k$	$r_1 = dr_1$	...	$r_x = dr_x$
⋮						
7						
8	A					
9	N					
10	N_1	...	N_k	N_{t+1}	...	N_u
11	$n_1 = dn_1$	...	$n_k = dn_k$	$n_{t+1} = dn_{t+1}$	...	$n_u = dn_u$
⋮						
12						
13	A					
14	M					
15	M_1	...	M_r	M_{r+1}	...	M_s
16	$m_1 = dm_1$	...	$m_r = dm_r$	$m_{r+1} = dm_{r+1}$	...	$m_s = dm_s$
⋮						

Fig. 16. ClassSheet of a relationship with all the key attributes being foreign keys.

	A			Mkey		
1	R			Mkey		
2				M_1	...	M_r
3				$m_1 = M.M_1$	...	$m_r = M.M_r$
4	Nkey					
5	N_1	...	N_k	N_{t+1}	...	N_u
6	$n_1 = N.N_1$	...	$n_k = N.N_k$	$n_{t+1} = dn_{t+1}$	...	$n_u = dn_u$
⋮						
7						
8	A					
9	M					
10	M_1	...	M_r	M_{r+1}	...	M_s
11	$m_1 = dm_1$	...	$m_r = dm_r$	$m_{r+1} = dm_{r+1}$	...	$m_s = dm_s$
⋮						

Fig. 17. ClassSheet of a relationship composed only by key attributes.

4.3 Mapping Strategy

In this section we present the mapping function between RID graphs and ClassSheets, which builds on the rules presented before. For that, we use the common strategic combinators listed below [48,73,74]:

$$
\begin{array}{llr}
nop & :: Rule & \text{-- identity} \\
\triangleright & :: Rule \rightarrow Rule \rightarrow Rule & \text{-- sequential composition} \\
\oslash & :: Rule \rightarrow Rule \rightarrow Rule & \text{-- left-biased choice} \\
many & :: Rule \rightarrow Rule & \text{-- repetition} \\
once & :: Rule \rightarrow Rule & \text{-- arbitrary depth rule application}
\end{array}
$$

In this context, *Rule* encodes a transformation from RID graphs to ClassSheets.

Using the rules defined in the previous section and the combinators listed above, we can construct a strategy that generates a ClassSheet:

$$genCS =$$
$$many\,(once\,(rule\ B)) \triangleright$$
$$many\,(once\,(rule\ A)) \triangleright$$

$many\ (once\ (rule\ A1)\ \oslash\ once\ (rule\ A2)\ \oslash\ once\ (rule\ A3))\ \triangleright$
$many\ (once\ (rule\ 2))\ \triangleright$
$many\ (once\ (rule\ 1))$

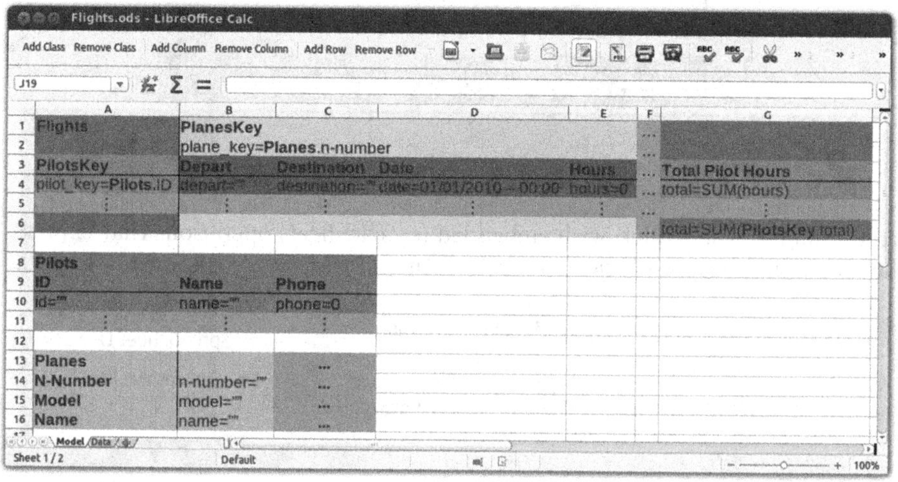

Fig. 18. The ClassSheet generated by our algorithm for the running example.

The strategy works as follows: it tries to apply *rule B* as many times as possible, consuming all the relationships with more than two relations; it then tries to apply *rule A* as many times as possible, consuming relationships with two relations; next the three sub-cases of *rule A* are applied as many times as possible consuming all the relationships with two relations that match some of the sub-rules; after consuming all the relationships and corresponding relations, the strategy consumes all the relations that are connected through a foreign key using *rule 2*; finally, all the remaining relations are mapped using *rule 1*.

In Fig. 18 we present the ClassSheet model that is generated by our tool for the flight scheduling spreadsheet.

4.4   Generation of Model-Driven Spreadsheets

Together with the definition of ClassSheet models, Erwig et al. developed a visual tool, VITSL, to allow the easy creation and manipulation of the visual representation of ClassSheet models [9]. The visual and domain specific modeling language used by VITSL is visually similar to spreadsheets (see Fig. 19).

The approach proposed by Erwig et al. follows a traditional compiler construction architecture [10] and generative approach [49]: first a language is defined (a visual domain specific language, in this case). Then a specific tool/compiler (the VITSL tool, in this case) compiles it into a target lower level representation: an *Excel* spreadsheet. This generated representation is then interpreted by a different software system: the *Excel* spreadsheet system through the *Gencel* extension [33]. Given that model representation, *Gencel* generates an initial spreadsheet instance

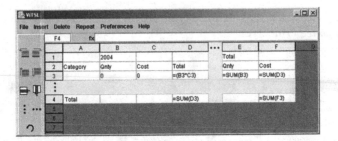

Fig. 19. Screen shot of the ViTSL editor, taken from [9].

(conforming to the model) with embedded (spreadsheet) operations that express the underlying business logic. The architecture of these tools is shown in Fig. 20.

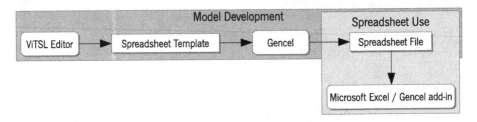

Fig. 20. ViTSL/*Gencel*-based environment for spreadsheet development.

The idea is that, when using such generated spreadsheets, end users are restricted to only perform operations that are logically and technically correct for that model. The generated spreadsheet not only guides end users to introduce correct data, but it also provides operations to perform some repetitive tasks like the repetition of a set of columns with some default values.

In fact, this approach provides a form of model-driven software development for spreadsheet users. Unfortunately, it provides a very limited form of model-driven spreadsheet development: it does not support model/instance synchronization. Indeed, if the user needs to evolve the model, then he has to do it using the ViTSL tool. Then, the tool compiles this new model to a new *Excel* spreadsheet instance. However, there are no techniques to co-evolve the spreadsheet data from the new instance to the newly generated one. In the next sections, we present embedded spreadsheet models and data refinement techniques that provide a full model-driven spreadsheet development setting.

4.5   Embedding ClassSheet Models in Spreadsheets

The ClassSheet language is a domain specific language to represent the business model of spreadsheet data. Furthermore, as we have seen in the previous section, the visual representation of ClassSheets very much resembles spreadsheets themselves. Indeed, the visual representation of ClassSheet models is a Visual Domain Specific Language. These two facts combined motivated the use of spreadsheet systems to define ClassSheet models [26], i.e., to natively embed ClassSheets in a spreadsheet host system. In this line, we have adopted the well-known techniques to embed Domain Specific Languages (DSL) in a host general purpose language [38, 44, 70]. In this way, both the model and the spreadsheet can be stored in the same file, and model creation along with data editing can be handled in the same environment that users are familiar with.

The embedding of ClassSheets within spreadsheets is not direct, since ClassSheets were not meant to be embedded inside spreadsheets. Their resemblance helps, but some limitations arise due to syntactic restrictions imposed by spreadsheet host systems. Several options are available to overcome the syntactic restrictions, like writing a new spreadsheet host system from start, modifying an existing one, or adapting the ClassSheet visual language. The two first options are not viable to distribute Model-Driven Spreadsheet Engineering (MDSE) widely, since both require users to switch their system, which can be inconvenient. Also, to accomplish the first option would be a tremendous effort and would change the focus of the work from the embedding to building a tool.

The solution adopted modifies slightly the ClassSheet visual language so it can be embedded in a worksheet without doing major changes on a spreadsheet host system (see Fig. 21). The modifications are:

1. identify expansion using cells (in the ClassSheet language, this identification is done between columns/rows letters/numbers);
2. draw an expansion limitation black line in the spreadsheet (originally this is done between column/row letters/numbers);
3. fill classes with a background color (instead of using lines as in the original ClassSheets).

The last change (3) is not mandatory, but it is easier to identify the classes and, along with the first change (2), eases the identification of classes' parts. This way, users do not need to think which role the line is playing (expansion limitation or class identification).

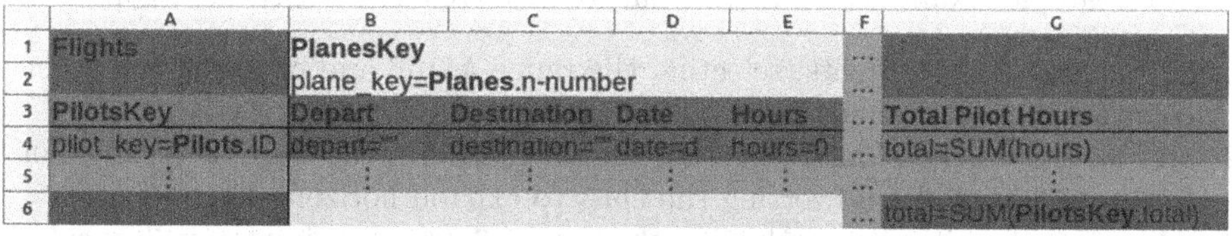

Fig. 21. Embedded ClassSheet for the flights' table.

We can use the flights' table to compare the differences between the original ClassSheet and its embedded representation:

– In the original ClassSheet (Fig. 9a), there are two expansions: one denoted by the column between columns E and F for the horizontal expansion, and another denoted by the row between rows 4 and 5 for the vertical one. Applying change 1 to the original model will add an extra column (F) and an extra row (5) to identify the expansions in the embedding (Fig. 21).

- To define the expansion limits in the original ClassSheet, there are no lines between the column headers of columns B, C, D and E which makes the horizontal expansion to use three columns and the vertical expansion only uses one row. This translates to a line between columns A and B and another line between rows 3 and 4 in the embedded ClassSheet as per change 2.
- To identify the classes, background colors are used (change 3), so that the class **Flights** is identified by the green[11] background, the class **PlanesKey** by the cyan background, the class **PilotsKey** by the yellow background, and the class that relates the **PlanesKey** with the **PilotsKey** by the dark green background. Moreover, the relation class (range B3:E5), called **PilotsKey_ PlanesKey**, is colored in dark green.

Given the embedding of the spreadsheet model in one worksheet, it is now possible to have one of its instances in a second worksheet, as we will shortly discuss. As we will also see, this setting has some advantages: for once, users may evolve the model having the data automatically coevolved. Also, having the model near the data helps to document the latter, since users can identify clearly the structure of the logic behind the spreadsheet. Figure 22a illustrates the complete embedding for the ClassSheet model of the running example, whilst Fig. 22b shows one of its possible instances.

To be noted that the data also is colored in the same manner as the model. This allows a correspondence between the data and the model to be made quickly, relating parts of the data to the respective parts in the model. This feature is not mandatory to implement the embedding, but can help the end users. One can provide this coloring as an optional feature that could be activated on demand.

Model Creation. To create a model, several operations are available such as addition and deletion of columns and rows, cell editing, and addition or deletion of classes.

To create, for example, the flights' part of the spreadsheet used so far, one can:

1. add a class for the flights, selecting the range A1:G6 and choosing the green color for its background;
2. add a class for the planes, selecting the range B1:F6, choosing the cyan color for its background, and setting the class to expand horizontally;
3. add a class for the pilots, selecting the range A3:G5, choosing the yellow color for its background, and setting the class to expand vertically; and,
4. set the labels and formulas for the cells.

The addition of the relation class (range B3:E4) is not needed since it is added automatically when the environment detects superposing classes at the same level (**PlanesKey** and **PilotsKey** are within **Flights**, which leads to the automatic insertion of the relation class).

---

[11] We assume colors are visible in the digital version of this paper.

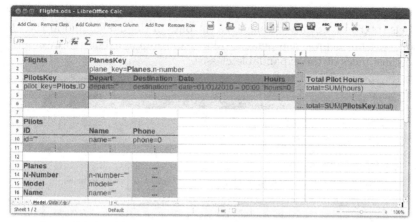

(a) Model on the first worksheet of the spreadsheet.

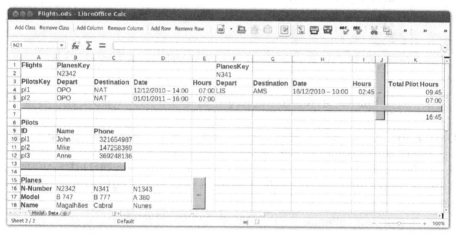

(b) Data on the second worksheet of the spreadsheet.

Fig. 22. Flights' spreadsheet, with an embedded model and a conforming instance.

Instance Generation. From the flights' model described above, an instance without any data can be generated. This is performed by copying the structure of the model to another worksheet. In this process labels copied as they are, and attributes are replaced in one of two ways: *(i)*, if the attribute is simple (i.e., it is like $a = \varphi$), it is replaced by its default value; *(ii)*, otherwise, it is replaced by an instance of the formula. An instance of a formula is similar to the original one defined in the model, but the attribute references are replaced by references to cells where those attributes are instantiated. Moreover, columns and rows with ellipses have no content, having instead buttons to perform operations of adding new instances of their respective classes.

An empty instance generated by the flights' model is pictured in Fig. 23. All the labels (text in bold) are the same as the ones in the model, and in the same position, attributes have the default values, and four buttons are available to add new instances of the expandable classes.

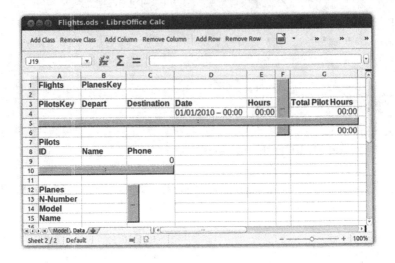

Fig. 23. Spreadsheet generated from the flights' model.

Data Editing. The editing of the data is performed like with plain spreadsheets, i.e., the user just edits the cell content. The insertion of new data is different since editing assistance must be used through the buttons available.

For example, to insert a new flight for pilot p11 in the **Flights** table, without models one would need to:

1. insert four new columns;
2. copy all the labels;
3. update all the necessary formulas in the last column; and,
4. insert the values for the new flight.

With a large spreadsheet, the step to update the formulas can be very error prone, and users may forget to update all of them. Using models, this process consists on two steps only:

1. press the button with label "···" (in column J, Fig. 22b); and,
2. insert the values for the new flight.

The model-driven environment automatically inserts four new columns, the labels for those columns, updates the formulas, and inserts default values in all the new input cells.

Note that, to keep the consistency between instance and model, all the cells in the instance that are not data entry cells are non-editable, that is, all the labels and formulas cannot be edited in the instance, only in the model. In Sect. 5 we will detail how to handle model evolutions.

Embedded Domain Specific Languages. In this section we have described the embedding of a visual, domain specific language in a general purpose visual spreadsheet system. The embedding of textual DSLs in host functional programming languages is a well-known technique to develop DSLs [44,70]. In our visual embedding, and very much like in textual languages, we get for free the powerful features of the host system: in our case, a simple, but powerful visual programming environment. As a consequence, we did not have to develop from scratch such a visual system (like the developers of ViTSL did). Moreover, we offer a visual interface familiar to users, namely, a spreadsheet system. Thus, they do not have to learn and use a different system to define their spreadsheet models.

The embedding of DSL is also known to have disadvantages when compared to building a specific compiler for that language. Our embedding is no exception: firstly, when building models in our setting, we are not able to provide domain-specific feedback (that is, error messages) to guide users. For example, a tool like ViTSL can produce better error messages and support for end users to construct (syntactic) correct models. Secondly, there are some syntactic limitations offered by the host language/system. In our embedding, we can see the syntactic differences in the vertical/horizontal ellipses defined in visual and embedded models (see Figs. 9 and 18).

5   Evolution of Model-Driven Spreadsheets

The example we have been using manages pilots, planes and flights, but it misses a critical piece of information about flights: the number of passengers. In this case, additional columns need to be inserted in the block of each flight. Figure 24 shows an evolved spreadsheet with new columns (F and K) to store the number of passengers (Fig. 22b), as well as the new model that it instantiates (Fig. 22a).

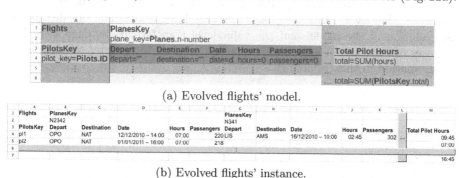

(a) Evolved flights' model.

(b) Evolved flights' instance.

Fig. 24. Evolved spreadsheet and the model that it instantiates.

Note that a modification of the year block in the model (in this case, inserting a new column) captures modifications to all repetitions of the block throughout the instance.

In this section, we will demonstrate that modifications to spreadsheet models can be supported by an appropriate combinator language, and that these model modifications can be propagated automatically to the spreadsheets that instantiate the models [28]. In the case of the flights example, the model modification is captured by the following expression:

$$addPassengers = once$$
$$(inside\ \texttt{"PilotsKey\_PlanesKey"}$$
$$(after\ \texttt{"Hours"}$$
$$(insertCol\ \texttt{"Passengers"})))$$

The actual column insertion is done by the innermost *insertCol* step. The *after* and *inside* combinators specify the location constraints of applying this step. The *once* combinator traverses the spreadsheet model to search for a single location where these constraints are satisfied and the insertion can be performed.

The application of *addPassengers* to the initial model (Fig. 22a) will yield:

1. the modified model (Fig. 24a),
2. a spreadsheet migration function that can be applied to instances of the initial model (e.g. Fig. 22b) to produce instances of the modified model (e.g. Fig. 24b), and
3. an inverse spreadsheet migration function to backport instances of the modified model to instances of the initial model.

In the remaining of this section we will explain the machinery required for this type of coupled transformation of spreadsheet instances and models.

5.1 A Framework for Evolution of Spreadsheets in Haskell

Data refinement theory provides an algebraic framework for calculating with data types and corresponding values [52,54,55]. It consists of type-level coupled with value-level transformations. The type-level transformations deal with the evolution of the model and the value-level transformations deal with the instances of the model (e.g. values). Figure 25 depicts the general scenario of a transformation in this framework.

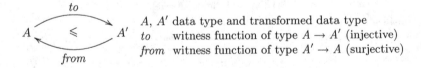

A, A' data type and transformed data type
to   witness function of type $A \to A'$ (injective)
from witness function of type $A' \to A$ (surjective)

Fig. 25. Coupled transformation of data type A into data type A'.

Each transformation is coupled with witness functions *to* and *from*, which are responsible for converting values of type A into type A' and back.

2LT is a framework written in Haskell implementing this theory [12,18]. It provides the basic combinators to define and compose transformations for data types and witness functions. Since 2LT is statically typed, transformations are guaranteed to be type-safe ensuring consistency of data types and data instances.

To represent the witness functions *from* and *to* 2LT relies once again on the definition of a *Generalized Algebraic Data Type*[12] (GADT) [43,61]:

data *PF a* **where**

id	:: *PF* $(a \to a)$	-- identity function
π_1	:: *PF* $((a, b) \to a)$	-- left projection of a pair
π_2	:: *PF* $((a, b) \to b)$	-- right projection of a pair
pnt	:: $a \to PF$ $(One \to a)$	-- constant
$\cdot \triangle \cdot$	:: *PF* $(a \to b) \to PF$ $(a \to c) \to PF$ $(a \to (b, c))$	
		-- split of functions
$\cdot \times \cdot$	:: *PF* $(a \to b) \to PF$ $(c \to d) \to PF$ $((a, c) \to (b, d))$	
		-- product of functions
$\cdot \circ \cdot$	:: *Type b* $\to PF$ $(b \to c) \to PF$ $(a \to b) \to PF$ $(a \to c)$	
		-- composition of functions
$\cdot^{\star}$	:: *PF* $(a \to b) \to PF$ $([a] \to [b])$	-- map of functions
head	:: *PF* $([a] \to a)$	-- head of a list
tail	:: *PF* $([a] \to [a])$	-- tail of a list
fhead	:: *PF* $(Formula1 \to RefCell)$	-- head of the args. of a formula
ftail	:: *PF* $(Formula1 \to Formula1)$	-- tail of the args. of a formula

This GADT represents the types of the functions used in the transformations. For example, π_1 represents the type of the function that projects the first part of a pair. The comments should clarify which function each constructor represents. Given these representations of types and functions, we can turn to the encoding of refinements. Each refinement is encoded as a two-level rewriting rule:

type *Rule* = $\forall$ *a* . *Type a* $\to$ *Maybe* (*View* (*Type a*))
data *View a* **where** *View* :: *Rep a b* $\to$ *Type b* $\to$ *View* (*Type a*)
data *Rep a b* = *Rep* { *to* = *PF* $(a \to b)$, *from* = *PF* $(b \to a)$ }

Although the refinement is from a type *a* to a type *b*, this can not be directly encoded since the type *b* is only known when the transformation completes, so the type *b* is represented as a *view* of the type *a*. A *view* expresses that a type *a* can be represented as a type *b*, denoted as *Rep a b*, if there are functions *to* :: $a \to b$ and *from* :: $b \to a$ that allow data conversion between one and the other. *Maybe* encapsulates an optional value: a value of type *Maybe a* either contains a value of type *a* (*Just a*), or it is empty (*Nothing*).

To better explain this system we will show a small example. The following code implements a rule to transform a list into a map (represented by $\cdot \to \cdot$):

listmap :: *Rule*
listmap $([a])$ = *Just* (*View* (*Rep* { *to* = *seq2index*, *from* = *tolist* }) (*Int* $\to a$))
listmap _ = *mzero*

---

[12] "It allows to assign more precise types to data constructors by restricting the variables of the datatype in the constructors' result types."

The witness functions have the following signature (for this example their code is not important):

$$tolist :: (Int \rightharpoonup a) \rightarrow [a]$$
$$seq2index :: [a] \rightarrow (Int \rightharpoonup a)$$

This rule receives the type of a list of a, $[a]$, and returns a view over the type map of integers to a, $Int \rightharpoonup a$. The witness functions are returned in the representation Rep. If other argument than a list is received, then the rule fails returning $mzero$. All the rules contemplate this last case and so we will not show it in the definition of other rules.

ClassSheets and Spreadsheets in Haskell. The 2LT was originally designed to work with algebraic data types. However, this representation is not expressive enough to represent ClassSheet specifications or their spreadsheet instances. To overcome this issue, we extended the 2LT representation so it could support ClassSheet models, by introducing the following GADT:

data *Type a* **where**
...

Value	:: $Value \rightarrow Type\ Value$	-- plain value
Ref	:: $Type\ b \rightarrow PF\ (a \rightarrow RefCell) \rightarrow PF\ (a \rightarrow b) \rightarrow Type\ a$	
	$\rightarrow Type\ a$	-- references
RefCell	:: $Type\ RefCell$	-- reference cell
Formula	:: $Formula1 \rightarrow Type\ Formula1$	-- formulas
LabelB	:: $String \rightarrow Type\ LabelB$	-- block label
$\cdot = \cdot$	:: $Type\ a \rightarrow Type\ b \rightarrow Type\ (a, b)$	-- attributes
$\cdot \mid \cdot$	:: $Type\ a \rightarrow Type\ b \rightarrow Type\ (a, b)$	-- block horizontal comp.
$\cdot \hat{\ } \cdot$	:: $Type\ a \rightarrow Type\ b \rightarrow Type\ (a, b)$	-- block vertical comp.
EmptyB	:: $Type\ EmptyB$	-- empty block
$\cdot$	:: $String \rightarrow Type\ HorH$	-- horizontal class label
$\mid \cdot$	:: $String \rightarrow Type\ VerV$	-- vertical class label
$\mid \cdot$	:: $String \rightarrow Type\ Square$	-- square class label
LabRel	:: $String \rightarrow Type\ LabS$	-- relation class
$\cdot \vdots \cdot$	:: $Type\ a \rightarrow Type\ b \rightarrow Type\ (a, b)$	-- labeled class
$\cdot : (\cdot)^{\downarrow}$	:: $Type\ a \rightarrow Type\ b \rightarrow Type\ (a, [b])$	-- labeled expand. class
$\cdot \hat{\ } \cdot$	:: $Type\ a \rightarrow Type\ b \rightarrow Type\ (a, b)$	-- class vertical comp.
SheetC	:: $Type\ a \rightarrow Type\ (SheetC\ a)$	-- sheet class
$\cdot \overset{\rightarrow}{}$	:: $Type\ a \rightarrow Type\ [a]$	-- sheet expandable class
$\cdot \mid \cdot$	:: $Type\ a \rightarrow Type\ b \rightarrow Type\ (a, b)$	-- sheet horizontal comp.
EmptyS	:: $Type\ EmptyS$	-- empty sheet

The comments should clarify what the constructors represent. The values of type *Type a* are representations of type a. For example, if t is of type *Type Value*, then t represents the type *Value*. The following types are needed to construct values of type *Type a*:

```
data EmptyBlock                                    -- empty block
data EmptySheet                                    -- empty sheet
type LabelB = String                                    -- label
data RefCell = RefCell1                          -- referenced cell
type LabS = String                              -- square label
type HorH = String                          -- horizontal label
type VerV = String                            -- vertical label
data SheetC a = SheetCC a                          -- sheet class
data SheetCE a = SheetCEC a              -- expandable sheet class
data Value = VInt Int | VString String | VBool Bool | VDouble Double
                                                        -- values
data Formula1 = FValue Value | FRef | FFormula String [Formula1]
                                                        -- formula
```

Once more, the comments should clarify what each type represents. To explain this representation we will use as an example a small table representing the costs of maintenance of planes. We do not use the running example as it would be very complex to explain and understand. For this reduced model only four columns were defined: *plane model*, *quantity*, *cost per unit* and *total cost* (product of *quantity* by *cost per unit*). The Haskell representation of such model is shown next.

$costs =$
$\quad | \ Cost : Model \ | \ Quantity \ | \ Price \ | \ Total ^{\wedge}$
$\quad | \ Cost : (model = ""\ | \ quantity = 0 \ | \ price = 0 \ | \ total =$
$FFormula \ "\times" \ [FRef, FRef])^{\downarrow}$

This ClassSheet specifies a class called *Cost* composed by two parts vertically composed as indicated by the ˆ operator. The first part is specified in the first row and defines the labels for four columns: *Model*, *Quantity*, *Price* and *Total*. The second row models the rest of the class containing the definition of the four columns. The first column has default value the empty string (""), the two following columns have as default value 0, and the last one is defined by a formula (explained latter on). Note that this part is vertical expandable. Figure 26 represents a spreadsheet instance of this model.

	A	B	C	D
1	Model	Quantity	Price	Total
2	B747	2	1500	=B2*C2
3	B777	5	2000	=B3*C3

Fig. 26. Spreadsheet instance of the maintenance costs ClassSheet.

Note that in the definition of *Type a* the constructors combining parts of the spreadsheet (e.g. sheets) return a pair. Thus, a spreadsheet instance is written as nested pairs of values. The spreadsheet illustrated in Fig. 26 is encoded in Haskell as follows:

$((Model\ , (Quantity, (Price, Total))),$
$[("B747", (2\qquad , (1500\ , FFormula\ "\times"\ [FRef, FRef]))),$
$\ \ ("B777", (5\qquad , (2000\ , FFormula\ "\times"\ [FRef, FRef])))])$

The Haskell type checker statically ensures that the pairs are well formed and are constructed in the correct order.

Specifying References. Having defined a GADT to represent ClassSheet models, we need now a mechanism to define spreadsheet references. The safer way to accomplish this is making references strongly typed. Figure 27 depicts the scenario of a transformation with references. A reference from a cell s to the a cell t is defined using a pair of projections, *source* and *target*. These projections are statically-typed functions traversing the data type A to identify the cell defining the reference (s), and the cell to which the reference is pointing to (t). In this approach, not only the references are statically typed, but also always guaranteed to exist, that is, it is not possible to create a reference from/to a cell that does not exist.

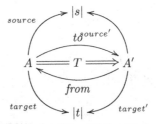

source Projection over type A identifying the reference
target Projection over type A identifying the referenced cell

$source' = source \circ from$
$target' = target \circ from$

Fig. 27. Coupled transformation of data type A into data type A' with references.

The projections defining the reference and the referenced type, in the transformed type A', are obtained by post-composing the projections with the witness function *from*. When *source'* and *target'* are normalized they work on A' directly rather than via A. The formula specification, as previously shown, is specified directly in the GADT. However, the references are defined separately by defining projections over the data type. This is required to allow any reference to access any part of the GADT.

Using the spreadsheet illustrated in Fig. 26, an instance of a reference from the formula *total* to *price* is defined as follows (remember that the second argument of *Ref* is the source (reference cell) and that the third is the target (referenced cell)):

costWithReferences =
Ref Int (fhead ∘ head ∘ (π₂ ∘ π₂ ∘ π₂) ∘ π₂) (head ∘ (π₁ ∘ π₂ ∘ π₂)* ∘ π₂) cost*

The *source* function refers to the first *FRef* in the Haskell encoding shown after Fig. 26. The *target* projection defines the cell it is pointing to, that is, it defines a reference to the the value 1500 in column *Price*.

To help understand this example, we explain how *source* is constructed. Since the use of GADTs requires the definition of models combining elements in a pairwise fashion, π_2 is used to get the second element of the model (a pair), that is, the list of planes and their cost maintenance. Then, we apply $(\pi_2 \circ \pi_2 \circ \pi_2)^*$ which will return a list with all the formulas. Finally *head* will return the first formula (the one in cell D2) from which *fhead* gets the first reference in a list of references, that is, the reference B2 that appears in cell D2.

Note that our reference type has enough information about the cells and thus we do not need value-level functions, that is, we do not need to specify the projection functions themselves, just their types. In the cases we reference a list of values, for example, constructed by the class expandable operator, we need to be specific about the element within the list we are referencing. For these cases, we use the type-level constructors *head* (first element of a list) and *tail* (all but first) to get the intended value in the list.

5.2 Evolution of Spreadsheets

In this section we define rules to perform spreadsheet evolution. These rules can be divided in three main categories: *Combinators*, used as helper rules, *Semantic* rules, intended to change the model itself (e.g. add a new column), and *Layout* rules, designed to change the visual arrangement of the spreadsheet (e.g. swap two columns).

Combinators. The semantic and the layout rules are defined to work on a specific part of the model. The combinators defined next are then used to apply those rules in the desired places.

Pull up all references. To avoid having references in different levels of the models, all the rules pull all references to the topmost level of the model. This allows to create simpler rules since the positions of all references are know and do not need to be changed when the model is altered. To pull a reference in a particular place we use the following rule (we show just its first case):

pullUpRef :: Rule
pullUpRef ((Ref tb fRef tRef ta) ⊦ b2) = **do**
    return (View idrep (Ref tb (fRef ∘ π₁) (tRef ∘ π₁) (ta ⊦ b2)))

The representation *idrep* has the *id* function in both directions. If part of the model (in this case the left part of a horizontal composition) of a given type has a reference, it is pulled to the top level. This is achieved by composing the existing projections with the necessary functions, in this case π_1. This rule has two cases (left and right hand side) for each binary constructor (e.g. horizontal/vertical composition).

To pull up all the references in all levels of a model we use the rule

$$pullUpAllRefs = many\ (once\ pullUpRef)$$

The *once* operator applies the *pullUpRef* rule somewhere in the type and the *many* ensures that this is applied everywhere in the whole model.

Apply after and friends. The combinator *after* finds the correct place to apply the argument rule (second argument) by comparing the given string (first argument) with the existing labels in the model. When it finds the intended place, it applies the rule to it. This works because our rules always do their task on the right-hand side of a type.

```
after :: String → Rule → Rule
after label r (label' ⌐ a) | label ≡ label' = do
    View s l' ← r label'
    return (View (Rep { to = to s × id, from = from s × id }) (l' ⌐ a))
```

Note that this code represents only part of the complete definition of the function. The remaining cases, e.g. ·ˆ·, are not shown since they are quite similar to the one presented.

Other combinators were also developed, namely, *before, bellow, above, inside* and *at*. Their implementations are not shown since they are similar to the *after* combinator.

Semantic Rules. Given the support to apply rules in any place of the model given by the previous definitions, we now present rules that change the semantics of the model, that is, that change the meaning and the model itself, e.g., adding columns.

Insert a block. The first rule we present is one of the most fundamentals: the insertion of a new block into a spreadsheet. It is formally defined as follows:

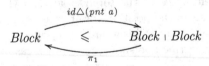

This diagram means that a horizontal composition of two blocks refines a block when witnessed by two functions, *to* and *from*. The *to* function, $id\triangle(pnt\ a)$, is a split: it injects the existing block in the first part of the result without modifications (*id*) and injects the given block instance *a* into the second part of the result. The *from* function is π_1 since it is the one that allows the recovery of the existent block. The Haskell version of the rule is presented next.

$insertBlock :: Type\ a \rightarrow a \rightarrow Rule$
$insertBlock\ ta\ a\ tx\ |\ isBlock\ ta \wedge isBlock\ tx = \mathbf{do}$
   $\mathbf{let}\ rep = Rep\ \{\ to = (id \triangle (pnt\ a)), from = \pi_1\ \}$
   $View\ s\ t \leftarrow pullUpAllRefs\ (tx \mid ta)$
   $return\ (View\ (comprep\ rep\ s)\ t)$

The function *comprep* composes two representations. This rule receives the type
of the new block *ta*, its default instance *a*, and returns a *Rule*. The returned
rule is itself a function that receives the block to modify *tx*, and returns a
view of the new type. The first step is to verify if the given types are blocks
using the function *isBlock*. The second step is to create the representation *rep*
with the witness functions given in the above diagram. Then the references are
pulled up in result type $tx \mid ta$. This returns a new representation *s* and a
new type *t* (in fact, the type is the same $t = tx \mid ta$). The result view has as
representation the composition of the two previous representations, *rep* and *s*,
and the corresponding type *t*.

   Rules to insert classes and sheets were also defined, but since these rules are
similar to the rule to insert blocks, we omit them.

Insert a column. To insert a column in a spreadsheet, that is, a cell with a label
lbl and the cell bellow with a default value *df* and vertically expandable, we first
need to create a new class representing it: $clas = |\ lbl : lbl\,\hat{}\,(lbl = df^{\downarrow})$. The label
is used to create the default value $(lbl, [\ ])$. Note that since we want to create an
expandable class, the second part of the pair must be a list. The final step is to
apply *insertSheet*:

$insertCol :: String \rightarrow VFormula \rightarrow Rule$
$insertCol\ l\ f@(FFormula\ name\ fs)\ tx\ |\ isSheet\ tx = \mathbf{do}$
   $\mathbf{let}\ clas = |\ lbl : lbl\,\hat{}\,(lbl = df^{\downarrow})$
   $((insertSheet\ clas\ (lbl, [\ ])) \triangleright pullUpAllRefs)\ tx$

Note the use of the rule *pullUpAllRefs* as explained before. The case shown in
the above definition is for a formula as default value and it is similar to the value
case. The case with a reference is more interesting and is shown next:

$insertCol\ l\ FRef\ tx\ |\ isSheet\ tx = \mathbf{do}$
   $\mathbf{let}\ clas = |\ lbl : Ref \perp \perp \perp (lbl\,\hat{}\,((lbl = RefCell)^{\downarrow}))$
   $((insertSheet\ clas\ (lbl, [\ ])) \triangleright pullUpAllRefs)\ tx$

Recall that our references are always local, that is, they can only exist with
the type they are associated with. So, it is not possible to insert a column that
references a part of the existing spreadsheet. To overcome this, we first create
the reference with undefined functions and auxiliary type ($\perp$). We then set these
values to the intended ones.

$setFormula :: Type\ b \rightarrow PF\ (a \rightarrow RefCell) \rightarrow PF\ (a \rightarrow b) \rightarrow Rule$
$setFormula\ tb\ fRef\ tRef\ (Ref\ \_\ \_\ \_\ t) =$
   $return\ (View\ idrep\ (Ref\ tb\ fRef\ tRef\ t))$

This rule receives the auxiliary type (*Type b*), the two functions representing the reference projections and adds them to the type. A complete rule to insert a column with a reference is defined as follows:

> *insertFormula* =
>   (*once* (*insertCol label FRef*)) ▷ (*setFormula auxType fromRef toRef*)

Following the original idea described previously in this section, we want to introduce a new column with the number of passengers in a flight. In this case, we want to insert a column in an existing block and thus our previous rule will not work. For these cases we write a new rule:

> *insertColIn* :: *String* → *VFormula* → *Rule*
> *insertColIn l* (*FValue v*) *tx* | *isBlock tx* = **do**
>   **let** *block* = *lbl* ˆ (*lbl* = *v*)
>   ((*insertBlock block* (*lbl, v*)) ▷ *pullUpAllRefs*) *tx*

This rule is similar to the previous one but it creates a block (not a class) and inserts it also after a block. The reasoning is analogous to the one in *insertCol*.

To add the column "Passengers" we can use the rule *insertColIn*, but applying it directly to our running example will fail since it expects a block and we have a spreadsheet. We can use the combinator *once* to achieve the desired result. This combinator tries to apply a given rule somewhere in a type, stopping after it succeeds once. Although this combinator already existed in the 2LT framework, we extended it to work for spreadsheet models/types.

Make it expandable. It is possible to make a block in a class expandable. For this, we created the rule *expandBlock*:

> *expandBlock* :: *String* → *Rule*
> *expandBlock str* (*label* : *clas*) | *compLabel label str* = **do**
>   **let** *rep* = *Rep* { *to* = *id* × *tolist*, *from* = *id* × *head*}
>   *return* (*View rep* (*label* : (*clas*)$^{\downarrow}$))

It receives the label of the class to make expandable and updates the class to allow repetition. The result type constructor is · : (·)$^{\downarrow}$; the *to* function wraps the existing block into a list, *tolist*; and the *from* function takes the head of it, *head*. We developed a similar rule to make a class expandable. This corresponds to promote a class *c* to *c*$^{\rightarrow}$. We do not show its implementation here since it is quite similar to the one just shown.

Split. It is quite common to move a column in a spreadsheet from on place to another. The rule *split* copies a column to another place and substitutes the original column values by references to the new column (similar to create a pointer). The rule to move part of the spreadsheet is presented in Sect. 5.2. The first step of *split* is to get the column that we want to copy:

$getColumn :: String \rightarrow Rule$

$getColumn \ h \ t \ (l' \char`^ b1) \ | \ h \equiv l' = return \ (View \ idrep \ t)$

If the corresponding label is found, the vertical composition is returned. Note that as in other rules, this one is intended to be applied using the combinator *once*. As we said, we aim to write local rules that can be used at any level using the developed combinators.

In a second step the rule creates a new a class containing the retrieved block:

do $View \ s \ c' \leftarrow getBlock \ str \ c$

$\quad$ **let** $nsh = | \ str : (c')^{\downarrow}$

The last step is to transform the original column that was copied into references to the new column. The rule *makeReferences :: String $\rightarrow$ Rule* receives the label of the column that was copied (the same as the new column) and creates the references. We do not shown the rest of the implementation because it is quite complex and will not help in the understanding of the paper.

Layout Rules. We will now describe rules focused on the layout of spreadsheets, that is, rules that do not add/remove information to/from the model, but only rearrange it.

Change orientation. The rule *toVertical* changes the orientation of a block from horizontal to vertical.

$toVertical :: Rule$

$toVertical \ (a \ | \ b) = return \ (View \ idrep \ (a \char`^ b))$

Note that since our value-level representation of these compositions are pairs, the *to* and the *from* functions are simply the identity function. The needed information is kept in the type-level with the different constructors. A rule to do the inverse was also designed but since it is quite similar to this one, we do not show it here.

Normalize blocks. When applying some transformations, the resulting types may not have the correct shape. A common example is to have as result the following type:

$A \ | \ B \char`^ C \ | \ D \char`^$
$E \ | \ F$

However, given the rules in [29] to ensure the correctness of ClassSheets, the correct result is the following:

$A \ | \ B \ | \ D \char`^$
$E \ | \ C \ | \ F$

The rule *normalize* tries to match these cases and correct them. The types are the ones presented above and the witness functions are combinations of π_1 and π_2.

```
normalize :: Rule
normalize (a ⋁ b ˆ c ⋁ d ˆ e ⋁ f) = do
    let to = id × π₁ × id ∘ π₁△π₁ ∘ π₂△π₂ ∘ π₁ ∘ π₂ × π₂
        from = π₁ ∘ π₁△π₁ ∘ π₂ × π₁ ∘ π₂△π₂ ∘ π₂ ∘ π₁△id × π₂ ∘ π₂
    return (View (Rep { to = to, from = from }) (a ⋁ b ⋁ d ˆ e ⋁ c ⋁ f))
```

Although the migration functions seem complex, they just rearrange the order of the pairs so they have the correct arrangement.

Shift. It is quite common to move parts of the spreadsheet across it. We designed a rule to shift parts of the spreadsheet in the four possible directions. We show here part of the *shiftRight* rule, which, as suggested by its name, shifts a piece of the spreadsheet to the right. In this case, a block is moved and an empty block is left in its place.

```
shiftRight :: Type a → Rule
shiftRight ta b1 | isBlock b1 = do
    Eq ← teq ta b1
    let rep = Rep { to = pnt (⊥ :: EmptyBlock)△id, from = π₂ }
    return (View rep (EmptyBlock ⋁ b1))
```

The function *teq* verifies if two types are equal. This rule receives a type and a block, but we can easily write a wrapper function to receive a label in the same style of *insertCol*.

Another interesting case of this rules occurs when the user tries to move a block (or a sheet) that has a reference.

```
shiftRight ta (Ref tb frRef toRef b1) | isBlock b1 = do
    Eq ← teq ta b1
    let rep = Rep { to = pnt (⊥ :: EmptyBlock)△id, from = π₂ }
    return (View rep (Ref tb (frRef ∘ π₂) (toRef ∘ π₂) (EmptyBlock ⋁ b1)))
```

As we can see in the above code, the existing reference projections must be composed with the selector π_2 to allow to retrieve the existing block *b1*. Only after this it is possible to apply the defined selection reference functions.

Move blocks. A more complex task is to move a part of the spreadsheet to another place. We present next a rule to move a block.

```
moveBlock :: String → Rule
moveBlock str c = do
    View s c' ← getBlock str c
    let nsh =⋁ str : c'
    View r sh ← once (removeRedundant str) (c ⋁ nsh)
    return (View (comprep s r) sh)
```

After getting the intended block and creating a new class with it, we need to remove the old block using *removeRedundant*.

removeRedundant :: *String* → *Rule*
removeRedundant s (*s'*) | *s* ≡ *s'* = **do**
  let *rep* = *Rep* { *to* = *pnt* (⊥ :: *EmptyBlock*), *from* = *pnt s'* }
  return (*View rep EmptyBlock*)

This rule will remove the block with the given label leaving an empty block in its place.

6   Model-Driven Spreadsheet Development in MDSheet

The embedding and evolution techniques presented previously have been implemented as an add-on to a widely used spreadsheet system, the OpenOffice/ LibreOffice system. The add-on provides a model-driven spreadsheet development environment, named MDSheet, where a (model-driven) spreadsheet consists of two type of worksheets: **Sheet** 0, containing the embedded ClassSheet model, and **Sheet** 1, containing the spreadsheet data that conforms to the model. Users can interact both with the ClassSheet model and the spreadsheet data. Our techniques guarantee the synchronization of the two representations.

In such an model-driven environment, users can evolve the model by using standard editing/updating techniques as provided by spreadsheets systems. Our add-on/environment also provides predefined buttons that implement the usual ClassSheets evolution steps. Each button implements an evolution rule, as described in Sect. 5. For each button, we defined a BASIC script that interprets the desired functionality, and sends the contents of the spreadsheet (both the model and the data) to our Haskell-based co-evolution framework. This Haskell framework implements the co-evolution of the spreadsheet models and data presented in Sect. 5.

MDSheet also allows the development of ClassSheet models from scratch by using the provided buttons or by traditional editing. In this case, a first instance/spreadsheet is generated from the model which includes some business logic rules that assist users in the safe and correct introduction/editing of data. For example, in the spreadsheet presented in Fig. 22, if the user presses the button in column J, four new columns will automatically be inserted so the user can add more flights. This automation will also automatically update all formulas in the spreadsheet.

The global architecture of the model-driven spreadsheet development we constructed is presented in Fig. 28.

Tool and demonstration video availability. The MDSheet tool [24] and a video with a demonstration of its capabilities are available at the SSaaPP – Spread-Sheets as a Programming Paradigm project's website[13].

In the next section we present in detail the empirical study we have organized and conducted to assess model-driven spreadsheets running through MDSheet.

---

[13] http://ssaapp.di.uminho.pt.

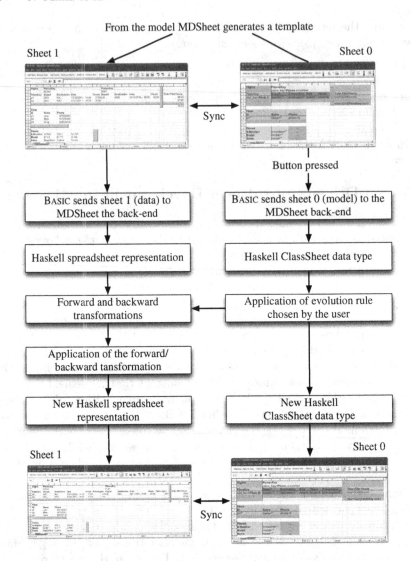

Fig. 28. Model-driven spreadsheet development environment.

Exercise 7. *Consider the spreadsheet and corresponding model defined in Exercise 5. First, write the ClassSheet model in the MDSheet environment. Second, update the spreadsheet instance with the data.*

7   Studies with School Participants

In this section we present the feedback we obtained from school participants regarding spreadsheets and their engineering. This feedback was solicited in two different moments and aimed at realizing the participants perspective on two different spreadsheet aspects.

For once, we asked participants to name, from the characteristics that have been natively incorporated in spreadsheet systems, the ones they realized as the most important. Also, we asked them to name the single feature they missed the most. The details on this inquiry are presented in Sect. 7.1, and its results were already presented to the participants during the summer school.

Secondly, we relied on the participants' feedback to identify possible improvements for our framework. This occurred after our tutorial sessions, and during a lab session, where participants volunteered to actually perform concrete spreadsheet engineering tasks under the framework that we have built and that we have described in this tutorial. The details on this experiment are described in Sect. 7.2.

In both cases, we believe that the generalization of the results we observe here would require a larger sample of participants, namely for statistical reasons. Nevertheless, we also believe that the volunteer nature and the interest demonstrated by the participants when providing concrete feedback is surely worth its analyzis and publishing.

7.1 Participants' Perspective on Spreadsheets

In the beginning of our tutorial, we asked for the participants cooperation in filling in an inquiry on the spreadsheet characteristics they understood as the most important and on the feature they would like to see incorporated in traditional spreadsheet systems. We chose this moment to do so, since we wanted to understand the participants' perspective unbiased from the materials we later exposed.

The inquiry that we conducted consisted in handing a paper form to each participant, asking:

1. *Please provide the three most important characteristics of spreadsheets, in (descending) order of preference.*
2. *Please provide the feature you miss the most in spreadsheet systems.*

Answers were completely open, in that no pre-defined set of possible answers was given.

Figure 29 shows the feedback we received with respect to the first (most important) characteristic identified by the school participants.

Out of a total number of 29 answers, 17 (almost 60 %) identify the simplicity in their usage as the most important characteristic of spreadsheets. Also, the tabular layout of spreadsheets, with 5 answers (exactly 17 %), and their underlying incremental engine, with 3 (10 %), were significantly acknowledged. Finally, their flexibility, multi-purpose, availability on almost any computer as well as their presentation-oriented nature were also mentioned, with 1 answer each (nearly 3 % of all answers).

Next, we follow this same analysis regarding the characteristics pointed out as the second most important of spreadsheets, and that are presented in Fig. 30.

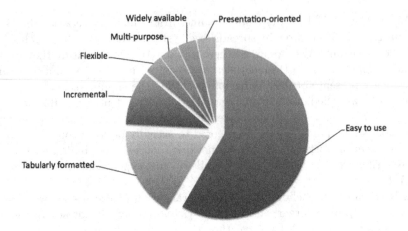

Fig. 29. Most important spreadsheet characteristic.

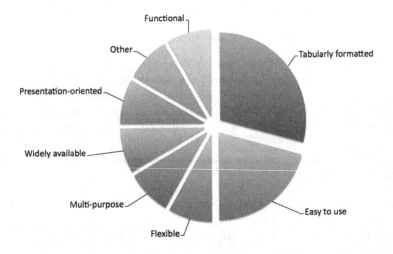

Fig. 30. Second most important spreadsheet characteristic.

In this case, we have received a total number of 24 answers. Out of these, the tabular nature of spreadsheets, with 7 answers (circa 30 %), and their simple usage, with 5 (around 10 %) are again the most pointed characteristics. Characteristics such as availability, multi-purpose, flexibility, functionality or presentation-orientation were all pointed out by 2 participants (i.e., by 8 % of all answers).

Regarding the answers that were given as the third most important spreadsheet characteristic, we have received a total of 20 valid answers, which are sketched in Fig. 31.

We observe a predominance of the availability and functionality of spreadsheets, with 4 answers each (i.e., 20 % of all answers each). The layout of

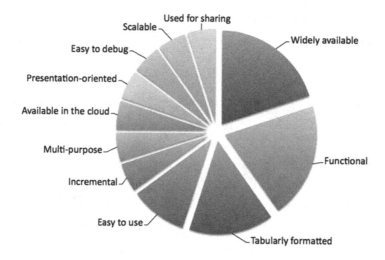

Fig. 31. Third most important spreadsheet characteristic.

spreadsheets was pointed by 3 participants (15 %) and all other characteristics were pointed out by a single participant (corresponding to 5 % of all answers).

Considering all the characteristics that were identified, irrespective to their order of preference, we obtain the results sketched in Fig. 32.

The top three identified characteristics were then the easiness of usage of spreadsheets, with 24 answers (33 %), their tabular format, 15 answers (21 %), and their availability, 7 answers (10 %).

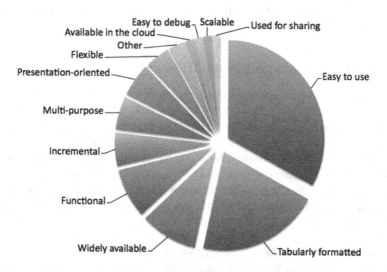

Fig. 32. Overall most important spreadsheet characteristic.

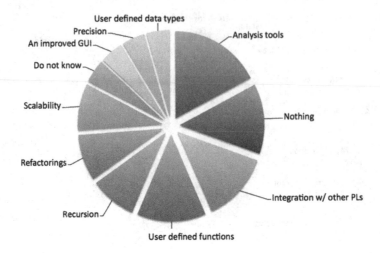

Fig. 33. The single most missed feature on spreadsheets.

Finally, regarding our pre-tutorial inquiry, participants were asked to identify the feature they missed the most on a spreadsheet system. The answers we received, in number of 23, are depicted in Fig. 33.

We see that analysis tools, integration with other programming languages, and user defined functions are the most missed features (with 4, 3 and 3 answers, respectively). Interestingly enough, 3 participants say that spreadsheet systems are fine in their current state, i.e., that they do not miss a single feature there. With 2 participants referring to them, recursion, refactorings, and a better scalability model are also identified as missing features. Finally, an improved graphical user interface, precision and user defined data types were also identified each by a single participant.

7.2   Participants' Perspective on MDSheet

In this section, we describe the simple experiment that we have devised in order to obtain feedback on the MDSheet framework from the participants. Five participants volunteered to join the experiment: 4 males and 1 female; all of them had never had contact with MDSheet prior to the summer school.

Our experiment consisted in executing three specific tasks. Prior to participants actually performing each one, we have ourselves demonstrated with equivalent actions. Also, the tasks that were solicited consisted of editing steps on an already built model to deal with a simple budget (registering incomes and expenses). These tasks followed the order:

1. Add an attribute to a class, being given its default value.
2. Add and attribute to a class, being its value defined by a given formula.
3. Remove an attribute from a class.

After the execution of each task, we made available a (web) form, where participants had the opportunity to answer the following questions:

(i) Did you find this functionality useful?
(ii) For this functionality, describe an advantage in using our environment.
(iii) For this functionality, describe a disadvantage in using our environment.
(iv) For this functionality, please give us a suggestion to improve our environment.
(v) Assuming that you are familiar with our environment, would you prefer to use standard *Excel* to complete this task? Please elaborate.

In the remaining of this section, we present our analysis on the feedback that was provided by participants.

Analyzing task 1. All participants found the functionality of adding attributes to a class useful. Also, they in general see as beneficial the fact that attributes may later be called by name, instead of by (alphabetical) column identifiers. In fact, this is in line with the results presented in [46] where authors showed that spreadsheet users create a mental model of the spreadsheet that helps them understand and work with the spreadsheet. These mental models are created using names from the real world as it is the case with our ClassSheet models.

In terms of disadvantages, they point out the fact that attribute names are not visible on the instances, and potential efficiency problems when using larger models. Some participants suggest that we should improve further our graphical user interface. Still, all participants state that they prefer using our environment over using a standard spreadsheet system for this type of action.

Analyzing task 2. All participants found the functionality of adding attributes whose values are given by a formula to a class useful. Indeed, they state that being able of defining formulas using attribute names is very intuitive and helpful. Also, they see as important the fact that a formula is defined only once, in the model, being automatically copied (and updated) wherever (and whenever) necessary at the instance level.

In terms of disadvantages, the one thing that is identified is that it would be better, when defining a formula, to be able to use the mouse to point to an attribute instead of having to type its name, as our tool in its current state demands. Actually, overcoming this disadvantage is the main suggestion for improvement that we receive here. For faster feedback, two participants state that they would prefer using *Excel* in the particular scenario that we have set and for this particular task. However, they also state that if they were dealing with a larger model, they would prefer MDSheet.

Analyzing task 3. Again, all participants found the functionality of removing an attribute from a class useful. All participants but one were particularly enthusiastic about the fact that all the necessary editions (e.g., in the scopes of all formulas affected by the deletion of the attribute) are automatically implemented.

Also, most participants found no disadvantages in using our framework for this type of tasks. Nevertheless, the issues that were raised here concern to the fact that using our model-based approach may sometimes restrict the flexibility of standard spreadsheets. The comments with respect to this task mainly suggest that we should make available a message confirming the will to delete data. Finally, no participant declared to prefer a standard spreadsheet system to accomplish a task such as this one.

Apart from feedback on accomplishing specific tasks, we also requested general feedback regarding MDSheet. Indeed, we asked each participant to choose the descriptions they believed were applicable to our framework from the following list. Any number of options was selectable.

Helpful	Not helpful	Useful for professional programmers
Usable	Requires specific knowledge	Useful for non-professional programmers
Intuitive	Counter intuitive	Can improve my productivity
Useless	Not useful in practice	Can not improve my productivity

The options that were selected, and the number of times they were selected is given next.

Helpful	4
Can improve my productivity	4
Useful for non-professional programmers	3
Usable	3
Intuitive	1
Requires specific knowledge	1

Finally, we asked for comments on MDSheet and for suggestions that could improve it. The most referred suggestion was to add an undo button to the framework. In another direction, one participant commented that our framework may be unfit for agile business practices.

As we explained before, this empirical study was performed in the laboratory sessions of our tutorial course. The number of participants in the study is small, and no statistical conclusions can be obtained from the study. However, we have conducted a larger study with end users where we evaluated their efficiency (measured as the time needed to complete a task) and effectiveness (measure as the number of errors produced in solving the task) using regular and model-driven spreadsheets [20]. Those results show that using our MDSD environment, end users are both more efficient and effective. In fact, those results just confirm the feedback we received from summer school participants.

8   Conclusion

This document presents a set of techniques and tools to analyze and evolve spreadsheets. First, it presents data mining and database techniques to infer a ClassSheet that represents the business logic of spreadsheet data. Next, it shows the embedding of the visual, domain specific language of ClassSheet in a general purpose spreadsheet system. Finally, it presents model-driven engineering techniques, based on data refinements, to evolve the model and have the instance automatically co-evolved. These techniques are implemented in the MDSheet framework: an add-on for a widely used, open source, spreadsheet system.

In order to validate both our embedding of a visual DSL and the evolution of our model-driven spreadsheets, we have conducted an empirical study with the summer school participants. The results show that regular spreadsheet users are able to perform the proposed tasks, and they recognize the advantages of using our setting when compared to standard spreadsheet systems.

The techniques and tools described in this paper were developed in the context of the SSaaPP - Spreadsheets as a Programming Paradigm research project. In the project's webpage, the reader may find the tools presented in this paper and other contributions in the area of spreadsheet engineering: namely the definition of a catalog of spreadsheet bad smells, the definition of a query language for model-driven spreadsheets, and a quality model for spreadsheets. They are available, as a set of research papers and software tools, at the following webpage:

http://ssaapp.di.uminho.pt

Acknowledgments. The theories, techniques and tools presented in this tutorial paper were developed under the project SSaaPP - SpreadSheets as a Programming Paradigm: a research project funded by the Portuguese Science Foundation (contract number FCOMP-01-0124-FEDER-010048). We would like to thank the members and consultants of this project who made important contributions for the results presented in this document, namely: Rui Maranhão Abreu, Tiago Alves, Laura Beckwith, Orlando Belo, Martin Erwig, Pedro Martins, Hugo Pacheco, Christophe Peixoto, Rui Pereira, Alexandre Perez, Hugo Ribeiro, André Riboira, André Silva, and Joost Visser.

References

1. Abraham, R., Erwig, M.: Header and unit inference for spreadsheets through spatial analyses. In: 2004 IEEE Symposium on Visual Languages and Human Centric Computing, pp. 165–172, September 2004
2. Abraham, R., Erwig, M.: UCheck: a spreadsheet type checker for end users. J. Vis. Lang. Comput. 18(1), 71–95 (2007)
3. Abraham, R., Erwig, M.: Goal-directed debugging of spreadsheets. In: VL/HCC, pp. 37–44. IEEE Computer Society (2005)
4. Abraham, R., Erwig, M.: Autotest: a tool for automatic test case generation in spreadsheets. In: Proceedings of the 2006 IEEE Symposium on Visual Languages and Human-Centric Computing (VL/HCC 2006), pp. 43–50. IEEE Computer Society (2006)
5. Abraham, R., Erwig, M.: Inferring templates from spreadsheets. In: Proceedings of the 28th International Conference on Software Engineering, pp. 182–191. ACM, New York (2006)
6. Abraham, R., Erwig, M.: Type inference for spreadsheets. In: Bossi, A., Maher, M.J. (eds.) Proceedings of the 8th International ACM SIGPLAN Conference on Principles and Practice of Declarative Programming, Venice, Italy, 10–12 July 2006, pp. 73–84. ACM (2006)

7. Abraham, R., Erwig, M.: Goaldebug: a spreadsheet debugger for end users. In: ICSE 2007: Proceedings of the 29th International Conference on Software Engineering, pp. 251–260. IEEE Computer Society, Washington, DC (2007)
8. Abraham, R., Erwig, M.: Mutation operators for spreadsheets. IEEE Trans. Softw. Eng. **35**(1), 94–108 (2009)
9. Abraham, R., Erwig, M., Kollmansberger, S., Seifert, E.: Visual specifications of correct spreadsheets. In: Proceedings of the 2005 IEEE Symposium on Visual Languages and Human-Centric Computing, VL/HCC 2005, pp. 189–196. IEEE Computer Society (2005)
10. Aho, A.V., Sethi, R., Ullman, J.D.: Compilers: Principles, Techniques and Tools. Addison Wesley, Reading (1986)
11. Alhajj, R.: Extracting the extended entity-relationship model from a legacy relational database. Inf. Syst. **28**(6), 597–618 (2003)
12. Alves, T.L., Silva, P.F., Visser, J.: Constraint-aware schema transformation. Electron. Notes Theor. Comput. Sci. **290**, 3–18 (2012)
13. Bricklin, D.: VisiCalc: Information from its creators, Dan Bricklin and Bob Frankston. http://www.bricklin.com/visicalc.htm. Accessed 5 Dec 2013
14. Bruins, E.: On Plimpton 322. Pythagorean numbers in Babylonian mathematics. Koninklijke Nederlandse Akademie van Wetenschappen **52**, 629–632 (1949)
15. Burnett, M., Cook, C., Pendse, O., Rothermel, G., Summet, J., Wallace, C.: End-user software engineering with assertions in the spreadsheet paradigm. In: Proceedings of the 25th International Conference on Software Engineering, ICSE 2003, pp. 93–103. IEEE Computer Society (2003)
16. Campbell-Kelly, M., Croarken, M., Flood, R., Robson, E.: The History of Mathematical Tables: From Sumer to Spreadsheets. Oxford University Press, Oxford (2003)
17. Codd, E.F.: A relational model of data for large shared data banks. Commun. ACM **13**(6), 377–387 (1970)
18. Cunha, A., Oliveira, J.N., Visser, J.: Type-safe two-level data transformation. In: Misra, J., Nipkow, T., Sekerinski, E. (eds.) FM 2006. LNCS, vol. 4085, pp. 284–299. Springer, Heidelberg (2006)
19. Cunha, J., Erwig, M., Saraiva, J.: Automatically inferring classsheet models from spreadsheets. In: IEEE Symposium on Visual Languages and Human-Centric Computing, VL/HCC 2010, pp. 93–100. IEEE Computer Society (2010)
20. Cunha, J., Fernandes, J., Mendes, J., Saraiva, J.: Embedding, evolution, and validation of model-driven spreadsheets. IEEE Trans. Software Eng. **PP**(99), 1 (2014)
21. Cunha, J., Fernandes, J.P., Ribeiro, H., Saraiva, J.: Towards a catalog of spreadsheet smells. In: Murgante, B., Gervasi, O., Misra, S., Nedjah, N., Rocha, A.M.A.C., Taniar, D., Apduhan, B.O. (eds.) ICCSA 2012, Part IV. LNCS, vol. 7336, pp. 202–216. Springer, Heidelberg (2012)
22. Cunha, J., Fernandes, J.P., Mendes, J., Martins, P., Saraiva, J.: Smellsheet detective: a tool for detecting bad smells in spreadsheets. In: Proceedings of the 2012 IEEE Symposium on Visual Languages and Human-Centric Computing, VLHCC 2012, pp. 243–244. IEEE Computer Society, Washington, DC (2012)
23. Cunha, J., Fernandes, J.P., Mendes, J., Saraiva, J.: Extension and implementation of ClassSheet models. In: Proceedings of the 2012 IEEE Symposium on Visual Languages and Human-Centric Computing, VLHCC 2012, pp. 19–22. IEEE Computer Society (2012)
24. Cunha, J., Fernandes, J.P., Mendes, J., Saraiva, J.: MDSheet: a framework for model-driven spreadsheet engineering. In: Proceedings of the 34th International Conference on Software Engineering, ICSE 2012, pp. 1412–1415. ACM (2012)

25. Cunha, J., Fernandes, J.P., Saraiva, J.: From relational ClassSheets to UML+OCL. In: Proceedings of the Software Engineering Track at the 27th Annual ACM Symposium on Applied Computing, pp. 1151–1158. ACM (2012)
26. Cunha, J., Mendes, J., Fernandes, J.P., Saraiva, J.: Embedding and evolution of spreadsheet models in spreadsheet systems. In: Proceedings of the 2011 IEEE Symposium on Visual Languages and Human-Centric Computing, VLHCC 2011, pp. 186–201. IEEE (2011)
27. Cunha, J., Saraiva, J., Visser, J.: Model-based programming environments for spreadsheets. Sci. Comput. Program. (SCP) **96**, 254–275 (2014)
28. Cunha, J., Visser, J., Alves, T., Saraiva, J.: Type-safe evolution of spreadsheets. In: Giannakopoulou, D., Orejas, F. (eds.) FASE 2011. LNCS, vol. 6603, pp. 186–201. Springer, Heidelberg (2011)
29. Engels, G., Erwig, M.: ClassSheets: automatic generation of spreadsheet applications from object-oriented specifications. In: Proceedings of the 20th IEEE/ACM International Conference on Automated Software Engineering, pp. 124–133. ACM (2005)
30. Erdweg, S., et al.: The state of the art in language workbenches. In: Erwig, M., Paige, R.F., Van Wyk, E. (eds.) SLE 2013. LNCS, vol. 8225, pp. 197–217. Springer, Heidelberg (2013)
31. Erwig, M.: Software engineering for spreadsheets. IEEE Softw. **29**(5), 25–30 (2009)
32. Erwig, M., Abraham, R., Cooperstein, I., Kollmansberger, S.: Automatic generation and maintenance of correct spreadsheets. In: Proceedings of the 27th International Conference on Software Engineering, pp. 136–145. ACM (2005)
33. Erwig, M., Abraham, R., Kollmansberger, S., Cooperstein, I.: Gencel: a program generator for correct spreadsheets. J. Funct. Program. **16**(3), 293–325 (2006)
34. Erwig, M., Burnett, M.: Adding apples and oranges. In: Adsul, B., Ramakrishnan, C.R. (eds.) PADL 2002. LNCS, vol. 2257, pp. 173–191. Springer, Heidelberg (2002)
35. Fisher II, M., Cao, M., Rothermel, G., Cook, C., Burnett, M.: Automated test case generation for spreadsheets. In: Proceedings of the 24th International Conference on Software Engineering (ICSE 2002), pp. 141–154. ACM Press, New York, 19–25 May 2002
36. Fisher II, M., Rothermel, G., Brown, D., Cao, M., Cook, C., Burnett, M.: Integrating automated test generation into the WYSIWYT spreadsheet testing methodology. ACM Trans. Softw. Eng. Methodol. **15**(2), 150–194 (2006)
37. Fisher II, M., Rothermel, G., Creelan, T., Burnett, M.: Scaling a dataflow testing methodology to the multiparadigm world of commercial spreadsheets. In: Proceedings of the 17th IEEE International Symposium on Software Reliability Engineering, Raleigh, NC, USA, pp. 13–22, November 2006
38. Gibbons, J.: Functional programming for domain-specific languages. In: Zsok, V. (ed.) Central European Functional Programming - Summer School on Domain-Specific Languages, July 2013
39. Hermans, F., Pinzger, M., van Deursen, A.: Automatically extracting class diagrams from spreadsheets. In: D'Hondt, T. (ed.) ECOOP 2010. LNCS, vol. 6183, pp. 52–75. Springer, Heidelberg (2010)
40. Hermans, F., Pinzger, M., van Deursen, A.: Supporting professional spreadsheet users by generating leveled dataflow diagrams. In: Proceedings of the 33rd International Conference on Software Engineering, ICSE 2011, pp. 451–460. ACM (2011)
41. Hermans, F., Pinzger, M., van Deursen, A.: Detecting and visualizing inter-worksheet smells in spreadsheets. In: Proceedings of the 2012 International Conference on Software Engineering, ICSE 2012, pp. 441–451. IEEE Press (2012)

42. Hermans, F., Pinzger, M., van Deursen, A.: Detecting code smells in spreadsheet formulas. In: ICSM, pp. 409–418 (2012)
43. Hinze, R., Löh, A., Oliveira, B.C.S.: "Scrap your boilerplate" reloaded. In: Hagiya, M. (ed.) FLOPS 2006. LNCS, vol. 3945, pp. 13–29. Springer, Heidelberg (2006)
44. Hudak, P.: Building domain-specific embedded languages. ACM Comput. Surv. **28**(4es), 196 (1996)
45. Jones, S.P., Blackwell, A., Burnett, M.: A user-centred approach to functions in excel. In: Proceedings of the 8th ACM SIGPLAN International Conference on Functional Programming, ICFP 2003, pp. 165–176. ACM (2003)
46. Kankuzi, B., Sajaniemi, J.: An empirical study of spreadsheet authors' mental models in explaining and debugging tasks. In: 2013 IEEE Symposium on Visual Languages and Human-Centric Computing, VL/HCC 2013, pp. 15–18 (2013)
47. Kuiper, M., Saraiva, J.: Lrc - a generator for incremental language-oriented tools. In: Koskimies, K. (ed.) CC 1998. LNCS, vol. 1383, pp. 298–301. Springer, Heidelberg (1998)
48. Lämmel, R., Visser, J.: A *Strafunski* application letter. In: Dahl, V. (ed.) PADL 2003. LNCS, vol. 2562, pp. 357–375. Springer, Heidelberg (2002)
49. Lämmel, R., Saraiva, J., Visser, J. (eds.): GTTSE 2005. LNCS, vol. 4143. Springer, Heidelberg (2006)
50. Luckey, M., Erwig, M., Engels, G.: Systematic evolution of model-based spreadsheet applications. J. Vis. Lang. Comput. **23**(5), 267–286 (2012)
51. Maier, D.: The Theory of Relational Databases. Computer Science Press, Rockville (1983)
52. Morgan, C., Gardiner, P.: Data refinement by calculation. Acta Inform. **27**, 481–503 (1990)
53. Nardi, B.A.: A Small Matter of Programming: Perspectives on End User Computing, 1st edn. MIT Press, Cambridge (1993)
54. Oliveira, J.: A reification calculus for model-oriented software specification. Form. Asp. Comput. **2**(1), 1–23 (1990)
55. Oliveira, J.N.: Transforming data by calculation. In: Lämmel, R., Visser, J., Saraiva, J. (eds.) Generative and Transformational Techniques in Software Engineering II. LNCS, vol. 5235, pp. 134–195. Springer, Heidelberg (2008)
56. Panko, R.R.: What we know about spreadsheet errors. J. End User Comput. (Special issue on Scaling Up End User Development) **10**(2), 15–21 (1998)
57. Panko, R.R.: Spreadsheet errors: what we know. what we think we can do. In: Proceedings of the European Spreadsheet Risks Interest Group (EuSpRIG) (2000)
58. Panko, R.R.: Facing the problem of spreadsheet errors. Decis. Line **37**(5), 8–10 (2006)
59. Panko, R.R., Aurigemma, S.: Revising the panko-halverson taxonomy of spreadsheet errors. Decis. Support Syst. **49**(2), 235–244 (2010)
60. Panko, R.R., Ordway, N.: Sarbanes-Oxley: What About all the Spreadsheets? CoRR abs/0804.0797 (2008)
61. Peyton Jones, S., Washburn, G., Weirich, S.: Wobbly types: type inference for generalised algebraic data types. Technical report, MS-CIS-05-26, University of Pennsylvania, July 2004
62. Powell, S.G., Baker, K.R., Lawson, B.: A critical review of the literature on spreadsheet errors. Decis. Support Syst. **46**(1), 128–138 (2008)
63. Rajalingham, K., Chadwick, D.R., Knight, B.: Classification of spreadsheet errors. In: Proceedings of the 2001 European Spreadsheet Risks Interest Group, EuSpRIG 2001, Amsterdam (2001)

64. Reinhart, C.M., Rogoff, K.S.: Growth in a time of debt. Am. Econ. Rev. **100**(2), 573–578 (2010)
65. Robson, E.: Neither Sherlock Holmes nor Babylon: a reassessment of Plimpton 322. Historia Mathematica **28**(3), 167–206 (2001)
66. Rothermel, G., Burnett, M., Li, L., Sheretov, A.: A methodology for testing spreadsheets. ACM Trans. Softw. Eng. Methodol. **10**, 110–147 (2001)
67. Ruthruff, J., Creswick, E., Burnett, M., Cook, C., Prabhakararao, S., Fisher II, M., Main, M.: End-user software visualizations for fault localization. In: Proceedings of the ACM Symposium on Software Visualization, San Diego, CA, USA, pp. 123–132, June 2003
68. Scaffidi, C., Shaw, M., Myers, B.: Estimating the numbers of end users and end user programmers. In: Proceedings of the 2005 IEEE Symposium on Visual Languages and Human-Centric Computing, pp. 207–214 (2005)
69. Stevens, P., Whittle, J., Booch, G. (eds.): UML 2003. LNCS, vol. 2863. Springer, Heidelberg (2003)
70. Swierstra, D., Azero, P., Saraiva, J.: Designing and implementing combinator languages. In: Swierstra, S.D., Oliveira, J.N. (eds.) AFP 1998. LNCS, vol. 1608, pp. 150–206. Springer, Heidelberg (1999)
71. Ullman, J.D., Widom, J.: A First Course in Database Systems. Prentice Hall, Upper Saddle River (1997)
72. Ullman, J.: Principles of Database and Knowledge-Base Systems, vol. I. Computer Science Press, Rockville (1988)
73. Visser, E.: A survey of strategies in rule-based program transformation systems. J. Symbolic Comput. **40**, 831–873 (2005)
74. Visser, J., Saraiva, J.: Tutorial on strategic programming across programming paradigms. In: 8th Brazilian Symposium on Programming Languages, Niteroi, Brazil, May 2004

The EDSL's Struggle for Their Sources

Gergely Dévai[✉], Dániel Leskó, and Máté Tejfel

Faculty of Informatics, Eötvös Loránd University, Budapest, Hungary
{deva,ldani,matej}@caesar.elte.hu

Abstract. Embedded Domain Specific Languages make language design and implementation easier, because lexical and syntactical analysis and part of the semantic checks can be completed by the compiler of the host language.

On the other hand, by the nature of embedding, EDSL compilers have to work with a syntax tree that stores no information about the source file processed and the location of the program entities within the source file. This makes it hard to produce user-friendly error messages and connect the generated target code with the source code for debugging and profiling purposes.

This lecture note presents this problem in detail and shows possible solutions. The first, lightweight solution uses macro preprocessing. The second one is based on syntax tree transformations to add missing source-related information. This is more powerful, but also more heavyweight. The last technique avoids the problem by turning the embedded language implementation to a standalone one (with own parser) after the experimental phase of the language development process: It turns out that most of the embedded implementation can be reused in the standalone one.

1   Introduction

As software systems become more and more complex, using appropriate languages that provide the right abstraction level and domain-specific optimization possibilities is crucial to keep the time-to-market short, the maintenance costs low and the product performance high.

These observations lead to the application of domain specific languages in many different application areas. On the other hand, building applications using DSLs adds new challenges: Designing new languages and creating well performing compilers is hard, integrating many different languages and tools into a project may be difficult and DSLs usually lack the rich tool support (debuggers, profilers, static analisers) that widely used general purpose programming languages have.

This paper addresses some of these challenges. In particular, we concentrate on embedded domain specific languages (EDSLs), that are implemented as special libraries in a general purpose programming languages (called the host languages). In this setup, language design is simplified to a great extent compared

Supported by EITKIC 12-1-2012-0001.

V. Zsók et al. (Eds.): CEFP 2013, LNCS 8606, pp. 300–335, 2015.
DOI: 10.1007/978-3-319-15940-9_7

to standalone language development. On the other hand, good quality error reporting, possibility of source level debugging and profiling is much harder.

This latter deficiency of EDSLs is due to the fact that the compilers of these languages have no access to the source code of the program (unless the host languages have special support for this). This paper presents three possible solutions for the problem. These were developed in different EDSL projects that the authors of this paper were involved in lately. One of these projects is Feldspar [2,8], which stands for Functional Embedded Language for Digital Signal Processing and Parallelism. It was originally initiated by Ericsson AB and run by Chalmers Univerity of Technology in Gothenburg and ELTE University in Budapest. The other project, called Miller [9], was initiated by Ericsson Hungary and is run at ELTE University. The objective of this project is to create a domain specific language for architectures with complex programmable memory hierarchies. The topic of the third project [7] is an embedded language to express formal specifications of programs and correctness proofs. All the three projects created embedded languages using Haskell as the host language.

The rest of this section introduces the concept of embedding and gives the details of the source code accessing problem. Section 2 presents a solution using preprocessing with standard tools, while Sect. 3 describes a more advanced possibility with syntax tree manipulation. Section 4 shows how to combine the development of an embedded language with its standalone version. Finally, Sect. 5 presents related work and a summary is given in the last section.

1.1 EDSLs

DSLs are usually categorized as *external* or *internal*. External DSLs are implemented as a stand alone language with own syntax and compiler, without any particular connection to any existing language. On the other hand, internal DSLs are created within the framework of another (usually general purpose) programming language, which is called the host language. The relation between an internal DSL and its host language can be of many sort. A detailed overview can be found in [17].

In this paper we consider a specific kind of internal DSL implementation strategy that Hudak [11] named as *domain specific embedded language (DSEL)* and is also called as *embedded domain specific language (EDSL)*.

An EDSL is a library written in the host language. EDSL programs are therefore programs in the host language that intensively use that library. The border between traditional libraries and EDSLs is not always clear, but it is an important feature of EDSLs that they have some kind of domain semantics in addition to their meaning as plain host language programs.

There are two types of EDSL: *shallow* and *deep* embeddings. In case of a shallow embedding, running the EDSL program as a host language program computes the result of the EDSL program. On the other hand, executing a program of a deeply embedded language as a host language program only creates the abstract syntax tree of the EDSL program. This AST is then usually further processed by the interpreter or compiler of the EDSL to execute the program or to generate target code. In the rest of the paper we will only focus on deeply embedded DSLs. Creating a deeply embedded DSL consists of the following steps:

- Definition of the data types of the abstract syntax tree. We will also refer to these data types as *internal representation.*
- Implementation of a front-end: a set of helper data types and functions that can be used to build up the abstract syntax tree. The purpose of this front-end is to provide a user-friendly way of writing EDSL programs. This frontend determines how EDSL programs will "look like", therefore one might say that it defines the EDSLs "syntax".
- Implementation of a back-end that processes the syntax tree: a code generator to transform the EDSL program to target code or an interpreter to execute it.

Compared to a standalone language, an EDSL is usually easier to develop:

- Since the EDSL has no own syntax, there is no need for lexer and parser: These tasks are done by the host language compiler.
- If the host language has expressive enough type system, it is also possible to encode much of the semantic rules of the EDSL in the types of the abstract syntax tree elements and frontend functions. This way the semantic analysis is partly done by the host language compiler too.
- The full power of the host language can be used to write meta programs on top of the EDSL. As EDSL programs are valid host language programs, EDSL program fragments can be freely combined and parametrized.

These advantages make embedding particularly suitable for language design experiments. More on this aspect will be presented in Sect. 4.

These observations are more-or-less true also for the comparison of EDSLs with other internal language implementation techniques, like Metaborg [4]. In case of Metaborg-style embeddings, one defines stand alone syntax for the DSL, but the DSL code fragments are written in host language source files. These mixed-language source files are then processed by the compiler of the DSL and the DSL fragments are translated to pure host language code. In the next step the compiler of the host language is used to create an executable.

Haskell is particularly well-suited to be a host language: Its syntax is minimal and is flexible enough to support different EDSL syntax styles. The type system of the language is advanced, allowing the language designer to encode many EDSL semantic rules in the types.

1.2 Accessing Source Code

Compilers of traditional, standalone languages have full access to the source files. Lexing and parsing keep track of the locations and string values of the tokens and the syntax tree can be annotated with this information. This annotation is then used for several different purposes:

- Quality error messages. The error messages contain exact (file, row, column) locations of the error. It may also name the entities (functions, variables etc.) that are involved in the error, using the same names that appear in the source file.
- Readable target code. Many DSL compilers translate the source code to another textual programming language instead of machine code. Programmers usually want to read this generated code and understand its connections to the original DSL code. To help this understanding process, it is helpful if the generated code uses the same names for variables, functions as the source. It may also be a good idea to add comments to the generated code showing connected DSL code fragments.
- Finding the connection between the source and target code is important not only for humans but also for software: In order to a show the active source code instruction during a debugging session or to show the values of variables it is necessary to provide the debugger with a mapping between the source and target code.
- The above mentioned mapping is also necessary to project profiling results back to the source level. This enables profilers to show performance bottlenecks in the source code or to provide runtime statistics on function or instruction level.

While any parsing based DSL development methods (standalone languages, Metaborg-style internal languages) have all the necessary information for the above tasks, EDSLs usually lack this information. The reason for this is simple: The EDSL compiler's input is the abstract syntax tree that was created by running the EDSL program as a host language program. As this syntax tree is not the result of parsing, location and textual information is not present. In order to have that in an EDSL syntax tree, the host language should provide constructs to ask for location and text of any program fragment. (See the note about the Scala language in the Related Work, Sect. 5.)

Summarizing Sects. 1.1 and 1.2, one is faced with the following tradeoff: On the positive side, EDSLs can use the host language compiler to solve lexical, syntactical and (partly) semantic analysis. Furthermore, the host language becomes a powerful meta programming layer on top of the EDSL. On the negative side, EDSL compilers usually lack source location and text information which prevents creating good quality error messages and connecting the generated target code for human understanding, debugging and profiling.

2   Preprocessing

2.1   Concept

Preprocessing is the process of scanning and modifying source code before the compiler inputs it. The most widely used preprocessor is the CPP (C preprocessor) which is used with many languages besides C and C++, including Haskell. It supports macro definitions (#define), conditional compilation (#if, #ifdef etc.), inclusion of other files into the source file (#include), which is also used instead of a proper modul system in C/C++.

There is a clone of the C preprocessor tailored a bit to the Haskell language: *cpphs* [1]. It accepts quotes and backticks in macro names to match the Haskell identifier lexical rules. However, operator symbols still cannot be used in macro names. Also, this tool is easier to integrate into compiler projects using Haskell as the implementation language than the traditional C preprocessor.

When compiling (or interpreting) Haskell sources using preprocessor directives, additional parameters are needed, for example:

```
ghci -cpp MyFile.hs
```

This will call the traditional C preprocessor, while the following uses cpphs:

```
ghci -cpp  -pgmPcpphs  -optP--cpp MyFile.hs
```

Preprocessing can also be used as a lightweight solution to the source code access problem of EDSLs. The transformation steps of an EDSL implementation can be summarized as follows:

- Extend the data types of the abstract syntax tree to be able to store source file names and line numbers, symbol names in the source etc.
- Add more parameters to selected interface functions to be able to pass these pieces of information.
- Create macros that generate these additional values automatically and publish these macros to the user instead of the original interface functions.

2.2 Example

This section presents examples on using the C preprocessor to reflect symbol names of the EDSL code in the generated target code and to make helpful error messages.

An Example EDSL. Consider the following language, called *Simple*, as an example. It contains the integer and boolean types, variables, basic arithmetic and logic operations and assignment.

Simple.hs

```
module Simple
    ( Simple
    , int , bool
    , (.=)
    , true , false
    , (&&), (||) , not
    , Num(..)
    , compile
    )
```

where

```
import Prelude hiding ((&&),(||),not)
import Simple.Frontend
```

An example program using this language is described in Example.hs.

Example.hs

```
import qualified Prelude
import Simple

correct :: Simple
correct = do ::
    x <- int
    x .= 10
    x .= x + 20 - 2 * x
    y <- bool
    y .= true && not y || false

wrong1 :: Simple
wrong1 = do
    x <- int
    (x - 1) .= (x + 1)
```

Compilation can be invoked as follows:

```
ghci Examples.hs
*Main> compile correct
int var0;
bool var1;
var0 = 10;
var0 = ((var0+20)-(2*var0));
var1 = ((true&&(!var1))||false);
```

The generated code contains generated variable names, which makes it harder to read and is really annoying in the error messages:

```
*Main> compile wrong1
Errors:
Non lvalue found on the left hand side of an assignment: (var0-1)
```

The task is to fix these problems, but first let us overview the implementation of the EDSL presented in the appendix before modifying it.

The Implementation of Simple. The implementation consists of three files in the *Simple* directory:

- *Representation.hs*: The data types of the abstract syntax tree of the language.
- *Frontend.hs*: The types and functions that can be used in *Simple* programs.
- *Compiler.hs*: Functions to check programs for errors and to generate target code.

A *Program* consists of *Declaration*s and *Instruction*s. A declaration contains a variable of some type *a*, where *a* is a *Supported* type of the language. An instruction is an assignment, consisting of two *Expression*s: the left and right hand sides of the assignment. Expressions are either *Literal*s, *Var*iables or compound expressions built up by arithmetic or logic operators.

Simple.Representation.hs

```
{-# LANGUAGE GADTs #-}

module Simple.Representation where

data Program =
    Program
    { declarations :: [Declaration]
    , instructions :: [Instruction]
    }

data Declaration where
    Declaration :: Supported a => Variable a -> Declaration

data Variable a = Variable String

class Supported a where
    declare :: Variable a -> String

data Instruction where
    Assign :: Expression a -> Expression a -> Instruction

data Expression a where
    Literal :: String -> Expression a
    Var     :: String -> Expression a
    Add     :: Expression Int
                -> Expression Int -> Expression Int
    Sub     :: Expression Int
                -> Expression Int -> Expression Int
    Mul     :: Expression Int
                -> Expression Int -> Expression Int
    And     :: Expression Bool
                -> Expression Bool -> Expression Bool
    Or      :: Expression Bool
                -> Expression Bool -> Expression Bool
    Not     :: Expression Bool -> Expression Bool
```

Note that expressions are typed, this means that type errors in *Simple* programs will be reported already by the Haskell compiler. Consider the following wrong3 program:

```
wrong3 :: Simple
wrong3 = do
    x <- int
    x .= true
```

The error message for this program is:

```
Examples.hs:31:10:
    Couldn't match expected type 'Prelude.Int'
                with actual type 'Prelude.Bool'
    Expected type: Simple.Representation.Expression Prelude.Int
      Actual type: Simple.Representation.Expression Prelude.Bool
    In the second argument of '(.=)', namely 'true'
    In a stmt of a 'do' block: x .= true
```

The frontend of the language instantiates the *Num* class for *Expression Int* to provide integer literals and basic arithmetic in the language. The *true* and *false* functions are the boolean literals and the standard (&&), (||) and not operations of the Haskell *Prelude* are redefined as the boolean operations of *Simple*.

Simple.Frontend.hs

```
{-# LANGUAGE FlexibleInstances , GADTs, RankNTypes #-}

module Simple.Frontend where


import Prelude hiding ((&&),(||),not)
import Control.Monad.State

import Simple.Representation
import Simple.Compiler

instance Num (Expression Int) where
    fromInteger n = Literal $ show n
    a + b = Add a b
    a - b = Sub a b
    a * b = Mul a b
    abs a = error "Function 'abs' is unsupported."
    signum a = error "Function 'signum' is unsupported."

true :: Expression Bool
true = Literal "true"

false :: Expression Bool
```

```haskell
false = Literal "false"

infixr 3 &&
(&&) :: Expression Bool -> Expression Bool -> Expression Bool
a && b = And a b

infixr 2 ||
(||) :: Expression Bool -> Expression Bool -> Expression Bool
a || b = Or a b

not :: Expression Bool -> Expression Bool
not a = Not a

data FrontendState =
    FrontendState
    { program       :: Program
    , uniqueid      :: Integer
    }

type Simple = State FrontendState ()

addVar :: Declaration -> Program -> Program
addVar d prg = prg { declarations = declarations prg ++ [d] }

int :: State FrontendState (Expression Int)
int = do
    st <- get
    let varName = "var" ++ show (uniqueid st)
    let v = Variable varName :: Variable Int
    put $ st
        { program = addVar (Declaration v) $ program st
        , uniqueid = uniqueid st + 1
        }
    return $ Var varName

bool :: State FrontendState (Expression Bool)
bool = do
    st <- get
    let varName = "var" ++ show (uniqueid st)
    let v = Variable varName :: Variable Bool
    put $ st
        { program = addVar (Declaration v) $ program st
        , uniqueid = uniqueid st + 1
        }
    return $ Var varName

addInstr :: Instruction -> Program -> Program
addInstr i prg = prg{ instructions = instructions prg ++ [i] }

infix 0 .=
```

```
(.=) :: Supported a => Expression a -> Expression a -> Simple
v .= e = do
    st <- get
    put $ st { program = addInstr (Assign v e) $ program st }

compile :: Simple -> IO ()
compile s = putStrLn $ show $ compile' result
  where
    result = program $ snd $ runState s empty
    empty = FrontendState (Program [] []) 0
```

The instructions in a *Simple* program are written in a monadic environment. The monad is called *Simple* and is a state monad with a state that collects the declarations and instructions of the program, and an *Integer* used to generate unique names for the declared variables.

The *int* and *bool* are monadic functions resulting in *Expression Int*s and *Expression Bool*s, so that they can be used to declare variables in the DSL programs. These functions *get* the actual state of the program, create a new *Declaration* with a *Variable* of the desired type inside, add this declaration to the program, increment the integer used as unique identifier in variable names and finally *put* the modified state back into the monad.

The *(.=)* operator can be used in the language to write an assignment operation. This function is also monadic, it adds the new assignment instruction to the state.

The *compile* function runs the state monad in order to obtain the abstract syntax tree of the program and calls the *compile'* function defined in the *Compiler* module to generate code.

As defined in *Compiler.hs*, the *Result* of the compilation is a list of *Strings*, which is either *Code* or *Errors*.

Simple.Compiler.hs

```
{-# LANGUAGE GADTs #-}

module Simple.Compiler where

import Control.Monad.State
import Data.List

import Simple.Representation

instance Supported Int where
    declare (Variable name) = "int" ++ name

instance Supported Bool where
    declare (Variable name) = "bool" ++ name

data Result = Code [String] | Errors [String]
```

```
instance Show Result where
    show (Code cs) = unlines cs
    show (Errors cs) = unlines $ "Errors:\n" : cs

type ResultM a = State Result a

addError :: String -> ResultM ()
addError s = do
    st <- get
    put $ case st of
        Code _ -> Errors [s]
        Errors es -> Errors $ es ++ [s]

addInstruction :: String -> ResultM ()
addInstruction s = do
    st <- get
    put $ case st of
        Code cs -> Code $ cs ++ [s]
        Errors es -> Errors es

compile' :: Program -> Result
compile' prg = snd $ runState (compile'' prg) empty
  where
    empty = Code []

compile'' :: Program -> ResultM ()
compile'' prg = do
    mapM compileDeclaration $ declarations prg
    mapM compileInstruction $ instructions prg
    return ()

compileInstruction :: Instruction -> ResultM ()
compileInstruction (Assign left right) = case left of
    Var name    -> do
        right' <- compileExpression right
        addInstruction $ name ++ " = "
                                ++ right' ++ ";"
    _                -> do
        left' <- compileExpression left
        addError $ "Non lvalue found on
                    the left hand side of an assignment:"
                    ++ left'

compileExpression :: Expression a -> ResultM String
compileExpression (Literal val) = return val
compileExpression (Var name) = return name
compileExpression (Add e1 e2) = binop "+" e1 e2
compileExpression (Sub e1 e2) = binop "-" e1 e2
compileExpression (Mul e1 e2) = binop "*" e1 e2
```

```
compileExpression (And e1 e2) = binop "&&" e1 e2
compileExpression (Or e1 e2) = binop "||" e1 e2
compileExpression (Not e) = do
    e' <- compileExpression e
    return $ "(!" ++ e' ++ ")"

binop :: String -> Expression a -> Expression a
                                -> ResultM String
binop op e1 e2 = do
    e1' <- compileExpression e1
    e2' <- compileExpression e2
    return $ "(" ++ e1' ++ op ++ e2' ++ ")"

compileDeclaration :: Declaration -> ResultM ()
compileDeclaration (Declaration v)
    = addInstruction $ declare v ++ ";"
```

Compilation is monadic, uses a state monad with the *Result* type as the state. The *addInstruction* and *addError* functions help adding new target code lines or error messages to the state. If an error occurs, the code lines generated so far and to be generated later are omitted and only the error messages are collected.

The *compileDeclaration*, *compileInstruction* and *compileExpression* monadic functions are used to generate code for declarations, instructions and expressions respectively. The *compileInstruction* function also reports an error when anything but a variable is found on the left hand side of an assignment.

Elimination of the Generated Variable Names. The first possible solution is to modify the language frontend so that programmers can set variable names that will appear in the generated code:

```
correct :: Simple
correct = do
    x <- int "x"
    x .= 10
    x .= x + 20 - 2 * x
    y <- bool "y"
    y .= true && not y || false
```

We can add a parameter of type *String* to the frontend functions *int* and *bool* and use this name instead of the generated one. The result of the compilation should now look like:

```
int x;
bool y;
x = 10;
x = ((x+20)-(2*x));
y = ((true&&(!y))||false);
```

On the other hand, this solution is inconvenient for the programmers and it is also easy to mess things up if the Haskell names and DSL names of variables diverge: x <- int "y".

This solution can be improved by creating a header file called `simple.h` and moving the import directives at the beginning of `Examples.hs` into it. The header has to be included in the example file: `#include "simple.h"`. From now on, compilation can be invoked passing `-cpp` option to *ghci* so that *ghci* calls the C preprocessor before parsing.

Two macros (`int` and `bool`) can be defined in the header file, each with one parameter. The macro call `int(x)` has to expand to `x <- int "x"`. Now, the examples can be rewritten so that they use the newly defined macros instead of the `int` and `bool` frontend functions:

```
correct :: Simple
correct = do
    int(x)
    x .= 10
    x .= x + 20 − 2 * x
    bool(y)
    y .= true && not y || false
```

This way the error messages reporting invalid assignments become a little bit more helpful, because they refer to the variables by their original names in the source code.

Adding File Names and Line Numbers to Error messages. First, a function

```
checkDeclarations :: [Declaration] -> ResultM ()
```

can be defined in `Compiler.hs` to find duplicate variable names in the declaration list. The function `addError` is useable to report error. We can call this function in the first line of the `compile''` function:

```
checkDeclarations (declarations prg)
```

Consider the following `wrong2` program:

```
wrong2 :: Simple
wrong2 = do
    x <- int
    x .= 0
    x <- int
    x .= 1
```

Now it should also result in an error message:

```
Variable x is redefined.
```

This error message could be more helpful if indicated the source file and the lines that caused the error:

```
Examples.hs, line 22: Variable x is redefined. Earlier definition
is in line 20.
```

In order to achieve this, the following modifications have to be implemented:

- Addition of two new parameters of types String and Int is needed to the functions int and bool to be able to pass the file name and the line number of the variable definition.
- The macros __FILE__ and __LINE__ has to be used in the definition of the int and bool macros to pass these new parameters.
- In Representation.hs, two new constructor parameters to the Variable constructor of types String and Int is needed. The compiler's code has to be adapted to this change.
- In the int and bool functions the two new parameters have to be used in the Variable constructor in order to store the file and line information in the abstract syntax tree.
- In the checkDeclarations function we have to use the new constructor parameters of Variable to extend the error message with useful information.

Better Error Messages About Assignments. The techniques seen in the previous section can be applied to make the error message about incorrect assignment instructions more user friendly. In order to do this, we need to turn the (.=) operator to a macro. This, unfortunately, will make the EDSL syntax less pretty:

```
correct :: Simple
correct = do
    int (x)
    let (x,  10)
    let (x,  x + 20 - 2 * x)
    bool (y)
    let (y,  true && not y || false )
```

On the other hand, we can make the assignment related error message look like this:

```
Examples.hs, line 14: Non lvalue found on the left hand side of an
assignment: (x-1)
```

In order to achieve this, we have to add new parameters to the (.=) function, implement the let macro in the header file, add new constructor parameters to Assign and use them in the error message inside the compileInstruction function.

Further Possibilities. The same technique can be used for example to simplify the definition of *Simple* programs. Instead of writing

```
correct :: Simple
correct = do
    ...
```

one might prefer using this syntax:

```
simple(correct)
...
```

This way we can further enrich the error messages with information about the function in which the error is located.

2.3   Evaluation

To summarize the techniques we have seen in this section, we conclude that the advantage of this solution is its simplicity and also that it only requires easy-to-use and standard tools like the C preprocessor.

On the other hand, all the well-known pitfalls of the textual replacement of macro expansion make this solution dangerous. Another disadvantage is that eventual Haskell error messages will refer to the code after macro expansion, while the user edits the one with macros.

The approach is also limited, and it affects the syntax of the EDSL as we have seen in the examples so far.

3   Syntax Tree Manipulation

In case of languages with own concrete syntax and a parser, it is easy to create a mapping between the source code and the target code, because the compiler gets the source file and analyses it from character to character, so it gets the position for each syntactical unit instantly and can store it in the syntax tree. But, as described in Sect. 1.2, this is not the case for embedded languages, they use the compiler of the host language to produce it's own embedded representation, the embedded compiler will not get any information about the source code.

This section presents a solution to this problem, which is more heavy weight than macro preprocessing used in Sect. 2, but is also more powerful. The idea is to perform a more advanced preprocessing, using the compiler of the host language. This way we gain access to the position of each syntactical unit, and can store it in the embedded syntax tree. For this, the we need to extend the internal representation (abstract syntax tree) and the frontend library. Using the extra location information, the compiler can create a mapping between the stored positions and the corresponding position of the target code.

3.1   Extended Compilation

Compiling an embedded source is done via the following process: The interpreter of the host language analyses the source code, the program is executed as a host language program and builds the internal representation of the DSL program. Than the EDSL compiler generates the target code from the internal representation.

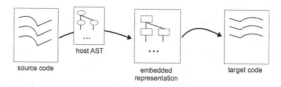

Compiling embedded source

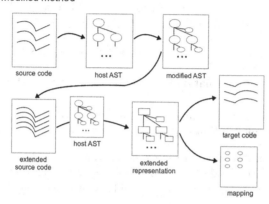

Modified method

Fig. 1. Compiling embedded source

In order to add location information to the internal representation, the compilation workflow becomes more complex. First of all we need the host syntax tree of the embedded source (the host AST). A transformation then gets the positions of all syntactical units and extends the host AST with further nodes that represent wrapper functions. If we transform the modified syntax tree back to embedded source, every necessary source position will appear. In this solution the interface library and the embedded representation need to be extended with the wrapper functions and the corresponding data types.

During the code generation we need to save each position from the node of the embedded syntax tree and match it up with the corresponding position of the target code to complete the mapping. Figure 1 illustrates the differences of the original and the extended compilation process.

3.2 Transformation

The first step of the described solution is the manipulation of the host AST. During this, each node representing a syntactical unit is labeled. The label function holds the source position of the syntactical unit that is being labelled. The result is an extended host AST, that can be easily transformed back to source code in which every syntactical unit's position appears as an argument of the corresponding label function. The transformation itself is independent of the embedded language, it depends only on the host language. Therfore it can be reused by any embedded language that uses the same host language.

3.3 Code Generation

Code generation also becomes a bit more complex, because it has to calculate the absolute position of parts of the generated target code and produce a mapping between the target and the embedded source. For this purpose, we need additional information to be able to generate code from each node of the embedded syntax tree: *the measure of the indentation*, *the absolute row and column position*, where the code generation should start from, *the absolute row and column positions*, where the code generation ends. This information, being spread among the nodes of the abstract syntax tree is categorized as follows:

- downward spread: information that every child node gets with the same value (*eg. measure of indentation*)
- upward spread: an information that the parents get from their child (*eg. generated target code*)
- state-like: an information that the node get from its parent and use it to calculate other information (*eg. absolute start row and column positions*)

The code generator uses wrapping nodes and other nodes in the abstract syntax tree differently: Nodes that represent language constructs are turned into target code, while wrapper nodes are used to produce the location mapping between the source and target files.

3.4 Embedding the *While* Language

The *While* language is a very simple imperative language which consists a sequence of simple statements such as assignment and control statements (if-then-else and while loop). Programmers can use logical constants and expressions eg. true, false, comparison, negation and basic arithmetic operations like addition, subtraction and multiplication. We choose this language, because it is not too complex, so we can focus on the mapping problem.

First of all, we need to define a data type, that describes the abstract representation of *While* language programs. A possible implementation of the embedded syntax is the following.

```
data Program where
    (:=)       :: Variable a -> Expr a -> Program
    Declare    :: [Variable a] -> Program
    Sequence   :: [Program] -> Program
    Loop       :: Expr Bool -> Program -> Program
    IfThenElse :: Expr Bool -> Program -> Program -> Program
    Skip       :: Program

Data Expr a where
    Plus    :: Expr Int -> Expr Int -> Expr Int
    And     :: Expr Bool -> Expr Bool -> Expr Bool
    Compare :: Expr Int -> Expr Int -> Expr Bool
```

```
Value :: (Show a) => a -> Expr a
Var   :: Variable a -> Expr a

data Variable a where
  Variable :: Name -> Variable a

type Name = String
```

The *Program* data type was defined as a generalised algebraic data type. This way it is possible to use type variables in the constructor parameters that do not appear as type variables of the *Program* data type itself.

So far, we defined the internal representation of the While language, but using directly the defined data constructors is not convenient. So we need to define an interface for the programmers, that hides the representation of the language and helps them to build the syntax tree conveniently.

```
class Compare a where
  (<) :: a -> a -> Expr Bool

class Equal a where
  (==) :: a -> a -> Expr Bool

class Logical a where
  (&&), (||) :: a -> a -> Expr Bool
  (!) :: a -> Expr Bool
```

We make *Expr Bool* an instance of these type classes so that programmers can write logical expressions in a convenient way. A question pops up here: Why did not we use the *Eq* type class that is provided by Haskell's Prelude module? The answer is simple, the type signature does not fit:

```
class Eq a where
  (==) :: a -> a -> Bool
```

In this case, if we want to examine if two integers or boolean values are equal, the result will be a *Bool*, but we need an *Expr Bool* instead. However, when it comes to arithmetic operations, we can use the *Num a* typeclass. If we make the *Expr Int* type an instance of the *Num a* type class we can even use integer literals in the arithmetic expressions of the DSL.

```
instance Num (Expr Int) where
  (+) = Plus
  (-) = Minus
  (*) = Mul
  fromInteger i = Value $ fromInteger i
```

In general, before the code generation process, the EDSL's compiler is allowed to make transformations on the embedded syntax tree to optimize it. This is not done in our case to make the example simple. Therefore the compilation phase contains only code generation.

```
class CodeGenerator a where
    generate :: a -> Int -> String
```

The *CodeGenerator* type class is used to generate target code from simple nodes. The *generate* function takes a node from the syntax tree and an indentation value and produces the corresponding target code. We use the *StateMonad*, to store the generated target code. The *code* function takes a *String* as an argument and puts it to the state of the monad. We give some example instances of the *CodeGenerator* typeclass:

```
instance CodeGenerator Program
  where
    generate ((:=) (Variable name) expr) indent = cSource
      where
        ((), cSource) = flip runState "" $ do
        code $ indenter indent ++ name
        code $ "=" ++ generate expr 0 ++ "\n;"
...
instance CodeGenerator (Expr a)
  where
    generate (Plus lhs rhs) indent = cSource
      where
        ((), cSource) = flip runState "" $ do
        code $ "(" ++ generate lhs 0 ++
        code $ ") + (" ++ generate rhs 0 ++ ")"
...
```

3.5 Extending the Language

So far we have presented a possible way to embed the *While* language into Haskell. However using the illustrated method the compiler does not have any information about the source code. In this part we extend our language, step-by-step, as mentioned in Sect. 3.1.

First, we extend the internal representation of the language and the frontend with wrapper nodes and functions. In the next step we apply a transformation, that manipulates the Haskell syntax tree in order to inject the positions of the syntactical units into the DSL program source code. Because we have extended the programmers' interface and the embedded representation, and during the transformation we did not break any syntactical rule of Haskell, the source code that is pretty printed from the transformed host syntax tree will result in valid code either in Haskell as well as in the (extended) *While* language.

New data constructors, so called wrapper nodes, are defined in the abstract syntax tree to store the positions of the embedded source. These constructors take a source position, and a node to be wrapped as an argument. In our case we need only three wrapper nodes:

```
type SrcLoc = ((Int, Int), (Int, Int))
type Name   = String

data Program where
...
    LabProg :: SrcLoc -> Program -> Program

data Expr a where
...
    LabExpr :: SrcLoc -> Expr a -> Expr a

data Variable a where
    Variable :: Name -> Variable a
    LabVar   :: SrcLoc -> Variable a -> Variable a
```

SrcLoc represents the wrapped node's position in the source. In the first tuple the start row and column positions are stored, while the second tuple stores the end row and column positions.

The frontend needs to be extended with functions that represent the wrapper nodes. For this purpose we created the *Label a* typeclass containing the *label* function, which takes a source position and a node from the embedded syntax tree. It wraps the node with the corresponding wrapper data constructor. Below is the definition of the *Label* typeclass and some of the necessary instances:

```
class Label a where
    label :: ((Int, Int), (Int, Int)) -> a -> a

instance Label Program where
    label = LabProg

instance Label (Expr a) where
    label = LabExpr
```

Using this modification the representation will be capable of storing information about the source code, but the question remains: How can we label the syntactical units with their source position? A tool is needed that can syntactically analyse Haskell source and build a syntax tree containing the necessary information. For this purpose we have chosen the *haskell-src-exts* package. After syntactically analysing the source, it can produce the host AST. All we need to do is to identify the syntactical units and extend them with new nodes that represent the previously defined *label* function.

First of all, we need a helper function that retrieves source information from a node of the Haskell syntax tree. For this purpose the *Location a* type class is defined:

```
class Location a where
    getStartLine :: a SrcSpanInfo -> Int
    getStartCol  :: a SrcSpanInfo -> Int
```

```
getEndLine    :: a SrcSpanInfo -> Int
getEndCol     :: a SrcSpanInfo -> Int
```

We instantiate this type class with the types that build the host syntax tree. Every node contains its position in the source code. The information is stored in a value with a type of *SrcSpanInfo*. The *haskell-src-exts* package provides helper functions to retrieve this information. Another function needs to be defined, to extend the syntax tree with further nodes, that represent the previously introduced *label* function. The new function has two arguments, the second will be the node that is to be wrapped, the first argument will be the source position of the wrapped node. The next example is simplified to make it easier to read:

```
wrap :: Exp SrcSpanInfo -> Exp SrcSpanInfo
wrap exp =
  (App
    (App
      (Var
        (UnQual (Ident "label"))
      )
      (Tuple
        [ Tuple [ startLinePosition
                , startColumnPosition ]
        , Tuple [ endLinePosition
                , endColumnPosition ]
        ]
      )
    )
    exp
  )
```

So far we have defined the transformation on a single node. We need to apply this on every node in the host AST. The *Transform a* type class is responsible for this. From the point of view of the transformation, the significant nodes are the nodes having type *Exp*, especially the function applications. The instance of the transformation function for nodes of other types is the identical mapping.

```
class Transform a where
    transform :: (a SrcSpanInfo) -> (a SrcSpanInfo)

instance Transform Exp
...

    transform x@(App _ _ _) = wrap $ transformRec x

transformRec (App inf fun arg) =
        App inf (transformRec fun) (transform x)
transformRec x = transform x
```

Note that the *transformRec* function can handle any function application with arbitrary number of arguments.

So far we managed to store each syntactical unit's position in the embedded representation, however we do not know the nodes' position in the generated target code. So our task is to calculate each node's position during the code generation. For this purpose we need additional information for each node:

- an absolute location, where the code generation starts (state information),
- an absolute location, where the code generation ends (upwards propagated information),
- and the measure of the indentation (downwards propagated information).

Upwards propagated information is stored in a record data structure. The *Result* record has three fields

- source: contains the generated target code so far,
- mapping: mapping generated so far
- position: the target's code absolute position generated from the latest node from the embedded syntax tree.

Now we can define the *DebugInfo* and *DebugInfo1* type classes which describe the modified code generation. The latter one is used when the current node contains a list.

```
type  Location  =  ( Int ,  Int )

class  DebugInfo  a  where
    generateDebugInfo  : :  a  ->  Int  ->  Location  ->  Result

class  ( DebugInfo  a )  =>  DebugInfo1  a  where
    generateDebugInfo '  : :  [ a ]  ->  Int  ->  Location  ->  Result
```

The original version of the code generator uses a *State monad*, where the state is the generated code, and the result value is unit. In the extended version, the *State monad* is used again, but the state will be a tuple with three members:

- the generated source so far,
- the absolute starting line position,
- the absolute starting column position.

We need to access these members during the whole process of code generation, so the entire procedure needs to be monadic.

Another monadic function is needed, that calculates the ending position of the code generated from the actual node of the embedded representation. With these helper functions the *DebugInfo a* typeclass can easily be implemented for the data types defined in the internal representation. However, as we pointed out earlier, wrapper nodes and language constructs are handled differently. In the case of a wrapper node our task is to call the monadic wrapper function with the wrapped node and lift the result into the monad. After that we need to retrieve the target code's position from the *Result* record's *position* field, pair it with the corresponding position in the source, then extend the list in the *mapping* field with this value. On the other hand, if we are dealing with a node that represents a language construct, the *code* function is used recursively for code generation on each of the children nodes.

At the end of the compilation, the *Result* record will contain the generated target code, and the mapping between the target code and the embedded source.

3.6   Example

Consider the following While program calculating the greatest common divisor of two *Int* number as an example.

```
gcd :: Program
gcd = (Declare [x, y]) ++
(Loop
    ((!)(x == y))
    (IfThenElse
      (x < y)
      (y := ((Var y) − (Var x)))
      (x := ((Var x) − (Var y)))
    )
)

x :: Variable Int
x = Variable "x"

y :: Variable Int
y = Variable "y"
```

From this source code the following target code can be generated.

```
int x;
int y;
while (!(x == y))
{
    if ((x < y))
    {
        y = (y) − (x);
    }
    else
    {
        x = (x) − (y);
    }
}
```

The following listing introduces the textual description of the modified AST created by adding new nodes representing the *label* functions.

```
gcd :: Program
gcd = label ((14, 7), (14, 123))
  ((label ((14, 8), (14, 22))
    (Declare (label ((14, 16), (14, 22)) [x, y])))
```

```
++
  (label ((14, 28), (14, 122))
  (Loop
    (label ((14, 34), (14, 45))
    ((!) (label ((14, 38), (14, 44)) (x == y))))
    (label ((14, 48), (14, 121))
    (IfThenElse (label ((14, 60), (14, 65)) (x < y))
      (label ((14, 68), (14, 92))
      (y :=
        (label ((14, 74), (14, 91))
          ((label ((14, 75), (14, 80)) (Var y)) −
            (label ((14, 85), (14, 90)) (Var x))))))
      (label ((14, 96), (14, 120))
      (x :=
        (label ((14, 102), (14, 119))
          ((label ((14, 103), (14, 108)) (Var x)) −
            (label ((14, 113), (14, 118)) (Var y))))))))))))
```

Using the extended version of the code generator and this modified AST we can get a final result which contains the same target code we have seen before and a mapping between the source code and the target code. The mapping can be represented, for example, by an XML file:

```xml
<root>
  <node>
    <startLine targetPosition="1" sourcePosition="14"/>
    <startColumn targetPosition="1" sourcePosition="7"/>
    <endLine targetPosition="13" sourcePosition="14"/>
    <endColumn targetPosition="1" sourcePosition="123"/>
  </node>
  <node>
    <startLine targetPosition="1" sourcePosition="14"/>
    <startColumn targetPosition="1" sourcePosition="8"/>
    <endLine targetPosition="3" sourcePosition="14"/>
    <endColumn targetPosition="0" sourcePosition="22"/>
  </node>
  ...
</root>
```

3.7 Summary

Debugging existing source code is not a simple task, even in case of general purpose languages. In case of domain specific languages, source level debugging is more complicated by the increased abstraction level. The generated target code can be debugged and the results have to be mapped back to the DSL level. This task is even harder in case of embedded programming languages, because the mapping between the generated target code and the source code is missing. This section presented a general method to extend an existing embedded language and its compiler to be able to produce this mapping.

The extension consists of the following elements:

- a transformation, that manipulates the host syntax tree,
- extended version of the internal representation and frontend containing wrapper nodes and functions,
- modified code generation to keep track of the location of the target code for each node in the abstract syntax tree.

The extended compilation workflow is able to produce the necessary mapping. The method can be used for every embedded language given that we have a tool to easily produce and maipulate the syntax tree of the host language.

4   Embedding and Parsing Combined

Using classical compiler technology makes the development of new DSLs hard. The new language usually changes quickly and the amount of the language constructs increases rapidly in the early period of the project. Continuous adaptation of the parser, the type checker and the back-end of the compiler is not an easy job.

As described in Sect. 1.1, *language embedding* is a technique that facilitates this development process. Not all general purpose programming languages are equally suitable to be host languages. Flexible and minimalistic syntax, higher order functions, monads, expressive type system are useful features in this respect. For this reason Haskell and Scala are widely used as host languages. On the other hand, these are not mainstream languages. As our experience from a previous project [2, 8] shows, using a host language being unfamiliar to the majority of the programmers makes it harder to make the embedded DSL accepted in an industrial environment.

Because of this, it is reasonable to create a standalone DSL as the final product of DSL projects. However, it would be beneficial to make use of the flexibility provided by embedding in the language design phase. This section of the paper presents our experience from an experiment to combine the advantages of these two approaches. The findings are based on a university research project initiated by Ericsson. The goal of the project is to develop a novel domain specific language that is specialized in the IP routing domain as well as the special hardware used by Ericsson for IP routing purposes.

The most important lessons learnt from the experiment are the following. It was more effective to use an embedded version of the domain specific language for language experiments than defining concrete syntax first, because embedding provided us with flexibility so that we were able to concentrate on language design issues instead of technical problems. The way we used the host language features in early case studies was a good source of ideas for the standalone language design. Furthermore, it was possible to reuse the majority of the embedded language implementation in the final product, keeping the overhead of creating two front-ends low.

This section is organized as follows. Section 4.1 introduces the architecture of the compiler. Then in Sect. 4.2 we analyse the implementation activities using statistics from the version control system used. Section 4.3 summarizes the learnt lessons.

4.1   Compiler Architecture

The architecture of the software is depicted in Fig. 2. There are two main dataflows as possible compilation processes: *embedded compilation* (dashed) and *standalone compilation* (dotted).

The input of the embedded program compilation is a Haskell program loaded in the Haskell interpreter. What makes a Haskell program a DSL program is that it heavily uses the *language front-end* that is provided by the embedded DSL implementation. This front-end is a collection of helper data types and functions that, on one hand, define how the embedded program looks like (its "syntax"), and, on the other hand, builds up the *internal representation* of the program. The internal representation is in fact the *abstract syntax tree (AST)* of the program encoded as a Haskell data structure.

The embedded language front-end module may contain complex functions to bridge the gap between an easy-to-use embedded language syntax and an internal representation suitable for optimizations and code generation. However, it is important that this front-end does not run the DSL program: It only creates its AST.

The same AST is built by the other, standalone compilation path. In this case the DSL program has it's own concrete syntax that is parsed. We will refer to the result of the parsing as *concrete syntax tree (CST)*. This is a direct representation of the program text and may be far from the internal representation. For this reason the transformation from the CST to an AST may not be completely trivial.

Once the AST is reached, the rest of the compilation process (optimizations and code generation) is identical in both the embedded and the standalone version. As we will see in Sect. 4.2, this part of the compiler is much bigger both in size and complexity than the small arrow on Fig. 2 might suggest.

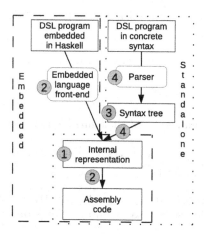

Fig. 2. Compiler architecture.

The numbers on the figure show the basic steps of the workflow to create a compiler with this architecture. The first step is to define the data types of the internal representation. This is the most important part of the language design since these data types define the basic constructs of the DSL. Our experience has shown that it is easier to find the right DSL constructs by thinking of them in terms of the internal representation then experimenting with syntax proposals.

Once the internal representation (or at least a consistent early version of it) is available, it is possible to create embedded language front-end and code generation support in parallel. Implementation of the embedded language front-end is a relatively easy task if someone knows how to use the host language features for language embedding purposes. Since the final goal is to have a standalone language, it is not worth creating too fine grained embedded language syntax. The goal of the front-end is to enable easy-enough case study implementation to test the DSL functionality.

Contrarily, the back-end implementation is more complicated. If the internal representation is changed during DSL design, the cost of back-end adaptation may be high. Fortunately it is possible to break this transformation up into several transformation steps and start with the ones that are independent of the DSL's internal representation. In our case this part of the development started with the module that pretty prints assembly programs.

When the case studies implemented in the embedded language show that the DSL is mature enough, it is time to plan its concrete syntax. Earlier experiments with different front-end solutions provide valuable input to this design phase. When the structure of the concrete syntax is fixed, the data types representing the CST can be implemented. The final two steps, parser implementation and the transformation of the CST to AST can be done in parallel.

4.2   Detailed Analysis

According to the architecture in Sect. 4.1 we have split the source code of the compiler as follows:

- *Representation:* The underlying data structures, basically the building data types of the AST.
- *Back-end:* Transforms the AST to target code. Mostly optimization and code generation.
- *Embedded front-end:* Functions of the embedded Haskell front-end which constructs the AST.
- *Standalone front-end:* Lexer and parser to build up the CST and the transformation from CST to AST.

The following figures are based on a dataset extracted from our version control repository[1]. The dataset contains information from 2012 late February to the end of the year.

---

[1] In this project we have been using *Subversion.*

Figure 3 compares the code sizes (based on the eLOC, effective lines of code metric) of the previously described four components. The overall size of the project was almost 9000 eLOC[2] when we summarized the results of the first year.

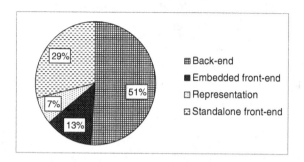

Fig. 3. Code size comparison by components.

No big surprise there, the back-end is without a doubt the most heavyweight component of our language. The second place goes to the standalone front-end, partly due to the size of lexing and parsing codes[3]. The size of the embedded front-end is less than the half of the standalone's. The representation is the smallest component by the means of code size, which means that we successfully kept it simple.

Figure 4 shows the exact same dataset as Fig. 3 but it helps comparing the two front-ends with the reused common components (back-end, representation).

The pie chart shows that by developing an embedded language first, we could postpone the development of almost 30 % of the complete project, while the so-called extra code (not released, kept internally) was only 13 %.

Figure 5 presents how intense was the development pace of the four components. The dataset is based on the log of the version control system. Originally it contained approximately 1000 commits which were related to at least one of the four major components. Then we split the commits by files, which resulted almost 3000 data-points, that we categorized by the four components. This way each data-point means one change set committed to one file.

It may seem strange that we spent the first month of development with the back-end, without having any representation in place. This is because we first created a representation and pretty printer for the targeted assembly language.

The work with the representation started at late March and this was the most frequently changed component over the next two-three months. It was hard to find a proper, easy-to-use and sustainable representation, but after the

---

[2] Note that this project was entirely implemented in Haskell, which allows much more concise code than the mainstream imperative, object oriented languages.

[3] We have been using the *Parsec* parser combinator library [12] of Haskell. Using context free grammars instead would have resulted in similar code size.

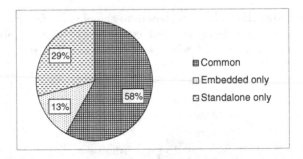

Fig. 4. Code size comparison for embedded / standalone.

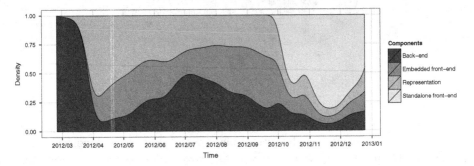

Fig. 5. Development timeline.

first version was ready in early April, it was possible to start the development of the embedded front-end and the back-end.

The back-end and code generation parts were mostly developed during the summer, while the embedded front-end was slightly reworked in August and September, because the first version was hard to use.

By October we almost finalized the core language constructs, so it was time to start to design the standalone front-end and concrete, textual syntax. This component was the most actively developed one till the end of the year. At the end of October we had a slight architecture modification which explains the small spike in the timeline. Approaching the year end we were preparing the project for its first release: Every component was actively checked, documented and cleaned.

4.3   Lessons Learnt

This section summarizes the lessons learnt from the detailed analysis presented in Sect. 4.2.

Message 1: Do the language experiments using an embedded DSL then define concrete syntax and reuse the internal representation and back-end! Our project started in January 2012 and in December the same year we released the first version of the language and compiler for the industrial partner. Even if this first version was not a mature one, it was functional: the hash table lookups of the multicast protocol was successfully implemented in the language as a direct transliteration from legacy code. Since state of the art study and domain analysis took the first quarter of the year, we had only 9 months for design and implementation. We believe that using a less flexible solution in the language design phase would not have allowed us to achieve the mentioned results.

Message 2: Design the language constructs by creating their internal representation and think about the syntax later! The temptation to think about the new language in terms of concrete syntax is high. On the other hand, our experience is that it is easier to design the concepts in abstract notation. In our case this abstract notation was the algebraic data types of Haskell: The language concepts were represented by the data types of the abstract syntax tree. When the concepts and their semantics were clear there was still large room for syntax related discussions[4], however, then it was possible to concentrate on the true task of syntax (to have an easy to use and expressive notation) without mixing semantics related issues in the discussion. This is analogous to model driven development: It is easier to build the software architecture as a model and think about the details of efficient implementation later.

Message 3: Use the flexibility of embedding to be able to concentrate on language design issues instead of technical problems! Analysis of the compiler components in Sect. 4.2 shows that the embedded front-end of the language is lightweight compared to the front-end for the standalone language. This means that embedding is better suited for the ever-changing nature of the language in the design phase. It supports the evolution of the language features by fast development cycles and quick feedback on the ideas.

Message 4: No need for a full-fledged embedded language! Creating a good quality embedded language is far from trivial. Using different services of the host language (like monads and do notation, operator precedence definition, overloading via type classes in case of Haskell) to customize the appearance of embedded language programs can easily be more complex then writing a context free grammar. Furthermore, advocates of embedded languages emphasize that part of the semantic analysis of the embedded language can be solved by the host language compiler. An example in case of Haskell is that the internal representation of the DSL can be typed so that mistyped DSL programs are automatically ruled out by the Haskell compiler. These are complex techniques, while we stated so far that embedding is lightweight and flexible — is this a contradiction? The goal of the embedded language in our project was to facilitate the language design process: It was never published for the end-users. There was no need for a mature, nicely polished embedded language front-end. The only requirement was to have an easy-to-use front-end for experimentation — and this is easy to

---

[4] *"Wadler's Law: The emotional intensity of debate on a language feature increases as one moves down the following scale: Semantics, Syntax, Lexical syntax, Comments."* (Philiph Wadler in the Haskell mailing list, February 1992, see [18].).

achieve. Similarly, there was no need to make the Haskell compiler type check the DSL programs: the standalone language implementation cannot reuse such a solution. Instead of this, type checking was implemented as a usual semantic analyser function working on the internal representation. As a result of all this, the embedded frontend in our project in fact remained a light-weight component that was easy to adapt during the evolution of the language.

Message 5: Carefully examine the case studies implemented in the embedded language to identify the host language features that are useful for the DSL! These should be reimplemented in the standalone language. An important feature of embedding is that the host language can be used to generate and to generalize DSL programs. This is due to the meta language nature of the host language on top of the embedded one. Our case studies implemented in the embedded language contain template DSL program fragments (Haskell functions returning DSL programs) and the instances of these templates (the functions called with a given set of parameters). The parameter kinds (expressions, left values, types) used in the case studies gave us ideas how to design the template features of the standalone DSL. Another example is the scoping rules of variables. Sometimes the scoping rules provided by Haskell were suitable for the DSL but not always. Both cases provided us with valuable information for the design of the standalone DSL's scoping rules.

Message 6: Plan enough time for the concrete syntax support, which may be harder to implement than expected! This is the direct consequence of the previous item. The language features borrowed from the host language (eg. meta programming, scoping rules) have to be redesigned and reimplemented in the standalone language front-end. Technically this means that the concrete syntax tree is more feature rich than the internal representation. For this reason the correct implementation of the transformation from the CST to the AST takes time. Another issue is source location handling. Error messages have to point to the problems by exact locations in the source file. The infrastructure for this is not present in the embedded language.

4.4 Plans vs Reality

Our original project plan had the following check points:

- By the end of March: State of the art study and language feature ideas.
- By the end of June: Ideas are evaluated by *separate* embedded language experiments in Haskell.
- By the end of August: The language with concrete syntax is defined.
- By the end of November: Prototype compiler is ready.
- December was planned as buffer period.

While executing it, there were three important diverges from this plan that we recommend for consideration.

First, the individual experiments to evaluate different language feature ideas were quickly converging to a joint embedded language. Project members working on different tasks started to add the feature they were experimenting with modularly to the existing code base instead of creating separate case studies.

Second, the definition of the language was delayed by three months. This happened partly because it was decided to finish the spontaneously emerged embedded language including the back-end, and partly because a major revision and extension to the language became necessary to make it usable in practice. As a result, the language concepts were more or less fixed (and implemented in the embedded language) by September. Then started the design of the concrete syntax which was fixed in October. At first glance this seems to be an unmanageable delay. However, as we have pointed out previously, it was then possible to reuse a considerable part of the embedded language implementation for the standalone compiler.

Third, we were hoping that, after defining the concrete syntax, it will be enough to write the parser which will trivially fit into the existing compiler as an alternative to the embedded language front-end. The parser implementation was, in fact, straightforward. On the other hand, it became clear that it cannot directly produce the internal representation of the embedded language. Recall what Sect. 4.3 tells about the template features and scoping rules to understand why did the transformation from the parsing result to the internal representation take more time than expected. Therefore the buffer time in the plan was completely consumed to make the whole infrastructure work.

In brief, we used much more time than planned to design the language, but the compiler architecture of Sect. 4.1 yet made it possible to finish the project on time.

4.5   Sustainability of the Architecture

It is still an open question if it is worth it to keep the presented compiler architecture while adding more language features.

Conclusions suggest to continue with the successful strategy and experiment with new language features by modifying, extending the embedded language and, once the extensions are proved to be useful and are stable enough, add them to the standalone language.

On the other hand, this comes at a cost: The consistency of the embedded and standalone language front-ends have to be maintained. Whenever slight changes are done in the internal representation, the embedded language front-end has to be adapted.

Furthermore, since the standalone syntax is more convenient than the embedded language front-end, it might not be appealing to experiment with new language concepts in the embedded language. It also takes more effort to keep in mind two different variants of the same language.

Even if it turns out that it is not worth maintaining the embedded language front-end and it gets removed from the compiler one day, its important positive role in the design of the first language version is indisputable.

5   Related Work

The embedding technique as used by this lecture notes originates from Hudak [11]. The first embedded languages, however, were interpreted and thus the strictly compilation-related issues discussed here were not causing problems. The foundations of compiled embedded languages are layed down in the seminal paper about the Pan image manipulation language [10]. About the optimization and compilation of Haskell functions over DSL types, the authors write: *"The solution we use is to extend the base types to support ≪ variables ≫. Then to inspect a function, apply it to a new variable [...] and look at the result."* The extension with a *named variable* is:

```
data FloatE = ... | VarFloat String
```

The problem of what the string value should be is not discussed in the paper. An obvious solution of generating arbitrary fresh strings for each parameter works well, but leads to generated variable names in the compiled code, making it hard to read and connect to the DSL source.

Obsidian is another compiled EDSL in Haskell, targeting graphics processors. Their authors claim [16] to build the language along the lines of Pan, mentioned above. The cited paper does not mention the problems discussed in this lecture notes, but there is a related code fraction in the Obsidian repository [15], related to standard C code emission:

```
getC :: Config
        -> Program a
        -> Name
        -> [( String ,Type )]
        -> [( String ,Type )]
        -> String
getC conf c name ins outs = ...
```

That is, the names of the function and the input/output paremeters are fine tuned when invoking the code generator function.

The authors of this lecture notes first met the source code access problem when working on the Feldspar compiler [8]. That project targeted the digital signal processing domain and the compiler produced C code. Since the project was running in an industry-university cooperation, there was emphasis on the generation of code that is readable and trackable back to the source code. If the compiler is invoked from the Haskell interpreter, the generated code uses generated variable names. On the other hand, Feldspar also has a standalone compiler that applies a solution close to the one described in Sect. 3 (Syntax tree manipulation): The compiler uses an off-the-shelf Haskell parser and uses it to collect all top level function names and the names of their formal parameters. Then a Haskell interpreter is started which loads the same source file, and then the compilation of each of the collected functions is initiated. As the function and parameter names are known this time, they are communicated to the compilation function and therefore the same identifiers show up in the target C code.

An emerging trend is to create embedded DSLs using the Scala language. The authors do not have much experience in Scala-based DSLs, but the reflection capabilities of the language seem to solve many of the problems discussed in this paper [13]: *"Scala reflection enables a form of metaprogramming which makes it possible for programs to modify themselves at compile time. This compile-time reflection is realized in the form of macros, which provide the ability to execute methods that manipulate abstract syntax trees at compile-time."* A EDSL compiler can use this feature to access the necessary source-related information while generating target code.

The Metaborg approach [4,5] (and many similar projects) extend the host language with DSL fragments using their own syntax. The applications are then developed using the mixed language and the DSL fragments are usually compiled to the host language. This approach requires a parsing phase to process the extended syntax, therefore the accessibility of the actual source code is not an issue.

Based on Spinellis's design patterns for DSLs [14], we can categorize our approaches. The preprocessing approach (see Sect. 2) is a combination of the lexical processing and piggybacking design patterns. The syntax tree manipulation based solution (see Sect. 3) uses the combination of the pipeline and the lexical processing approaches. Finally, the combined embedding&parsing approach internally uses an embedded front-end, which is a realization of a piggyback design pattern, where the new DSL uses the capabilities of an existing language. While the final version of the language, which employs a standalone front-end, is a source-to-source transformation.

5.1 Embedding and Parsing Combined

Combining the embedded and the parsing approach is the most advanced solution in our paper, therefore this subsection is devoted to somewhat similar approaches and related works.

Thomas Cleenewerck states that *"developing DSLs is hard and costly, therefore their development is only feasible for mature enough domains"* [6]. Our experience shows that if proper language architecture and design methodology is in place, the development of a new (not mature) DSL is feasible in 12 months. The key factors for the success are to start low cost language feature experiments as soon as possible, then fix the core language constructs based on the results and finally expand the implementation to a full-fledged language and compiler.

Frag is a DSL development toolkit [20], which is itself a DSL embedded into Java. The main goal of this toolkit is to support deferring architectural decisions (like embedded vs. external, semantics, relation to host language) in DSL software design. This lets the language designers to make real architectural decisions instead of ones motivated by technological constraints or presumptions. In case of our embedding&parsing approach (see Sect. 4) there were no reason to postpone architectural decisions: It was decided early in the project to have an external DSL with a standalone compiler. What we needed instead was to postpone their realization and keep the language implementation small and simple in the first few months to achieve fast and painless experiment/development cycles.

Another approach to decrease the cost of DSL design is published by Bierhoff, Liongosari and Swaminathan [3]. They advocate incremental DSL development, meaning that an initial DSL is constructed first based on a few case studies, which is later incrementally extended with features motivated by further case studies. This might be fruitful for relatively established domains, but our experience shows that the language design iterations are mostly heavier then simple extensions. We believe that creating a full fledged first version of the language and then considerably rewriting it in the next iterations would have wasted more development effort than the methodology we applied.

David Wile has summarized several lessons learnt about DSL development [19]. His messages are mostly about how to understand the domain and express that knowledge in a DSL. Our current paper adds complementary messages related to the language implementation methodology.

6   Summary

This paper deals with the problem that EDSLs' compilers have no access to their source code, which would be important for good quality error messages, debugging and profiling. Three different solutions are outlined.

Section 2 discussed how to use standard source code preprocessing tools like the C preprocessor to add the missing location information to the abstract syntax tree of the EDSL.

Next, in Sect. 3, we have generalized the preprocessing solution: The method presented there extends the AST with and the language frontend with wrappers and reuses the host language compiler to inject the location information into the EDSL's AST. The code generator is then able to produce a mapping to connect the generated target code with the corresponding source code fragments.

Finally, Sect. 4 evaluates a language development methodology that starts the design and implementation with an embedded language, then defines concrete syntax and implements support for it. The main advantage of the method is the flexibility provided by the embedded language combined by the advantages of a standalone language. Experience from a project using this methodology shows that most of the embedded language implementation can be reused for the standalone compiler.

References

1. cpphs: Haskell implementation of the C preprocessor. http://projects.haskell.org/cpphs/
2. Axelsson, E., Claessen, K., Dévai, G., Horváth, Z., Keijzer, K., Lyckegård, B., Persson, A., Sheeran, M., Svenningsson, J., Vajdax, A.: Feldspar: a domain specific language for digital signal processing algorithms. In: 2010 8th IEEE/ACM International Conference on Formal Methods and Models for Codesign (MEMOCODE), pp. 169–178. IEEE (2010)

3. Bierhoff, K., Liongosari, E.S., Swaminathan, K.S.: Incremental development of a domain-specific language that supports multiple application styles. In: OOPSLA 6th Workshop on Domain Specific Modeling, pp. 67–78 (2006)

4. Bravenboer, M., de Groot, R., Visser, E.: MetaBorg in action: examples of domain-specific language embedding and assimilation using stratego/XT. In: Lämmel, R., Saraiva, J., Visser, J. (eds.) GTTSE 2005. LNCS, vol. 4143, pp. 297–311. Springer, Heidelberg (2006)

5. Bravenboer, M., Visser, E.: Concrete syntax for objects: domain-specific language embedding and assimilation without restrictions. SIGPLAN Not. **39**(10), 365–383 (2004)

6. Cleenewerck, T.: Component-based DSL development. In: Pfenning, F., Macko, M. (eds.) GPCE 2003. LNCS, vol. 2830, pp. 245–264. Springer, Heidelberg (2003)

7. Dévai, G.: Embedding a proof system in haskell. In: Horváth, Z., Plasmeijer, R., Zsók, V. (eds.) CEFP 2009. LNCS, vol. 6299, pp. 354–371. Springer, Heidelberg (2010)

8. Dévai, G., Tejfel, M., Gera, Z., Páli, G., Gyula Nagy, Horváth, Z., Axelsson, E., Sheeran, M., Vajda, A., Lyckegård, B., et al.: Efficient code generation from the high-level domain-specific language feldspar for dsps. In: ODES-8: 8th Workshop on Optimizations for DSP and Embedded Systems (2010)

9. Dévai, G., Tejfel, M., Leskó, D.: Embedding and parsing combined for efficient language design (accepted for publication at icsoft-ea) (2013)

10. Elliott, C., Finne, S., De Moor, O.: Compiling embedded languages. J. Funct. Program. **13**(3), 455–481 (2003)

11. Hudak, P.: Building domain-specific embedded languages. ACM Comput. Surv. **28**(4es), 196 (1996)

12. Leijen, D., Meijer, E.: Parsec: direct style monadic parser combinators for the real world. Electron. Notes Theor. Comput. Sci. **41**(1) (2001)

13. Miller, H., Burmako, E., Haller, P.: Reflection. http://docs.scala-lang.org/overviews/reflection/overview.html

14. Spinellis, D.: Notable design patterns for domain-specific languages. J. Syst. Softw. **56**(1), 91–99 (2001)

15. Svensson, J.: Obsidian source code repository. https://github.com/svenssonjoel/Obsidian

16. Svensson, J., Sheeran, M., Claessen, K.: Obsidian: a domain specific embedded language for parallel programming of graphics processors. In: Scholz, S.-B., Chitil, O. (eds.) IFL 2008. LNCS, vol. 5836, pp. 156–173. Springer, Heidelberg (2011)

17. Tratt, L.: Domain specific language implementation via compile-time meta-programming. ACM Trans. Program. Lang. Syst. (TOPLAS) **30**(6), 31 (2008)

18. Wadler, P.: Wadler's "Law" on language design. Haskell mailing list (1992). http://code.haskell.org/~dons/haskell-1990-2000/msg00737.html

19. Wile, D.: Lessons learned from real dsl experiments. Sci. Comput. Program. **51**(3), 265–290 (2004)

20. Zdun, U.: A dsl toolkit for deferring architectural decisions in dsl-based software design. Inf. Softw. Technol. **52**(7), 733–748 (2010)

Hardware Specification with CλaSH

Jan Kuper(✉)

University of Twente, Enschede, The Netherlands
j.kuper@utwente.nl

Abstract. CλaSH is a recently developed system to specify and synthesize hardware architectures, strongly based on the functional programming language Haskell. Different from other existing approaches to describe hardware in a functional style, CλaSH is not defined as an embedded language inside Haskell, but instead, CλaSH uses Haskell *itself* to specify hardware architectures. In fact, every CλaSH specification is an executable Haskell program. Hence, the simulation of a hardware architecture is immediate, and all abstraction mechanisms that are available in Haskell are maintained in CλaSH, insofar they are directly applicable to the specification of hardware.

This paper describes several examples of specifications of hardware architectures in CλaSH to illustrate the various abstraction mechanisms that CλaSH offers. The emphasis is more on the CλaSH-*style* of specification, than on the concrete technical details of CλaSH. Often, the specifications are given in plain Haskell, to avoid some of the specific CλaSH details that will be indicated in a separate section.

The given examples include regular architectures such as a ripple carry adder, a multiplier, vector and matrix multiplications, finite impulse response filters, and also irregular architectures such as a simple Von Neumann style processor and a reduction circuit. Finally, some specific technicalities of CλaSH will be discussed, among others the processing pipeline of CλaSH and the hardware oriented type constructions of CλaSH.

1 Introduction

In this paper we describe the hardware specification environment CλaSH, which is based on the functional programming language Haskell. The perspective from which a CλaSH specification views a hardware architecture is that of a *Mealy Machine*, that is, as a function of two arguments – one representing the state of a component and the other the input – which yields two results – the new state and the output. We will show several examples in CλaSH, ranging from matrix product and FIR-filters, to a simple processor and a reduction circuit.

Since hardware architectures have specific properties, some extensions have to be added to Haskell, and furthermore, not every Haskell program can be translated into hardware. For example, the data type of *lists*, which is often

Jan Kuper—This work is partly supported by EU project POLCA, FP7-ICT-2013-10, grant agreement no. 610686.

V. Zsók et al. (Eds.): CEFP 2013, LNCS 8606, pp. 336–380, 2015.
DOI: 10.1007/978-3-319-15940-9_8

used in a functional setting, is not suitable to describe architectures since a list may vary in length during a computation, whereas hardware is fixed in size. Besides, data dependent recursion is not possible in CλaSH, since that requires transformations that are not (yet) included in the CλaSH compiler.

In the rest of this paper we first shortly discuss some related work (Sect. 2), after which we outline the pattern along we will specify architectures (Sect. 3). Then, in Sect. 4 we first describe some regular architectures and in Sect. 5 we describe some irregular architectures. in both sections we give examples of state *less* architectures and state*ful* architectures. Finally, in Sect. 6 we give an informal description of some aspects of CλaSH itself.

2   Related Work

The most well-known specification languages for digital hardware are VHDL and Verilog. Also in industry, the design of digital architectures is mostly expressed in VHDL and Verilog. However, abstraction mechanisms available in these languages are not very strong and it is cumbersome to generalize a given specification for different input/output types, or to parameterize for the functionality in a sub-component. Over the years several attempts are made to improve the abstraction mechanisms in these languages, leading to concepts such as *generics* and *generate statements*. With *generics* a design can be formulated exploiting – a limited form of – polymorphism such that one may use the same design for different types (see [9]).

However, full abstraction is reached only to a limited extent by these extensions, such that using them is still quite verbose and error-prone. Besides, these extensions are not fully supported by synthesis tools. This is widely recognized by the hardware design community, and there are many attempts to base hardware design on standard programming habits, notably on imperative languages such as C/C++ or Java, leading to so-called *high level synthesis*. A well known example of this approach is *System-C*, for an overview we refer to [6].

The perspective from which both VHDL and Verilog, as well as high level synthesis languages view a hardware architecture is — at least partially — imperative in nature. On the other hand, we argue that the concept of digital hardware is closer to a *function*, than to an imperative *statement*: a digital circuit may be viewed as a structure that transforms an input signal into an output signal, exactly what a function in mathematics does, though in the case of a function one speaks of arguments and results rather than input signals and output signals.

This observation makes it likely that a functional language might be better suitable to specify hardware architectures than languages which are partly based on an imperative perspective. Besides, abstraction mechanisms available in functional programming languages are high, and include features such as higher order functions, polymorphism, lambda abstraction, and pattern matching. This observation was made several times before, dating back to the early eighties of the 20th century, and is expressed in papers such as [4,10,15]. Since then several languages are proposed which approach the specification of hardware architectures from a functional perspective, some of the most important ones being Lava [3,8], Bluespec [13], ForSyDe [14]. For an overview of several of these languages see [5].

Most of these functional hardware description languages, however, are *embedded languages* inside a functional programming language, which has certain limitations concerning the abstraction mechanisms that are available in a functional language. For example, choice constructs that most functional language offer, such as guards, pattern matching and case constructs, are not easily exploitable in embedded languages, and give rise to more verbose formulations.

On the other hand, the method described in this paper, called CλaSH, uses the functional programming language Haskell *itself*. Hence, all above mentioned abstraction mechanisms that are available in Haskell are automatically also available in CλaSH. It falls outside the scope of this introduction into CλaSH to go into further details concerning a comparison with other functional hardware description languages.

3   Basic Program Structure for Hardware Descriptions

In this section we will give a first introduction to the general principles according to which a CλaSH specification is built up.

3.1   Mealy Machine and Simulation

Below we assume that a hardware architecture consists of memory elements together with a combinatorial circuit, and that it is connected to input and output ports. The values in the memory elements form the *state* of the architecture, whereas the combinatorial circuit generates its *functionality*. At every clock cycle, the input signals and the values from the memory elements are going into the combinatorial circuit, defined by some function f, which results in output signals and in new values in the memory elements. Thus, the general format of the function f is that f has *two* arguments (the state and the input) and the result of f consists of two values as well (the updated state and the output):

$$f \ s \ x \ = \ (s', y) \tag{1}$$

where s denotes the current content of the state, x is the input, s' is the updated value of the state, and y is the output of the circuit described by f[1]. Clearly, both the new state s' and the output y must be defined separately, but we will come to that later. Here only the top-level structure of the definition of a hardware specification function f is relevant.

This function f describes the *structure* of the architecture, in addition we need a function to *simulate* the described architecture. The simulation works by executing the hardware function f repeatedly, on every clock cycle. The following function *simulate* realizes this simulation process:

$$simulate \ f \ s \ (x{:}xs) = \ y \ : \ simulate \ f \ s' \ xs$$
$$\textbf{where}$$
$$(s', y) \ = \ f \ s \ x$$
$$simulate \ f \ s \ [] \quad = \ []$$

---

[1] Note that we follow the convention used in Haskell, and write $f \ s \ x$ instead of $f(s, x)$.

This definition consists of *two* clauses, where the difference is in the third argument (x:xs vs [], see below). The function *simulate* can be used for simulation purposes by applying it to a given initial value of the state and a given list of concrete arguments and executing that in Haskell.

The function *simulate* has *three* arguments, which can be described as follows:

- the first argument is a *function* f, which determines the functionality of some hardware architecture as described above. We emphasize that f is just a formal parameter of the function *simulate*, i.e., with every usage of *simulate* this parameter f will be instantiated to the functionality of a concrete hardware architecture.

  Since *simulate* has a function as argument, *simulate* is called a "higher order function".

- the second argument is the *state* s, which contains all the values in all memory elements in the architecture. Note that s need not be a simple parameter, consisting of just one integer (say). Instead, s may be a structured parameter which consists of several parts representing various memory elements.

- the third argument of the function *simulate* is the *list of inputs*, denoted by the "patterns" x:xs and [], respectively. The second pattern denotes the empty list, so the second clause only will be chosen when the input is empty, i.e., when all input values are processed by the first clause (in case an input list is finite).

  The first pattern x:xs denotes a non-empty list of input values, so the first clause is chosen as long as the input still contains values. The colon ":" breaks the input in its first element x and the rest xs (suggesting the plural of one x, and pronounced as x-es). The value x will be dealt with during the present clock cycle, and xs will be dealt with in future.

  Here too, x may be a compound value, consisting of several parts which all come in parallel during the same clock cycle.

In the result of *simulate* the values y and s' are used, which are calculated by the function f. The result of f then consists of a *pair* (s', y) of two things: the output y (which again may consist of several parallel values), and the new state s'. This corresponds to the idea of a *Mealy machine*, as depicted in Fig. 1.

The global result of the *simulate*-function now is the output y followed by (indicated by ":") a recursive call of the function *simulate*, but with the new state s' and the rest of the input xs. That means that the function *simulate* repeats itself, each time with the state resulting from the previous execution of *simulate*, and with the rest of the input sequence. Thus, the total result of the function *simulate* is a list of outputs generated by a repeated evaluation of the architecture f, meanwhile updating the state at every step.

Note that the function *simulate* simulates a clock cycle at every recursive call. Note also that we assume that at every clock cycle a new input value x is available, though that can be weakened by choosing a *Maybe* type for the input values, indicating that x can be a meaningful value, or *Nothing*.

3.2   A Simple Architecture Example

In this section we will give an example of definition of a concrete architecture by means of a function f according to the pattern as shown in Eq. (1). We will also show the simulation of this architecture, using the function *simulate* as defined above.

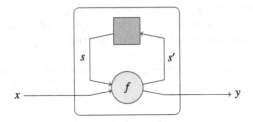

Fig. 1. Mealy machine

Suppose we have to calculate the dot product of two vectors x and y of integers, i.e., we have to calculate the following expression:

$$\sum_{i=1}^{n} x_i \cdot y_i.$$

Suppose further that we have only one multiplier and one adder available. Then we clearly need a memory element *acc* to accumulate intermediate results of the addition, and which should initially contain the value 0. In Fig. 2 the architecture is shown that does the job: at each clock cycle the inputs x_i and y_i are first multiplied, and then added to the value in the accumulator *acc*. The result of this is put both back into the accumulator, and on the output.

Description in a Functional Language. The function `macc` (for "multiply-accumulate", see Fig. 2), which expresses the above behavior, may be defined as follows:

$$macc :: Int \rightarrow (Int, Int) \rightarrow (Int, Int)$$
$$macc\ acc\ (x, y) = (z, z)$$
$$\textbf{where}$$
$$z = acc + x * y$$

On the first line in this definition the *type* of the function *macc* is mentioned, which expresses that *macc* is a *function* with an *Int* as its first argument, a pair *(int,int)* as its second argument, and a pair *(int,int)* as its result.

We remark that the structure of the function *macc* matches the structure of the function f in Eq. (1) and of the function f in the definition of *simulate*. That is to say, where in the definition of *simulate* the pair (s', y) is calculated by *using* the function f, now the function *macc* is *defined* such that it can be used in the role of f.

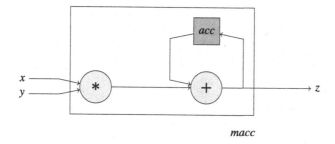

macc

Fig. 2. Multiply-accumulate

To explain the correspondence between *macc* and *f* in greater detail, we observe that

- the first argument *acc* is the state of the architecture, and corresponds to *s* in the expression "*f s x*" in the function *simulate*. In the case of *macc*, the state consists of a single number only,
- the second argument (x, y) is the input that arrives at each clock cycle, and corresponds to the parameter *x* in the expression "*f s x*" in the function *simulate*. In this case the input consists of two numbers,
- the result (z, z) matches the pair (s', y) in the definition of *simulate*, so in this example both the output and the new content of the state are the same value *z*. For reasons of readability we use a where-clause to define *z*, though we might have written directly

$$macc \ acc \ (x, y) \ = \ (acc + x * y, acc + x * y).$$

Suppose we want to simulate and test this architecture with the vectors:

$$x = \langle 1, 2, 3, 4 \rangle$$
$$y = \langle 5, 6, 7, 8 \rangle$$

Then the input for the architecture is a sequence of parallel *x* and *y* values, as follows (in Haskell notation as a list of 2-tuples):

$$input \ = \ [(1, 5), \ (2, 6), \ (3, 7), \ (4, 8)]$$

The initial value of the accumulator is 0, so in Haskell we can now simulate this by evaluating:

$$simulate \ macc \ 0 \ input$$

The output of the simulation then is:

$$[5, 17, 38, 70]$$

The last value is the dot product of the two vectors *x* and *y*.

Description in VHDL. In order to illustrate some differences between a functional language and a standard hardware specification language, we describe the same multiply-accumulator in VHDL. One possible specification is as follows (leaving out the standard initial LIBRARY and USE statements):

```
ENTITY macc IS
   PORT (x, y : IN  integer;
         z    : OUT integer;
         rst,
         clk  : IN  std_logic);
END macc;

ARCHITECTURE behaviour OF macc IS
   SIGNAL acc : integer;
   SIGNAL zi  : integer;
BEGIN
   zi  <= acc + x * y;

   acc <= 0   when rst='0'              else
             zi when rising_edge(clk);

   z   <= zi;
END behaviour;
```

Assuming that the reader is not familiar with VHDL, we make some remarks about this specification. First of all we remark that, in order to keep the VHDL code as short as possible, we omitted the size of the type integer from the above code.

Second, we remark that in VHDL it is not allowed to read from an OUT signal, hence inside the architecture a local signal zi (for "z-internal") is defined which is used for both the OUT signal z and for the accumulator acc.

We further remark that the **when** statement is shorthand notation for a concurrent **process**.

Concerning a comparison between CλaSH and VHDL we restrict ourselves to some obvious differences. A more detailed comparison falls outside the scope of this text.

A first difference of course is the huge difference in syntactical notation: what is a "type" in Haskell corresponds to a certain extent to an "entity" in VHDL, and what is a "function definition" in Haskell, corresponds more or less to an "architecture" in VHDL. We remark that in a functional language the concept of "type" is wider than in VHDL, for example, in a functional language for every type a and b, the type $a \rightarrow b$ is the type of all functions from a to b.

As a second difference we mention that in the VHDL-specification time and space are mixed in the sense that references to the clock (clk) are present on the same level in the code as the description of the functionality of the architecture. In the functional specification, on the other hand, time and space are strictly separated: the clock is represented by the recursion in the *simulate* function, whereas the circuit itself is described in the "architecture function" (such as *macc*).

Note that in VHDL also a reset (`rst`) is present, whereas in the functional specification a reset is not expressed. Without going into details we mention that adding a reset to the functional specification is done on the level of the *simulate* function as well, by distinguishing it as a special type of input value. That means that for a reset too it holds that in VHDL it is part of the code describing the architecture, whereas in a functional description it is dealt with on a separate level.

A third difference has to do with the way how we understand the code: in a functional specification we are strictly talking about *values* of variables, such that a functional description is very close to a mathematical, structural description. In VHDL one is more tempted to understand the code as a description of *behavior*, i.e. what actions take place under certain conditions. In the *macc*-example one might say that the outcome of the expression *macc acc* (x, y) *is* the value (z, z), whereas in VHDL one has to perform an action of putting the value of an expression on a signal (channel).

4   Regular Architectures

In this section we will discuss several examples of regular architectures, and illustrate the power of higher order functions to specify such architectures. In particular we will define a ripple carry adder, a multiplier, and several variants of an FIR-filter. Besides, we will show that the fact that functions are *first class citizens* in Haskell can be used to parameterize architecture specifications beyond the level of numerical constants, i.e., we show that we can parameterize an architecture with respect to the functionality of its subcomponents.

4.1   Introduction

To introduce the topic of this approach we start with the dot product as already discussed in Sect. 3.2. First we repeat the definition of the dot product:

$$ \boldsymbol{x} \bullet \boldsymbol{y} \; = \; \sum_{i=0}^{n-1} x_i \cdot y_i \tag{2} $$

and mention that in Sect. 3.2 the dot product was calculated by an architecture which performed one multiplication and one addition per clock cycle. Consequently, there were as many clock cycles needed as there were elements in the vectors to calculate the full dot product. It is however also possible to execute the calculation of the dot product in a single clock cycle, by using more multipliers and adders. In Fig. 3 the architecture is shown that calculates a dot product in one clock cycle — assuming of course that all adders and multipliers also take a single clock cycle. Clearly, there are hardware limitations to the number of components that can be reasonably executed in a single clock cycle. Besides, the more components are combined in a so-called *combinatorial path*, the more energy it takes. However, we will ignore such aspects here and concentrate on the structure of the architecture and its specification.

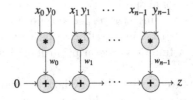

Fig. 3. Dot product

As can be seen from Fig. 3, this is a rather regular structure, in which the same combination of operations is repeated several times. In words the dot product can be described as follows: multiply the corresponding values pairwise, and add the results. In Haskell there exist the functions *zipWith* and *foldl* which perform exactly these operations. Before we come to the definition of the dot-product and the convolution example in Haskell, we first give the meaning in hardware of some standard higher order functions.

Some standard higher order functions. We show the architectures indicated by the standard higher order functions: *map*, *zipWith*, and *foldl*. Note that the architectures hold for any function f and for any operation $\star$.

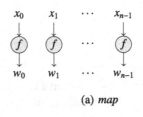

(a) *map*

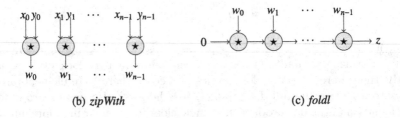

(b) *zipWith*   (c) *foldl*

Fig. 4. Some standard higher order functions

(a) *map*. The function *map* applies a function to all elements in a given list of elements, for example:

$$map \ (+1) \ [3, 5, 8, 6] = [3+1, 5+1, 8+1, 6+1]$$
$$= [4, 6, 9, 7]$$

Here, the function (+1) is applied to all the numbers is the list $[3, 5, 8, 6]$. The meaning of *map* as an architecture specification is shown in Fig. 4(a).

(b) *zipWith*. The function *zipWith* combines two sequences of elements by applying a given binary operation or function to the elements of the lists pairwise. For example:

$$zipWith \ (+) \ [3, 5, 8, 6] \ [4, 6, 9, 2] = [3+4, 5+6, 8+9, 6+2]$$
$$= [7, 11, 17, 8]$$

The architectural meaning of *zipWith* is shown in Fig. 4(b). Note that both *map* and *zipWith* are strongly parallel.

(c) *Variants of fold*. There are several variants of *fold*: *foldl, foldr, foldl1, foldr1*. Here we only show *foldl* (for *fold-left*), which intuitively works as follows (see Fig. 4(c)):

$$foldl \ (+) \ 0 \ [7, 11, 17, 8] = (((0 + 7) + 11) + 17) + 8$$
$$= 43$$

The "left" nature of these operations is indicated by the brackets, saying that the operation (addition in this case) proceeds from left to right through the list.

We remark that for associative operations it is more efficient to give the architecture of a *fold* function the form of a tree, but in the context of this text we ignore such issues of efficiency.

Below we first describe some regular architectures which do not have state and after that we describe some regular architectures which do have state. In particular, in Sect. 4.2 we describe matrix operations and elementary arithmetical architectures, and in Sect. 4.3 we describe some variants of FIR-filters.

4.2 Regular Stateless Architectures

In this section we describe again the dot product of two vectors, followed by matrix-vector multiplication and matrix-matrix multiplication.

Dot Product. Combining the architectures of the functions *foldl* and *zipWith*, we can describe the dot product from Fig. 3 as follows:

$$\boldsymbol{x} \ .*. \ \boldsymbol{y} \ = \ foldl \ (+) \ 0 \ (zipWith \ (*) \ \boldsymbol{x} \ \boldsymbol{y})$$

Equivalently, in a somewhat more elaborate notation we may define ($\boldsymbol{w}$ and z refer to Fig. 3):

$$\boldsymbol{x} \ .*. \ \boldsymbol{y} = z$$
$$\textbf{where}$$
$$\boldsymbol{w} \ = \ zipWith \ (*) \ \boldsymbol{x} \ \boldsymbol{y}$$
$$z \ = \ foldl \ (+) \ 0 \ \boldsymbol{w}$$

We choose for ".∗." as notation for the dot product, since the notation "•" cannot be typed directly on a keyboard. We remark that both definitions are valid Haskell definitions, and thus executable in a simulation.

CλaSH translates specifications given in terms of higher order functions like *zipWith* and *foldl*, and in the case of the definition of the dot product, it indeed yields the architecture as shown in Fig. 3.

Matrix-Vector Product. We continue the usage of higher order functions by discussing a matrix vector product, an example being given in Fig. 5.

$$\begin{pmatrix} 11 \ 12 \ 13 \\ 21 \ 22 \ 23 \\ 31 \ 32 \ 33 \\ 41 \ 42 \ 43 \end{pmatrix} \times \begin{pmatrix} 1 \\ 2 \\ 3 \end{pmatrix} = \begin{pmatrix} 74 \\ 134 \\ 194 \\ 254 \end{pmatrix}$$

Fig. 5. Matrix-vector product

A fairly standard way to deal with matrices is to consider them as a sequence of rows, thus the matrix in Fig. 5 actually is represented in Haskell as

$$[[11, 12, 13], \ [21, 22, 23], \ [31, 32, 33], \ [41, 42, 43]]$$

That is to say, a row in the matrix is in fact an *element of* the matrix.

Now note that the i-th element of the result of the matrix-vector multiplication is obtained by taking the dot product of i-th row with the vector. For example,

$$[21, 22, 23] \ .\ast. \ [1, 2, 3] \ = \ 134.$$

Hence, the result vector is computed by applying the dot product with the vector $[1, 2, 3]$ to every row in the matrix. And thus, since the matrix is a list of rows, this can be done by the *map* function. In other words, if xss is a matrix (seen as a list of lists, hence the notation "xss"), and ys is a vector, then the matrix-vector multiplication mxv can be defined as

$$mxv \ xss \ ys \ = \ map \ (.\ast.ys) \ xss$$

Matrix-Matrix Product. This can even further be extended to matrix-matrix-multiplications, see Fig. 6.

To define matrix-matrix multiplication in Haskell, let xss and yss be two matrices, then matrix-matrix multiplication is obtained by multiplying the matrix xss with every *column* of matrix yss, which gives the *columns* of the result matrix. Thus, when we first *transpose* the matrix yss, and transpose the result back, then the above reasoning applies to the rows of yss. Hence, the multiplication of matrix xss with matrix yss (denoted as the function mxm) may be defined as

$$mxm \ xss \ yss \ = \ transpose \ (map \ (mxv \ xss) \ (transpose \ yss))$$

We invite the reader to test these definitions in Haskell.

Generating Architectures by CλaSH. In order to offer the above definitions on vector and matrix operations to CλaSH, we first have to add an empty state arguments, e.g., as in

$$mxv' \ s \ (xss, ys) = (s, zs)$$
$$\textbf{where}$$
$$zs = mxv \ xss \ ys$$

Note that the state s remains unchanged, so it can be anything we like, the most obvious choice being $s = ()$. Note further, that the input of the architecture formally is one item (xss, ys) again, though it consists of many elements. Extended in this way, CλaSH translates these definitions into hardware architectures, performing the described operations directly in hardware. For matrix-vector multiplication of the size as in Fig. 5 the resulting architecture looks as follows, exactly as intended:

We leave it to the reader to draw the architecture for matrix-matrix multiplication (Fig. 7).

A Ripple-Carry Adder. The ripple-carry adder is a standard way to add integer numbers, and is an immediate translation to binary number representations of the usual way in which we add numbers by hand. For example:

$$\begin{array}{r} 1\ 1\ 0\ 1\ 0 \\ 1\ 0\ 1\ 0\ 1\ 1 \\ \hline 1\ 0\ 0\ 0\ 1\ 0\ 1 \end{array}$$

Clearly, we need the elementary logical gates for *and*, *or*, and *xor*:

$$
\begin{array}{lll}
0 \wedge 0 = 0 & 0 \vee 0 = 0 & 0 \otimes 0 = 0 \\
0 \wedge 1 = 0 & 0 \vee 1 = 1 & 0 \otimes 1 = 1 \\
1 \wedge 0 = 0 & 1 \vee 0 = 1 & 1 \otimes 0 = 1 \\
1 \wedge 1 = 1 & 1 \vee 1 = 1 & 1 \otimes 1 = 0
\end{array}
$$

We remark that Haskell recognizes Unicode, so the above definitions are valid Haskell definitions.

The most common way to define a ripple-carry adder is by means of a half adder and a full adder, where a half adder takes two input bits, and a full adder additionally also the carry-bit from the right neighbor. In both cases the result is the *pair* of the sum-bit of the input bits and the carry-bit. In Fig. 8 we give the

$$
\begin{pmatrix} 11 & 12 & 13 \\ 21 & 22 & 23 \\ 31 & 32 & 33 \\ 41 & 42 & 43 \end{pmatrix}
\star
\begin{pmatrix} 1 & 4 & 7 & 10 \\ 2 & 5 & 8 & 11 \\ 3 & 6 & 9 & 12 \end{pmatrix}
=
\begin{pmatrix} 74 & 182 & 290 & 398 \\ 134 & 332 & 530 & 728 \\ 194 & 482 & 770 & 1058 \\ 254 & 632 & 1010 & 1388 \end{pmatrix}
$$

Fig. 6. Matrix-matrix product

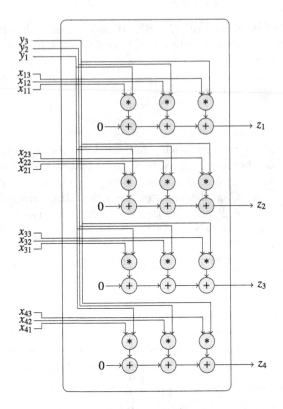

Fig. 7. Architecture for matrix-vector product

x y	(c, s)
0 0	(0, 0)
0 1	(0, 1)
1 0	(0, 1)
1 1	(1, 0)

$$ha\ (x, y) = (c, s)$$
where
$$c = x \wedge y$$
$$s = x \otimes y$$

Fig. 8. Half adder

truth table of the half-adder, the Haskell definition which calculates this truth table, and the architecture which is specified by the Haskell definition. In Fig. 9 we do the same for the full adder.

We will say that the Haskell definition of the full adder has *two* arguments (the pair of input bits (x, y), and the carry bit c), and *two* results (the pair of the carry bit c' and the sum bit s). Although this is a somewhat inconsistent formulation since we consider a pair on the input side as *one* value and on the output side as *two* values, we nevertheless choose for that formulation, since it gives us the possibility to connect the full adders using a general *mapAccumL* function:

x y c	(c', s)
0 0 0	(0, 0)
0 0 1	(0, 1)
0 1 0	(0, 1)
0 1 1	(1, 0)
1 0 0	(0, 1)
1 0 1	(1, 0)
1 1 0	(1, 0)
1 1 1	(1, 1)

$$fa\ c\ (x, y) = (c', s)$$
where
$$c' = (x \land y) \lor (x \land c) \lor (y \land c)$$
$$s = x \otimes y \otimes c$$

Fig. 9. Full adder

the function *mapAccumL* can combine a sequence of functions of this structure into a combined function that gets a *list* and a starting value *a* as arguments. Figure 10 shows the Haskell definition and the corresponding architecture of the function *mapAccumL*. Note that the function *mapAccumL* is a combination of the function *map* and an *accumulation* (from the *left*, hence its name).

$$mapAccumL\ f\ a\ xs = (a', zs)$$
where
$$(as, zs) = unzip\ (zipWith\ f\ (a{:}as)\ xs)$$
$$a' \quad = last\ as$$

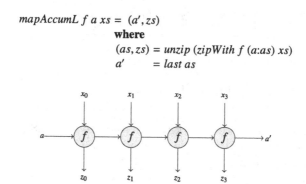

Fig. 10. *mapAccumL*

As a short explanation of the recursive structure in the where clause of the definition of *mapAccumL*, we remark that the list *as* is developed element by element: the first element a_0 is calculated by applying *f* to *a* and the first element x_0 of *xs*. Then the second element a_1 is calculated by applying *f* to a_0 and x_1, and so on. The function *unzip* is needed, since *zipWith* results in a list of pairs, and we need the lists of all first elements *as* and all second elements *zs* of these pairs.

Already now we remark that $mapAccumL\ f$ has the same structure as needed for f: it gets *two* arguments (a starting value a and a list of inputs xs), and it results in *two* values as well (a final result a' and the list of intermediate results zs). We will use this fact later, in Sect. 4.2.

In order to define the ripple-carry adder in Haskell, assume that xs and ys are the bit representations of two integer numbers x and y, where the first elements of xs and ys are the *least* significant bits, and the last elements are the *most* significant bits. Assumed is further that xs and ys are extended with leading zeroes to a given fixed length (say 16 or 32).

Now the ripple carry adder rca can be defined by combining full adders fa by the function $mapAccumL$ with starting value 0 (the initial carry bit) and the list corresponding pairs of bits from xs and ys as inputs. The result of $mapAccumL$ is the pair of the list of intermediate sum bits ss and the last carry bit c. Clearly, to get the result of the ripple carry adder rca, the sum bits ss and the last carry bit c have to be concatenated.

$$rca\ xs\ ys = ss \mathbin{+\!\!+} [c]$$
$$\textbf{where}$$
$$xys\ \ \ = zip\ xs\ ys$$
$$(c, ss) = mapAccumL\ fa\ 0\ xys$$

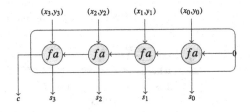

Fig. 11. Ripple-carry adder

As the matrix operations, we remark that in order to let CλaSH generate hardware from the definition of the ripple carry adder, we have to extend the definition of rca with an empty state argument (Fig. 11).

An Elementary Multiplier. We conclude the stateless architectures with the definition of an elementary multiplier. Again, we start from the way we would multiply two binary numbers by hand, as in:

$$
\begin{array}{r}
1\,1\,0\,1\,0 \\
1\,0\,1\,1 \times \\
\hline
1\,1\,0\,1\,0 \\
1\,1\,0\,1\,0 \\
0\,0\,0\,0\,0 \\
1\,1\,0\,1\,0 \quad + \\
\hline
1\,0\,0\,0\,1\,1\,1\,1\,0
\end{array}
$$

Assume that two 4-bit numbers x and y are given, whose bit sequences are xs and ys where x_0 and y_0 are the least significant bits:

$$x_3 \; x_2 \; x_1 \; x_0$$
$$\underline{y_3 \; y_2 \; y_1 \; y_0} \; \times$$

An elementary multiplier can be constructed by using the ripple-carry adder as defined in Sect. 4.2 and is as shown in Fig. 12.

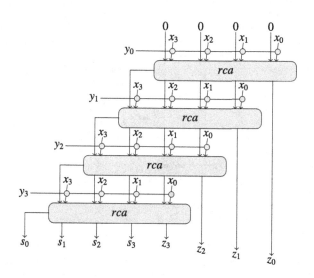

Fig. 12. Elementary multiplier

First note that every horizontal line either consists of the bits from xs or it consists of zeroes only, depending on the question whether the corresponding y-bit is 1 or 0. To calculate this we have to calculate

$$map \; (\wedge y_i) \; xs$$

on every line before the results are given to a ripple-carry adder, which then adds it to the first four bits of the previous line, taking all zeroes at the first line. Note that a ripple-carry adder yields one bit more than the length of the inputs, and the last bit z_i of that result is given to the total result immediately – just as in the case of the calculation by hand. To get the total result, these last bits resulting from all ripple-carry adders have to be concatenated with the first four bits from the last ripple-carry adder.

Before we give the Haskell code for this elementary multiplier, we observe that every line itself again is a function of the form as requested by the *mapAccumL* function:

– every line has *two* inputs: the list ss of the first four sum bits from the previous line (four zeroes on the first line), and the bit y_i indicating whether the bit sequence xs should be added or whether there should be zeroes instead,

– and it has *two* outputs: the first four sum bits going to the next adder, and the last bit z going straight to the final result.

Note that at every line the bit y_i makes the choice whether or not to use the bit sequence xs. That means that the sequence xs can be considered *the same* at every line, i.e., it is a *global* input which is the same at every line. This global pattern is shown in Fig. 13.

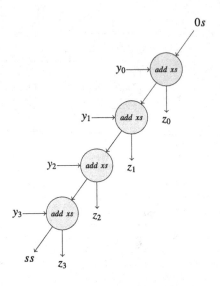

Fig. 13. Multiplier pattern

The Haskell definitions can now be given as follows:

$$add \ xs \ ss \ y = \ (ss', z)$$
$$\textbf{where}$$
$$z{:}ss' \ = \ rca \ ss \ (map \ (y\wedge) \ xs)$$

The function *add* takes xs as its first argument, meaning that *add* xs is a *function* which takes sum bits ss and a single bit y, and applies the ripple-carry adder to ss and $map \ (\wedge y) \ xs$. Note that the first bit of the result of the function *rca* is the least significant bit, so that is the bit that has to be separated from the rest. This is done by the pattern matching $z{:}ss'$ in the where-clause.

Note also that *add* xs is the actual addition function that is performed at every line, and furthermore, *add* xs answers the pattern as described above. hence, *add* xs can be given to the *mapAccumL* function:

$$mul \ xs \ ys = \ zs \ +\!\!\!+ \ ss$$
$$\textbf{where}$$
$$zeroes \ = \ replicate \ (length \ xs) \ 0$$
$$(ss, zs) \ = \ mapAccumL \ (add \ xs) \ zeroes \ ys$$

Here, the function *replicate* produces the initial sequence of zeroes, to start the additions. Clearly, the sum bits coming from the *mapAccumL* function, and the individual z values that were given to the final output now have to be concatenated in order to turn the result into a single number. We mention again that the first bit of this number is the least significant bit.

The reader is invited to test the above definitions in Haskell, and even more so, to experiment with CλaSH to see that these definitions actually can be translated into hardware and, e.g., put on an FPGA.

We conclude with the remark that this elementary multiplier is not very efficient. More efficient, for example, is the Baugh-Whooley multiplier, but we leave it as an exercise to define this multiplier.

4.3   Regular Architectures with State

In this section we return to the dotproduct, but now we assume that there is an ongoing stream of input values and we repeatedly need the dotproduct of an initial part of the input stream with a fixed vector of co-efficients. So, this is a "sliding window" over the input stream, and the computational technique we will discuss is called *convolution*. With the right choice of co-efficients, this technique can be used to filter high or low tones from a music stream, it can be used for video processing, in astronomy, etcetera. In such situations one often speaks of *FIR-filters* (for "Finite Impulse Response" filters). In this section we will discuss the derivation of some variants of FIR-filters, and show their architectures and their specifications in Haskell.

We start with the formula that expresses the convolution function. Let h be a vector of n co-efficients, and let $x_0, x_1, x_2, \ldots, x_t, \ldots$ be a stream of input values, with the index t indicating the moment in time that the value arrives. The FIR-filter determined by the vector h is called an n-tap FIR filter, and its output y_t at time t is defined as

$$ y_t \;=\; \sum_{i=0}^{n-1} h_i * x_{t-i} \tag{3} $$

So the FIR-filter calculates at every moment t the dotproduct of the co-efficients h and the last n input values $x_t, \ldots, x_{t-n+1}$. For $n = 4$, Fig. 14 shows three time steps, where the dashed lines follow the values x_i from one time moment to the next (for reasons of space we join multiplication of h_i and x_{t-i}, and addition into one computational component). Note that y_3 is the first correct result of the convolution.

Above, time was introduced with respect to the moments that the input values x_i arrive, but it does not say anything on the *scheduling of the computation* of the results y_i. Even though Fig. 14 suggests that the computation is done on an architecture that consists of (in this case) four computing units doing a multiplication and an addition, it in fact only expresses the dependencies between the computations. Concerning the actual scheduling of the computations, there are many different possibilities, which each give rise to a different architecture.

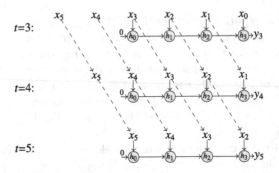

Fig. 14. Convolution on a stream

The remaining parts of this section discuss some of these possible architectures and the way they can be derived from the dependencies expressed in Fig. 14.

FIR-Filter: Variant 1. A straightforward way to schedule the data dependencies from Fig. 14 is to schedule *horizontally*, as indicated by the thick black lines in Fig. 15. All operations between two thick black lines are executed within the same time frame. In the context of this text we will assume that a time frame takes one clock cycle. Hence, data that moves from one time frame to the next has to be remembered, i.e., at every position where a data line crosses a time line, a memory element will be introduced. In Fig. 15 the data lines that cross a time line, are the dashed lines indicating the traversal of the input values x_i. For example, at the end of the first time frame, input x_3 has to be put in a memory element before it will be multiplied by h_1. That is realized by memory element u_1 in the right hand side of Fig. 15. In the same way memory elements u_2 and u_3 can be explained. For memory element u_0 the same reasoning holds, but as will be noted, it would not have been necessary to extend the time line as far to the left as we did. In that case, an input value x_i would be multiplied with h_0 in the same clock cycle as x_i arrives.

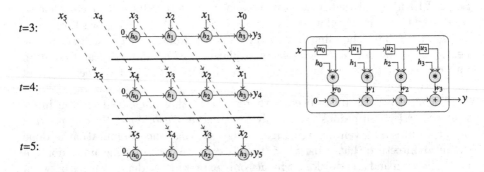

Fig. 15. FIR-filter, variant 1

As can now be seen from Fig. 15, the dot product of the convolution has to be applied to the co-efficients hs and to all values us in the memory elements, i.e., the architecture has to calculate the expression

$$hs \ .*. \ us$$

Besides, the values in the memory elements us all have to be shifted one position to the right, and the next value x_i has to be put in u_0. For this we define the operation $+\!\!>\!\!>$, saying that a value has to be "shifted into" a sequence of memory elements:

$$x +\!\!>\!\!> us \ = \ x : init \ us$$

For example:

$$5 +\!\!>\!\!> [1, 2, 3, 4] \ = \ [5, 1, 2, 3]$$

Since the co-efficients hs are constant during the operation of the FIR-filter on an input stream, we take those as a parameter to the FIR-filter. Hence, the *first* argument of the FIR-filter consists of the co-efficients hs, the *second* argument is the state us, and the *third* argument is the next input value x. As before, the result consists of the updated state us' and the output value y. That leads to the following definition of the first variant of the FIR-filter:

$$fir1 \ hs \ us \ x \ = \ (us', \ y)$$

where

$$us' = x +\!\!>\!\!> us$$
$$y \ \ = hs \ .*. \ us$$

Note that $fir1 \ hs$ matches the pattern of an architecture description as required by the function *simulate*, thus $fir1 \ hs$ indeed defines an architecture. That coincides with the intuition, that the co-efficients hs are part of the architecture of the FIR-filter.

FIR-Filter: Variant 2. For the second variant of the FIR-filter we choose the time frames as indicated by the thick lines in Fig. 16. Note that now an input value x_i is multiplied with all co-efficients hs within the same time frame, expressed in the right hand side of Fig. 16 by the fact that an input value x is not delayed by a memory element before all multiplications with the co-efficients hs.

The data lines that cross the time lines are now the connections that are between the computational units. Thus, the result of each computational unit has to be put in a memory element before it is given to the next computational units. That is realized by the memory elements vs between the computational units in the right hand side of Fig. 16.

In this variant, the dotproduct operation by itself is not performed within a single time slice, so we cannot use the standard dotproduct function. Instead, we observe that the results ws are pairwise added to the values from the memory elements vs (plus 0 in front). That is to say, the additions correspond to a *zipWith* operation. However, the *zipWith* with + results in a sequence of *four* values, the

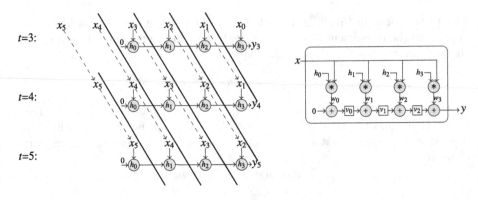

Fig. 16. FIR-filter, variant 2

last of which is the output y, and the initial three are the new content of the memory elements vs. Finally, we remark that the fact that all co-efficients hs are multiplied with the same x-value is expressed by the map function.

This gives rise to the following Haskell definition:

$$fir2\ hs\ vs\ x\ =\ (vs',\ y)$$

where

$$ws\ =\ map\ (*x)\ hs$$
$$vs''\ =\ zipWith\ (+)\ (0{:}vs)\ ws$$
$$vs'\ =\ init\ vs''$$
$$y\ \ \ =\ last\ vs''$$

We leave it to the reader to check that y indeed is the dot product of four consecutive inputs.

FIR-Filter: Variant 3. In the third variant we choose a different slope of the time lines, and again, we check where the data lines and the time lines cross. Now note that there are *two* crossings in the lines for x_i before it reaches the next computational unit, expressed by two memory elements u_{2i-1} and u_{2i} in the right hand side of Fig. 17. As with variant 2, there again is one memory element v_i between the computational units.

To define this architecture in Haskell, we define an operation to select a sequence of elements (indicated by a list of indexes is) from a list:

$$xs\ !!!\ is\ =\ map\ (xs!!)\ is$$

For example:

$$[2, 1, 6, 4, 3]\ !!!\ [0, 2, 4]\ =\ [2, 6, 3]$$

Finally, note that the state now consists of two lists us and vs of memory elements. This leads to the following definition:

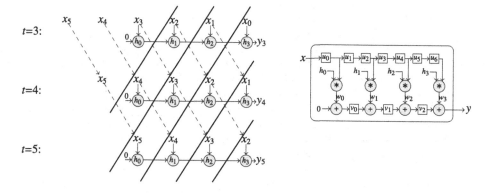

Fig. 17. FIR-filter, variant 3

$$fir3 \; hs \; (us, vs) \; x \; = \; ((us', vs'), \; y)$$
$$\textbf{where}$$
$$ws \qquad = zipWith \; (*) \; hs \; (us!!![0, 2..])$$
$$vs'' \qquad = zipWith \; (+) \; (0{:}vs) \; ws$$
$$(us', vs') = (x \; {+}{\gg} \; us, \; init \; vs'')$$
$$y \qquad\quad = last \; vs''$$

Again we leave it to the reader to check that indeed this architecture produces the dotproduct of the co-efficients hs and four consecutive values from the input stream. Apart from checking that by hand, one may also run the function *simulate* on the architecture *fir3 hs* for a given list hs of co-efficients, and some input stream xs.

FIR-Filter: Variant 4. As a last variant we discuss variant 4, in which the input stream goes from right to left. Furthermore, observe that there are only two computational units in the same time frame. We remark that these units are not consecutive, i.e., either the first and the third, or the second and the fourth computational unit are in the same time frame. The consequence is that not all elements of the input stream will be meaningfully processed, thus the input stream has to be interleaved with arbitrary values. We leave it as an exercise to the reader to check the crossings of the data lines and the time lines, and to connect these to the memory elements in the right hand side of Fig. 18.

We mention that the notation $us \lll{+}x$ means that x is "shifted into" the list us from the right. It is defined as follows:

$$us \lll{+}x \; = \; tail \; us \; {+}\!\!{+} \; [x].$$

For example:

$$[1, 2, 3, 4] \lll{+} \; 5 \; = \; [2, 3, 4, 5]$$

Now the Haskell definition should be straightforward:

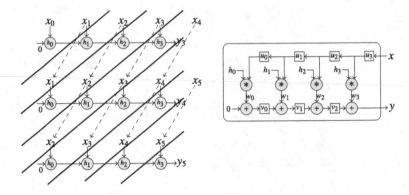

Fig. 18. FIR-filter, variant 4

$$\textit{fir4 hs } (us, vs) \; x \;\; = \;\; ((us', vs'), \; y)$$
$$\textbf{where}$$
$$\begin{aligned} ws &= zipWith \; (*) \; hs \; us \\ vs'' &= zipWith \; (+) \; (0{:}vs) \; ws \\ (us', vs') &= (us \lll{+}x, \; init \; vs'') \\ y &= last \; vs'' \end{aligned}$$

Concluding Remarks. The above architectures are derived by a systematic method, starting from the data dependencies generated by the mathematical formula of the dotproduct of a list of co-efficients and an equally long initial part of the input stream. By varying on the division in time frames, the concrete architectures can be developed by introducing memory elements on the crossings of data lines and time lines.

The major difference between these architectures consists of the number and positioning of memory elements, and may cause some difference in delay of the output and in maximum clock frequency. For example, in variant 1 there is a long combinatorial path, going from the input through the first multiplication, followed by four additions. Clearly, the output is available in the same clock cycle as in which the last input arrived (or very quickly after that), but the consequence of such a long combinatorial path may be that the clock frequency will be low.

In variant 2 the maximal length of the combinatorial paths is much shorter, but there still is the need to deliver the input value to many operations in parallel, taking a lot of energy and possibly a low clock frequency. In variant 3, on the other hand, all combinatorial paths are rather short, so the clock frequency can be high, but there is a longer delay between the last input and the moment that the output becomes available.

Such issues are examples of the considerations which may be relevant which architecture suits a given situation best. This question falls outside the scope of this text which is mainly aiming at the correspondence between an architecture and its Haskell specification.

We conclude with a possible generalization that is made possible by the high level abstraction mechanisms the Haskell offers: *parameterization*. It is possible to generalize each of the above architectures with the functionality of subcomponents. We will illustrate this for variant 1 of the FIR-filter above. If we abstract away from the concrete functionalities of the subcomponents, and instead turn them into arguments of the architecture, we get a higher level architecture, shown in the following Haskell code:

$$genfir1\ (f, g, a, hs)\ us\ x\ =\ (us',\ y)$$

$$\textbf{where}$$

$$us' = x \mathbin{+\!\!\gg} us$$
$$ws = zipWith\ f\ hs\ us$$
$$y\ = foldl\ g\ a\ ws$$

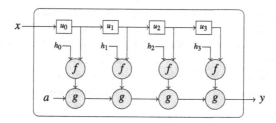

Fig. 19. Parameterized filter

In this code not only the co-efficients hs are taken as parameters, but also the functionalities f and g, and the initial value a in the application of *foldl*. The corresponding architecture is shown in Fig. 19.

Note that we can now define

$$fir1\ hs\ us\ x\ =\ genfir\ ((*), (+), 0, hs)\ us\ x$$

It is equally well possible to define a *pattern matcher*, which selects subsequences from an input stream that match a given pattern hs:

$$pattm\ hs\ us\ x\ =\ genfir\ ((==), (\&\&), True, hs)\ us\ x$$

This definition leads to the architecture in Fig. 20.

5   Irregular Architectures

In this section we turn to an example of an irregular architecture, the *Sprockell*: a *S*imple *pro*cessor in Has*kell* (see Fig. 21). It is an instruction set architecture

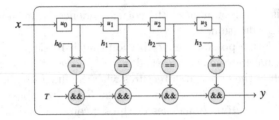

Fig. 20. Pattern matcher

which has many simplifications in comparison with a real processor, for example, we will assume that the execution of an instruction as well as fetching data from memory takes only one clock cycle, there is no pipelining, there are no cache memories, there is no I/O. We assume a program memory that is separated from data memory, and only one program can be executed at the same time. Nevertheless, the architecture together with its instruction set are Turing complete, so it is a non-trivial processor.

The aim of showing it here is to demonstrate the natural character of its specification by means of mathematical functions, which are all executable in Haskell. The irregular character shows itself by the fact that no usage of higher order functions is made, i.e., there is no repeating pattern in the architecture. On the other hand, the way the definitions are given does show a regular pattern, most definitions are just straightforward case-expressions.

5.1   The Sprockell

In Fig. 21 it can be seen that the program memory (pmem) contains a list of instructions (see below for the complete instruction set). The decode function $\mathcal{D}$ decodes these instructions one by one and sends signals onto all its outgoing wires. The formulation "sends signals onto all its outgoing wires" is represented in the definition of the function $\mathcal{D}$ by the fact that the result of $\mathcal{D}$ for every instruction is a record consisting of 13 fields, where every field corresponds to one of the outgoing wires of the decoder.

The Sprockell is a *load-store* architecture, where the load function $\mathcal{L}$ is able to load data from various sources into some register in the register bank $\mathcal{R}$. The sources of these data can be a constant value delivered by the decoder, it can be the output of the alu, or it can be a value from some address in data memory. Which value the load function has to choose, is determined by a special code sent to the load function by the decoder. Clearly, also the address of the register in which the load function has to put the value, is coming from the decoder.

The store function $\mathcal{S}$ saves a value in data memory. As with the load function, this value may come from different sources: it may be a constant sent by the decoder, or it may be a value from some address in the register bank. Here too, the decoder delivers the information which value to choose, which register to read, and which address in data memory to save to.

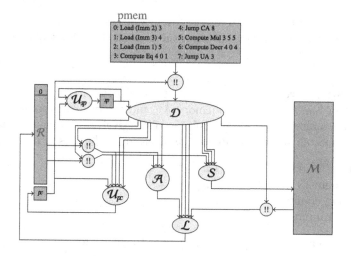

Fig. 21. Sprockell

The alu $\mathcal{A}$ performs an operation, indicated by an opcode, on two values from the register bank, and sends its result to the load function $\mathcal{L}$.

The last elements we mention in this introductory description are the program counter and the stack pointer. As always, the program counter tells which instruction from program memory should be fetched for the decoder (shown in Fig. 21 by the indexing operation !! from Haskell). The program counter is stored in a register which is updated by the function $\mathcal{U}_{pc}$, the program counter update function, based on information from again the decoder. For the stack pointer the same holds: it is stored in a register that is updated by the stack pointer update function $\mathcal{U}_{sp}$.

So, all in all the state of the architecture consists of the register bank $\mathcal{R}$, data memory $\mathcal{M}$, and two registers for the program counter pc, and for the stack pointer sp. The Sprockell itself is defined as a function which transforms its state every clock cycle, based on the instruction that has to be executed. In the sections below we will formalize the above intuitive descriptions of the various subcomponents and combine them in the definition of the Sprockell as a whole.

We remark that in order to save space and to have some visual recognition based on the names of the components, we choose for a more mathematical formulation. However, this formulation may be readily translated into Haskell in a word for word fashion, by choosing names fro the symbols, such as *alu* for $\mathcal{A}$, *load* for $\mathcal{L}$, *dataMemory* for $\mathcal{M}$, etcetera. Since Haskell recognizes Unicode, one might also choose to leave some of the symbols unchanged, and the result will nevertheless be an executable Haskell program, and simulation can be done with the same function *simulate* as before.

The specification given below is complete in the sense that it can also be mapped onto real hardware, e.g., onto an FPGA. However, in order to give the code to CλaSH to be translated into synthesizable code, still some mainly minor transformations have to be executed on the Haskell code. We will come back to that issue in Sect. 6.

Memory Structure. As mentioned above, the *state* of the Sprockell consists of the register bank $\mathcal{R}$, the data memory $\mathcal{M}$, and the two registers *pc* and *sp* for the program counter and the stack pointer, respectively. For reasons of simplicity we choose to let all values be integers, and $\mathcal{M}$ and $\mathcal{R}$ be lists of integers:

Register bank:	$\mathcal{R}$	$:: [Int]$
Data memory:	$\mathcal{M}$	$:: [Int]$
Program counter:	pc	$:: Int$
Stack Pointer:	sp	$:: Int$

Note that for real hardware it is not sufficient to choose for integers, nor for lists of integers: for integers one has to choose the number of bits with which the integers will be represented, and also for lists one has to make a choice for the length of the list. We will come back to this in Sect. 6.

To update the register bank or the data memory we define an update operation $<\!\!\sim$ to put a value v on position i in a list:

$$xs \;<\!\!\sim\; (i, v) = \; ys \; +\!\!+ \; [v] \; +\!\!+ \; zs$$
$$\textbf{where}$$
$$(ys, \_ \!:\! zs) = \; splitAt \; i \; xs$$

Applying this operation to the register bank or to the data memory has the following limitations:

- register 0 of the register bank always contains the value 0, so putting a value in this register means that the value will be lost,
- before putting a value in the data memory, it has to be enabled for writing.

The Alu $\mathcal{A}$. Concerning the functional components in the *Sprockell*, we start with the alu function $\mathcal{A}$. As can be seen in Fig. 21, the alu has three input signals. Thus, the function $\mathcal{A}$ that specifies the alu has three arguments. The first of these arguments is the opcode *opc* which decides which operation the alu should perform, the other two arguments x and y are the values on which this operation should be performed. The opcodes are defined as an *embedded language*, i.e., as an algebraic data type in Haskell, which can be extended as desired:

data $OpCode = NoOp \mid Id \mid Incr \mid Decr \mid Neg \mid Add \mid Sub \mid Mul \mid Eq \mid Gt \mid \cdots$

The meaning of these opcodes become clear in the definition the alu function $\mathcal{A}$, which is a simple case-expression, defined by *pattern matching* on the opcode:

$$\mathcal{A} \ opc \ x \ y = \textbf{case } opc \textbf{ of}$$

$$
\begin{aligned}
NoOp &-> 0 \\
Id &-> x \\
Incr &-> x + 1 \\
Decr &-> x - 1 \\
Neg &-> -x \\
Add &-> x + y \\
Sub &-> x - y \\
Mul &-> x * y \\
Eq &-> tobit \ (x == y) \\
Gt &-> tobit \ (x > y)
\end{aligned}
$$

$$\vdots$$

where

$tobit \ True = 1$

$tobit \ False = 0$

Note that in Haskell the relation ">" results in a boolean, so the function *tobit* is needed to transform this into an integer.

The Load Function $\mathcal{L}$. The *load* function $\mathcal{L}$ has several input values:

– we choose to let the result of the load function $\mathcal{L}$ be the updated register bank as a whole, so also the register bank $\mathcal{R}$ itself is an argument to the load function,
– three values from which the function $\mathcal{L}$ has to choose to put into the register bank: an immediate value c coming from the decoder, a value from data memory d, or the output z from the alu,
– a code *ldc* to tell the load function which value to put in the register bank, or not to load anything at all,
– of course, the register r in which to put the value.

The codes which value to load is defined in an embedded language *LoadCode*:

$$\textbf{data } LoadCode \ = \ NoLoad \mid LdImm \mid LdAddr \mid LdAlu$$

Now the definition of the load function $\mathcal{L}$ again is a straightforward case-expression, though the case where no value has to be loaded into the register bank is defined in a separate clause:

$$
\begin{aligned}
\mathcal{L} \ NoLoad \ \mathcal{R} \ r \ (c, d, z) &= \ \mathcal{R} \\
\mathcal{L} \ ldc \ \mathcal{R} \ r \ (c, d, z) &= \ \mathcal{R} <\!\!\sim (r, v)
\end{aligned}
$$

$$\textbf{where}$$

$$
v = \textbf{case } ldc \textbf{ of}
$$

$$
\begin{aligned}
LdImm &-> c \\
LdAddr &-> d \\
LdAlu &-> z
\end{aligned}
$$

The Store Function $\mathcal{S}$. The *store* function $\mathcal{S}$ has the following input arguments:

- as with the load function $\mathcal{L}$, we choose to let the result of the store function $\mathcal{S}$ be the updated data memory as a whole, so also the data memory $\mathcal{M}$ itself is an argument to the function $\mathcal{S}$,
- two values from which the function $\mathcal{S}$ has to choose to put into the register bank: an immediate value c coming from the decoder, or a value x from data memory,
- a code *stc* to tell the store function which value to put in the data memory, or not to store anything at all,
- of course, the address a at which to store the value.

The codes which value to store are again defined in an embedded language *StoreCode*:

$$\textbf{data } StoreCode \ = \ NoStore \mid StImm \mid StReg$$

Again, the definition of the store function $\mathcal{S}$ is a straightforward case-expression, taking the *NoStore* case as a separate clause leaving the data memory $\mathcal{M}$ unchanged:

$$\mathcal{S} \ NoStore \ \mathcal{M} \ a \ (c,x) \ = \ \mathcal{M}$$
$$\mathcal{S} \ stc \ \mathcal{M} \ a \ (c,x) \ = \ \mathcal{M} <\!\!\sim (a,v)$$
$$\textbf{where}$$
$$v = \textbf{case } stc \textbf{ of}$$
$$StImm \ -\!\!> c$$
$$StReg \ -\!\!> x$$

The Program Counter Update Function $\mathcal{U}_{pc}$. The program counter is updated by the function $\mathcal{U}_{pc}$, based on a jump code to be provided by the decoder. The jump codes are defined in an embedded language *JumpCode*:

$$\textbf{data } JumpCode \ = \ NoJump \mid UA \mid UR \mid CA \mid CR \mid Back$$

The meaning of the jump codes is as follows:

- *NoJump*: just go to the next instruction,
- in *UA, UR, CA, CR* the U/C stand for *Unconditional* and *Conditional*, respectively, i.e., jump in any case, or based on the value x (0 or 1) of a condition. A/R stand for *Absolute* and *Relative*, respectively, i.e., jump to instruction with number n, or jump a n instructions forward (backward in case n is negative) from the current instruction,
- *Back* says that the program counter can jump back to a previously remembered instruction, to be used in case of, e.g., return from a subroutine.

The program counter update function now again is straightforwardly defined by a case-expression (ipc is the program counter, *jmpc* the program counter code, y the previously stored program counter):

$$\mathcal{U}_{pc} \; (jmpc, x) \; (n, y) \; pc \; = \textbf{case} \; jmpc \; \textbf{of}$$

	NoJump	$-> pc+1$
	UA	$-> n$
	UR	$-> pc+n$
	CA	$\mid \quad x==1 \qquad -> \quad n$
		$\mid \quad \textbf{otherwise} -> \; pc+1$
	CR	$\mid \quad x==1 \qquad -> \quad pc+n$
		$\mid \quad \textbf{otherwise} -> \; pc+1$
	Back	$-> y$

The Stack Pointer Update Function $\mathcal{U}_{sp}$. The stack is a dedicated sequence of memory locations in the data memory, starting at a freely to determine memory address. The idea of defining the stack pointer update function should be clear by now, and we give the definitions straight away. The stack pointer update code:

$$\textbf{data} \; SPCode \; = \; Up \mid Down \mid None$$

The stack pointer update function, where sp is the stack pointer, and spc the stack pointer code:

$$\mathcal{U}_{sp} \; spc \; sp \; = \textbf{case} \; spc \; \textbf{of}$$

	Up	$-> sp+1$
	$Down$	$-> sp-1$
	$None$	$-> sp$

The Instruction Set. Also the *instruction set* is defined as an embedded language, called *Assembly*:

$$\textbf{data} \; Assembly = \textbf{Compute} \; OpCode \; Int \; Int \; Int$$
$$\mid \; \textbf{Jump} \; JumpCode \; Int$$
$$\mid \; \textbf{Load} \; Value \; Int$$
$$\mid \; \textbf{Store} \; Value \; Int$$
$$\mid \; \textbf{Push} \; Int$$
$$\mid \; \textbf{Pop} \; Int$$

The type *Value* consists of two sorts of values: immediate values (constants) and values indicated by their address in data memory. It is defined as follows:

$$\textbf{data} \; Value = Addr \; Int$$
$$\mid \; Imm \; Int$$

The following table describes the meaning of the instructions:

Compute $opc \; i_0 \; i_1 \; i_2$: the alu will perform the operation opc on the values from registers i_0 and i_1, and the result will be put in register i_2,

Jump $jmpc \; n$: the program counter will be changed by the number n, based on the jump code $jmpc$,

Load $(Imm \; n) \; j$: the value n will be loaded into register j,

Load (*Addr i*) *j:* the value from address *i* in data memory will be loaded into
    register *j*,
Store (*Imm n*) *j:* the constant *n* will be stored in data memory at address *j*,
Store (*Addr i*) *j:* the value from register *i* will be stored in data memory at
    address *j*,
Push *i:* the value from register *i* will be pushed onto the stack,
Pop *i:* the top value of the stack ill be loaded into register *i*.

The program memory is a list of assembly instructions, i.e., the program memory
has type [*Assembly*].

The Decode Function $\mathcal{D}$. The *decode* function $\mathcal{D}$ translates an instruction
into signals for all other functions in the Sprockell. That is to say, the function
$\mathcal{D}$ gets two arguments: the stack pointer *sp* and an assembly instruction α, and
produces a record consisting of 13 fields, as shown in Fig. 21 This record type
represents the "machine code" and is defined as:

$$
\begin{aligned}
\textbf{data } MachCode \ = \ MachCode \ \{ & \ ldCode \quad :: LoadCode, \\
& \ stCode \quad :: StoreCode, \\
& \ opCode \quad :: OpCode, \\
& \ jmpCode :: JumpCode, \\
& \ spCode \quad :: SPCode, \\
& \ jmpN \quad \ :: Int, \\
& \ immvalR :: Int, \\
& \ immvalS :: Int, \\
& \ reg0 \qquad :: Int, \\
& \ reg1 \qquad :: Int, \\
& \ addr \qquad :: Int, \\
& \ toreg \qquad :: Int, \\
& \ toaddr \quad :: Int \ \}
\end{aligned}
$$

We define an empty record for the machine code $\mathbf{C_0}$:

$$
\begin{aligned}
\mathbf{C_0} = MachCode \ \{ & \ ldCode{=}NoLoad, \ stCode{=}NoStore, \ opCode{=}NoOp, \\
& \ jmpCode{=}NoJump, \ spCode{=}None, \ jmpN{=}0, \\
& \ immvalR{=}0, \ immvalS{=}0, \\
& \ reg0{=}0, \ reg1{=}0, \ addr{=}0, \ toreg{=}0, \ toaddr{=}0 \ \}
\end{aligned}
$$

The function $\mathcal{D}$ now is defined by updating the empty machine code $\mathbf{C_0}$ for
every instruction separately, by using a case-expression. Note that the fact that
the instruction set is defined as an embedded language, offers the possibility of
pattern matching on each instruction:

$$
\begin{aligned}
\mathcal{D} \ sp \ \alpha \ = \ & \textbf{case } \alpha \textbf{ of} \\
& \textbf{Compute } opc \ i_0 \ i_1 \ i_2 \ {-}{>} \ \mathbf{C_0} \ \{ \ ldCode{=}LdAlu, \ opCode{=}opc, \ reg0{=}i_0, \ reg1{=}i_1, \ toreg{=}i_2 \ \} \\
& \textbf{Jump } jc \ n \qquad\quad {-}{>} \ \mathbf{C_0} \ \{ \ jmpCode{=}jc, \ jmpN{=}n, \ reg0{=}1, \ reg1{=}6 \ \} \\
& \textbf{Load } (Imm \ n) \ j \qquad {-}{>} \ \mathbf{C_0} \ \{ \ ldCode{=}LdImm, \ immvalR{=}n, \ toreg{=}j \ \} \\
& \textbf{Load } (Addr \ i) \ j \qquad {-}{>} \ \mathbf{C_0} \ \{ \ ldCode{=}LdAddr, \ addr{=}i, \ toreg{=}j \ \} \\
& \textbf{Store } (Imm \ n) \ j \qquad {-}{>} \ \mathbf{C_0} \ \{ \ stCode{=}StImm, \ immvalS{=}n, \ toaddr{=}j \ \} \\
& \textbf{Store } (Addr \ i) \ j \qquad {-}{>} \ \mathbf{C_0} \ \{ \ stCode{=}StReg, \ reg0{=}i, \ toaddr{=}j \ \} \\
& \textbf{Push } i \qquad\qquad\quad {-}{>} \ \mathbf{C_0} \ \{ \ stCode{=}StReg, \ spCode{=}Up, \ reg0{=}i, \ toaddr{=}sp{+}1 \ \} \\
& \textbf{Pop } i \qquad\qquad\quad\ {-}{>} \ \mathbf{C_0} \ \{ \ ldCode{=}LdAddr, \ spCode{=}Down, \ addr{=}sp, \ toreg{=}i \ \}
\end{aligned}
$$

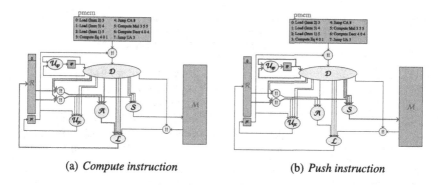

(a) *Compute instruction*   (b) *Push instruction*

Fig. 22. Examples of the effect of instructions (color figure online)

In order to illustrate the definition of the decoder, we give two examples. In Fig. 22(a) it is shown which extra signals (marked with red) in comparison to the empty machine code are activated by the decode function $\mathcal{D}$ to execute the *compute* instruction. From the corresponding clause in the definition of $\mathcal{D}$ we derive that these extra signals are:

- two register addresses by which the values for the alu $\mathcal{A}$ are selected,
- the opcode signal directly to the alu $\mathcal{A}$,
- two signals to the load function $\mathcal{L}$, saying that the outcome z of $\mathcal{A}$ has to be put in the register bank, and to which register that value has to be put.

Likewise, Fig. 22(b)can be compared to the clause in the decode function $\mathcal{D}$ to see that the following signals are added to the empty machine code for the *push* instruction:

- the value from register i has to be selected,
- the store function $\mathcal{S}$ should know that the value x from the register bank has to be put in data memory $\mathcal{M}$, and that it has to be stored on top of the stack, i.e., at address $sp+1$,
- since an element is put on top of the stack, the stack pointer has to be increased by one, such that the stack pointer again points to the top element of the stack.

We leave it to the reader to check the decoding of the other instructions.

The Sprockell Function. Finally we come to the function *sprockell*, in which all the above defined functions are composed together. We first remark that the function *sprockell* is of the pattern as described by a Mealy Machine (see Sect. 3):

- it is parameterized with a sequence as of instructions in the program memory,
- its state $(\mathcal{R}, \mathcal{M}, pc, sp)$ consists of the register bank, the data memory, and the program counter and stack pointer,
- the input is irrelevant, since for these lecture notes we chose to leave the processor without I/O. The input may be interpreted as a clock tick,
- the result consists of the updated state and some output, which can be freely defined, e.g., as a specific memory element to follow the changes.

$$sprockell \ \alpha s \ (\mathcal{R}, \mathcal{M}, pc, sp) \quad \_\ = \quad ((\mathcal{R}', \mathcal{M}', pc', sp'), \ out)$$

$$
\begin{aligned}
\textbf{where} \\
MachCode\{..\} &= decode \ sp \ (\alpha s!!pc) \\
\mathcal{R}^+ &= \mathcal{R} \ +\!\!+ \ [pc] \\
(x, y) &= (\mathcal{R}^+!!reg0, \ \mathcal{R}^+!!reg1) \\
z &= \mathcal{A} \ \ opCode \ x \ y \\
d &= \mathcal{M}!!addr \\
\mathcal{R}' &= \mathcal{L} \ \ ldCode \ \mathcal{R} \ toreg \ (immvalR, d, z) \\
\mathcal{M}' &= \mathcal{S} \ \ stCode \ \mathcal{M} \ toaddr \ (immvalS, x) \\
pc' &= \mathcal{U}_{pc} \ (jmpCode, x) \ (jmpN, y) \ pc \\
sp' &= \mathcal{U}_{sp} \ \ spCode \ sp \\
\\
out &= \cdots
\end{aligned}
$$

Note that the first line of the where-clause says that we may use the field names of the machine code record as if they were normal variables. The next line defines an "extended register bank" such that we can also choose the value of the program counter by indexing this extended register. That is practical in case a value of the program counter is saved on the stack in case of subroutine calls.

The variables x and y are defined as the values from the register bank at addresses $reg0$ and $reg1$, which come from the machine code vector, i.e., they are chosen by the decoder. The variable z results from applying the alu $\mathcal{A}$ to these values x and y, and applying the operation indicated by $opCode$, again afield from the machine code record. Likewise, d is the value from the data memory $\mathcal{M}$.

In the last four lines the various parts of the state are updated by applying the corresponding update functions to their arguments.

Simulation. The Sprockell can now be simulated by choosing an appropriate sequence α sof instructions, and appropriate values for the initial register bank and data memory. Clearly, the expected values to fill register bank and data memory are zeroes. The program counter should start at 0, and the stack pointer at that value that indicates the address in data memory where the stack starts. Now the processor may be simulated by the following expression:

$$simulate \ (sprockell \ \alpha s) \ (\mathcal{R}_0, \mathcal{M}_0, pc_0, sp_0) \ [0..]$$

The list of instructions in the program memory in Fig. 21 calculates the value of 2^3. It puts 2 in register 3, 3 in register 4, and puts the result in register 5. If we define out above as

$$(pc, \mathcal{R}!!1, \mathcal{R}!!3, \mathcal{R}!!4, \mathcal{R}!!5)$$

then the simulation gives the following sequence of 5-tuples:

$$
\begin{aligned}
&[(0,0,0,0,0), \ (1,0,2,0,0), \ (2,0,2,3,0), \ (3,0,2,3,1), \\
&(4,0,2,3,1), \ (5,0,2,3,1), \ (6,0,2,3,2), \ (7,0,2,2,2), \ (3,0,2,2,2), \\
&(4,0,2,2,2), \ (5,0,2,2,2), \ (6,0,2,2,4), \ (7,0,2,1,4), \ (3,0,2,1,4), \\
&(4,0,2,1,4), \ (5,0,2,1,4), \ (6,0,2,1,8), \ (7,0,2,0,8), \ (3,0,2,0,8), \\
&(4,1,2,0,8), \ (8,1,2,0,8), \ (*** \ \text{Exception} : \text{Prelude.}(!!) : \ \text{index too large}
\end{aligned}
$$

The first line contains the initialization of the values 2, 3, 1 in the registers 3, 4, 5 (respectively), and the other lines all start with the result of instruction 3 which computes whether register 4 equals zero. Note that the values in the registers are the values *before* the instruction indicated by the program counter (on the first position each 5-tuple) is executed.

Note also that instruction 3 puts the result in register 1, since that is the register where the conditional jump looks to decide whether it should jump or not (as determined by the choice *reg0*=1 in the definition of the decode function for the jump instruction).

Finally, note that the simulation ends by an "index too large" error, since instruction 4 will cause that the program counter gets the value 8, whereas the largest index of the sequence is 7. Clearly, that is not the most elegant solution, but in the framework of these lecture notes, we don't elaborate this point any further.

Concluding Remarks. Above we described a non-trivial processor in order to show the naturality by which the components and the total processor can be specified and simulated using Haskell. A further step would be to define a programming language for the Sprockell, which can also be done by embedded languages, a simplified example being:

```
type Variable   = String
data Expression = ···
data Program    = Program [Statement]
data Statement  = Assign Variable Expression
                | If Expression [Statement] [Statement]
                | While Expression [Statement]
```

We leave it to the reader to work out the details, including the definition of a *compiler*, which now can be defined as a function from these types to a list of instructions, i.e., to the type [*Assembly*]. Clearly, the compiler also needs a lookup table in which it is registered on which memory location the value of a variable is put.

5.2 Composition of Stateful Components

In the previous section we described the Sprockell processor as an example of an irregular architecture. All subcomponents of the Sprockell are stateless, which makes the composition of these subcomponents straightforward, as can be seen in de definition of the function *sprockell*. In this section we will discuss an example of an irregular architecture which is a composition of stateful subcomponents. The example we choose for that is a reduction circuit as described in [7].

The issue with the composition of subcomponents with state is that the fact that the state is an explicit argument and an explicit result of an architecture definition causes that also the component that contains these subcomponents must have the state of these subcomponents as an argument. The reason is that each clock cycle the resulting state of a component has to be fed back to the same component as an argument. The consequence is that all states of all subcomponents — and of subcomponents of subcomponents, etcetera — are arguments and results of the top-level architecture. Because of the negative effect of this on the readability of an architecture specification, we wish to hide the state of subcomponents and suppress the visibility of state on a higher level then the subcomponent to which the state belongs.

The Haskell feature that we use for this is called *arrows*. We will only show the usage of arrows in the example below, for a deeper understanding of the concept we refer to the Haskell website (www.haskell.org) where several introductions to the concept can be found.

The Reduction Circuit. The intention of the reduction circuit presented here is to add — on an FPGA — sequences of numbers which enter in order, for example:

$$a_1, \ldots, a_k, \ b_1, \ldots, b_m, \ c_1, \ldots, c_n, \ \ldots$$

Thus, all numbers a_i have to be added, all numbers b_i have to be added, etcetera.

There are a few aspects that have to be taken into account:

- every number is marked with the row to which it belongs, but all numbers belonging to the same row arrive consecutively,
- every number is a floating point number, meaning that addition is a pipeline and takes several clock cycles,
- every clock cycle a number arrives and has to be processed immediately.

Clearly, the combination of the last two points make this a tricky problem, and many architectures are published to do the reduction efficiently. The architecture we will present uses the possibilities of the pipelined adder to process several additions in parallel such that all additions can be executed streamingly. The global idea of the architecture is shown in Fig. 23:

- there is a pipelined floating point adder receiving two numbers at a time, which then travel through the adder upwards until at the top they are completely added. Meanwhile the adder may receive new numbers, possibly belonging to a different row. In the figure the adder is working on four additions, two belonging to row a, and two belonging to row b.
- when the adder finished adding two numbers, the result is put in the partial result memory on a location reserved to the row to which this result belongs. In the figure this is row a, whereas an intermediate result of row b is stored on another location. One clock cycle later, the adder will produce a next intermediate result of row b, and together with the partial b-result from memory, that will be sent to the adder.
- there is an input buffer (a FIFO buffer) where the numbers are received in-order, one-by-one. From this input buffer, the numbers are sent to the pipelined floating point adder, either two at the same time (as shown in the Fig. 23), or one together with a result from the adder belonging to the same row.

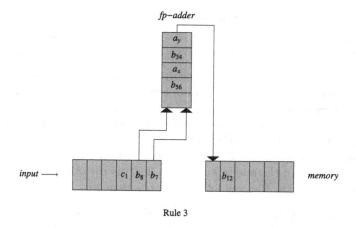

Fig. 23. Reduction circuit, schematic

There are five rules concerning the priority of the number combinations to be sent to the adder:

1. a number from the adder together with a previous result of the same row in memory,
2. a number from the adder together with the first number from the input buffer if it belongs to the same row,
3. the first two numbers from the input buffer if they belong to the same row,
4. the first number from the input buffer if it is the last of a row, together with 0,
5. no number at all if none of the above rules apply.

We refer to [7] for a more extensive description of the algorithm and for a proof that no pipeline stalls and no buffer overflows occur.

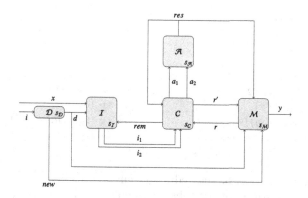

Fig. 24. Reduction circuit, architecture

In Fig. 24 the components $\mathcal{I}$, $\mathcal{A}$, $\mathcal{M}$ correspond to the input buffer, the pipelined adder, and the intermediate result memory, respectively. In addition to these components there are two more components:

- a *discriminator* $\mathcal{D}$ which adds a marker to each number for the row it belongs to. Note that this information is also sent to the partial result memory to make a reservation for a location for the intermediate results of a row. When the end result of a row is completely calculated, the corresponding marker can be re-used for the numbers of a later row.
- a *controller, $\mathcal{C}$* which checks the above rules and decides which combination of numbers to send to the adder, and which informs the other components how this choice influences the content of these components.

Each component has its own internal state, called $\mathcal{S}_D$, $\mathcal{S}_I$, etcetera. As an example, we mention that the input buffer $\mathcal{I}$ receives every clock cycle a number x together with its marker d. It sends its first two numbers i_1 and i_2 (or an *undefined* value in case there is only zero or one cell of the input buffer filled) to the controller and receives in return (in the same clock cycle) the number *rem* telling whether there were 0, 1, or 2 of the values i_1 and i_2 used and which have thus to be removed from the state of the input buffer.

   Without going into the internal details of the other components, we remark that they all are defined according to the pattern of a Mealy Machine, i.e., they have the form

$$f \; state \; input \; = \; (state', \; output)$$

Now the state of the reduction circuit $\mathcal{RC}$ as a whole is the combination of the states of all its subcomponents, i.e.,

$$s_{RC} \; = \; (s_D, \; s_I, \; s_A, \; s_C, \; s_M)$$

The reducer as a whole is a composition of the nested states and can be defined as follows:

$$
\begin{aligned}
&reducer \; s_{RC} \; (x, i) \; = \; (s'_{RC}, \; y) \\
&\textbf{where} \\
&(s_D, \; s_I, \; s_A, \; s_C, \; s_M) \; = \; s_{RC} \\
&(s'_D, (new, d)) && = && \mathcal{D} \; s_D \; i \\
&(s'_I, (i_1, i_2)) && = && \mathcal{I} \; s_I \; (x, d, rem) \\
&(s'_P, res) && = && \mathcal{P} \; s_P \; (a_1, a_2) \\
&(s'_R, (r, y)) && = && \mathcal{R} \; s_R \; (new, d, res, r') \\
&(s'_C, (a_1, a_2, rem, r')) && = && \mathcal{C} \; s_C \; (i_1, i_2, res, r) \\
&s'_{RC} \; = \; (s'_D, \; s'_I, \; s'_A, \; s'_C, \; s'_M)
\end{aligned}
$$

Note that the total state of the reduction circuit first has to be unpacked in the 5-tuple of the states of its subcomponents, after which every individual subcomponent is applied to its own state and the corresponding inputs (we leave it to the reader to check these inputs with Fig. 24). The outcome of the application of each subcomponent is a tuple of its updated state, and its outputs, after which the updated state of the reduction circuit as a whole again is the 5-tuple of the internal states of the various subcomponents.

Though straightforward, this is a cumbersome notation, the technique that CλaSH uses to avoid it is by means of Haskell's *arrow* abstraction mechanism, written as follows (the input of the circuit consists of (x, i), and the output of y, the total of a row):

$$
\begin{aligned}
reducer \; = \; & \textbf{proc} \; (x, i) \; -> \; \textbf{do rec} \\
(new, d) \quad & <- \; (\, D \;^{\sim\!\sim\!\sim}\; s_D^0 \,) \; -< i \\
(i_1, i_2) \quad & <- \; (\, I \;^{\sim\!\sim\!\sim}\; s_I^0 \,) \; -< (x, d, rem) \\
res \quad & <- \; (\, P \;^{\sim\!\sim\!\sim}\; s_P^0 \,) \; -< (a_1, a_2) \\
(r, y) \quad & <- \; (\, R \;^{\sim\!\sim\!\sim}\; s_R^0 \,) \; -< (new, d, res, r') \\
(a_1, a_2, rem, r') \quad & <- \; (\, C \;^{\sim\!\sim\!\sim}\; s_C^0 \,) \; -< (i_1, i_2, res, r)
\end{aligned}
$$

$$\textbf{returnA} \; -< \; y$$

The internal state of each component is now maintained by the arrow mechanism, where the notation $^{\sim\!\sim\!\sim}$ instantiates a component with an adequately defined initial component s_x^0. The comparison of this specification with Fig. 24 shows an immediate correspondence between specification and figure.

The totally worked out code of the reduction circuit can be found on the CλaSH website, clash.ewi.utwente.nl.

6   CλaSH

In the previous sections we gave several examples of architectures using Haskell as a specification language, illustrating several aspects of such specifications. We showed that Haskell has many powerful features which are very suitable for the description of hardware architectures. First of all, the mathematical perspective of the language suits the concept of transforming a signal by means of a digital circuit, since that concept is close to th e concept of a function. But also several more concrete features of Haskell are very powerful, for example, polymorphism turned out to be a very pleasant feature when it comes to a first structural design, as well as the possibility of higher order functions in case of regular architectures. Furthermore, the flexibility in choice constructs, the possibility of exploiting embedded languages, and the derivation of types are practical. Finally, we mention the immediate possibility of simulating a design as a very practical feature.

However, in order to produce real hardware from these specifications, for example on an FPGA, we still have to modify the Haskell code in order to make it suitable for processing by CλaSH. Since every CλaSH specification also is an executable Haskell program, these modifications boil down to some rather standard adaptations. In Sect. 6.1 we will describe some of these steps. In Sect. 6.2 we will sketch the processing pipeline of CλaSH, and give an informal idea of the rewrite mechanism that CλaSH performs in order to produce synthesizable code. Finally, in Sect. 6.3 we will mention some further issues where CλaSH still has to be improved.

6.1 Transforming Haskell Code into CλaSH Code

The modifications of Haskell code into code that can be processed by CλaSH, can be distinguished in three different issues, discussed below:

- Bringing the Haskell code into a specific form that can be dealt with during CλaSH simulation and translation,
- Issues concerning types, in particular number types and list types,
- Issues that have to do with typical hardware deliberations, such as fixed point arithmetic versus floating point arithmetic.

CλaSH Syntactical Form

Types. Several types that are natural in Haskell have to be modified in order to be usable for hardware. The limitation stems from the fact that on hardware one has to choose explicitly how many wires to use, for example, the designer has to decide on the bit width of the involved number types. Besides, in order to use the available area on an FPGA optimally, a designer will often choose for a non-standard bit width of integers, such as 18 bit integers.

Number Types. CλaSH offers several typing constructs to express these choices, the most important ones being *Signed* and *Unsigned* for integer numbers. In addition the bit width of these numbers has to be indicated, for example *Signed*16 for 16 bit signed numbers.

List Types. The same holds for lists: in Haskell a list may vary in length during the evaluation of a program. On hardware, however, that is not possible, so the designer has to make a choice for the length of a "list". For this, CλaSH offers *vector* types, of the following pattern: *Vector* ⟨*width*⟩ ⟨*type*⟩, where the width should be, e.g., 16, 24, etcetera, and the type may be any type that is acceptable on hardware.

Polymorphism. One further point concerning this issue is polymorphism: often a specification in Haskell holds for many different types, for example, the specification of FIR-filters in Sect. 4.3 hold for any number type, they hold for *Int*, *Integer*, *Float*, etcetera, alike. As mentioned above, for hardware a choice has to be made, but it often is sufficient to make this choice at the top level of the specification. For many types of subexpressions of the specification, the types will be derived by the compiler.

Algebraic Types. As we saw in Sect. 5, a very powerful usage of algebraic types is to define *embedded languages*. CλaSH is able to translate these types into bit patterns, which can be mapped onto hardware. These bit patterns are efficient in the sense that parts of the bit pattern can be re-used for other constructors from the same algebraic type.

Further Transformations. The above transformations stem from the need to adapt Haskell code to specific hardware requirements, such as decisions on bit widths of number types. Some other transformations that may have to be necessary have to do with design choices concerning the performance and the precision of the designed hardware. A typical example of such a choice concerns the choice for floating point or fixed point arithmetic, which has to do with a trade off between the usage of area and time on the actual hardware. In Haskell everything is done in floating point, so if the design has to use fixed point arithmetic, the Haskell code has to be adapted correspondingly.

A comparable issue arises with some arithmetical operators which may be complex in hardware, such as division. In Haskell itself, which is evaluated as software, the designer does not need to think about such issues. But in order to avoid the complexity in hardware, and possibly slow execution of such operators, a designer may choose for an approximation of such an operator.

6.2   The Processing Pipeline of CλaSH

The process performed by CλaSH is a pipeline and consists of several stages (see Fig. 25):

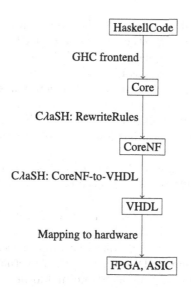

Fig. 25. CλaSH pipeline

GHC Frontend. The first step is done by the standard Haskell compiler *GHC*, or by *GHCi*, the interactive variant of *GHC*. *GHC* takes care of aspects such as syntax analysis, desugaring, parsing, and type checking. Also type derivation is taken care of by *GHC*.

Besides, *GHC* translates the CλaSH specification into the *Core* language, a *GHC* internal language which is a fully fledged functional language, but has only a limited number of syntactical constructions. That is to say, the result of *GHCI* is a *Core* expression which is equivalent to the original specification, but which is easier to deal with because of its greater syntactical simplicity.

CλaSH Rewrite Rules. This phase in the CλaSH pipeline is the first step of the CλaSH kernel itself: to rewrite a specification into a *normal form* (CoreNF) which makes the hardware architecture explicit in detail. In fact, this CλaSH normal form is close to a so-called *netlist* formalism, which is used in techniques to produce actual hardware from a specification. Informally put, a netlist formalism describes a graph in which every wire is mentioned. The CλaSH normal form has the following structure:

$$
\lambda x. \textbf{ let}
$$
$$
\begin{aligned}
y_0 &= e_0 \\
y_1 &= e_1 \\
y_2 &= e_2 \\
&\vdots
\end{aligned}
$$
$$
\textbf{in}
$$
$$
z
$$

Thus, the CλaSH normal form is a lambda expression with zero or more formal parameters which correspond to the inputs of the specified component. The body is a **let** expression with a sequence of local definitions, in which every defining expression e_i is a simple expression, i.e., an expression with only variables as subexpressions. Every variable defined in this let-expression corresponds to a wire in the actual hardware. Finally, the **in** part of the let-expression also is a single variable, which corresponds to the output of the component. In fact, every wire in the CλaSH normal form has a name, and thus the CλaSH normal form is close to a netlist format.

Below we will give an informal example of this part of the pipeline to show that the normal form indeed is close to the hardware architecture.

CoreNF to VHDL. The second step of the CλaSH kernel is the translation the CλaSH normal form into VHDL. The reason to choose for VHDL as a target language is that VHDL is a standardized hardware specification language, and many tools exist that map VHDL specifications to actual hardware, such as an FPGA. In fact, the expression in CλaSH normal form already is in a structural sense already very close to VHDL.

Mapping to Hardware. This is the last phase in the pipeline and consists of the usage of the tools that are available for VHDL to take care of the actual mapping of the specification onto hardware. For example, the synthesis of an FPGA is realized by these VHDL tools.

Example of the Rewrite Step. Assume we specify a simple alu, using pattern matching, as follows:

$$alu\ ADD = (+)$$
$$alu\ MUL = (*)$$
$$alu\ SUB\ = (-)$$

So the alu is only able to add, to multiply, and to subtract numbers, i.e., the embedded language for the opcodes is as follows:

$$\textbf{data}\ OpCode\ =\ ADD\ |\ MUL\ |\ SUB$$

Note, however, that no matter how simple the specified alu is, the specification is polymorphic and higher order. It is polymorphic in the sense that it works for any number type, and higher order because it is defined in terms of the *functions* $(+)$, $(*)$, $(-)$ only, without using individual variables for numbers.

Intuitively, the hardware architecture specified by this definition is clear, and shown in Fig. 26.

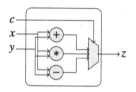

Fig. 26. The specified alu

The first step in the rewrite process is the GHC frontend which removes the syntactic sugar of pattern matching and turns de definition into a lambda-abstraction:

$$alu = \lambda c.\ \textbf{case}\ c\ \textbf{of}$$
$$ADD \rightarrow (+)$$
$$MUL \rightarrow (*)$$
$$SUB \rightarrow (-)$$

The first rewrite step chosen by CλaSH will be *η-expansion*, i.e., to add lambda abstractions and corresponding arguments:

$$alu\ =\ \lambda c.\ \lambda x.\ \lambda y. \left(\begin{array}{l} \textbf{case}\ c\ \textbf{of} \\ ADD \rightarrow (+) \\ MUL \rightarrow (*) \\ SUB \rightarrow (-) \end{array} \right) x\ y$$

The result of η-expansion is that all inputs of the alu (c, x, y) now correspond to formal parameters of the specification.

Since the case-expression is of function type, the next step is *application propagation*, i.e., to move the arguments x, y into the case-expression:

$$alu = \lambda c\, x\, y\textbf{case } c \textbf{ of}$$
$$ADD \to (+)\; x\; y$$
$$MUL \to (*)\; x\; y$$
$$SUB \to (-)\; x\; y$$

The next step might be called *letification*, i.e., the body of the lambda term is turned into a let-expression, by introducing a name z for the expression as a whole and having that name as the only term in the body of the let-expression. The result is that the output of the architecture (see Fig. 26) corresponds to this variable z. For reasons of readability we write the arithmetical operations in an infix way:

$$alu = \lambda c\, x\, y\textbf{let}$$
$$z = \textbf{case } c \textbf{ of}$$
$$ADD \to x + y$$
$$MUL \to x * y$$
$$SUB \to x - y$$
$$\textbf{in}$$
$$z$$

Finally, all subexpressions that are not single variables will be *extracted* and defined separately, resulting in a name for every single wire in the architecture:

$$alu = \lambda c\, x\, y\textbf{let}$$
$$p = x + y$$
$$q = x * y$$
$$r = x - y$$
$$z = \textbf{case } c \textbf{ of}$$
$$ADD \to p$$
$$MUL \to q$$
$$SUB \to r$$
$$\textbf{in}$$
$$z$$

The resulting expression now is in CλaSH normal form, and corresponds to Fig. 26 to the extent that all wires got names with, e.g., p being the wire that results from the addition component.

6.3   Final Remarks

As described and illustrated in these lecture notes, CλaSH is a system to specify hardware. It is based on Haskell, and translates Haskell definitions of a specific form into synthesizable VHDL, which can be mapped to, e.g., an FPGA. However, CλaSH is still under development, thus these lecture notes are not the final text on CλaSH, for an in-depth presentation of CλaSH we refer to [2]. Further examples of architectures specified of in CλaSH can be found in, e.g., [1,12,17,18], whereas some first introductions may be found in [1,11,16].

As an example of a topic on which CλaSH still has to be extended is the usage of recursive definitions. At the moment there is no systematic treatment of recursive specifications in CλaSH yet, it is future work to fill in that gap.

References

1. Baaij, C.P.R., Kooijman, M., Kuper, J., Boeijink, W.A., Gerards, M.E.T.: CλasH: Structural descriptions of synchronous hardware using haskell. In: Proceedings of the 13th EUROMICRO Conference on Digital System Design: Architectures. Methods and Tools, Lille, France, pp. 714–721. IEEE Computer Society, USA, September 2010

2. Baaij, C.P.: Digital Circuits in Cλash – Functional Specification and Type-Driven Synthesis. Ph.D. thesis, University of Twente, The Netherlands (2014, forthcoming)

3. Bjesse, P., Claessen, K., Sheeran, M., Singh, S.: Lava: Hardware design in Haskell. In: Proceedings of the Third ACM SIGPLAN International Conference on Functional Programming, pp. 174–184. ACM (1998)

4. Cardelli, L., Plotkin, G.D.: An algebraic approach to vlsi design. In: Gray, J.P. (ed.) Proceedings of the first International Conference on Very Large Scale Integration, pp. 173–182. Academic Press (1981)

5. Chen, G.: A short historical survey of functional hardware languages. ISRN Electronics (2012)

6. Coussy, P., Morawiec, A. (eds.): High-level Synthesis. From Algorithm to Digital Circuit. Springer Publishers, New York (2008)

7. Gerards, M.E.T., Baaij, C.P.R., Kuper, J., Kooijman, M.: Higher-order abstraction in hardware descriptions with Cλash. In: Kitsos, P. (ed.) Proceedings of the 14th EUROMICRO Conference on Digital System Design, DSD 2011, Oulu, Finland, pp. 495–502. IEEE Computer Society, USA (2011)

8. Gill, A., Bull, T., Kimmell, G., Perrins, E., Komp, E., Werling, B.: Introducing kansas lava. In: Morazán, M.T., Scholz, S.-B. (eds.) IFL 2009. LNCS, vol. 6041, pp. 18–35. Springer, Heidelberg (2010)

9. IEEE Standard: VHDL Language Reference Manual. IEEE (2008)

10. Johnson, S.: Applicative programming and digital design. In: Proceedings of the 11th ACM SIGACT-SIGPLAN Symposium on Principles of Programming Languages, pp. 218–227. ACM (1984)

11. Kuper, J., Baaij, C.P.R., Kooijman, M., Gerards, M.E.T.: Architecture specifications in CλaSH. In: Kaźmierski, T.J., Morawiec, A. (eds.) System Specification and Design Languages. LNEE, vol. 106, pp. 191–206. Springer, New York (2011)

12. Niedermeier, A., Wester, R., Rovers, K.C., Baaij, C.P.R., Kuper, J., Smit, G.J.M.: Designing a dataflow processor using cλash. In: 28th Norchip Conference, NORCHIP 2010, Tampere, Finland, p. 69. IEEE Circuits and Systems Society, November 2010

13. Nikhil, R.: Bluespec: A general-purpose approach to high-level synthesis based on parallel atomic transactions. In: Coussy, P., Morawiec, A. (eds.) High-Level Synthesis - From Algorithm to Digital Circuit, pp. 129–146. Springer, Netherlands (2008)

14. Sander, I., Jantsch, A.: System modeling and transformational design refinement in ForSyDe. IEEE Trans. Comput. Aided Des. Integr. Circuits Syst. **23**, 17–32 (2004)
15. Sheeran, M.: μFP, a language for VLSI design. In: Proceedings of the 1984 ACM Symposium on LISP and Functional Programming, pp. 104–112. ACM (1984)
16. Smit, G.J.M., Kuper, J., Baaij, C.P.R.: A mathematical approach towards hardware design. In: Athanas, P.M., Becker, J., Teich, J., Verbauwhede, I. (eds.) Dagstuhl Seminar on Dynamically Reconfigurable Architectures, Dagstuhl, Germany. Dagstuhl Seminar Proceedings, vol. 10281, p. 11. Internationales Begegnungs- und Forschungszentrum für Informatik (IBFI), Dagstuhl, Germany, December 2010
17. Wester, R., Baaij, C.P.R., Kuper, J.: A two step hardware design method using cλash. In: 22nd International Conference on Field Programmable Logic and Applications, FPL 2012, Oslo, Norway, pp. 181–188. IEEE Computer Society, USA, August 2012
18. Wester, R., Sarakiotis, D., Kooistra, E., Kuper, J.: Specification of apertif polyphase filter bank in cλash. In: Communicating Process Architectures 2012, Scotland, pp. 53–64. Open Channel Publishing, United Kingdom, August 2012

Functional Web and Mobile Development in F#

Adam Granicz[✉]

IntelliFactory, Budapest, Hungary
adam.granicz@intellifactory.com
http://intellifactory.com

Abstract. In these lecture notes we present examples of F# mobile web applications using WebSharper [1], an open source F# web framework. In the first part of the tutorial, we provide a quick walkthrough of the relevant WebSharper features and concepts. WebSharper, through its extensions, can provide type-safe interfaces to various JavaScript libraries. We will make use of extensions to jQuery Mobile [2] and Sencha Touch [3], and demonstrate how to develop F# mobile web applications with these libraries.

1 WebSharper

WebSharper [1] is a mature, open source web framework for F#, that enables developers to author F# web applications using various functional web abstractions such as formlets and sitelets, and provides automatic and faithful translation to JavaScript.

WebSharper can be used as a standalone tool, although most developers prefer to use it as an extension to one of the mainstream integrated development environments (IDEs), such as Visual Studio and/or MonoDevelop. We assume working with the Visual Studio integration in this paper, and the reader is referred to Sect. 1.8 to learn more about the available toolsets and templates in that bundle.

The WebSharper team has also been hard at work to provide an online IDE for WebSharper and F# development, and the first releases of CloudSharper [10], an online IDE with these goals in mind, offer a friction-less way to get started online.

WebSharper applications can be fully client-side (HTML + JavaScript), or can have an optional server side that the client side code can call upon. These client-server calls are simple F# function calls with each participating function annotated to denote the tier it's designed to run under.

The following snippet demonstrates seamless client-server RPC calls:

```
namespace Testing

module Server =
    [<Rpc>]
    let ServerFunction (...) =  ...
```

© Springer International Publishing Switzerland 2015
V. Zsók et al. (Eds.): CEFP 2013, LNCS 8606, pp. 381–406, 2015.
DOI: 10.1007/978-3-319-15940-9_9

```
module Client =
    [<JavaScript>]
    let ClientFunction (...) =
        ...
        Server.ServerFunction (...)  // Call the server
```

1.1 Overview of the WebSharper Programming Model

WebSharper builds on F# and can largely be seen as a library of extensions providing various web abstractions, enabling developers to embed entire web applications, including client and server-side functionality into F#.

This single-language, uniform programming model avoids many of the shortcomings of mainstream, script-based web development, and empowers developers with numerous functional constructs that dramatically simplify implementing web applications.

WebSharper applications are built as a two step process. The first step involves executing the F# compiler to produce a dynamically linked library, also known as a .NET assembly. This assembly will contain quotation data for annotated components such as those marked for client-side execution in JavaScript, and meta information such as client-side dependencies (JavaScript and CSS resources) required to be in scope when code is served in WebSharper contexts from the given assembly. This quotation data is embedded automatically by the F# compiler, as all WebSharper-related code attributes inherit from ReflectedDefinition, the main F# attribute class that instructs the F# compiler to embed the corresponding reified syntax tree representation into the containing assembly.

The second build step invokes the WebSharper compiler, passing all references and the main application assembly, and various other command line options that drive compilation, and executes the code generation logic relevant to the execution model selected. In every compilation path, F# to JavaScript code generation uses the quotation data embedded in target and referenced assemblies. Using this representation as opposed to the more raw .NET intermediate language (CIL) representation has the added benefit of producing code that is sufficiently high level and maintains stronger ties to the original source code by retaining its shape and characteristics.

Code Generation for Sitelets. One key execution model for WebSharper applications is based on WebSharper sitelets (see Sect. 1.6), an abstraction that represents web applications as values in the F# type system. Sitelets provide an elegant shorthand notation for building larger WebSharper applications, and also cater for developing more advanced capabilities such as responding to REST requests [9] or enabling user authentication on part of or the entire application under development. The main sitelet can be marked as a sitelet entrypoint in its assembly (one per assembly) using a wrapper type and an assembly-wide attribute. The required code makes a reference to an Action discriminated union type that the sitelet is said to "implement," containing union cases that represent the different functional areas/aspects of the resulting web application, MySitelet, referencing the sitelet to be exposed, and MyActions, containing a list of Action union cases to generate client-side code for:

```
[<Sealed>]
type Action =
    | ...


type MyApplication() =
    interface IWebsite<Action> with
        member this.Sitelet = MySitelet
        member this.Actions = MyActions

[<assembly: Website(typeof<MyApplication>)>]
do ()
```

WebSharper sitelets can be "online" or "offline", with the former representing web applications that are made up of a server side as well as a client side. For online sitelets, the explicit facility to control the generated client-side code and markup (via MyActions in the above snippet) is ignored, and instead no static markup is produced, as this is a chore that is performed on request by the sitelet handler embedded into the host web server. Online sitelets can be deployed and run in any web server implementation that supports ASP.NET or OWIN, the Open Web Interface for .NET.

Offline sitelets, also called HTML sitelet applications, consist of HTML markup and client-side code, and can be fully encapsulated by a set of generated HTML and JavaScript files and their related static artifacts such as images and style sheet files. This means that offline sitelet applications, once generated, can be embedded into any web server, not just those that support ASP.NET. When building offline sitelet applications, the WebSharper compiler generates all markup into separate HTML pages and embeds references to generated JavaScript files for each piece of dynamic functionality. This follows the exact same pattern as the content served via online sitelets in a sitelet-aware web application container.

Code Generation for Non-sitelet HTML Applications. An alternate execution model for client-only applications is generating plain JavaScript code that can be included in an HTML page. These applications are made up of ordinary client-annotated F# functions and effectful value bindings that execute as soon as their generated JavaScript file is referenced and loaded. Therefore, these applications must manually control the point of generated script inclusion into host markup. Despite this, such low-level control is often useful and desirable, and from the perspective of other high-level language to JavaScript translation users, this mode of operation is straightforward and helps to get started with WebSharper for novice users.

1.2 F# to JavaScript Translation

WebSharper can produce verbose and minified JavaScript output, driven by a command-line switch to the WebSharper compiler, or by a web application configuration setting in online sitelet applications. The latter enables developers to change verbosity settings while the application at hand is running, making it easier to keep deployed applications optimized in their ordinary course of operation, dropping back to a more verbose configuration when targeted debugging and investigation is necessary.

The verbose output retains the identifiers/names and nested structure of the original F# code, thereby greatly assisting in debugging. At the time of writing, there are plans to support source maps to link the original F# code to the generated code more tightly, but this is not yet available. Without source maps, developers must rely on the verbose syntax to navigate the generated code, which in practice turns out to be easy to get used to. However, unless debugging issues in WebSharper extensions to various JavaScript libraries or missing resources, one rarely has a reason to investigate the generated code more closely.

WebSharper translation performance and memory consumption is proportional to the size of the input program (the parts that are marked for client-side execution) and to the number of WebSharper extension/stub libraries used. In general, WebSharper compilation times are similar to those of the F# compiler for the same code base. For instance, a WebSharper solution consisting of about 100 lines of F#/WebSharper code is compiled under a second, while a larger, enterprise-grade application of about 25,000 lines of F#/WebSharper code is compiled in about 10 seconds on a mainstream development machine with an Intel i5 quadcore CPU.

Compilation proceeds by constructing a call graph over the entire set of referenced assemblies, and uses standard graph algorithms to traverse this graph to infer dependencies and other meta information, and to generate JavaScript code in a modular fashion (one file per assembly) given the main entry points of the application. While it is possible to reduce the generated code to only those fragments that are actually used in the given application, WebSharper makes no such optimization as of writing this tutorial, and instead outputs client-side code that reflects all the capabilities in the referenced assemblies and the main application. This makes the JavaScript output modular and reusable (in both verbose and minified form) in other consuming applications as well, at the expense of containing potentially unused code. This makes smaller WebSharper applications relatively more verbose in terms of the generated code, but this quickly balances out as the size of the application grows.

Unused generated code increases load times, but have no effect on the runtime performance. There are, however, code generation characteristics that should be taken into consideration. Most importantly, as discussed earlier, WebSharper generates JavaScript from F# quotations as opposed to intermediate language (IL) representation. This has the immediate effect that WebSharper projects are tied to the F# compiler and to F# as a source language, instead of being able to work from other .NET Common Language Runtime (CLR) languages such as C# and Visual Basic. While we have plans to enable other languages to be used with WebSharper in subsequent releases, the ways of interoperability envisioned are not via IL code.

Not relying on the .NET Common IL (CIL) representation also means that none of the optimizations that are otherwise performed by the F# compiler (or other .NET front-end compilers in future releases) are included in the JavaScript code generation. Some optimizations are performed by WebSharper itself, such as eliminating intermediate lambda expressions and applying a sophisticated inlining mechanism, overall giving a good balance of high-level and optimized code. One notable major compromise is the missing tailcall optimization on top-level functions, however, tailcalls are optimized for local/inner functions.

The example below demonstrates the optimizations performed by WebSharper.

```
namespace Bundle1

open IntelliFactory.WebSharper

[<JavaScript>]
module Client =
    let Foo x = x+1
    let Bar x y = if x = y then x+1 else y+1
    let F x =
        let bar (x, y) = if x = y then x+1 else y+1
        1+bar (x, Foo x)
    let Main =
        let foo = Bar 1
        1 + Bar 1 (foo 2)
```

Note in particular that:

- Namespaces and modules are compiled to inner scopes
- Top-level functions are mapped to JavaScript functions with the same arity
- Top-level bindings are mapped to Runtime.Fields calls and are evaluated in the order of their declaration
- Simple local functions are inlined
- Local functions taking tuples are converted to single-arity functions and are called with an array of arguments via Runtime.Tupled.

The actual generated JavaScript code for the above snippet is inlined below:

```
Runtime.Define(Global,{
  Bundle1:{
  Client:{
   Bar:function(x,y)
   {
    return x===y?x+1:y+1;
   },
```

```
F:function(x)
{
 return 1+(Runtime.Tupled(function(tupledArg)
 {
  var x1,y;
  x1=tupledArg[0];
  y=tupledArg[1];
  return x1===y?x1+1:y+1;
 }))([x,Client.Foo(x)]);
 },
 Foo:function(x)
 {
  return x+1;
 },
 Main:Runtime.Field(function()
 {
  return 1+Client.Bar(1,Client.Bar(1,2));
 })
 }
 }
});
```

The internal conversion from tuples to heterogeneous arrays gives a straightforward embedding for tuples and a predictable performance in extracting tuple elements, however, in many cases the `Runtime.Tupled` machinery in local function calls could be optimized out.

1.3   Other Considerations

No WebSharper application is complete without adding the appropriate style sheets and presentation layer artifacts. These can be generated from F# code, or more often simply included in the markup that serves as a dynamic template for sitelets or legacy ASP.NET applications. Section 1.8 contains an example of the templating mechanism used in most WebSharper sitelet applications. This approach makes it possible to embed typed placeholders in external markup template files, which are in turn bound dynamically at runtime and instantiated from the sitelet handler with programmed content.

Dynamic templating has the significant advantage of requiring no recompilation upon changing the template files themselves. This enables a quick and seamless workflow to adjust and fine-tune the templates, and developers and designers only need to agree on the placeholder names and types used in these templates.

Dynamically-bound templates, however, may mismatch their consuming sitelet code. Such mismatch is discovered on the first request to a page that misuses the underlying template, e.g. specifies a different number and/or type of placeholders than those embedded in the actual template. Older versions of WebSharper also supported static templates, which were converted to F# code during compilation to ensure that all occurrences of template placeholders are addressed as expected. This, however, proved to be too inconvenient and slowed development considerably with the frequest design changes that each application is expected to undergo, and the static templating approach was thus removed from subsequent releases of WebSharper.

1.4   Code Annotations

There are required and optional custom attribute annotations that drive how F# code gets compiled to JavaScript. To participate in client-side code, a code entity must be annotated with either the `JavaScript` attribute or one of the attributes inheriting from `AbstractInlineAttribute`. To customize the name in the compiled JavaScript output, it might also be annotated with an attribute inheriting from `AbstractNameAttribute`. Both of these abstract attributes and their descendant attribute types discussed in this section are placed automatically in scope when the `IntelliFactory.WebSharper` namespace is opened.

The JavaScript Attribute. The `JavaScript` attribute marks members for compilation into JavaScript. It is the single most important attribute in Web-Sharper. The annotated members are translated to JavaScript by the WebSharper compiler by inspecting and translating their F# bodies, extracted from quotations that are embedded into the containing assembly by the F# compiler, triggered by the presence of `ReflectedDefinitionAttribute`, a superclass of the `JavaScript` attribute, and all other WebSharper-related attributes.

Naming Attributes. These attributes influence the member names output in JavaScript code. The base class, `Naming.AbstractNameAttribute`, allows to create custom attributes with arbitrary logic for determining the compiled name. This is useful in various context-dependent translation scenarios, such as to avoid name clashes and shadowing.

   A simple implementation, the `Name` attribute, explicity sets the JavaScript-compiled names of members and types. For example, in the snippet below, both `Date` and `Date.GetDate` output a specific JavaScript identifier when used.

```
[<Stub>]
[<Name "my.package.Date">]
type Date =
    /// Returns the day of the month.
    [<Name "getDate">]
    member this.GetDate() = 0
```

Inlining Attributes. Inlining attributes mark functions for inline compilation to JavaScript. The base class, `Inlining.AbstractInlineAttribute`, allows to create custom attributes with arbitrary macro-expansion logic. Three common forms are provided: `InlineAttribute`, `ConstantAttribute` and `StubAttribute`.

– `InlineAttribute` - a simple attribute that specifies that members are to be compiled inline. This attribute either complements `JavaScriptAttribute`, or serves standalone with a JavaScript template string. The following two forms are equivalent:

```
[<Inline>]
[<JavaScript>]
let Add (x: int) (y: int) = x + y

[<Inline "$x + $y">]
let Add (x: int) (y: int) = 0
```

The syntax of the template string is regular JavaScript. Variables that start with $ are treated as placeholders. There are named ($x), positional ($0), and special ($this,$value) placeholders. To use an actual variable that starts with a $ sign, duplicate the sign, as in $$x.

– `ConstantAttribute` - allows members to compile to constant literals. Its most common use is to annotate union cases. For example:

```
type Align =
    | [<Constant "left">]   Left
    | [<Constant "center">] Center
    | [<Constant "right">]  Right
```

With these annotations, `Align.Left` is compiled as literal ''left'', and pattern-matching against any union case is compiled as an equality test against the corresponding literal.

This pattern is especially useful for providing type safety in JavaScript code where literals are used as a segmentation device, or where the list of literals is closed. By bringing these to F# as discriminated unions or constant literals one can eliminate the potential for spelling errors or forgetting to handle all "cases" of the literal list.

– `StubAttribute` - commonly marks types that expose JavaScript-implemented functionality to WebSharper. `StubAttribute` is useful for enabling WebSharper code to consume and interoperate with legacy and third-party JavaScript code.

Methods and fields on types marked with `StubAttribute` that are not marked with special translation attributes such as `JavaScriptAttribute` are translated by-name. Methods do not have to have a meaningful body, but should be correctly typed.

The example below exposes to F# code some of the functionality of the `Date` object as present in most JavaScript environments (as specified in the ECMA-262 standard).

```
[<Name [| "Date" |]>]
[<Stub>]
type Date() =
```

```
/// Returns the day of the month.
member this.getDate() = 0

/// Returns the day of the week.
member this.getDay() = 0

/// Returns the year.
member this.getFullYear() = 0
```

1.5   HTML Combinators

WebSharper provides two sets of HTML combinators to construct HTML content: one for client-side use to dynamically create DOM nodes in JavaScript, and another for constructing markup on the server side. While these two sets of combinators are largely equivalent in the way of their construction, they differ in how they can include JavaScript functionality.

Constructing HTML. The following list summarizes the basic HTML combinators and their usage (Table 1):

Table 1. Basic HTML Combinators

Symbol	Definition	Comment
$html ::=$	`Div	P	...`	HTML constructors
$attr ::=$	`Attr.Class "..."	` `Attr.HRef "..."	...`	HTML attributes
$attrs ::=$	`[ `$attr_1$` ; ...; `$attr_n$` ] — [ ]`	Sequencing
$htmlnode ::=$	$html\ attrs$	HTML nodes
$node ::=$	$htmlnode$	Nodes without subnodes
	$htmlnode -< nodes$	Nodes with subnodes
	$htmlnode -- node$	Nodes with a single subnode
	`Text "..."`	Text nodes

Client-side HTML combinators are contained under `IntelliFactory.Web-Sharper.Html`, while the server-side equivalents are in the `IntelliFactory.Html` namespace. It is common practice in WebSharper applications to separate client and server functionality into separate F# modules, opening the appropriate HTML combinator namespace within those modules.

Embedding Client-Side Behavior. Adding event handlers to client-side HTML is straightforward using the builtin `OnClick`, etc. primitives in the `Pervasives` module, opened automatically with the core `IntelliFactory.WebSharper` namespace.

The following snippet shows the syntax to attach an event handler to a DOM node:

```
Button [Text "Click"]
|>! OnClick (fun _ _ ->
    JavaScript.Alert "Hello World!"
)
```

Here, the |> operator, as opposed to the common F# forward pipe (|>) operator, is used to attach the given event handler to a DOM element, returning that same element. This operator is simply defined as:

```
let (|>!) x f = f x; x
```

Adding client-side functionality to server-side markup, on the other hand, requires special treatment. This consists of defining a new server-side control type, deriving from the Web.Control WebSharper control type, wrapping the desired functionality, and embedding an instance of this server-side control in client-side markup. This type marks crossing the client-server boundary in sitelets, a server-side representation of web application values, and are necessary to generate correct HTML/JavaScript interaction from them. The examples in this tutorial employ this technique to embed client-side behavior.

1.6   Sitelets

A sitelet is a WebSharper abstraction to represent web applications. Sitelets are F# values, and they can be programmatically created (using Sitelet.Content, Sitelet.Infer, and Sitelet.Protect) and composed into larger sitelets (using Sitelet.Sum).

Sitelets use the server-side HTML combinators to represent HTML markup, and can embed WebSharper controls, as described in the previous section. Sitelets define how requests are mapped to responses by providing a bijection through a so-called action type: a discriminiated union type that contains various shapes to represent the connection between requests and responses.

Consider the following simple action type, representing a web application with two entry points:

```
type Action =
    | Home
    | ContactUs
```

To see the basic sitelet combinators in action, we can create a sitelet for this application as follows:

```
module Site =
    let HomePage = ...
    let AboutPage = ...
```

```
let Main =
    Sitelet.Sum [
        Sitelet.Content "/" Action.Home HomePage
        Sitelet.Content "/about" Action.About AboutPage
    ]
```

Here, `Sitelet.Content` creates a singleton sitelet that "listens" on a particular URL translating GET requests to that URL to one of the shapes of the action type the sitelet is parameterized over, and maps a given response content to it. `Sitelet.Sum` simply combines sitelets into larger ones, aggregating the URL space and the action type coverage by the resulting sitelet.

In scenarios that involve action type cases carrying parameters, one can use `Sitelet.Infer` to create/infer sitelets, enabling access to the carried values.

```
type Action =
    | [<CompiledName "home">] Home
    | ContactUs
    | Echo of string

module Site =
    let HomePage = ...
    let AboutPage = ...
    let EchoPage s = ...

    let Main =
        Sitelet.Infer (fun action ->
            match action with
            | Action.Home ->
                HomePage
            | Action.ContactUs ->
                AboutPage
            | Action.Echo msg ->
                EchoPage msg
        )
```

With `Sitelet.Infer`, URLs are inferred for each action case, and these in turn can be obtained via a sitelet context when creating content. This makes the need to control actual URLs less relevant and it also avoids hard-coded URLs that point inside the application.

There are, however, situations where being able to override the inferred URLs is required. This can be easily accomplished by adding a `CompiledName` attribute on the affected action case, as shown in the snippet above. Further refinements, such as multiple URLs pointing to the same content, are possible by combining sitelets appropriately.

More complex scenarios, such as handling non-GET HTTP requests or managing unbounded URLs are beyond the scope of this tutorial, and the reader is referred to [5] for more information.

1.7   Formlets and Piglets

WebSharper formlets [6] are an implementation of the formlet abstraction described in [7], providing an F# embedding with various enhancements such as dependent formlets and flowlets, a wizzard-like presentation of a sequence of related formlets.

Formlets provide a composable, type-safe, and declarative way of specifying user interfaces that take user input. Consider the following WebSharper formlet, which implements a two-page flowlet: a simple input box with Submit and Reset buttons followed by printing the typed value back to the user.

```
Formlet.Do {
    let! x =
        Controls.Input ""
        |> Enhance.WithTextLabel "Enter something"
        |> Validator.IsNotEmpty "Can't be empty"
        |> Enhance.WithSubmitAndResetButtons
        |> Enhance.WithFormContainer
    return!
        Formlet.OfElement (fun _ ->
            H1 [Text x]
        )
}
|> Formlet.Flowlet
```

Here, the formlet in the first page, represented by the binding to x, results in a string value typed into the text box. It only accepts if the attached validator is not blocking and the Submit button has been clicked. Numerous other enhancements and validators are available in the standard formlet library, and custom ones can be constructed easily.

Composing formlets into larger ones follows the general form, where Formlet_1 ... Formlet_n are sub-formlets and v_1 ... v_n are their results:

```
Formlet.Yield (fun v_1 ... v_n -> [combined result])
<*> Formlet_1
...
<*> Formlet_n
```

Here, the type of the combined result will drive the type of the resulting formlet. A short example to implement a formlet to input a "person" is as follows:

```
type Person = {
    Name: string
    Age: int
}

[<JavaScript>]
```

```
let PersonFormlet () : Formlet<Person> =
    let nameF =
        Controls.Input ""
        |> Validator.IsNotEmpty "Empty name not allowed"
        |> Enhance.WithValidationIcon
        |> Enhance.WithTextLabel "Name"
    let emailF =
        Controls.Input ""
        |> Validator.IsInt "Valid age required"
        |> Enhance.WithValidationIcon
        |> Enhance.WithTextLabel "Age"
    Formlet.Yield (fun name age -> {Name = name; Age = int age})
    <*> nameF
    <*> emailF
    |> Enhance.WithSubmitAndResetButtons
    |> Enhance.WithLegend "Add a New Person"
    |> Enhance.WithFormContainer
```

Formlets enable ultra-rapid user interface development by relieving the developer from having to worry about presentation-level details. In fact, the snippet above can be changed to take a list of "person" records by a single line of code: by applying `Enhance.Many` to the composed formlet before further enhancements.

WebSharper Pluggable Interactive GUIlets [8], or piglets for short, are another powerful user interface abstraction offered on the WebSharper tool stack. Piglets cater to the full customizability of the formlet markup, making it possible to reuse the same declarative piglet definition across multiple content delivery channels, for instance for tablets, mobile phones and full web front-ends. The reader is encouraged to study piglets in more detail in the paper referenced above.

1.8   Visual Studio Integration

WebSharper can be installed as a Visual Studio extension, supplying build automation and various WebSharper templates for use with Visual Studio. Below we give a short description of two of the main Visual Studio templates, used in most WebSharper applications and in this very tutorial as well.

HTML Sitelet Applications. This template is designed to contain a typical HTML/JavaScript application written in F#. It contains an F# file `Main.fs`, that implements a simple web application as a WebSharper sitelet. The pages of this web application use an external HTML "designer" template file `Main.html`, also found in the template.

The plumbing to inject content into this designer template is defined in the `Skin` module, which implements, among others, the `WithTemplate` function to instantiate pages, with their placeholder content represented as the record type `Skin.Page`. Placeholders can be string or `Content.HtmlElement` values, a WebSharper representation for HTML DOM nodes.

The snippet below contains the templating logic. Note the reference to the HTML template source file. The content substitution mechanism implemented in WebSharper builds on a simple, non-intrusive approach: the content placeholders in the template markup are simple HTML elements with special HTML5 data attributes. These attributes drive whether content is inserted inside or replaces the placeholder node, using data-hole and data-replace, respectively.

```
module Skin =
    open System.Web

    type Page =
        {
            Title : string
            Body : list<Content.HtmlElement>
        }

    let MainTemplate =
        Content.Template<Page>("~/Main.html")
            .With("title", fun x -> x.Title)
            .With("body", fun x -> x.Body)

    let WithTemplate title body : Content<Action> =
        Content.WithTemplate MainTemplate <| fun context ->
            {
                Title = title
                Body = body context
            }
```

In addition to the data-attributes just described, WebSharper can also interpret simple string placeholders using the $name syntax. A rudimentary designer template is included in the project template and is shown below:

```
<!DOCTYPE html>
<html>
<head>
    <title>${title}</title>
    <meta name="generator" content="websharper"
          data-replace="scripts" />
</head>
<body>
    <h1>${title}</h1>
    <div data-hole="body">
    </div>
</body>
</html>
```

HTML Bundle Applications. Similar to HTML sitelet applications, the HTML bundle application template is designed to enable fully offline HTML/ JavaScript applications. The key difference to its sitelet-based alternative is that HTML bundle applications do not require a sitelet to be defined, and instead can express the main application logic directly. This typically takes the form of executing an initialization function compiled from F# to JavaScript, that brings the static designer template markup to life. The word *bundle* derives from the fact that this application template produces and packages all the necessary scripts into a self-containing bundle that uses a sophisticated, lazy-loaded set of include scripts and a single HTML page. Therefore, bundle applications are often used to implement Single Page Applications (SPAs).

An example bundle application is shown below. Note that defining a sitelet is not required, and that the content insertion logic is explicit.

```
namespace MyApp

open IntelliFactory.WebSharper
open IntelliFactory.WebSharper.Html

[<JavaScript>]
module Client =

    let Main =
        let input = Input [Text ""]
        let label = Div [Text ""]
        Div [
            input
            label
            Button [Text "Click"]
            |>! OnClick (fun _ _ ->
                label.Text <- input.Value)
        ].AppendTo "entry"
```

For this code to execute properly, the containing HTML page has to take care of loading the generated scripts (by default, generated under `Content/ project.min.js`) and it must contain the placeholder element ("entry" in this example). A sample host HTML page is shown below:

```
<!DOCTYPE html>
<html lang="en">
<head>
    <title>My Application</title>
    <meta charset="utf-8" />
    <meta name="viewport"
        content="width=device-width,initial-scale=1.0" />
    <link rel="stylesheet" type="text/css"
        href="Content/MyApp.css" />
```

```
</head>
<body>
    <div id="entry"></div>

    <script type="text/javascript"
            src="//code.jquery.com/jquery-1.10.2.min.js">
    </script>
    <script type="text/javascript"
            src="Content/MyApp.min.js"></script>
</body>
</html>
```

2 Example: jQuery Mobile

In this section, we walk through a small WebSharper application that uses jQuery Mobile [2] for its user interface. jQuery Mobile is an extension of jQuery [4] and is one of the first HTML/JavaScript libraries designed to implement a familiar mobile look and feel in consuming applications. It is heavily markup-based, using HTML5 data attributes to erect a simple page-based structure with embedded mobile controls, driving their appearance and eye candy such as transition effects.

2.1 SlideApp.fs

Our example uses the HTML Sitelet Application Visual Studio template described in the previous section. The main client-side functionality, placed in Slide App.fs, implements a PageManager type that can manage a set of UI pages that can be scrolled (via a left or right swipe event) horizontally. The final application is depicted in Fig. 1.

```
[<IntelliFactory.WebSharper.Pervasives.JavaScript>]
module SlideApp

open IntelliFactory.WebSharper
open IntelliFactory.WebSharper.JQuery
open IntelliFactory.WebSharper.JQuery.Mobile
open IntelliFactory.WebSharper.Html

[<AutoOpen>]
module private Internal =

    let JQM = Mobile.Instance

    type Transition =
        | NoTransition
        | SlideLeft
```

```
   | SlideRight
   | SlideDown
   | SlideUp

   member this.Reverse =
       match this with
       | SlideUp
       | SlideLeft -> true
       | NoTransition
       | SlideDown
       | SlideRight -> false

   member this.Name =
       match this with
       | NoTransition -> "none"
       | SlideLeft
       | SlideRight -> "slide"
       | SlideUp
       | SlideDown -> "slidedown"
```

The actual page manager wraps jQuery Mobile page elements. It provides an abstraction from keys of a given type to actual DOM elements that represent pages of the UI. The `SwitchTo` member performs a visual shift of a given

Fig. 1. A Simple WebSharper Application Using jQuery Mobile

kind from the current page to a given page specified by its key value using
`Mobile.Instance.ChangePage` from the jQuery Mobile binding.

```
type PageManager<'P when 'P : equality>() =

    let rendered = Dictionary<'P, Element>()
    let mutable setupPage : 'P -> Element = fun _ -> Div []

    member this.SwitchTo (p: 'P, ?trans: Transition) =
        if not (rendered.ContainsKey p) then
            rendered.[p] <- setupPage p
            JQuery.Of("body").Append(rendered.[p].Body).Ignore
            (rendered.[p] :> IPagelet).Render()
        let trans = defaultArg trans NoTransition
        JQM.ChangePage(JQuery.Of(rendered.[p].Body),
            ChangePageConfig(
                Transition = trans.Name,
                Reverse = trans.Reverse))

    member this.Setup(setup: PageManager<'P>->'P->Element) =
        setupPage <- setup this
```

We also provide a series of helper functions: `PageDiv` to create a jQuery
Mobile page element with the given content, `OnSwipeLeft` and `OnSwipe Right`
for binding event handlers to the corresponding swipe events, `Header` to create a
header element, and `PageCarousel` to create a left-right carousel from a sequence
of page contents.

```
let PageDiv content =
    Div [HTML5.Attr.Data "role" "page"] -< content
    |>! OnAfterRender (fun el ->
        Mobile.Page.Init (JQuery.Of el.Body))

let OnSwipeLeft f (e: #IPagelet) =
    JQuery.Of(e.Body).On("swipeleft", fun _ -> f e; true)

let OnSwipeRight f (e: #IPagelet) =
    JQuery.Of(e.Body).On("swiperight", fun _ -> f e; true)

let Header x = Div [HTML5.Attr.Data "role" "header"] -< x
```

`PageCarousel` returns for a given set of pages a function that computes its
page-per-page representation. For each page of index i, it constructs a page element with a header of left/right buttons to switch to the previous/next page, and
with the specified content given for that page. Switching between neighboring
pages is also attached via the corresponding swipe events.

```
let PageCarousel (pages: seq<string * #seq<Element>>) =
    let pages = Array.ofSeq pages
    let n = pages.Length
    fun (pm: PageManager<int>) (i: int) ->
        let i = i % n
        let ``i-1``= (i+n-1) % n
        let ``i+1``= (i+1) % n
        let title, content = pages.[i]
        let prevTitle, _ = pages.[``i-1``]
        let nextTitle, _ = pages.[``i+1``]
        let goPrev() = pm.SwitchTo(``i-1``, SlideLeft)
        let goNext() = pm.SwitchTo(``i+1``, SlideRight)
        PageDiv [
            yield Header [
                Button [
                    HTML5.Attr.Data"icon" "arrow-l"
                    HTML5.Attr.Data "iconpos" "left"
                    Text prevTitle
                ]
                |>! OnClick (fun _ _ -> goPrev())
                H1 [Text title]
                Button [
                    HTML5.Attr.Data "icon" "arrow-r"
                    HTML5.Attr.Data "iconpos" "right"
                    Text nextTitle
                ]
                |>! OnClick (fun _ _ -> goNext())
            ]
            yield! content
        ]
        |>! OnSwipeLeft (fun _ -> goNext())
        |>! OnSwipeRight (fun _ -> goPrev())
```

Finally, Init constructs the skeleton of our application: a carousel with three pages, each displaying a single button that once clicked takes the user back to the home page. Customizing the content of each page is straightforward, simply by giving a different content list to start with.

```
let Init() =
    let carousel = PageManager<int>()
    let home = PageManager<unit>()
    let homeButton() =
        Button [Text "Home"]
        |>! OnClick (fun _ _ -> home.SwitchTo((), SlideDown))
    let carouselPages =
        [
            "Timeline", [
```

```
                homeButton()
            ]
            "My tweets", [
                homeButton()
            ]
            "Mentions of me", [
                homeButton()
            ]
        ]
    carousel.Setup(PageCarousel carouselPages)
    home.Setup(fun _ () ->
        PageDiv [
            yield Header [H1 [Text "Home"]]
            yield! carouselPages |> List.mapi (fun i (title,_) ->
                Button [Text title]
                |>! OnClick (fun _ _ ->
                    carousel.SwitchTo(i, SlideUp)))
        ])
    home.SwitchTo(())
```

2.2 Main.fs

With the page skeleton in place, the rest of the application code simply needs to
embed the main page as a client-side functionality into a single-page sitelet. For
this, we define a server-side control that initializes the page functionality into a
div placeholder once it has been rendered.

```
namespace MyApplication

open IntelliFactory.WebSharper
open IntelliFactory.WebSharper.Sitelets

type Action = | Index

module Client =
    open IntelliFactory.WebSharper.Html

    [<Sealed>]
    type Control() =
        inherit Web.Control()
        [<JavaScript>]
        override this.Body =
            Div []
            |>! OnAfterRender (fun _ ->
                SlideApp.Init())
            :> _
```

Our single index page is an instantiation of a barebones designer HTML file in `Main.html`, similar in content to that of the HTML Sitelet template discussed earlier.

```
module Pages =
    type Index = { Body: Content.HtmlElement list }

    let IndexTemplate =
        Content.Template(__SOURCE_DIRECTORY__ + "/Main.html")
            .With("body", fun x -> x.Body)

    open IntelliFactory.Html

    let Index =
        Content.WithTemplate IndexTemplate <| fun ctx ->
            { Body = [Div [new Client.Control()]] }
```

Once all the pieces are defined, we can create our sitelet to represent the entire application as follows:

```
[<Sealed>]
type MyWebsite() =
    interface IWebsite<Action> with
        member this.Actions = [Action.Index]
        member this.Sitelet =
            Sitelet.Content "/" Action.Index Pages.Index

[<assembly: Website(typeof<MyWebsite>)>]
do ()
```

3   Example: Sencha Touch

While jQuery Mobile provides a good set of common mobile functionality and look and feel, its markup-based mode of operation is often inflexible when customizations need to be implemented. Therefore, users often desire to work in various application frameworks implemented in JavaScript. One such framework is Sencha Touch [3], an open-source, royalty-free JavaScript library that implements a wide array of UI elements and mobile functionality. Through its API, consuming applications can implement custom user interfaces and application logic, embed arbitrary HTML/HTML5 content, and use other, external JavaScript libraries.

With the matching WebSharper extension, developers can author Sencha Touch applications entirely in F#. In this section, we walk through a simple application using Sencha Touch, shown in Fig. 2 as developed in IntelliFactory's CloudSharper, an online Integrated Development Environment (IDE) for F# and WebSharper.

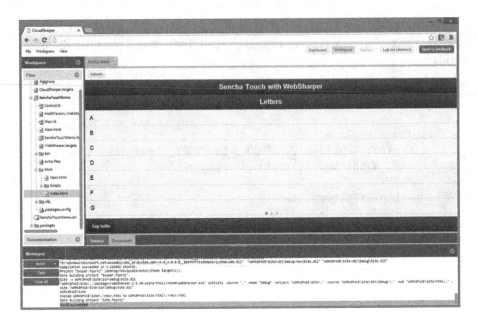

Fig. 2. An Enhanced Sencha Touch Application Running in CloudSharper

3.1   Control.fs

The core application functionality consists of assemblying a Sencha Touch `Ext.`
`Application` value. To help with this objective, we provide a `MakeList` function,
that creates a Sencha Touch container, similar to a jQuery Mobile page, with a
title bar docked on the top, and a list view that lists the given data values.

```
module Control

open IntelliFactory.WebSharper
open IntelliFactory.WebSharper.Html5
open IntelliFactory.WebSharper.Html
open IntelliFactory.WebSharper.SenchaTouch

[<JavaScript; AutoOpen>]
module ExtHelpers =
    let Comps a = a : Ext.ComponentCfg[]

    let MakeList title data =
        Ext.ContainerCfg(
            Layout = "fit",
            Items = Comps [|
                Ext.TitleBarCfg(
                    Docked = "top",
```

```
                     Title = title
                )
                Ext.dataview.ListCfg(
                    ItemTpl = "{title}",
                    Data = As(Array.map (fun i -> {title=i}) data)
                )
            |]
        )
```

Sencha Touch applications can be initialized by a single function that is called at launch time. In our application, this function creates a full screen carousel container, and initializes its slidable pages with three sets of data values: letters, numbers, and punctuation characters.

```
[<JavaScript>]
let OnLaunch () =
    Ext.ContainerCfg(
        Fullscreen = true,
        Layout = "fit",
        Items = Comps [|
            Ext.TitleBarCfg(
                Docked = "top",
                Title = "Lists in Carousel"
            )
            Ext.carousel.CarouselCfg(
                Items = Comps [|
                    MakeList "Letters" <|
                        [|"A";"B";"C";"D";"E";"F";"G";"H";
                          "I";"J";"K";"L";"M";"N";"O";"P";
                          "Q";"R";"S";"T";"U";"V";"W";"X";
                          "Y";"Z"|]
                    MakeList  "Numbers" <| As [| 0 .. 20 |]
                    MakeList "Punctuation" <|
                        [|".";",";"?";"!";"»";":";";";
                          "-";"\"";"/";"(";")"|]
                |]
            )
        |]
    )
    |> fun cfg -> Ext.Container cfg |> ignore
```

We embed this client-side functionality into a server-side control, which in turn can be embedded into a sitelet page, a routine task now that we have completed a similar exercise in the previous section. With Sencha Touch, a stateful call to Ext.Application with the correct ApplicationCfg value does the trick, however, we still need to return a dummy DOM element from the server-side control's Body function.

```
type AppControl() =
    inherit Web.Control()

    [<JavaScript>]
    override this.Body =
        Ext.app.ApplicationCfg(Launch=OnLaunch) |> Ext.Application
        upcast Div []
```

3.2 Main.fs

Given the server-side function to create the entire Sencha Touch application, we can simply wrap it into an empty designer HTML file in a single-page sitelet, exactly in the same way as we did in the previous example. We omit that code here, as it largely follows the same format, except for the actual control that is embedded.

4 Related Work

There are three main broad topics, ideas presented in this tutorial. The first topic concerns using modern, high-level programming languages. such as F#, and generating JavaScript code from these languages in order to facilitate a more robust and maintainable way of developing web and mobile web applications. The main motivations are two-fold: benefiting from a stricter type system (JavaScript is weakly typed), and/or a shorter, more maintainable source syntax.

In the examples we presented, we gained a great deal of brevity from the concise syntax of F#, as expressed in terms of lines of code (LOC) of source language code versus generated JavaScript code. Savings averaged a factor of 5-7. Furthermore, entire classes of potential bugs were eliminated by the use of a sound type system and safer language features, and development was further accelerated by the code assistance features available for F#, such as code completion and type checking.

The ubiquitous nature of JavaScript (the "assembly language of the web") has yielded JavaScript translators for nearly all mainstream programming languages. Notable examples include GWT for Java, Scala.js for Scala, ClojureScript for Clojure, WebSharper and FunScript for F#, Haste for Haskell, Script# for C#, Ocamljs and Opa for OCaml, Hop for Scheme, PythonJS for Python, among many-many others.

Next to language-to-JavaScript translators and web frameworks, there are a growing number of new web programming languages that similarly target generating JavaScript code. These include those that require explicit translation by a corresponding tool, such as Elm [11], Roy, Dart, and others, and those that are implemented in and implicitly converted to JavaScript, such as TypeScript, LiveScript, CoffeeScript and its variants, and many others.

The second central topic to our tutorial is using functional programming constructs and abstractions to model various aspects of web development. We briefly presented our F# implementation [6] for formlets [7] and mentioned piglets [8], a similar, but more flexible abstraction for modeling type-safe, composable user interfaces. Formlets are widely implemented in various functional languages, including Haskell, OCaml, F# and Scala. The WebSharper formlet library we briefly introduced is one of the most advanced implementations available, providing explicit facilities for dependent formlets, enabling to encode dependencies among form elements, and flowlets, a type-safe representation for wizard-like sequences of formlets.

A unique functional programming-inspired construct we presented were sitelets (Sect. 1.6), enabling developers to compose web applications as F# values. Sitelets give a robust answer to modeling Model-View-Controller (MVC) applications by encapsulating routers and controllers into a single notation, and yielding important added benefits such as safe URLs and type-safe URLs by using a combination of an abstract URL representation, pattern matching, and F# active patterns [12]. Similar approaches are available in Happstack and Yesod with Haskell, and in Play with Scala.

And last, we have hinted to the applicability of online/web IDEs to cater to and facilitate such functional web development, and showcased CloudSharper, an online IDE for developing F# and WebSharper applications in one of running examples. While an increasing number of online IDEs are available for scripting languages such as PHP or JavaScript/HTML, including Cloud9, Visual Studio Online, Codio, and others, CloudSharper remains in the top tier by providing code assistance for a strongly-typed language.

5   Conclusions

In this tutorial, we presented the fundamentals of WebSharper-based F# mobile web development using two notable HTML/JavaScript mobile libraries: jQuery Mobile and Sencha Touch. Both examples we developed are self-contained and are fully expressed in F#. The corresponding WebSharper extensions can be obtained from [1], and the reader is encouraged to experiment more with these and other extensions to enjoy the truly remarkable and highly productive alternative to mainstream web and mobile web development that WebSharper enables.

Acknowledgements. The author would like to thank his IntelliFactory colleagues Loic Denuziere and Andras Janko for their help with the examples in this tutorial, and Anton Tayanovskyy for writing most of Sect. 1.4.

References

1. Granicz, A., Tayanovskyy, A., Denuziere, L., Janko, A., et al.: The WebSharper website. http://websharper.com, Accessed 10 December 2013
2. The jQuery Mobile website. http://jquerymobile.com, Accessed 10 December 2013
3. The Sencha Touch website. http://www.sencha.com/products/touch. Accessed 10 December 2013

4. The jQuery website. http://jquery.com, Accessed 10 December 2013
5. Syme, D., Granicz, A., Cisternino, A.: Expert F# 3.0. Apress, Berkeley (2012)
6. Bjornson, J., Tayanovkyy, A., Granicz, A.: Composing reactive GUIs in F# using WebSharper. In: Hage, J., Morazán, M.T. (eds.) Implementation and Application of Functional Languages. LNCS, vol. 6647. Springer, Heidelberg (2011)
7. Cooper, E., Lindley, S., Wadler, P., Yallop, J.: An Idioms Guide to Formlets. Technical report, University of Edinburg (2008)
8. Denuziere, L., Rodriguez, E., Granicz, A.: Piglets to the rescue. In: 25th Symposium on Implementation and Application of Functional Languages, IFL. Nijmegen, The Netherlands (2013)
9. Fielding, R.T.: Architectural styles and the design of network-based software architectures. Ph.D. thesis, University of California, Irvine (2000)
10. Granicz, A., Tayanovskyy, A., Denuziere, L.: Experience Report: Developing a Cloud-Based Integrated Environment for F# Web and Mobile Applications. InformatikaKorszeru Technikai, IKT 2012. Dunaujvaros, Hungary (2012)
11. Czaplicki, E., Chong, S.: Asynchronous functional reactive programming for GUIs. In: The Proceedings of the 34th ACM SIGPLAN Conference on Programming Language Design and Implementation, PLDI 2013, pp. 411–422. Seattle, WA, USA (2013)
12. Syme, D., Neverov, G., Margetson, J.: Extensible pattern matching via a lightweight language extension. In: The Proceedings of the 12th ACM SIGPLAN International Conference on Functional Programming, ICFP 2007. Freiburg, Germany (2007)

Zipper-Based Modular and Deforested Computations

Pedro Martins[1]([✉]), João Paulo Fernandes[1,2], and João Saraiva[1]

[1] High-Assurance Software Laboratory (HASLAB/INESC TEC),
Universidade do Minho, Braga, Portugal
{prmartins,jas}@di.uminho.pt
[2] Reliable and Secure Computation Group ((rel)ease),
Universidade da Beira Interior, Covilhã, Portugal
jpf@di.ubi.pt

Abstract. In this paper we present a methodology to implement multiple traversal algorithms in a functional programming setting. The implementations we obtain s of highly modular and intermediate structure free programs, that rely on the concept of functional zippers to navigate on data structures.

Even though our methodology is developed and presented under *Haskell*, a lazy functional language, we do not make essential use of laziness. This is an essential difference with respect to other attribute grammar embeddings. This also means that an approach similar to ours can be followed in a strict functional setting such as *Ocaml*, for example.

In the paper, our technique is applied to a significant number of problems that are well-known to the functional programming community, demonstrating its practical interest.

Keywords: Deforested computation · Generic programming · Functional programming

1 Introduction

Functional programs are often constructed by gluing together smaller components, using intermediate data structures to convey information between components. These data structures are constructed in one component and later consumed in another one, but never appear in the result of the whole program. This compositional style of programming has many advantages for clarity and modularity, but gives rise to a maintenance problem due to the extra data that must be created and consumed. The usual solution is to remove intermediate data structures by combining smaller components into larger ones, thereby ruining modularity. In this paper we develop a technique for avoiding this tradeoff: we implement modular functional programs without defining intermediate data structures.

Consider the problem of transforming a binary leaf tree t_1 into a new tree t_2 with the exact same shape as t_1, but with all the leaves containing the minimum value of t_1. This problem is widely known as *repmin* [1], and is often

© Springer International Publishing Switzerland 2015
V. Zsók et al. (Eds.): CEFP 2013, LNCS 8606, pp. 407–427, 2015.
DOI: 10.1007/978-3-319-15940-9_10

used to illustrate important aspects of modern functional languages [2–4]. In this paper, *repmin* is also used as a first running example, and we start by presenting different solutions for it. In order to solve *repmin*, we start by defining a representation for binary leaf trees:

```
data Tree = Leaf Int | Fork Tree Tree
```

In a strict, purely functional setting, solving this problem requires a two traversal strategy. First, we need to traverse the input tree in order to compute its minimum value:

```
tmin :: Tree -> Int
tmin (Leaf n)   = n
tmin (Fork l r) = min (tmin l) (tmin r)
```

Having traversed the input tree to compute its minimum value, we need to traverse that tree again. We need to replace all its leaf values by the minimum value:

```
replace :: Tree -> Int -> Tree
replace (Leaf _)   m = Leaf m
replace (Fork l r) m = Fork (replace (l ,m))
                            (replace (r ,m))
```

In order to solve *repmin*, we now only need to combine functions *tmin* and *replace* appropriately:

```
transform :: Tree -> Tree
transform t = replace t (tmin t)
```

There are many advantages in structuring our programs in this modular way. Considered in isolation, functions *tmin* and *replace* are very clear, simple, they are easy to write and to understand, so they have a great potential for reuse. Furthermore, each function can be focused in performing a single task, rather than attempting to do many things at the same time.

In this particular solution, given the simplicity of *repmin*, the input tree t serves as input to both functions *tmin* and *replace*. In general, however, modular programs are given by definitions such as $prog = f.g$, where $prog :: a \to c$, $g :: a \to b$ and $f :: b \to c$. This means that these programs use an intermediate structure, of type b, that needs to be more informative than the input one, of type a. This fact forces the programmer to define and maintain new data structures which are constructed as the program executes. The construction of these structures that never appear in the result of the whole program adds overhead that makes maintenance hugely difficult, which gets worse as the program increases both in size and in complexity.

In the above solution, it is also the case that the scheduling of computations was left to the programmer. Indeed, in order to implement *transform*, we realized that the minimum of the input tree needs to be computed before the replacement is possible. Although the scheduling in this case is trivial, for more realistic problems, the scheduling of computations may not be a simple task. For example, the optimal pretty printing algorithm presented in [5] is implemented by four traversal functions, whose scheduling is extremely complex. Moreover, those four functions rely on three (user-defined) gluing intermediate structures to convey information between the different traversals.

In a lazy functional setting such as *Haskell* an alternative solution to *repmin* can be formulated. In his original paper, [1] showed how to derive such a solution from the two traversal solution seen before. He derives the program:

```
repmin :: Tree -> Int -> (Tree, Int)
repmin  (Leaf n)   m = (Leaf m,   n)
repmin  (Fork l r) m = (Fork t₁ t₂ , min m₁ m₂)
   where  ( t₁ , m₁) = repmin l m
          ( t₂ , m₂) = repmin r m
transform :: Tree -> Tree
transform t = nt
   where (nt, m) = repmin t m
```

This program is *circular*: we can see that, in the definition of the *transform* function, m is both an argument and a result of the *repmin* call. Although this definition seems to induce both a cycle and non-termination of this program, the fact is that, in a lazy setting, the lazy evaluation machinery is able to determine, at runtime, the right order to evaluate it. In this type of programs, the work associated with the scheduling of computations is, therefore, transferred from the programmer to the lazy evaluation machinery.

We may also notice that the circular version of *transform* does not construct or use any intermediate data structure, and this is a characteristic of all circular programs: since they define a single function to perform all the work (*repmin*, in the example), the definition of intermediate data structures to glue different functions loses its purpose. In fact, circular programming may be considered an advanced technique for intermediate structure deforestation [3].

In a circular program, the definition of a single function, on the other hand, forces us to encode together all the variables used in the program. Indeed, if we needed to use more arguments or to produce more results in our example, these would all have to be defined in *repmin*. As a consequence, the definition of such a function needs to be concerned with using and computing many different things. In this sense, we observe that circular programs are not modular.

Circular programs are also known to be difficult to write and to understand and even for experienced functional programmers, it is not hard to define a *real* circular program, that is, a program that does not terminate. The execution of such programs is, furthermore, restricted to a lazy execution setting, since such a setting is essential to schedule circular definitions. This means that we are not able to execute the latter version of *transform* in a strict language such as *Ocaml*, for example.

In summary, we notice some characteristics of these approaches: the first version of *transform* is highly modular and its execution is not restricted to a lazy setting, but relies on gluing data types and function scheduling, whereas the second one is free of intermediate structures and requires no explicit scheduling by the programmer but is hard and "non-natural" to write such circular programs, and even for an advanced lazy functional programmer it is hard to write a program which is not completely circular, i.e., which terminates.

In this paper, we develop a framework for implementing multiple traversal algorithms in a functional setting. Programs in our framework combine the best of the two *transform* solutions: they are modular, intermediate structure free and do not require explicit scheduling by the programmer. This is achieved by thinking of our programs in terms of Attribute Grammars (AGs), i.e., by implementing AGs as first class elements in our language. In this sense, our work may also be thought of as an AG embedding.

In the literature, one may find other approaches with similar goals; [2,4] are two notable examples. An essential difference with respect to these approaches is that our framework does not make essential use of laziness, so that it can easily be implemented in a strict setting such as *Ocaml*. A more detailed comparison to related work is presented in Sect. 6.

The framework we propose relies heavily on the concept of functional zippers, originally proposed by [6]. As we will see later, our use of functional zippers is such that they provide an elegant and efficient mechanism for navigating on tree structures, but also to hide that navigation.

In a previous work [7], we have presented an embedding of Attribute Grammars in a functional setting, together with modern AG extensions, and shown how these can be used to implement the semantics of programming languages. In this work, we show how such setting can also be useful as an alternative to traditional implementations on a functional setting, by creating programs that are more modular and structured.

This paper is organized as follows. In Sect. 2, we review the standard concept of functional zippers. In Sect. 3, we show how standard zippers can be used to express a modular attribute grammar to solve the *repmin* problem. Our approach is then used in Sects. 4 to 5 to express attribute grammar solutions to programming problems more realistic than *repmin*, as well as a generic solution to *repmin*. In Sect. 6 we describe works that relate to ours, and finally in Sect. 7 we draw our conclusions.

2   The Zipper

The zipper data structure was originally conceived by Huet [6] to solve the problem of representing a tree together with a subtree that is the focus of attention, where that focus may move left, right, up or down the tree.

In our work we have used the generic zipper library of [8]. It works for both homogeneous and heterogeneous datatypes, and data-types for which an instance of the *Data* and *Typeable* type classes [9] are available can be traversed.

In order to introduce the concept of zipper, we consider again the representation for binary leaf trees in *Haskell*:

```
data Tree = Leaf Int | Fork Tree Tree
```

and one of its possible instances with its visual representation:

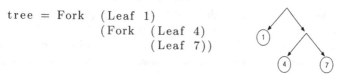

```
tree = Fork   (Leaf 1)
              (Fork   (Leaf 4)
                      (Leaf 7))
```

We may notice that, in particular, each of *tree*'s subtree occupies a certain location in *tree*, if we consider it as a whole. That location may be represented by the subtree under consideration and by the rest of the tree, which is viewed as the context of that subtree. For instance, the context of *Leaf* 4 in *tree* is

```
Fork   (Leaf 1)
       (Fork   focus
               (Leaf 7))
```

where *focus* marks a hole which corresponds exactly to the spot where *Leaf* 4 appears in *tree*. One of the possible ways to represent this context is as a path from the top of the tree to the hole. To reach *Leaf* 4 in *tree*, we need to go down the right branch and then down the left one.

Using this idea, we can easily reach *Leaf* 4 in *tree* using the generic zippers provided by [8]. We start by encapsulating *tree* into a zipper:

```
a = to_Zipper tree
```

where a has the type $a :: Zipper\ Tree$. With this, it is simple to traverse a and the position of the tree where *Leaf* 4 is:

```
b = let  d = fromJust (down a)
    in   fromJust (down' d)
```

In this operation, we go to the rightmost child using *down*, and then to the leftmost child using *down'*. Since all the functions of this library wrap the result inside a data type to make them total, we also have to unwrap the result every time a function is called. We do so simply by using the function $fromJust$[1].

The result of this operation has the type $b :: ZipperTree$, meaning that b is a zipper like a, with the difference of having a different *focus*. With this said, if we ask for the focus of b, using the function *getHole*:

```
let focus = getHole b :: Maybe Tree
focus = Leaf 4
```

In this formalism, the semantics are dependent on information that is immediately above or below of a certain tree position, concept which is directly provided by zippers and the associated navigation functions.

The zipper data structure provides an elegant and efficient way of manipulating locations inside a data structure. Zippers are particularly useful for performing incremental edits on tree structures. Zippers have already been used in

---

[1] We are not really checking for totality, otherwise we would have to test each function call against a set of possible results. For simplicity we are just assuming the function produced a result and we are directly unwrapping it with $fromJust$.

the implementation of filesystems [10] and window managers [11], but they are applicable anytime there is a focal point for edits. In the implementation of a filesystem, the current working directory is the focal point of attention, and in a window manager it is the window with focus.

In the next section, we show how we abstract this library of zippers by creating a set of constructors that resemble more closely the traditional formalism to implement AGs.

2.1 Abstracting the Generic Zippers

The generic zipper library presented on previous section provides a useful set of functions to navigate throughout data types. However, it is our intention to abstract as much as possible from this library and create a setting where *Haskell* constructors are as similar as possible to the typical primitives used in Attribute Grammars. In this section we present a set of functions that allows the easy navigation of data types, that does not require further testings for the user (for example, we abstract over totality checks) and leverages the implementation to one much closer to AGs.

Let us consider a concrete data type to represent programs in an Algol 68-like language restricted to expressing declarations and uses of variables. Programs in this language consist of instruction blocks, where each instruction declares a variable, uses a variable or defines a nested instruction block. A small example of a program in this language is

p = [decl ' y; [decl ' w; use ' x;] use ' y;]

In order to represent programs in the Algol 68 language, we define the following *Haskell* data-type. This data-type will be used, in Sect. 4, to implement a semantic analyzer for that language:

```
data Root = Root Its
       deriving (Typeable , Data)
data Its  = ConsIts It Its | NilIts
       deriving (Typeable , Data)
data It   = Decl String | Use String | Block Its
       deriving (Typeable , Data)
```

In this representation, p is defined as:

```
p = Root (ConsIts  (Decl "y")
                (ConsIts  (Block  (ConsIts  (Decl "w")
                          (ConsIts  (Use "x") NilIts )))
                (ConsIts  (Use "y") NilIts )))
```

Our goal now is to navigate on elements of type P in the same way that we traversed elements of type *Tree*, in Sect. 2. Using our Attribute Grammar-based approach, instead of writing concrete location navigation functions, the user is only required to declare the data types to traverse as deriving from the *Data* and *Typeable* type classes, which are provided as part of GHC's[2] libraries. This

---

[2] The Glasgow Haskell Compiler, http://www.haskell.org/ghc/.

means we will be immediately able to navigate through the data types *Root*, *Its* and *It* using the zipper-provided functions.

Suppose that we want to traverse the previous *Algol* phrase to the identifier of the variable that is being used in the nested block of p. The first thing to do is to get p inside a zipper:

g_1 :: Zipper Root
g_1 = to_{Zipper} (Root p)

In order to reach the desired nested block on the program p, we now need to go down from the root location created in $g1$. We do this using function .$, as follows:

g_2 = g.$1 :: Zipper Root

Data type locations do not need any information about the types of their children, but neither does the user. Because we are embedding *Algol* in *Haskell*, and *Haskell* has a strong type system, type correctness is always necessarily enforced meaning a phrase of *Algol* is always type-valid. And because the zipper does not need any contextual information, regarding what is above or below a given position, this information is abstracted from the user as well. Of course, one must be aware of the position of a tree where certain computation needs to be performed, but our setting adds an increased level of abstraction comparing with traditional *Haskell* programs while retaining the same core language features such as type safety or referential transparency.

Retuning to our example, the value held by the location g_2 is one position below the initial focus on the zipper, which was *Root*. As expected, $g2$ yields:

```
g₂ = ( ConsIts   ( Decl  "y" )
                 ( ConsIts   ( Block   ( ConsIts   ( Decl "w" )
                             ( ConsIts   ( Use  "x" )  NilIts )))
                 ( ConsIts   ( Use  "y" )  NilIts )))
```

We need to continue going down on p, if we want to edit the declaration of the variable "w":

g_1 = g_2 . $2

With $g3$:

```
g₁ = ConsIts   ( Block   ( ConsIts   ( Decl  "w" )
                         ( ConsIts   ( Use  "x" )  NilIts )))
               ( ConsIts   ( Use  "y" )  NilIts )
```

Notice that function .$ is a generic function, that applies to locations on any data type that derives from *Typeable* and *Data*. It is not even the case that. $ applies only to data-types that have the same number of children. What is more, *Root* has a single data-type child, *Its*, and that *Its* may have two children, *It* and *Its*. When .$ is applied with a constructor that has more than one child, it will go down to the user-defined one. This is precisely how the original Attribute Grammars formalism works: semantics on a tree site depend on the parent if they are inherited, or on specific children that in our setting are numerically defined.

We can see that the declaration of variable $"w"$ occurs in the first (left) child of the current location. This means that if we apply function .$1 to g_3 we will immediately go to the correct child:

$$g_4 = g_1 . \$1$$

Location g_4 holds, as expected, the nested block of instructions that occurs both in p, and in g_3:

$$g_4 = \text{Block (ConsIts } \quad (\text{Decl } "w")$$
$$(\text{ConsIts } \quad (\text{Use } "x") \quad \text{NilIts}))$$

We continue our navigation performing another *go down* step to access the instructions in the nested block on g_4,

$$g_4 = g_4 . \$1$$

obtaining:

$$g_4 = \text{ConsIts } \quad (\text{Decl } "w")$$
$$(\text{ConsIts } \quad (\text{Use } "x") \quad \text{NilIts})$$

An important remark is that in this block (g_5) we declare a variable $"w"$ but use a variable $"x"$; intuitively, the identifiers of these two variables should probably match. The zipper library we use provides primitives to change the parts of a tree. In this example, we could easily correct the wrong assignment of $"x"$ (or declaration of $"w"$). We do not worry about this as this is not a traditional behavior of Attribute Grammars.

Attribute Grammars as a formalism is extremely suitable to perform tree transformations, but such operations are typically implemented by designing a set of attributes that traverses the tree and whose result is a new, refactored one. With this in mind, using AGs we would not change ou zipper, we would instead create a new, corrected tree (as we do in Sects. 3 and 5). Nevertheless, such operation is possible and the functions provided in the generic zipper library we use are compatible with our abstraction of tree navigation functions with (.$), serving as a reminder of the adaptability of our approach.

In the next sections, we show how the generic zipper framework introduced in this section can be used to solve different programming problems.

3   The Repmin

In [1], it was originally proposed to solve *repmin* using a circular program, i.e., a program where, in the same function call, one of its results is at the same time on of its arguments. With his work, Bird showed that any algorithm that performs multiple traversals over the same data structure can be expressed in a lazy language as a single traversal circular program.

Furthermore, using circular programming, the programmer does not have to concern himself with the definition and the scheduling of the different traversal functions and, because there is a single traversal functions, neither does the programmer have to define intermediate gluing data structures to convey information between traversals.

Writing circular programs, however, forces the programmer to encode together all the arguments and results that are used in the circular call. When functions have many arguments as well as many results, it is often preferable to express multiple traversal algorithms in terms of attribute grammars (AGs), that have been proved to be strongly related to circular programs [12,13]. The AG programming paradigm does not force the programmer to encode all the aspects together.

Returning to our example, in [4], the authors identified three components for solving *repmin*: computing the minimal value, passing down the minimal value from the root to the leaves and constructing the resulting tree. In this section, we review the Attribute Grammar for *repmin* that was introduced by [14], and show how each of the three components identified by [4] in that grammar can be embedded in *Haskell* using our approach.

The attribute grammar for *repmin* starts by defining the underlying data structure, i.e., binary leaf trees. The attribute grammar fragments presented in this section follow the standard AG notation of [14]. In this notation, we straightforwardly use the *Tree* datatype from Sect. 2.

Having defined the structure, we need to define functionality. We start by reviewing the AG component that computes the minimal value of a tree:

```
SYN Tree [smin : Int]
SEM   Tree  | Leaf lhs.smin =  @v
            | Fork lhs.smin =  @left.smin
                                  'min'
                               @right.smin
```

This component declares, using the *SYN* keyword, that elements of type *Tree* synthesize an attribute *smin* of type *Int*. Then, a *SEM* sentence defines how *smin* is computed: when the current tree is a leaf, clearly its minimal value is the leaf value itself; when it is the fork of two other trees (the *left* and the *right* subtrees), we compute the minimal values of each subtree (i.e., their *smin* attribute), and then their minimal value (function *min*). In this notation, *lhs* refers to the left-hand side symbol of the production and @ prefixes a reference to a field.

Our zipper-based embedding of this component is defined as:

```
smin :: Zipper Root -> Int
smin t = case constructor t of
         "Root" -> smin (t.$1)
         "Leaf" -> lexeme t
         "Fork" -> min (smin (t.$1)) (smin (t.$2))
```

Function *constructor*, given in Sect. 3.1, maps any element to a textual representation of its constructor. Function *lexeme* is also defined in Sect. 3.1 to compute the concrete value in any leaf of a tree.

We can see that the embedding of *smin* that we obtain very much directly follows from its AG specification.

Having implemented the first of the three components that solve *repmin*, we now consider the remaining two. We start by implementing the construction of the result of *repmin*, a tree with all leaves being the minimum of the original one.

```
SYN   Tree [sres : Tree]
SEM   Tree  | Leaf lhs.sres  = Leaf @lhs.ival
            | Fork lhs.sres  = Fork @left.sres @right.sres
```

We are now defining an attribute *sres*, again synthesized by elements of type *Tree*. This attribute definition may again be mapped to our setting very easily. We obtain the following implementation:

```
sres :: Zipper Root -> Tree
sres t = case constructor t of
            "Root" -> sres ( t.$1 )
            "Leaf" -> Leaf (ival t)
            "Fork" -> Fork (sres (t.$1)) (sres (t.$2))
```

The implementation of *sres* places in each leaf of a tree the value of the *ival* attribute. This value corresponds to the minimal value of the global tree, that still needs to be passed down to all the nodes in the tree. This corresponds exactly to the third component that we still need to implement. In order to bind the minimal value being computed (attribute *smin*) with the minimal value that is passed down through the tree (attribute *ival*), it is common, in the AG setting, to add a new data-type definition,

```
DATA Root | Root tree : Tree
```

and a new semantic rule,

```
SEM   Root | Root tree.ival = @tree.smin
```

Passing down *ival* then becomes:

```
INH   Tree [ival : Int]
SEM   Tree | Fork left  .ival = @lhs.ival
                  right .ival = @lhs.ival
```

In our setting, we closely follow this approach and always introduce a new data type that marks the topmost position of the tree, in this case, "*Root*".

When the current location corresponds to the top one, we have to define the values of *smin* to *ival* in this particular position. In our setting, we then define the attribute *ival* as follows (we use the location navigation function *parent* to access the parent of a tree location):

```
ival :: Zipper Root -> Int
ival t = case constructor t of
            "Root" -> smin t
            "Leaf" -> ival (parent t)
            "Fork" -> ival (parent t)
```

Notice that we do not explicitly distinguish between inherited and synthesized attributes. Like in modern attribute grammar systems [14,15], inherited attributes, such as *ival*, correspond to attributes that are defined in parent nodes.

Having defined the three components that allow us to solve the *repmin* problem, we may now define a semantic function that takes a tree and produces a *repmined* tree, using these components:

```
semantics :: Root -> Tree
semantics t = replace (toZipper t)
```

Regarding this implementation, we may notice that it has the best properties of the two *transform* solutions presented in Sect. 1. First, it is modular, since the global computational effort has been separated into several components, and does not rely on laziness, like the first *transform* implementation. Second, it constructs no intermediate structure and it requires no explicit scheduling: notice that *smin, replace* and *ival* were defined with no particular focus on the order they need to be computed.

In this section, we have presented a solution to the *repmin* problem in terms of an attribute grammar. Our solution is expressed in *Haskell* and closely follows common attribute grammar notation. We showed that we can easily intermingle separate concerns with the implementation's basic functionality, which itself has been split into different components. Therefore, we believe that our framework is very appropriate for static aspect oriented programming [16] in a functional language.

3.1 Boilerplate Code

Our goal with this paper was to address concerns of the expression problem without relying in an opaque and possibly complex pre-processor. A disadvantage of this approach is that some code that may be considered boilerplate code needs to be manually defined. Function *constructor*, that we have used throughout the paper to map an element to a textual representation of its constructor, is a function clearly in this set: it goes down all the possible constructors and tries to match them with a given element.

```
constructor :: Zipper Root -> String
constructor a = case (getHole a :: Maybe Tree) of
        Just (Fork _ _) -> "Fork"
        Just (Leaf _)   -> "Leaf"
            otherwise -> case (getHole a :: Maybe Root ) of
                    Just (Root _) -> "Root"
```

For each individual argument, *constructor* matches an element wrapped up in a zipper against the constructors of the data-type *Tree*. In this example, *constructor* matches an element against the constructors *Fork, Leaf* and *Root*, creating a *String* representation of them.

The other function that we have used and that could easily be given by a pre-processor is function *lexeme*, that computes the value in any leaf of a tree. In the leaves of our running example's trees, we only have elements of on one data constructor, *Leaf*, and these elements are always of type *Int*. So, it suffices to define:

```
lexeme :: Zipper Root -> Int
lexeme t = let Leaf v = fromJust (getHole t :: Maybe Tree)
           in  v
```

As we said, the functions defined in this section could easily be given by a pre-processor. Indeed, we could have implemented a simple program to go through the Haskell's abstract syntax tree that we obtain by parsing the data-types definitions of Sect. 3 and finding all its constructors (for *constructor*) and all its leaves (for *lexeme*). We, however, opted not to use this pre-processor approach because we wanted to give clear and transparent definitions for all the functions involved in our framework that also could be edited in a simple way by any programmer. What's more, the use of a pre-processor is often considered a disadvantage when one needs to choose to re-use a tool or a setting against some others.

4   The Algol 68 Scope Rules

In this section we present an attribute grammar that uses the tree navigating mechanism of the generic zipper presented in the previous sections to implement the Algol 68 scope rules [17]. These rules are used, for example, in the Eli system [18] to define a generic component for the name analysis task of a compiler.

We wish to construct a modular and deforested program to deal with the scope rules of the block structured language introduced in Sect. 2.1. If the reader recalls the running example, named "p", there was an identifier "x" which was visible in the smallest enclosing block, with the exception of local blocks that also contain a definition of "x". In the latter case, the definition of "x" in the local scope hides the definition in the global one. In a block an identifier may be declared at most once. In Sect. 2.1, p is a simple example of a program we want to analyze. The following program illustrates a more complex situation where an inner declaration of "y" hides an outer one.

```
p'= [ use'   y; decl' x;
            [ decl' y; use' y; use' w;]
      decl' x; decl' y;  ]
```

Programs such as p or p' describe the basic block-structure found in many languages, with the peculiarity that declarations of identifiers may also occur after their first use. According to these rules, p' contains two errors: a) at the outer level, the variable "x" has been declared twice, and b) the use of the variable "w", at the inner level, has no binding occurrence at all.

We aim to develop a program that analyses *Algol* programs and computes a list containing the identifiers which do not obey the scope rules. In order to make it easier to detect which identifiers are being incorrectly used in a program, we require that the list of invalid identifiers follows the sequential structure of the program. Thus, the semantic meaning of processing p' is $[w, x]$.

Because we allow use before declaration, a conventional implementation of the required analysis leads to a program which traverses the abstract syntax tree twice: once to accumulate the declarations of identifiers and construct an environment, and again to check the uses of identifiers using the computed environment. The uniqueness of names is detected in the first traversal: for each newly encountered declaration we check whether the identifier has already been declared at the current level. In this case an error message is computed. Of course the identifier might have been declared at an outer level. Thus we need to distinguish between identifiers declared at different levels. We use the level of a block to achieve this. The environment is a partial function mapping an identifier to its level of declaration.

As a consequence, semantic errors resulting from duplicate definitions are computed during the first traversal of a block and errors resulting from missing declarations in the second one. A straightforward implementation of this program may be sketched as[3]:

```
semantics :: P -> Errors
semantics p = missing_decls (duplicate_decls p)
duplicate_decls :: P -> (P', Env)
missing_decls    :: (P', Env) -> Errors
```

In this implementation, a *"gluing'"* data structure, of type P', has to be defined by the programmer and is constructed to pass the detected errors explicitly from the first to the second traversal, in order to compute the final list of errors in the desired order. To be able to compute the missing declarations of a block, the implementation also has to explicitly pass the names of the variables that are used in a block between the two traversals of the block. This information must therefore also be in the P' intermediate structure.

We start by defining an *Haskell* datatype that describes *Algol* syntactically, whose data constructors will be, similarly to AGs, used as semantic points on which functions (read attributes) will be defined.

```
data Root = Root Its

data Its = ConsIts It Its
         | NilIts

data It = Decl String
        | Use String
        | Block Its
```

Next, we implement the same analysis but in terms of an attribute grammar that does not rely on the construction of any intermediate structure.

As stated before, the language presented in this chapter does not force a *declare − before − use* discipline, which means a conventional implementation of the required analysis naturally leads to a program that traverses each block twice: once for processing the declarations of identifiers and constructing an environment and a second time to process the uses of identifiers (using the computed environment) in order to check for the use of non-declared identifiers.

---

[3] The interested reader may find in [17,19] strict and circular solutions to solve these scope rules.

An algorithm for processing this language as to be designed in two traversals:

- On a first traversal, the algorithm has to collect the list of local definitions and, secondly, detect duplicate definitions from the collected ones.
- On a second traversal, the algorithm has to use the list of definitions from the previous step as the global environment, detect the use of non-defined variables and finally combine the erros from both traversals.

Next, we will define the semantics of the grammar. For every block we compute three things: its environment, its lexical level and its invalid identifiers. The environment defines the context where the block occurs. It consists of all the identifiers that are visible in the block. The lexical level indicates the nesting level of a block. Observe that we have to distinguish between the same identifier declared at different levels, which is a valid declaration (for example, "*decl y''*" in p'), and the same identifier declared at the same level, which is an invalid declaration (for example, "*decl x*" in p'). Finally, we have to compute the list of identifiers that are incorrectly used, i.e., the list of errors.

The Attribute Grammar that analyses a phrase of *Algol* will be composed by:

- An environment, attribute *env*, which consists of all the identifiers that are visible in the block: *type Env* $= [(String, Int)]$.
- A lexical level, attribute *lev*, which indicates the nesting level of a block: *type Level* $= Int$.
- The invalid identifiers, attribute *errs*, which contains the list of identifiers that are incorrectly used: *type Errors* $= [String]$.

We start by defining the construction of the environment of an *Algol* program. Every block inherits the environment of its outer block. Therefore, we associate an inherited attribute *dcli*, that carries an environment, to the non-terminal symbols *Its* and *It* that define a block. The inherited environment is threaded through the block in order to accumulate the local definitions and in this way synthesizes the total environment of the block. We associate a synthesized attribute *dclo*, that also carries the environment, to the non-terminal symbols *Its* and *It*, which defines the newly computed environment.

In our solution, we defined semantic *Haskell* functions which pattern match on data constructors. For the readers familiar with Attribute Grammars, there is an obvious mapping between *Haskell* functions and attributes, and between data constructors and grammar productions. The attributes *dcli* and *dclo* are declared as follows:

```
dcli :: Zipper Root -> [(String, Int)]
dcli z = case (constructor z) of
           "Root"-> []
           "NilIts"-> case (constructor (parent z)) of
                        "ConsIts"-> dclo ((parent z).$1)
                        "Block"  -> env (parent z)
                        "Root"   -> []
           "ConsIts"-> case (constructor (parent z)) of
```

```
                    "ConsIts"-> dclo ((parent z).$1)
                    "Block"  -> env (parent z)
                    "Root"   -> []
        "Block"  -> dcli (parent z)
        "Use"    -> dcli (parent z)
        "Decl"   -> dcli (parent z)

dclo :: Zipper Root -> [(String, Int)]
dclo z = case (constructor z) of
         "ConsIts"-> dclo (z.$2)
         "NilIts" -> dcli z
         "Use"    -> dcli z
         "Decl"   -> (value z, lev z) : (dcli z)
         "Block"  -> dcli z
```

The only production that contributes to the synthesized environment of a phrase of *Algol* is *Decl*. The single semantic equation of this production makes use of the semantic function ':' (written in infix notation) to build the environment. Note that we are using the *Haskell* type definition presented previously. The use of pairs is used to bind an identifier to its lexical level. The single occurrence of pseudo-terminal *Name* is a syntactically referenced in the equation since it is used as a normal value of the semantic function. All the other semantic equations of this fragment simply pass the environment to the left-hand side and right-hand side symbols within the respective productions.

Now that the total environment of a block is defined, we pass that context down to the body of the block in order to detect applied occurrences of undefined identifiers. Thus, we define a second inherited that also carries the environment, called *env*, to distribute the total environment. It should be noticed that attribute *dclo* can be used to correctly compute the required list of errors. We choose to distribute the list of declarations in a new attribute to demonstrate our techniques, as with this approach we force a two traversal (strict) evaluation scheme. Although this approach is not really needed in the trivial *Algol* language, it is a common feature when defining real languages. *Env* is defined as:

```
env :: Zipper Root -> [(String, Int)]
env z = case (constructor z) of
          "NilIts"-> case (constructor (parent z)) of
                      "Block"  -> dclo z
                      "ConsIts"-> env (parent z)
                      "Block"  -> dclo z
          "ConsIts"-> case (constructor (parent z)) of
                      "Block"  -> dclo z
                      "ConsIts"-> env (parent z)
                      "Root"   -> dclo z
          "Block"  -> env (parent z)
          "Use"    -> env (parent z)
          "Decl"   -> env (parent z)
          "Root"   -> dclo z
```

The first semantic equation of *Block* specifies that the inner blocks inherit the environment of their outer ones. As a result, only after computing the environment of a block is it possible to process its nested blocks. That is, inner blocks will be processed in the second traversal of the outer one.

The total environment of the inner blocks, however, is the synthesized environment (attribute *dclo*), as defined for *Block*. It is also worthwhile to note that the equations:

```
"Root"   -> dclo z
"Block"  -> dclo z
```

induce a dependency from a synthesized to an inherited attribute of the same symbol.

Every block has a lexical level. Thus, we introduce one inherited attribute *lev* indicating the nesting level of a block. The *Haskell* primitive function '+' is used to increment the value of the lexical level passed to the inner blocks:

```
lev :: Zipper Root -> Int
lev z = case (constructor z) of
          "Root"   -> 0
          "NilIts" -> case (constructor $ parent z) of
                  "Block"  -> (lev (parent z)) + 1
                  "ConsIts"-> lev (parent z)
                  "Root"   -> 0
          "ConsIts"-> case (constructor (parent z)) of
                  "Block"  -> (lev (parent z)) + 1
                  "ConsIts"-> lev (parent z)
                  "Root"   -> 0
          "Block"  -> lev (parent z)
          "Use"    -> lev (parent z)
          "Decl"   -> lev (parent z)
```

Finally, we have to synthesize one attribute defining the (static) semantic errors. We define a second synthesized attribute: *errs*. The attribution rules for this semantic domain are shown next:

```
errs :: Zipper Root -> [String]
errs z = case (constructor z) of
          "Root"   -> errs (z.$1)
          "NilIts" -> []
          "ConsIts"-> (errs (z.$1)) ++ (errs (z.$2))
          "Use"    -> mBIn (value z) (env z)
          "Decl"   -> mNBIn (value z, lev z) (dcli z)
          "Block"  -> errs (z.$1)
```

There are two semantic functions that we need to define: *mBIn* and *mNBIn*. The definition of these functions must be included in the grammar specification. For this reason, attribute grammar specification languages provide an additional notation in which semantic functions can be defined. Generally, this notation is simply a standard programming language. We are embedding AG's so we use plain *Haskell* for these functions. Thus, the two semantic functions look as follows:

```
mBIn :: String -> [(String, Int)] -> [String]
mBIn name [] = [name]
mBIn name ((n,l):es) = if (n==name) then []
                                    else mBIn name es

mNBIn :: (String, Int) -> [(String, Int)] -> [String]
mNBIn tuple [] = []
mNBIn pair (pl:es) = if (pair==pl) then [fst pair]
                                   else mNBIn pair es
```

We may now define a program that implements the semantic analysis described, simply by inspecting the *errs* attribute computed at the topmost location of the program:

```
semantics :: P -> [String]
semantics p = errs (to_Zipper p)
```

This program can be used to compute the list of errors occurring in the p and p' programs presented before. As expected, we obtain:

```
semantics p  = ["x"]
semantics p' = ["w","x"]
```

5   Breadth-First Numbering

The running examples presented so far have shown that zippers provide a modular and intermediate structure free environment for implementing multiple traversal algorithms in a functional setting. A key aspect of the implementations seen earlier in the paper is that they make no essential use of laziness. In fact, all of these implementations could be *straightforwardly* translated and implemented in a strict setting. This property does not hold for the example that we study in this section.

Consider the problem, described in detail in [20], of breadth first numbering a binary tree, or *bfn* for short. A sample input/output to such problem is sketched next.

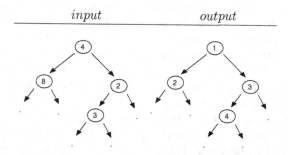

In order to tackle this problem, we follow the approach taken by [20]. To implement *bfn*, the author computes a list of integers representing the first available index on each of the levels of the input tree. This list is initially the infinite list of ones and is updated as it goes down the tree to produce the numbering.

In order to implement this algorithm we will need three attributes. Attribute *slist* will be used to compute the list of indexes and *ilist* to pass that list down the tree. Attribute *replace* will hold the result of breadth-first numbering a tree. Attributes *slist* and *replace* have the same definition for any tree, regardless of whether it is the topmost one or one of its subtrees. In this example, we follow Okasaki by using binary trees instead of binary leaf trees:

```
data Tree = Fork Int Tree Tree | Empty
            deriving (Typeable, Data)
```

Attributes *slist* and *replace* are defined as follows, for any *tree* location:

```
slist :: Zipper Root -> [Int]
slist z = case (constructor z) of
            "Fork" -> (head (ilist z) + 1) : (slist (z.$3))
            "Empty"-> ilist z
```

```
replace :: Zipper Root -> Tree
replace z = case (constructor z) of
              "Empty"-> Empty
              "Fork" -> Fork (head (ilist z))
                        (replace (z.$2)) (replace (z.$3))
              "Root"-> replace (z.$1)
```

The third attribute, *ilist*, is a little bit more tricky. We have to defined *ilist* for the upmost location on the input tree, which we do by testing if the parent is the "*Root*". We then define the following values for *ilist*:

```
ilist :: Zipper Root -> [Int]
ilist z = case (constructor (parent z)) of
            "Root"     -> [1] ++ (slist z)
            {- If z is the third child, it is the rightmost one-}
            otherwise -> case (z.|3) of
                          True  -> slist (fromJust (left z))
                          False -> tail (ilist (parent z))
```

Notice the very peculiar relationship between attributes *ilist* and *slist* at the top level: *ilist* is defined as the list whose head is 1 and whose tail is *slist*, and *slist* is defined as the list whose head is the head of *ilist* incremented by 1 and whose tail is the *slist* value computed for the right subtree of the current tree. Then, if we try to compute, for example, the value of *ilist* in a strict setting, this will cause the value of *slist* to be fully computed. But *slist* can not be computed until *ilist* is itself computed. Therefore, in a strict setting, these computations can not be ordered, and this particular program can not be directly implemented in such a setting. In a lazy setting, however, the use of *head*, the standard operator that selects the first element of a list, makes it possible for the above program to terminate. So, even though our approach does not fundamentally dependent on laziness, attribute definitions that use laziness can be accommodated.

It is now simple to obtain a bfn transformer for binary trees:

```
transform :: Tree -> Tree
transform t = replace (to_Zipper (Root t))
```

6   Related Work

In this paper, we have shown how the zipper data structure can be used to implement multiple traversal algorithms in a functional language. The implementations we obtain are modular, do not require the use of intermediate data structures and do not fundamentally rely on laziness. That is to say that our implementations benefit from the best of the two traditional ways of expressing multiple traversal programs described in the introduction.

Uustalu and Vene [21] use zippers in their approach to embed computations using comonadic structures, with tree nodes paired with attribute values. However, the zipper approach they use does not appear to be generic and must be individually instantiated for each new structure. They also rely on laziness to avoid static scheduling.

Zippers are also used by Badouel *et al.* [22], where zipper transformers define evaluations. This approach relies on laziness and their zipper representation is not generic. This is also the case of [23], that similarly requires laziness and forces the programmer to be aware of a cyclic representation of zippers.

Yakushev *et al.* [24] use mutually recursive data types, for which operations are described with a fixed point strategy. In this work, data structures are translated into generic representations, used for traversals and updates, and translated back after. This solution implies the extra overhead of the translations, and also requires advanced features of *Haskell* such as type families and rank-2 types.

We have showed previously how zippers can be used to embed AGs on a functional setting, together with modern extensions [7,25]. Even though our library is defined in *Haskell*, a lazy language, we do not make essential use of laziness, making the approach extendable to strict languages.

With this work we further extend the functionalities of functional zippers and show these can be used as a substitute to traditional programming techniques in a functional setting: while we do not rely on laziness, we present a setting where the programmer can abstract from function scheduling and intermediate data types and focus on more modular programs.

7   Conclusions

In this paper we presented a zipper-based approach to elegantly and modularly express circular programs in a functional setting. Our approach does not rely on laziness such as circular programs do, and does not force the programmer to deal with intermediate data structures nor to schedule multiple traversal functions. Our solution uses functional zippers as a mechanism to allow generic tree traversals upon which traversal functions are defined.

We have further proof-tested our approach by embedding other languages in *Haskell*, using implementations that avoid functions scheduling and intermediate data structures. These, together with the examples from this paper, can be found in www.di.uminho.pt/~prmartins or in the cabal package *zipperAG*.

As future work we plan to study both the design and implementation of our embedding when compared to other techniques. Thus, we plan to study how our embedding compares to first class AGs [2,26]. Circular programs are known to have some performance overhead due to lazy evaluation. We want to study the performance of the zipper embedding, and how the strictification techniques persented in [27] could be adapted to our setting.

References

1. Bird, R.: Using circular programs to eliminate multiple traversals of data. Acta Informatica **21**, 239–250 (1984)
2. de Moor, O., Backhouse, K., Swierstra, S.D.: First-class attribute grammars. Informatica (Slovenia) **24**(3), 329–341 (2000)
3. Fernandes, J.P., Pardo, A., Saraiva, J.: A shortcut fusion rule for circular program calculation. In: Proceedings of the ACM SIGPLAN Haskell Workshop, pp. 95–106 (2007)
4. Viera, M., Swierstra, D., Swierstra, W.: Attribute grammars fly first-class: How to do aspect oriented programming in haskell. In: Proceedings of the 14th ACM SIGPLAN International Conference on Functional Programming (ICFP 2009), pp. 245–256 (2009)
5. Swierstra, D., Chitil, O.: Linear, bounded, functional pretty-printing. J. Func. Programm. **19**(01), 1–16 (2009)
6. Huet, G.: The zipper. J. Func. Programm. **7**(5), 549–554 (1997)
7. Martins, P., Fernandes, J.P., Saraiva, J.: Zipper-based attribute grammars and their extensions. In: Du Bois, A.R., Trinder, P. (eds.) SBLP 2013. LNCS, vol. 8129, pp. 135–149. Springer, Heidelberg (2013)
8. Adams, M.D.: Scrap your zippers: A generic zipper for heterogeneous types. In: Proceedings of the 6th ACM SIGPLAN Workshop on Generic Programming, WGP 2010, pp. 13–24. ACM, New York (2010)
9. Lämmel, R., Jones, S.P.: Scrap your boilerplate: A practical design pattern for generic programming. In: Proceedings of the 2003 ACM SIGPLAN International WorkShop on Types in Language Design and Implementation, (TLDI 2003), pp. 26–37. ACM (2003)
10. Kiselyov, O.: Tool demonstration: A zipper based file/operating system. In: Haskell Workshop. ACM Press, September 2005
11. Stewart, D., Janssen, S.: XMonad: A tiling window manager. In: Haskell 2007: Proceedings of the 2007 ACM SIGPLAN Workshop on Haskell. ACM Press (2007)
12. Johnsson, T.: Attribute grammars as a functional programming paradigm. In: Functional Programming Languages and Computer Architecture, pp. 154–173 (1987)

13. Kuiper, M., Swierstra, D.: Using attribute grammars to derive efficient functional programs. In: Computing Science in the Netherlands CSN 1987, November 1987
14. Swierstra, S.D., Azero Alcocer, P.R., Saraiva, J.: Designing and implementing combinator languages. In: Swierstra, S.D., Oliveira, J.N. (eds.) AFP 1998. LNCS, vol. 1608, pp. 150–206. Springer, Heidelberg (1999)
15. Swierstra, D., Baars, A., Löh, A.: The UU-AG attribute grammar system (2004)
16. Kiczales, G., Lamping, J., Mendhekar, A., Maeda, C., Lopes, C.V., Loingtier, J.M., Irwin, J.: Aspect-oriented programming. In: ECOOP, pp. 220–242 (1997)
17. Saraiva, J.: Purely functional implementation of attribute grammars. Ph.D. Thesis, Department of Computer Science, Utrecht University, The Netherlands, December 1999
18. Kastens, U., Pfahler, P., Jung, M.T.: The eli system. In: Koskimies, K. (ed.) CC 1998. LNCS, vol. 1383, pp. 294–297. Springer, Heidelberg (1998)
19. Fernandes, J.P.: Design, implementation and calculation of circular programs. Ph.D. Thesis, Department of Informatics, University of Minho, Portugal, March 2009
20. Okasaki, C.: Breadth-first numbering: lessons from a small exercise in algorithm design. ACM SIGPLAN Notices 35(9), 131–136 (2000)
21. Uustalu, T., Vene, V.: Comonadic functional attribute evaluation. In: Trends in Functional Programming, Intellect Books, vol. 10, pp. 145–162 (2005)
22. Badouel, E., Fotsing, B., Tchougong, R.: Yet another implementation of attribute evaluation. Research Report RR-6315, INRIA (2007)
23. Badouel, E., Fotsing, B., Tchougong, R.: Attribute grammars as recursion schemes over cyclic representations of zippers. Electron. Notes Theory Comput. Sci. 229(5), 39–56 (2011)
24. Yakushev, A.R., Holdermans, S., Löh, A., Jeuring, J.: Generic programming with fixed points for mutually recursive datatypes. In: Proceedings of the 14th ACM SIGPLAN International Conference on Functional programming, pp. 233–244 (2009)
25. Martins, P.: Embedding attribute grammars and their extensions using functional zippers. Ph.D. Thesis, Universidade do Minho (2014)
26. Viera, M., Swierstra, S.D., Swierstra, W.: Attribute grammars fly first-class: how to do aspect oriented programming in haskell. SIGPLAN Not. 44(9), 245–256 (2009)
27. Fernandes, J.P., Saraiva, J., Seidel, D., Voigtländer, J.: Strictification of circular programs. In: Proceedings of the 20th ACM SIGPLAN Workshop on Partial Evaluation and Program Manipulation. PEPM 2011, pp. 131–140. ACM, New York (2011)

Tasklets: Client-Side Evaluation for iTask3

László Domoszlai[1][(✉)] and Rinus Plasmeijer[2]

[1] Department of Programming Languages and Compilers,
Eötvös Loránd University, Budapest, Hungary
dlacko@gmail.com
[2] Software Technology Department, Radboud University, Nijmegen, The Netherlands
rinus@cs.ru.nl

Abstract. iTask3 is the most recent incarnation of the iTask framework for the construction of distributed systems where users work together on the internet. It offers a domain specific language for defining applications, embedded into the lazy functional language Clean. From the mere declarative specification a complete multi-user web application is generated. Although the generated nature of the user interface (UI) entails a number of benefits for the programmer, it suffers from the lack of possibility to create custom UI building blocks. In this paper, we present an extension to the iTask3 framework which introduces the concept of *tasklets* for the development of custom, interactive web components in a single language manner. We further show that the presented tasklet architecture can be generalized in such a way that arbitrary parts of an iTask application can be executed on the client.

1 Introduction

The iTask framework was originally developed as a dedicated web-based Workflow Management System (WFMS). Its most recent incarnation, iTask3 [14], however, extends its boundaries beyond classical WFMS and offers a novel programming paradigm for the construction of distributed systems where users work together on the internet.

According to the iTask paradigm, the unit of application logic is a *task*. Tasks are abstract descriptions of interactive persistent units of work that have a typed value. When a task is executed, it has an opaque persistent value, which can be observed by other tasks in a controlled way. In iTask, complex multi-user interactions can be programmed in a declarative style just by defining the tasks that have to be accomplished. The specification of the tasks is given by a domain specific language embedded in the pure, lazy functional language Clean. Furthermore, the specification is given on a very high level of abstraction and does not require the programmer to provide any user interface definition. Merely by defining the workflow of user interaction, a complete multi-user web application is generated, all the details e.g. the generation of web user interface, client-server communication, state management etc. are automatically taken care of by the framework itself.

© Springer International Publishing Switzerland 2015
V. Zsók et al. (Eds.): CEFP 2013, LNCS 8606, pp. 428–445, 2015.
DOI: 10.1007/978-3-319-15940-9_11

Developing web applications such a way is straightforward in the sense that the programmers are liberated from these cumbersome and error-prone jobs, such that they can concentrate on the essence of the application. The iTask system makes it very easy to develop interactive multi-user applications. The down side is that one has only limited control over the customization of the generated user interface, but for this type of applications, this is often acceptable. However, the experiment with real world applications, e.g. the implementation of the Netherlands Coast Guard's Search and Rescue (SAR) protocol [10,11], indicated that even if the functional web design is satisfactory, custom building blocks may be required for the purpose of user-friendliness. A good example is the aforementioned SAR workflow, where Google MAPS widgets complemented the otherwise functional web application to visualize the locations of incidents.

To overcome this shortcoming, in this paper we present an extension for the iTask3 system which enables the development of such widgets, the so called *tasklets*. Tasklets are seamlessly integrated into iTask to preserve the elegance of functional specification by hiding the behavior behind the interface of a task. Tasklets are developed in a *single-language*, declarative manner and in accordance with the *model-view-controller* user interface design (MVC) [9]. MVC decouples the application logic (the controller), the application data (the model) and the presentation data (the view) to increase flexibility and reuse. Technically speaking, tasklets are embedded applications which behavior is encoded in Clean written event handler functions. The event handlers are executed in the browser, where, they have unrestricted access to client-side resources. Using browser resources the tasklet can create custom appearance and exploit functionality available only in the browser (e.g. HTML5 GeoLocation API), utilizing the event-driven architecture the tasklet can achieve interactive behavior. With this extension, iTask gains similar characteristics to *multi-tier* programming languages like Links [4] or Hop [15,16], in the sense that the same language is used to specify code residing on multiple locations or tiers, such as the client and the server.

We further show that the presented tasklet facility can be used to improve the responsiveness of an iTask application by enabling the execution of ordinary tasks (virtually any part of an iTask application) in the browser instead of the server. This, amongst other things, helps with avoiding the latency of communication, thus providing smoother user experience. Executing an iTask task in the browser demands much more than executing an ordinary function. Tasks have complex, interactive behavior and e.g. observable intermediate values which requires communication with other tasks; therefore the execution must obey a certain *evaluation strategy*. We will obtain general client-side execution support by encoding this evaluation strategy in a tasklet.

In this paper we make the following contributions:

- The iTask framework is extended to enable the development of client-side, interactive UI components in a single-language, declarative manner. These components can be used to increase the expressiveness of the functional iTask applications, and to provide functionality which is available only in the browser.

This facility, called tasklet, is designed in such a way to fit as seamlessly as possible into the iTask formalism, that is to be opaque for the developer of the functional specification and to retain the advantageous generated nature of user interfaces of iTask applications as much as possible;

– Tasklets foster the model-view-controller user interface design to separate the application logic, the application data and the presentation data. The separation of these roles helps with increasing code flexibility, reuse and maintainability;

– We further show that the tasklet architecture is versatile enough to pave the way for the evaluation of almost all tasks at the client-side. Executing tasks in the browser helps with avoiding client-server communication to reduce server load and provide smoother user experience. This feature also creates the preconditions for running iTask applications offline in a browser which is a desired direction of future development;

– Finally, tasklets utilize a special compilation technique to enable the execution of arbitrary expression of an iTask application in the browser without shipping of unnecessary code. This technique is based on run-time deserialization of Clean expressions and involves on the fly compilation to JavaScript. By minimizing the amount of client code, this approach has the definite advantages of reducing communication cost and memory usage in the browser. Moreover it makes it possible to dynamically tune the set of tasks executed in the browser by the current server load or other run-time information.

The remainder of this paper is organized as follows: in Sect. 2 we start with a short overview of the iTask framework and develop a non-trivial, but necessarily simplified example of a flight check-in application to give a taste of iTask. In Sect. 3 we introduce the tasklet architecture and demonstrate its usage by developing a tasklet to enrich the example of the previous section. Some real-world use cases studies are discussed in Sect. 4. In Sect. 5 we briefly discuss the design of the tasklet architecture, then we generalize it in Sect. 6 to enable the execution of legacy tasks; some common restrictions on its applicability is also given in this section. After a discussion of related work in Sect. 7, we conclude in Sect. 8.

The iTask framework has been created in Clean. A concise overview of the syntactical differences with Haskell is in [2]. We assume the reader is familiar with the concept of generic programming and uniqueness typing.

2   Introduction to iTask

The most recent incarnation of the iTask system, iTask3, is a prototype framework for programming workflow support applications in Clean using a new programming paradigm built around the concept of a *task*. iTask uses a combinator-based embedded domain specific language (EDSL) to specify compositions of interdependent tasks. From these specifications, complete multi-user web applications are generated.

```
:: Task a        // Task is an opaque, parameterized type constructor

// Exception handling:
throw     :: e                              → Task a | iTask a & iTask, toString e
catchAll :: (Task a) (String → Task a) → Task a | iTask a

// Sequential composition:
(>>=) infixl 1 :: (Task a) (a → Task b) → Task b | iTask a & iTask b
(>>|) infixl 1 :: (Task a) (Task b)     → Task b | iTask a & iTask b
return       :: a                       → Task a | iTask a

// Parallel composition:
(||-) infixr 3 :: (Task a) (Task b)     → Task b | iTask a & iTask b

// User interaction:
viewInformation  :: String m     → Task m | iTask m
enterInformation :: String       → Task m | iTask m
enterChoice      :: String (c o) → Task o | OptionContainer c & iTask o
```

Fig. 1. Combinators and primitive tasks used in the paper

Tasks are abstract descriptions of interactive persistent units of work that are represented by the opaque type `Task a`, where a denotes the type of the value that will be, eventually, delivered by the task when it is executed. Tasks can be combined *sequentially*. The infix functions `return` and `>>=` are standard monadic combinators. Task f `>>=` s, first performs task f, then the value produced by f can be used by task s to compute any new task expression. The combinator `>>|` works similarly, but it drops the value of the first task during composition. Task `return` v produces value v without any effect. Tasks also can be performed in *parallel*. In this paper only the rather special `||-` combinator is used; it groups two tasks in parallel and return the result of the right task.

The primitive task `enterInformation` is a *generic editor*, a type-driven task which generates a web form for the arbitrary (first-order) type m and allows the user to enter and edit a value of that type. Similarly, `enterChoice` allows the user to choose from a set of values of type o. The selectable values must be disposed in a container, the type of which is an instance of the type class `OptionContainer`. Predefined instances of the `OptionContainer` class are the list type and a simple tree type to enable hierarchical selection. Finally, `viewInformation` is used to display a given value of the type m. The first argument of these functions is a brief description of what the end-user is expected to do. Most type definitions of the iTask combinators contain a closure at the end of their type signature, e.g. `| iTask m`. This closure imposes a type restriction on the type variable m. It means, that m can be arbitrary type, provided that some generic functions, necessary for the iTask run-time system, must have instances for the given type.

A task can raise an exception in case it can no longer produce a meaningful value. Any value can be thrown as exception by the `throw` function, provided that it can be serialized as a string. Exceptions can be caught by `catchAll` the first argument of which is a task that will possibly raise an exception, and its second argument is a task to handle it.

In Fig. 1, the small set of combinators and primitive tasks of the iTask DSL is presented which are used throughout this paper (for reasons of presentation, the types have been slightly simplified). The full language definition and its semantics can be found in [14].

In the rest of this section, we demonstrate the expressive power of iTask presenting an overly simplified, but still realistic example of a flight check-in application. The application will operate on the following types:

```
:: Seat = Seat Int Int    // Seat information: row, seat number in the row
:: Seats :== [Seat]
```

```
:: Booking = { bookingRef   :: String      // Unique booking reference number
             , firstName     :: String      // Passenger's first name
             , lastName      :: String,     // Passenger's last name
             , flightNumber  :: String,     // Flight number
             , pid           :: Hidden String,  // Unique number of passenger's ID
             , seat          :: Maybe Seat   // Seat information
             }
```

```
:: Flight  = { flightNumber :: String      // Unique flight number
             , free          :: Seats       // List of free seats
             }
```

The `Booking` type describes a booking for a flight. It contains a unique reference number, the flight number, and data of the passenger, including the unique number of the ID document (`pid`). This latter is wrapped in the Hidden type to indicate for the framework that it is not supposed to be displayed on any of the screens. For the sake of brevity, the last field, `seat`, encodes seat information and also indicates whether the passenger is checked-in. If a seat number is present, the passenger is already checked-in, otherwise has not been yet. The `Flight` record type describes a simplified view of flight data; in our case it contains only the unique flight number and the list of vacant seats.

To concentrate on the essence of the application, the implementation of the following functions, comprising the data tier, are omitted:

```
// Find flight and booking records by flight number and reference number accordingly
findFlight  :: String → Task (Maybe Flight)
findBooking :: String → Task (Maybe Booking)
// Returns a list of booking records fulfilling a condition given by the first argument
listBookings :: (Booking → Bool) → Task [Booking]
// Update datasets and returns the up-to-date booking record
commitCheckIn :: Booking Seat → Task Booking
```

To keep the example as concise as possible, a very simple exception controlled mechanism is used to handle errors; when an exception occurs the application prints the error message and restarts the workflow. Therefore, the main task, checkIn, is responsible for handling exceptions only. The task does not return any meaningful value (Void), its semantics is based on side-effect:

```
checkIn :: Task Void
checkIn = catchAll workflow (λmsg → viewInformation "Error:" msg >>| checkIn)
```

Thanks to exceptions, the top level workflow can be straightforwardly decomposed to a sequence of tasks:

```
workflow = enterInformation "Please enter booking information:"          1
    >>= λbi   → lookUpBooking bi                                          2
    >>= λmbB  → verifyBooking mbB                                         3
    >>= λb    → findFlight b.Booking.flightNumber                        4
    >>= λf    → chooseSeat f                                              5
    >>= λseat → commitCheckIn b seat                                     6
    >>= viewInformation "Check-in succeeded:"                            7
    >>| checkIn                                                          8
```

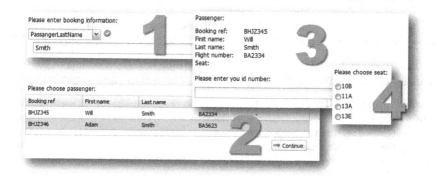

Fig. 2. The flight check-in screens

First, the user is asked to provide booking information (line 1). The entered information is used to look up the booking record (line 2), then the identity of the user and other prerequisites are verified (line 3). After looking up the related flight record in line 4, the user is asked to choose seat (line 5). Finally, the check-in is committed to the database and the updated booking record is displayed (line 6–7). In the last line, the workflow is restarted to continue with a new check-in procedure.

The generic enterInformation function in line 1, generates a user interface for the BookingInfo type; this type is inferred by looking at the type of lookUpBooking. According to this type, the passenger is asked to provide the booking reference number or her last name:

```
:: BookingInfo = BookingReference String | PassangerLastName String
```

In lookUpBooking, if a reference number was provided, the booking record is looked up. Otherwise the user is asked to choose (using enterChoice) one of the booking records in which the passenger's last name matches and contains no seat information. The function returns Nothing if a booking record could not be found:

```
lookUpBooking :: BookingInfo → Maybe Booking
lookUpBooking (BookingReference ref) = findBooking ref
lookUpBooking (PassangerLastName ln)
    =    listBookings (λb → b.lastName==ln && isNothing b.seat)
      >>= λbs → case bs of
              [] = return Nothing
              fs = enterChoice "Please choose passenger:" fs >>= return o Just
```

In the next step, the found booking record is validated. If some simple conditions hold, the passenger is kindly asked to prove her identity:

```
verifyBooking :: (Maybe Booking) → Booking
verifyBooking Nothing        = throw "Passenger cannot be found"
verifyBooking (Just b) | isJust b.seat = throw "Passenger is already checked-in"
verifyBooking (Just b) =  viewInformation "Passenger:" b
                ||-
                      enterInformation "Please enter you id number:"
   >>= λid → if (fromHidden b.pid==id) (return b) (throw "Identification...")
```

The final missing piece, the chooseSeat function, lets the passenger choose a seat using enterChoice by the list of free seats stored in the Flight record:

```
chooseSeat :: (Maybe Flight) → Seat
chooseSeat (Just f)
    = enterChoice "Please choose seat:" (map toString (sort f.free))
      >>= return o fromString
chooseSeat Nothing = throw "Flight information cannot be found"
```

Figure 2 shows the screenshots of the application. As it can be seen, the user interfaces are automatically generated from the type of the tasks only. Nevertheless they commonly look fine and intuitive to use. The only exception in this example is the fourth screen shown; choosing a seat from a list of seat numbers is anything but user friendly. In the next section we develop a more intuitive UI component, a tasklet, for choosing a seat by looking at the layout of the airplane.

3   Introduction to Tasklets

Tasklets are designed for the development of interactive web components in a single-language manner. With this extension iTask3 becomes a multi-tier programming language since all the different tiers of the web application can be programmed in the single language Clean.

However, despite the common basis, there are many important differences to most multi-tier programming languages. First of all, tasklets are *not* for the development of complete, customized applications. It is designed to develop independent *components* to be attached to the generated trunk of an iTask application. As such, we decided not taking the usual lightweight, view-centric web development approach but enforce the *model-view-controller* user interface design in tasklet development. We believe that the separation of roles suits better the development of components and it is more consistent with the objectives of iTask. This heavyweight approach also fits better for a lazy, purely functional language like Clean, where the expression of side-effects needs special attention.

Tasklets are designed to be *independent* in the sense that no facility is provided to initiate communication with other server or client components. One can argue that this imposes limitations, however in our experience, it suits well typical tasklets and enjoy an important advantage: this way the communication between the client and server components can be completely *implicit*. Any argument can be passed to a tasklet by enclosing it into a closure of the tasklet and the result is automatically shipped to the server when it is needed. The developer does not even have to be aware of programming different tiers. The accessible resources are statically controlled by the unique type that appears in the signature of the function.

Tasklets are defined by the means of the `Tasklet st val` record type. It has two type parameters denoting the type of the internal state (the *model*) of the tasklet (`st`) and the type of its result value (`val`):

```
:: Tasklet st val = { generatorFunc :: (*World → *(TaskletHTML st, st, *World))
                    , resultFunc    :: (st → TaskValue val)
                    }
:: TaskValue a    = NoValue | Value a Stability
:: Stability   :== Bool
```

During initialization, `generatorFunc` is executed on the server to provide the initial state and user interface of the tasklet. Its only argument, a value of the unique type `*World`, allows access to the external environment. The current value of the tasklet is calculated when necessary by `resultFunc` from its internal state. The result type, `TaskValue a`, an iTasks system type, expresses that the result of a task execution can be an actual value (`Value`) which is *stable* or *unstable*, or can indicate no meaningful value (`NoValue`). For the explanation of value stability, please refer to [14], in this paper we always use stable return values, which basically tells the task engine that the computation of the actual task is finished. The user interface (the *view*) and its behavior (the *controller*) are defined by the `TaskletHTML` structure:

```
:: TaskletHTML st = { html          :: HtmlDef
                    , eventHandlers :: [HtmlEvent st]
                    }
:: HtmlDef = ∃a: HtmlDef a & toHtml a

:: HtmlEvent st = HtmlEvent HtmlElementId EventType (EventHandlerFunc st)
:: EventType    = OnClick | OnMouseOver | OnMouseOut | ...
:: EventHandlerFunc st :== (st JSValue *JSWorld → *(st, *JSWorld))
```

The actual user interface (`html` field) can be given by any data structure provided that it has an instance of the function class `toHtml`. In the following, we will use an overly simplified ADT to create HTML definitions which suits

well our straightforward example, however may not satisfying for more complicated ones. Core iTask already supports the generation of high-level web forms
based on the iData [12] toolkit. In this case full, low-level control over the definition of HTML elements is needed. This can be done in an abstract, monadic
way like in Wash [19] or by an XML like domain specific language similar to
that of Hop. Furthermore, the MVC concept enables that the three components
can be developed separately, and specifically allowing the View to be developed
by non-programmers. For this reason, some template mechanism also could be
considered to be added similar to e.g. Yesod [17] or Snap [3]. However, providing
any particular tool here would beyond the scope of this paper.

The run-time behavior, the *controller* part, of a tasklet is encoded in a list
of event handler functions (eventHandlers field). Event handlers are defined
using the HtmlEvent type. Its only data constructor has three arguments: the
identifier of an HTML element, the type of the event and the event handler
function. During the instantiation of the tasklet on the client, the event handler
function is attached to the given HTML element to catch events of the given type.

The event handler functions work on the JavaScript event object (a value
of type JSValue in Clean) and the current internal state of the tasklet. They
also have access to the HTML Document Object Model (DOM) to maintain
their appearance. The DOM is a shared object from the point of event handlers,
therefore it can be manipulated only the way as IO done in Clean, through
unique types. That is, accessing the DOM is possible only using library functions
controlled by the unique *JSWorld type. This type is used in a similar way as
the type *World on the server. Introducing a new type to have IO on the client
has the advantage that reflects for the different purposes of client and server
side code. The server code can access all resources of the server computer, like
the file system, not available on the client; at the same time, the client code has
external access to a resource accessible only on the client: the DOM.

Following the tasklet definition, a wrapper task must be created to hide the
behavior of the tasklet behind the interface of a task:

```
mkTask :: (Tasklet st a) → Task a
```

The life cycle of a tasklet starts when the value of the wrapper task is requested.
First, generatorFunc is executed on the server to provide the initial state and
user interface of the tasklet. Then, the initial task state and the event handlers
defined in Clean are on the fly compiled to JavaScript and, along with the UI
definition, shipped to the browser. In the browser, the HTML markup is injected
into the page and the event handlers are attached. As events are fired, the related
event handlers catch them, and may modify the state of the tasklet and the
DOM. If the state is changed, resultFunc is called to create a new result value
that is sent to the server immediately. The life cycle of the tasklet is terminated
by the framework when the result value is finally taken by another task.

3.1 Seat Choosing by Map

To clarify the usage of tasklets, we enrich our example with the aforementioned seat chooser component. So far the passenger was to choose a seat from the list of available seats by their designation. The new idea is to allow the user choosing by looking at a simplified seat map of the airplane as it is shown in Fig. 3. For this, the Flight record is extended with layout information:

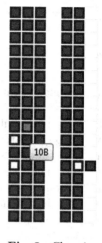

```
:: Flight  = { ...
           , rows   :: Int    // Number of rows
           , layout :: [Int]  // Layout of a row
           }
```

The rows and layout fields contain the number of rows on the plane and the layout of the rows, respectively. If the layout value is [2,3], rows consist of 5 seats in 2 groups: 2 seats, corridor, 3 seats.

Fig. 3. Choosing a seat

The signature of chooseSeat does not have to be changed, we simply redefine its body:

```
chooseSeat (Just f) = mkTask seatChooserTasklet where
```

The internal state of the tasklet in this simple case is Maybe Seat. This expresses that a seat is already chosen or has not been yet. At the beginning it is Nothing (second value of the result of generatorFunc). According to resultFunc, the tasklet results in the chosen seat if its state is not empty, otherwise no meaningful value is propagated.

```
seatChooserTasklet :: Tasklet (Maybe Seat) Seat
seatChooserTasklet =
    { generatorFunc = (λworld  → (TaskletHTML gui, Nothing, world))
    , resultFunc   = maybe NoValue (λv → Value v True)
    }
```

The rowLayout function transforms the row layout description to a list of seat numbers where corridors are denoted by -1:

```
rowLayout = intercalate [-1] (numbering 1 f.layout)
numbering i [] = []
numbering i [x:xs] =[take x [i..] : numbering (i+x) xs]
```

The result of this function can be straightforwardly mapped to HTML elements in genRowUI. In this example, we use only one data constructor of an overly simplified ADT to create HTML markup. The different kind of seats and the corridors are all mapped to HTML div elements using the DivTag data constructor. It has two list arguments, the first contains the description of the attributes, like TitleAttr, IdAttr and StyleAttr, and the second one contains child elements. For the sake of readability and simplicity the style attributes corridorStyle, freeStyle, occupiedStyle and newRowStyle are neglected.

```
genRowUI (Seat _ -1) = DivTag [corridorStyle] []
genRowUI seat | elem seat f.free
    = DivTag [TitleAttr (toString seat), IdAttr (genSeatId seat), freeStyle] []
    = DivTag [TitleAttr (toString seat), occupiedStyle] []

seatMap = DivTag [] (intercalate [DivTag [newRowStyle] []]
         [map (λs → genRowUI (Seat r s)) rowLayout \\ r ← [1 .. f.rows]])
```

The genRowUI function also takes into account whether the seat is still vacant or not. If a given seat has not been occupied yet, it gets different color and a HTML id attribute for the later attachment of event handlers. Finally, function seatMap generates and merges the markups of different lines. The special style attribute newRowStyle forces the browser to wrap subsequent div elements to the next line. The function genSeatId generates unique identifiers for HTML id attributes from a value of type Seat.

Now that we have defined the actual user interface, it is time to assign behavior to it. A seat should be chosen by simply clicking on it, furthermore, we would like the free, selectable seats to be highlighted when the mouse pointer is over them.

```
attachHandlers seat =
    [ HtmlEvent (genSeatId seat) OnClick (setState (Just seat))
    , HtmlEvent (genSeatId seat) OnMouseOver (setColor "red")
    , HtmlEvent (genSeatId seat) OnMouseOut (setColor "white")]

setState nst _ _ w = (nst, w)
setColor clr st e w = (st, setObjectAttr e "target.style.backgroundColor" clr w)
```

Three event handlers are attached to each div element representing free seat. Clicking on one of them, the internal state of the tasklet is changed to indicate the corresponding seat. This triggers the execution of resultFunc which creates a value result to send to the server. As for highlighting, the color of the event target is changed on moving mouse over and out.

Setting the state is done by creating a closure of the setState function. It is an event handler function which does nothing more than return its first argument as the new state. The OnMouseOver and OnMouseOut event handlers also create a closure of the function setColor which simply set the background color of the target of the event. This is done by the setObjectAttr library function which sets an attribute of a JavaScript object. This function has a side effect thus the *JSWorld type appears in its signature. It takes a reference to an external object (JSValue), the name of an attribute and an arbitrary value. The value is converted to its JavaScript equivalent then the attribute of the object is set.

```
setObjectAttr :: JSValue String a *JSWorld → *JSWorld
```

The tasklet run-time system is shipped with a library which contains a large set of interface functions, similar to that of setObjectAttr. These functions enable tasklets to directly interface with the enclosing JavaScript environment, e.g. to access the HTML Document Object Model (DOM), create arbitrary JavaScript objects (including HTML elements), read/write/create object attributes, or execute methods of JavaScript objects. This low level, general library provides unrestricted access to the JavaScript environment, and enables the development of arbitrary higher level, special purpose libraries on top of it.

Finally, the last piece is the `TaskletHTML` record to assign the view (the HTML markup) and controller (the event handlers) components:

```
gui = { html        = HtmlDef seatMap
      , eventHandlers = concatMap attachHandlers f.free
      }
```

4   Use Case Studies

In this chapter, two real-world use cases of the presented tasklet architecture are discussed to prove its usefulness. Both examples are taken from ongoing projects of the iTask development team, and part of the current version of the iTask system.

The first of these projects aims the port of the Clean integrated development environment, the Clean IDE, to the iTask system. With this development, we believe to achieve a web based multi user development environment, and to be able to refine the semantics of the iTask combinators in the same time. The iTask system excel at generating traditional graphical user interfaces, however, there is one component, namely the *source code editor*, which cannot be generated in any way. Thus, we decided to develop a tasklet based

on the CodeMirror JavaScript text editor component. The tasklet we gained is well customizable using a standard functional API, and seamlessly fits into the generated user interface.

The goal of the second project, called Tonic, is to develop an infrastructure to graphically represent the definition and behavior of tasks. It translates a textual iTask specification into a graphical one, called a *blueprint*. The Clean compiler has been adjusted to generate blueprints, and a standalone application, a Tonic viewer, written in iTask, is developed to visualize them.

Such a blueprint is basically a general *graph*, which consists of special kind of annotated nodes and edges. To be able to draw graphs, a general tasklet is developed. This tasklet is able to create a graphical

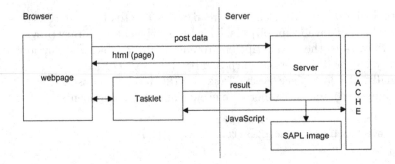

Fig. 4. The architecture of client-side execution

representation of a graph `Graph n e`, provided that a `GraphletRenderer n e` instance for the given node and edge types exist. The graph is given in a standard, functional way, while the renderer must provide a description understandable by the D3 JavaScript library, on which the tasklet is based.

5   The Architecture of Client-Side Execution

The client-side execution architecture is designed in such a way that the two groups of functions, executed on the client versus executed on the server, are not designated during compilation. Instead of this, two images of the same application are produced by the Clean compiler: the server executable running in native code and an intermediate representation that can be compiled to JavaScript (see Fig. 4). For the intermediate representation, the so called Simple Application Programming Language (SAPL) [7], a core, lazy functional language is utilized. It is used to execute arbitrary Clean expressions in the browser as follows:

0. There are two images produced by the Clean compiler: a server image (native code, executable) and a SAPL image (intermediate representation);
1. The executable on the server is started;
2. Instead of evaluating an expression on the server, one can decide, at run-time, to evaluate it on the client instead. This can in principle be done for any expression;
3. The expression to evaluate on the client is at run-time converted to an equivalent SAPL expression;
4. This SAPL expression is passed to the run-time linker specially developed for this purpose. The linker collects the dependencies of the expression recursively using the SAPL image of the application;
5. The result is run through a caching mechanism to filter out SAPL code already processed in a previous session;
6. The remaining SAPL code is on the fly compiled to efficient JavaScript code by a newly developed SAPL-to-Javascript compiler [6];
7. The generated JavaScript code can be used e.g. by tasklets to perform computation in the browser.

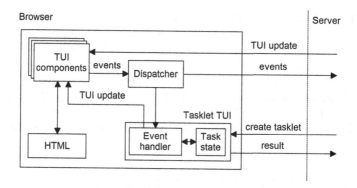

Fig. 5. The generalized tasklet architecture

Therefore arbitrary Clean expressions of an iTask application can be executed in the browser. Furthermore this is done by minimizing the necessary JavaScript code shipped to the client which has the advantages of reducing communication cost and memory usage of the browser.

6   Task Evaluation on the Client

Executing tasks is an intricate job compared to executing ordinary functions because tasks have interactive behavior which needs life cycle management. The difficulties can be understood by seeing the big picture of task *evaluation logic*.

A task basically consists of a *state* and a state *transition function*. When the state transition function is executed, it produces (1) a new state (2) an abstract description of the user interface of the task (hereafter Task User Interface, TUI) and (3) an observable task value. Based on this, task execution involves the following steps:

1. The state transition function is executed on the server to create the user interface and the result value;
2. The result value can be observed by other tasks; they can decide to continue with this current value. In that case the observed task is terminated;
3. The user interface information is sent to the browser to display;
4. If any event occurs on the client, it is passed to the state transition function on the server and the procedure continues with step 2.

The standard way tasks are evaluated closely fits the architecture of tasklets: (1) there is a distinct state to work on (2) the state transition function generates a new state and user interface just as we need in `generatorFunc` (3) the user interface generates events (4) event handlers modify the state and the user interface (see step 4). The consequence of this perfect fit is that it is possible to define *one* general tasklet creator to run *any* task exclusively in the browser:

```
runOnClient :: (Task a) → Task a
```

The result of the `runOnClient` task is a tasklet in which the state transition function of the enclosed task is utilized in `generatorFunc` and in the event handlers. Neglecting any details, at this point the tasklet API was slightly *generalized* to enable these functions to create and interact with TUI elements in addition to HTML. When the value of `runOnClient anyTask` is requested, the state transition function of `anyTask` is called on the server to create the initial user interface and state of `anyTask`. These, and the JavaScript counterpart of the event handlers (implicitly containing the state transition function) are sent to the browser. Figure 5 summarizes the client part of the generalized architecture:

1. In the browser the TUI elements are displayed;
2. The events emitted by the TUI are passed to an event dispatcher function which can decide if the target of the event runs on the server or on the client;
3. In the latter case the event is forwarded directly to the wrapper tasklet running on the client instead of being sent to the server;
4. The event handler of this tasklet executes the state transition function of `anyTask` on the client to create a new state, result value and TUI definition;
5. If the result value is changed, it is shipped back to the server;
6. The user interface is updated by the TUI definition resulted by the state transition function and the procedure continues with step 2.

6.1   Limitations

As for the current implementation there are some restrictions to the applicability of the tasklet architecture. Some of them derives from the limitation of the Clean to SAPL compiler and give constraints on the application of Clean language elements: (1) tasks evaluated on the client can only produce higher order functions as intermediate value. Higher order values cannot be returned as final result, because the de-serialization of SAPL expressions into a Clean executable is possible only in the case of first order values; (2) certain tasks are intended to be executed on the server e.g. when a database is accessed, or global information is shared between distributed tasks. Such tasks cannot easily be shipped to the client, still a general solution is possible using a server side mediator service which is being under development.

7   Related Work

The iTask3 system with the tasklet extension is a unique multi-tier programming language. In contrast to most web programming languages where the functionality is view-centric, built around the user interface, iTask proposes an *inverted* development model: the trunk of an iTask application is generated by a functional specification then augmented with custom web components.

Several other languages address multi-tier programming. In the imperative world the most modern approach is the Google Web Toolkit (GWT) [1], Google Dart [5] and Node.js [18]. GWT utilizes a Java to JavaScript compilation technique for building complex browser-based applications. GWT fosters classical

GUI programming where widgets can be developed using a programming model comparable to that of tasklets.

The Dart language and the Node.js framework take a different approach. They enable multi-tier programming by providing a run-time environment of their languages for both client and server side. The language of Node.js is JavaScript, which is native in the web browsers; the framework also provides a run-time environment, including IO libraries, for the server side. Dart is a programming language developed by Google specially designed for web application engineering. On the client, it compiles to JavaScript, on the server it is executed by a Dart virtual machine. However, these systems have a more general approach than iTask and tasklets, they still share the idea of using the same language on both client and server side and implicitly bridging the communication between them.

Hop [15,16] uses a declarative approach. It is a dedicated web programming language with a HTML-like syntax built on the top of Scheme. Hop uses two compilers, one for compiling the server side program and one for compiling the client-side part. The client side part is only used for executing the user interface. Hop uses syntactic constructions for indicating client and server part code. The application essentially runs on the client and may call services on the server. In contrast, an iTask application essentially runs on the server and may execute services, tasklets, on the client.

Links [4] and its extension Formlets is also a functional language-based web programming language. Links compiles to JavaScript for rendering HTML pages, and SQL to communicate with a back-end database. In a Links program, the keywords `client` and `server` force a top-level function to be executed at the client or server respectively.

The iTask framework differs from the latter two by fostering a non view-centric approach even in the component development. Links and Hop have extended syntax for embedding XML descriptions in the language; this is used to mix the user interface definition and the behavior of the application. During tasklet development the model-view-controller user interface design is enforced to separate these roles.

Another important difference is that tasklets blur the boundaries of different tiers. Links uses location annotations, Hop utilizes special syntactic construction to denote the target tier of a given function or expression. In tasklets this is implicit (basically the controller role runs in the browser) but unconcerned. If a function is pure, it does not matter where it is executed. If it is not pure, the available resources are controlled statically by the signature of the function. Furthermore, the communication between the tiers is also implicit for tasklets.

As for iTask, there are earlier implementations of similar features utilizing a Java written SAPL interpreter [7] as a browser plug-in. The iEditors [8] enables the development of interactive web UI elements as tasklets do, however, it does not allow direct access to browser resources, therefore its applicability is restricted to functionality provided by the plug-in. As a consequence, it does not have the single-language property either, because for some functionality the plug-in has to be extended using Java. There also had been client-side task evaluation attempts for an early version of iTask using the same plug-in based interpretation technology [13]. However, our approach, to give one general solution for both of the problems is a novel strategy.

8   Conclusion

In this paper we have presented a number of contributions to the iTask3 system, a web-enabled combinator library written in the lazy functional language Clean. In iTask, complex, multi-user web applications are generated from a mere functional specification. However, up to now, the system lacks the possibility to create custom, interactive web components.

We introduced *tasklets*, an extension to iTask3, for the development of interactive web components in a single-language manner. With this extension iTask3 becomes a unique multi-tier programming language which offers an unusual web development model based on the enrichment of a generated trunk program. Furthermore, in contrast to most multi-tier programming languages, the extended iTask framework enforces the model-view-controller user interface design in component development and blurs the boundaries of different tiers.

For the execution of Clean code in the browser, a special client-side execution facility was developed. It is designed in such a way that instead of evaluating an expression on the server, one can decide, at run-time, to evaluate it on the client. The expression is compiled to JavaScript on the fly.

Finally, we showed that the presented tasklet facility can be generalized to enable the execution of ordinary tasks in the browser instead of the server by turning an arbitrary task into a tasklet. This, amongst other things, can be used to improve the responsiveness of an iTask application by avoiding the latency of communication.

Acknowledgements. The research was partially carried out as part of the EITKIC 12-1-2012-0001 project, which is supported by the Hungarian Government, managed by the National Development Agency, financed by the Research and Technology Innovation Fund and was performed in cooperation with the EIT ICT Labs Budapest Associate Partner Group.

References

1. The Google Web Toolkit site. http://code.google.com/webtoolkit/
2. Achten, P.: Clean for Haskell98 programmers - A quick reference guide, 13 July 2007. http://www.st.cs.ru.nl/papers/2007/achp2007-CleanHaskellQuickGuide.pdf
3. Collins, G., Beardsley, D.: The snap framework: A web toolkit for haskell. IEEE Internet Comput. 15(1), 84–87 (2011)
4. Cooper, E., Lindley, S., Yallop, J.: Links: Web programming without tiers. In: de Boer, F.S., Bonsangue, M.M., Graf, S., de Roever, W.-P. (eds.) FMCO 2006. LNCS, vol. 4709, pp. 266–296. Springer, Heidelberg (2007)

5. DART. Dart : structured web programming (2011)
6. Domoszlai, L., Bruël, E., Jansen, J.M.: Implementing a non-strict purely functional language in Javascript. Acta Univ. Sapientiae. Informatica **3**(1), 76–98 (2011)
7. Jansen, J.M., Koopman, P., Plasmeijer, R.: Efficient interpretation by transforming data types and patterns to functions. In: Proceedings of 6th Symposium on Trends in Functional Programming, TFP 2006 (2006)
8. Jansen, J.M., Plasmeijer, R., Koopman, P.: iEditors: extending iTask with interactive plug-ins. In: Proceedings of 20th International Conference on Implementation and Application of Functional Languages, IFL 2008 (2011)
9. Krasner, G.E., Pope, S.T.: A cookbook for using the model-view controller user interface paradigm in Smalltalk-80. J. Object Oriented Program. **1**(3), 26–49 (1988)
10. Lijnse, B., Jansen, J.M., Nanne, R., Plasmeijer, R.: Capturing the Netherlands coast guard's SAR workflow with iTasks. In: Proceedings of the 8th International Conference on Information Systems for Crisis Response and Management, ISCRAM 2011 (2011)
11. Lijnse, B., Jansen, J.M., Plasmeijer, R.: Incidone: A task-oriented incident coordination tool. In: Proceedings of the 9th International Conference on Information Systems for Crisis Response and Management, ISCRAM 2012 (2012)
12. Plasmeijer, R., Achten, P.: iData for the world wide web – programming interconnected web forms. In: Hagiya, M. (ed.) FLOPS 2006. LNCS, vol. 3945, pp. 242–258. Springer, Heidelberg (2006)
13. Plasmeijer, R., Jansen, J.M., Koopman, P., Achten, P.: Declarative Ajax and client side evaluation of workflows using iTasks. In: Proceedings of 14th International Symposium on Principles and Practice of Declarative Programming, PPDP 2008, July 2008
14. Plasmeijer, R., Lijnse, B., Michels, S., Achten, P., Koopman, P.: Task-oriented programming in a pure functional language. In: Proceedings of the 14th Symposium on Principles and Practice of Declarative Programming, PPDP 2012, pp. 195–206. ACM, New York (2012)
15. Serrano, M., Gallesio, E., Loitsch, F.: Hop: a language for programming the web 2.0. In: ACM SIGPLAN Conference on Object-Oriented Programming, Systems, Languages, and Applications, OOPSLA 2006 (2006)
16. Serrano, M., Queinnec, C.: A multi-tier semantics for hop. Higher-Order Symbolic Comput. **23**, 409–431 (2010)
17. Snoyman, M.: Developing web applications with Haskell and Yesod. O'Reilly Media Inc (2012)
18. Surhone, L.M., Tennoe, M.T., Henssonow, S.F.: Node.Js. Betascript Publishing, Mauritius (2010)
19. Thiemann, P.: WASH/CGI: Server-side web scripting with sessions and typed, compositional forms. In: Proceedings of 4th International Symposium on Practical Aspects of Declarative Languages, PADL 2002, January 2002

DSL for Grammar Refactoring Patterns

Ivan Halupka[✉]

Technical University of Košice, Letná 9, 04200 Košice, Slovakia
ivan.halupka@tuke.sk

Abstract. Grammar refactoring is a significant cornerstone of grammarware engineering, aimed at adjusting a formal grammar to specific requirements derived from the application environment, without affecting the language that a grammar generates. In our research, we focus on tackling the problems related to formal specification and automated application of well-known and newly-discovered refactoring procedures. One of our research results is a language for specification of the refactoring patterns to which we refer to as pLERO. In this paper, we present an extension of pLERO language aimed at expanding the scope of its applicability to additional classes of refactoring problems, such as folding and unfolding of grammar productions.

Keywords: Grammarware engineering · Grammar refactoring · Structural patterns · pLERO language

1 Introduction

Grammar refactoring is a non-trivial process of changing the form in which a formal grammar is expressed, with preserving the language that a grammar generates. Two or more formal grammars that generate the same language are called equivalent. The objective of the classical grammar refactoring is adjusting the form in which a grammar is expressed to specific requirements considering the future purpose of a grammar. In our research we focus on context-free grammars, since they are the most commonly used formal apparatus for expressing the abstract syntax of programming languages.

Although grammar refactoring is both of theoretical and of practical significance, for various subdomains of gramarware engineering it is still weakly understood and poorly practiced [1]. A current gap between state-of-art and state-of-practice can be clearly seen in the compiler design, where current state-of-art provides limited number of specialized refactoring procedures. This, in turn forces language designers to perform the majority of the refactoring procedures manually on the basis of their intuition. This is a problem mainly because such refactoring can be significantly difficult and error prone, while results in many cases cannot be verified, since proving equivalence of two grammars is in general an undecidable problem.

In our previous work, we addressed this issue by proposing two approaches to automated grammar refactoring, more specifically a probabilistic approach based

© Springer International Publishing Switzerland 2015
V. Zsók et al. (Eds.): CEFP 2013, LNCS 8606, pp. 446–458, 2015.
DOI: 10.1007/978-3-319-15940-9_12

on evolutionary algorithm, called *mARTINICA* (metrics Automated Refactoring Task-driven INcremental syntactIC Algorithm) [2,3], and a deterministic approach based on formal specification language called *pLERO* (pattern Language of Extended Refactoring Operators) [4,5].

pLERO is the domain-specific language for specification of refactoring and other transformations on context-free grammars. The core idea behind the approach is to provide universal formal apparatus for automated application of the knowledge of grammar engineers. The main purpose of pLERO is to uniformly define deterministic solutions to recurring refactoring problems, such as left recursion removal and elimination of epsilon productions. To these solutions we refer to as grammar refactoring patterns.

pLERO is currently being developed in two distinct dialects, namely a imperative and a declarative. Refactoring patterns written in the imperative dialect of pLERO are more process-centric, meaning that they are intended for the specification of particular steps of a refactoring process, while refactoring patterns written in the declarative dialect are more result-centric and facilitate the understanding of a grammar's structural changes. Detailed description of the imperative dialect of pLERO can be found in [4], while description of the declarative dialect of pLERO can be found in [5]. Refactoring patterns expressed in both dialects currently operate on grammars expressed in BNF notation.

In this paper we consider the declarative dialect of pLERO and present its extension aimed at addressing the following aspects of a pattern's formal specification:

- Parameterization of patterns, since the recently published [5] specification of pLERO only included support for expressing parameterless refactoring transformations.
- Matching of the negative grammar structures, meaning expressing structural preconditions that grammar should not fulfill in order to be transformable by a pattern, as opposed to previous version of pLERO, where only matching of positive grammar structures could be formally specified.
- Equivalence precondition for grammatical structures whose properties are expressed at multiple levels of abstraction.
- Iteration over structurally different grammar productions.

2 Grammar Refactoring Patterns

Refactoring patterns are the only first-class citizens of the pLERO language, specifying structural transformations of grammar's productions, and as such they can be considered generic schemes of refactoring operations.

A grammar refactoring pattern consists of a nonempty set of transformation rules, and a set of declarations. Each transformation rule defines alternation of grammar's production rules which exhibit some structural properties, while each declaration specifies additional properties of formal structures that occur in some of the transformation rules. We understand the term 'structural property of production rule' as the ordering of symbols and symbol types production.

For instance, a production rule may exhibit the structural property that its right-hand side starts and ends with a nonterminal symbol.

A transformation rule consists of two parts, namely a *predicate* defining the structure of some subset of a grammar's production rules, and a *transformation* describing the way in which this structure should be changed. Although predicates and transformations have different purposes, they are both expressed in similar fashion using the formalism of *meta-production rules*. The predicate is specified by exactly one meta-production rule, while the transformation is defined by a set of meta-production rules.

Each meta-production rule specifies chosen structural properties exhibited by some subset of the grammar's productions. A meta-production rule is divided into a left-hand side describing left-hand side of a grammar's production rule, and a right-hand side specifying structure of a right-hand side of a grammar's production rule. The left-hand side of a meta-production rule comprises exactly one *pattern variable*, while the right-hand side of a meta-production rule is a sequence of *pattern variables*.

Each pattern variable defines a homogeneous sequence of grammar symbols, and as such consists of a *variable name* and a *variable prefix*. The variable prefix describes a type of grammar symbols that can occur in sequences assigned to a pattern variable, and the three possible variable prefixes are: $'t'$ denoting terminal, $'n'$ denoting nonterminal and $'s'$ denoting both terminal and nonterminal, while each of these prefixes can be followed by $'*'$, denoting sequences of arbitrary length, or $'\{m\}'$ denoting sequences of exactly $'m'$ symbols. The variable name serves as an identifier of a specific sequence of grammar symbols, and it enables us using this sequence in other parts of a transformation rule in which the pattern variable occurs (local pattern variable). It also enables us using this sequence in other transformation rules or declarations (global pattern variable) and adding a new nonterminal to the grammar (new pattern variable).

Each pattern specification in pLERO must follow the same notion template, as shown in Fig. 1, which has suffered minor changes since its publication [5] due to extension of pLERO language itself.

More detailed description of the pLERO language, the pattern matching and the pattern application processes can be found in [5]. In what follows we only discuss pattern declarations and ways of pattern parameterization, since these are parts of the language that have been subjected to change.

3   PLERO Extension

3.1   Pattern Parameterization

The main idea behind our previous refactoring approach to which we refer to as mARTINICA [2,3] was to perform grammar transformation on the basis of certain mathematically expressed objectives, while the refactoring process consisted of a series of incremental applications of the refactoring operators. In this case, we operated with a constant set of refactoring operators, which were implemented

```
pattern [pattern_name]
        (argument₁ annotation₁,
            ...
        argumentₖ annotationₖ)
{
    [declaration₁];
    [declaration₂];
        ...
    [declarationₙ];
    [transformation_rule₁];
    [transformation_rule₂];
        ...
    [transformation_ruleₘ];
}
```

Fig. 1. Template of a pattern notation

in the Java language. Initially pLERO was designed as complementary to this approach, with the intention of providing a simple DSL in which language developers can specify their own refactoring procedures and incorporate them in the base of refactoring operators. Patterns defined using the pLERO formalism were not parameterized, since in mARTINICA parameters are mostly generated randomly, and thus it was decided that any input arguments that were needed for refactoring were to be generated by the pLERO pattern matching environment.

However, the following two factors motivated us to incorporate support for pattern parameterization in the pLERO formalism:

– Recognition of the potential of pLERO to be used as formalism for preservation of newly discovered refactoring procedures and as a stand-alone tool for their application.
– Need for passing grammar-specific data that cannot be randomly generated or inferred from grammar's productions, such as start symbol.

Each refactoring pattern may have an arbitrary number of parameters. Each pattern parameter consists of an argument and an annotation. An argument can be a meta-production rule denoting the production rule of a specific structure, a pattern variable denoting specific sequence of symbols or an integer variable denoting the length of a sequence of symbols. Each argument has annotation describing its meaning, and each pattern variable occurring in arbitrary argument is considered to be a global pattern variable whose value cannot be altered during the pattern matching process. The types of the pattern arguments do not need to be declared, since they are inferred during the matching process. The way in which parameters are specified can be seen in Fig. 1.

3.2 Declarations

In this section we present five declarations within the pLERO language: variables, new symbols, join, equivalence and nonequivalence. The first two were part of the most recently published version of pLERO, however they were never closely examined, and the rationale behind them was never provided, which is the main reason why we also include their descriptions in this section.

Global Variables. In general, pattern variables with the same name and prefix occurring in different transformation rules represent distinct sequences of symbols. One advantage of such approach is the relatively large separation of concerns between individual transformation rules, which leads to a high level of structural integrity for production rules matched against specific predicate. This constraint also lowers the risk of the accidental structural corruption. However, in terms of generating the language, structurally diverse production rules may be closely interlinked. Preservation of grammar's equivalence may require that transformation of production rules exhibiting some structure must be conditioned by transformation of productions with different structures. Moreover, such production rules may have common substructures that need to be preserved or handled in a similar fashion, independently of structural differences that are observable when considering production rules as a whole.

In our experience, this scenario is actually quite common and such interlinkage is present in almost every meaningful refactoring pattern. A trivial example of such a connection between structurally different productions can be found in the pattern specifying the well-known procedure of immediate left-recursion removal. If a left-recursive nonterminal is reachable in any derivation, in order for the grammar to terminate, it must contain both left-recursive and non left-recursive productions of such nonterminal. In the process of left-recursion elimination both left-recursive and non-left-recursive productions need to be transformed, while the transformation pattern is different for each of these two structural classes of production rules. On the other hand, the recursive nonterminal on the left-hand side of each transformed production needs to be preserved, independently of the other structural properties.

In order to resolve this issue, we allowed sharing of pattern variables between transformation rules, however all shared variables must be explicitly declared using the *'variables'* keyword and the template notion, as depicted in Fig. 2. Pattern variables that are not specified using variables declaration and that are not implicitly global (such as pattern arguments) are interpreted as local pattern variables.

Generated Nonterminals. A refactoring process often involves the incorporation of new nonterminal symbols in a grammar. An example of a refactoring procedure, always leading to the incorporation of one new nonterminal in a grammar is the application of refactoring operator to which is referred to as pack [2,3]. This operator and its formal specification are more closely examined in Sect. 5.2

```
variables:
    [prefix₁].[variable_name₁],
    [prefix₂].[variable_name₂],
        ...
    [prefixₙ].[variable_nameₙ];
```

Fig. 2. Variables declaration template

Names of nonterminals that need to be incorporated in a grammar could be passed as pattern arguments, or could be set to constants using equivalence declaration. However, this could lead to a naming conflict with existing non-terminals, which can break the structure of the entire language generated by a grammar. In order to resolve this issue, we created a declaration generating non-conflicting names of nonterminal symbols. This declaration is specified using the *'new symbols'* keyword and the template for it is depicted in Fig. 3. Each nonterminal pattern variable that is specified in a new symbols declaration represents a nonterminal with unique name that is not part of the original grammar, and as a consequence of this, variables declared in such fashion cannot be present in predicate, but only in the transformation part of a transformation rule.

```
new symbols:
    n.[variable_name₁],
    n.[variable_name₂],
        ...
    n.[variable_nameₙ];
```

Fig. 3. New symbols declaration template

Production Alternatives. In the process of derivation the sentences of a language every nonterminal symbol in each derivation can be expanded by arbitrary production rule whose left-hand side is this nonterminal. This means that from a language standpoint, multiple productions with the same nonterminal on their left-hand side are alternatives directing the way in which language sentences develop. However, in BNF notation these alternatives are expressed as separate productions, and moreover from a structural standpoint, they may significantly differ among themselves.

In our experience, during the execution procedure of the various refactoring transformations, it is required that productions with equivalent left-hand sides be treated jointly, as alternatives occurring in one production whose left-hand side is particular nonterminal. An example of such transformations is the application of well-known refactoring operators, which is referred to as fold and unfold [6]. In terms of BNF, unfolding means the replacement of specific nonterminal on the right-hand side of an arbitrary production with all right-hand sides of productions whose left-hand side is this nonterminal, while unfolding presents inverse transformation to fold and its execution is conditioned by existence of productions containing each alternative, as the only structural difference between them. The problem with the approach above is that during the language design phase any form of iteration (with the exception of iteration deriving from pattern recognition process) was excluded from pLERO, mainly for the reasons of simplicity and computational complexity.

We addressed this issue by proposing a declaration creating special kind of iterator over productions whose left-hand side is the same nonterminal and which exhibit particular structural properties. This declaration is specified using the 'join' keyword and the template notion, as depicted in Fig. 4. The pattern variable before the 'where' keyword represents a nonterminal over which iterator is created, while the meta-production rule after the 'where' keyword describes the structure of productions included in the iterator. All pattern variables included in this declaration are implicitly global, and in case of their occurrence in a predicate they specify the need for matching against all possible pattern bindings in the iterator. On the other hand, if they occur in a transformation, they specify the creation of productions which contain all possible pattern bindings in the iterator.

```
join n.[variable_name]
    where [meta_production_rule];
```

Fig. 4. Join declaration template

Notice that this declaration combines right-hand sides of production rules whose left-hand side is a same nonterminal into one production rule of EBNF notation, whose left-hand side is this nonterminal and whose right-hand side consists of right-hand sides of the combined productions between which EBNF alternative meta-operator has been put.

Equivalence and Nonequivalence. Various refactoring procedures can be performed only in the case of structural equivalence or nonequivalence of particular sequences of grammar symbols. In most cases, the first case is not an issue, since in pLERO, the precondition of the structural equivalence can be specified by using same pattern variables for equivalent structures, alternatively declaring these variables as global. However, there is an exception when this solution cannot be used, and that is in the case when one sequence of symbols needs to be expressed using two or more distinct sequences of pattern variables. For example, when we specify refactoring operator which is referred to as pack, the production rule that needs to be transformed is passed as a pattern argument, which is typed as meta-production rule denoting arbitrary production. However, the transformation rule which specifies this operator needs to operate on more fine-grained structures of the production that is passed as pattern argument, since the application of the pack operator in general case requires dividing the production in three parts (symbols before packed sequence, packed sequence itself and symbols after packed sequence). Some refactoring procedures may also require that a grammar does not exhibit some structural properties, for example if refactoring precondition is that grammar must be in Chomsky normal form, then one of structural preconditions is that grammar does not include epsilon productions.

The mentioned refactoring problems present our motivation to extend pLERO with declarations of equivalence and nonequivalence. The equivalence precondition for two sequences of pattern variables (separated by 'and' keyword) is specified by keyword 'equivalence', and notion template, as depicted in Fig. 5, while nonequivalence precondition for two sequences of variables is specified in similar fashion, by replacing 'equivalence' keyword with 'nonequivalence'. All pattern variables used both in equivalence and nonequivalence declaration are implicitly global.

```
equivalence  [prefix_1].[variable_name_1]
                    ...
             [prefix_k].[variable_name_k]
     and
             [prefix_n].[variable_name_n]
                    ...
             [prefix_m].[variable_name_m];
```

Fig. 5. Equivalence declaration template

4 Related Work

We were not able to find related research considering grammar refactoring patterns; however, any refactoring approach closely aimed for solving refactoring issues of a particular problem domain [7–9] can in some sense be considered a pattern.

Lämmel presented a suite of fifteen grammar transformation operators, four considering grammar construction, five considering grammar destruction and six considering grammar refactoring [6]. These operators are in large degree tailored for solving issues of two specific problem domains e.g. grammar adaptation and grammar recovery.

Lämmel and Zaytsev recently introduced a suite of four refactoring operators, specifically aimed for tackling refactoring tasks occurring in the process of grammar extraction from multiple diverse sources of information [10].

5   Discussion

This section examines the process of formal specification of two chosen refactoring operators using the pLERO language. The following discussion elaborates on difficulty of specifying solutions to commonly occurring refactoring problems using formal apparatus provided by previous version of pLERO. Subsequently, it describes a way in which proposed language extensions tackle these issues and thus provides justification of the new language features with relation to the purpose of the pLERO language.

Domain-specific languages trade generality for expressiveness in a limited domain [11]. We believe that a relative comparative advantage of using domain-specific language over formal apparatus provided by general-purpose languages should be evaluated in the terms of balance between the generality and the expressiveness of the language. Therefore, in our view, the growth of domain-specific language's expressive power is generally not a sufficient reason for its extension. In an ideal case, domain-specific languages should only be extended in situations in which a particular extension does not have a significant negative impact on the balance between the generality and the expressiveness of the language in the domain (in the opposite case, benefits of its usage over using a general-purpose language may be questioned).

In order to demonstrate, that the proposed language extensions fulfill this condition, we have also implemented both discussed refactoring operators in Java. However, comparison of expressive powers of different languages may be difficult, especially since to the best of our knowledge, there is no generally accepted methodology for performing such task. Therefore we decided to compare a number of language statements used to implement refactoring operators in both languages. For the analysis of Java code, we used tool Resource Standard Metrics (available at http://msquaredtechnologies.com), while in pLERO we evaluated this metric as sum of number of transformation rules and number of declarations. In the analysis of Java source code, we included only Java methods that implement logic of refactoring operator, while other parts of source code, such as grammar parser and grammar model were excluded from the analysis.

5.1   Case A: Unfold

Unfold is the refactoring operator that replaces each occurrence of a nonterminal on the right-hand side of some production rule with all possible combinations of right-hand sides of production rules whose left-hand side is this nonterminal. For instance, consider the grammar containing set of three production rules $\{A \rightarrow \text{`}a\text{'} B \text{`}a\text{'}, B \rightarrow \text{`}a\text{'}, B \rightarrow \text{`}b\text{'}\}$. In case we unfold the nonterminal B, the resulting grammar will contain four production rules $\{A \rightarrow \text{`}a\text{'} \text{`}a\text{'} \text{`}a\text{'}, A \rightarrow \text{`}a\text{'} \text{`}b\text{'} \text{`}a\text{'}, B \rightarrow \text{`}a\text{'}, B \rightarrow \text{`}b\text{'}\}$.

The unfolding operator is widely used in various procedures of grammarware engineering, such as post-processing of inferred grammars, and grammar convergence. Grammar inference is a process of extracting a correct grammar for unknown target language from a finite set of language examples [12]. The problem is that majority of approaches to grammar inference primarily aim at extracting a grammar of a correct language, focusing on issues related to over-generality and over-specialization of inferred grammar [13], while the form in which the extracted grammar is presented remains only a secondary concern if addressed at all. In this case, the unfolding operator may be repeatedly used on a grammar with the aim of reducing the count of grammar's nonterminal symbols, or reducing depths of derivation trees constructed for sentences of language generated by a grammar. Grammar convergence is a method of establishing and maintaining the connection between grammar knowledge contained within heterogeneous software artifacts. In this case, the unfolding operator is preferably used in the process of transformation of software artifacts, predominantly because it leads to semantics-preserving grammar transformations [10].

The Java method used to implement the unfolding operator consists of 37 language statements spanning over 47 effective lines of code, while the specification of the unfolding operator in pLERO required only 2 language statements. This pLERO specification is depicted in Fig. 6 and it consists of the proposed join declaration and the transformation rule that defines transformation on productions containing the unfolded nonterminal on their right-hand sides.

```
pattern Unfold
    (n.A 'Unfolded nonterminal')
{
    join n.A where n.A ::= s*.x;
    n.B ::= s*y1 n.A s*y2
           -> n.B ::= s*y1 s*.x s*.y2;
}
```

Fig. 6. Unfold pattern specification

Since there is an arbitrary number of productions whose left-hand side is the unfolded nonterminal, and all such productions need to be considered in each application of unfolding operator, it is clear that some form of iteration over grammar's productions is required. Iterations derived from multiple applications of pattern are in this case not sufficient. The rationale behind this claim can be derived from the fact that between two consequent applications of pLERO pattern no states are preserved, and thus the iterations derived from multiple applications of pattern must preserve grammar equivalence in each step of refactoring procedure. In the case of formal specification of unfolding operator this condition cannot be satisfied without using the 'join' declaration, since grammar equivalence is preserved only if all productions containing the unfolded nonterminal on their left-hand side are used in the transformation, and since number of such productions is arbitrary, they generally cannot be matched in a single transformation step.

5.2   Case B: Pack

Pack is the refactoring operator that replaces the specific sequence of symbols contained within right-hand side of some production rule with newly created nonterminal, and creates new production whose left-hand side is this nonterminal and right-hand side is this sequence of symbols. Such sequence can be defined by the position of its initial symbol within production's right-hand side and by its length. For instance, consider the grammar containing set of two production rules $\{A \rightarrow \text{'}a\text{'}\text{'}a\text{'} B \text{'}a\text{'}\text{'}a\text{'}, B \rightarrow \text{'}a\text{'}\text{'}b\text{'}\}$. In case we pack sequence of three symbols, starting from the second symbol of the first production the resulting grammar will contain three production rules $\{A \rightarrow \text{'}a\text{'} NT \text{'}a\text{'}, NT \rightarrow \text{'}a\text{'} B \text{'}a\text{'}, B \rightarrow \text{'}a\text{'}\text{'}b\text{'}\}$, while NT will correspond with newly created nonterminal.

Pack may be used in various situations, with aim of reducing length of grammar's productions, reducing number of direct child nodes for each node of constructed derivation trees and improving grammar comprehension. The Java method used to implement the unfolding operator consists of 18 language statements spanning over 25 effective lines of code, while the specification of the unfolding operator in pLERO required only 4 language statements. This pLERO specification is depicted in Fig. 7 and it consists of three declarations and one transformation rule.

```
pattern Pack
    (n.A ::= s*.x 'Packed production',
     int.I 'Initial package symbol',
     int.L 'Package length')
{
    variables s{int.I}.y1, s{int.L}.p,
              s*.y2;
    equivalence s*.x and
              s{int.I}.y1 s{int.L}.p s*.y2;
    new symbols n.B;
    n.A ::= s{int.I}.y1 s{int.L}.p s*.y2
         -> n.A ::= s{int.I}.y1 n.B s*.y2,
            n.B ::= s{int.L}.p;
}
```

Fig. 7. Pack pattern specification

The general form of the pack operator, specifying pack operator for all possible sequences of symbols on right-hand side of production rule cannot be specified without parameterization of patterns since pLERO does not provide any other formalism for exact specification of sequences of symbols with variable length and ambiguous structural properties. By ambiguity in the above sentence we understand, the inability to exactly identify some sequence of symbols within production on the basis of definition provided by predicate of transformation rule. However, specific forms of pack operator (for instance, applying pack operator on sequence of three symbols starting from the second symbol of a production) can be described without parameterization of patterns, but since the count of such situations is infinite, the pack cannot be specified as their unification. The same applies for the equivalence declaration, since general form of pack operator also cannot be specified without it, and the reason for this is that arbitrary structure of production within pattern argument could not be unambiguously matched against specific structure of transformation rule describing the pack operator.

6   Conclusion

The most significant contribution of this paper is the contribution to automated grammar evolution. As such, our refactoring approach presents an appropriate basis for creation of new theory concerning automated task-driven grammar refactoring, while the provided patterns as well as some other experimental results [3,5] demonstrate the correctness and the applicability of our approach. We believe that the proposed extensions significantly increase the applicability of pLERO language for specification of various patterns occurring in the domain of grammar refactoring, while preserving relative balance between languages generality and expressive power.

In the future we would like to focus on increasing the abstraction power of the pLERO language, so it would formalize other knowledge considering refactoring problems and context of their occurrence, such as consequences of pattern's application on grammar's quality attributes. We would also like to adopt our approach to EBNF notation, which is structurally richer and would cause pattern matching to be more deterministic.

Acknowledgments. This work was supported by project VEGA 1/0341/13 *Principles and methods of automated abstraction of computer languages and software development based on the semantic enrichment caused by communication.*

References

1. Klint, P., Lämmel, R., Verhoef, C.: Toward an engineering discipline for grammarware. ACM Trans. Softw. Eng. Methodol. (TOSEM) **14**(3), 331–380 (2005)
2. Halupka, I., Kollár, J.: Evolutionary algorithm for automated task-driven grammar refactoring. In: Proceedings of International Scientific Conference on Computer Science and Engineering (CSE 2012), pp. 47–54. Technical University of Košice, Slovakia (2012)

3. Halupka, I., Kollár, J., Pietriková, E.: A task-driven grammar refactoring algorithm. Acta Polytech. **52**(5), 51–57 (2012)
4. Kollár, J., Halupka, I.: Role of patterns in automated task-driven grammar refactoring. In: 2nd Symposium on Languages, Applications and Technologies (SLATE 2013), pp. 171–186. Schloss Dagstuhl-Leibniz-Zentrum fuer Informatik, Dagstuhl (2013)
5. Kollár, J., Halupka, I., Chodarev, S., Pietriková, E.: pLERO: language for grammar refactoring patterns. In: 4th Workshop on Advances in Programming Languages (WAPL 2013), Kraków, Poland (in print)
6. Lämmel, R.: Grammar adaptation. In: Oliveira, J.N., Zave, P. (eds.) FME 2001. LNCS, vol. 2021, pp. 550–570. Springer, Heidelberg (2001)
7. Louden, K.: Compiler Construction: Principles and Practice. PWS Publishing, Boston (1997)
8. Lohmann, W., Riedewald, G., Stoy, M.: Semantics-preserving migration of semantic rules during left recursion removal in attribute grammars. Electron. Notes Theoret. Comput. Sci. (ENTCS) **110**, 133–148 (2004)
9. Kraft, N., Duffy, E., Malloy, B.: Grammar recovery from parse trees and metrics-guided grammar refactoring. IEEE Trans. Softw. Eng. **35**(6), 780–794 (2009)
10. Lämmel, R., Zaytsev, V.: An introduction to grammar convergence. In: Leuschel, M., Wehrheim, H. (eds.) IFM 2009. LNCS, vol. 5423, pp. 246–260. Springer, Heidelberg (2009)
11. Mernik, M., Heering, J., Sloane, A.M.: When and how to develop domain-specific languages. ACM Comput. Surv. **37**(4), 316–344 (2005)
12. Stevenson, A., Cordy, J.R.: Grammatical inference in software engineering: an overview of the state of the art. In: Czarnecki, K., Hedin, G. (eds.) SLE 2012. LNCS, vol. 7745, pp. 204–223. Springer, Heidelberg (2013)
13. D'ulizia, A., Ferri, F., Grifoni, P.: A learning algorithm for multimodal grammar inference. IEEE Trans. Syst. Man, Cybern. - Part B **41**(6), 1495–1510 (2011)

Design and Implementation of Queries for Model-Driven Spreadsheets

Jácome Cunha[1,2], João Paulo Fernandes[1,3], Jorge Mendes[1], Rui Pereira[1](✉),
and João Saraiva[1]

[1] HASLab/INESC TEC, Universidade do Minho, Braga, Portugal
{jacome,jpaulo,jorgemendes,ruipereira,jas}@di.uminho.pt
[2] CIICESI, ESTGF, Instituto Politécnico do Porto, Porto, Portugal
[3] RELEASE, Universidade da Beira Interior, Covilhã, Portugal

Abstract. This paper presents a domain-specific querying language for model-driven spreadsheets. We briefly show the design of the language and present in detail its implementation, from the denormalization of data and translation of our user-friendly query language to a more efficient query, to the execution of the query using Google. To validate our work, we executed an empirical study, comparing *QuerySheet* with an alternative spreadsheet querying tool, which produced positive results.

Keywords: Spreadsheets · Model-driven engineering · Querying

1 Introduction

Nowadays, spreadsheets can be considered one of the most popular programming system around, particularly in the field of business applications, and one of the largest domain specific programming languages. With their availability on any computing device (PC, smart-phone, etc.) and in the cloud, visual simplicity, low learning curve for new users, and flexibility when it comes to what can be written in a spreadsheet, the amount of users per year increases drastically. Although spreadsheets begin as a simple, single-user software artifact, they may evolve into a large and complex data-centric software [1]. In these cases, manipulating a large amount of data in a traditional matrix structure becomes an arduous task. This issue arises in spreadsheets, unlike the traditional database systems, due to one considerable flaw: the absence of a data query language.

The problem of querying data is not new, having decades worth of attention within the database community. Yet, only recently has it been seriously considered in the context of spreadsheets. And even then, these attempts to replicate a

This work is part funded by ERDF - European Regional Development Fund through the COMPETE Programme (operational programme for competitiveness) and by National Funds through the FCT - Fundação para a Ciência e a Tecnologia (Portuguese Foundation for Science and Technology) within projects FCOMP-01-0124-FEDER-010048, and FCOMP-01-0124-FEDER-022701. The first author was funded by FCT grant SFRH/BPD/73358/2010.

© Springer International Publishing Switzerland 2015
V. Zsók et al. (Eds.): CEFP 2013, LNCS 8606, pp. 459–478, 2015.
DOI: 10.1007/978-3-319-15940-9_13

traditional database querying system have several drawbacks of their own. Most impose restrictions on how the data must be stored, organized, and represented, and some even have a hard-to-read query language.

To solve these problems, we propose a query language based on the Structured Query Language (SQL) where users can easily construct queries right in their spreadsheet environment, without the need of complicated configurations, or extra programs other than a simple add-on. Both SQL and spreadsheets can be seen as domain-specific functional programming languages [2]. Our approach builds upon a model-driven spreadsheet development environment, where the queries would be expressed referencing entities in ClassSheet models, instead of the actual data, allowing the user to not have to worry about the arrangement of the spreadsheet's data, but only what information is present.

This allows spreadsheet evolution to occur in the data or the arrangement of entities within a spreadsheet model, without invalidating previously constructed queries, as long as the entities continue to exist. The query results are then shown as an inferred spreadsheet model, and a new worksheet in conformance with the model. This system was named *QuerySheet* [3,4], and will be shown further on.

Our goal is to make spreadsheet querying more humanized, understandable, robust, and productive. In order to validate our achievements, we executed an empirical study with real end users. Their experiences, productivity, and feedback in using the *QuerySheet* system were recorded and are now presented.

The results observed from this study were positive, as we will discuss further on. Also, we plan to take on the user's feedback to further improve our framework.

This paper is organized as follows: Sect. 2 presents existing techniques to query spreadsheets, detailing two specific approaches. In Sect. 3, a simple introduction to model-driven spreadsheets is given. Section 3 explains the spreadsheet querying system we propose, and shows an example of that envisioned system. In Sect. 4 we present queries for model-driven spreadsheets. We then present in Sect. 5 the design and implementation of our model-driven spreadsheet system, along with a small demonstration of the actual tool in Sect. 6. Section 7 details our empirical study and presents the results. And finally, Sect. 8 presents our concluding thoughts and future work.

2   Spreadsheets and Queries

Before we present techniques to query spreadsheets, let us introduce a spreadsheet to be used as a running example throughout this document. Figure 1 presents a spreadsheet to store information about the budget of a company. This spreadsheet contains information about the Category of budget use (such as Travel or Accommodation) and the Year. The relationship between these two entities gives us information on the Quantity, the Cost, and the Total Costs.

As previously stated, there have been attempts to query spreadsheets using some form of SQL. Two widely known names followed this path to create a

	A	B	C	D	E	F	G	H	I
1	Budget		Year			Year			
2			2005			2006			
3	Category	Name	Qnty	Cost	Total	Qnty	Cost	Total	Total
4		Travel	2	525	1050	3	360	1080	2130
5		Accomodation	4	120	480	9	115	1035	1515
6		Meals	6	25	150	18	30	540	690
7	Total				1680			2655	4335

Fig. 1. Spreadsheet data for a Budget example

spreadsheet querying system: Microsoft and Google, with their MS-Query Tool and Google QUERY Function respectively. The following subsections will give a brief description of each of these approaches.

2.1 MS-Query Tool

Microsoft's Query tool, or MS-Query, is the database query interface used by Microsoft Word and Excel, a utility which imports databases, text files, OLAP cubes, and other spreadsheet representations (such as csv). While these are the main uses, it can be used to query data from a spreadsheet, placing the data into an intermediate database-like table to be able to apply the query and represent the findings, but in turn brings some restrictions.

To be able to query the spreadsheet data, the data itself must be in a single tabular format, with the headers present in the first row. In other words, they require the data to be denormalized [5] if the user wishes to completely represent his spreadsheet information. In most cases, users tend to use their spreadsheet for more than one entity in a single worksheet, not joining all the information into one single unified table (as we can see in our running example in Fig. 1). This requirement prohibits the freedom to represent the spreadsheet data how a user wishes.

Figure 2 shows the necessary denormalized representation of the data in our running example, having the headers of each attribute explicitly represented in a single row, just so we may be able to query the data using the MS-Query tool.

As one may notice, the representation of the data in this way is much harder for someone to read, manage, and analyze, and if looking at a real-life spreadsheet, which might have the number of columns reaching the hundreds, it can become even more difficult. Along with the previously mentioned problem, a user with this representation, may not expand his information horizontally, but only vertically, to conform to the table format needed to query, allowing even less freedom to represent the data.

2.2 Google QUERY Function

Google provides a QUERY function (GQF) which allows users, using a SQL-like syntax, to perform a query over an array of values. An example would be their Google Docs spreadsheets, where the function is built-in.

	A	B	C	D	E	F	G	H
1	Year	Total(Year)	Name	Qnty	Cost	Total	Total(Category)	Total(Grand)
2	2005	1680	Travel	2	525	1050	2130	4335
3	2005	1680	Accomodation	4	120	480	1515	4335
4	2005	1680	Meals	6	25	150	690	4335
5	2006	2655	Travel	3	360	1080	2130	4335
6	2006	2655	Accomodation	9	115	1035	1515	4335
7	2006	2655	Meals	18	30	540	690	4335

Fig. 2. Spreadsheet data for a Budget example (denormalized)

In this setting, a query is a two part function, consisting of a *range* as its first argument, to state the range of the data cells to be queried, for example A1:B6. The second part consists of the *query string* itself, using a subset of the SQL language, with column letters. The function's input also assumes the first row as headers, and each column of the input can only hold values of certain types. An example function is shown in Listing 1.1. This function can actually be written on the spreadsheet itself, allowing on-the-spot results.

Listing 1.1. Google QUERY function example

```
=query(A1:F53;"SELECT A, B, F WHERE D > 5")
```

While being a powerful query function, it still has its flaws. The function shares the same problems as MS-Query in regards to the data representation. Much like MS-Query, to run the function, the data needs to be represented with a single header row, without relationships between the entities, in other words, also denormalized (as already shown in Fig. 2).

Along with the difficulty of managing the data in such a way, the function has another flaw. Instead of writing the query using column names/labels, one must use the column letters (as shown in Listing 1.1) to write the query. Even with the small sized example we have been using, column letters and not names can get confusing, counter-intuitive, and almost impossible to understand what the query is supposed to do, without having the data sheet alongside. Moreover, Google queries do not truly support evolution, since they do not adapt/evolve when the spreadsheet data evolves. That is to say, by adding a new column to the spreadsheet, we may turn a query invalid or incorrect because the data changed positioning in the spreadsheet.

3   Model-Driven Spreadsheet Engineering

To overcome the issues identified in Sect. 2, and to design a language and system which match the previously defined criteria, we turned to model-driven engineering methodologies [6,7]. Model-driven engineering is a development methodology in software development that uses and exploits domain models, or abstract representations of a piece of software, a solution to the handling of complex and evolving software systems. This has been applied to spreadsheets, making model-driven spreadsheets possible [8,9], and even a model-driven spreadsheet environment [10,11].

One of these spreadsheet models is ClassSheets [12,13], a high-level and object-oriented formalism, using the notion of classes and attributes, to express business logic spreadsheet data. Using ClassSheets, we can define the business logic of a spreadsheet in a concise and abstract manner. This results in users being able to understand, evolve, and maintain complex spreadsheets by just analyzing the (ClassSheet) models, avoiding the need to look at large and complex data.

	A	B	C	D	E	F	G
1	Budget		Year			...	
2			year=2005			...	
3	Category	Name	Qnty	Cost	Total	...	Total
4		name="abc"	qnty=0	cost=0	total=qnty*cost	...	total=SUM(total)
5						...	
6	Total				total=SUM(total)	...	total=SUM(Year.total)

Fig. 3. ClassSheet model for a Budget example

To showcase ClassSheets, we present in Fig. 3 a ClassSheet model for the Budget example shown in Fig. 1. In this ClassSheet model, a **Budget** has a **Category** and **Year** class, expanding vertically and horizontally, respectively. The joining of these gives us a **Quantity**, a **Cost**, and the **Total** of a **Category** in a given **Year**, each with its own default value. The **Total** in column G gives us the total of each **Category** and the **Total** in column A gives us the total of each **Year**.

This ClassSheet model specifies the business logic of the budget spreadsheet data from our running example. In model-driven engineering, we would say that the spreadsheet data (Fig. 1) *conforms to* the model (Fig. 3), as shown in Fig. 4.

Using models, we can also have a safe way to practice software evolution [14], a term defining the process of changing an existing software system or program, due to needs, rules, and other factors, is updated, or in other words evolves,

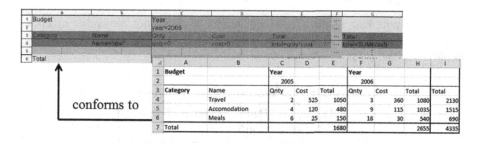

Fig. 4. Spreadsheet model and example in conformity

to continue to be useful in its environment. Evolution, and other techniques (such as spreadsheet model embedding and bidirectionality) are present in the model-driven spreadsheet framework MDSheet [11,15]. A fully detailed explanation of ClassSheets can be found in [Our DSL"13 ClassSheets tutorial].

4   Model-Driven Spreadsheet Querying

Querying spreadsheets should be simple and intuitive as it is in the database realm. Using a simple SQL-like query language, users should be able to easily construct queries right in their spreadsheet environment, without the need of complicated configurations or extra programs. This language should be humanized, avoiding the use of computer-like terms as column letters, and use some form of labels or descriptive tags to point to attributes and entities. In fact, this is in line with the results presented in [16] where authors showed that spreadsheet users create a mental model of the spreadsheet that helps them understand and work with the spreadsheet. These mental models are created using names from the real world as it is the case with our ClassSheet models.

To do this, a good approach would be to build upon a model-driven spreadsheet development environment, where we can take advantage of ClassSheets, allowing the queries to be expressed referencing the entities in ClassSheet models instead of the data's positioning. This would allow the user to not have to worry about the arrangement of the spreadsheet's data, but only what information is present. This is almost identical to how a database administrator or analyst would look at the relational model of a database to construct queries, and not the data itself.

4.1   Querying Model-Driven Spreadsheets: An Example

To show how we envision the model-driven spreadsheet querying system, we will show an example.

Using our previous Budget model from Fig. 3, and the Budget data from Fig. 1, we will try to answer two simple questions:

> Query1: What was our budget use in 2005?
> Query2: What was our total quantity per year?

By simply looking at our ClassSheet model, if we do not remember or know the structure of our spreadsheet data, we would be able to write the following simple SQL-like queries:

Listing 1.2. Model-driven query for Query1

```
SELECT Name, Qnty, Cost, Total
WHERE Year = 2005
```

Listing 1.3. Model-driven query for Query2

```
SELECT  Year ,  Sum( Qnty )
GROUP  BY  Year
LABEL  Sum( Qnty )  " Total  Qnty"
```

These queries will produce the following results shown in Table 1 and Table 2 respectively.

Table 1. Results for Query1

Name	Qnty	Cost	Total
Travel	2	525	1050
Accommodation	4	120	480
Meals	6	25	150

Table 2. Results for Query2.

Year	Total Qnty
2005	12
2006	30

The two equivalent Google QUERY functions would be Listings 1.4 and 1.5 respectively:

Listing 1.4. Google QUERY function for Query1

```
=query ( A1 : H7 ; "SELECT  C,  D,  E,  F WHERE A  =  2005" )
```

Listing 1.5. Google QUERY function for Query1

```
=query ( A1 : H7 ; "SELECT  A,  sum (D)
GROUP  BY  sum (D)  LABEL  sum (D)  ' Total  Qnty ' " )
```

Using this model-driven approach, we eliminate the work of using column letters when writing the query, and the need of restricting the user's data to a specific format. This way, the user can maintain the original spreadsheet, without having to conform to data representation restrictions, and analyze it with references to the entities and attributes presents.

So as one can see, our approach hopes to make querying spreadsheets more:

- *Humanized* - Now we can represent attributes and data areas (models) using human designated names, instead of column letters.
- *Understandable* - Now we can actually understand and easily read the queries, knowing exactly what they do.
- *Robust* - Unless attributes in the query are removed or renamed, the queries can still correctly function even with spreadsheet data/model evolutions.
- *Productive* - No need to manually think through what spreadsheet area our data is inn, or what column letter is a given attribute.

These four topics are what we strived to achieve. To validate these topics, we executed an empirical study, which is presented in Sect. 7 with more details.

5   Design and Implementation

In this section we explain how the model-driven query language system we envisioned has been materialized. Figure 5 presents the overall architecture of our system which we have implemented on top of MDSheet [10].

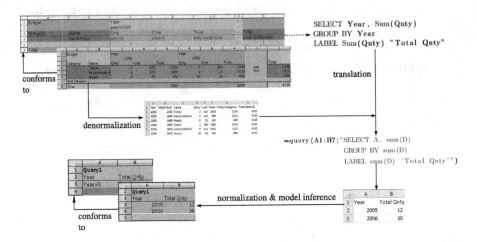

Fig. 5. The model-driven query system

In MDSheet all mechanisms to handle models and instances are already created. This is our starting point: in the left part of the figure we show a spreadsheet instance and its corresponding model. The second required part is the query over the model/instance. This will be explained in detail in the next Subsect. 5.1. The spreadsheet instance is then denormalized, as we will explain in Subsect. 5.2, and the query over the model is translated into a Google query, as explained in Subsect. 5.3. The Google query and the denormalized data are sent to Google and the result received is shown in the bottom-right part of the figure, described in Subsect. 5.4. Finally, a new model is inferred so the result can be used as input to a new query, as explained in Subsect. 5.5. This last step is necessary since we want the queries to be composable, and new models to be generated from queries.

Before presenting the algorithms that are used by our query mechanism, let us introduce our Haskell representation of models and instances.

data *Class = Class Name Expansion [Attribute] HName VName*
data *Expansion = Horizontal | Vertical | Both | None*
data *Attribute = Attribute Name [Value]*
data *Value = Value Val InstanceH InstanceV*
data *Layout = Layout [(Name, ClassName)]*

These are the four main data types for querying in our framework. The *Class* data type holds the *Class*'s *Name*, *Expansion* direction (either *Horizontal*, *Vertical*, *Both*, or *None*) a list of *Attribute*(s), and its horizontal/vertical class name if it has one (*HName*/*VName*). Each attribute also has a *Name*, and a list of *Values*, in which each Value has the value in a cell (*Val*), and its horizontal and vertical instance (*InstanceH* and *InstanceV*). These instances are used to know which relational classes to combine with. The *Layout* data type has the header information of the denormalized data, including the attribute's *Name* and class name (*ClassName*).

We can show the top function of our system. It receives the user's query, along with the worksheet being used. It then passes through all the processes previously mentioned (denormalization, translation, execution, and inference) and returns the new model and instance.

$$
\begin{aligned}
&querysheet :: Query \rightarrow Worksheet \rightarrow (Model, Instance) \\
&querysheet\ query\ worksheet = \\
&\quad \textbf{let}\ (model, inst) && = getModelInstance\ worksheet \\
&\qquad (denormData, layout) && = denormalize\ model\ inst \\
&\qquad googleQueryFun && = translate\ query\ layout \\
&\qquad queryResults && = runGQF\ googleQueryFun\ denormData \\
&\qquad (newModel, newInstance) && = inferClassSheet\ queryResults \\
&\quad \textbf{in}\ (newModel, newInstance)
\end{aligned}
$$

In the next Subsections we will explain in more detail each of the steps of our algorithm.

5.1 Model-Driven Query Language

The Model-Driven Query Language (MDQL) is very similar to the standard SQL language, while also allowing some of the GQF's clauses such as LIMIT and LABEL. To create the MDQL, we used advanced engineering techniques, namely generalized top-down parsers and strategic programming to traverse trees.

The syntax of our query language is defined in the grammar shown in Listing 1.6. As we can see, instead of selecting column letters in the SELECT clause, the user can select the ClassSheet attributes he/she wishes to query, while also allowing him/her to further specify, as to avoid any naming conflicts which may occur, alternative ways of naming the attribute such as:

- stating its name - (**Cost**)
- stating the attribute along with its classes' name (**Year.Total**)
- stating both classes ((**Year, Category**).**Total** or (**Category, Year**).**Total**)
- stating all the attributes in a given class (**Category.***)

Listing 1.6. Part of the model-driven query language syntax

```
SELECT [DISTINCT] (* | attr₁, ...,agg(attrₓ), ...)
 [FROM ClassSheet₁, [JOIN ClassSheet₂], ...]
 [WHERE conditions]
 [GROUP BY attr₁, ...]
 [ORDER BY attr₁ [ASC|DESC], ...]
 [LIMIT numRow]
 [LABEL attr₁ 'new_attr₁', ...]
 [WITH HISTOGRAM]
attr ::= attribute
     | Class.*
     | (Class₁, Class₂).*
     | Class.attribute
     | (Class₁, Class₂).attribute
agg ::= Sum(attr)
     | Count(attr)
     | Avg(attr)
     | Min(attr)
     | Max(attr)
conditions ::= attr logic attr
             | attr logic 'string'
             | attr logic number
logic :: = < | > | <= | >= | == | !=
```

The MDQL also has a FROM clause, very reminiscent from the same clause in SQL, which allows the user to choose which ClassSheet model(s) to use for the query, in cases where more than one ClassSheet is present in a spreadsheet. Also note that as in SQL we allow JOIN operations between two ClassSheets (nonexistent in the GQF). We also have the LIMIT clause to limit the amount of results returned by a given number, and LABEL to rename attributes to a given name, both originating from GQF clauses. The WHERE, GROUP BY, and ORDER BY clauses work the same as in SQL, applying filters such as where an attribute is equal to a given name (e.g. Category.Name = 'Travel'), grouping values to apply an aggregation function, and ordering by a given attribute either ascendant (ASC) or descendant (DESC), all three respectively. Finally, the DISTINCT clause was also implemented (also nonexistent in the GQF) to remove duplicated results which may occur, and WITH HISTOGRAM is used to state if the user wishes the results produce a histogram chart to visually show the results.

Since this language is very similar to SQL, it allows users who already know basic SQL to simply jump into query writing in this system, avoiding the need to learn a new language, allowing us to adapt the most used query language instead of creating one, while also allowing queries to be more elegant, concise, robust and understandable for spreadsheets, along with being easy to learn since the

SQL-language is often described as "English-like" because many of its statements read like English [17].

5.2   Denormalization of Spreadsheet Data

As mentioned before, to be able to use the Google Query Function, the data must be in a single matrix format, with the headers present in the first row. In consequence of this restriction, for a user to be able to write all the queries possible with the data, every bit of data from the spreadsheet has to be written in this single matrix structure. To do so, the data has to be in a redundant state, combining the data from multiple tables together, reminiscent of a JOIN between tables in databases, thus duplicating the data. In other words, we have to denormalize our spreadsheet data [18].

To correctly do this, we must first obtain all the necessary and critical information from the ClassSheet models, and their attributes/data. To begin, we obtain this information from the MDSheet framework (atleast in this context), such as which ClassSheet classes exist, their names, their expansion direction (horizontally, vertically, both, or none at all) and most importantly the attributes in each class.

After obtaining the ClassSheet models and data, we begin the denormalization process, where we denormalize the models used in the query, and join the relational models with their corresponding horizontal and vertical classes. This denormalization process is automatic, and can always be done on the ClassSheet data, as long as we have the ClassSheet model and the conformed data. A fragment of that denormalization process can be seen next.

$$denormalize :: Model \rightarrow Instance \rightarrow (Data, Layout)$$
$$denormalize\ model\ inst =$$
$$\mathbf{let}\ \ allClasses \qquad = merge\ model\ inst$$
$$relationClasses = findRelations\ allClasses$$
$$res \qquad\qquad = relationDenorm\ relationClasses\ allClasses$$
$$ssdata \qquad\quad = getData\ res$$
$$layout \qquad\quad = getLayout\ res$$
$$\mathbf{in}\ (ssdata, layout)$$

As we can see, the first step is to merge the model and instance information together into an intermediate representation we use. Using that intermediate representation, we find the relational classes, for example (Category, Year), and then denormalize the data in the relation, and obtain the spreadsheet data and layout. The true process of denormalizing the data is presented next.

$$relationDenorm :: [\,Class\,] \rightarrow [\,Class\,] \rightarrow Table \rightarrow Table$$
$$relationDenorm\ [\,]\ ac\ tab = tab$$
$$relationDenorm\ ((\,Class\ n\ exp\ attrs\ hName\ vName) : cs)\ ac\ tab =$$
$$\mathbf{let}\ \ hClass\ = getClass\ hName\ ac$$
$$vClass \qquad = getClass\ vName\ ac$$

$$classResJoin \; = rJoin \; (Class \; n, exp, attrs, hName, vName) \; hClass \; vClass$$
$$tabRes \qquad = addTable \; classResJoin \; tab$$
$$table \qquad\; = relationDenorm \; cs \; ac \; tabRes$$
$$\mathbf{in} \; \; table$$

$$rJoin :: Class \to Class \to Class \to Class$$
$$rJoin \; (Class \; n \; exp \; (attr : as) \; hName \; vName) \; hClass \; vClass =$$
$$\quad \mathbf{let} \; \; hAttrs \; = getHInstances \; attribute \; (getAttributes \; hClass)$$
$$\qquad vAttrs \; = getVInstances \; attribute \; (getAttributes \; vClass)$$
$$\qquad clas \; \; = (Class \; n \; exp \; ((attr : as) \; +\!\!+ \; hAttrs \; +\!\!+ \; vAttrs) \; hName \; vName)$$
$$\quad \mathbf{in} \; \; clas$$

We obtain, through the class names, the appropriate classes, which we then use to correctly match and join the information from the relational classes. This process happens in the *rJoin* function, where we use the *HInstances* and *VInstances* to properly match the relational class, with its two "parent" classes.

A more detailed explanation of the denormalization process, along with examples, and description of certain problems automatically solved, can be found in [15].

5.3   Translation to Google Query

The main reason we chose not to develop a new querying engine, but re-utilize the QUERY function's querying engine, is because we do not want to try to compete with Google in terms of performance and speed where Google has shown dominance in developing querying engines.

To properly run the GQF, our model-driven queries must adhere to the *Visualization API Query Language* [19], specified by Google. So, for our model-driven queries to function correctly, a translator was made to transform the model-driven queries to their equivalents for the GQF. To do so, we took advantage of a strategy language to control transformations and pattern matching, to translate and inspect the query respectively.

The translator automatically calculates the *range* from the ClassSheet models selected, in the FROM clause for example, by using a lookup function to find what is the new range of data after the denormalization process. It also substitutes the attribute names to their corresponding column letters in the denormalized data, without the user having to do so. After parsing the user's query, and verifying that each attribute chosen by the user exists, and has no conflicts, such as any ambiguous attribute names due to the attribute name repeating in more than one ClassSheet (which may be solved by adding the class name beforehand as shown in Sect. 5.1), we apply another lookup function on each attribute, and calculate the column letter corresponding to each attribute. A fragment of one of the lookup functions (for translating an attribute with its class name) can be seen in the following:

$$lookUp :: (Name, ClassName) \to Layout \to String$$
$$lookUp \; p \; (Layout \; l) =$$

let *allIndices* = *elemIndices p l*
in if (*length allIndices*) ≡ 1
    then *intToColumn* (*head allIndices*)
    else "ERROR"

Using the *lookUp* function, we find the matching header, and if there is one and only one occurrence, we translate the index number to its appropriate column letter (for example 0 = A, AA = 27). If more than one occurrence occurs, or no occurrences, we send an error.

Now having both the denormalized data and translated model-driven query ready, we can send the spreadsheet data to Google Spreadsheets, run the GQF and afterwards retrieve the results for the user to view in its spreadsheet.

5.4 Google Spreadsheets

To be able to send the spreadsheet data to Google Spreadsheets and run the GQF, we turned to the *Google Spreadsheets API version 3.0* [20], an API which enables developers to be able to create applications that can read, write and modify the data in Google Spreadsheets. It allows us to manage the worksheets in a Google spreadsheet, manage cells in a worksheet by position, and also allows us to create spreadsheets, worksheets, insert and delete data, and retrieve a single worksheet or a spreadsheet, along with authorizing requests and authentication.

So before we acquire the query results, we begin by creating a temporary worksheet which will be filled with the denormalized data, followed by creating a second temporary worksheet where the query function string is sent to. When the query function is inserted into a cell, it calculates the results, and now that second worksheet contains the query results. Finally, the results are retrieved, the temporary worksheets removed and an inference technique is ran before presenting it to the user.

5.5 ClassSheet Inference

In order to make the queries composable, that is, to allow the output of a model-driven query as the input of another model-driven query we must provide the results from the GQF with a model. Without having a model, it is impossible to make a query on a result of another query. Previous work in this field introduced a technique to automatically infer a ClassSheet model from spreadsheet data [21]. Thus, applying this technique on the results obtained from the GQF, we can now infer the correct ClassSheet model and have it alongside the queried results. For example, applying the inference technique to the results from Query2 presented in Table 2, we would obtain the ClassSheet model shown in Fig. 6, and now present the user the results alongside its model.

	A	B
1	**Query1**	
2	Year	Total Qnty
3	Year=0	TotalQnty=0
4	⋮	⋮

Fig. 6. Model automatically inferred from the spreadsheet data shown in Table 2

6   QuerySheet

The model-driven query language and the techniques proposed in the previous sections are the building blocks used to construct a tool, integrated in MDSheet and OpenOffice/LibreOffice, named *QuerySheet* [4].

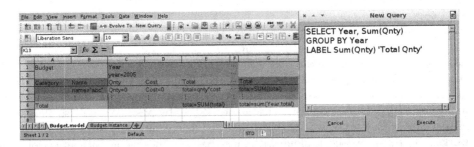

Fig. 7. A model-driven spreadsheet representing Budget information

To demonstrate *QuerySheet*, we will be using the same running ClassSheet model, shown on the left in Fig. 7. Suppose we wanted to answer our previous question:

– What was our total quantity per year?

In *QuerySheet*, we can express the query based on the ClassSheet model. The tool provides a *New Query* button, which opens a text box to allow the user to define a query. As we can see in Fig. 7 on the right, we have the query for our first question, and as expected, the query looks very much like SQL, using the same keywords and syntactic structure. Moreover, we now use the ClassSheet entities to identify the attributes to be queried.

When executing the query, *QuerySheet* passes through all the phases explained in the previous Sections and shown in Fig. 5, while also generating the result as a ClassSheet-driven spreadsheet. In fact, two new worksheets are added to the original spreadsheet: one containing the spreadsheet data that results from the query (Query1.instance), and the other contains the ClassSheet model (Query1.model), as shown in Fig. 8. This whole process is depicted in Fig. 9.

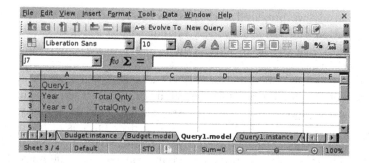

Fig. 8. A model-driven spreadsheet inferred from Query1

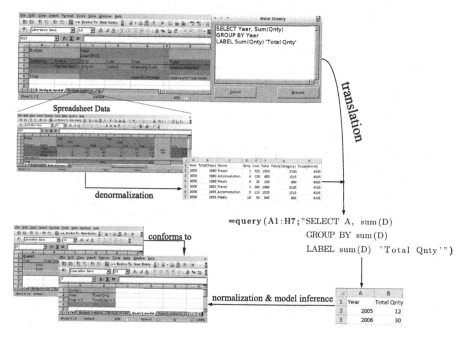

Fig. 9. The architecture of *QuerySheet*

7   Empirical Evaluation

To validate our query system, a study was planned and executed, to obtain results of end-user's experiences, productivity, and feedback. We ran this study one participant at a time. This allowed us to see each participant using our system and learn the difficulties participants were having and how to improve the system to overcome them.

For this study, we had seven students participating, all with basic or minimal knowledge of SQL, who are studying informatics/computer sciences, ranging from Bachelor to PhD students.

For this study we prepared a tutorial to teach them how to use Google's QUERY function and the *QuerySheet* system with a series of exercises using both systems. When the users were comfortable with each system, the actual study was performed.

In the actual study, a real-life spreadsheet was used, which we obtained, with permission to use, from the local food bank in Braga. We then explained to the students how the information was represented, and how to properly read the spreadsheet, in this case, information regarding distributions of basic products and institutions. This specific spreadsheet had information on 85 institutions and 14 different types of basic products, giving way to over 1190 lines of unique information.

We also denormalized the information for the students (since we wanted to study the end-user's interaction with the two different systems, and already knew that denormalizing over 1000 lines of information would take a long time), and also prepared the spreadsheet model and conformed instance in the MDSheet environment. Since we can not show the actual spreadsheet due to revealing private information, only the spreadsheet model (the same one used in the study) is presented below in Fig. 10.

	A	B	C	D	E	F	G
1	Distribution			Product	name=""	...	
2					code=""	...	
3	Institution				stock=0	...	
4	code=""	name=""	lunch=0	dinner=0	distributed=0	...	
5	:	:	:	:	:		:
6						...	

Fig. 10. A model-driven spreadsheet representing institutions, products, and distributions, used in the empirical evaluation

As we can see in the model, and hence the actual spreadsheet, the **Distribution** class is composed of a **Institution** class and a **Product** class. The **Institution** class has its **Code** (Institution's Code), **Name** (Intitution's Name), **lunch** (units used for lunch and snacks) and **dinner** (units used for lunch and dinner). The **Product** class has a **Name** (Product's Name), a **Code** (Product's Code), and **Stock** which represents the amount of that specific product they have in stock. The relationship between both classes gives us information on the quantity **Distributed** of a specific **Product** to a specific **Institution**.

For the study, a series of four questions were asked to the students, regarding the information present in the distributions spreadsheet:

1. What is the total distributed for each product?
2. What is the total stock?
3. What are the names of each institution without repetitions?
4. Which were the products with more than 500 units distributed, and which institution were they delivered to?

For each question, they would answer it using Google's QUERY function, and the *QuerySheet* system, alternating between starting with one then the other (the starting system would also alternate between students, so one would begin alternating starting with *QuerySheet*, and another would begin alternating starting with Google's QUERY function). This alternation was introduced in the study so the potential learning from answering a question in one system could not interfere with the results. Since different participants started by answering the same question using different querying systems, the potential learning can be ignored for both systems.

The students were asked to write down the time after carefully reading each question, and the time after the queries were executed with no errors (the correctness of the queries and results were analyzed afterwards), repeating for each system, so they would read the question, write down initial time, write down concluding time, and repeat starting with reading the question once again.

Along with writing down the time, after each question, and having answered it using both systems, the students were asked to choose which system they felt was more: Intuitive, Faster (to write the queries), Easier (to write the queries), Understandable (being able to explain and understand the written queries).

After finishing answering the questions, the students answered which system they preferred and why, and what advantages/disadvantage existed between the systems. Some of the comments can be seen below:

- *"The usage of models helped alot in building the queries. And not having to calculate the range saves time and headaches."*
- *"Using attribute names instead of column letters is simple and natural."*
- *"QuerySheet is much more intuitive to use, as simple as looking at the model and attribute names and then I could begin writing queries."*

The results were gathered and analyzed, and are now presented in Fig. 11. The left side (Y-Axis) represents the number of minutes the students took to answer the questions. The bottom side (X-Axis) represents the Question the students answered. The green bars represent the Google QUERY function, and the blue bars represent the *QuerySheet* system.[1]

As we can see, users using the *QuerySheet* system spent significantly less time to write the queries to answer the questions, ranging from as much as 90 % less to 40 % less, averaging out to 68 % faster.

Regarding the system they felt was more Intuitive, Faster, Easier, and Understandable, almost all chose the *QuerySheet* system.

We also analyzed the results and queries written, and in the cases where the queries/results were incorrect, almost all were with the Google QUERY function system, ranging from incorrect column letters chosen, to incorrect ranges.

Furthermore, the written questions at the end also gave us positive feedback. Users stated that using the *QuerySheet* system was much easier to write the query, being able to look at the model to understand the logic behind the information, and not having to deal with calculating the ranges, or worry about

---

[1] We assume colors are visible through the digital version of this document.

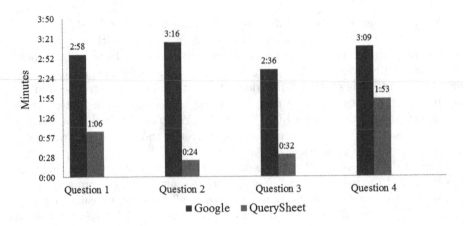

Fig. 11. A chart detailing the information gathered from the empirical evaluation

positing of information, while being easier to understand what is being written and in turn was more intuitive.

With the user feedback, we were also able to understand what is still needed in *QuerySheet*, such as having a way to store the previous queries for future use. Along with the direct user feedback, we also realized that a basic knowledge of SQL is needed, as expected, to be able to correctly answer the questions. Users who incorrectly wrote queries in the *QuerySheet* system always incorrectly wrote them in Google's QUERY function, due to bad query construction. One of the comments received was to have an interface to build the query visually and not descriptively written, something we already believed would be helpful and needed for a user not used to SQL writing.

8   Conclusion

In this paper, we presented the design and implementation of a query language for model-driven spreadsheets. We designed the query language focusing primarily on how expressive, friendly, readable, and intuitive the queries would be to the users. As our study showed we were able to implement a system that can in fact be used to query spreadsheets in a way users are comfortable with.

Indeed we created a query system that can be used to further knowledge extraction from the spreadsheets. For instance, an interesting way to take advantage of it, is to use it for detecting smells in spreadsheets [22–24], similarly to Fowler's idea of detecting bad smells in source code [25]. With our query language, a user can easily detect a specific bad smell on a spreadsheet, before having to handle possibly critical data. This can even be simplified using a predefined set of template queries.

8.1   Future Work

Even with the good results and responses in regards to the work already accomplished, some interesting directions of future research were identified.

Although the empirical results we have presented are interesting, they were the result of a study with only seven participants. We are already planing a second study, this time with more participants so we can confirm our initial results, and provide a more thorough analysis.

Currently, each time a user executes a query, the data is denormalized on-the-spot. A possible way to improve this is to have it so that this full on denormalization is done only once in the beginning, and further changes to data and/or models are changed incrementally, either during the changes, or in the next query execution. An interesting topic which can bring in another level of functionality to the framework, and take advantage of an incremental denormalization, would be synchronization with the query results and original data. By this we mean, allowing a user to, e.g., update the information of one of his/her employees from a previous query result, and in turn this update would reflect upon the original data which the results came from. Acting almost as if the results were a View Table on the original spreadsheet data, possibly using techniques from [26] regarding ways to solve the update-view problems.

References

1. Chambers, C., Scaffidi, C.: Struggling to excel: A field study of challenges faced by spreadsheet users. In: Hundhausen, C.D., Pietriga, E., Díaz, P., Rosson, M.B. (eds.) VL/HCC, pp. 187–194. IEEE (2010)
2. Wadler, P.: Xquery: a typed functional language for querying xml. In: Jeuring, J., Jones, S.L.P. (eds.) AFP 2002. LNCS, vol. 2638, pp. 188–212. Springer, Heidelberg (2003)
3. Cunha, J., Mendes, J., Fernandes, J.P., Pereira, R., Saraiva, J.: Querying model-driven spreadsheets. In: IEEE Symposium on Visual Languages and Human-Centric Computing. IEEE CS, San Jose (2013)
4. Belo, O., Cunha, J., Fernandes, J.P., Mendes, J., Pereira, R., Saraiva, J.: Querysheet: A bidirectional query environment for model-driven spreadsheets. In: IEEE Symposium on Visual Languages and Human-Centric Computing, VLHCC 2013. IEEE CS, San Jose (2013)
5. Maier, D.: The Theory of Relational Databases. Computer Science Press, Rockville (1983)
6. Schmidt, D.C.: Guest editor's introduction: Model-driven engineering. Computer 39(2), 25–31 (2006)
7. Bézivin, J.: Model driven engineering: an emerging technical space. In: Lämmel, R., Saraiva, J., Visser, J. (eds.) GTTSE 2005. LNCS, vol. 4143, pp. 36–64. Springer, Heidelberg (2006)
8. Ireson-Paine, J.: Model master: an object-oriented spreadsheet front-end. In: Computer-Aided Learning using Technology in Economies and Business Education (1997)
9. Abraham, R., Erwig, M., Kollmansberger, S., Seifert, E.: Visual Specifications of Correct Spreadsheets. In: VL/HCC 2005: IEEE Symposium on Visual Languages and Human-Centric Computing, pp. 189–196. IEEE Computer Society (2005)

10. Cunha, J., Fernandes, J.P., Mendes, J., Saraiva, J.: MDSheet: A framework for model-driven spreadsheet engineering. In: Proceedings of the 34th International Conference on Software Engineering, pp. 1412–1415. ACM (2012)

11. Mendes, J.: Evolution of model-driven spreadsheets. Master's thesis, University of Minho (2012)

12. Engels, G., Erwig, M.: ClassSheets: automatic generation of spreadsheet applications from object-oriented specifications. In: Proceedings of the 20th IEEE/ACM International Conference on Automated Software Engineering, pp. 124–133. ACM (2005)

13. Bals, J.C., Christ, F., Engels, G., Erwig, M.: Classsheets - model-based, object-oriented design of spreadsheet applications. In: Proceedings of the TOOLS Europe Conference (TOOLS 2007), Zürich (Swiss), vol. 6, pp. 383–398, October 2007. Journal of Object Technology

14. Mens, T., Demeyer, S. (eds.): Software Evolution. Springer, New York (2008)

15. Pereira, R.: Querying for model-driven spreadsheets. Master's thesis, University of Minho (2013)

16. Kankuzi, B., Sajaniemi, J.: An empirical study of spreadsheet authors' mental models in explaining and debugging tasks. In: 2013 IEEE Symposium on Visual Languages and Human-Centric Computing (VL/HCC), pp. 15–18 (2013)

17. Melton, J.: Database language sql. In: Bernus, P., Mertins, K., Schmidt, G. (eds.) Handbook on Architectures of Information Systems. International Handbooks on Information Systems, pp. 103–128. Springer, Heidelberg (1998)

18. Shin, S.K., Sanders, G.L.: Denormalization strategies for data retrieval from data warehouses. Decis. Support Syst. **42**(1), 267–282 (2006)

19. Google: Google query function (2013). https://developers.google.com/chart/interactive/docs/querylanguage. (Accessed on November 2013)

20. Google: Google spreadsheet api (2013). https://developers.google.com/google-apps/spreadsheets. (Accessed on November 2013)

21. Cunha, J., Erwig, M., Saraiva, J.: Automatically inferring classsheet models from spreadsheets. In: IEEE Symposium on Visual Languages and Human-Centric Computing, pp. 93–100. IEEE CS (2010)

22. Cunha, J., Fernandes, J.P., Martins, P., Mendes, J., Saraiva, J.: Smellsheet detective: A tool for detecting bad smells in spreadsheets. In: Erwig, M., Stapleton, G., Costagliola, G. (eds.) VL/HCC, pp. 243–244. IEEE (2012)

23. Cunha, J., Fernandes, J.P., Ribeiro, H., Saraiva, J.: Towards a catalog of spreadsheet smells. In: Murgante, B., Gervasi, O., Misra, S., Nedjah, N., Rocha, A.M.A.C., Taniar, D., Apduhan, B.O. (eds.) ICCSA 2012, Part IV. LNCS, vol. 7336, pp. 202–216. Springer, Heidelberg (2012)

24. Hermans, F., Pinzger, M., van Deursen, A.: Detecting and visualizing inter-worksheet smells in spreadsheets. In: Proceedings of the 2012 International Conference on Software Engineering, ICSE 2012. IEEE Press, Piscataway (2012)

25. Fowler, M.: Refactoring: Improving the Design of Existing Code. Addison-Wesley Longman Publishing Co., Inc., Boston (1999)

26. Bohannon, A., Vaughan, J.A., Pierce, B.C.: Relational lenses: A language for updateable views. In: Principles of Database Systems (PODS) (2006). Extended version available as University of Pennsylvania technical report MS-CIS-05-27

Rea: Workflows for Cyber-Physical Systems

Dávid Juhász$^{(\boxtimes)}$, László Domoszlai, and Barnabás Králik

Department of Programming Languages and Compilers, Faculty of Informatics,
Eötvös Loránd University, Budapest, Hungary
juhda@caesar.elte.hu, dlacko@pnyf.inf.elte.hu, kralikba@elte.hu

Abstract. Cyber-Physical Systems (CPSs) are distributed systems composed of computational and physical processes, often containing human actors. In a CPS setting, the computational processes collect information about their physical environment via sensors and react upon them using actuators in order to realize a change in the physical world.

In the approach presented in this paper, a CPS application is described as a hierarchical workflow of loosely-coupled tasks whose execution can be constrained with various conditions. We have designed a framework (Péα) of a minimal set of combinators implementing features relevant to CPS programming. The details are revealed through an illustrative example defined in our fully functional implementation embedded into an extended version of the Erlang distributed functional programming language.

Keywords: Cyber-physical system · Task-oriented programming · Workflow · Domain-specific language

1 Introduction

Cyber-Physical Systems (CPSs) are around us. The information systems that influence our lives so much are getting integrated, and increasingly interact with activities and processes of the real world. There are many application domains where Cyber-Physical Systems have appeared. However, from the programmers' perspective, Cyber-Physical Systems also constitute a well-defined domain. Programming such systems requires a certain set of techniques, and many CPS applications share a certain set of requirements. Therefore, we aim to discover methodologies for developing CPS applications and provide support for CPS programming.

The approach we have taken is based on a recent programming paradigm, task-oriented programming (TOP), in which computations are defined as workflows of simpler computational steps usually called primitive tasks. We designed a hierarchical workflow language (Péα), whose features are presented in this paper. The language provides a minimal set of combinators that are relevant to CPS programming.

Péα is a domain-specific workflow language the first incarnation of which is an embedding into an extended version of the distributed functional programming language Erlang. We choose Erlang due to its built-in capabilities

© Springer International Publishing Switzerland 2015
V. Zsók et al. (Eds.): CEFP 2013, LNCS 8606, pp. 479–506, 2015.
DOI: 10.1007/978-3-319-15940-9_14

of seamless distribution. Moreover, TOP and functional programming makes it able to orchestrate a complex application from loosely coupled building blocks. This seems to be a crucial characteristic for easing the testing and verification of such complex systems.

To demonstrate the capabilities of our framework, a small scale example has been worked out the implementation of which poses all the challenges with which developers of large scale CPS applications have to cope. Besides implementing a workflow application for the example, we have tailored a special piece of hardware to run the application and give a real-world demonstration. Different features of Péα are revealed through the step-by-step construction of a control application for that example.

We have two contributions presented in this paper:

- We designed Péα, a distributed, hierarchical workflow system for building CPS applications from loosely coupled tasks whose execution can be constrained with various conditions.
- We implemented a fully functional Péα framework as an embedding into an extended version of Erlang.

The rest of the paper is structured as follows. The problem domain at hand, Cyber-Physical Systems, is summarized in Sect. 2. Section 3 describes the principles of Péα followed by a review of an illustrative example in Sect. 4. The workflow application controlling the device described there is revealed using the actual syntax of the Péα implementation embedded into Erlang in Sect. 5. Related work is discussed in Sect. 6 and, finally, Sect. 7 concludes the paper.

2   Cyber-Physical Systems

Cyber-Physical Systems [14] are networks of computational and physical processes, often containing human actors. In a CPS setting, the computational processes collect information about their physical environment via sensors and react upon them using actuators in order to realize a change in the physical world. Some examples, to illustrate the vast diversity of the application domains, are as follows: automated production lines, automated transportation systems, infantry fighting vehicles, robotic surgery, smart home and smart city applications.

Nevertheless, those very different application domains have common attributes raising issues that are to be addressed. Computational devices involved in a CPS are typically embedded devices, i.e. limitations on power consumption and performance have to be considered. There is a network of computational devices working to reach a common goal, which needs an efficient goal-driven distribution of data and computation among those nodes. Physical environment is to be taken into account when defining the behaviour of the system, which also should be able to react in a physical way. To that end, handling sensors and actuators has to be an essential piece of the building blocks upon which a CPS application is built. A special part of the applications' physical environment is the segment of human beings. Making humans able to interact with a smart system in a comfortable way is to be settled as well. Last but not least, most of the CPSs are critical systems on which even human lives might depend.

There are also other requirements with which CPSs' software must deal, e.g. real-time constraints, robustness, fault-tolerance, failure recovery, adaptivity, safety and security.

Our first step towards answering the aforementioned challenges is P$\acute{e}\alpha$ presented in this paper. Its current implementation addresses the basic questions of CPS development. More sophisticated software features – e.g. failure recovery, adaptivity or a limited scope of timing constraints – could be easily implemented using current features. Other issues – such as precise worst-case execution time and resource consumption estimation – need more research to be done.

3 P$\acute{e}\alpha$ – A language for Cyber-Physical Workflows

In P$\acute{e}\alpha$, the behaviour of a CPS application is described as a workflow of loosely coupled tasks whose execution can be constrained with various conditions, where tasks are composed by combinators that are applicable to CPS programming. Principles and considerations behind the design of P$\acute{e}\alpha$ are published in [12].

The basics of task-oriented programming are summarized in Sect. 3.1. The details of P$\acute{e}\alpha$ compared to the general principles of TOP are exposed in Sect. 3.2, and a short description on the DSL implementation in Erlang is provided in Sect. 3.3. A more detailed elaboration of P$\acute{e}\alpha$'s features is provided through an example in Sect. 5.

3.1 Task-Oriented Programming

Task-Oriented Programming (TOP) [18] is a novel programming paradigm for the development of distributed multi-user applications which extends pure functional programming with a notion of tasks and operations for composing programs from tasks. Its four main concepts are as follows:

– *Tasks:* Tasks are abstract descriptions of interactive persistent units of work that have a typed value. Other tasks can observe the *current* value of a task. The observed current value can be of three kinds: (1) the task has no observable value; (2) the current value of the task is *unstable*, it may change in the future; (3) the current value of the task is *stable*, it is the final value of the task.
– *Many-to-many Communication with Shared Data:* When multiple tasks are executed simultaneously, they may need to share data among each other. In TOP, typed abstract interfaces, the so-called *Shared Data Sources* are provided to read, write and update shared data atomically. When one task modifies shared data, the other tasks can observe this change.
– *Generic Interaction:* A TOP framework generates user interfaces *generically* for any type of data used by tasks. This means that the framework can be asked to manage single interactions such as entering, updating or displaying some data, and it takes care of all the related job automatically, e.g. generating a user interface, client-server communication, state management, etc.

- *Task Composition:* TOP defines a small carefully designed set of core combinator functions from which complex patterns can be constructed. These are: (1) *dynamic* sequential composition, where dynamic means that the subsequent task can be dependent of the current value of some initial task; (2) parallel composition: the simultaneously executed tasks have read only access to the current values of their siblings to be able to monitor each other.

3.2   Tasks and Combinators in P$\mathcal{E}\alpha$

A P$\mathcal{E}\alpha$ *task* corresponds to that of TOP, dynamic sequential and parallel compositions are supported as well. Instead of shared data sources, P$\mathcal{E}\alpha$ provides the pipe construct for tasks to observe the current value of another task. Note that the functionality of a shared data source can be easily simulated by using pipes. P$\mathcal{E}\alpha$ has some primitives for interacting with the user via a form-based user interface. The implementation of this might seem rudimentary - but keep in mind that P$\mathcal{E}\alpha$ is supposed to be used (mostly) in headless embedded systems.

In P$\mathcal{E}\alpha$, a constant value can be turned into a task with the function return; while a complex computation defined by a host-language function can be transformed into a task by using the function task_create. Such tasks are called *primitive tasks*, as they are the smallest building blocks of workflows. More complex tasks, that are considered *workflows*, can be created by combining already defined ones using *combinators*. Besides stable and unstable values, a task in P$\mathcal{E}\alpha$ can result in a special kind of final value, exception, which stops the execution of subsequent tasks.

The system provides predefined primitive tasks. Two general ones are the following: (1) delay blocks for a given amount of time, then results in a special stable value timeout; (2) current_node returns the name of the Erlang virtual machine it is executed in. GUI operations, pipes and message passing among simultaneously executed tasks have their predefined primitive tasks as well.

Primitive tasks are considered atomic operations, which typically do not have unstable values. The predefined task show_form, which handles the user interaction with a GUI form, is an exception to this as it raises unstable values in correspondence with state changes of GUI elements. Nevertheless, the function task_create, which is provided for workflow developers to create their own application-specific primitive tasks, supports only the creation of tasks without unstable values.

Combinators that can be used to compose tasks to build more complex ones in P$\mathcal{E}\alpha$ are shown in Fig. 1. We introduce a graphical representation of the combinators in order to ease understanding of program logic for domain experts. There is a 1-to-1 mapping between elements of the graphical notation and elements of the language - thus, executable code can be generated from such diagrams in a straightforward manner.

The *sequence combinator* simply executes two tasks in a sequence, passing the result of the first task to the second one. It is the only combinator which raises new unstable values: the inner result of the sequence becomes an unstable value when produced by the first task. All the other combinators propagate

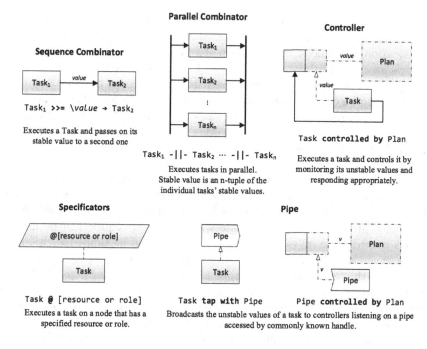

Fig. 1. Combinators in Péα

or process the unstable values raised by instances of the sequence combinator. While stable values are passed on according to the control flow, unstable values are propagated backward in the control flow graph.

The *parallel combinator* is to use when concurrency is required in a workflow. The combinator operates in the fork-join model: all the subtasks are executed in parallel and the whole construct would finish when all parallel tasks are finished. The unstable and stable values of the parallel combinator is a list consisting of those of the subtasks. A task executed by the parallel combinator is able to observe the actual state of its siblings through a pipe created by the combinator. Moreover, parallel tasks are able to send messages to each other according to the roles associated to them.

A *controller* executes a task and processes its unstable values. Each unstable value raised inside of the observed task triggers the execution of the so-called plan, which is a task with a special result. The stable value of a plan can be of two kinds: (1) an `unstable` result indicates that the observed task can continue and the value resulted by the plan is propagated as unstable value to other tasks observing the controller; (2) a `stable` result means that the observed task is to be stopped and the value resulted by the plan is the result of the controller. If the observed task completes without the controller stopping it, the result of the controller is that of the observed task. Hierarchies of tasks can be defined by means of nested controllers. Note that the unstable values of a plan are ignored by the executing controller. Though a plan could be constructed with controllers inside, such a practice would lead to workflows of bad design.

Péα provides *specificators* to constrain the execution of tasks according to a number of conditions. Currently, specificators defining constraining conditions on the location and time of the execution of a task are built in to Péα. The usage of the *resource specificator* is shown in Fig. 1. When executing a task annotated with a resource specificator, the runtime environment ensures that the annotated task is going to be executed on a node which provides the specified resource(s). Note that we can say *role* when talking about a number of resources connected to each other and provided always together, e.g. a node running on a kettle provides the resources *heating elements* and *thermometers*, and is referred to as a node of the role `kettle`.

A *pipe* can be used to observe the state of a task which is in an unconnected part of the control flow graph – namely in a parallel branch of execution. Note that unstable values are propagated backward in the control flow, thus sibling tasks cannot observe each other's state without pipes. A pipe can be used in two ways according to its two endpoints: (1) a task can be tapped with a pipe, in which case the unstable values of the tapped task are propagated through the pipe, and the behaviour of the tapped task does not change locally; (2) the receiving end of a pipe can be observed by a controller, so making it possible for the remote state to be taken into account. Data flow paths unrelated to the control flow can be introduced in a workflow this way.

More details about the combinators and their usage are discussed in Sect. 5.

3.3   Implementation as an Embedding into Erlang

A fully functional implementation of the system is developed as a domain-specific language embedded into an extended version of the Erlang [1] functional programming language. Erlang has been chosen as a host language for the first implementation of Péα since it is a widely used programming language for implementing highly scalable, distributed, reliable, and fault-tolerant software systems [6]. Even though having appropriate properties for implementing the designed features, Erlang is certainly not suitable as a host language for embedding DSLs into and does not support code mobility.

To mend the above mentioned flaws, Péα workflows are implemented in an extended version of the Erlang language. Programs in this language are translated back to simple Erlang in one single step, then compiled and run as usual Erlang applications. The required transformations are implemented twice with two different software transformation tools separately to compare their capabilities. One of the tools is a fork of RefactorErl [4], which is a static analysis and refactoring toolkit for Erlang. The other one is a standalone tool developed using the Spoofax language workbench [9], which is a general-purpose toolkit for implementing (domain specific) languages.

The combinators of Péα are implemented as regular Erlang functions, but are provided for workflow developers as operators of the language. Custom operators cannot be defined nor overridden in pure Erlang. However, the extended language gives us a natural way to let arbitrary function names be used in prefix or infix form. Even precedences can be assigned to them. Appropriately exploiting these features, even mixfix operators can be expressed.

Using resource specificators requires the framework to transmit tasks between separate Péα nodes. Sending tasks between Erlang virtual machines is not trivial. More often than not, a task consists of primitive tasks defined by means of anonymous Erlang functions. Erlang does not support sending such functions out of the virtual machine in which it is defined. To overcome this limitation, we extended Erlang with so-called portable functions. These are supported by a transformation which turns anonymous functions into complex data terms representing the computations along with their dependencies attached.

Further details on the language extension are revealed in [8].

4   Illustrative Example

Having described our problem domain, Cyber-Physical Systems, and the basics of our framework, an illustrative example, the implementation of which poses all the challenges with which developers of large scale CPS applications have to cope, is discussed. The problem and the hardware abstraction layer of the solution are revealed in the current section, while the control logic implemented as a Péα workflow is presented in Sect. 5.

4.1   Bringing Water to Boil

The example is about an interactive, computer-controlled, networked, safe and fault tolerant kettle. Features include letting the user define when she would like to have hot or boiling water; how hot exactly should the water be; automatic fault detection and correction by using hot spares of hardware components; cutting off heating when water reached the desired temperature and maintaining that level of temperature until water is consumed or unit is turned off.

The kettle is a wireless device connecting to a network. Other devices connected to the same network can monitor and control the kettle. This scenario is shown in Fig. 2. Currently, only one device is allowed to be in control of the kettle at a given time; nevertheless any number of devices could monitor its status.

In that small scale Cyber-Physical System, the control application may be executed on separate devices in a distributed manner – among which there could

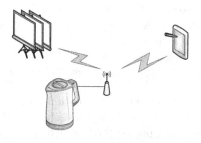

Fig. 2. Wireless access to the kettle

be embedded systems as well. The kettle itself is an embedded device in such a system. The application measures specific properties of the physical world via thermometers and reacts upon changes via actuators – namely by turning coils on and off.

Some details about the hardware and the software environment running on it are exposed in Sect. 4.2; its Péα interface – as a set of application-specific primitive tasks - is described in Sect. 4.3. Main parts of the control application are elaborated in Sect. 5.

4.2   The Hardware

Our tailor-made piece of hardware, "The Budapest Kettle", consists of multiple coils and thermometers which are directly controlled by a custom circuit. The controller application runs on a tiny, WiFi-capable router built into the kettle, which is thus able to take part in a distributed network of Péα nodes.

The heater tank contains 3 off-the-shelf electric kettles built into one common enclosure along with 3 thermometer chips. The coils and the temperature measurement units are directly connected to a self-designed interface board with relays, data converters and an 8-bit microcontroller. The main computing unit of the kettle is a travel router with a MIPS24Kc processor. The serial communication link provided by the interface board is connected to the router via a Serial over USB adapter.

The firmware of the interface board has also been developed in our lab. The router runs a copy of OpenWRT, an embedded Linux distribution for routers, on which Péα is executed by a stripped down version of Erlang R16B01 release.

More details about the hardware and the software code are provided on our website: http://cps.elte.hu/kettle.

4.3   Low-Level Control

Without exposing the actual protocol implemented by the interface board, a short summary on the features is given.

- The board can read the current values from thermometers and return a list of raw measurements – voltage levels –, that need to be converted to degrees Celsius according to the specification of the used thermometers.
- The board can be instructed to change the states of relays connected to it, so switching individual coils on and off.
- Last but not least, the board is able to provide information about the project during which the research and development have been carried out.

The interface board has a serial communication port connected to the embedded router via USB using a Serial to USB converter, which yields a serial device on the Linux system. Connecting to the serial device directly from Erlang is not so easy to do because the Erlang virtual machine does not allow blocking functions. Therefore, natively implemented functions (NIFs) have to be used to realize such functionality. There is a publicly available Erlang module, `srly`, providing direct access to serial devices. However, it uses platform-specific features in NIFs that make it incompatible with the architecture of our embedded router's CPU. Thus, communication is performed through TCP, which needs a Serial-TCP bridge running on the router.

For safety reasons, the board automatically cuts off the power supply of the coils when there is no communication for a considerable length of time.

The controller module, `kettle_controller`, is implemented as an instance of Erlang OTP's `gen_tcp` behaviour, which connects to the Serial-TCP bridge on *localhost* and runs as a service in the Erlang virtual machine. A Péα node running on a kettle has the role `kettle`, which indicates that the service implemented by the module `kettle_controller` is provided for the workflows executed on the node.

Péα applications are able to interact with the kettle via the interface functions exported from the module `kettle_controller`. The two relevant interface functions of `kettle_controller` are wrapped into primitive tasks, that are utilised by the kettle controller application.

- `read_temperature` receives measurements from thermometer chips, converts them to actual temperature values and returns a list of them.
- `set_relays` is a unary function whose argument is a list of 3 logical values indicating for each coil if it has to be provided with power supply.

5 The Control Application

In this section, we define the main parts of an application controlling the kettle described in Sect. 4. The application is revealed step-by-step from a trivial solution to a complex one which has the features listed previously. The different capabilities of our system are also explained along the way.

Only snippets of the full program code are presented in the paper. Fully functional workflow applications are available for download on our web page.

5.1 Simply Bring Water to Boil

The very first version of the control application does not provide any sophisticated features, it only brings the water to boil. All the coils are switched on at the beginning, then switched off when the water temperature has reached its boiling point.

The Trivial Solution. The entry point of the workflow listed in Code 1 is the function `main`, which executes the workflow defined in `control_workflow` on a Péα node having the role `kettle`. On such a node, the `kettle_controller` module is available, thus kettle-specific operations of the control application can be executed. The remote execution combinator `@!`, which is a resource specificator, ensures that exactly one kettle will be selected to execute the workflow.

```
kettle_plan() ->
 fun!(V) ->
  case V of
   #task_value{value = {ok, Ts}} ->
    effective_temperature(Ts) >>= fun!(T) ->
    Error_Threshold = 3,
    if
     T > 100 - Error_Threshold ->
      kettle_controller:set_relays([off,off,off]) >>|
      stable({done, T});
     true ->
      unstable(T)
    end
  end end
 end.

temperature_reading() ->
 iterate(fun!() ->
  kettle_controller:read_temperature() >>= fun!(Ts) ->
  continue(Ts) end end).

control_workflow() ->
 kettle_controller:set_relays([on,on,on]) >>|
 temperature_reading() controlled by kettle_plan().

main() ->
 execute(control_workflow() @! [kettle]).
```

Code 1. Simply bring water to boil

The control workflow consists of two tasks combined with a sequential combinator which discards the result of its first component, i.e. it is not used by the rest of the computation. First, all three coils are switched on. After that, the actual temperature of the water is monitored. The latter is implemented by a controller which executes temperature_reading controlled by kettle_plan.

As the temperature must be measured continuously in order for the application to be able to cut the power when the water starts to boil, measuring is implemented as an iterative task. The iterative combinator iterate is provided with a nullary function which defines a workflow reading the actual temperature and returning it wrapped into a continue value. The resulted value indicates that the workflow belonging to iterate is to be executed again. In that workflow, the original variant of the sequential combinator is used, which makes it possible to use the result of the first task later on. Note that temperature values returned by read_temperature are propagated towards the plan of the controller as unstable values.

```
temperature_reading() ->
 iterate(fun!() ->
  kettle_controller:read_temperature() >>= fun!(Ts) ->
  delay(timer:seconds(1)) >>|
  continue(Ts) end end).
```

Code 2. Delaying subsequent sensor readings

The plan in this case is very straightforward. It receives the actual temperature reading as a task value and lets the application run until the temperature has reached the boiling point. The hardware interface returns a list of readings from all of the temperature sensors. This list is then transformed into one value by the task effective_temperature. That task can compute the average of the values or perform more sophisticated computations with the list, e.g. discarding extreme values or sudden changes from a given sensor. In general, such design decisions are made by domain experts.

Having an effective temperature computed, there is one simple question to answer: is the water boiling yet? If the temperature is within the range of the boiling point – considering an error threshold –, the coils are switched off and a stable value is returned. Otherwise, the water is deemed to require more heating. Note that returning a stable value indicates that the controlled task is to be ended, and the workflow would continue its execution with subsequent tasks.

In our example, as there are no subsequent tasks after the controller in the workflow, the kettle control application is terminated.

Slowing down the Sampling Rate. In the previous version of the workflow, temperature is read continuously, which yields an overflow of sensory data. Instead, the sampling can be made coarser by delaying subsequent sensor readings. Again, it is up to domain experts to decide the right sampling rate. In the case of the kettle, a 1 Hz sampling rate is sufficient to safely detect water temperature.

The extended version of task temperature_reading is listed in Code 2. In this version, an extra task is put between the sensor reading and continue. One of the predefined primitive tasks in Péα is delay, which blocks for the given amount of time, then returns a special value, timeout.

Note that higher level timing combinators, e.g. setting a timeout for tasks and rerun tasks periodically, can be easily defined by the means of delay and basic Péα combinators.

Note that sensory data is propagated to the associated plan as soon as sequential combinators raise unstable values. The set delay only postpone later readings.

```
form("kettle monitor",
  [label(11, "Temperature:"), label(temp, ""),
   label(12, "Coils:"), label(heat, ""),
   label(comment, "")], []).
```

Code 3. Declarative description of the monitor form

```
kettle_workflow() ->
  create_form(monitor_form()) @! [iot_monitor] >>= fun!(Form) ->
  par([
    show_form(Form),
    control_workflow(Form) @! [kettle]
  ]) end.
```

Code 4. The new entry point of the control workflow

5.2 Monitoring Status

The next step is to somehow visualise the status of the kettle. This is achieved in a simple way, by using predefined Péα GUI form components.

Creating a Monitor Form. First of all, a form is to be defined. Péα supports the declarative description of forms, as shown in Code 3. The form function needs three arguments: the title of the form, a list of the form components and a list of actions corresponding to buttons in the form — the rest is handled by the framework.

In our example, the actual temperature and status of coils are committed to the form with some comments, e.g. indicating that the water has reached the desired temperature, or that something went wrong.

Having a form description generated by form, a form instance must be created on a capable Péα node and then shown on that particular node. The instantiation of forms is performed by the task create_form, which creates a form on the local node and returns a descriptor which can be used anywhere inside the Péα network to reach the instance. A form instance can be shown, updated and stopped.

Let us consider the beginning of the life-cycle of a form as presented in Code 4. A form is created on a node with role iot_monitor, then displayed by show_form, which is run with control_workflow in parallel. That is because show_form is blocking until the form is stopped, closed or one of its actions is selected by clicking on a button. Nevertheless, the form descriptor is now passed to control_workflow as it is needed to update the components of the form.

A task updating temperature value in a form can be seen in Code 5. The temperature value is converted into text, with which an update request is generated using form_update. The update then can be realized by update_form fed with a form descriptor and an update request. A form can be updated before and while it is shown, but not afterwards.

```
temperature_writer(Form) ->
 fun(T) -> task_create(fun!()->
  Text = io_lib:format("~p", [T]),
  Update = form_update([label_update(temp, Text)]),
  update_form(Form, Update)
 end) end.
```

Code 5. Writing temperature to a form

```
create_form(monitor_form()) @ [iot_monitor].
```

Code 6. A task creating a number of monitor forms

Implementing other form updates are left as an exercise to the reader.

For this version of the workflow to be ready, kettle_plan also needs some modification to keep the information on the monitor form up-to-date: a few update requests for the values on the form have to be inserted in certain points; and the form is also to be stopped just before returning the final stable value from the plan. This latter can be done by using the primitive task stop_form fed with the form descriptor.

Note that the remote execution combinator @, which is an other kind of resource specificator beside @!, executes an instance of a task on each such node that provides the required resource(s). Thus, the task of Code 6 results in a list of form descriptors by creating a monitor form on each iot_monitor node connected to the Péα network. Maintaining a number of forms would require only a slight extension of the workflow to issue update requests for all of the forms instead of just one of them.

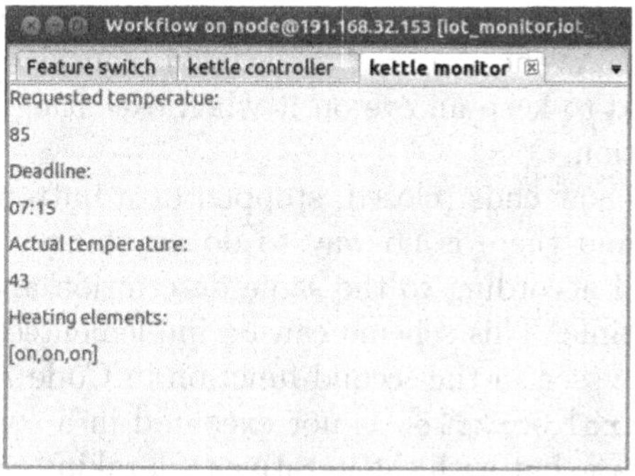

Fig. 3. The final shape of the kettle monitor form

```
monitor_form_plan () ->
 fun!(#task_value{value = [#task_value{value = FV}, _]}) ->
   case get_action (FV) of
    closed ->
     stable (continue (FV));
    stopped ->
     stable (FV);
    _ ->
     unstable (FV)
   end;
   (V) -> V
 end.

controlled_monitor_form () ->
 iterate (fun! () ->
   create_form (monitor_form ()) @! [iot_monitor] >>= fun! (Form) ->
   par ([
    show_form (Form),
    form_updater (Form)
   ]) controlled by monitor_form_plan ()
  end
 end).

kettle_workflow () ->
 par ([
   {monitor, controlled_monitor_form ()},
   control_workflow () @! [kettle]
 ]).
```

Code 7. Recreating the monitor form iteratively

The Form is Important. The definition of a monitor form does not contain any actions (see Code 3), so show_form will never return because a button was pressed. Nevertheless, the user is able to close the form by clicking the 'x' at the top of the tab (see Fig. 3). Although one form cannot be forced to remain open against the user's will, the user can be forced to deal with the form by recreating it over and over again. As the status of the kettle is considered to be important, the user will be forced to keep an eye on it when executing further revisions of the workflow application.

Once a form somehow ends (closed, stopped or a button has been clicked), its life-cycle is over and there is no way to do anything with it. A new form has to be instantiated according to the same description and the new instance is to be shown next time. This scheme can be implemented using the iterative combinator, as can be seen in the second function in Code 7.

In this case, control_workflow is not executed in a common parallel construct with a show_form, but with the iterative task taking care of recreating the monitor form if needed. Moreover, that task has the role monitor, which makes other tasks executing in the same parallel environment able to send it messages by using the predefined primitive task send_role_msg. Utilising message passing facilities of P*éα* is necessary because the dynamically changing form descriptor is required for updating the status information.

Inside the iterative task, the descriptor of the form actually displayed is available, thus the form_updater task is able to directly issue updates on that form. The implementation of form_updater consists simply in iteratively receiving messages by means of the predefined task receive_msg, and executing the proper form updaters that were already used in the previous version of the application. On the other side, form updaters are replaced with tasks sending appropriate messages to the role monitor from control_workflow.

The plan controlling the parallel task inside the iterative combinator seems a bit complicated because parallel combinators are propagating a list of task values inside an unstable value. Thus, pattern matching against a list of an appropriate length is necessary. The result of a displayed form is of the record form_value, which contains an action and the final values of the form components. The action can be one of the user-defined actions belonging to the form or one of two special values: closed and stopped. The former indicates that the form has been closed by the user, whilst the latter indicates that the form has been stopped by the application itself. In the case of monitor_form_plan, the iterative task is to be rerun if the user closed the form, i.e. it returns a continue value if the resulted action is closed.

Note that form updates are causing unstable values of the record form_value raised with action updated, which is why the last branch is present in the conditional expression. Also note that different instances of the monitor form might appear on separate iot_monitor nodes as the node is selected before each instantiation. One could force the form to be recreated on the same node by two means: (1) moving the remote execution operator outside of the iterative combinator or (2) selecting an iot_controller node outside of the iterative construct and execute create_form on that particular node every time by using the remote execution combinator. The difference between the two alternatives is whether the whole iterative task or only the form instantiations are to be executed on the selected node.

5.3   Detecting Failures

The application is now able to report its status – at least the actual temperature of the water and whether each one of the heating elements is on or off. But the application is unable to detect any kind of failures; for example, the application is going to wait indefinitely for the water to boil if only broken heating elements are switched on. In order to detect erroneous situations, the workflow must be aware of its *history*, that is, whether some events and states occurred recently. Such functionality can be implemented in P*éα* by using a controller with an *accumulator*. To detect broken coils, only two parts of the workflow need to be changed, whose new version can be found in Code 8.

In the function control_workflow, the controller construct is extended with an accumulator using the construct with accumulator with an initial value of 0.

```
kettle_plan () ->
 fun!(Old, V) ->
  case V of
   #task_value{value = {ok, Ts}} ->
    effective_temperature(Ts) >>= fun!(T) ->
    send_role_msg(monitor, {temp, T}) >>| task_create(fun!() ->
    Error_Threshold = 3,
    if
     T > 100 - Error_Threshold ->
      shutdown("Water boiled.") >>|
      stable({done, T});
     Old - T > Error_Threshold ->
      shutdown("Heating element broken!")>>|
      stable({error, T});
     true ->
      unstable(max(Old, T), T)
    end
  end) end end
 end.

control_workflow() ->
 change_heating_element_status([on,on,on]) >>|
 temperature_reading()
  controlled by kettle_plan() with accumulator 0.
```

Code 8. Control plan mainaining an accumulator

Now the plan has two arguments, the first one is the actual value of the accumulator and the second is the unstable value propagated from the controlled task. In the case of returning an unstable result, two values have to be defined: a new accumulator value and a value which is to be propagated as an unstable value upwards in the controller hierarchy.

As can be seen in the code listing, the plan sends messages in order to inform the form updater running under the role monitor about the actual temperature.

The definition of the task shutdown is not listed in Code 8 as its implementation is really simple: it turns all the coils off and instructs the form updater to write its actual argument into the comment label of the monitor form. Note that the form updater here also takes care of stopping the form after setting the comment.

The logic implemented by the plan is able to detect when the water temperature is dropping, thus determining if coils are broken. The accumulator value is always set to the maximum of the previous value and the actual reading in order to prevent the water from cooling down slowly unnoticed, which could otherwise happen when the temperature difference of subsequent measurements is under the value Error_threshold.

```
control_form(T, D) ->
 form("kettle controller",
  [label(l1, "Temperature:"), textfield(t, T),
   label(l2, "Deadline:"), textfield(d, D)],
  [action(ok, "Ok"), action(cancel, "Cancel")]).
```

Code 9. Declarative description of the control form

```
{T, D} = {97, ""},
pipe() >>= fun!(P) ->
par([
 {monitor, controlled_monitor_form()},
 {control, controlled_control_form(T,D,P) @! [iot_controller]}
  '
 control_workflow(T, D, P) @! [kettle]
]) >>|
destroy_pipe(P) end.
```

Code 10. The task starting up the application

5.4   The Human in the Loop

The application up to now is only slightly interactive, as it can show its status to the user, but the user cannot influence the behaviour of the kettle. The next version of the workflow allows the user to parameterise via a form.

The new form has two input fields: temperature and deadline. In the example, only the value from the former is used, however the deadline could also be similarly utilised with further modification of the controller plan.

Creating a Control Form. The definition of the control form is listed in Code 9. The form has two input fields, whose initial values are given as arguments of the function, and two actions to indicate whether the actual input values have to be submitted to the control plan or reverted to the most recent ones. The form is to be recreated every time it ends until the workflow is finished, which is easily done with an iterative task.

First, let us consider the changes needed in the already familiar parts of the application. On one hand, the monitor form should reflect the current user values registered by the application. This is easily achieved by putting two new labels on the form and extending the form updater with a new kind of message. On the other hand, the control logic must go through deeper changes.

The start of the workflow can be seen in Code 10. The initial user request (T for temperature and D for deadline) is set programatically in the first line, but the control form could be executed to obtain a real input instead. First of all, notice that the plan monitoring the temperature also must monitor input values to be aware of the user's current wishes. The task measuring the temperature could be moved inside a parallel construct along with a task managing the control form, i.e. inside `control_workflow`; but that would cause the whole user control logic to run on the kettle, while the control form must be present on some other `iot_controller` node. In order to avoid that pitfall, the task responsible for the control form is combined with the same parallel combinator than the monitor form and the control logic.

Now the values coming from the user must be passed to the control plan, for which the pipe construct is to be used. A pipe can be created with the predefined primitive task `pipe` and must be destroyed with `destroy_pipe`. Between the execution of those two tasks, the created pipe can be used for propagating values between tasks that are residing in parallel parts of the same workflow. Task values normally are propagated according to the control flow: stable values forward and unstable values backward. Pipes can be used to open one-way tunnels between parallel control flow paths to propagate task values.

On the receiving side, a pipe behaves very similarly to usual tasks as it raises unstable values. However, it would never end on its own. The usage of values propagated via a pipe is shown in Code 11. The pipe is used as any normal task: it gets executed in parallel with temperature reading. The plan `pipe_filter` is only turning form values with an action other than 'ok' into `novalue`, so making the implementation of `kettle_plan` simpler.

Instead of the simple parallel construct used previously, a special form of it is utilised in `control_workflow`. Controlling a parallel construct may be cumbersome when determining which component of the parallel construct triggered the raise of a new list of values. In the case of the example at hand, different things have to be done according to whether the pipe or sensor reading gave a new unstable value. For such situations, P$\acute{e}\alpha$ provides a parallel combinator with a tightly coupled monitor whose plan is fed with a triplet instead of a list consisting of recent task values. The triplet provided for the plan consists of (1) an index, (2) the kind of the third component of the triplet and (3) a value coming from the task corresponding to the index. Remember that a task's value can be of three kinds: `unstable`, `stable` and `exception`.

Now, the accumulator belonging to `kettle_plan` is a three-tuple: the recent temperature extended with the currently requested temperature and deadline. The implementation of the plan is straightforwardly derived from its previous version. Some clarification is required only when processing a form value supplied by the pipe. The action and new user input is taken out from the form value in the first line of the corresponding branch. Then user input must be converted from strings to numbers. Note that the action is ensured to be 'ok' at that point by `pipe_filter`.

Now let us see the iterative task handling the control form in Code 12. The implementation is very similar to that of the monitor form, the only main difference is the usage of a pipe. On the side where values are issued, a pipe can be connected to a task using the `tap with` operator. A task tapped with a pipe behaves exactly as a normal one; tapping is completely transparent.

```
kettle_plan () ->
 fun!({RT, RD, Old}, V) ->
  case V of
   #task_value{value = {1, unstable, {ok, Ts}}} ->
    effective_temperature(Ts) >>= fun!(T) ->
    send_role_msg(monitor, {temp, T}) >>| task_create(fun!() ->
    Error_Threshold = 3,
    if
     T > RT - Error_Threshold ->
      shutdown("Water temperature at the desired level.") >>|
      return(stable({done, T}));
     Old - T > Error_Threshold ->
      shutdown("Heating element broken!") >>|
      return(stable({error, T}));
     true ->
      return(unstable({RT, RD, max(Old, T)}, T))
    end end) end;
   #task_value{value = {2, unstable, #form_value{} = FV}} ->
    {ok, T, D} = get_action_and_values(FV),
    {T2, D2} = {convert_temperature(T), convert_time(D)},
    send_role_msg(monitor, {request, T, D})>>|
    return(unstable({T2, D2, Old}, Old));
   _ ->
    V
  end
 end.

control_workflow(T, D, Pipe) ->
 change_heating_element_status([on,on,on]) >>|
 controlled_par([
  temperature_reading(),
  Pipe controlled by pipe_filter()
 ], kettle_plan(), {T, D, 0}).
```

Code 11. Control logic of the kettle

The task running in parallel with the form waits for one message indicating that the form should be stopped. When that message is received, the plan controlling the parallel construct returns a non-continue stable value. Also note that the accumulator here belongs to the iterative task in order to access the most recent user input when recreating the control form. An iterative task maintaining an accumulator must be built from a unary function whose argument is the actual value of the accumulator. The initial value can be defined with the operator with accumulator, just like in the case of a controller.

Dealing with Erroneous Input. Converting text typed by the user inside the control plan is not good practice. There are many theoretical reasons for that. The most practical one is that the user could not be informed about an erroneous input because of the pipe being unidirectional. In the following revision of the

```
controlled_control_form(T, D, Pipe)  ->
 iterate(fun!({T, D}) ->
  create_form(control_form(T, D)) >>= fun!(Form) ->
  par([
   show_form(Form) tap with Pipe,
   receiver()
  ]) controlled by control_form_plan(T, D)
 end end) with accumulator {T, D}.
```

Code 12. Iterative task for handling user input

```
to_integer(S) ->
 case string:to_integer(S) of
  {error, R} -> throw({to_integer, R, S});
  {T, _} -> T
 end.

convert_input(FV) -> task_create(fun!() ->
 {A, T, D} = get_action_and_values(FV),
 case A of
  ok ->
   {ok, {convert_temperature(T), convert_time(D)}};
  _ ->
   {A, {}}
 end end).

get_and_convert_input(Form) ->
 show_form(Form) >>= fun!(FV) ->
 convert_input(FV)
 end.          •
```

Code 13. Converting user input

workflow, the conversion of user inputs is moved from the control plan to a task executed immediately after the input is over.

The workflow needs to be modified at three points. Task show_form is to be replaced with get_and_convert_input of Code 13 in the iterative task related to the control form. Then pipe_filter and kettle_plan is to be adjusted to the value format resulting from convert_input. Finally, the plan controlling the control form is to be modified to handle exceptions.

The input has to be converted only when the action is 'ok', and can be ignored otherwise. The implementation of the two converter functions are not interesting, but note that they utilise the function to_integer. If the given string cannot be converted to an integer, an exception is thrown. Exceptions are wrapped into a task value of kind exception automatically as long as they are thrown inside

```
fun!(V) ->
  case V of
  % other branches
  #task_value{value = [#task_value{stability = exception},_]}->
    stable(continue({T, D, "Wrong format!"}));
  _ ->
    V
  end
end.
```

Code 14. Pattern matching against an exception

a task. The plan controlling the form then can catch the exception in Code 14. In this case, the form is extended with a new label for giving feedback to the user about errors, and the accumulator tuple also has a third slot for storing the text of that label.

It Could Be Shut Down. So far, the kettle can be shut down only by the application itself, however the user must be able to stop it at any time. Therefore, make the control form is extended with a new action, 'shutdown'.

From now on, the plan controlling the form is to return a non-continue stable value when the form returns with the action 'shutdown', thus keeping the form from being recreated again. On the receiving side of the pipe, some simple modifications are also in order. The plan pipe_filter must keep values triggered by the action 'shutdown' also intact, besides the ones triggered by the 'ok' button. Then, the control plan has to check whether the value coming from the pipe is a new user input or a shutdown request. In the latter case, task shutdown is to be executed to end the workflow.

Once again, these modifications are left as an exercise to the reader.

5.5 Keeping the Water Warm

The last feature of the kettle allows the water to stay warm until it is consumed; this latter fact being indicated by clicking the 'shutdown' button.

Up to now, the workflow used to end when the temperature reached the desired level. Now, it will follow a different plan which maintains the temperature and falls back to the heating plan if the user changes their mind and sets a higher temperature. Only the control logic requires modifications, other parts of the workflow remain the same.

Changing Plans on Demand. We need to find a way to change plans on demand. A straightforward-looking approach would call for creating a complex plan which starts with deciding which scenario is active actually: heating the water or maintaining its temperature. The accumulator is to be extended with

```
kettle_status_reading(Pipe, ControlFun, InitAcc) ->
 controlled_par([
  temperature_reading(),
  Pipe controlled by pipe_filter()
 ], ControlFun, InitAcc).

heating(Pipe) ->
 recent_piped_value(Pipe) >>= fun!({A, I}) ->
 case A of
  shutdown ->
   return({shutdown, nil});
  _ ->
   {T, D} = I,
   change_heating_element_status([on,on,on]) >>|
   kettle_status_reading(Pipe, heating_plan(), {T, D, 0})
 end end.

control_workflow(Pipe) ->
 iterate(fun!() ->
  heating(Pipe) >>= fun!(Res) ->
  case Res of
   {done, T} ->
    keeping_warm(T, Pipe);
   _ ->
    return(Res)
  end
 end end).
```

Code 15. Changing of plans

a flag indicating the actual scenario in this case. The plan itself would consist of a case expression with a number of patterns, which comes obviously with some thinking.

However, a more verbose approach is presented here to discuss other issues. The relevant parts of the revised implementation are shown in Code 15.

The task running on the kettle is defined by control_workflow as an iterative task. It starts with heating after which keeping_warm, a task maintaining the user-defined temperature, would be executed if the heating was successful. That second part can result in a continue value if the water needs more heating due to the user having changed the desired temperature to a higher value. Otherwise, a non-continue value would be returned eventually.

The two tasks, heating and keeping_warm, are very similar, thus only heating is revealed in the provided code snippet. The only difference is in the second branch of the case expression: in the task keeping_warm, there is no need for turning the coils on, and, of course, a different plan with a proper initial accumulator value is to be passed as actual argument to kettle_status_reading.

There is an issue, however, that must be addressed in this approach due to starting separate controllers, one in heating and another one in keeping_warm. After one controller is ended and before the next one is started, there is a tiny period of time in which no controller is monitoring the pipe and values propagated by it could be missed. The predefined task recent_piped_value, which results in the value that has been most recently gone through the pipe, is to be used in order to mitigate the impact of such unfortunate circumstances.

Note that, in this case, the task convert_input requires the most recent user input with each 'cancel' action, thus being able to set the initial accumulators of control plans.

The plan for heating is exactly the same as in the previous versions of the workflow. The other plan is a bit more complicated. Its detailed implementation is not presented here, but we provide a short discussion on it. Its implementation consists of two main cases:

- If new user input is received, there are three different scenarios: (1) if the requested temperature is below of the current one, the controller needs to update its accumulator; (2) if the requested temperature is set to a higher value, the iterative task is to be restarted to heat up the water; (3) in case of a 'shutdown' action, the plan returns a stable value which ends the whole application.
- There are also three different scenarios when the execution of the plan is triggered by a new temperature measurement: (1) if temperature is higher than necessary, coils have to be turned off; (2) if temperature is below of the desired level with a given threshold, the coils have to be switched on; (3) if the coils are already on, a hardware failure can be detected just like earlier, in which case the plan results in a stable value ending the whole workflow.

Stop Wasting Energy. The final revision of the application is able to shut down the kettle if there was no user interaction for a long time while maintaining water temperature. This needs only the modification of control_workflow, in which timing constraints can be defined in an elegant way by using Péα combinators. The new version of that task is presented in Code 16.

Note that the combinators used in this revision to define timing constraints are predefined in Péα, but could be implemented in a couple of lines with the help of the primitive tasks and combinators mentioned in the paper.

The combinator or after lets keeping_warm run for 5 min. If the task does not end within the given time, the combinator stops it and executes the other task provided after the do operator, i.e. the sequentially combined task would be executed after 5 min. A warning message is sent to monitor form, then keeping_warm is executed again. That second running of keeping_warm is to be timed out by the combinator timeout after after another 5 min. That timeout will eventually end the workflow as it results in a value which is not wrapped into a continue.

It is also noteworthy that such timeouts could be implemented inside the plan which controls kettle_status_reading in the task keeping_warm. In that

```
control_workflow(Pipe) ->
 iterate(fun!() ->
  heating(Pipe) >>= fun!(Res) ->
  case Res of
   {done, _} ->
    keeping_warm(Pipe) or after timer:minutes(5) do
     send_role_msg(monitor, {cmt, "Hot water is ready!"}) >>|
    keeping_warm(Pipe) timeout after timer:minutes(5);
   _ ->
    return(Res)
  end
 end end).
```

Code 16. Keeping the water warm for a limited time

case, however, the high level control structure would be less clear. Elapsed time would have to be computed and meticulously kept track of within the plan by passing it around explicitly.

6   Related Work

The design of Péα is based on the principles of task-oriented programming, more specifically on the iTask System [18]. As the domain on which our research is focused is different from that of iTasks, Péα implements a modified set of TOP principles to fit the requirements of Cyber-Physical Systems. For example, we do not really need to generate user interfaces automatically. However, letting the system operate in a distributed manner is first principle for us.

Workflows are used for modelling and organizing business processes [11] for a very long time, because such graphical tools are easy for managers and other non-programmer persons to understand. Besides programming CPSs with Péα, our aim is to provide a tool for non-programmer domain-experts to create their very own applications easily. Therefore, ideas worked out for widely used workflow languages are also to be considered as possible extensions for the front-end of our system.

Reactive programming has recently gained popularity in developing event-driven and interactive applications [2]. Péα, in fact, makes it easy to express concepts of functional reactive programming (FRP). If we drop the notion of stable values outside plans, we would get a system highly similar to FRP. The matching operation of function composition would then be the controller; the matching notion of signals would be that of streams of unstable values.

There are many different approaches and tools to model, design and program Cyber-Physical Systems. The current and planned features of Péα are implemented by some of them to some extent. However, none of them integrates a sufficient set of features to build and orchestrate a comprehensive application connected to different cyber-physical domains. Some of the existing tools are dedicated to particular vertical domains; others need not only engineers but experienced software craftsmen to utilise their capabilities. In fact, both of these are true for most contemporary toolkits. The emerging need for a comprehensive tool which integrates the orthogonal design concerns of Cyber-Physical Systems is well known [20]. One way to ease the actual situation is defining design methodology in terms of existing tools and techniques. A thing which is more or less done already, for example [5] contains the very high-level principles of such an integrated methodology. Nevertheless, that combined design apparatus would be better used to identify the different aspects of the CPS design process and then implement one consistent tool supporting those separate concerns.

The main industrial parties also have their standardized methodologies for systems design, which nowadays can be considered as CPS design standards. For example, one of the standards of automotive industry is EAST-ADL [3] describing the different concerns have to included in any design documents. Nevertheless, implementation issues of the designed systems have a separate standard, AUTOSAR [21].

The Orc Programming Language [10] is advertised as a tool for CPS applications which heavily involve human interaction. The language is based on a concurrency calculus of the same name, extended with a functional core. The language can be used to distribute computation among many nodes dynamically, which truly makes it suitable for CPS programming. However, it supports features that make the language impure and hard to reason about. Compared to P$\acute{e}\alpha$, Orc does not support reactive programming; user interfaces can be defined only with external tools involved; and the implicit parallelism inherited from the base calculus, which is present throughout the language, makes it hard to understand its semantics without significant background knowledge.

One way to create cyber-physical applications quickly based on existing services is writing glue code for those services. A tool that makes gluing web services together possible is described in [19]. The paper proposes two ways to define the glue application: writing Python code, which needs a considerable body of knowledge on programming in Python; and defining the glue logic in a 2D tabular workspace, which is also not so straightforward according to the experience of the authors of this paper. The system is called event-driven, yet it needs manual synchronisation of each event in the glue application. Moreover, the control logic itself is to be developed as a web service.

There is a workflow engine, ERWF [7], with high-level goals similar to ours. The research is aiming at creating a framework for describing the computational part of user-centric Cyber-Physical Systems as workflows and execute them on embedded systems in a real-time manner. Despite the similar vision, the implementations could not be more different. ERWF is implemented using the Real Time Application Interface of Linux, which makes the system able to execute tasks taking time constraints into account – a feature that lacks from P$\acute{e}\alpha$ when this paper is being written. It is noteworthy that the decision about task execution is based on probabilistic approximation of worst-case execution time. Moreover, definition of ERWF tasks involves low-level features like global variables for data sharing and wait/notify primitives for synchronisation, which makes programming the system really hard and error-prone. The low-level workflows of ERWF are not comparable with those of Péα.

Besides the somewhat general tools, which require solid programming knowledge to harness them, there are domain-specific ones as well. Those tools are easy to use for domain-experts, but the area where they can be applied is very limited.

Regiment [15] is a DSL to program sensor networks on the global level rather than individual sensor nodes. The approach in which the global network program is automatically translated into node-local programs is called macroprogramming. Regiment is a good tool for macroprogramming sensor networks, however it is not flexible enough for solving general CPS problems. Dynamic behaviour of applications, dynamically changing network configuration and rapid queries, which are present in Péα as the propagation of unstable values, cannot be implemented with Regiment.

There is a tool described in [13] which supports designing energy efficient buildings in a model-driven way. An UML-like modelling DSL is provided to define all the facilities that affect the energy consumption of a building. The tool can be used to make the building more energy efficient through the model-driven design process. Having the construction done, the sensors deployed throughout the premises is to be controlled by a distributed application generated by the tool and collecting data about the energy consumption. The data collected is then used to create different kinds of reports. The application has nothing to do with controlling the building, yet it could be a good basis for such a reactive system.

Not only buildings, but every mission-critical systems have to be monitored to check their behaviour. Copilot [16,17] is a real-time monitoring tool with the ability to oversee temporal properties of running systems in a non-intrusive way. The recent version of Copilot is able to trigger callbacks in the system in certain situations as well. That kind of monitoring tool comes in handy for auditing legacy systems. However, monitor and control functionality is better included into new applications by design, which can be implemented simply in Péα.

7   Conclusion

A workflow system, Péα, specifically designed for programming Cyber-Physical Systems is presented in this paper. Péα is based on the principles of task-oriented programming, nevertheless it restricts some of its features while extending its capabilities with new ones to suit the system to the needs of CPS programming. A working Péα framework is implemented in an extended version of the Erlang distributed functional programming language.

The features of the current implementation are revealed through a small scale illustrative example, the implementation of which poses all the challenges with which developers of large scale CPS applications have to cope.

The first version of our workflow system, as it is published in this paper, addresses the basic issues of CPS programming and provides a good basis for continuing research and adding more sophisticated features to the system in order to solve further open questions of the field of CPS programming.

A referee asked if there would be a second "incarnation" of P$\acute{\varepsilon}\alpha$. Having the first version of this paper submitted, we started to work on implementing P$\acute{\varepsilon}\alpha$ in Scala using the Akka library. Scala has a rich static type system, which can be leveraged to ease the development of P$\acute{\varepsilon}\alpha$ workflows by preventing many issues that occurs as runtime errors in the Erlang implementation, and raising static type errors instead. Moreover, Akka implements the actor model of Erlang, which makes it easy for us to port the Erlang implementation into Scala. Although the embedding into Scala is not completed at the time when this paper is finalised, we believe that the changes that are forced by the strong type system of Scala would result in a new incarnation of P$\acute{\varepsilon}\alpha$ that can be used in a more concise way than the original version presented in this paper.

Acknowledgement. The authors would like to thank Dr Christian Rinderknecht for his comments and discussion. They are also grateful to the anonymous referees for their suggestions.

The research was carried out as part of the EITKIC_12-1-2012-0001 project, which is supported by the Hungarian Government, managed by the National Development Agency, financed by the Research and Technology Innovation Fund and was performed in cooperation with the EIT ICT Labs Budapest Associate Partner Group (www.ictlabs.elte.hu).

References

1. Armstrong, J.: Programming Erlang: Software for a Concurrent World. Pragmatic Bookshelf, Raleigh (2007)
2. Bainomugisha, E., Carreton, A.L., Van Cutsem, T., Mostinckx, S., De Meuter, W.: A survey on reactive programming. ACM Comput. Surv. **45**(4), 52:1–52:34 (2013). https://doi.acm.org/10.1145/2501654.2501666
3. Blom, H., Lönn, H., Hagl, F., Papadopoulos, Y., Reiser, M.O., Sjöstedt, C.J., Chen, D.J., Kolagari, R.T.: EAST-ADL - An Architecture Description Language for Automotive Software-Intensive Systems. Technical report the EAST-ADL 2 Consortium (2012)
4. Bozó, I., Horpácsi, D., Horváth, Z., Kitlei, R., Kőszegi, J., Tejfel, M., Tóth, M.: Refactorerl - source code analysis and refactoring in erlang. In: Proceedings of the 12th Symposium on Programming Languages and Software Tools, Tallin, Estonia, pp. 138–148, October 2011. ISBN 978-9949-23-178-2
5. Broman, D., Lee, E.A., Tripakis, S., Törngren, M.: Viewpoints, formalisms, languages, and tools for cyber-physical systems. In: Proceedings of the 6th International Workshop on Multi-Paradigm Modeling, MPM 2012, pp. 49–54. ACM, New York (2012). http://doi.acm.org/10.1145/2508443.2508452
6. Cesarini, F., Thompson, S.: Introduction. In: ERLANG Programming, pp. 1–3. O'Reilly Media Inc., USA (2009)
7. Chen, W.C., Shih, C.S.: Erwf: Embedded real-time workflow engine for user-centric cyber-physical systems. In: International Conference on Parallel and Distributed Systems, pp. 713–720 (2011)
8. Horpácsi, D.: Extending erlang by utilising refactorerl. In: Proceedings of the Twelfth ACM SIGPLAN Workshop on Erlang, Erlang 2013, pp. 63–72. ACM, New York (2013). http://doi.acm.org/10.1145/2505305.2505314

9. Kats, L.C.L., Visser, E.: The Spoofax language workbench. Rules for declarative specification of languages and IDEs. In: Rinard, M. (ed.) Proceedings of the 25th Annual ACM SIGPLAN Conference on Object-Oriented Programming, Systems, Languages, and Applications, OOPSLA 2010, Reno, NV, USA, October 17–21, pp. 444–463 (2010)

10. Kitchin, D., Quark, A., Cook, W., Misra, J.: The orc programming language. In: Lee, D., Lopes, A., Poetzsch-Heffter, A. (eds.) FMOODS 2009. LNCS, vol. 5522, pp. 1–25. Springer, Heidelberg (2009)

11. Ko, R.K., Lee, S.S., Lee, E.W.: Business process management (bpm) standards: A survey. Bus. Process. Manage. J. 15(5), 744–791 (2009)

12. Kozsik, T., Lőrincz, A., Juhász, D., Domoszlai, L., Horpácsi, D., Tóth, M., Horváth, Z.: Workflow description in cyber-physical systems. Stud. Univ. Babes-Bolyai Ser. Info. LVIII(2), 20–30 (2013). http://www.cs.ubbcluj.ro/~studia-i/2013-2/052-Horvath.pdf

13. Kurpick, T., Pinkernell, C., Look, M., Rumpe, B.: Modeling cyber-physical systems: Model-driven specification of energy efficient buildings. In: Proceedings of the Modelling of the Physical World Workshop, MOTPW 2012, pp. 2:1–2:6. ACM, New York (2012). http://doi.acm.org/10.1145/2491617.2491619

14. Lee, E.A.: Cyber physical systems: Design challenges. Technical report UCB/EECS-2008-8, EECS Department, University of California, Berkeley, January 2008. http://www.eecs.berkeley.edu/Pubs/TechRpts/2008/EECS-2008-8.html

15. Newton, R., Morrisett, G., Welsh, M.: The regiment macroprogramming system. In: Proceedings of the 6th International Conference on Information Processing in Sensor Networks, IPSN 2007, pp. 489–498. ACM, New York (2007). http://doi.acm.org/10.1145/1236360.1236422

16. Pike, L., Goodloe, A., Morisset, R., Niller, S.: Copilot: a hard real-time runtime monitor. In: Barringer, H., Falcone, Y., Finkbeiner, B., Havelund, K., Lee, I., Pace, G., Roşu, G., Sokolsky, O., Tillmann, N. (eds.) RV 2010. LNCS, vol. 6418, pp. 345–359. Springer, Heidelberg (2010). http://dblp.uni-trier.de/db/conf/rv/rv2010.html#PikeGMN10

17. Pike, L., Wegmann, N., Niller, S., Goodloe, A.: Copilot: Monitoring embedded systems. Innov. Syst. Softw. Eng. 9(4), 235–255 (2013). http://dx.doi.org/10.1007/s11334-013-0223-x

18. Plasmeijer, R., Lijnse, B., Michels, S., Achten, P., Koopman, P.: Task-oriented programming in a pure functional language. In: Proceedings of the 14th Symposium on Principles and Practice of Declarative Programming, PPDP 2012, pp. 195–206. ACM, New York (2012). http://doi.acm.org/10.1145/2370776.2370801

19. Srbljić, S., Škvorc, D., Popović, M.: Programming languages for end-user personalization of cyber-physical systems. AUTOMATIKA: časopis za automatiku, mjerenje, elektroniku, računarstvo i komunikacije 53(3), 294–310 (2012)

20. Sztipanovits, J.: Composition of cyber-physical systems. In: ECBS, pp. 3–6. IEEE Computer Society (2007). http://dblp.uni-trier.de/db/conf/ecbs/ecbs2007.html#Sztipanovits07

21. Voget, S.: Autosar and the automotive tool chain. In: Proceedings of the Conference on Design, Automation and Test in Europe, DATE 2010, pp. 259–262. European Design and Automation Association, 3001 Leuven, Belgium (2010). http://dl.acm.org/citation.cfm?id=1870926.1870988

Author Index

Printed in the United States
By Bookmasters